Advancing Social Justice
Through Clinical Practice

Titles of Related Interest from Lawrence Erlbaum and Associates, Inc.

Giuseppe Costantino, Richard H. Dana, & Robert G. Malgady • *TEMAS (Tell-Me-A-Story) Assessment in Multicultural Societies*

Charles J. Gelso & Jeffrey A. Hayes • *Countertransference and the Therapist's Inner Experience: Perils and Possibilities*

Lawrence G. Calhoun & Richard G. Tedeschi • *Handbook of Posttraumatic Growth: Research & Practice*

Arthur J. Clark • *Empathy in Counseling and Psychotherapy: Perspectives and Practices*

Uwe P. Gielen, Jefferson M. Fish, & Juris G. Draguns • *Handbook of Culture, Therapy, and Healing*

Joel Paris • *Half in Love with Death: Managing the Chronically Suicidal Patient*

Zipora Shechtman • *Group Counseling and Psychotherapy with Children and Adolescents: Theory, Research, and Practice*

Lisa L. Weyandt • *An ADHD Primer, Second Edition*

Klaus Grawe • *Neuropsychotherapy: How the Neurosciences Inform Effective Psychotherapy*

David Blustein • *The Psychology of Working: A New Perspective for Career Development, Counseling, and Public Policy*

Dewey G. Cornell • *School Violence: Fears Versus Facts*

Edwin L. Herr, Dennis E. Heitzmann, & Jack R. Rayman • *The Professional Counselor as Administrator: Perspectives on Leadership and Management of Counseling Services Across Settings*

Katherine D. Arbuthnott & Dennis W. Arbuthnott • *The Mind in Therapy: Cognitive Science for Practice*

John Pellitteri, Robin Stern, Claudia Shelton, & Barbara Muller-Ackerman • *Emotionally Intelligent School Counseling*

L. DiAnne Borders & Lori L. Brown • *The New Handbook of Counseling Supervision*

Cynthia E. Glidden-Tracey • *Counseling and Therapy with Clients Who Abuse Alcohol or Other Drugs: An Integrative Approach*

Richard H. Dana • *Multicultural Assessment: Principles, Applications, and Examples*

Bruce Wampold • *The Great Psychotherapy Debate: Models, Methods, and Findings*

Advancing Social Justice Through Clinical Practice

Edited by

Etiony Aldarondo
University of Miami

LEA
2007

LAWRENCE ERLBAUM ASSOCIATES, PUBLISHERS

Mahwah, New Jersey   London

Lawrence Erlbaum Associates, Inc., Publishers
10 Industrial Avenue
Mahwah, New Jersey 07430
www.erlbaum.com

Cover design by Kathryn Houghtaling Lacey

Cover art by Sebastián Picker © 2006,
The Fight for Justice, oil on canvas.
Reproduced with permission.

Library of Congress Cataloging-in-Publication Data

Advancing Social Justice Through Clinical Practice

ISBN 978-0-8058-5517-3 — ISBN 0-8058-5517-3 (cloth)
ISBN 978-0-8058-5518-0 — ISBN 0-8058-5518-1 (pbk)
ISBN 978-1-4106-1517-6 — ISBN 1-4106-1517-0 (e book)

Copyright information for this volume can be obtained by contacting the Library of Congress.

Books published by Lawrence Erlbaum Associates are printed on acid-free paper,
and their bindings are chosen for strength and durability.

Printed in the United States of America
10 9 8 7 6 5 4 3 2

Brief Contents

Contents

PART III: COMMUNITY BUILDING FOR WELLNESS AND JUSTICE

PART IV: TEACHING AND TRAINING FOR SOCIAL ACTION

Foreword

George W. Albee
University of Vermont

Last fall, I received invitations to attend a day of remembrance for Professor Ignacio Martín-Baró to be held at Stirling University in Scotland. I also received an invitation from Professor Aldarondo to write the Foreword for this volume. I accepted the Scottish invitation because the meeting was imminent. At 83, my energy for new commitments is increasingly limited, so I put off responding to Professor Aldarondo.

I prepared for the meeting in Scotland by learning all I could about Professor Martín-Baró and his writing. I was thrilled and inspired by his thoughts about establishing an international psychological group concerned with mental health and human rights, which, he argued, were inextricably bound together. I was pained to learn that he and five other fellow Jesuit professors had been murdered in 1988 on the campus of the University of Central America in San Salvador. Their housekeeper and her 15-year-old daughter were also shot. The perpetrators were a death squad of the ruling military. The crime: speaking out against the oppression of the country's poor and supporting a liberation theology.

I then agreed to write this "Foreword." Those of us who believe in the importance of the bond between mental health and human rights must come together in an alliance with groups everywhere who share this belief. We must make serious efforts to help students in our field learn the importance of this connection and find the courage to oppose the mainstream that stresses adjustment to the status quo. Contemporary psychological education and practice emphasizes efforts at helping clients deal with internal interpersonal conflicts without reference to an external social world filled with injustice and toxic social experiences. Our practice is largely limited to clients who are covered by insurance with an invalid psychiatric diagnostic system that invents so-called mental diseases that are said to be a result of defective brains. The evidence? Pronouncements of authorities (funded by drug companies) who control the education of the professionals working in the field. The research supporting this biological/chemical defect model is financed largely by pharmaceutical firms who control funding, publication, and information to the public. Back before the Reagan triumph, mental disorders were sometimes seen as resulting from the stresses of poverty, unemployment, and living in a world replete with discrimination against those outside the mainstream. With the ascendance of a conservative social order favoring those with economic power, the model explaining emotional distress shifted from social stress to brain disease. Let me give two examples.

When President Jimmy Carter established a Commission on Mental Health back in the 1970s, his wife, Rosalynn Carter, was to chair the Commission. This turned out to violate some regulation, so she served as Honorary Chair. She was very active in the work of the Commission and supported its findings that found poverty, unemployment, and social stresses as major contributors to the causation of mental/emotional problems.

On the dust jacket of our 1981 Vermont conference volume, *Prevention Through Political Action and Social Change*, she wrote:

> It is clear that the impact of poverty, racism, and discrimination in all its forms adversely affects the mental health of millions. . . . Too often, the pressing need for services distracts our efforts from those primary prevention activities which in the long run can have far greater impact on the mental health of our people.

But Ms. Carter, like most Americans, respects the findings of scientists. American's top psychiatrists, including those appointed to head the National Institute of Mental Health, have changed the explanatory model. Now it is brain disease that causes "mental illness."

Seventeen years after the statement she made above, on July 17, 1998, while on the NBC News, Rosalynn Carter was asked about her long-standing interest in the field of mental health. She now lined up with the new position of the national mental health leadership. She said: "We now know that mental illnesses are due to problems with the brain. We can treat brain disease." But reliable scientific research has failed to find the alleged brain defects and chemical imbalances. Lack of objective evidence does not deter the experts.

At the 1999 White House Conference on Mental Health, the keynote speaker, H. Koplewicz, argued that "childhood psychiatric disorders" are brain diseases. He denied any role for social-environmental factors. He said:

> It's hard to believe that until 20 years ago, we still believed that inadequate parenting and bad childhood traumas were the cause of psychiatric illness in children. And in fact, even though we know better today, that antiquated way of thinking is still out there, so that people who wouldn't dream of blaming parents for other types of disease, like their child's diabetes or asthma, still embrace the notion that somehow absent fathers, working mothers, over-permissive parents are the cause of psychiatric illness in children. [No one says this!] And the only way we can change that is through more public awareness. I mean, essentially, these are no-fault brain disorders. These diseases are physiological; they respond to medicine.

This statement contradicts both scientific and clinical evidence accumulated over decades. It is so bizarre we cannot take it seriously. But many do—they respect authority.

It was Marx who taught us that the ruling ideas of a society are those that support the ruling class. So it should not surprise us to see explanations of mental disorders that support and protect the ruling class of an exploitative society from any responsibility for causing mental–emotional problems. Instead, it is easier to attribute the causes to brain disease and/or defects in biology or chemistry. These organic explanations of every form of mental problem—including crime and delinquency, alcohol and drug addiction, and all forms of child and adult distress—make social change unnecessary. If underpaid workers, exploited and undervalued women, uneducated minorities, the unemployed, the aged, all have high rates of mental disorders, alcoholism, drug addiction, and crime, these pathologies are due to defective biology/chemistry. They are not the fault of the system, say the ruling elite.

The system is replete with faults. Social injustices erode or eliminate human rights. Our society grows increasingly divided between the small group of "haves" and the growing group of "have-nots." We don't need research to prove that water runs downhill! Nor do we need research to reveal the growing enrichment of the rich and the growing impoverishment of the poor. Well-paying jobs are disappearing as heavy industry leaves and jobs are outsourced.

This book is a welcome addition to the literature opposing the current unjust system. The editor, Etiony Aldarondo, has brought together an impressive group of people whose writing has been assembled in one volume of wide-ranging contributions that support the essential unity of mental health and social justice. As one steeped in the culture and values of public health, I must note the long-held public health dictum: No pathological condition has ever been eliminated by intervention with individuals one at a time. In other words, no disease or disorder has ever been treated out of existence. The benefit of working with individuals damaged by the exploitative system is that we learn the nature and causes of injustice that produce toxic social stresses. Then we must move beyond treating individuals to unified efforts to change the system. However, as we lead our students to fully understand the urgent need for the struggle to achieve social justice, we must also be sure of their awareness of their risks. Large corporations have little or no conscience. In their quest for profits they do not hesitate to exploit, to pollute, and to destroy opposition. Remember Professor Martín-Baró and his colleagues.

—George W. Albee
Past President, American Psychological Association
and American Association for Applied and Preventive Psychology
Professor Emeritus
University of Vermont

Preface

The idea for this book owes much to my early clinical experiences with poor and working-poor families at the Gándara Mental Health Center in Springfield, the Family Center of the Berkshires in Pittsfield, the Cambridge Hospital's Latino Mental Health Clinic at Harvard Medical School, and the Philadelphia Child Guidance Clinic at the Philadelphia Children's Hospital. It was not unusual in casual discussions among colleagues to acknowledge some of the handicapping social realities influencing our clients—for example, substandard housing conditions, unemployment, racism, sexism, homophobia, community violence, and abuses of power by employers. Unfortunately, these observations rarely found their way into our "clinical formulations," and almost never became part of our "treatment plans." We were familiar with the social injuries (Sennett & Cobb, 1980; e.g., alienation, demoralization, despair) presented by our clients, but because these injuries were often ameliorated by medication, family therapy, and traditional psychological interventions, we felt we had done our job—at least until our clients returned for additional services. Our familiarity with these social injuries masked the political nature of our clients' troubles, which we were not prepared to address.

The inability to address these issues reveals significant training deficiencies in our professions. As clinicians and human service providers we are taught to attend to the distress of individuals seeking our help. We have learned to do this very well. We are respectful, caring, mindful of their experiences, and supportive of their effort to feel better and to construct a life that works. We know how to help them modify ways of being and relating to others that may be destructive to themselves and to those around them. The reality, however, is that our goodwill and individual-oriented clinical skills are a poor match for the persistent effects of harsh social realities in the lives of those seeking our assistance. Without adequate socialization and appropriate conceptual models and strategies to understand and transform the conditions that make them vulnerable, too many clinicians experience a failure of confidence and imagination that not only tempers their motivation to assume social action roles but also confines them to managing people's distress and leaves them open to feelings of demoralization and burn-out.

As a clinical supervisor and teacher of counseling psychology students, mental health counselors, family therapists, and domestic violence workers, I have endeavored to narrow the gap between clinicians' abilities to respond to the debilitating psychosocial realities of our citizens and the dominant practices in our field. In this process, I have come to see clinicians' learning of social justice-oriented models and their development of skills to carry on this work as limited by several factors, including the individualistic ideology of dominant approaches to therapy, the progressive privatization of our craft, a lack of appropriate training materials, and a tenuous sense of connection to a community of human service providers committed to this endeavor. This book is a modest attempt to offset some of these limitations.

In my experience, assuming a social justice orientation to clinical work enhances the ability of human service providers from different theoretical persuasions to reduce distress and improve the lives of those they serve. It helps psychodynamic and humanistic clinicians discern between handicapping conditions derived from psychosocial factors and conditions derived from intrapsychic and interpersonal factors. It helps cognitive-behavioral clinicians explore the fit between individuals' cognitive schemas and the rationality of the social order. It helps family therapists expand their systemic frameworks to include the effects of social factors in family life. Moreover, it helps them all develop strategies for solving mental health problems that incorporate sociopolitical elements in addition to their preferred emotional, intellectual, or interpersonal ones.

The outline and style of writing in this book reflect my desire to make the material accessible to novice and seasoned clinicians as well as to professors and training directors considering ways to integrate social justice-oriented models into their training programs and services. I believe that all disciplines within the metal health profession can play an important role in the promotion of social justice and that each discipline has the potential to generate unique insights into how to do so. To this end, this book includes chapters written by leading social workers, family therapists, clinical psychologists, community psychologists, psychiatrists, and counseling psychologists committed to the integration of social justice values in their practice and training endeavors.

The chapters in Part I, "Steps Toward a Social Justice Therapeutic Practice," are designed to offer a mix of historical, ethical, and experiential foundations for the development of social justice-based practices. These three chapters will help practitioners and students learn about social justice traditions in the mental health professions, become aware of practical and ethical dilemmas brought forth by making the promotion of social justice central to our work, and get an idea of the personal challenges and rewards awaiting those who chose to integrate social justice ambitions into their clinical endeavors.

Part II, "Liberating Visions of Clinical Practice," involves an exploration of conceptual frameworks, clinical tools, and strategies used by social justice-oriented practitioners in different localities and under different institutional constraints. Contributors analyze the corrosive effect of social injustices and internalized forms of oppression for individuals and relationships. Then they present ways of intervening in the lives of people, couples, and families that do not downplay the historical and social conditions affecting them, or needlessly pathologize their response to these conditions.

The chapters in this section cover only a limited number of specific ways in which social justice-oriented clinicians work[1] but the analyses and suggestions contained in them demonstrate the strong relationship between the structural conditions in people's lives, the psychological distress they experience, and the need to include them both as units of analysis and intervention. To be sure, this relationship has long been known and largely ignored in the mental health professions (e.g., Albee, 1986; Danto, 2005; Jacoby, 1975; Lerner, 1991; Wakefield, 1988).

The chapters in Part III, "Community Building for Wellness and Justice," focus on ways in which mental health professionals can create inclusive social systems that are not only responsive to individual and communal needs but that also prime people for greater involvement in community affairs. Recognizing that the promotion of social justice requires that mental health professionals extend their reach outside traditional clinical settings into the environments where people live, play, and work, contributors address the relationship between mental health policy and social justice aspirations and highlight collaborative work done with families, community-based organizations, religious organizations, schools, and medical institutions.

The chapters in Part IV, "Teaching and Training for Social Action," discuss various skills and competencies required of mental health professionals aspiring to be agents of both individual and social transformation and outline organizational and training structures supportive of their development. To date, training objectives and practices related to social justice competencies have varied widely across and within disciplines in the mental health professions, with training programs in social work having historically paid more attention to social justice concerns than any other discipline in our field, and more recently an increasing number of counseling psychology programs making a concerted effort to address this gap. Still, the integration of social justice concerns and practices into traditional training programs remains one of the biggest challenges to the development of social justice-oriented practices in the mental health professions.

In a democratic society eager for solutions, we ought to welcome the development of the mental health professional as a citizen-professional, who uses his or her clinical skills and knowledge to relieve human suffering and to redress social inequities. I hope that by putting together and disseminating the ideas of some of the most accomplished social justice-oriented clinicians in the field today, this book will serve to empower clinicians to act while also advancing the growth of a new generation of mental health professionals who will be prepared for the promotion of social justice as an important part of their work.

REFERENCES

Albee, G. W. (1986). Toward a just society: Lessons from observations on the primary prevention of psychopathology. *American Psychologist, 41*, 891–897.
Danto, E. A. (2005). *Freud's free clinics: Psychoanalysis and social justice, 1918–1938.* New York: Columbia University Press.
Finn, J. L., & Jacobson, M. (2003). *Just practice: A social justice approach to social work.* Peosta, Iowa: Eddie Bowers Publishing Co.

---

[1]See, for example, Janet Finn and Maxine Jacobson's (2003) *Just Practice* and Colleen Lundy's (2004) *Social Work and Social Justice.*

Jacoby, R. (1975). *Social amnesia: A critique of contemporary psychology from Adler to Laing.* Boston: Beacon Press.

Lerner, M. (1991). *Surplus powerlessness: The psychodynamics of everyday life—And the psychology of individual and social transformation.* Atlantic Highland, NJ: Humanities Press International.

Lundy, C. (2004). Social work and social justice. Peterborough, Ontario: Broadview Press.

Sennet, R., & Cobb, J. (1980). *The hidden injuries of class.* London: Farber & Farber.

Wakefield, J. (1988). Psychotherapy, distributive justice, and social work: Part II—Psychotherapy and the pursuit of justice. *Social Service Review, 62,* 353–382.

Acknowledgments

This book would not have been possible without the inspiration, support, and contributions of many people. The passionate and thoughtful support for the integration of social justice values and practices in clinical training offered by students in the counseling theories seminar at Boston College provided much of the impetus for this project. The care and attention to detail by Keven Henze and Steve Gilbert was crucial as we identified potential authors and shaped the proposal for the book. I then moved to the University of Miami, where members of the social justice-based practices research group, Susana Blanco, Dulce Jane, Carla Mayorga, and Stephanie Triarhos, reviewed and discussed each chapter and offered suggestions on how to make the material responsive to the needs and concerns of training clinicians. I am grateful for their hard work and for having had the opportunity to go through this process in their company.

The authors are truly exceptional people. Their unwavering enthusiasm for this book and their willingness to address even our most picky requests for revisions with a balanced sense of professionalism and personalism made this a much more rewarding and enriching process that I ever anticipated it to be.

Susan Milmoe's initial commitment to this project made Lawrence Erlbaum Associates an easy choice as publisher. Following her retirement, the advice and guidance offered by Steve Rutter, Nicole Buckman, and Sondra Guideman made the final editing and production of the book a smooth process. My special thanks to Elsa Efran for her careful proofreading and thoughtful indexing.

I am also indebted to my wife, Maria Carlo, for daring to dream with me without letting her feet leave the ground. More importantly, she lived this undertaking as another family project and gracefully made room for my anxieties and obsessions whether we were at home, in the hospital, visiting relatives, or on vacation.

This book seeks a safer, more humane, and just world. I dedicate it to my son, Diego, his best friend, Ian, and to his cousins, Alanna, Brianna, Isabela, Sara Gabriela, Marina, and Jorge. I am hopeful that as they grow they will come to realize that such a world cannot be taken for granted. I also want to dedicate this book to George Albee, who passed away a few months before this project came to fruition. I am honored to have his words and spirit serving as a foreword to this book. He inspired many social justice-oriented clinicians of my generation and would undoubtedly inspire many more to come.

—Etiony Aldarondo

STEPS TOWARD A SOCIAL JUSTICE THERAPEUTIC PRACTICE

1

Rekindling the Reformist Spirit in the Mental Health Professions

Etiony Aldarondo
University of Miami

Vladimir: Let us not waste our time in idle discourse. Let us do something, while we have the chance! It is not everyday that we are needed. Not indeed that we personally are needed. . . To all mankind they were addressed, those cries for help still ringing our ears! But at this place, at this moment of time, all mankind is us.

Pozzo: Help!

Vladimir: Whether we like it or not. Let us make the most of it, before it is too late!. . . It is true that when with folded arms we weigh the pros and cons we are less a credit to our species. The tiger bounds to the help of his congeners without the least reflection, or else he slinks away into the depths of the thickets. But that is not the question. What are we doing here, that is the question. And we are blessed in this, that we happen to know the answer. Yes, in this immense confusion one thing alone is clear. We are waiting for Godot to come.

Estragon: Ah yes!

Samuel Beckett, from *Waiting for Godot* (Knowlson, 1993, p. 73)

When Samuel Beckett wrote *Waiting for Godot* in the late 1940s, the world was going through a time of considerable confusion and apprehension not unlike our current times. World War II made clear that we have an extraordinary capacity for destruction, which is only surpassed by our desire for power and domination. Beckett knew then what many mental health providers learn as they witness people's suffering and attempt to help them live better lives, that our commitment and effort to promote wellness and happiness seem absurd in a society so capable of negating them. We live in a society with unprecedented levels of material comfort, luxury, and safety. Ours is also a society where half of the citizens are expected to meet criteria for a mental illness at some point in their lives and where "[p]sychosocial problems are the single most common reason for consulting a doctor, and the largest group of drug prescriptions are for psychoactive drugs or painkillers to help us cope with depression, anxiety, sleeplessness, and so on" (Wilkinson, 2005, p. 4).

Care, justice, equality, and dignity are foundational values of our society that are embraced by the mental health professions (i.e., clinical psychologists, counseling psychologists, family therapists, psychiatrists, psychiatric nurses, and social workers). We know this and try to practice these values while being aware that a small number of families own the overwhelming majority of the country's financial assets; that the income and wealth inequality in the United States is wider than it has been for 50 years; that poverty and inequality are the strongest determinants of health problems in our nation; that more than a third of our people do not have medical insurance; that about a third of the insured do not have enough to cover the cost of medication; that the average life expectancy is much shorter for people living in poor communities compared with those of the richest neighborhoods; that mental health problems are extremely unevenly distributed across our communities according to class, race, and gender; that people of color are significantly overrepresented in our prisons; that children in public schools spend much of their classroom time preparing for "high-stake tests," whereas children in private schools enroll in "enriched" curriculums; that women continue to earn considerably less than their male counterparts and that more than a third of them will be victims of domestic violence during their lifetime; and so on.[1] There is no question, as Kovel (1981) asserts, to practice psychotherapy in our society "is to be enmeshed in contradictions" (p. 252).

Over the years, I have come to believe that good mental health professionals are neither strangers to the pervasive presence of inequality and injustice in our society nor are they naïve about its effects in the inner life of people. Most competent clinicians try to do the best they can in a context that favors restrictive biologically oriented services while state and federal governments aim to thin down their historical responsibility to care for their most disenfranchised citizens. Not surprisingly under these conditions, an increasing number of therapists from different persuasions, like Vladimir in Beckett's play, have been asking out loud "what are we doing here?" (e.g., Albee, 2000; Doherty, 1995; Fratarolli, 2001; Hillman & Ventura, 1992; Miller, 2004; Richards, 2004; Richardson, Fowers, & Guignon, 1999).

This brings me back to Beckett's *Waiting for Godot*. The play consists of two similar acts. Vladimir and Estragon meet beside a bare tree to wait for Mr. Godot. They vaguely remember doing this before, but don't dwell on it. We know, however, that they have been there before. They share some general concerns in their lives and amuse each other with stories. They want help for a problem, which they hope will be resolved by Godot. Then they meet Pozzo, the owner of the area, and Lucky, his slave, pulled by his master with a piece of rope tied to his neck. Pozzo amuses the waiting pair before cruelly ordering Lucky to entertain them. After enduring considerable abuse from his master, Lucky produces a stream of meaningless words. Vladimir and Estragon demand better treatment of Lucky, who responds with anger and attacks them, kicking Estragon. Vladimir and Estragon then help Pozzo get an agitated Lucky under the control of his master. Pozzo and Lucky leave, and a young fearful boy who had witnessed much of this brutal event comes by to tell Vladimir and Pozzo that Mr. Godot "won't come this evening but surely tomorrow."

Act II takes place the next day. Vladimir and Estragon wait near the tree, which now has leaves. Estragon does not remember much of what happened the day be-

[1]See Richard Hofrichter's (2003) *Health and Social Justice*, Thomas LaVeist's (2005) *Minority Populations and Health*, Richard Wilkinson's (2005) *The Impact of Inequality*, and the *2001 U.S. Department of Health and Human Services supplement to the first Surgeon General's report on Mental Health*, for in-depth discussions of health disparities in the United States.

fore. They chat and keep each other busy while waiting for Godot to show up. Vladimir gets a better hat and Estragon a more comfortable pair of boots. Pozzo and Lucky walk by, but this time Pozzo is blind and Lucky is mute. The boy comes back again to let them know that Godot would not be coming today but tomorrow. Vladimir and Estragon, feeling despair, talk about leaving for good or coming back tomorrow, which is what we are led to believe will happen.

Beckett knew not only of the profound paradox faced by Vladimir and Estragon, but also of the deforming consequences social injustices and internalized oppression have on our individual, relational, and communal life. Lucky's voice is lost, the slave master can no longer see, Estragon forgets, and Vladimir tries to make sense of it all. They all need help, but who would do it? Why? Doing nothing is an option that brings only minimal comfort to Vladimir and Estragon but to no one else.

In my interpretation of Beckett's play, Pozzo and Lucky are like many people who end up in our offices and clinics looking for help—some do not see how their actions are oppressive and destructive to themselves and those around them, and others seem unable to articulate their struggles and suffering. Estragon embodies people in insurance companies, mental health agencies, and training programs who have a very short memory for social inequality and injustice and as a result are not troubled by focusing on their comfort first. Vladimir represents a large number of good mental health professionals who know that something is wrong, feel like it is their responsibility to do something about it, but are not clear about what to do and are missing the encouragement, training, and support to risk doing something that may be better than waiting for Godot to come with the one solution, the one study, or the one policy that would make things better. This book was designed in part to assist and empower these clinicians to act.

To be sure, the preference to circumvent the humanistic inclination to act when faced with social injustices and inequities is not unique to mental health professionals. Indifference to the misery of others and failure to take corrective action are forms of "passive injustice" all too common in our society (Shklar, 1990). However, unlike other participants in our society, mental health professionals have proclaimed a commitment not only to witness and decrease human suffering, but also to promote human values of equality and justice. And, our ability to fulfill this commitment is constantly being tested within the current system of mental health care.

This book attempts to transcend the conclusion to Beckett's drama within the mental health professions by disseminating the insights of clinicians and trainers who have been making a deliberate effort to address both individual suffering and social inequities fueling this suffering. Writing from various vantage points within the system of mental health care in the United States, these authors aim to rekindle a reformist spirit, long present in our professions, while offering an array of conceptual and practical tools for the development of social justice-oriented therapeutic practices. As prelude to the book, this chapter presents a brief history of efforts made by social justice-oriented clinicians to promote forms of mental health practice responsive to the social realities of those we serve.

SOCIAL JUSTICE LEGACIES IN THE MENTAL HEALTH PROFESSIONS

For many clinicians and students today, the expression of social justice concerns and aspirations in the field of mental health is synonymous with the work done by feminist therapists and community psychologists. That this would be the case is not surprising because, for decades, these groups have persistently reminded us of the need to understand people's lives within the social contexts in which they develop, highlighted the political nature of mental health problems, and advocated an activist stance for human services providers and scholars (e.g., Brown, 1993, 1994; Rappaport, 1981). Moreover, feminist therapists and community psychologists continue to play a leadership role in the development of social justice-oriented theories and practices (e.g., Enns, 2004; Nelson & Prilleltensky, 2005; Prilleltensky & Nelson, 1997; see also chapters by Perilla, Lavizzo, and Ibanez, and by Goodman and her colleagues in this volume).

The history of social justice oriented practices within the mental health professions, however, is considerably broader in scope. Every major discipline in our field today includes important social justice legacies, which have remained largely absent from our institutional memory (e.g., Cushman, 1992; VandenBos, Cummings, & DeLeon, 1992). Lack of awareness about this history is, in our view, a significant obstacle to the growth and development of social justice-oriented theories and practices. We present here a selective review of social justice legacies in social work, psychoanalysis, counseling psychology, psychiatry, and family therapy with the dual purpose of helping readers appreciate the commitment and struggles of previous generations of social justice-oriented clinicians and locating the contributions included in this volume within their appropriate historical traditions.

Social Work

Social work is arguably the discipline with the strongest tradition of commitment to social justice concerns and ambitions among the mental health professions. According to social work historians (Reisch & Andrews, 2002; Specht & Courtney, 2000), the field was born in the context of the charities and correction movement and the settlement houses of the late 19th century and their efforts to promote charitable giving for the poor, community and trade union organizing, and safety, health, and labor legislation among other things. Later during the Great Depression of the 1930s, social workers formed the rank and file movement (Fisher, 1936, 1980), which was critical of New Deal programs aiming to reduce social unrest without directly addressing the social inequities of the time. In addition, rank and file members "organized unions among social service workers, published a radical journal, *Social Work Today* (1934–1942), initiated local political discussion groups, and supported labor unions and organizations of unemployed workers" (Gil, 1998, p. 83).

During the 1940s and 1950s, the reformist spirit of many social workers was tempered in part by the government's effort first to undermine suspected "left-wing groups" and later in the McCarthy era to persecute anyone suspected to be communist or "communist sympathizer."[2] Facing negative consequences for themselves and their loved ones, many social workers, like many other dissenting voices at the time, kept their social justice concerns and aspirations to themselves (Reisch & Andrews, 2002).

In the 1960s, the social justice spirit of social workers was again openly expressed. As Gil (1998) says, in the 1960s

---

[2]See Albert Fried's (1997) *McCarthyism* for a discussion of the creation of the House Un-American Activities in 1938 and the Alien Registration Act of 1940.

a social justice orientation reemerged among social workers, under the influence of civil rights, peace, and feminist movements. Social workers became involved in community organizing in antipoverty and Model Cities programs, and in the Welfare Rights movement. These unconventional practice experiences led to a renewal of a radical critique of capitalist society and culture . . . The critique stimulated the founding of local networks of radical human service workers and of a socialist journal, *Catalyst*, which, was published by a social workers' collective for about ten years before being reorganized in 1998, as *The Journal of Progressive Human Services*. (p. 84)

In the past three decades, even as a mix of corporate and socially conservative ideologies has swayed the country and the privatization of social work services has grown (Specht & Courtney, 2000; Wakefield, 1988), concerns about equality and justice have continued to fuel the development of structural, radical, empowerment, and anti-oppressive models of social work (e.g., Bailey & Brake, 1976; Finn & Jacobson, 2003; Gil, 1998; Gutierrez, Parsons, & Cox, 1998; Lundy, 2004; Mullaly, 2002). Although there are theoretical and practical differences between these models, they all highlight the debilitating role played in the mental health of our citizens by power imbalances built into the structure of our society and the importance of unmet material needs for psychological well being; they call for social workers to assist their clients in understanding the nature of these imbalances, developing skills to deal with oppressive social realities, redressing the negative impact of these dynamics in their personal and interpersonal lives, and promoting the development of strategies that link individual and social change. Chapters by Almeida et al., Kamya, Ackerson and Korr, and Reeser in this volume build on this reformist tradition in social work and expand on its implications for family therapy, narrative therapy, policy development, and training.

Psychoanalysis

Although many students and young clinicians today associate psychoanalytic theory and practice with the promotion of an ideology seemingly irrelevant to social justice concerns and aspirations, the development of psychoanalysis in Europe prior to World War II, psychoanalytic critiques of society in the United States in the aftermath of the war, and more recent social critiques of psychoanalytic practices[3] provide testimony to a reformist spirit present throughout the history of the psychoanalytic movement.

The development of psychoanalysis in the years between World War I and World War II was characterized by strong links to political activism on behalf of the poor. "Freud always believed that psychoanalysis would release the reasoning abilities in oppressed individuals and that personal insight (combined with critical thinking) naturally led to psychological independence" (Danto, 2005, p. 302). For that to happen, Freud said in 1918, "treatment shall be free. The poor man should have just as much right to assistance for his mind as he now has to the life-saving help offered by surgery" (as cited by Danto, pp. 2–3). During the 1920s and 1930s socially minded psychoanalysts created free clinics where experienced analysts and students donated their time to serve people who could not afford psychoanalysis. According to Danto (2005), "[a]t least one fifth of the work of the first and second generation of psychoanalysts went to indigent urban residents" (p. 2).

---

[3]See Jacoby (1975), Kovel (1980, 1988), and Wachtel (1999, 2002).

   In the aftermath of the war, many psychoanalysts in Europe immigrated to the United States where the practice of psychoanalysis was controlled and regulated by the medical profession and the government was actively discouraging reformist attitudes and practices. In spite of these obstacles, during the 1950s and 1960s analysts such as Fromm (1955), H. S. Sullivan (1953), Fenichel (1967), and Reich (1946) wrote about the restrictions placed by socioeconomic structures on the psychological development of its citizens, promoted forms of social psychoanalysis (Jacoby, 1983), and advocated for the use of psychoanalysis as a tool for social reform (Lasch, 1984).

   In recent decades, even as the influence of psychoanalytic theory and practice has greatly diminished, periodic calls have been made for the integration of individual and social levels of analysis and interventions in psychoanalytic practice. From Kovel's (1981) "transcendent praxis," to Frosh's (1987) interpretation of the politics of psychoanalysis, to Wachtel's (1997) "cyclical psychodynamics" runs a commitment to account for the multiple ways in which material and social realities of inequality become internalized as unconscious beliefs, aspirations, and scripts that dominate individual life and become important sources of everyday unhappiness. For these analysts and a new wave of clinicians exploring the roles psychoanalysis might play in bringing about social justice (e.g., Dimen, 2004; Javier & Moskowitz, 2002; Richards, 2004), uncovering and challenging these limiting social scripts is seen as both personally liberating and the foundation for a broader transformation of social relations. Clinical applications of some these insights are illustrated in the works by Comas-Diaz, Roy, and Green in this volume.

Counseling Professions

   The counseling profession[4] is anchored in a foundation of lifespan development, strength-oriented, and multicultural models of human behavior, which has made responding to oppressive, toxic, and dehumanizing social conditions a recurrent, if underdeveloped, part of its history. Through its evolution in the areas of vocational, school, and mental health counseling, the counseling profession has demonstrated concern for the needs of marginalized and underserved populations and a strong disposition to assist and advocate on their behalf.

   Social justice commitments were evident in the seminal contributions of Frank Parsons (Parsons, 1909). In the early 20th century, when social tensions brought forth by industrialization and immigration "and injustices rampant through abuse by those with growing wealth and power called out for reform. . . Parsons became a reformer with a mission" (Sweeney, 2001, p. 8). Concerned by the lack of resources and opportunities afforded to impoverished youth in Boston, Parsons helped found vocational guidance and advocacy organizations such as the Boston's Vocational Bureau and the Breadwinners Institute. Not only did Parsons pioneer efforts to advocate for the poor and the working class (Hartug & Blustein, 2002), but his model of vocational counseling also"became the foundation on which modern career counseling is based" (Kiselica & Robison, 2001, p. 390).

   In spite of the enormous influence Parson's work would go on to have in the counseling profession, his concerns about social inequality and his inclination for

---

[4]The counseling profession includes closely related disciplines such as counselor education, mental health counseling, and counseling psychology.

social action were met with ambivalence by a young profession mired with issues of identity and economic viability. This ambivalence notwithstanding, social justice commitments were evident in individual efforts of advocacy counseling on behalf of socially disadvantaged groups such as the poor, war veterans, women, individuals with disabilities, the elderly, and racial and ethnic minorities (Fouad, Gerstein, & Toporek, 2005).

During the 1960s, heightened awareness about social injustices brought about by the civil rights and anti-war movements, together with the Community Mental Health Act of 1963 and the Economic Opportunity Act of 1964, helped direct the attention of the field to the disadvantaged and the poor. This led to the emergence of a social critique of the field and calls for the inclusion of social action as an important dimension of counseling (e.g., Banks & Martens, 1973, Lewis, Lewis, & Dworkin, 1971; Tucker, 1973; Warnath, 1973).

During the 1980s and early 1990s the reformist spirit of the counseling profession was displaced by a strong push to medicalize and privatize counseling services. However, even as these conservative forces were operating, many counseling psychologists in academia made multicultural, gender, and other social issues the focus of their work and, in doing so, helped create conditions for rapprochement with activist counseling psychologists who had continued to work at the margins of the profession.

Over the past 10 years, the shared social justice aspirations and commitments of research and activist counseling psychologists have received greater attention by the field and are quickly becoming a vital part of the field's identity. The strength of the social justice reformist spirit in counseling is now evident in the focus of national conferences (e.g., 2001 National Counseling Psychology Conference, annual counseling and social justice conferences being held at the University of Wisconsin-Madison and at George Mason University), the structure of professional organizations (e.g., the new Counselors for Social Justice division of the American Counseling Association), and in the professional literature (e.g., Blustein, McWhirter, & Perry, 2005; Goodman et al., 2004; Lee & Walz, 1998; Toporek, Gerstein, Fouad, Roysircar, & Israel, 2005; Utsey, Bolden, & Brown, 2001; Vera & Speight, 2003). Social justice counseling perspectives on work, school, community life, and graduate training are found in chapters led by Blustein, Kenny, Goodman, Vera, McWhirter, and Arredondo in this volume.

Psychiatry

Psychiatry in contemporary American society is popularly viewed as the diagnosis and medical treatment of biologically determined mental illnesses. However, this characterization obscures the fact that, through much of its history, psychiatrists have held very different opinions about the potential causes and appropriate solutions to mental health problems. Moreover, many psychiatrists have highlighted the importance of toxic social conditions in mental health and argued for the prevention and transformation of these conditions.

The mental hygiene movement of the 1910s and 1920s served as foundation for the evolution of modern psychiatry in the United States. Increased awareness about the poor treatment and conditions at insane asylum facilities, generated by Clifford Beers' (1980) autobiographical account and the advocacy efforts of the organization he helped start, The National Committee for Mental Hygiene, helped usher American psychiatry out of the asylums and into an era of more humane treatment and care of patients in mental hospitals. During this time "American psychiatrists had more or less adopted Adolf Meyer's biopsychosocial perspective, which defined mental health and mental health disorder in social and behavioral terms as adjustment to society" (Pols, 2001, p. 385). Without denying the potential importance of biological determinants of health, mental hygienists believed it necessary to take a proactive approach in promoting mental health outside of mental hospitals. They promoted prevention initiatives for people at risk of developing mental health illness.

Historian Hans Pols (2001) points out that the commitment and resolve of this group of psychiatrist grew stronger in the 1930s when,

> [t]hey were alarmed at the enormous increase in suicide, crime, debilitating unhappiness, insecurity, anxiety, and interpersonal conflict during the Depression. Accordingly mental hygienists redoubled their efforts to stem the tide of mental illness. They designed programs of community mental hygiene that aimed to enhance the mental health of the population as a whole . . ." (p. 375)

Some leading mental hygiene psychiatrists of the time openly advocated for social reform measures that would go beyond individualized therapy approaches and would include collaboration with business, education, and religious institutions (e.g., Hincks, 1935). Moreover, other psychiatrists such as former medical director of NCMH Frankwood E. Williams (1930, 1932) became more interested in the relationship between the economy and mental health problems and argued that the latter reflected toxic dynamics in the former. Accordingly, this group considered their professional responsibility to advocate for the transformation of capitalist values and practices to promote mental health (Pols, 2001).

Following the Depression, American psychiatrists became increasingly focused on strengthening their ties to the medical profession. Licenses, certifications, funding requirements, and the introduction of psychotropic medications further promoted a biological conception of mental illness and the need for medical treatment (Kovel, 1980; Pols, 2001). Within this context, the circulation of reformist ideas was limited and carried out primarily by psychoanalysts, as described earlier in this chapter.

The Second World War brought forth renewed awareness within psychiatry of the relationship between mental health and the quality of living conditions, leading them to expand the reach of psychiatry into the management of peoples' distress with ordinary social life. By the 1960s, however, the inability of traditional medical psychiatry to abate increased citizens' demand for services, combined with a paucity of reliable and valid medical knowledge to guide psychiatric treatment and the financial backing of the government, turned psychiatrists' attention to the design of community mental health centers and outpatient programs to deal with mental health problems.

The 1960s also witnessed the emergence of various "anti-psychiatry" critics to the medical model of psychiatric care. The anti-psychiatrists included an ideologically diverse group of writers such as Thomas Szasz and R. D. Laing, who among other things, questioned the existence of mental illness, considered illegitimate the dominant psychiatric treatments of the day (e.g., drugs, electroconvulsive therapy), argued that traditional psychiatric care subverted people's autonomy, and challenged the authority of psychiatrists as purveyors of the mental health needs of the nation (Miller, 1986; Segwick, 1982). Unfortunately, as Ingleby (2006) points out, the one-sided and indiscriminate anti-psychiatry critique was misused by policymakers wanting to reduce government support for psychiatric services and easily dismissed by the psychiatric establishment.

In the second half of the 1960s, a more complex social critique and treatment alternative was presented by a "radical psychiatry" group concerned with the overly narrow biological focus of psychiatry and its failure to take into account the interrelationship of harmful social conditions and internalized oppression (Steiner, 1975). Since then, radical psychiatry has quietly evolved into a sophisticated social justice-oriented framework for clinical practice (Roy & Steiner, 1988; see also Roy's chapter in this volume).

Technological advancements in neuroscience, massive investments in research and public relations by the pharmaceutical industry, and the streamlining of mental health services for financial motivations, paved the way for the dramatic dominance of the biological approach to psychiatry witnessed since the 1980s. Yet, the limited utility of classical psychiatric care to respond to the multidimensional nature of mental health problems has served as impetus for a growing number of practicing psychiatrists to generate alternative ways to conceptualize and deliver psychiatric services. Chief among these are proponents of "critical psychiatry" (e.g., Double, 2006; Ingleby, 2004) who argue for greater appreciation of the relationship between mental health problems and sociocultural realities, "more attention to the different ways in which service users understand their experiences", and social action to both limit the control of psychiatry by the pharmaceutical industry and allied corporations (Thomas & Bracken, 2004, p. 368) and reduce the misuses of power caused by casting social, moral, and political problems as medical problems (Ingleby, 2006). Chapters by Pakman and Rojano in this volume describe two approaches to psychiatric care consistent with this emerging trend.

Family Therapy

When family therapy began to take its place as a legitimate branch within the mental health field in the late 1950s and early 1960s it carried with it the social justice reformist spirit of social workers, psychiatrists, and psychologists interested in developing mental health theories and practices relevant to the needs of ordinary individuals and families. Consistent with the sociopolitical developments of the time, many of these clinicians favored an anthropological stance to mental health and an appreciation for social issues such as subjugation, prejudice, and poverty (Green, 1998; Minuchin, Montalvo, Guerney, Rosman, & Shumer, 1967). However, in search for a distinct professional identity, family therapists quickly shifted their focus from concerns about the social basis for health and mental health problems to interpersonal dynamics within the family.

By the late 1970s the field of family therapy was easily recognized for its innovative interpersonal approaches to therapy. Although many of these approaches promoted a systemic view of mental health problems, they tended to ignore the social environments within which families developed. During this time, feminist family therapists began to challenge the field for failing to consider the lived experiences of women and children raised in contexts characterized by power imbalances and social inequality (e.g., Hare-Mustin, 1978). In the ensuing decade, feminist scholars made numerous proposals to address sexist biases in family therapy theories and increase their relevance for the promotion of a more equitable and just society (e.g., Bograd, 1984; Goldner, 1985, 1987; Luepnitz, 1988; Walters, 1985; Wheeler, Avis, Miller, & Chaney, 1985). Moreover, they asked family therapists to evaluate the structure of our society, the ways in which they support the status quo, and their responsibility to help transform these structures.

The 1980s also gave rise to multicultural perspectives in family therapy attentive to the needs of multiproblem, poor, minority families (e.g., Boyd-Franklin, 1989; Falicov, 1983; McGoldrick, 1998; McGoldrick, Pearce, & Giordano, 1982). Since then, these perspectives have evolved into an "expanded" cultural framework and social analysis of family life,[5] which openly addresses what McGoldrick (1998) refers to as "the unspoken secrets that have structured the culture-, race-, class-, and gender-biased hierarchies that are the underpinnings of our society" (pp. 4–5). During this time narrative approaches to family therapy have become increasingly popular among social justice-oriented family therapists (e.g., Waldegrave, 1990; White & Epston, 1990). Chapters by Almeida and her colleagues, Green, and Kamya in this volume present some of the most sophisticated thinking to date emerging from this tradition.

Finally, over the past several years as a growing number of family therapists strive to generate theories and practices more relevant to needs of our society, a family-centered community perspective has begun to emerge, in which family therapists are engaged in the work of building community and creating social change (e.g., Boyd-Franklyn & Bry, 2000; Doherty & Beaton, 2000). The works of Doherty and Carroll and Rojano in this volume present cutting-edge work in this area.

TOWARD AN OPEN CONSPIRACY FOR SOCIAL JUSTICE

As this survey of social justice legacies in the mental health professions illustrates, the recognition that social realities are important determinants of distress that must be addressed as part of our efforts to promote the wellness of those we serve, have been present since the early days of our professions. Social justice concerns and the will to act on behalf of those at the bottom of the social hierarchy were shared by many of the founding figures of our field. However, as each discipline grew and developed as a profession, social justice ideals and their auspicious reformist potential were restricted by the needs of the professions (i.e., profit, authority, prestige, etc.).

One unfortunate consequence of this process has been the failure to integrate social justice-oriented theories and practices into our training programs and clinical work. This lack of knowledge places unnecessary limitations on the ability of mental health professionals to promote the well-being of those we serve. Without a clear appreciation of the social justice dimensions of our work, it is relatively easy to confuse harmful effects of social conditions with psychological and interpersonal deficits or to focus on interpersonal and intrafamilial dynamics without understanding how these dynamics reflect the influence of social factors.

Failure to integrate social justice values and practices into our training programs has other adverse consequences for mental health professionals—it favors a context

[5]See Aponte (1994), Inclan (2003), and Minuchin, Minuchin, Colapinto, and Greenan (2006).

in which it seems natural to separate our commitments and obligations as professionals from our commitments and obligations as citizens and to subordinate the latter to the former. Not surprisingly, we have grown accustomed to keeping our social commitments optional and our clinical work safely neutral. We comfortably assume that what is good for our professions must also be good for society and inconspicuously confuse the expansion of markets for our interventions with the search for legitimate solutions to people's distress. This separation of responsibilities does not invite accountability to our fellow citizens for the choices we make on their behalf such as excessively relying on a medical model of mental health practice of questionable scientific and clinical validity (see Albee, 1998; Kutchins & Kirk, 1997; Rogers & Pilgrim, 2003). This state of affairs also increases the chances that our efforts, albeit well intentioned, may end up legitimizing ways of thinking and forms of practice supportive of a *status quo* which is disproportionately harmful to the less privileged members of our communities (Prilleltensky, 1994; Wilkinson, 2005).

The trouble is, in part, that professional mental health organizations and graduate training programs recognizing both individual and social influences in psychopathology and mental health have made a compromise. To deny the importance of inequitable social realities in mental health leaves them vulnerable to accusations of racial, gender, and social class insensitivity. On the other hand, to highlight the effects of harmful social realities and dynamics threatens to undermine the claim of mental health practice as a legitimate form of medical care upon which our current system for the compensation of services is based. Thus, rather than risking to prepare clinicians to understand and transform social inequities inimical to wellness and mental health, our professional organizations and training programs choose to subordinate the effects of social realities to individual biology and psychology. Within this context, it is easy to understand why even socially minded clinicians are often unfamiliar with social justice models and practices that have emerged in the shadows of their dominant medical model-inspired counterparts.

This situation reminds us again of the strong hold that the market economy has on mental health practice. However, to paraphrase Kovel's (1980, p. 101) words, it is pointless to wring one's hands about the sad state of today's training and practice without taking account of the opportunity for change that this represents. The medicalization and privatization of mental health services have shown to be insufficient to improve the quality of life and mental health of significant portions of our population. This, in turn, has helped create new pockets of resistance across the mental health professions. As the boundaries of our professions get reconfigured and the distinction between public and private practice fades away, a growing number of clinicians and human service providers are figuring out new ways to realize the aspirations of earlier generations of social justice-oriented clinicians.

The emerging perspectives, many of which are showcased in this volume, are profoundly feminist, multicultural, systemic, and spiritual, yet they are fueled more by a vision of an equitable and just society than by theoretical commitments. These perspectives are inviting clinicians to openly address the inequities at the core of our society. They invite us to refine our roles as human services providers to be more in line with the social realities in the lives of those we serve. They urge us to make our work relevant to their lived experiences. They invite us to deliberately redress the balance between professing our craft as clinicians and professing our humanity as citizens. They stress the urgency and responsibility of mental health professionals to humanize institutions and bureaucratic structures that oppress people. Moreover, going back to Beckett's play, these social justice perspectives would not only embolden and guide Vladimir to act but would help him realize, as Pogo did long ago that, "we have found the enemy and the enemy is us."

REFERENCES

Albee, G. W. (1998). Fifty years of clinical psychology: Selling our soul to the devil. *Applied and Preventive Psychology, 7,* 189–194.

Albee, G. W. (2000). Critique of psychotherapy in American society. In C. R. Snyder & R. E. Ingram (Eds.), *Handbook of psychological change: Psychotherapy processes & practices for the 21st century* (pp. 689–706). New York: Wiley.

Aponte, H. J. (1994). *Bread & Spirit: Therapy with the new poor.* New York: Norton.

Bailey, R., & Brake, M. (1976). *Radical social work.* New York: Pantheon.

Banks, W., & Martens, K. (1973). Counseling: The reactionary profession. *Personnel and Guidance Journal, 51,* 457–462.

Beers, C. W. (1980). *A mind that found itself: An autobiography.* Pittsburgh: University of Pittsburgh Press. (Original work published 1908)

Blustein, D. L., McWhirter, E. H., & Perry, J. C. (2005). An emancipatory communitarian approach to vocational development theory, research, and practice. *The Counseling Psychologist, 33,* 141–179.

Bograd, M. (1984). Family systems approaches to wife battering: A feminist critique. *American Journal of Orthopsychiatry, 54,* 558–568.

Boyd-Franklin, N. (1989). *Black families in therapy: A multisystems approach.* New York: Guilford Press.

Boyd-Franklyn, N., & Bry, B. H. (2000). *Reaching out in family therapy: Home-based, school, and community interventions.* New York: Guilford Press.

Brown, L. S. (1993). Anti-domination training as a central component of diversity in clinical psychology education. *The Clinical Psychologist, 46,* 83–87.

Brown, L. S. (1994). *Subversive dialogues: Theory in feminist therapy.* New York: Basic Books.

Cushman, P. (1992). Psychotherapy to 1992: A historically situated interpretation In D. K. Freedheim (Ed.), *History of psychotherapy: A century of change* (pp. 21–64). Washington, DC: American Psychological Association.

Danto, E. A. (2005). *Freud's free clinics: Psychoanalysis and social justice, 1918–1938.* New York: Columbia University Press.

Dimen, M. (2004). Between mind and matter: In search of the Marx/Freud Synthesis. *Psychoanalysis, Culture, & Society, 9,* 52–62.

Doherty, W. J. (1995). *Soul searching: Why psychotherapy must promote moral responsibility.* New York: Basic Books.

Doherty, W., & Beaton, J. M. (2000). Family therapists, community, and civic renewal. *Family Process, 39,* 149–161.

Double D. B. (Ed). (2006). *Critical psychiatry: The limits of madness.* New York: Palgrave Macmillan.

Enns, C. Z. (2004). *Feminist theories and feminist psychotherapies: Origins, themes, and diversity* (2nd ed.). New York: The Haworth Press.

Falicov, C. (1983). *Cultural perspectives in family therapy.* Rockville, MD: Aspen Systems.

Fenichel, O. (1967). Psychoanalysis as the nucleus of a future dialectical-materialistic psychology. *American Imago, 24,* 290–311.

Finn, J. L., & Jacobson, M. (2003). *Just Practice: A social justice approach to social work.* Peosta, IA: Eddie Bowers Publishing Co.

Fisher, J. (1936). *The rank and file movement in social work: 1931–1936.* New York: New York School of Social Work.

Fisher, J. (1980). *The response of social work to the Depression.* Cambridge, MA: Schenkman.

Fouad, N. A., Gerstein, L. H., & Toporek, R. L. (2005). Social justice and counseling psychology in context. In R. L., Toporek, L. Gerstein, G. Roysircar, N. Fouad, & T. Israel (Eds.), *Handbook for social justice in counseling psychology* (pp. 1–27). Thousand Oaks, CA: Sage.

Fouad, N. A., McPherson, R. H., Gerstein, L. H., Blustein, D. L., Elman, N., Helledy, K. I., et al. (2004). Houston 2001: Context and legacy. *The Counseling Psychologist, 32,* 15–77.

Frattaroli, E. (2001). *Healing the soul in the age of the brain: Becoming conscious in an unconscious world.* New York: Viking Press.

Fried, A. (1997). *McCarthyism: A documentary history*. New York: Oxford University Press.

Fromm, E. (1955). *The sane society*. New York: Holt, Rinehart, & Winston.

Frosh, S. (1987). *The politics of psychoanalysis*. New Haven, CT: Yale University Press.

Gil, D. G. (1998). *Confronting injustice and oppression*. New York: Columbia University Press.

Goldner, V. (1985). Feminism and family therapy. *Family Process, 24,* 31–47.

Goldner, V. (1987). Instrumentalism, feminism, and the limits of family therapy. *Journal of Family Psychology, 1,* 109–116.

Goodman, L., Liang, B., Helms, J. E., Latta, R. E., Sparks, E., & Weintraub, S. R. (2004). Training counseling psychologists as social justice agents: Feminist and multicultural principles in action. *The Counseling Psychologist, 32,* 793–837.

Green, R. J. (1998). Race and the field of family therapy. In M. McGoldrick (Ed.), *Re-visioning family therapy* (pp. 93–110). New York: Guilford..

Gutierrez, L. M., Parsons, R. J., & Cox, E. O. (1998). *Empowerment in social work practice: A sourcebook*. Pacific Grove, CA: Brooks/Cole.

Hare-Mustin, R. (1978). A feminist approach to family therapy. *Family Process, 17,* 181–194.

Hartug, P. J., & Blustein, D. L. (2002). Reason, intuition, and social justice: Elaborating on Parsons' career decision-making model. *Journal of Counseling and Development, 80,* 41–47.

Hillman, J., & Ventura, M. (1992). *We have had a hundred years of psychotherapy—and the world's getting worse*. San Francisco: Harper.

Hincks, J. E. (1935). The next quarter century. *Mental Hygiene, 19,* 69–77.

Hofrichter, R. (Ed.). (2003). *Health and social justice: Politics, ideology, and inequity in the distribution of disease*. San Francisco: Jossey-Bass.

Inclan, J. (2003). Class, culture, and gender in immigrant families. In L. B. Silverstein & T. H. Goodrich (Eds.), *Feminist family therapy: Empowerment in social context*. Washington, DC: American Psychological Association.

Ingleby, D. (Ed.). (2004) *Critical psychiatry: the politics of mental health* (3rd ed.). London: Free Association Books.

Ingleby, D. (2006). Transcultural mental health care: The challenge to positivist psychiatry. In D. B. Double (Ed.), *Critical psychiatry: The limits of madness*. New York: Palgrave Macmillan.

Jacoby, R. (1975). *Social amnesia: A critique of contemporary psychology from Adler to Laing*. Boston: Beacon Press.

Jacoby, R. (1983). *The repression of psychoanalysis*. New York: Basic Books.

Javier, A. R., & Moskowitz, M. (2002). Introduction: Notes from the trenches. *Psychoanalytic Psychology, 19,* 144–148.

Kiselica, M. S., & Robison, M. (2001). Bringing advocacy counseling to life: The history , issues, and human dramas of social justice work in counseling. *Journal of Counseling and Development, 79,* 387–397.

Knowlson, J. (1993). *The theatrical notebooks of Samuel Beckett, Volume I: Waiting for Godot*. New York: Grove Press.

Kovel, J. (1980). The American mental health industry. In D. Ingleby (Ed.), *Critical psychiatry: The politics of mental health* (pp. 72–101). New York: Pantheon.

Kovel, J. (1981). *The age of desire: Case stories of a radical psychoanalyst*. New York: Pantheon.

Kovel, J. (1988). *The radical spirit: Essays on psychoanalysis and society*. London: Free Association Books.

Kutchins, H., & Kirk, S.A. (1997). *Making us crazy, DSM: The psychiatric bible and the creation of mental disorders*. New York: The Free Press.

Lasch, C. (1984). *The minimal self*. New York: Norton.

LaVeist, T. A. (2005). *Minority populations and health: An introduction to health disparities in the United States*. San Francisco: Jossey-Bass.

Lee. C. C., & Walz, G. R. (1998). *Social action: A mandate for counselors*. Alexandria, VA: American Counseling Association.

Lewis, M. D., Lewis, J. A., & Dworkin, E. P. (1971). *Counseling and the social revolution. Personnel and Guidance Journal* (special issue), *49*(9).

Luepnitz, D. A. (1988). *The family interpreted: Feminist theory in clinical practice*. New York: Basic Books.

Lundy, C. (2004). *Social work and social justice*. Peterborough, Ontario: Broadview Press.

McGoldrick, M. (1998). Re-visioning family therapy through a cultural lens. In M. McGoldrick (Ed.), *Revisioning family therapy: Race, culture, and gender in clinical practice* (pp. 3–19). New York; Guilford Press.

McGoldrick, M., Pearce, J., & Giordano, J. (1982). *Ethnicity and family therapy*. New York: Guilford Press.

Miller, P. (1986). Critiques of psychiatry and critical sociologies of madness. In P. Miller & N. Rose (Eds.), *The power of psychiatry* (pp. 12–42). Cambridge, MA: Polity Press.

Miller, R. B. (2004). *Facing human suffering: Psychology and psychotherapy as moral engagement*. Washington, DC: American Psychological Association.

Minuchin, S., Minuchin, P., Colapinto, J., & Greenan, D. E. (2006). *Working with families of the poor*. New York: Guilford Press.

Minuchin, S., Montalvo, B., Guerney, B. G., Jr., Rosman, B. L., & Schumer, F. (1967). *Families of the slums: An exploration of their structure and treatment*. New York: Basic Books.

Mullaly, B. (2002). *Challenging oppression: A critical social work approach*. Ontario: Oxford University Press.

Nelson, G., & Prilleltensky, I. (2005). *Community psychology: In pursuit of liberation and well-being*. New York: Palgrave Macmillan.

Parsons, F. (1909). *Choosing a vocation*. Boston: Houghton-Mifflin.

Pols, H. (2001). Divergences in American psychiatry during the Depression: Somatic psychiatry, community mental hygiene, and social reconstruction. *Journal of the History of the Behavioral Sciences, 37,* 369–388.

Prilleltensky, I. (1994). *The morals and politics of psychology*. Albany, NY: SUNY Press.

Prilleltensky, I., & Nelson, G. (1997). Community psychology: Reclaiming social justice. In D. Fox & I. Prilleltensky (Eds.), *Critical psychology* (pp. 166–184). Thousand Oaks, CA: Sage.

Rappaport, J. (1981). In praise of paradox: A social policy of empowerment over prevention. *American Journal of Community Psychology, 9,* 1–25.

Reich, W. (1946). *The mass psychology of fascism*. Harmondsworth, England: Penguin.

Reisch, M., & Andrews, J. (2002). *The road not taken: A history of radical social work in the United States*. New York: Brunner-Routledge.

Richards, B. (2004). What is psychoanalysis for? *Psychoanalysis, Culture, & Society, 9,* 149–158.

Richardson, F. C., Fowers, B. J., & Guignon, C. B. (1999). *Re-envisioning psychology: Moral dimensions of theory and practice*. San Francisco: Jossey-Bass.

Rogers, A., & Pilgrim, D. (2003). *Mental health and inequality*. New York: Palgrave Macmillan.

Roy, B., & Steiner, C. (Eds.). (1988). *Radical psychiatry: The second decade*. San Francisco: Bay Area Radical Therapy Collective.

Segwick, P. (1982). *Psycho politics: Laing, Foucalt, Goffman, Szasz and the future of mass psychiatry*. New York: Harper & Row.

Shklar, J. N. (1990). *The faces of injustice*. New Haven, CT: Yale University Press.

Specht, H., & Courtney, M. E. (2000). *Unfaithful angels: How social work has abandoned its mission*. New York: The Free Press.

Steiner, C. (1975). *Readings in radical psychiatry*. New York: Grove Press.

Sullivan, H. S. (1953). *The interpersonal theory of psychiatry*. New York: Norton.

Sweeney, T. J. (2001). Counseling: Historical origins and philosophical roots. In D. C. Locke, J. E. Myers, & E. L. Herr (Eds.), *The handbook of counseling* (pp. 3–26). Thousand Oaks, CA: Sage.

Thomas, P., & Bracken, P. (2004). Critical psychiatry in practice. *Advances in Psychiatric Treatment, 10,* 361–370.

Toporek, R. L., Gerstein, L. H., Fouad, N. A., Roysircar, G., & Israel, T. (2005). *Handbook for social justice in counseling psychology*. Thousand Oaks, CA: Sage.

Tucker, S. J. (1973). Action counseling: An accountability procedure for counseling the oppressed. *Journal of Non-White Concerns in Personnel Guidance, 2,* 35–42.

U.S. Department of Health and Human Services (2001). *Mental health: Culture, race, and ethnicity—A supplement to mental health: A report of the Surgeon General*. Rockville, MD: U.S. Department of Health and Human Services, Substance Abuse and Mental Health Services Administration, Center for Mental Health Services.

Utsey, S. O., Bolden, M. A., & Brown, A. L. (2001). Visions of revolution from the spirit of Frantz Fanon. In J. G. Ponterotto, J. M. Casas, L. A. Suzuki, & C. M. Alexander (Eds.), *Handbook of multicultural counseling* (pp. 311–336). Thousand Oaks, CA: Sage.

VandenBos, G. R., Cummings, N. A., & DeLeon, P. H. (1992). A century of psychotherapy: Economic and environmental influences In D. K. Freedheim (Ed.), *History of psychotherapy: A century of change* (pp. 65–102). Washington, DC: American Psychological Association.

Vera, E. M., & Speight, S. L. (2003). Multicultural competence, social justice, and counseling psychology: Expanding our roles. *The Counseling Psychologist, 31,* 253–272.

Wachtel, P. L. (1997). *Psychoanalysis, behavior therapy, and the relational world*. Washington, DC: American Psychological Association.

Wachtel, P. L. (1999). *Race in the mind of America*. New York: Routledge.

Wachtel, P. L. (2002). Psychoanalysis and the disenfranchised: From therapy to justice. *Psychoanalytic Psychology, 19,* 199–215.

Wakefield, J. (1988). Psychotherapy, distributive justice, and social work: Part II—Psychotherapy and the pursuit of justice. *Social Service Review, 62,* 353–382.

Waldergrave, C. (1990). Just therapy. *Dulwich Centre Newsletter, 1,* pp. 5–46.

Walters, M. (1985). Where have all the flowers gone: Family therapy in the age of the Yuppie. *The Family Therapy Networker, 9,* 38–41.

Warnath, C. F. (1973). The school counselor as institutional agent. *The School Counselor, 20,* 202–208.

Wheeler, D., Avis, J., Miller, L. A., & Chaney, S. (1985). Rethinking family therapy education and supervision: A feminist model. *Journal of Psychotherapy and the Family, 1,* 53–71.

White, M., & Epston, D. (1990). *Narrative means to therapeutic aims.* New York: Norton and Norton.

Wilkinson, R. G. (2005). *The impact of inequality: How to make sicker societies healthier.* New York: The New Press.

Williams, F. E. (1930). *Some social aspects of mental hygiene.* Philadelphia: American Academy of Political and Social Science.

Williams, F. E. (1932). Out from confusion. *Survey, 68,* 225–227, 244, 248, 253.

2

Counseling for Wellness and Justice: Foundations and Ethical Dilemmas

Isaac Prilleltensky
University of Miami

Paul Dokecki
Gina Frieden
Vanderbilt University

Vivian Ota Wang
National Institute of Health

Wellness is a positive state of being, brought about by the simultaneous, balanced, and synergistic satisfaction of personal, relational, and collective needs. For wellness to take place in each one of these domains, and for it to flourish at the intersection of them all, justice ought to be present in each and every one of them. Wellness cannot flourish in the absence of justice, and justice is devoid of meaning in the absence of wellness. We demonstrate in this chapter the strength of the wellness–justice nexus, and we offer recommendations for aligning counseling practices with the need to promote wellness and justice at the same time.

The first part of this chapter elucidates the connections between wellness and justice at the personal, relational, and collective levels of analysis. In light of that background, the second part distills ethical dilemmas associated with prevailing counseling practices. We explore how dominant modes of practice contend with the need to advance wellness and justice at the personal, relational, and collective levels at the same time. Each practice is subjected to scrutiny for its success or failure in promoting wellness and justice.

Following a critique of existing forms of counseling, the third part of this chapter outlines innovative practices that may fulfill the requirement for promoting wellness and justice, at the same time, at all the levels. This is a high calling and not without obstacles or dilemmas. Hence, we subject our own recommendations to close scrutiny as well. We debate each recommendation and offer potential solutions to the various dilemmas we encounter along the way.

In recent years, an increasing number of mental health professionals and scholars have presented convincing arguments in favor of a value-based approach to

*This chapter was co-written while Dr. Ota Wang held a faculty position at Vanderbilt University. The views expressed are those of Vivian Ota Wang. No official endorsement by the NIH or the Department of Health and Human Services is intended or should be inferred.

counseling. This perspective asserts that, as counselors, we bring a set of values to work, that if we don't challenge the societal status quo, we tacitly support it, and if we concentrate exclusively on intrapsychic dynamics, we run the risk of neglecting the social origins of suffering and distress. A great deal of scholarship has demonstrated that professionals cannot neutralize their personal values, that passivity in light of injustice amounts to complicity, and that the value of individualism reigns supreme in society and the mental health professions (Dokecki, 1996; Prilleltensky, 1994, 1997; Prilleltensky & Nelson, 2002; Ota Wang, 2004).

In this chapter, we go beyond well-established critiques of dominant mental health practices: We strive to tackle the ethical dilemmas that stem from knowing that (a) we are value-laden professionals, (b) we wish to challenge the societal status quo, and (c) unless we address the societal sphere our efforts will be forever undermined by larger forces. But after a momentary celebration of our newly gained insights, a whole new set of questions and dilemmas arise: What right do we have as counselors to suggest to our clients to join a social cause? What responsibility do we have as professionals to address social causes of oppression when our training is primarily in helping individuals? What are the limits of our expertise when we try to work at the personal, relational, and collective levels at the same time? These questions have rarely been asked. By framing wellness in light of justice and by linking personal satisfaction to relational and collective concerns, we open a whole new field of ethical inquiry. All of a sudden, it is no longer the sanctity of the relationship between counselor and client that is the sole refractor of ethical concerns, but the very context within which that relationship is situated.

Our hope is that this chapter challenges not only counselors who may need their consciousness raised, but also challenges those of us who already understand the connection between wellness and justice. With every new realization, there is a new ethical dilemma with which to contend. We want to be explicit about the new dilemmas that arise from linking wellness with justice and from linking the personal with the relational and the collective.

FOUNDATIONS

Webs of Personal, Relational, and Collective Wellness

Individuals experience wellness when three primary sets of needs are fulfilled: personal, relational, and collective (Prilleltensky, Nelson, & Peirson, 2001a, 2001b; Schneider Jamner & Stokols, 2000). Research demonstrates that needs for hope, optimism (Seligman, 2002), intellectual stimulation, cognitive growth (Shonkhoff & Phillips, 2000), mastery, control (Marmot, 1999; Rutter, 1987), physical health (Smedley & Syme, 2000), mental well-being (Nelson, Lord, & Ochocka, 2001; Nelson & Prilleltensky, 2005), meaning, and spirituality (Kloos & Moore, 2001; Powell, Shahabi, & Thoresen, 2003) are vital for the experience of personal wellness. But these needs cannot be met in isolation. Many of them, like hope, optimism, meaning, and mental health, require the presence of supportive relationships.

Relational wellness is characterized by affection, caring, compassion, bonding, support (Cohen, Underwood, & Gottlieb, 2000; Gottman & DeClaire, 2001; Ornish, 1997; Rhoades & Eisenberg, 2002; Stansfeld, 1999); respect for diversity (Dudgeon,

Garvey, & Pickett, 2000; Goodman, 2001; Trickett, Watts, & Birman, 1994); and meaningful participation in family, work, and civic life (Klein, Ralls, Smith-Major, & Douglas, 2000; Nelson, Lord, & Ochocka, 2001; Putnam, 2000, 2001).

Though essential, personal and relational needs are insufficient for the development of wellness. Without the satisfaction of collective needs, personal wellness can exist in limited form only. We require "well-enough" social and political conditions, free of economic exploitation and human rights abuses, to experience quality of life (Felice, 2003; George, 2002; Korten, 1995, 2000; Sen, 1999a, 1999b). Health, safety, self-determination, and opportunities for growth are predicated on adequate health care, access to safe drinking water, crime-free environments, just distribution of resources, and economic prosperity (Carr & Sloan, 2003; Frey & Stutzer, 2002; Keating & Hertzman, 1999; Kim, Millen, Irwin, & Gersham, 2000; Marmot & Wilkinson; 1999; Wilkinson, 1996).

Based on that evidence, wellness seems to travel through the links that connect the personal with the relational and the collective. Figure 2.1 positions wellness at the center of intersecting circles or nodes. If we pull out any one node, the web unravels. A strong personal node (e.g., self-esteem, mastery, control, hope) cannot stand in lieu of weak relational (e.g., caring and compassion, social support) or collective nodes (e.g., access to health care, safety nets, equality). The three nodes of wellness must be balanced in their relative strength. They support each other and rely on each other (Lustig, 2001; Nelson, Lord, & Ochocka, 2001). The ability of strong nodes to compensate for weak ones is limited and overrated. A case in point is the presumed ability of personal growth, skills, and resilience to outweigh adverse societal factors affecting health (Marmot & Wilkinson; 1999; Smedley & Syme, 2000; Wilkinson, 1996).

Diverse yet converging bodies of knowledge demonstrate the interlocking ties among personal, relational, and collective wellness. Putnam's research in the United States (2000, 2001) illustrates how participation in civic life benefits individuals beyond the actors involved. Compared to communities and states with low social capital or civic participation, communities where members volunteer more in churches,

FIG. 2.1. The synergy and balance of personal, relational, and collective needs in wellness.

hospitals, schools, and civic associations enjoy higher levels of relational wellness (e.g., bonding and bridging), and higher levels of collective wellness (e.g., better educational, health, and welfare outcomes). Social capital has even positive effects for diversity, measured in Putnam's research by tolerance of affirmative action policies. Similar collective effects were also found in Switzerland for political participation and economic prosperity (Frey & Stutzer, 2002).

Marmot's (1999; Marmot & Feeney, 1996) research offers yet another window into the web of wellness. Following thousands of British civil servants for more than 20 years, Marmot discovered that the people with less amount of personal control over their jobs—menial workers and unskilled labor—were dying at four times the rate of those with the most control: managers and executives. The group with the highest degree of autonomy (managers) had half the mortality rate of the second group (professionals), a third compared with the next group (assistants), and a fourth of the group with the least amount of autonomy (unskilled). Workplace relationships and class divisions interacted with personal control and flexibility to create differential rates of personal health and mortality.

TABLE 2.1
Relationship Between Wellness and Justice in Personal,
Relational, and Collective Domains

Wellness Is Enhanced by the Balanced Satisfaction of Needs	Justice Is Enhanced, and Contributes to Wellness, by the Power, Capacity, and Opportunity To:
Personal Needs	
• Control and self-determination	• Experience voice and choice throughout life
• Mastery, learning, and growth	• Experience stimulation and growth-enhancing events
• Hope and optimism	• Experience positive events in life and avoid learned helplessness
• Physical health	• Obtain food, shelter, safety, and health care
• Psychological health	• Engage in supportive, and avoid abusive, relationships and obtain wellness-enhancing resources
• Meaning and spirituality	• Explore the meaning of life and transcendence free of ideological repression
Relational Needs	
• Caring and compassion	• Experience nurturing relationships free of physical, emotional, or psychological abuse
• Affection, bonding, and social support	• Engage in mutually supportive relationships
• Solidarity and sense of community	• Share experiences with others without oppressive norms of conformity
• Democratic participation	• Participate in community life and resist passivity
• Respect for diversity	• Uphold one's unique identity without fear of discrimination or reprisals
Collective Needs	
• Equality	• Struggle for and benefit from fair and equitable distribution of resources, obligations, and power
• Freedom	• Pursue and benefit from individual and collective liberty
• Environmental sustainability	• Ensure a clean and sustainable environment

Note. Adapted from Prilleltensky and Fox (in press).

Webs of Wellness and Justice

Justice refers to the fair and equitable allocation of burdens, resources, and opportunities in society (Miller, 1999). As may be seen in the right-hand column of Table 2.1, the fulfillment of personal, relational, and collective needs depends on having the power, capacity, and opportunity to experience certain rights and entitlements. For example, to meet the need for control and self-determination, we should be able to experience voice and choice throughout life. To enjoy equality, we have to have access to power, capacity, and opportunities to benefit from a fair distribution of resources and obligations in society. To choose an example from the relational domain, respect for diversity is a need that cannot be fulfilled unless we have the power, capacity, and opportunity to uphold our unique identity without fear of discrimination or reprisals. The key phrase in each one of these examples is *power, capacity, and opportunity*. Without them we do not have the means to experience or even struggle for justice. Without justice, we could not satisfy a requisite for the fulfillment of personal, relational, and collective needs.

Power, capacity, and opportunity create the conditions for the pursuit of justice. Child abuse is characterized by abuse of power, which, in turn, deprives children of their rights to safety and psychological health (See Dokecki, 2004, for an analysis of clergy sexual abuse showing that abuse of power is central). Domestic abuse operates in a similar way. At the collective level, oppression and discrimination are perpetuated by the unchallenged abuse of power, whereas freedom and equality are promoted by conditions in which individuals and groups have the opportunity to benefit from certain rights and the obligation to live with certain responsibilities.

Sen (1999a, 1999b) illustrates the interdependence and web-like quality of the relationship between capability and opportunity. He does so by elucidating the connections among five factors involved in human development: (a) political freedoms, (b) economic facilities, (c) social opportunities, (d) transparency guarantee, and (e) protective security:

> Each of these distinct types of *rights* and *opportunities* helps to advance the general *capability* of a person. They may also serve to *complement* each other. . . . Freedoms are not only the primary ends of development, they are also among its principal means. In addition to acknowledging, foundationally, the evaluative importance of freedom, we also have to understand the remarkable empirical connection that links freedoms of different kinds with one another. Political freedoms (in the form of free speeches and elections) help to promote economic security. Social *opportunities* (in the form of education and health facilities) facilitate economic participation. Economic facilities (in the form of *opportunities* for participation in trade and production) can help to generate personal abundance as well as public resources for social facilities. Freedoms of different kinds can strengthen one another. (Sen, 1999b, pp. 10–11; emphasis added)

Table 2.1 denotes particular *conditions* of justice that ought to be met for each personal, relational, or collective need to be satisfied. The question is: Who is responsible for creating these *conditions*? Some claim that it is up to the individual to create the necessary conditions for the pursuit of justice and the fulfillment of personal, relational, and collective needs, whereas others ascribe responsibility to government, the community, or any other source external to the person (Etzioni, 1998). In general terms, responsibility for creating the conditions of justice and wellness may be assigned to sources internal or external to the person. Whereas individuals bear certain responsibility for creating these conditions, their capacities are largely determined by the external conditions and opportunities they are presented with in the first place. Hence, we claim that justice and wellness are a function of both *capacity* and *opportunity;* where capacity refers to sources internal to the person and opportunity to sources external to the person. As Sen (1999a, 1999b) demonstrated, capacity and opportunity are inextricably entwined. They exist in a dialectical relationship. This is why we define power as having both the capacity and opportunity to pursue a particular course of action (Prilleltensky, in press). To reduce power to either one of these two components would be to ignore the influence of the environment or the human potential for change. But just as we cannot ignore either component, we cannot inflate their importance either. Environments do not improve physical or mental health without the active participation of the individual, nor do individuals alter their habits without some kind of environmental change (Smedley & Syme, 2000; Stokols, 2000, 2003).

Depending on certain conditions, some groups have more power, capacity, and opportunity to meet their needs than others (Prilleltensky, in press). Conditions of privilege, class, race, gender, and physical or psychological abilities create inequality and oppression in interpersonal, organizational, and collective situations (Moane, 1999; Shulman Lorenz & Watkins, 2003). Thus, power differentials get in the way of achieving equality, justice, fairness and democratic participation (Carr & Sloan, 2003; Prilleltensky 2003).

Now we face a new question: How do we facilitate the empowerment of those with fewer capacities and resources in society? Political education and political literacy are part of the answer. Indeed, they are a *sine qua non* of empowerment and, transitively, of wellness. Awareness of power differentials is the first step in removing barriers to wellness. At the relational level, power may be a key factor in staying or leaving an abusive relationship. At the collective level, political power may lead one group to overcome apartheid and another to achieve equality in pay for women and minorities.

The state of Kerala in India provides a useful illustration of how collective power can transform conditions of inequality, which, in turn, can enhance wellness. Women's power and bonds of solidarity created positive ripple effects in Kerala at the three levels of wellness (Franke & Chasin, 2000). Since the beginning of the century, women in this poor state began to organize into social movements that demanded tenant protection, nutrition programs for children, land reform, and community development. Through the organizing process women experienced a psychological sense of empowerment. But solidarity resulted not only in enhanced personal control and a sense of mastery; it also led to meaningful social change. Public health indices such as literacy, infant mortality, and longevity have been higher in Kerala than in the rest of India for many years (Franke & Chasin, 2000).

We can summarize what we have learned so far in the image of two webs. The first web weaved together personal, relational, and collective wellness. The second one weaved the multilevel concept of wellness with justice. For justice and wellness to take place we learned that both *capacity* and *opportunity* are crucial. Whereas capacity refers to personal capabilities, opportunity refers to conditions that enable the person to act on his or her behalf for the pursuit of individual or collective wellness. And just as personal, relational, and collective wellness complement each other, so do capacity and opportunity. Within this framework, any type of counseling practice should take into account the complementary nature of (a) the various components of wellness, (b) wellness and justice, and (c) capacity and opportunity.

PRACTICE AND ETHICAL DILEMMAS

In this section, we review counseling practices in light of the webs of wellness and justice. Following a critique of dominant approaches we recommend justice-based practices. In both cases we provide a detailed analysis of (a) practices, (b) justification, (c) associated dilemmas, and (d) possible resolutions. Although we strive to articulate sound justice-based alternatives, we do not expect them to be free of ethical dilemmas. Hence, we subject our very own prescriptions to the same rigorous analysis that we apply to current practices.

Current Practices

We examine in this section a number of current counseling practices in light of the connections among personal, relational, and collective wellness and the nexus between justice and wellness. We make an effort to understand how counselors justify their practice and how they resolve associated ethical dilemmas.

Current counseling Practice #1: Counselors concentrate on the personal and relational domains of wellness and tend to neglect the collective sphere.

There is a long and glorious, albeit sometimes controversial, history of members of the counseling profession providing services to individual persons in their offices or in family or group settings. This is undoubtedly the predominant mode of professional counseling practice concerned with mental health issues, and for good reason. The extremely important goal of this prevailing approach to counseling may be described as the enhancement of human wellness at the personal and relational levels.

Justification for counseling Practice #1: Counselors are trained in helping individuals and small groups, and it is often beyond their expertise to address issues of justice and other psychopolitical matters and to intervene at the community level in the collective sphere.

Psychology is the discipline that has most strongly influenced the development of the theory and practice of counseling. The most influential domains within psychology have been personality theory and research and developmental psychology and—perhaps to a lesser degree—social psychology, usually the social psychology of small groups and group dynamics. These psychological domains focusing on individuals and their immediate social environment have yielded an enormous amount of useful and important knowledge over the last 100 or so years, the kind of knowledge that has abundant practical implications. Most current counselors were probably initially attracted to the counseling profession by the image of individual, family, or group counselors applying these insights from psychology to help people in need gain access to the secrets of their troubled lives. Such counselors help provide insights into the dynamics and processes of personality, human development, and social relationships.

Counseling's reliance on a predominantly individual- and small group-focused body of theory and research resulted in the profession's focus on the personal and relational domains. Personally, counselors form therapeutic alliances with clients to enable and empower them to develop self-control and self determination; to master their world by learning coping skills and thereby developing socially and emotionally to their potential; to foster feelings of hope and optimism; to improve their psychological and physical health; and to find meaning in their lives and get in touch with the spiritual dimension of their existence. Relationally, counselors collaborate with clients to enable and empower them to become more caring and compassionate; to develop bonds of affection and bonding and utilize networks of social support; to be able to enter relationships characterized by solidarity with others that enhance their psychological sense of community; to be able to participate meaningfully in group democratic decision-making settings; and to enhance their willingness to relate to a wide variety of people who are different from them, and initially threatening, by appreciating the value of diversity in a meaningful social life. Ethical pursuit of these personal- and relational-level goals is a noble and praiseworthy endeavor, absolutely essential in a world that threatens personal identity and integrity and alienates people from others, often frustrating the universal human quest for community (Nisbet, 1953/1990; Sarason, 1974)

Ethical dilemmas associated with Practice #1: *The emphasis on helping individuals and small groups sometimes undermines the importance of recognizing and addressing the societal factors that are often more responsible for personal problems than are personality dynamics and small group processes.*

We live in a culture that localizes responsibility for success and failure on the individual. Counseling practice is not beyond or above this culture. Instead of recognizing people's experiences as embedded in a context, people's lives are told as if they were the sole creators of their destiny. When counseling practice reinforces this ideology of self-blame or self-credit, a surreptitious "blame-the-victim" orientation subtly engulfs the counseling enterprise.

Blaming the victim is a common societal practice of seeing the victims of insidious political, economic, and social processes as having caused their own problems. For example, one of us (Dokecki, 1999) recently reviewed two books by Tod Sloan (1996a, 1996b), a critical and community psychologist, who has systematically traced the role of broader societal factors in threatening personal and relational wellness. Sloan developed a detailed framework that analyzes modernity and its specific processes and traces these influence on human development and their possible contribution to the genesis of psychopathology. He argued, echoing Habermas's critical theory, that the plight of many people in the workforce who feel overwhelmed and inadequate—for example, in experiencing the stress of needing to balance career and family demands—to a significant degree is a function of modernity's colonization of the lifeworld. This is a corrosive process whereby the system of material production invades the personal and intersubjective realms. It is "a mechanism by which advanced capitalist society stabilizes itself. Its crises in the economic sphere are deflected into the lifeworld realms of culture, society and personality. Among the prices paid for this stability are the loss of meaning, the destruction of solidarity [community] and psychological crisis" (Sloan, 1996a, p. 65, as quoted in Dokecki, 1999).

Dokecki (1999) had occasion to write about his daughters, who are successful career women; two are "married-with-children" systems engineers in large corporations, and another was a lawyer litigating her way up the ladder in a busy law firm. When they speak about their professional life, their pride in their accomplishments has overtones of anguish and stress about the uncertainties of work life in the highly competitive and rapidly changing corporate world, and especially about work life's relentless encroachment on personal and family life, their lifeworld. As a consequence, they beat up on themselves for their inability to cope effortlessly and gracefully with their demanding modern lives. They might be considered typical of many clients in counseling. On reading Sloan's books, Dokecki had the urge to be "parent-as-bibliotherapist" and leap to the computer to send his books to them via Amazon.com. These volumes would help them understand that their guilt and anguish come primarily not from their lack of self efficacy but from their blaming the victim, in this case themselves, for situations spawned by the values and forces of modernity. If the situation of these upper-middle-class women alerts us to the power of psychopolitical factors affecting human wellness, how much more should it suggest to counselors that they take seriously the long-known and well-established findings about the relationship between psychopolitical factors such as race, minority group status, and social class, on the one hand, and the problems of living encountered in the mental health system, on the other.

Possible resolution of the ethical dilemmas associated with Practice #1: Recognize the limitations of individual and small group-level counseling and circumscribe its practice to cases in which the origin and the resolution of clients' problems lie within their immediate personal and interpersonal context.

Because practicing within the limits of one's competence is one of counselors' primary ethical obligations, it can be argued that they should have enough psychopolitical knowledge to be able to recognize cases where their individual- and small-group focus is not adequate to cases where social injustice factors are strongly implicated. They might, then, either refuse to take such cases because they lie outside their expertise or make referrals to counselors who have well-developed psychopolitical knowledge and associated intervention skills. This would require, at the very least, that counselor education programs take on the task of raising the consciousness of emerging professionals about the relationship between personal and relational wellness and societal political, economic, and social forces. Beyond consciousness-raising, counselors-in-training should also be exposed to the theoretical and research literature that addresses the psychopolitical dimensions of human development. An additional benefit to developing this expanded awareness would be the enrichment of traditional counselors' understanding of the human situation, in all its levels and complexities, which would make them more sensitive to clients' total life experiences and, thereby, better equipped to deliver even traditional modes of counseling services. There is a role for accreditation and professional bodies in this regard. The more we institutionalize psychopolitical training in curricula, the higher the chances that counselors will have their consciousness raised about these issues.

Current counseling Practice #2: Counseling work tends to be reactive and focused on person-based solutions, to the relative neglect of both proactive and community-based solutions. Counselors are reluctant to connect clients to social causes and social movements because their participation in them may divert attention away from personal issues that need to be resolved first.

Many, if not most, practitioners operate in a reactive mode. They wait until clients come to them with problems and provide person-based interventions. This is the typical mode of service delivery; two people sitting in an office behind closed doors trying to equip the counselee with insights and new behaviors that will resolve or alleviate the presenting problem. Even when counselors are aware of the external webs that entrap the client, their practice remains focused on the individual in front of them. Furthermore, even when they know that the origins of the problems remain untouched by their *modus operandi,* their practice seldom changes. This "wait-in-the-office-for-the-next-client" approach does not entertain change agent roles for therapist or client. When enacted, social change roles are typically performed outside working hours. We explore next why this may be the case.

Justifications for Practice #2: In some cases, clients do need to look inside and change something within them. Participation in social issues may reinforce externalizing tendencies and prevent an in-depth examination of psychological issues. Counseling is based on client demand. People tend to be reactive about their personal problems. We cannot blame counselors for people's lack of proactive thinking.

It is quite possible that counselees need to concentrate on personal issues: anger management, grieving, phobias, or anxiety. Involvement in social issues may not assist them in solving these problems. In some cases, it may even distract them or induce further distress. These are reasonable explanations for some, but not all cases of exclusive office-based work.

It is harder to find justifications for the reactive nature of much counseling. Counselors may claim that agencies expect them to see clients-one-after-the-other-in-the-office. Waiting lists are long and the need for services is great. How can we afford the time to do proactive work when people are hurting now in front of us? Though justifiable to a certain extent, this argument has to be weighed against another one: No mass disorder afflicting human kind has ever been eliminated, or brought under control, by treating the affected individual (Albee, 1998). Treating victims of child or domestic abuse does not end abuse, much like treating victims of HIV/AIDS does not stop the epidemic. If counseling agencies never allow practitioners to engage in proactive work, who is going to do it? The fact that "this-is-the-way-we've-always-done-counseling" provides little justification for neglecting preventive work. Although prevention in mental health is slowly taking root, investments pale in comparison to resources channeled to treatment and rehabilitation (Nelson, Prilleltensky, Laurendeau, & Powell, 1996; Nelson, Prilleltensky, & Peters, 2003). The most advanced provinces in Canada and states in the United States invest less than 2% of their health, mental health, human, and community service budgets in prevention. Most resources are allocated to hospitals, beds, reactive treatments, and rehabilitation.

The fact that the population tends to be reactive about mental health issues is hardly a justification for not engaging in prevention. Once we have professional knowledge about an aspect of mental health it behooves us to act on it. Knowing that the general public does not recognize the merits of prevention should only strengthen our conviction to promote it.

Dilemmas associated with Practice #2: If we leave it up to the population to be proactive we may never quite engage in the promotion of wellness. Counselors have a responsibility, personally and collectively, to pursue justice at the collective level so that wellness may flourish at all levels. Participation in social issues may be personally empowering and generative. There may never be a point where citizens are sufficiently free of psychological issues to join a social movement in a state of perfect mental health. If we wait until that state arrives, nobody would be justified in joining movements for social justice.

There are two main dilemmas associated with the dominant practice of wait-in-the-office. The first one concerns the neglect of prevention. Although counselors may not have the authority within their agencies to redefine their roles, or decide on priorities, it is their responsibility to do something that will begin to address the neglect of prevention. Blaming the professional status quo is not an excuse. Once we possess knowledge about a better treatment, or, better yet, about how to prevent mental health problems, it is our professional duty to act on it. If managers, supervisors, or administrators do not shift priorities towards prevention, then it is up to the workers to initiate change processes that would bring the urgent need for prevention to the attention of colleagues and superiors. Failing to act on knowledge that may prevent future cases of abuse or addictions because "it's-not-the-we've-always-done-it" is hardly defensible.

The second dilemma stems from the hesitation to encourage clients to join social movements or groups that tackle injustice or exploitation. Although we just acknowledged that, in some cases, such involvement may be counterindicated, the caveat surely does not apply to all cases of counseling. Furthermore, in some instances people benefit from participation in advocacy or social change groups (Lord & Hutchison, 1993; Nelson, Lord, & Ochocka, 2001). Neglect of such practice seems unwarranted, potentially denying clients of a positive experience and the community of a contribution towards social justice.

Possible resolution of ethical dilemmas associated with Practice #2: *Agencies may create opportunities for clients to join groups engaged in the promotion of social justice and community wellness. This is not instead of therapy or counseling but in addition to them. Counseling agencies can allocate a group of counselors to do preventive work. If further training is required, agencies need to take responsibility for providing the necessary skills to work proactively.*

A young woman with eating disorders may gain a great deal by participating in groups that educate about the negative effects of advertising and organize boycotts against exploitive advertising. Some consciousness-raising groups have been found to assist participants in gaining power and control over distress caused by social factors such as advertising, consumerism, labeling, and discrimination (Collins, 1990; Community Mental Health Project, 1998). It is possible for agencies to offer participation in social action groups that promote both wellness and social justice. There is no need to see justice and wellness as divorced from each other. On the contrary, we have to see how closely related they are.

It is a vestige of reductionism that we treat mental health problems in microscopic terms. The more we learn about networks in general and about webs of wellness in particular, the more we realize that we can no longer afford to treat mental health problems in isolation from social problems (Barabasi, 2002; Nelson & Prilleltensky, 2005). Seeing networks instead of atoms, webs instead of nodes, and connections instead of fragments will generate new ways of thinking and new ways of practicing counseling. We hope some of these ways involve community-based prevention and social action for social justice. Agencies need not wait for a paradigmatic revolution before they offer clients an opportunity to work with others on social issues connected to psychological distress (Prilleltensky & Prilleltensky, 2003a, 2003b, 2003c).

Current counseling Practice #3: *Training and research focus on single levels of analysis: individual, family, or group.*

Traditional counseling training programs have centered on the development of individual and group counseling skills. Less attention has been paid to prevention as an important component of wellness-based practice. The philosophy of many training models was historically guided by a focus on helping individuals, couples, families, and groups. These models strived to maximize people's potential and resolve difficulties in intrapersonal and interpersonal functioning. Although community counseling advocates a paradigm shift toward community building and prevention, research and practice promoting effective interventions at the community level remain largely ignored.

New standards addressing the importance of training in multicultural competencies is helping to move the field toward more engagement in advocacy and community involvement. However, these influences are still in the background. Predominant models remain largely focused on individual counseling skills and strategies.

Justification for Practice #3: Although there is little disagreement in theory about the importance of focusing on multiple levels of analysis and interventions, the demand for person-centered orientations is so high that other approaches must take a back seat.

Three main forces inhibit a multilevel orientation in counseling. First, even as researchers and educators become more vocal about the need for community-based practice, social and market forces impact how training may be carried out. These forces focus on crisis management and remediation. The growing impact of managed health care and licensure requirements dictate what populations may be seen and by whom. This creates questions about the marketability of counselors who are not well versed in psychopathology.

The second impediment is closely aligned to the first. If counselors are going to treat conditions such as depression, anxiety, or eating disorders as part of their practice, then training that does not require core competencies in diagnosing and treating mental disorders is deemed inadequate. Students who are unfamiliar with the current language of mental health care cannot be powerful advocates for people in distress. Even if counselors do not want to treat more serious disorders, they must have awareness of the biopsychosocial forces that interact with counseling practice.

The final concern arises in the content and structure of training and in the person–environment fit of students entering counseling programs. Van Hesteren and Ivey (1990) argued for the need for counselors to be trained as developmental specialists, capable of working with psychopathology through a developmental orientation. Understanding how to help people in crisis and, in addition, how to be proactive and how to work across levels is, to say the least, very challenging. In 2-year training programs, there is little if any time left to explore multilevel interventions. Although some students have had life experiences that challenged them to be reflective, many others feel overwhelmed about aspects of themselves they hadn't encountered before. The personal challenge leaves little time or mental energy for contemplating what is just and fair in society.

Dilemma associated with Practice #3: Research and training programs that neglect multiple levels of analysis and the needs of a diverse society will become increasingly irrelevant.

If the current trend continues, fewer and fewer individuals will have access to helping professionals. Counseling will be available only to those who have the means to access services. Programs that are ill-equipped to address the needs of underserved and diverse populations through prevention, advocacy, community organizing, or counseling will fall short in their training missions. Counselor educators who do not commit to addressing needed changes in policies, standards, and training experiences, need to rethink the current imbalance. Without this commitment, counseling programs will continue to serve less vital roles in communities, and access to care will be limited to a select few.

Possible resolution of ethical dilemmas associated with Practice #3: Counselor educators and researchers must take a more proactive stance in revising the curriculum and research agendas to include multilevel orientations and interventions.

Research and training agendas should include more emphasis on the webs of wellness. No single level can account for wellness or suffering. Although there are market forces pressing for single-level-type interventions, the mental health field has accumulated sufficient knowledge to challenge the received wisdom that "resilient" people can ultimately overcome the ill effects of unfavorable environments. Nothing short of a paradigm shift will ensure that counseling practice and research pay equal attention to the personal, relational, organizational and collective domains of wellness. This will require a concerted effort on the part of educators, practitioners, and researchers, not to mention professional associations.

Current counseling Practice #4: Counselors concentrate on cognitive and intrapsychic dynamics at the expense of power dynamics of oppression and discrimination affecting the individual.

Counseling has been seduced by scientific empiricism and reductionism to deal with life complexities by narrowly focusing on individual or small group-based interventions (e.g., Corsini & Wedding, 1995; Prochaska & Norcross, 1994). Consequently, counseling has primarily focused on enabling clients to function more effectively as individuals in a decontextualized context. This stance has resulted in a de-emphasis of understanding interactions within the context of social factors in lieu of understanding individual implicit affective processes.

Justification for Practice #4: The many social, political, cultural, and economic factors that affect mental health are at best very difficult to change. Because counseling is predicated on the notion that individuals can change, counselors concentrate on the individual, the unit of analysis they feel empowered and able to change.

As a means of empowerment, counseling has focused on helping an individual answer the age-old questions of "Who am I?" and "Why is _____ happening to me?" Racial-cultural identity development models have been considered "one of the most promising approaches to the field of multicultural counseling/therapy" (Sue & Sue, 1999, p. 123). Racial-cultural identity development has had valuable clinical utility by highlighting that a person's life experiences, as well as the counseling process itself, are influenced by the racial-cultural identity of the players (Carter, 1995; Helms, 1984, 1990).

By definition, racial identity attitudes are "the psychological or internalized consequences of being socialized in a racially oppressive environment and the characteristics of self that develop in response to or in synchrony with either benefiting from or suffering under such oppression" (Helms, 1996, p. 147). The critical roles and functions of racial-cultural identity development models have rested on their utility of: (1) advancing understanding of self-identification processes employed among members of all racial-cultural groups; (2) their emphasis on the individual within a social-cultural environmental context; and, (3) how personal self-understanding and self-concept have been unduly influenced by interpretations or perceptions of interactions with others. To this end, integrated cognitive-affective learning that has focused on introspection and reflective self-evaluation when examining one's own identities, beliefs, and attitudes has been shown to be a powerful and effective method of growth in counseling (Carter, 1995, Johnson, 1987; Ota Wang, 1998; Pinderhughes, 1989; Tomlinson-Clarke & Ota Wang, 1999; Sue & Sue, 1999).

Dilemma associated with Practice #4: The convenience of working with individuals is not enough justification for a professional practice. In some respects, it is like looking for the penny where there is more light, rather than looking for it where it got dropped. People may be more inclined to look for solutions where there is more light, akin for looking for a penny where illumination is better. But if the penny got dropped where it is dark, it will be of no use searching for it where there is light. In some respects intervening at the individual cognitive and psychodynamic level is easy, but this intervention may not be strong enough to reverse the effects of oppressive relationships and environments. We can apply individual and cognitive techniques, because it is what we have and what we know, it is our light in the "penny" analogy. But it is possible that other interventions techniques may be more suitable, even if we weren't trained in them in graduate school.

Because people's lives are a complex kaleidoscope of experiences that influence what they believe and do, focusing merely on individual experiences leaves individuals trying to understand their lives out of context. On a narrow level, understanding people from a racial-cultural identity perspective has meant understanding individual selves alone and with a limited number of other people. Racial identity is influenced by powerful social, cultural, and political contexts. These environments can and often do impose real physical and psychological barriers to development. These barriers include conformity, prejudice, and oppression. To varying degrees, people have been overtly or covertly subjected to these obstructions and their messages about desirability or unacceptability in society. With regards to conformity, the prevalence of societal, institutional, or self-imposed ideals to do the expected (e.g., White, blonde, blue-eyed people are smarter than those who have darker complexions; men are better at business, science, and math than women; engineers, physicians, and lawyers are smarter than those who work in the social sciences or the arts, etc.) have often resulted in feelings of inferiority for those who haven't fit those ideals of superiority. Beyond limiting individuals, these illusory ideals have also prevented other members of society from recognizing and benefiting from the value of the diversity around them.

With respect to prejudice, those who hold the power in society and in institutions have denied equity to people who are different from themselves by conveying messages such as "you can only achieve the goods" of society if you are like us, or "you can't be like us if your phenotype, gender, values, or sexual orientation are not the same as ours." Because prejudice has promoted the idea that certain groups and cultures are superior to others, its destructive forces have kept members of various racial-cultural groups artificially separated.

With regards to oppression, this barrier has been more socially and personally destructive than the former two barriers. In addition to being pressured into becoming something *they are not*, and prevented from fully participating in society, people have been exploited for *being who they are* as racial-cultural people.

Possible resolution of ethical dilemma associated with Practice #4: Make power differentials central to the practice of counseling. Even in cases where the client may have little influence over the immediate oppressive environment, there is merit in naming the issue of oppression and exploitation and looking for ways to eliminate it.

An Ecological Person–Process–Context model can account for social, cultural, and political systemic structures in which specific individual, community, and societal content and processes affecting the individual can be better understood (Bronfenbrenner, 1986). For example, this model allows the examination of *who* a person is by providing a structure to examine how individual and collective intra/intergroup processes and social interactions influence psychological identity and social development. Furthermore, this model allows for an examination of power dynamics affecting personal and community development.

This contextual approach has been successful in allowing counseling trainees to gain multicultural counseling competence (Tomlinson-Clarke & Ota Wang, 1999). By paying greater attention to the multiple individual and collectives forces impinging on personal affective, cognitive, and physical contexts, this model suggests a person's behavior is the result of psychological processes that are interacting with his or her environmental ecology or life space. Thus, the complexity of an intrapsychic worldview is accounted for within a social, cultural, and political reality that takes seriously oppression and power differentials.

Justice-Based Practices

Based on the "Foundations" section, where we established that personal, relational, and collective wellness are dependent on the presence of justice, we formulate recommendations for new practices that overcome the limitations associated with current modalities of helping. This is not to say that justice-based practices are problem-free. They may resolve some existing dilemmas but they may create new ones. It would be naive to think that we can offer justice-based practices that do not harbor incipient ethical dilemmas. Therefore, it is our job to think about best justice-based practices, but we need to do so with a critical and self-reflective attitude.

Justice-based counseling Practice #1: Counselors pay equal attention to the personal, relational, and collective domains of wellness. No attempt is made to privilege one domain until the context of a particular client or a specific client population has been thoroughly examined. Whereas personal and relational issues may be salient for some clients, justice concerns at the collective level may be dominant for others.

In addition to the consciousness raising suggested earlier, this approach to counseling would also require counselors to have both in-depth psychopolitical theoretical knowledge and an expanded set of intervention techniques capable of addressing clients' human development needs at all levels.

Heflinger and Dokecki (1989) provided a useful framework for dealing with multiple levels of intervention. They suggested that the helping professions conceptualize their task of promoting wellness and human development using a systems-oriented framework. Such framework calls for a variety of interrelated practices. Available services should include both direct face-to-face encounters with clients and community-level interventions with the significant persons and organizations that constitute clients' social ecology. Beyond these direct and indirect services on behalf of individual clients, counselors also ought to be active in addressing collective matters on behalf of certain client groups (e.g., persons with mental handicaps, children with developmental disabilities, families and children victimized by poverty). These collective-oriented interventions would include activities such as conducting participative action research, joining in class action suits, engaging in community organizing, and attempting to influence public policy. In these kinds of professional activities, "the intent remains that of helping people, but service is a secondary goal: Increasing knowledge about the problem or influencing system change is the primary emphasis" (Heflinger & Dokecki, p. 144). Although few people would be capable enough to engage in all these activities within the ethical bounds of their competence, counselors might specialize in one or more of them, with the important proviso that they understand that they are part of a system in which they are expected to collaborate with colleagues with other specialties. Such a system would be capable of addressing human development and wellness holistically at the interrelated personal, relational, and collective levels.

Justification for justice-based counseling Practice #1: The justice-oriented practice of counseling assumes that the personal is political. You can run but you can't hide from the psychopolitical dimensions of human development. Moreover, if counselors ignore psychopolitical reality, they may be practicing unethically, either because they intentionally or unintentionally always blame clients for their own problems, or because they base their interventions on incomplete assessment of the full range of relevant factors that affect human development.

Much of the material in this chapter so far forms the rationale for this practice. As mentioned earlier, counselors operating in a justice-oriented service system work toward understanding clients in their full human complexity at their multiple levels of existence, increasing the likelihood that even standard modes of counseling will be more adequate to clients' needs and situations.

Ethical dilemmas associated with justice-based Practice #1: It is possible that the values of justice-based counseling may not be consistent with the values of certain clients, raising the possibility that it may undermine their personal autonomy because the counselor would, explicitly or implicitly, challenge what clients value and believe in. It is also possible that the processes of justice-based counseling may violate expectations certain clients have that counseling will be conducted according to the current and prevailing mode of practice, and they may find the situation to be aversive and unacceptable.

Justice-based counselors have had their consciousness raised to a point where they may be viewed by some as countercultural in both values and mode of delivering service. To be avoided is a Procrustean-bed approach to counseling where clients are bent out of shape and coerced to fit a justice agenda not of their own making or choosing.

Possible resolution of ethical dilemmas associated with justice-based Practice #1: It is absolutely essential that clients be fully informed about the values and processes they will encounter in justice-based counseling before they enter the counseling process.

Helping move society toward conditions that strengthen the personal autonomy of all persons is a key value and goal of justice-based counseling. Freedom of choice entailing fully informed consent is central to this value; therefore, it is imperative that justice-based counseling not violate its own central value by imposing its own agenda and mode of operating on clients, thereby compromising their personhood. Justice-based counselors have an obligation to educate people about why their value system and approach to counseling is valuable and worth choosing over other forms of counseling.

Justice-based counseling Practice #2: Counselors offer opportunities to engage themselves and their clients in groups and/or causes that promote social justice. Counselors pay equal attention to reactive and proactive practices.

Although community members are subject to negative societal influences, they need not be passive recipients of toxic messages. They can become agents of change to transform the conditions that perpetuate their own suffering or the suffering of others (Prilleltensky & Nelson, 2002; Prilleltensky & Prilleltensky, 2003b). Women who suffer from eating disorders may choose to combat images of femininity that are unhealthy. By engaging in a public act of defiance, they are likely to help themselves and others who may be subject to similar negative influences. This would not replace the need for individual counseling, but would be a much welcome addition. We recommend that counseling agencies offer clients opportunities to work with others on socially related maladies such as addictions, violence, discrimination, and eating disorders. Drinking alcohol is promoted as a way to happiness, slim figures as a way to success, and competition as a way to be "number one."

There is no need for counseling agencies to divorce themselves from the need to tackle social issues. If mental health is inextricably intertwined with the health of the society as a whole, there is no justification to always refer social concerns elsewhere, such as welfare agencies or political parties. There is no justification for the promotion of wellness in fragments (Barabasi, 2002; Nelson & Prilleltensky, 2005). Wellness comes in webs, not capsules.

Counselors, needless to say, are not passive citizens either. We encourage them to join in the effort to minimize the negative influence of destructive norms of violence, conformity, and consumerism, and in the struggle to build healthier societies.

Justification for Practice #2: *Wellness and justice are intertwined. Wellness requires justice, and justice without wellness has no meaning. Actions to improve wellness should reflect this state of interdependence.*

Little argument can be anticipated against this postulate. The struggle to enact new practices will lie not in conceptual appeal but rather on the force of habit and inertia. "Wait-in-the-office" and "this-is-the-way-we've-always-done-it" approaches curtail the imagination. We suggest the gradual introduction of new services and practices. If 100% of counselors in an agency do office-based reactive counseling 100% of the time, can we not change it? How about shifting these percentages from 100 to 80? The balance can be used to start social action or health groups that deal with social, not personal, ills. Periodic evaluations of new practices may gradually improve efforts and may even lead to the institutionalization and expansion of innovative practices.

Dilemmas associated with Practice #2: *Clients may dislike or reject new practices that seem to deviate from the implicit contract and expectations of individual counseling. Furthermore, group work may be counterindicated for some clients. Finally, counselors may feel ill-prepared to undertake social justice work.*

These are all valid concerns. However, with the introduction of every new service or modality of treatment, there is always an educational process. Professionals explain to clients the rationale behind the new intervention. It may take some time for counseling clients to recognize social justice work as related to their mental health concerns, but so is the case with the introduction of any innovation in society. In fact, the sooner the new practices are in place, the sooner the public will begin to realize that mental health is related to justice, as portrayed in detail in Table 2.1.

Social justice work may not be for everybody. This is understandable. The same may be said about therapy or counseling, but very few counselors seem to raise this as an issue. At present, the worry is not that social justice work may not be for everybody, but rather that nobody is offered this opportunity when seeking services.

It is true that for some people joining social justice groups may not be advised. And there is always the possibility that group leaders will use their authority to proselytize. But that risk is also present in individual counseling. Precautions that work in the latter should apply to the former. People seeking counseling are vulnerable and should be protected from anyone seeking to take advantage of their precarious state for any personal or political advantage.

Counselor training deserves serious consideration. No assumption should be made that every good counselor can do social justice work. Workshops and professional development opportunities would have to be offered to counselors interested in pursuing in practice the connection between wellness and justice.

Finally, the question of client confidentiality comes up. It is possible that clients would object to participating in social justice groups because that might disclose the fact that they are in "counseling" or "therapy." Although this is a potential concern, agencies can devise plan where social action groups consist of people from all walks of life, and they would not have to be identified as groups for clients of therapy. As with any suggestion made by counselors, professionals would have to make sure that clients do not just "follow the doctor's orders" but that they understand the value of the proposal. Recommending to clients to join an action group is not unlike recommending that they join a self-help group. It is an ancillary to counseling and therapy; in this case, an ancillary that may be empowering and may have positive communal effects at the same time.

Possible resolution of ethical dilemma associated with Practice #2: Selection procedures will have to be put in place to make sure that the right clients and the right leaders participate in social justice groups.

We make no claim that social justice work is for everybody. We should be definitely concerned about overinclusion. At present, social justice is rarely, if ever, offered as an adjunct to counseling. As we introduce this type of intervention gradually, we will have to make sure that it is beneficial to all those who join, and that it is coordinated by competent professionals.

Justice-based counseling Practice #3: Counselor educators provide experiences that promote advocacy, action-based research, prevention, community wellness, and social justice.

The need to provide training experiences that facilitate trainees' development as self-directed and self-aware advocates for social change is essential. Programs need to include training in multicultural competencies, advocacy, and the creation of partnerships with grass-roots organizations. Internships need to take place in settings that support the acquisition and development of these skills. Accrediting bodies and certification boards need to make sure that multilevel and justice-based interventions are appreciated, supported, and valued in training requirements.

Counseling programs must also be developmental and encourage learners to think in critical and contextual ways. Learning is not just about skill acquisition. To address competencies only as a cluster of skills—diagnostic or multicultural—is to miss the larger agenda. Education for development must go to the very core of how people construct their notions of wellness, justice, and power. Otherwise, the mission becomes bogged down in trying to do it all (a quantitative demand) rather than trying to do it well (a qualitative demand):

> The developmental approach is to realize that there are many different values and worldviews; that some are more complex than others; that many of the problems at one stage of development can only be defused by evolving to a higher level; and that

only by recognizing and facilitating this evolution can social justice be finally served. (Wilbur, 2000, p. 42)

Justification for justice-based Practice #3: *Training that promotes wellness encourages synergistic and systemic interventions that promote the common good. Issues such as oppression, discrimination, and inequality raise awareness of how social norms can become obstacles to human potential.*

Counselor trainees who can serve as social change agents at the individual, group, and community levels can champion the need for continuity of care. The continuum of care begins with the person and goes upstream all the way to the policy level. Wellness and justice are related to the need for changes in state and federal legislation. Evidence-based practice, as part of the overall training agenda, can be formative in helping programs become more effective in advocating for just and fair policies. We need to expand the definition of evidence-based practice to include evidence that addressing social issues can have beneficial effects on the counselee and possibly the community at large at the same time. At present, evidence-based practice is very narrowly defined, usually to signify manualized approaches to delivery.

Dilemmas associated with justice-based Practice #3: *Counseling has been criticized for being too diffuse in its professional identity (Hanna & Bemak, 1997; Myers, 1995).*

By trying to be all things to all people, the profession of counseling is at risk of losing its credibility. By trying to train counselor trainees in multiple levels, the risk exists of rushing the process and creating fragmented, rather than coherent, philosophies about helping. Programs' missions may end up doing just the opposite of what they were designed to do. Rather than training for wellness, programs will demand more with fewer resources, creating stress for students, faculty, and training sites.

These are valid, but not fatal, points. Any innovation requires adjustments on the part of players: students, professors, and practitioners. In our view, counselors' identity need not be undermined by the innovations, but rather challenged. There is a difference between challenged and undermined. A good challenge brings about renewal, not mortality. It would be most unfortunate if the only argument for stopping innovation would be that the status quo is all we know.

Possible resolution of ethical dilemma associated with Practice #3: *Care will need to be given to how changes are incorporated into a curriculum that promotes wellness and justice.*

Advocating for resources must go hand in hand with advocating for change in training. Innovative programs that link wellness and justice to a continuum of care need to design learning objectives that are contextually based and developmentally sound. This requires a competent faculty skilled in both multicultural and developmental approaches. Although the foundations of most training programs already advocate these positions, few programs are well equipped to carry out an ambitious agenda and do it well. Collaborating with professionals in related fields can add expertise where needed. Although changes will not occur instantly, a gradual shift in orienting educators, students, and professionals to these important goals can lead to substantial improvements over time.

Justice-based counseling Practice #4: *Counselors pay equal attention to intrapsychic forces, injustice, and power dynamics potentially oppressing clients from the* inside and the outside. Internalized oppression is often a manifestation of external oppression. The former cannot be eradicated without addressing the latter.

If counseling is a discipline that hopes to understand, to nurture, and to value its diversity, it has to be able to identify and eliminate conformity, prejudice, and oppression within its practices. Developing programs with goals of recognizing, respecting, and learning from the interactions between intrapsychic, individual, and collective cultural similarities and differences will combat stereotypes that have often resulted in the exploitation, coercion, and oppression of all racial-cultural people. The role of power and injustice in the creation and perpetuation of internalized oppression and external oppression must be attended to in training and practice.

Justification for justice-based Practice #4*: Eliminate the "tyranny of the shoulds."*

Despite color-blind and value-free illusions, conformist trends have often led the disenfranchised to live what W. E. B. Dubois termed "tyranny of the shoulds":

> . . . a peculiar sensation, this double consciousness, this sense of always looking at one's self through the eyes of others, of measuring one's soul by the tape of the world that looks on in amused contempt and pity. One ever feels his two-ness—an American, a Negro; two souls, two thoughts, two unreconciled strivings; two warring ideals in one dark body, whose dogged strength alone keeps it from being torn asunder (1903/ 1989, p. 3).

At some level, adaptations to a "socialized" mirage may have enabled some visible racial-cultural people to exist in threatening environments while letting those people from more privileged groups "off the hook" by allowing them to pat themselves on the back for helping "those" underprivileged people.

The lack of justice-based counseling practices will unnecessarily limit a person's ability to achieve his or her full potential, resulting in personal and group self-doubt, alienation, and isolation from essential personal and spiritual resources and support.

Dilemma associated with justice-based Practice #4: *Rhetoric of diversity and justice simplifies issues and does not translate into action.*

If cultural pluralism and empowerment have been effective in equity and inclusion of underserved visible racial-cultural groups, "Why are all the Black kids sitting together in the cafeteria?" (see Tatum, 1997). Several reasons can account for this continued separatist phenomenon. Overall, attention to inclusiveness and pluralism has not provided meaningful principles for the elimination of oppression in society. We have not moved far beyond obvious axioms such as all humans have language, families, region, political and social systems, emotions, and values. Our consciousness has often been limited to simplistic caricatures about service delivery and cultural norms (e.g., Lynch & Hanson, 1992; Sue & Sue, 1999). Furthermore, a partial consciousness of oppression has converted members of visible racial-cultural groups into overgeneralized, homogenized stereotypes, allowing individual variation of clients within certain groups to be neglected.

The situation in counseling is reflective of the situation in the culture. As Helms and Richardson (1997) have asserted, "most of the traditional counseling and psychotherapy theoretical orientations favored in the United States claim to honor the unique psychological characteristics of the client, but, in fact, ignore the differential psychological consequences to clients (and therapists) of being continuously socialized in a variety of sociodemographic groups" (p. 60).

Possible resolution of ethical dilemma associated with justice-based Practice #4: *Going beneath the surface in training and action.*

What has been lacking in counselor education has been an interactive framework that incorporates a multicultural perspective challenging students' affective understanding of their own beliefs, attitudes, and assumptions. Who they are as racial-cultural people, and how social, historical, and political processes have influenced their professional development are key questions for trainees. Needless to say, the same questions apply to trainers.

Educators will need to continue developing training programs to incorporate cognitive/affective racial-cultural self-exploration so counselors will be prepared for a realistic variety of interactions with clients representing varying aspects of human diversity (Carter, 1995; Pinderhughes, 1989; Sue & Sue 1999; Tomlinson-Clarke & Ota Wang, 1999). The onion of cultural and political experience has many layers. Peeling off only the top layer can be deceiving. If we only deal with racism and oppression at the surface level, we may create the impression that we're making progress whereas, in fact, we're only impeding it by creating the illusion that our talk will change realities.

CONCLUSION

Personal, relational, and collective wellness can be neither studied nor pursued in isolation from each other. Moreover, no form of wellness can be promoted in the absence of justice. In this chapter, we have demonstrated the close links that exist among the three domains of wellness, and the nexus that connects all forms of wellness with justice. This conceptual foundation afforded us some criteria to evaluate current professional practices. Our assessment indicates that many practices are still primarily reactive, person-centered, and only superficially concerned with issues of power and oppression. In light of this unsatisfactory state of affairs, we proceeded to formulate a set of recommendations for justice-based counseling. Based on the wellness–justice nexus, we proposed four new practices designed to move counseling towards more proactive, holistic, and politically aware approaches. Our new practices are not unproblematic. But the claim that new practices ought to be perfect before they are implemented is just as unacceptable as claiming that imperfect practices of the day ought to be eliminated altogether. In the end, we have to weigh the risk of launching promising, but yet unproven, practices against the threat of perpetuating well-known but wanting approaches.

REFERENCES

Albee, G. W. (1998). The politics of primary prevention. *Journal of Primary Prevention, 19,* 117–127.

Barabasi, A. (2002). *Linked: The new science of networks.* Cambridge, MA: Perseus.

Brofenbrenner, U. (1986). Recent advances in research on the ecology of human development. In R. K. Silbereisen, K. Eyferth, & G. Rudinger (Eds.), *Development as action in context: Problem behavior and normal youth development* (pp. 287–309). Heidelberg and New York: Springer-Verlag.

Carr, S., & Sloan, T. (2003). (Eds.). *Poverty and psychology: Emergent critical practice.* Boston, MA: Kluwer/Plenum.

Carter, R. T. (1995). *The influence of race and racial identity in psychotherapy: Toward a racially inclusive model.* New York: Wiley.

Cohen, S., Underwood, L. G., & Gottlieb, B. H. (Eds.). (2000). *Social support measurement and intervention: A guide for social and health scientists.* Oxford, England: Oxford University Press.

Collins, P. H. (1990). *Black feminist thought: Knowledge, consciousness, and the politics of empowerment.* New York: Routledge.

Community Mental Health Project. (1998). Companions on a journey: The work of the Dulwich Centre Community Mental Health Project. In C. White & D. Denborough (Eds.), *Introducing narrative therapy* (pp. 1–16). Adelaide, South Australia, Australia: Dulwich Centre Publications.

Corsini, R. J., & Wedding, D. (1995). *Current psychotherapies* (5th ed.). Itasca, IL: F. E. Peacock Publishers, Inc.

Dokecki, P. (1996). *The tragi-comic professional: Basic considerations for ethical reflective-generative practice.* Pittsburgh: Duquesne University Press.

Dokecki, P. R. (1999). Making life choices amid the ruins of modernity. *The Community Psychologist, 22,* 15–17.

Dokecki, P. (2004). *The clergy sexual abuse crisis: Reform and renewal in the Catholic community.* Washington, DC: Georgetown University Press.

Dubois, W. E. B. (1903/1989). *The soul of Black folks.* New York: Bantam Classic.

Dudgeon, P., Garvey, D., & Pickett, H. (Eds.). (2000). *Working with indigenous Australians: A handbook for psychologists.* Perth, Western Australia: Gunada Press.

Etzioni, A. (Ed). (1998). *The essential communitarian reader.* Boulder, CO: Rowman & Littlefield.

Felice, W. (2003). *The global new deal: Economic and social human rights in world politics.* New York: Rowman and Littlefield.

Franke, R., & Chasin, B. (2000). Is the Kerala model sustainable? Lessons from the past, prospects for the future. In G. Parayil (Ed.), *Kerala: The development experience* (pp. 16–39). New York: Zed Books.

Frey, B., & Stutzer, A. (2002). *Happiness and economics: How the economy and institutions affect human well-being.* Princeton, NJ: Princeton University Press.

George, R. E. (2002). *Socioeconomic democracy: An advanced socioeconomic system.* London: Praeger.

Goodman, D. (2001). *Promoting diversity and social justice.* London: Sage.

Gottman, J., & DeClaire, J. (2001). *The relationship cure.* New York: Crown.

Hanna, F.J., & Bemak, F. (1997). The quest for identity in the counseling profession. *Counselor Education and Supervision, 36,* 196–204.

Heflinger, C. A., & Dokecki, P. R. (1989). A community psychology framework for participating in mental health policy making. *Journal of Community Psychology, 17,* 141–154.

Helms, J. E. (1984). Toward a theoretical explanation of the effects of race on counseling: A Black and White model. *The Counseling Psychologist, 12,* 153–165.

Helms, J. E. (1990). *Black and White racial identity: Theory, research, and practice.* Westport, CT: Greenwood Press.

Helms, J. E. (1996). Toward a methodology for measuring and assessing racial as distinguished from ethnic identity. In G. R. Sodowsky & J. C. Impara (Eds.), *Multicultural assessment in counseling and clinical psychology* (pp. 143–192). Buros-Nebraska Series on Measurement and Testing, University of Nebraska-Lincoln.

Helms, J. E., & Richardson, T. Q. (1997). How "multiculturalism" obscures race and culture as differential aspects of counseling competency. In D. B. Pope-Davis & H. L. K. Coleman (Eds.), *Multicultural counseling competencies: Assessment, education, training, and supervision* (pp. 60–79). Thousand Oaks, CA: Sage.

Johnson, S. D. (1987). Knowing that versus knowing how: Toward achieving expertise through multicultural training for counseling. *The Counseling Psychologist, 15,* 320–331.

Keating, D. P., & Hertzman, C. (Eds.). (1999). *Developmental health and the wealth of nations: Social, biological, and educational dynamics.* New York: Guilford Press.

Kim, J. K., Millen, J. V., Irwin, A., & Gersham, J. (Eds.). (2000). *Dying for growth: Global inequality and the health of the poor.* Monroe, ME: Common Courage Press.

Klein, K., Ralls, R. S., Smith-Major, V., & Douglas, C. (2000). Power and participation in the workplace: Implications for empowerment theory, research, and practice. In J. Rappaport & E. Seidman (Eds.), *Handbook of community psychology* (pp. 273–295). New York: Kluwer Academic/Plenum.

Kloos, B., & Moore, T. (Eds.). (2001). Spirituality, religion, and community psychology II: Resources, pathways and perspectives [Special issue]. *Journal of Community Psychology, 29*(5).

Korten, D. (1995). *When corporations rule the world.* San Francisco: Berrett-Koehler/Kumarian Press.

Korten, D. (2000). *The post-corporate world.* San Francisco: Berrett-Koehler/Kumarian Press.

Lord, J., & Hutchison, P. (1993). The process of empowerment: Implications for theory and practice. *Canadian Journal of Community Mental Health, 12*(1), 5–22.

Lustig, N. (2001). Introduction. In N. Lustig (Ed.), *Shielding the poor: Social protection in the developing world* (pp. 1–20). Washington, DC: Brookings Institution Press/Inter-American Development Bank.

Lynch, E. W., & Hanson, M. J. (Eds.). (1992). *Developing cross-cultural competence.* Baltimore, MD: Paul Brookes Publishing Co.

Marmot, M. (1999). Introduction. In M. Marmot & R. Wilkinson (Eds.), *Social determinants of health* (pp. 1–16). New York: Oxford University Press.

Marmot, M., & Feeney, A. (1996). Work and health: Implications for individuals and society. In D. Blane, E. Bruner, & R. Wilkinson (Eds.), *Health and social organization* (pp. 235–254). London: Routledge.

Marmot, M., & Wilkinson, R. (Eds.). (1999). *Social determinants of health.* New York: Oxford University Press.

Miller, D. (1999). *Principles of social justice.* Cambridge, MA: Harvard University Press.

Moane, G. (1999). *Gender and colonialism: A psychological analysis of oppression and liberation.* London: Macmillan.

Myers, J. E. (1995). Specialties in counseling: Rich heritage or force for fragmentation? *Journal of Counseling and Development, 74,* 115–116.

Nelson, G., Lord, J., & Ochocka, J. (2001). *Shifting the paradigm in community mental health: Towards empowerment and community.* Toronto: University of Toronto Press.

Nelson, G., & Prilleltensky, I. (Eds.). (2005). *Community psychology: In pursuit of liberation and well-being.* New York: Palgrave Macmillan.

Nelson, G., Prilleltensky, I., Laurendeau, M. C., & Powell, B. (1996). A survey of prevention activities in mental health in the Canadian provinces and territories. *Canadian Psychology, 37*(3), 161–172.

Nelson, G., Prilleltensky, I., & Peters, R. DeV. (2003). Prevention and mental health promotion in the community. In W. L. Marshall & P. Firestone (Eds.), *Abnormal psychology: Perspectives* (2nd ed., pp. 462–479). Scarborough, Canada: Prentice Hall/Allyn and Bacon.

Nisbet, R. A. (1953/1990). *The quest for community: A study in the ethics of order and freedom.* San Francisco: ICS Press.

Ornish, D. (1997). *Love and survival: The scientific basis for the healing power of intimacy.* New York: Harper and Collins.

Ota Wang, V. (1998). Curriculum evaluation and assessment of multicultural genetic counselor education. *Journal of Genetic Counseling, 7*(1), 87–111.

Ota Wang, V. (2004). The ecology of life spaces: The I am–We are phenomena in racial identity based education and training. In R. T. Carter (Ed.), *The handbook of racial and cultural psychology and counseling* (pp. 78–96). Thousand Oaks, CA: Sage.

Pinderhughes, E. (1989). *Understanding race. ethnicity, and power in clinical practice.* Chicago: Free Press.

Powell, L., Shahabi, L., & Thoresen, C. (2003). Religion and spirituality: Linkages to physical health. *American Psychologist, 58,* 36–52.

Prilleltensky, I. (1994). *The morals and politics of psychology: Psychological discourse and the status quo.* Albany, NY: State University of New York Press.

Prilleltensky, I. (1997). Values, assumptions, and practices: Assessing the moral implications of psychological discourse and action. *American Psychologist, 47,* 517–535.

Prilleltensky, I. (2003). Understanding, resisting, and overcoming oppression: Toward psychopolitical validity. *American Journal of Community Psychology, 31,* 195–202.

Prilleltensky, I. (in press). The role of power in wellness, oppression and liberation: The promise of psychopolitical validity. *Journal of Community Psychology.*

Prilleltensky, I., & Fox, D. (in press). Psychopolitical literacy for wellness and justice. *Journal of Community Psychology.*

Prilleltensky, I., & Nelson, G. (2002). *Doing psychology critically: Making a difference in diverse settings.* London: MacMillan/Palgrave.

Prilleltensky, I., Nelson, G., & Peirson, L. (Eds.). (2001a). *Promoting family wellness and preventing child maltreatment: Fundamentals for thinking and action.* Toronto: University of Toronto Press.

Prilleltensky, I., Nelson, G., & Peirson, L. (2001b). The role of power and control in children's lives: An ecological analysis of pathways towards wellness, resilience, and problems. *Journal of Community and Applied Social Psychology, 11,* 143–158.

Prilleltensky, I., & Prilleltensky, O. (2003a). Towards a critical health psychology practice. *Journal of Health Psychology, 8,* 197–210.

Prilleltensky, I., & Prilleltensky, O. (2003b). Reconciling the roles of professional helper and critical agent in health psychology. *Journal of Health Psychology, 8,* 243–246.

Prilleltensky, I., & Prilleltensky, O. (2003c). Synergies for wellness and liberation in counselling psychology. *The Counseling Psychologist, 20*(10), 1–9.

Prochaska, J. O., & Norcross, J. C. (1994). *Systems of psychotherapy—A transtheoretical analysis* (3rd ed.). Pacific Grove, CA: Brooks/Cole.

Putnam, R. (2000). *Bowling alone: The collapse and revival of American community.* New York, NY: Simon & Schuster.

Putnam, R. (2001). Social capital: Measurement and consequences. *Isuma: Canadian Journal of Policy Research, 2,* 41–51.

Rhoades, L., & Eisenberg, R. (2002). Perceived organizational support: A review of the literature. *Journal of Applied Psychology, 87,* 698–714.

Rutter, M. (1987). Psychosocial resilience and protective mechanisms. *American Journal of Orthopsychiatry, 57,* 316–331.

Sarason, S. B. (1974). *The psychological sense of community: Perspectives for community psychology.* San Francisco: Jossey-Bass.

Schneider Jamner, M., & Stokols, D. (Eds.). (2000). *Promoting human wellness.* Berkeley, CA: University of California Press.

Seligman, M. E. (2002). *Authentic happiness.* New York: Free Press.

Sen, A. (1999a). *Beyond the crisis: Development strategies in Asia.* Singapore: Institute of Southeast Asian Studies.

Sen, A. (1999b). *Development as freedom.* New York, NY: Anchor Books.

Shonkhoff, J., & Phillips, D. (Eds.). (2000). *From neurons to neighbourhoods: The science of early childhood development.* Washington, DC: National Academy Press.

Shulman Lorenz, H., & Watkins, M. (2003). Depth psychology and colonialism: Individuation, seeing through, and liberation. *Quadrant, 33,* 11–32.

Sloan, T. (1996a). *Damaged life: The crisis of the modern psyche.* London and New York: Routledge.

Sloan, T. (1996b). *Life choices: Understanding dilemmas and decisions.* Boulder, CO: Westview Press.

Smedley, B. D., & Syme, S. L. (Eds.). (2000). *Promoting health: Intervention strategies from social and behavioral research.* Washington, DC: National Academy Press.

Stansfeld, S. (1999). Social support and social cohesion. In M. Marmot & R. Wilkinson (Eds.), *Social determinants of health* (pp. 155–178). New York: Oxford University Press.

Stokols, D. (2000). The social ecological paradigm of wellness promotion. In M. S. Jamner & D. Stokols (Eds.), *Promoting human wellness* (pp. 21–37). Los Angeles: University of California Press.

Stokols, D. (2003). The ecology of human strengths. In L. Aspinwall & U. Staudinger (Eds.), *A psychology of human strengths: Fundamental questions and future directions for a positive psychology* (pp. 331–343). Washington, DC: American Psychological Association.

Sue, D. W., & Sue, D. (1999). *Counseling the culturally diverse: Theory and practice* (3rd ed.). New York: Wiley.

Tatum, B. D. (1997). *"Why are all the Black kids sitting together in the cafeteria?" and other conversations about race.* New York: Basic Books.

Tomlinson-Clarke, S., & Camilli, G. (1995) An exploratory investigation of counselor judgments in multicultural research. *Journal of Multicultural Counseling and Development, 23,* 237–245.

Tomlinson-Clarke, S., & Ota Wang, V. (1999). A paradigm for racial-cultural training in the development of counselor cultural competencies. In M. S. Kiselica (Ed.), *Confronting prejudice and racism during multicultural training* (pp. 155–167). American Counseling Association.

Trickett, E. J., Watts, R. J., & Birman, D. (Eds.). (1994). *Human diversity: Perspectives on people in context.* San Francisco: Jossey-Bass.

Van Hesteren, F., & Ivey, A.E. (1990). Counseling and development: Toward a new identity for a profession in transition. *Journal of Counseling and Development, 68,* 524–528.

Wilbur, K. (2000). *Integral psychology: Consciousness, spirit, psychology and therapy.* Boston: Shambhala.

Wilkinson, R. G. (1996). *Unhealthy societies: The afflictions of inequality.* London: Routledge.

3

Social Justice Concerns and Clinical Practice

Lane A. Gerber
Seattle University

*If the small is problematic, the large has its problems too. It tends to encourage a
sense of contempt for anything that is not as large as itself, so that soon one's work
with the mentally ill, or the homeless, or the battered can come to seem futile when
set against the large numbers of homeless and battered and mentally ill who wan-
der the streets beyond the reach of one's acts of concern; so that soon one is not doing what one might because one is defeated by not doing what one should, and the
process of closing off sets in and soon one is wrapped in a numbing, life-threatening
indifference.*

—Chernin (1993, p. 91)

EARLY MEMORIES

An early memory of mine involves coming into the living room of my family's house
when I was a boy and seeing my mother watching television and crying. Before I
could ask what was the matter, she told me to sit down and watch what was going
on. She was watching the Army–McCarthy hearings in Washington, DC. Members of
the army were being interrogated by then-Senator Joseph McCarthy about their
possible connections with Communists. My mother was watching this and mutter-
ing angrily through her tears, "It isn't right. Look at this, Lane. Listen to that evil
man."

At some point during this phase of the process, Senator McCarthy turned his
venom toward a young attorney who was associated with the law firm of the opposing attorney, Joseph Welch. He began a personal attack on the young attorney, ac-
cusing him of belonging to the Lawyers Guild, which McCarthy arbitrarily branded a
Communist or Communist-leaning organization. Joseph Welch, the attorney representing accused men in the army, appalled and angered at McCarthy's attempt to
impugn the honesty of anyone and everyone who opposed him, confronted McCarthy and in a very emotional exchange said, "Have you no decency, sir?" Welch's

comment, standing up for the men unfairly accused by Senator McCarthy, gladdened my mother's heart. She turned to me with resolve and now, with tears of joy in her eyes, said, "Remember this, Lane."

This was a very powerful experience for me. Yet in another way, it was simply one of many experiences and examples that I witnessed throughout my growing-up years. Given that my grandparents' generation fled from pogroms in Russia when they were young, stories of my grandparents seeing Cossacks burn their village or kill members of their community, or in the case of my mother's mother, kill her grandfather as she walked hand in hand with him, were as much a part of me as the air that I breathed. And, of course, the history of my religion/culture included centuries of wanderings, pain, and loss in addition to the richness of relationships, stories, and ethical teachings. Doing something to help heal the world ("*tikkun olam*") was an expectation that was part of the upbringing for many of us. If asked "what we wanted to do when we grew up," a typical response was "I want to help people." We assumed everyone wanted to "help" in some way, too. Thus, a central part of my motivation comes from my earliest days in my family and community.

Along with this, I learned through stories and examples that the world is bigger than my family, community, or even country—and that we all effect each other for better and for worse. So, "pay attention," I would be told, "be aware, see what you can do to help." And this was part of what I brought to my graduate training.

It has been a challenge being a clinician born just before World War II; whose grandparents fled pogroms against the Jews in Russia at the turn of the 20th century; who was trained during the 1960s, and has been practicing and teaching from the late 1960s until the present; who has tried to integrate clinical work and social justice, and wanted somehow to do individual psychotherapy and also to use my background and training to address broader social concerns. As they do for many of us, family background, early experiences, and ideals framed my desire to "help" others.

This chapter traces my background and motivation; describes some of the roadblocks I experienced in my graduate training, professional life, and in myself; and discusses some ways I found to express my efforts for social justice in my clinical work and my teaching and supervising. My process in searching for ways to engage both of my passions was, fortunately or unfortunately, a process of trial and error and success. And it has always been striking to me that during these tumultuous years in human history, there were such few professional paths and so little attention paid in the literature of psychotherapy to the social and political events that influenced all of our lives. The following is not be a program to follow, but rather a personal narrative, and an explication of some stories I have witnessed as psychotherapist and teacher. These experiences have sometimes enabled me and/or others to take small steps (some of which have evolved into larger steps) along a path whose destination was integrating social justice concerns with clinical work. I hope that by "giving a feel" for my process, I can help readers understand the sometimes complex, personal journey toward integration that they may undertake.

HISTORICAL CONTEXT AND EARLY BARRIERS

My graduate school clinical training was bracketed between President John Kennedy's assassination near the beginning of my training and Robert Kennedy's just as I completed my dissertation. These events and the feelings they aroused were on everybody's lips—including the students and faculty's—yet were seldom mentioned in our classrooms or consultation sessions. Although both students and faculty were active socially and politically during this time, keeping one's beliefs about political and social issues separate from one's professional role was reinforced during graduate school. When the patients I saw during this time talked about the assassinations, civil rights issues, or simply the politics of everyday life, my supervisors regarded the material as important and interesting, but "not therapy material."

Another assumption, perhaps rationalization, that many had regarding any linkage or integration of social-political issues with psychotherapy was that successful psychotherapy enabled the client to be more open to the world. This openness, it was assumed, would include social and political events and their meanings, so that as clients would feel a greater sense of empowerment, they also would work toward greater openness in society as well as themselves. There was nothing else that was needed to be done or should be done. Good therapy work would do it all. Thus, those of us who were active in civil rights and/or in political, social, or environmental causes but disagreed with the assumptions just discussed felt that there was no "appropriate" way to include or integrate our personal commitments into our professional lives. We were frustrated and disillusioned in our newfound work, yet there was so much to learn if one wanted to do good clinical work, and besides, much seemed to be changing in the world outside of the therapy office. So maybe our generation would change the old therapy assumptions, too.

The birth of the community mental health movement in the late 1960s enabled some of my generation, and those after us, to do our clinical work within a structure that was, at least originally, aimed at understanding, being part of, and working with the community, its needs, and expressions. At the same time during the 1970s, and especially the 1980s and later, psychotherapy as practiced by nonphysicians was enjoying exponential growth. Many psychologists and social workers opted for private practice in some form, concentrating on growing their practices and growing themselves as clinicians. Many of these people started out as clinicians in community mental health centers. There, they gained experience after having completed their degrees. Then they went into private practice. Additionally, doctoral programs for clinicians suddenly boomed, and more and more people were trained in large professional schools. Thus, there were crosscurrents of community growth and power as well as a burgeoning of individuals aiming to enter the individual private practice of psychotherapy.

All of the these developments happened during historical periods that also included the Cold War between the United States and the Soviet Union, the related manufacturing and deployment of nuclear weapons, the war in Vietnam, the emergence of feminist therapy and family therapy, the rise of Pol Pot in Cambodia and genocide of perhaps 2 million Cambodians, the growing awareness of our environment, the growing awareness of the interconnectedness of all life on our planet, the continuing strife in the Middle East, the growth of political conservatism in this country (with its disdain for the public realm), and the beginning of a continuous erosion in funding for many social programs and for community mental health.

For many of us raised with some awareness and commitment to social justice, these events increased our desire to bring our values and commitments into our professional lives. How to do this was the question. We had an inability to imagine, and imagine in a way that would satisfy our idealistic dreams, how to include this awareness within the clinical work and clinical training we did.

What actions I did take always seemed terribly insufficient to me as I started doing them. As time went on, however, and I examined my own grandiose expectations, as well as looked around at what others were and were not doing in the world, I finally saw the different ways in which change can happen and values can be expressed. It took me some time to appreciate that change happens not only through the efforts of the relative few doing unusual deeds or birthing new and powerful movements, but also by the many who are putting their energies and time to work in small ways. "The small, it might be said, spins the threads that weave the net that catches the world. This world-net we cast, almost unknowingly, from our gathering together of individual acts, holds as a value that which is intimate, immediate, participatory, and personally engaged" (Chernin, 1993, p. 91).

FIRST LESSONS AND MORE BARRIERS

During the 1970s and early 1980s, many of us were involved in social justice and peace groups. Typically, these involvements were separate from work. During the 1970s and 1980s, as nuclear-arms buildups occurred in both the United States and the Soviet Union, and as our populations increasingly seemed to live in the shadows of "mutually assured destruction" doctrines, I wondered how it was that conversations about these horrors seemed to grow outside our office doors but were rarely admitted into our therapy offices. I wondered, what is our responsibility as people who are also psychotherapists?

At the time, there was a large majority of mental health professionals who supported a nuclear-weapons freeze and who were very concerned about nuclear warfare. Despite this fact there was almost nothing published on how political-societal aspects of the self might be included, or at least not excluded, in clinical practice. Was this lack of inclusion because of clinical concerns about trying to maintain "value-free" work (Walsh, 1989), or because of clinicians' own use of denial and helplessness (Segal, 1988)? On the one hand, there was justifiable concern about clinicians who were caught up in society-wide denials of the urgency of social and political matters (Prilleltensky, 1989). On another side were well-respected clinicians thinking exclusively that anything that a patient might say about such matters was strictly a reflection of their own early, internal conflicts. A final and very important caveat was, of course, that therapists could "contaminate" the therapeutic situation or use therapy to direct patients to areas that were not their (i.e., patients') concerns but those of their therapists (Mack, 1988). Given all this, it was difficult to imagine how to proceed.

Although these and other pros and cons swirled in my head, my experience as a boy watching the Army–McCarthy hearings with my mother returned to me again and again. One of the most important lessons (Lesson #1) I discovered during the process was to ask myself, when I was alone as well as in the company of others I trusted, "Why do I want to do this work?" As a result of my reflections and my conversations with other trusted colleagues about what was important to us in doing our work, I found myself siding with Jacobs (1998), who wrote that therapists have "not paid sufficient attention to the ways in which our patients, by pursuing through love and work their own happiness, have failed to identify themselves with the larger community, now seriously at risk" (p. 177). I decided that I would ask each new patient I saw sometime during the first several history-taking sessions about any feelings that they had about the community in which they lived and any social or political happenings in the country and world that they felt were significant as regards their mood or state of being.

Given the coverage in newspapers and on TV about nuclear, economic, and social issues, I wondered if they had any feelings about any of this that they would like to talk about. I asked this in the context of other questions concerning their personal history, family of origin, job, reasons for entering psychotherapy, and so on. The patient could respond to the question or not. I did this during the first few sessions when the patient and I have a chance to size each other up and to confirm or change our decisions to work together in therapy. So if a patient felt uneasy about my questions, he or she could choose not to continue to work with me (Gerber, 1990).

Over the next 2 years, I saw 18 new patients and tried to track their progress. In addition, I met regularly with a supervisor-consultant with whom I would review my work in an effort to prevent any influencing or steering of the therapy conversation away from what the client brought in to issues that were of concern to me and not them. This was clearly not a large sample, and it may be that people referred to me were referred because of my involvement with these issues. Out of this group, only one person terminated therapy, and he did so after he was offered a promotion in another area of the country. I did notice that 13 out of this group did talk more about death, and issues of power and powerlessness, and of feeling alone or "cut off" in the world. These patients' therapies also led to more talk of anger, to convictions to use their energies toward what was important to them as a way of respecting their own lives and life in general. That is, there seemed to be increased connections to life and to others that one generally hopes for in therapy.

Approximately three quarters of this group brought up something in their therapies related to the social-political world—a particular presidential action, votes on congressional policies, test bans, school bond levies, and so on—how they felt about such issues, how they understood the politics of involvement in their communities, their own temperamental proclivities for such engagement, and often their sense of being overwhelmed by "all that there is to do in the world." Most of my clients, whether they reflected a lot or a little on these matters in therapy, said that they were glad that they had a place that was "legal" to bring up such matters when they were on their mind.

I was pleased that I had started asking these few questions at the beginning of therapy work. It seemed to me that there were possibilities for broadening the scope of my understanding of the person I was sitting with in psychotherapy by allowing room for social and political aspects of personality into psychotherapy without making the process one that smacked of proselytizing or of using a client's time for my issues. And, all of this happened as some others began writing about this area (Cushman, 1990; Jacoby, 1983; Lifton, 1976, 1979; Mack, 1984; Marmor, 1988; Prilleltensky, 1989), and as multicultural awareness, increased international travel, and technological changes such as the computer and the Internet began to be born. So maybe my questions weren't so strange and different. Taking this small step of asking one question during the initial history-taking part of therapy work with new clients over this period of time opened up more possibilities in the therapy work (which was Lesson #2—one small step can open more steps), and gave me and others the sense that perhaps it was possible to include the social-political self into clinical work. At the same time, of course, asking these kinds of questions of patients during the beginnings of our possible longer term work together also seemed so terribly insufficient given all that was happening in the world.

I continued incorporating this question in the beginning of the therapy I was doing with new patients, I also had been seeing a middle-aged woman, "Ms. R.," in therapy for about 1 year, with whom I hadn't asked any of these questions at the start of our work. One day she came in for her session and talked about passing a homeless woman and daughter on the street. She said, "I didn't know what to do. There are more and more of these people around. What is happening here?" (Gerber, 1992, p. 628).

After I reflected on the impact that the homeless woman and her daughter had on her, she continued on about how she felt looking into their faces and wondering where they would go at night. She kept coming back to the look on their faces, then abruptly said, "I don't know why I'm thinking about it. She isn't the first I have seen. . . . Oh, I don't know. That's not why I'm coming here to talk to you. That's not what we are supposed to do here" (Gerber, 1992, p. 628).

I was really struck by her comment that such material is not "what we're supposed to do here." I commented on her being so clearly affected by the homeless woman and daughter, continuing to picture them in her mind, and also her statement at the beginning of our work together that she came in because she was depressed and because she felt like no one really listened to her or took what she was saying seriously. I wondered what she meant about what we were and weren't supposed to be talking about in our work, and did she want me to take her words seriously.

She replied that she felt that she was supposed to be talking about her feelings about her family or her personal history or her work, but not something that felt like a "social problem." Therapy was for "personal problems" not "social problems" and "outside things weren't relevant." That is, this client was talking about the big separation most of us make between the "outside world" and the "inside world"—a separation that can make it almost impossible for many of us to even think about our involvement in the outside world, whether or not we are in therapy.

In following sessions, Ms. R. alternated between talking about her fear of abandonment as a child, and all the hurt and scared feelings she carried inside herself, and the image of the homeless woman's face. As she continued we began making the connection between her own feelings of being abandoned, without a sense of feeling "at home" in the world, and the pain that she felt when she saw abandoned and homeless women and children on the street. That is, we were reflecting on the connection between her personal history and the apparent present state of many people in the world.

As her therapy progressed, Ms. R. talked about many important memories and aspects of her personal history. These included a sense of powerlessness she felt in her family and in the world. As she was talking about this in another session, she added that she saw another homeless woman and child on the streets, stopped to give them some money and asked how the woman was doing. The woman told her that someone had stolen their blanket and they were cold. Ms. R. then went home and found some old blankets and returned to give them to the woman on the street. Ms. R. said that she needed to do this and to look at the woman and not avert her eyes.

It was striking to me how Ms. R.'s interaction with the homeless woman and child led to a greater awareness of her early life experiences and how she felt with others as a young girl and as an adult. Ms. R. continued in therapy, feeling a somewhat greater sense of her own power, uncovering memories, using information from the transference and countertransference to make meaningful and satisfying progress for herself. She also continued her involvement with homeless women on the street. Doing "outside" work didn't preclude "inner" work or vice versa.

In my responses to Ms. R., I included her responses to "outside social problems" as an aspect of her responses to the world of which she is part; that is, legitimate aspects of the psychotherapy dialogue. My sense was that, by not excluding the "external" world and the manifest content of her dreams but instead adding to these the traditional "inner" and latent content, more aspects of her personhood were included in our work.

At professional meetings and within the graduate program where I teach, I talked about this work. Often I was accused of turning clients' therapies into a pursuit of my interests alone. Or, I was told that if I didn't present myself as neutral, then of what value would my interpretations be? So, my experience doing this was very mixed, although asking one question at the intake process certainly didn't seem like I was wildly pushing some agenda. Still, the strong reaction of some of my colleagues chastened me and served as a barrier for a while as I rethought and talked with others about what I was doing.

A conversation with some colleagues who were also interested in trying to understand the self historically in the changing contexts of the world began and has continued for more than a decade. I learned again an old and powerful lesson that conversation/discussion with colleagues about what we read, and what we were aiming at, was a rich and important source of support and encouragement that I and the others very much needed to prevent ourselves from feeling very isolated (Lesson #3). It was in my work with Ms. R., and in talking about such examples with other colleagues and students, that I began to feel that perhaps small acts can begin to spin threads that can be woven together (Lesson #4).

These original colleagues, joined by some graduates of our master's program, included in our conversations articles and books that might be germane to sociopolitical aspects of the self, social justice work, and clinical work. These ongoing discussions were and have been rich and fulfilling, I believe, for all of us. At the same time, doing this reading and talking about such matters seemed so terribly overwhelming. Were we doing this reading to become better informed? Were we doing this reading because we wanted to "do something" that would promote a greater integration of social justice ideals and psychotherapy—two realms of possible healing that seemed to us to be kin to each other? And if we did want to do something, what is it we thought we could accomplish in a world so vast and so filled with pain and turmoil? Frequently we got stuck on such questions. The problems and their remedies seemed so much beyond our abilities, our imaginings, and our temperaments. We felt overwhelmed, powerless, and numb.

Over time, however, we learned to trust each other, so when it was suggested that each of us talk about all the detailed fantasies that we had concerning our "fixing the world," we readily agreed. This conversation in which we revealed aloud to ourselves and to each other what we had fantasized about was alternately very serious and then very humorous as so many of our grandiose fantasies were expressed. It turned out that there were many like me from family backgrounds where we had been entrusted the task of saving the larger world. We were able to ruefully smile together, be both embarrassed and proud, laugh, and then move out of our stuck place. And, in the future, when one or more of us began talking about "why we wanted to do this work" as though nothing less than saving the world would be "doing enough," we could put our arms around each other and nod our heads indicating that we understood, and then wonder together what small pieces are there for us to do. This ongoing, personal–professional conversation, this compassionate and challenging conversation (which included examining our grandiosities), and the periodic inclusion of the question "Why do we want to do this work?" enabled us to work one thread at a time.

What we could try to do, for example, was consider a serious problem "close to home"—the diminishing allocation of funds to community mental health centers in the Seattle area. We could write letters to legislators and to newspapers. We did that again and again. Then we decided that we could meet with others in the mental health professions and band together to go to the state capital and meet with legislators. And a few of us did that. That felt awkward to us, but useful. Some of us discovered that we were inexperienced doing such things. We were still naïve about how to do such demonstrations and meetings with legislators. Some of us were impatient, or typically not suited temperamentally to doing these things. We again felt some blockage as we experienced doing anything other than a "big" action would be meaningless . . . yet "big" things seemed beyond our power to do. Others felt like that was where they could make an impact. So some of the group continued meeting with legislators, others went other directions. But all of us kept meeting regularly as a group.

I, influenced by the "Army–McCarthy" hearings, my parents' teachings, and what happened to "our people" in the Holocaust of World War II, felt caught between these two extreme alternatives. I very much wanted to do something that would make a difference for large and growing numbers of people who had few resources themselves. At the same time, I felt embarrassed by the seeming grandiosity of my intentions given the scope of the problem and my lack of knowledge of what I could really do that might make some difference.

As we continued talking about what we wanted to do and where our motivations came from, it suddenly dawned on us that feeling again like only big actions and commitments could make any difference was exactly one of the main reasons we felt stuck. We finally came to terms with the fact that the more we argued and talked about who was suited for what, and what kind of involvement held significance for anyone, the less we did. We resolved that we would act in various ways depending on our temperaments, our family needs, and our personal styles—and that we would continue to report in to each other in the group. This was a basic and obvious lesson (Lesson #5) that we needed to discover—and experience for ourselves—that there are different ways to act, and that different ways appeal to different temperaments and personal styles and the combination of different actions and styles are often helpful in accomplishing goals.

A few years later, one of us found an article (Chernin, 1993) that said some of this more succinctly. "Most people with a sense of social responsibility, who nevertheless do not act, are often (if unknowingly) measuring the acts of concern they might spontaneously undertake against a social imperative that immediately dwarfs them" (p. 18).

"The small is problematic, but it is redeemed by its capacity to generate consequence" (Chernin, p. 18).

One result of the prior discussions in our group was a decision to offer clinical service in ways that we knew how to do. Given the continuing decreases in funding for mental health services in local mental health centers, the closing of some centers, and an increased number of patients unable to obtain services, there was a big and growing need to provide low-cost, long-term therapy for those needing and wanting those services. Thus, as I talked with some of our ongoing group, and then with two other faculty members and two graduates of our program, the idea of the Psychotherapy Cooperative was birthed. The members of the "Co-op" group wanted to put our intentions and values into practice, as well as talk about issues of psychotherapy and social justice. For approximately 9 years now, this group, the Psychotherapy Cooperative, has offered pro bono services to the community. The "Co-op" has been a small but steady resource that has offered a setting for clients who want to do long-term psychotherapy but do not have medical insurance and/or cannot afford to be seen at mental health agencies in the area. Each therapist offers 3 hours a week of therapy and meets with a faculty consultant for 1 hour per week. All therapy and consultation services are volunteered.

This small enterprise that started by seeing a handful of clients has grown so that the original group of graduates who provided the psychotherapy will now become supervisors to another batch of graduates who will start to provide services. In this way we grow the availability of services provided to a larger number of clients, continue supervision for all, and keep ourselves in small cohesive groups of manageable size.

As this project has slowly grown, it has brought me into contact with others in the community who are doing work out of their own disciplines and skill (e.g., people working in street ministries, schools, shelters, etc.). In this way some of us from the Co-op met a minister who had strong clinical training and abilities and who had established with others a mental health ministry for homeless men and women in the area. Besides serving as resources for each other, we were also able to begin internship programs for graduate students at shelters for homeless people and for those on the street. In this way, the small step of beginning the Psychotherapy Co-op also led to being able to have graduate students in internships multiply the care given by community workers to people who had been receiving little care. We learned again that a single small step can indeed interconnect with and lead to other steps (Lessons #2 and #4). And although one's initial actions at the very start of a project are much less than one's grandiose fantasies, those actions have more positive repercussions than one can imagine (Lesson #6).

LESSONS FROM SURVIVORS

Concomitant with the time that I started including a question about any social-political concerns in my beginning sessions with new clients, I also began to do some work with a community that at first I knew little about. The time was the mid-1980s, following the War in Vietnam, this country's secret bombings in Cambodia, and the terrible genocide carried out there by the Khmer Rouge under the leadership of Pol Pot. Many Southeast Asian people, including many Cambodians, tried to flee their countries in an effort to survive and to raise their families in safety. A number of movies, such as *The Killing Fields*, were seen by millions of people. This was another instance when many of us in mental health work wanted "to do something" that would be useful or helpful. But what was that? The probability was that up to 2 million people were killed by the Khmer Rouge. How does one understand that? What can one do?

For some of us in our continuing reading/discussion/support group, there was an urge to "do something." At the same time, we didn't understand the culture, language, and religion of the others. Wasn't it more than a little presumptuous to think that we could help in a situation like this? And what was it we thought we could do? And besides, wasn't it hard enough just trying to live our lives with our family and our profession? Where is the time and energy to do anything about something else and something so vast? Again, our feelings moved back and forth between wanting to do something that was "enough" and feeling powerless, overwhelmed, and wanting to distance ourselves.

Again, we in the group sat with the question of "Why do we want to do this work?" Especially because all of us were busy with our work and families. And because few of us had much understanding of Southeast Asian culture. Why did we want to do *this* work? For me, there was the call not just from present-day refugees in pain, but also the internal call from my refugee grandparents' generation. What would they say to me if I could talk to them now? Talking out all of this in our group was enormously helpful to all of us in the group. There was space and safety to talk about our fantasies of what we would like to do, our grandiosity about doing something "big," and our guilt and powerlessness and busy schedules if we did nothing.

One lesson we learned was a confirmation that all of us in the group were in this together regardless of who among us would be directly involved. The importance of the group as a place of support and of challenge in which to confront ourselves and clarify our own motivations, especially those that continued to spring from the question of "Why do we want to do this work?" (e.g., of working with Southeast Asian refugees, or the Psychotherapy Co-op, or the more general project of trying to integrate social justice and our psychotherapy work) cannot be overestimated. And, because we know each other well, and know each other's families, there is also always the question of what is realistic for each of us, and for the group itself, to hold.

My decision in the process just discussed was to investigate a refugee medical clinic in the area and get more information about what went on, what would be helpful to them, and how I would feel about any possible involvement. This led to my sitting in with the medical director of the refugee clinic of a large public hospital that serves this county, as she talked with a Cambodian woman, via an interpreter, about the woman's pain, disabilities, and injuries that came during her imprisonment in one of the Khmer Rouge "work" camps. That one conversation led to another with myself, the woman, and an interpreter. I found that I wanted to learn more about the cultures, history, and traditions of Southeast Asia, so I soon found a Vietnamese man who had lived through the war in his country and was then trained as a social worker. He agreed to be my consultant, and so began another phase of my learning and training.

After being at the refugee clinic for more than 1 year, I placed an ad in one of the local professional journals and had the great fortune of finding another person who had traveled internationally, knew something about Southeast Asian cultures, and was interested in giving some time to this "talking" part of the clinic. Growing slowly, one step at a time, we became a group of three psychologists, one social worker, three master's degree-level counselors, two acupuncturists, two massage therapists, and then two graduate student interns. We added cooking groups, sewing groups, and story-telling groups.

When I asked these people why they had responded to my ads and notices, they simply said that they wanted to do something for the larger society in addition to the professional work they were already doing. They had felt stuck in a place of wanting to be more involved in the community, but didn't know where they could be or what they really had to offer. They appreciated the opportunity to be involved. And, after they had worked in the clinic for 6 months, they all said that they got so much more from the work than they gave.

I learned two more lessons from this. The first was how many people want to "do something more" than they are doing for the greater society and for the social justice values they hold (Lesson #7). It seemed to me that there was a small town of folks who wanted to do something like this. They had been stuck, as I had been, between their fantasies of "really doing something" and their sense of feeling powerless and overwhelmed by the enormity of the pains to be addressed.

The second lesson I learned relates to what I was told by my new colleagues after they had been at the clinic about 6 months. Although the patients thanked us and talked about us very favorably in their communities, we wondered how it was that the refugees continued to thank us when it seemed that we were the ones who got so much that was (and is) life-sustaining from seeing them? (Lesson #8). The following two examples illustrate some of the meaning generated in these relationships. They also demonstrate how social-political awareness and social justice seem to flow so naturally from this work. Finally, they continue the discussion of "Why do we do this work?"

HEARING EACH OTHER'S CRY

The patient I had seen in my very first visit to the refugee clinic became a patient I continued to see. She had suffered much pain and loss, including seeing two of her children killed in front of her, during the Khmer Rouge reign and then afterwards in a refugee camp in Thailand. After we had talked together for some time, she told me, during a particularly anxious period she was going through, of a memory that she had. She was in a refugee camp in Thailand and at one point the Khmer Rouge attacked the camp, as they had done on other occasions. This particular time, the fighting and exploding shells and artillery fire were quite intense and the refugees fled the camp, trying to make their way into the jungle. My patient, "N.," was part of this "flood of people" trying to escape. Everyone was frightened that they would be killed. As N. fled with two of her children and some friends from the camp, she saw a woman sitting by the side of the road and rocking her infant in her arms. She was moaning and crying and rocking back and forth. With all of this going on, N. told her children to go with the family friends into the jungle while N. went over to the woman by the side of the road. The shooting continued and the road was littered with people who had been shot. N. draped her body over the woman who was trying to nurse her child. Finally, the shooting stopped and N. could see that she and the woman were the only ones still alive on the road to the jungle. She thought that her children made it safely to the jungle because they had left early. She also saw that the infant at the woman's breast was dead.

During the telling of this very intense memory, all three of us in the office, N., the interpreter, and I, had tears in our eyes. I was amazed by many parts of the story—chief among them was N., this woman I knew who was partially disabled, and was depressed and anxious much of the time, stopping on her way to possible safety in the jungle to drape her body across those of the woman and her dead infant in the midst of rockets and automatic weapons fire. I knew she wasn't (at least at that time) very devout, so why did she stop?

She told me that she knew what it was like to suffer the loss of one's children. She said that as she ran down the road toward the jungle, she saw this woman's face. She said that she could not ignore that face, that cry, that mother and child. She said that the sight of those faces "called" to her. She could not ignore that call.

> "But weren't you afraid for yourself when you stopped?" I asked. She said that she and the woman trembled together, but that she had to do what she did. "The woman was in pain. I knew that crying and pain, too. That made us related to each other," she said. She continued telling me that during the Khmer Rouge time, no one in the Khmer Rouge-controlled work-concentration camps could talk with each other. If people did talk with each other about their hunger or pain, they would be killed. So they worked and often died beside each other, but could say nothing. "We all suffered, but we suffered in ourselves. We could not talk. The suffering was useless. When people hear each other's pain and talk with each other, then the suffering reminds them that they are all the same; they are all people." We all have pain. We must hear that and see that in each other or we are not people. (Gerber, 1996, p. 298)

HEARING THE CRY: A SECOND STORY

Approximately 7 years ago, a young woman who is an interpreter and a paraprofessional therapist approached a couple of us about starting a group for those Cambodian survivors who wanted to talk and write about their experiences before, during, and after the Cambodian genocide. She said that she and some others didn't want to merely exist while feeling dead inside, but they wanted "to live and become healthy and grow." She said that she needed to do this for herself, and for those people who had died in Cambodia and in the camps, and for their children who were now living in this country. Although this country was safer, she worried about being in a country with different traditions where spiritual values were so absent in the day-to-day culture and where materialistic ones were common.

The other therapist who was asked to be in this group wondered with me about whether these people who had survived unimaginable conditions would be able to do such a group. Certainly many people in pain cannot bear to tell their stories, and, in the process, re-live such horror and death. The remarkable fact is that, indeed, some of these people can, in the face of so much that has been done to crush any sense of meaning and religion and values from their lives, try to create again some sort of meaning and life for themselves and their community.

The other therapist and I talked regularly with each other about the survivors group as it began and continued meeting. We were trying to better understand what we were witnessing. We felt like we lacked the words to describe what we heard and why, in the midst of such pain as we heard, did we feel that there was something so transformative for us? Why were we so drawn to these people and their stories? Did we feel guilty that we had not and were not doing enough in the world? Did we feel guilty because, even after September 11th, we were feeling relatively safe in this country? Were we doing it because of recent events in order to learn about situations that might, more and more, befall this country? As we wondered about these questions we realized that something more emerged for all of us. As we wondered what kept hope alive for the survivors with whom we worked, our conversations led us into a deeper sense of community with each other and a deeper exploration of what enabled us to keep our own hopes alive in a world that felt (and feels) increasingly frightening and vulnerable.

During one of the sessions of the survivors group, one of the participants, a Cambodian man in his 50s, said, "As long as I can talk to people about what happened to us, then I am alive. They [i.e., the Khmer Rouge] have not silenced me. I live and raise my new family and tell them about what happened and that we have survived to live." Hearing such a statement made the other Cambodian survivors as well as the two of us volunteers feel a renewed sense of hope.

The survivors' fear, however, continues now, especially after September 11th, the increased awareness of terrorism, the deportation of refugees who had been in this country for some years, the increased use of police powers and encroachment of our civil liberties by the attorney general and president of this country, and the war in Iraq. Another of the Cambodian survivors in our group spoke to me again about what he had described to all of us a few years earlier about the torture he heard and saw others endure in Cambodia. He talked again about how helpless he felt and how terribly scared he was. He spoke of his own torture as having been done in an isolated place; there was, he remembered,

> no one to hear me. No one knew what was happening to me. I thought I would die. I wanted to die. I tried to remember people who loved me, but my pain was too harsh. And then I thought of going to the temple when I was a boy. The monks liked me and taught me even though I was very young. . . . I didn't believe that Buddha would come save me, but I did think about the monks praying with me and that helped me during the torture. I remembered that the monks and Buddha talk about suffering and I thought the monks would care if they heard me. I think that kept me alive. They knew that we suffer and that we must hear each other. They cared for me. I, too, must care for others and not let them be alone with their pain. We must do that for each other or we will all die.

Clearly there is something about what we hear from these Cambodian survivors that makes us feel that although there is, of course, death and pain in their memories, there is also life. We do know that witnessing them and what they say and how they are, despite the nightmares and headaches that we volunteers have after hearing such memories, feels like a privilege. To try to hear the call of another and to try to recognize their suffering in whatever limited way that we can feels like choosing life over death. And in this process of choosing life, we feel like we become more human and reaffirm our ethical power in the face of a world in which destruction seems to rule. "It is this attention to the Other which across the cruelties of our century . . . can be affirmed as . . . a supreme ethical principle . . . Properly speaking, the inter-human lies in a non-indifference of one to another, in a responsibility of one for another" (Levinas, 1988, pp. 158–159).

WHY DO WE DO THIS WORK?

A short time after the Cambodian man spoke about being heard as a boy by the monks and about the need to hear each other and care for each other or we shall die, I talked with a physician colleague who also works with refugees. I wondered with her why she had chosen to work with refugees. She wasn't sure why she did this work except that the work was "more interesting, more alive" for her than working with other populations. She also told me, however, that a friend of hers had previously suggested to her that she did this work because of her need "to be adored." That is, with a group of people as scared and needy as the refugees from Southeast Asia and Western Africa with whom we work, there can be stronger expressions of thanks when one does something to try to help them than when one works with "typical" Western patients.

This understanding of our motivation to help being based solely or chiefly on a model of self-interest seemed very limited to me. Although we all like to feel special or needed or praised, this certainly didn't seem like the whole story.

My colleague continued her reflection, saying,

> All these people are considered "Other" by society. Some of them tend to be at the extremes of "Otherness," but all of us have felt "Other" at some point in our lives. I know I have. I think we all know what it's like to some extent and we recognize the "Other's" pain as having been ours, too. So we want to reach out to them. . . . I think we all want a world in which everyone can feel that they belong.

It took a good deal of time for us to capture some of the feelings that motivated us to work with the patients that we do. It was extremely difficult to put these feelings into words. For example, as we talked about wanting to help these patients who were in so much pain and had experienced so much loss feel better and be more able to help themselves, we wondered whether our desire to help was really rooted in making ourselves feel better. So, does helping others make us feel more loved, more powerful, more special, and is that why we do this work? We admitted that these factors certainly can be part of our motivation, yet certainly not what felt like the biggest part. We wondered about what seemed like the lack of words, the lack of vocabulary for helping others "because that's how things should be." Wasn't it possible that a strong part of one's motivation came from having compassion for others as well as from "self-interest"? Yet why was this so hard to put into words? And why when we did talk about our caring and compassion did we feel naïve and silly? Interestingly enough, we acknowledged to each other how much more easily the Cambodian survivors spoke of compassion and care for others than did we.

I wondered if Robert Wuthnow (1991) was correct in saying, "In an individualistic society . . . caring is sometimes seen as an abnormality. We do not even believe in sharing too deeply in the suffering of others. Our individual autonomy is too important. If caring for others becomes too demanding, we get out. We call it an obsession" (p. 219). Does this mean that if it is hard to find "culturally acceptable words for motives related to compassion, if we sense that when we speak in this way, people close their ears to us, then not only is our understanding of the range of human motives narrowed, but our present and future behaviors also can be limited"?(p. 82).

Yet, the lessons, the confirmations in the work of the Psychotherapy Co-op, and the work with the Cambodian refugees are that, despite all the indifference and pain that are part of our human heritage, the desire to hear and respond to "the Other" lives. Although there are many obstacles to our hearing and responding, there is still the possibility for hearing another, being heard, and coming into life. The imagination of the listener is moved by hearing testimony-narrative, and then more compassionate action can occur. Just as words and values are needed to sustain our compassion and our humanity, so is responsible action.

LESSONS FROM TRAINING: WHAT I LEARNED

Teaching the values and ethics of social justice without anticipating some of the barriers students might encounter in their clinics, and without teaching what actions and alternatives support the values of social justice is to create despair in our trainees as opposed to hope (Lesson #9). This has likely always been true, but it is especially relevant in these times of economic upheaval, moral emptiness, and personal isolation.

HOW I LEARNED

Ten years ago, a student in our graduate program sought me out to discuss his internship experience in one of the community mental health centers in the area. This particular internship site had been considered one of the "plum offers," and he had been very happy to have been offered it. It was one of the few places left in the area that had continued to offer long-term therapy to its clients regardless of their ability to pay. It also offered a good deal of supervision and consultation to its trainees.

The student, like many other students over the last several years, had recently been told by the internship site that, because of financial pressures within the county, there was less money available to fund mental health services. Therefore, contracts with managed care companies (for obtaining county money based on a county-wide managed care model) were now a necessity for the agency's survival. He was told it was time for therapists to be more efficient and more responsible for their work. He was told that he was a "provider" of services to "consumers" and that he must be "productive." His supervisor said, "This is only right so that others can make sure that the services provided are appropriate and efficient and not a waste of time and money . . . consumers have no right to complain since most of the cost of therapy is covered by someone else."

He also was told that complaining about the way things were wasn't going to get him or his consumers anything. In fact, he was told he was going to be evaluated on the basis of his "productivity" (i.e., the number of therapy hours he actually did each week and the number of new patients he was able to see each week) and his ability to carry out the mandate of the agency—and nothing else. Talking during any consultation he got, if he got any, was not to be about the switch to the current system, nor was he to talk about any of this to the people he saw in psychotherapy. "Talking with others about this just impedes the work you and they do. It prevents everybody from being productive and makes the consumers discontent without accomplishing anything."

Finally he was told that the agency was giving him clinical experience, for which he should be grateful. If he wanted a good recommendation from them, he had better get to work and "not think about other things." If he didn't like it, of course, "there are many others looking for positions like yours who would love for you to leave."

This last statement really scared the student. He pictured a world of others like himself who were desperately hungry to start their careers, who had sizable amounts of student loans to pay back, and would do anything to survive. He not only felt scared but also isolated and alone. He had been made to feel like it was dangerous to talk with his peers or faculty about all this. His only alternative was to fight for himself by himself. He had come to me in shame and humiliation because although he had been trying to fight, he felt that he no longer could do this by himself. Although he experienced this as a statement of his inadequacy, he was too tired and overwhelmed and confused to do otherwise. And, in addition, he was disillusioned.

Hearing his comments, and then those of others, made me realize that we on the faculty had given him and others words and theories and values during their 1st-year courses—courses that had evoked excitement and increased their idealism. What we hadn't done was adequately prepare them for the specific realities they might find in the clinics. These realities were how the economy and the conservative turn of politics have impacted mental health care, how the dynamics of power have shifted in some clinics, what alternative responses—and their attendant risks—there might be to talking with a supervisor like the one just described, how we can learn from each other's experience, and so on.

HOW STUDENTS AND FACULTY RESPONDED

The first thing that happened was that there were a series of meetings between students and faculty. One meeting was for students in their clinical internships and faculty. Another meeting was for graduates of our program and our faculty. A third meeting was for our 1st-year students and our faculty. These meetings were jointly arranged by the student just mentioned and myself. Part of the decision to initiate all these meetings came from remembering my earlier experience working with Southeast Asian refugees, wondering if anyone else was interested in this, and getting many people who wanted to do this work (Lesson #7). That is, the sense that the "one" often stands for many more.

The purpose of the meeting with students in their internships was to hear their comments about their internship experiences, especially in regards how they felt to shift from the excited idealism of their more academic first year, to the clinical setting of their second year. What we heard was a great deal of despair. Learning "first-hand" about therapy process and client–therapist interpersonal dynamics was exciting, but they felt they had also become part of a machine designed to grind down their spirit. They particularly disliked some of the new vocabulary they were learning—words like "providers" and "consumers" as well as the emphasis on speed rather than care. They felt naïve and ill-prepared for such a world, and wondered if this was what they really wanted to do. They said that they wanted to do the work of therapy, and particularly to groups that were underserved, but all said that they heard much too much about the "bottom line," and "keeping their mouths shut," and "finishing the paperwork."

More meetings were held and more information shared between students and faculty, including many comments about why they wanted to do this work. They spoke of the therapeutic process as exciting and growth producing and intimate. And they spoke of their caring, their desire to "be with" an other, and of "trying in some little way to make things better in the world." They spoke about their commitment to helping others. And, again, they spoke of their disappointments at feeling like there probably wouldn't be much room for these dreams to become reality in the work for which they were training.

Others felt like there was so much to learn about psychotherapy process and the therapeutic relationship that they didn't have the internal psychological space or energy to "try to cure the world" (in the words of one student). I certainly understood what that student was saying, but I also took those remarks as meaning that I had plenty of work to do in trying to improve my teaching. I needed to improve the way I conveyed understanding a client as a being in and shaped by "external" forces in the larger world, as well as being in and shaped by the intimate world of family. I needed to improve my teaching about human beings as beings in context—whether we talk about the social-political historical factors that help shape our being, or the social-political historical factors that shape the clinics where we are interning, the clients whom we are seeing, and the therapeutic interactions that we are part of.

As a result of many of these conversations and meetings, some of the alumni of the program who were involved with social justice concerns spoke with our interning students about possible alternative actions that clinicians could take both in and out of their clinics. The alumni felt highly valued by the students in the clinics and therefore continuing conversations were established, and numerous smaller conversations and relationships were kindled. In addition, a tradition began with some 2nd-year graduate students having continuing discussions and conversations with 1st-year students about all these matters.

Faculty doing supervision as well as some faculty teaching the 1st-year class began talking with students about why they wanted to do this work. And as these reflections on their varied motivations continued, conversations could be started about what barriers might be encountered in the clinics, in the graduate program, in themselves. (Establishing safe and supportive environments for these discussions was, of course, most important.) Slowly, as students moved into the 2nd year, discussions could begin to include possible alternative actions to be taken, possible risks involved, power dynamics, getting needed support for themselves, and reflecting on and learning from what resulted when actions were taken, and so on. In these ways, many of our students, graduates of the program, and clinical and nonclinical faculty talked with each other, tried to learn from each other, and tried to define what was helpful and what was not.

As noted, not all of the faculty or students involved themselves in these discussions. Those students and faculty not involved cited busy schedules, other priorities, or simply "not believing that they needed to do this." Although, on the one hand, I was disappointed that not all of us were involved in this process (and I continue to try to learn from and respect these decisions), on the other hand, I was pleased that many of us were making a start and were committed to the process.

WHAT HAPPENED TO THE STUDENT

The exhausted and frightened student just mentioned sat with his outrage and his fears for several weeks. He talked about his situation during supervision with me and with his classmates. He talked about why he wanted to do this work and how his motivations have developed and changed over time. During this process of reflection and dialogue, a different response slowly emerged. The student decided to object whenever anyone at the agency called the people he saw in therapy "consumers." With fear and trepidation he said at his agency, "I am not a commodity to be bought and sold. I am not a salesperson. Please don't call the clients I see 'consumers.'" Initially he said that this was a "small" decision and action, but it evoked lectures from his supervisor that were frightening and made him feel like he was "stepping off the edge of the known universe."

A larger decision involved telling all his clients that county-managed care requirements and agency policy mandated that their number of visits be time-limited, and that he could no longer promise strict confidentiality to them and for their records. The student said that he wanted to try to do what he felt was ethical. To keep all he knew secret from his clients would be, to paraphrase Cushman (1995), "exercising power while disguising power" (p. 283). To go along with the agency's rules would mean that the psychotherapist was collaborating with a system where economics was more important than the compassionate, responsible listening to the individuals who are to be served by the system. Eventually, all of this resulted in a switch in internship sites. It also resulted in the series of meetings, conversations, and course changes among students, graduates of the program, and the faculty just described.

Of course, the process is not finished. It is just begun and is ongoing. Along this path, faculty who valued social justice and ethical concerns learned more about what we weren't providing in our course work and training. We were humbled in the process, but were also energized. On this 50th anniversary of Senator Joseph McCarthy's finally meeting his match, we continue to learn and work at further integrating strong, ethical clinical training and our concerns for social justice.

TO LIFE: WHY WE DO THIS WORK

It is becoming clear we live in an age of traumatic change for the self and for the place of persons in society and in the narrative of culture. Lifton (1967, 1976) teaches us that the lessons of social justice and of witnessing those defined as "Other" can help create meaning and sustain life during this time when community and public/social welfare seem largely to have fallen apart. What the survivors of this traumatic age teach is related to the responsibility for our compassionate hearing of the "Other's" call.

Prilleltensky (1996) urges the helping professions to look at the individual and also beyond the individual and focus on the larger human community and the political-social structures that impede human life: "To reclaim the search for the good society, we must invoke the concepts of the moral sphere, political literacy, and political action. . . . We should ask ourselves whether our apathetic bystanding does not violate the moral sphere" (p. 319). The testimony of homeless people, refugee survivors, families, and children who are excluded from clinical services because of economics and a disintegrating mental health system is necessary for understanding the community and our future. Otherwise, this information will be omitted from our common history, depriving us of the opportunity to learn from each other and change that which acts as a barrier to life. When survivors no longer speak, or when there is nobody to hear, when mental health and social services especially for certain groups are minimized or eliminated, our awareness and compassion for the needs and concerns of others are eliminated, too. And, the potential for social change that informed such hearing and such knowledge is also eliminated. Hearing and responding to the "Other's" call gives definition and meaning to the do-er, whose response opens one to something larger and beyond oneself. Our historical period, characterized by consumerism and "bottom lines," assumes that filling ourselves with material goods is all that is necessary to sustain life. The gift of responsibility, of hearing the "Other's" call, offers an opportunity to restore connection to something beyond ourselves and to restore the sacred into everyday life and actions. Thus, do we also restore our own humanity and consecrate our everyday abilities of hearing and seeing: "The small, it might be said, spins the threads that weave the net that catches the world" (Chernin, 1993, p.91).

REFERENCES

Chernin, K. (1993). The politics of the small. *Tikkun, 8,* 15–91.

Cushman, P. (1990). Why the self is empty: Toward a historically situated psychology. *American Psychologist, 45,* 599–611.

Cushman, P. (1995). *Constructing the self, constructing America.* Reading, MA: Addison-Wesley.

Gerber, L. (1990). Integrating political-societal concerns in psychotherapy. *American Journal of Psychotherapy, 44,* 471–483.

Gerber, L. (1992). Intimate politics: Connectedness and the social-political self. *Psychotherapy, 29,* 626–630.

Gerber, L. (1996). We must hear each other's cry: Lessons from Pol Pot survivors. In C. Strozier & M. Flynn (Eds.), *Genocide, war, and human survival* (pp. 297–305). London: Rowman, Littlefield.

Jacobs, D. (1988). Love, work, and survival. In H. Levine, D. Jacobs, & L. Rubin (Eds.), *Psychoanalysis and the nuclear threat* (pp. 173–187). Hillsdale, NJ: The Analytic Press.

Jacoby, R. (1983). *The repression of psychoanalysis.* New York: Basic Books.

Levinas, E. (1969). *Totality and infinity.* Pittsburgh: Duquesne University Press.

Levinas, E. (1988). Useless suffering. In R. Bernasconi & D. Wood (Eds.), *The provocation of Levinas: Rethinking the other* (pp. 100–135). London: Routledge.

Lifton, R. J. (1967). *Death in life: Survivors of Hiroshima.* New York: Basic Books.

Lifton, R. J. (1976). *The life of the self.* New York: Harper.

Lifton, R. J. (1979). *The broken connection: On death and the continuity of life.* New York: Basic Books.

Mack, J. (1984). Resistances to knowing in the nuclear age. *Harvard Educational Review, 54,* 260–270.

Mack, J. (1988). The threat of nuclear war in clinical work. In H. Levine, D. Jacobs, & L. Rubin (Eds.), *Psychoanalysis and the nuclear threat* (pp. 189–214). Hillsdale, NJ: The Analytic Press.

Marmor, J. (1988). Psychiatry in a troubled world: The relation of clinical practice and social reality. *American Journal of Psychotherapy, 58,* 484–491.

Prilleltensky, I. (1989). Psychology and the status quo. *American Psychologist, 44,* 797–802.

Prilleltensky, I. (1996). Human, moral, and political values for an emancipatory psychology. *The Humanistic Psychologist, 24,* 307–324

Segal, H. (1988). Silence is the real crime. In H. Levine, D. Jacobs, & L. Rubin (Eds.), *Psychoanalysis and the nuclear threat* (pp. 35–58). Hillsdale, NJ: The Analytic Press.

Walsh, R. (1989). Toward a psychology of human survival: Psychological approaches to contemporary threats. *American Journal of Psychotherapy, 43,* 158–180.

Wuthnow, R. (1991). *Acts of compassion.* Princeton, NJ: Princeton University Press.

LIBERATING VISIONS
OF CLINICAL PRACTICE

4

Radical Psychiatry: An Approach to Personal and Political Change

Beth Roy
Private Practice San Francisco

Another world is not only possible, she is on her way. On a quiet day, I can hear her breathing.

—Arundhati Roy (2003)

In 1973, I arrived in California and discovered that a good friend had become a lay psychotherapist, working with a group called "Bay Area Radical Psychiatry." I was doubtful. A socialist and passionate critic of therapy, I believed most individual distress grew out of oppressive social conditions. To treat the individual, I was convinced, was to become distracted from the real deal: transforming society. Young and passionate, I scoffed at the possibility that therapy could be anything more than a Band-Aid on a seriously bloody wound.

At the same time, I respected the views of my friend. Becky Jenkins was a "red-diaper baby" (the child of left-wing activists), someone whose commitment to social justice I knew to be consistent and thoughtful. "Just come see the work," she cajoled, and I could think of no convincing reason to decline. So I sat in on a group session she conducted . . . and I was moved, fascinated, and engaged. I can't say I was an immediate convert, but a door opened a few inches, and I continued to observe the work, listening with a more thoughtful ear. Increasingly, I came to see possibilities for bringing together personal and political change, bridging a dichotomy that had always before tilted me in an activist and antitherapy direction.

I also needed a job. A single mom who had lived outside the United States for many years, I lacked the essentials—a credit card, a history of employment, a clear career path. Still, I was resisting taking on work out of sync with my values. So, I agreed to join the collective of Radical Psychiatrists practicing in the San Francisco Bay Area.

Thirty-plus years later, I am still practicing. Mostly I do group therapy and conflict resolution, the two most direct outgrowths of the social theory that is the basis of the work. But some individual therapy has crept in over the years, as well as some couple counseling and family work, although in an atypical form. I also train and supervise therapists. I view all of it as political activity; indeed, I believe all therapy is political, no matter how it views itself. In the case of Radical Psychiatry, the politics are explicit, openly stated in the theoretical underpinnings, deeply imbedded in the practice.

IN THE SPIRIT OF THE TIMES

On Tuesday, Wednesday, and Thursday evenings, groups of six to eight people convene in my office. We call them problem-solving groups, not therapy, in an effort to get away from a medical mindset for the work we do. I lead both women's groups and a gender-mixed group. Based on a model of cooperation, each member sets her or his own goals for the work. Time is shared through an explicit process created by each group of people to suit their sensibilities. Members take turns talking about whatever is on their minds that night. While I actively guide the work, intervening in ways particular to my role as leader, members interact intently, making observations, giving feedback, sharing their own life experience, registering feelings, asking questions, growing relationships, nurturing, supporting, and critiquing, all within a framework of respectful speech and self-determination. Groups are the heart of the practice, for reasons both pragmatic and theoretical.

Radical Psychiatry began in collectivity. It was the beginning of the 1970s. Movements for social change were thick in the air: civil rights, free speech, antiwar, lifestyle change, gay liberation, and feminism. Berkeley and San Francisco were flooded with young people, drawn from towns all over the country by stories of flower-child utopia in the Bay Area. They crashed in cheap "pads," smoked pot on the streets, experimented with free sex—and some of them fell apart both physically and emotionally. Far away from home, confronting unfamiliar realities of poverty, unskilled in recognizing or solving the social problems that come along with revolutionary new personal behavior, they fell ill with malaise ranging from unattended respiratory infections to unheard-of sexual diseases. Right along with the open and welcoming love fest the flower children so progressively proposed, many people also encountered conventional jealousies, conflicts, competitiveness, unrequited love, proscribed anger, and, most surprising of all, loneliness and a sense of inadequacy.

The Berkeley Free Clinic formed to address physical problems, and a loose-knit group of progressive therapists came forward to address the emotional ones. Radical Psychiatry eventually evolved from this latter group. This part of the story is hearsay for me. It predated my return to the country. The version I carry in my mind is that a group of people formed to create a new approach to psychological work built in the spirit of the times on the foundation of a social theory. Hogie Wyckoff, a student at the University of California at Berkeley, brought new understandings of Marxism joined with her passionate feminism; Claude Steiner his years of experience leading Transactional Analysis groups; Bob Schwebel a critique of his graduate studies in psychology and an interest in designing noncompetitive games; Joy Marcus her talents as a poet; Becky Jenkins her roots in the political left and the arts. There were contributors who came from Quaker backgrounds and Catholic and Jewish ones, from experiences in many of the social movements of the times, from wealthy families and poor ones, from every part of the country. Racial diversity was lacking; typical of the "ghetto-ized" times, the new movement was largely White. Some originators were psychologists, others were social workers; most had no professional training and eagerly embraced new means of developing skills based on an apprenticeship model. Bonded by a common desire to be of service in some way that reflected the radical spirit of the times, the founders set to work to articulate the principles of a political psychology, and to live those principles in the process as they constituted themselves a collective.

The first and perhaps most productive commitment of the group was to be realistic as well as idealistic. Working collectively meant exercising a will to challenge power in all its forms; but having articulated a desire for cooperation, the group quickly found that they did not in fact know how to do it. Instead, they recognized how deeply schooled they were in practices of competitiveness, just like the people they sought to serve, just like most Americans. To be cooperative required both a theory of cooperation and a way to embody it in practice.

From the beginning, then, practical needs combined with ideology to shape a theoretical agenda resting on three legs: a social-constructionist description of psychology, a visionary procedure for cooperation, and a realistic understanding of power.

WHERE SOCIETY AND PSYCHE INTERSECT

Radical Psychiatry theory begins with the simplest of premises: people are good. We do the best we can under the conditions we are given. Those conditions are social in nature, and because they are severely stressed for most of us, they stress and distort human experience. The first step, therefore, is to name the material conditions in which emotional and interpersonal life is lived.

Operationally, that set of ideas runs counter to embedded assumptions of more conventional therapies. We resist explanatory notions of pathology, of addictive or self-destructive behavior, or of biochemical flaws, believing that, in their cultural and professional popularity, they overshadow a view from a more political and material angle. If people act peculiarly, if they are hostile or depressed or anxious, we postulate that there are describable reasons for those behaviors. Starting with an understanding of alienation, we study the ways social dynamics become deeply imbedded in individual psyches and lead to feelings, ideas, and behaviors that limit a sense of what is possible, sometimes causing people to act against their own best interests in a manner that may seem irrational but, seen in a larger context, is not. Instead, such behaviors, and the feelings that intertwine them, are products of oppression and its internalization.

It is in the interrelationship of material facts and internalized oppression that the work of "therapy" lies. I put quotation marks around "therapy" because it suggests a process of healing when, in fact, I'm talking about a process of change. Language is a boundary, a fence walling off alternative ways of thinking. None of us is nor ever has been a psychiatrist, in the professional sense of the word. But in the early days of our work, we reclaimed "psychiatry," noting that the Greek meaning translates into "soul healing," a practice, we insisted, that is everybody's business. In that sense, the process of group is not about sick psyches; it is about injured spirits.

ALIENATION AND CHANGE, SOCIAL AND PERSONAL

We equate human distress with alienation, and we attribute alienation to an interactive combination of three factors: *oppression, mystification,* and *isolation.*

First, *oppression* is a fundamental experience of all but a very few individuals living in hierarchical societies. Oppression is coercion in its many forms, evident and opaque, physical and subtle, that induce or force us to accept less than fully human lives: disassociated work, unhappy relationships, absent communities, conflict-ridden families, and other familiar features of the times.

Given that the human will is strong, and strongly leans toward well-being, why do we comply with oppression? We would be less likely to submit if we knew we were being oppressed. But, especially in modern capitalist societies, oppression is *mystified,* the second element making for alienation. We are told lies about the prevailing social conditions. Through popular culture, interpersonal transactions, legend, and myth, we are told that we live in the best of all possible systems, that we are free individuals and have free choice, that the best succeed and the inadequate fail. If we are unhappy, therefore, it is our own fault, the product of some moral inadequacies: laziness perhaps, or stupidity or some other unredeemable flaw. Material oppression thus becomes internalized in moral terms, and the network of ideas forms an ideology so deeply learned as to become unquestioned, transmuted into invisible assumptions.

This approach to understanding the interaction of society and psyche has been elaborated by numbers of 20th-century scholar-activists. Frantz Fanon (1963) described its political course in the framework of colonialism, whereas Phyllis Chesler (1989) analyzed women's relationship to psychiatry in terms of internalized oppression. Perhaps the most compelling exploration, because it focuses on cultural dynamics of mystification in an attempt to conceptualize and create counterculture as a revolutionary act, is the work of Antonio Gramsci (1979). We are immersed in a sea of ideas and practices that, taken together, form the boundaries within which we can question social reality, indeed within which we can think. The work of social change, and by extension of personal change, is involved with an ability to think outside that frame. "I don't know who discovered water," some clever person said, "but I'm pretty sure it wasn't a fish." Much of the work of Radical Psychiatry is aimed at naming those assumptions about self and society that limit the possibilities for action, and then quite literally rethinking them, transforming them into a redefinition of the possible.

The route to accomplishing that process is honest interaction. *Isolation* is the third condition necessary to the perpetuation of alienation. There are many ways to think about the functional impact of isolation, how it is enacted and what it accomplishes. We can start with the role of shame (Scheff, 1990). A key element in constructing any social order, shame holds the whip that keeps individuals within the fence of acceptable behavior. Although every society produces some version of shame, each society does so differently: that which is shameful here is no big deal somewhere else. In modern America, the effective values, those standards the violation of which cause the cheek to burn and the voice to falter, are different for people in different social locations—gender, class, race, and so on—but they all tend to cluster around individualism. The ultimate judgments on an individual's character are about autonomy, independence, effectiveness, and success: At least, those are the measuring sticks for men. Women's standards have grown closer to men's as gendered economic roles have begun to converge, but they still involve what were once complementary measures such as an ability to put others' needs before one's own, to nurture and bolster rather than assert and initiate. Now women still find these relational injunctions deeply settled within their sense of self-worth, but they are in conflict with the more masculine commands that fuel competitive success in the capitalist world of work: to be able to stand alone in the world, to look out for oneself, and so on.

Thus oppression, mystification, and isolation interact to produce the distressed and disempowered individual whom conventional psychiatry sees as pathological. If human distress is actually a form of alienation, then the work of therapy becomes a project of changing the conditions that alienate. The early Radical Psychiatry theorists captured that agenda in two formulae:

Alienation = Oppression + Mystification + Isolation

Contact + Awareness + Action → Change (Liberation?)

The first step toward "soul healing" is to bring people together. Many of the social movements of the day were vividly demonstrating how powerful a force the telling of life stories could be. Women's consciousness-raising groups were an explicit model, as was with Eric Berne's work with groups. The simple act of people gathering in small batches to talk honestly about their lives was the core organizing form for the burgeoning women's liberation movement. Meanwhile, the Black power movement challenged ideas as fundamental as beauty; "Black is beautiful" had a galvanizing impact on African American people's sense of self-worth, raising to consciousness the inhibiting force of standards of beauty for all people.

The second step in the process is thus a potential outgrowth of the first, to construct a different understanding of life and oneself in society. I say "potential" because we all have had experiences of being in groups that compound alienation rather than relieving it. Groups, as we usually find them, are a powerful force for oppression. Families, our first group experience, often both enforce roles on every member and mystify the oppressive nature of those roles through a moral discourse grounded in cultures of secrecy. Families talk about privacy when actually they promote shame by imposing silence, a self-protective construct in a competitive and judgmental world. Classrooms, that familiar childhood exposure to groups, institutionalize more subtle familial lessons about competition; we are endlessly, explicitly judged and ranked against our classmates. Job sites capitalize on the pedagogy of competitiveness, adding the major incentive of insecurity: If we don't stack up well, we suffer unemployment. Meanwhile, friendship groups and communities created for recreation and social support instead reproduce secrecy and competition, the only rules of interaction we know. How many times do people "hear it through the grapevine," experiencing the shame of being the last to know that which has been whispered elsewhere first.

THE COOPERATION THEORY

No wonder then that so many people shy away from groups. Simple contact has the potential to be as oppressive as it can be liberatory. The early Radical Psychiatry collective lived that problem even as they tried working consensually to create the new practice. A major element of the work was clearly to unlearn one way of relating to others, and, in its stead, learn to cooperate. One of the earliest projects was, therefore, to identify the basic components of cooperation, to create a theory that might guide practice. What the collective came up with was pretty simple: a commitment to honesty and to respectful, noncoercive interaction. These precepts were captured in the form of a *cooperation contract* consisting of three agreements:

- No secrets or lies
- No power plays
- No self-sacrifice

Seemingly obvious, in the real world, these rules test core questions about relationships. They require two crucial pre-conditions: a reasonable approximation of equal power and a shared will toward equal rights. Failing these conditions, simple acts of honesty can be high-risk business. I've noted how destructive secrets can be in families and communities. But secrecy has a function: where there is a danger of coercion, through force or judgment, it is wise to use information strategically. Information, as has been well demonstrated in the modern communications era, is power, a tool both for those in positions of superiority and of suppression. Withholding information can be a means for imposing ones' will on others or for self-protection. In either case, it precludes cooperation.

To dramatize the importance of information, we call secrets "lies of omission." Keeping secrets is not generally seen as a "bad thing," whereas telling lies is. But we contend that secrets are every bit as destructive when people are striving to conduct relationships cooperatively. Withholding information is, in fact, a power play.

A power play is defined as any act designed to get another person to do something he or she would not otherwise choose to do. In subtle or overt form, it is coercion. To agree to eliminate power plays is to sign on for negotiation, persuasion, consensus.

The third rule, no self-sacrifice, is in some ways the most difficult to enact. Giving up one's rights and interests is also, in a more convoluted way, an act of coercion, a secret decision to withhold information and produce an outcome that might well be different if everyone were involved in the process. We look at the phenomenon in terms of a concept taken from Transactional Analysis, the Rescue (or Drama) Triangle. Rescue is similar to co-dependency, but with a crucial difference that makes it a more useful tool for analyzing power. It describes three roles: *Rescuer, Victim,* and, its distinguishing feature, *Persecutor.* To Rescue is to do more than your share of the work around some transaction, or to do something you really don't want to do—two variations on a theme of self-sacrifice. Rescue often takes the form of an implicit and unchallenged division of labor. A prototypic example grounded in gender dynamics is given to us by common ways heterosexual couples find themselves handling life's work. Same-sex couples may experience seemingly similar dynamics, but with crucial and illustrative differences (Rabenold, 1988). Similarly, although the couple I describe are White and working-class, their story may well ring familiar to people of many other social identities.

Simon is a skilled carpenter; he spends his weekends and evenings renovating the basement of the house that he owns with Wendy. They desperately need more space now that they have two small kids, and, what with mortgage payments and repaying the loan Wendy's parents gave them for the down payment, they couldn't possibly afford to pay for labor. At first, Simon liked the creative challenge, but the pleasure has long since worn thin and all he wants is to be finished.

Meanwhile, Wendy is left with a lot more child care than she really wants to do, in addition to her part-time sales job at the department store. She's a dedicated mom, but all the work of getting kids up and out in the morning, bathed and settled at night, is draining her. She tries to talk with Simon about it, without a lot of success. He sees her complaints as criticism, "attack" is his word for it, and, in truth, feels helpless to do anything about it anyway.

Simon *Rescues* by tending to physical space; Wendy, by taking charge of both the domestic and emotional environments. He fixes things, she takes care of the household and relationships. Each of them has become *Victimized* by their Rescue, suffering losses and pain. But each also falls into the Rescue role because she or he sees the other as a Victim. Wendy couldn't possibly learn to wield a hammer, could she? And Simon is hopeless around the struggles and maneuvers of breakfast and bedtime. But both parents have long since become burned out, and they take their fatigue and depletion out on each other. They *Persecute,* Wendy by indignant nagging, Simon by refusing to talk and eventually turning his bottled up emotional energy into outbursts of angry shouting. Wendy feels martyred, Simon beleaguered. Each is both right and wrong.

Wendy has no constructive way to voice her feelings, and they come out as anger at Simon, especially when he insists he's working harder than she is. She falls into the competitive pattern of trying to top his sense of oppression. Moreover, she senses that the work she does is not visible as work to him. After all, he remembers his mother's doing all the same work without complaining. Isn't it just part of life? Whereas Simon's own work in the basement yields very tangible results on a daily basis.

But Simon too feels helpless. He can't see a way to get off the treadmill of working 8-to-5 as a nonunion carpenter and then coming home to more work. He feels responsible for supporting his family, knowing that his manual skills earn more money than Wendy could possibly command. But he also experiences an endless series of demands on him, with little enough encouragement to meet them and far too little appreciation for what he does.

Each looks to the other to solve the pressing problems, each knowing, at some level, the impossibility of that quest. They have some friends and relatives to whom they occasionally complain, but nowhere on the social horizon does anything promise to deliver the effective help they need and deserve. In this respect, they are actual victims of an unkind social system, of class and of the nuclear family, as well as psychological Victims insofar as they have come to a false conviction that the problems lie in their own and the other's inadequacies, and the remedies lie beyond their powers.

POWER

This example is typical of a gendered division of labor, still very common in today's heterosexual relationships when both women and men work for wages but men on average earn more money and women still do more than 50% of domestic labor (Hochschild, 1989). It is also prototypical of Rescue as a power dynamic. A social structure that results in scarcity (in this case, of money and labor) combines with a limited vision of alternatives (neither Wendy nor Simon can look up from the task at hand long enough to have a creative idea) and a poverty of interconnection with others (the failure of community is a core cause of their problems and, at the same time, deprives them of the awareness that their problems are not unique to them, not about their own failings as individuals but socially induced) to produce a set of ingrained roles that are functional but highly distressing as well. Neither has an apparent source of power to take control over her or his life.

Power is a problematic concept. It dons so many costumes that it is difficult to identify, elusive to name. One handicap is that we tend to think of power as a thing, as something to possess (Birkhoff, 2000). Moreover, people struggling to be cooperative most often think of it as a *bad* thing and, in consequence, shy away from naming it or dealing with it directly.

I find it more useful to think about power as a process, operating on many levels, a dynamic between and among people, multilayered and ever-shifting. There are five arenas (at least) in which power is transacted: *internal, interactional, organizational, cultural, structural*. Like any schema, this one is less than exhaustive, carving complex reality up into discrete categories. Like many schemas, this one also has analytic usefulness, but we need to remember that power is operating on all these levels simultaneously, the various arenas interacting in such a way as to mutually construct each other continuously.

Starting with the most external, *structural* power accrues from institutional arrangements, the inevitable context within which all human experience is lived. Wendy and Simon exist within several defining social structures: the nuclear family, urban life bereft of meaningful communities, institutions of work based on wage labor, political policies that fail to provide adequate child-rearing support, and so on. These structures remain largely invisible to them; they take them for granted, deeply obscured as they are by the cultural hegemony within which they swim.

Problems that result from negotiating these structures are compounded by *cultural* practices. Most obviously, gender shapes Wendy and Simon's experience. They fall into roles for which they have been securely socialized. The structures of their own families of origin mediated socially inscribed gender identities and practices—shaping Simon for instrumentality, Wendy for relationship. Lessons in gender solidify into character structures, metaphorically and literally embodied, and enacted in the form of silent agreements: "I'll do this, you do that, even if neither of us likes it." In the process, power is distributed, and because of structural inequities, the distribution is rarely equal. Wendy's lack of economic power disadvantages her in a world without assured support more severely than Simon's lack of emotional prowess.

Gendered cultural arrangements interact with other social identities—race, ethnicity, sexual orientations, disability, generation, and so on—to parse power relations in complex ways. Children of immigrants, for instance, very often struggle with tensions between American standards of individualism and a strong sense of responsibility to their elders, especially when racial discrimination is at play. When to break free of parents and when loyally to advocate for them and for the larger community can be conflicting choices. Young people, perhaps confronting their own barriers to well-being in a racist society, are keenly aware of the even greater hurdles confronting the first generation who may lack English-language skills as well as cultural knowledge needed to negotiate new systems.

Similarly, gender relations among people of color can be severely strained by the different forms of racism men and women face. African American women speak of having to choose between their own dissatisfactions in relationships with Black men and the greater condemnation heaped on the latter by White society. Can the women afford to be critical and risk colluding with a whole array of damaging stereotypes of Black men?

Many of these quandaries manifest *organizationally,* showing up most evidently in the dealings of people of color with institutions, both state and civil. In the aftermath of the police killing of Amadou Diallo in New York, a social worker in the Bronx, who lived near where the young African immigrant was shot, talked with me about her experience with police intervention in domestic violence in her community. She was part of a campaign to encourage women to dial 911. But when they did, police—several times in quick succession—shot and killed the offending men. "We wanted our men restrained, not dead," she said. Women stopped calling the police, leaving them with less power to protect themselves, less power to insist their men learn nonviolent ways, and less help from the larger community. Decisions about how to take power, where its limits lie, are thus informed and enforced by particular social experiences.

Organizational power relations are most clearly identified in workplace and civil institutions, such as schools and churches. Hierarchies in these settings tend to be both overt—named in the form of titles and offices—and covert. Who speaks first and often in meetings, who gets the coffee, how it is decided that one person will travel to a conference while another of apparently equal rank stays back to finish the office work—all these unspoken roles and responsibilities transact power in ways both intricate and, most often, mystified.

The family, too, is an organization in which parallel power dynamics are acted out, interlacing age and gender to form compelling lessons in hierarchy. Parents order children around, older siblings dominate younger ones through "play," brothers rough-house with sisters and overwhelm them frequently, and so on. Meanwhile, Rescue dynamics—children who decide to cause parents no trouble because they can see how overwhelmed they are, or how drunk; parents who wear themselves out keeping a neat house or paying the mortgage, and then tyrannize everyone to pick up the crumbs or turn out the lights—form countercurrents of power, parsing domination and submission in different ways at different moments.

Simultaneously, racialized lessons in power are also being taught, explicitly through language, implicitly through very fundamental transactions. In her book *Black Looks: Race and Representation*, bell hooks (1992) describes "The Oppositional Gaze." "I remember being punished as a child for staring," she writes, "for those hard intense direct looks children would give grown-ups, looks that were seen as confrontational, as gestures of resistance, challenges to authority" (p. 115). She goes on to note the contradiction and locate it historically:

> Yet, when punished, the child is told by parents, "Look at me when I talk to you." Only, the child is afraid to look. Afraid to look, but fascinated by the gaze. There is power in looking.
>
> Amazed the first time I read in history classes that White slave-owners (men, women, and children) punished enslaved Black people for looking, I wondered how this traumatic relationship to the gaze had informed Black parenting and Black spectatorship. (p. 115)

What seems, at first glance, to be a transaction negotiating generational power—the gaze can flow from parent to child, but not the other way—is in addition a piece of the construction of race relations, continued through time. That it is a product of trauma gives it weight and substance. That it teaches something about current realities of oppression and danger gives the lesson immediacy and function. Direct looks in public spaces can be dangerous for Black adults as well, subject to interpretation in a racialized climate as confrontational, and consequently violently punished.

White children learn thoroughly implicit lessons about their racial identity as well. The very absence of mention of Whiteness communicates the expectation that their experiences are the norm, that which is to be expected without note. My own parents were courageous integrationists in a southern city during Jim Crow. I very clearly understood lessons in justice. But, at the same time, I witnessed the prevalence of Black domestic labor and the rarity of Black professional people in our community. I witnessed my father's assumption that he could lift a telephone and be heard by the mayor or the chief of police when trouble was afoot, and I knew his access was a function of his race, gender, and class. Brave and outspoken as she was, my mother never made the same bold kinds of phone calls. By association and contrast, through emulation and opposition, I formed my own relationship to those social attributes and to the power dynamics they constructed.

Culture and social location commonly intermingle, manifested as power struggles in all kinds of relationships, in ways sometimes banal and often troubling. Krista and Wanda keep bumping up against an all-too-familiar impasse in their 1-year-old lesbian relationship. From Wanda's perspective, Krista suddenly vanishes at some point in a disagreement. Krista describes her mode as "being easy in the front and, in the back, going my own way." She chooses that roundabout route when she feels overpowered, which she does regularly during negotiations, or what she experiences as fights, because Wanda is skillfully verbal, acutely self-knowing. Both women are White, close in age, and probably equally in love with each other. But Krista's methodology was forged in Germany, in a family that never talked about themselves or their relationships and that imposed very strong expectations of a very conventional, heterosexual sort on their daughter. Early on, she learned silence was a potent means of self-protection and a cover for going her own way. Wanda, meanwhile, grew up with a single mom who talked openly and elaborately with her only child. When she found herself in a lesbian community where "process" was valued, she excelled.

Another example: culture and social structure shape parental expectations, sometimes spoken, sometimes implied, which, in turn, shape children's strategies for taking power. My father was the child of immigrants from Eastern Europe. Working on the lower East Side of Manhattan in sweatshops, his parents looked to their first-born son as the economic hope of the family. He became a doctor. From time to time, people asked him when he'd decided on a medical career, and he always replied, "As soon as I was old enough to understand what my mother was telling me." Heavily shaped by culture, often dictated by the requirements of negotiating disadvantaged social locations or protecting privileged ones, instructions to children are communicated through the most nuanced of *interactions:* a parent's raised eyebrow, a derisive comment about a neighbor overheard in the elevator, praise heaped on someone else's son or daughter. Like my father, some children never consider the possibility of disobeying. Others rebel, choosing paths as divergent from their given road-maps as they can possibly find. Only later may they realize that their direction was nonetheless set by their parents' values, just in reverse, through opposition.

Strategies for survival and well-being track children into adulthood. They both offer strengths and simultaneously trap people in behaviors they wish to change. Eduardo works hard to support his family, following the example set by his father in a rural setting in El Salvador. But unlike the village men, Eduardo emulates, he lacks the shared responsibility of a farming community as well as the ready companionship of an extended family. Needing the relief and support those structures provided his father, Eduardo escapes responsibility Friday nights by drinking heavily and gambling with his male friends. But his wife Alejandra shares his isolation; no close-at-hand community of women to help her with domestic chores, brush her hair during the hot afternoon break, share gossip and laughter over the evening cooking. She, too, works for wages all day and then comes home to a "second shift." Eduardo cannot see clearly all that she does, but he nonetheless knows its overload and he sympathizes with her. She rages at him for his Friday-night disappearing act, angry that he's not home to help and even more that he loses significant sums of money. He regularly promises to reform, but come Friday night he's ready to burst with fatigue and disquiet and knows no other way to care for himself. Lacking language to say all that to Alejandra, he simply does not go home after work on Friday.

Wendy's most powerful tool is language; she can talk Simon to a standstill. But Simon literally disarms her by refusing the conversation she seeks to impose. When he sets his mouth, refuses to meet her eyes, turns back to his hammer and nails, he exercises power effectively: he forces Wendy to abandon verbal processes, and she knows of no alternative. On the other hand, when Wendy insists Simon wash the dishes after dinner and then follows in his path, wiping up crumbs and splotches he's overlooked, she is wielding her greater housekeeping skills in a moral battle. Power transactions are infinitely creative, ranging from the most subtle (a cast of the eyes) to the most overt (a throw of the fist).

Violence is, of course, the ultimate power play. For that reason, any work on building cooperative relationships depends on the absence of any threat of violence. Men resort to violence as a form of dominance often paradoxically born of the sensation of powerlessness. It is not a sign of evil, nor even sometimes of entitlement. It is what men are trained to do—use the physical body as their means to take control over an unwieldy environment. Its consequence, though, is to reinforce relations of privilege and disadvantage that are systemically constructed. Domestic violence negates the possibility of doing any constructive cooperative work, until a clear and realistic commitment to nonviolence has been made. The work we know how to do is grounded in a framework that values equality of power as a pragmatic good: relationships work badly when people live in fear. All our work is premised on the possibility of conscious change, and that includes the reality that men who batter can learn alternatives. Innovative work has been done by groups of men helping batterers reform, based in principles of group support and the premise that using physical force is a choice that can be changed.

Finally, power operates *internally*. We all accrue beliefs about what we can and cannot do, where we have permission to act, when we have agency to effect change. If Wendy has secretly formed the belief that she is not smart enough to support herself and her children without Simon, she is more likely to resist doing those things that might, in fact, help her acquire the skills she needs to negotiate the world of money. If Simon believes he is inadequate to form nurturing relationships with his children, he is more likely to fade away from the troubled moments of the day and choose play times to be with them instead. Each is dependant on the other for what she or he perceives to be an inadequacy in herself or himself. Without the necessity of taking on those tasks, each is deprived of the experiences that would form an ability to perform.

INTERNALIZED OPPRESSION: "THE PIG"

The theory of internalized oppression is at the heart of Radical Psychiatry practice. A great deal of what happens in "therapy" is about naming and challenging this pervasive set of attitudes. In the early days of Radical Psychiatry, as antiwar and Black-power movements raged in the streets, the collective nicknamed internalized oppression "The Pig." It is the internalized police officer that keeps us in our socially prescribed place. The name has advantages and disadvantages. It is punchy, usable both as verb ("I Pig myself as much as others") and noun ("My Pig says I should . . ."). It lends itself to therapeutic metaphor; we can name the Pig, reveal the Pig, fight the Pig, unlearn the Pig. It suggests that the struggle is about something external that nonetheless has great power to enforce rules of the most intimate sort. But it is, itself, Pig, a slur on police officers—not to mention on pigs. Yet it remains a piece of solidified history, difficult to relinquish however much it may breed discomfort. Because it is an extant therapeutic form, and because cognitive dissonance can be a constructive experience, helping to heighten consciousness, I continue to use the disquieting nomenclature here—as I do in my practice, with explanation and apology, and an open invitation to "rename the Pig."[1]

The Pig is an ideological construct that is learned through articulated messages, interpersonal interaction, and cultural hegemony. I've already written about how Wendy and Simon's assumed models of gender are reinforced by the interactions between them and with their children. Clearly, those stereotypes of gendered behavior are compounded with great frequency by media and other cultural forms. A few years ago, some students of mine did a visual research project on gender and racial messages contained in advertising images. They found that the majority of male models in shiny magazines were posed face-forward, chin up, photographed in some action. Women, on the other hand, rarely faced the camera, usually lounged passively, often with downcast eyes. Most of the female models were White, all showing great expanses of bare flesh. The rare woman of African or Asian heritage usually posed in some sort of "exotic" attire. All the White men were fully clothed; the only African American male model they found was also the only example of near-nude male cheesecake. Imagistic symbolism changes over time, sometimes quite rapidly. Today male flesh has become a good deal more prevalent, and boldness in women has been redefined as sexy.

Messages about who we are and how we are supposed to behave take two forms: injunctions and attributions. Injunctions tell us how to behave ("Be strong; don't cry"; "Be sweet; don't be angry"). Attributions tells us what's wrong with us if we disobey ("You're a sissy!"; "My, you're selfish!"). Gendered messages suit us for heterosexuality. They find their way, of course, into same-sex relationships, but they ideally fit people for the sort of relationship that Wendy and Simon illustrate, constructing a coercive interdependency that adds iron to marriage vows.[2]

---

[1]Other nomenclature I've heard people use is "The Critic," "The Demon," and the "Voice of Internalized Oppression." Roberto Vargas, a colleague who created approaches to therapy and to organizational development suited to Chicano communities, uses the term *El No,* a phrase I like a lot. Navajos use a concept called *nayee,* which refers to anything that stands in the way of a good life.

[2]As times change, paradoxically, that rigidity also induces fractures; today's heterosexual relationships often embody enormous tensions between new ideals of equality, emotional intimacy, friendship, and sexuality on the one hand, and the actual capacities men and women bring with them to fulfill those expectations. The structure of relationship has failed to change as rapidly as the ideals, with the end result of disappointment, anger, and, eventually, grief.

Injunctions and attributions support the construction of all sorts of social hierarchies. Intelligence and diligence are two fundamental categories of internalized oppression. The many interactions children of color encounter in school, for instance, in which they are signaled that their intelligence is suspect because their cultural expression falls outside a White teacher's expectations, or their assumptions about life clash with a standardized curriculum, construct power-diminishing responses—self-doubt, for instance, or rebelliousness—that undercut the attainment of skills for survival in White-dominated society (Bourgois, 1995). The examples can be multiplied endlessly.

The Pig may make complex accusations of inadequacy or wrongdoing, but in Western capitalist society, they tend to boil down to seven categories: stupid, lazy, crazy, sick, ugly, bad. When all these beliefs about oneself exist simultaneously, people are frequently suicidal; the seventh message is "deserves to die."

Because these messages are learned, they can be unlearned. It is a defining characteristic of the Pig that it is false. Its very grammatical structure gives rise to its internal impossibility: it is categorical and abstract. When Wendy has trouble keeping track of her bank balance, the voice of the Pig echoes in her mind saying she is stupid. But it excludes from her consciousness evidence of her brilliance in knowing what her children need, indeed what they feel and think. It discounts the intelligence needed to multitask in the ways she does as a matter of course. It ignores the fact that she was never taught how to balance a checkbook, nor that she lost her confidence in her math abilities at the age of 11 when the message became palpable that girl math whizzes were not attractive.

Power in general, and internalized oppression in particular, are processes we negotiate. We are not passive objects waiting to be molded into solid shapes that can never be undone. In fact, the genesis of the Pig often lies in a very particular sort of negotiation. As children, we realize very soon where the limits to our power lie, and we construct strategies for dealing with the ensuing problems. In the midst of parental conflict, for example, some children opt to make themselves invisible, others to make a distracting fuss; still others try to mediate. To each of these strategies is attached certain conclusions: "I'm not strong enough to make a difference." "I fall apart when trouble hits." "The fate of the world depends on my intervention." The first becomes embodied as a sense of futility, the second as a sense of fragility, the third as a sense of overburdened responsibility. Each of these premises is tested in other venues, becoming refined or reinforced. These conclusions, once useful, later become counterproductive when altered conditions call for different, more self-affirming strategies and skills.

It is fundamental to the practice of Radical Psychiatry that very deeply ingrained beliefs and behaviors can be altered, that the processes of negotiation by which they were formed continue throughout life, giving hope for both personal and social change.

PROBLEM-SOLVING GROUP

It is to promote and support such change that Radical Psychiatry practice assumes the form of problem-solving groups. Group is itself a small example of social change, bringing together community support, skill learning, and a very intentional process of unlearning powerlessness while experiencing conscious forms of power-sharing, to challenge both internal and external barriers to well-being.

From start to finish, power is negotiated between group leaders and group members. Fees, for instance, are kept as low as feasible. (We continue to contend, rhetorically, that no one should have to pay for "therapy"; it should be a readily accessible form of community support.) Many of us use a sliding scale, inviting clients to set their own fees within a range that, in my case, has grown ever wider over the years, as I've raised the top but not the bottom.

Not everything about group is negotiable: the basic structure is a given—how long group lasts (mine are 2 hours long), how many people belong (six or seven), who joins when a place opens up (although I certainly take into consideration needs for particular representation to provide support for particular current members). I'm happy, though, to talk through the reasoning behind these choices, and on occasion I've been persuaded to expand or contract the length, to add more or fewer people. Transparency and flexibility both serve the purpose of keeping me true to an intention to use the power of leadership humanely and openly.

On the other hand, the content of people's work is very much their own, including their judgment of what they need to change about their lives and when they're ready to leave the group. (We do not insist on elaborate "termination" processes, trusting that few people turn away from a good and helpful thing as long as it continues to be useful.)

"Work" in group takes many forms—problem-solving, expressing emotion, role-playing, sorting out in-the-room feelings and relationships, and more. A typical exchange may look something like this:

Trina (a newcomer to group): I am so scattered, I drive myself crazy! I am just so dumb I can't keep track of where I'm supposed to be and what I'm supposed to have with me. I showed up for my big presentation at work without the transparencies I was supposed to show, and now I'm really afraid I'm going to get fired.

Sylvia (an older group member): Wow, is it ever hard for me to imagine you as "dumb"! I remember your talking a couple of weeks ago about how much you had to handle as the child of immigrants: keeping track of all sorts of paperwork, translating for your parents, getting yourself and your siblings to school. You got bad grades because you were exhausted by all that, but you were clearly not stupid then and you're certainly not now! I've been knocked out by the great feedback you give us in group!

Beth (the group leader): It makes real sense that you'd feel overwhelmed and at some point check out, Trina, just as Sylvia said. Your Pig says you're stupid, but that was the way you were defined at school, which was clearly both racist- and class-biased. Also, maybe it was a pretty smart strategy—at least back then—to decide you were stupid. Given how much people depended on you, maybe it gave you a little protection. But now that view of yourself is clearly demeaning and getting in your way.

When Trina came into group, she told us she wanted to improve her self-esteem. The first act in group is to define the immediate goal of the work, what is inaccurately called a contract.[3] It is a simple positive statement that serves several pur-

---

[3]Much of the jargon of Radical Psychiatry is taken from commercial dealings, a peculiar contradiction with the value basis of the work. Some of that usage reflects the historic influence of Transactional Analysis. I look forward to a future project to reform the descriptive vocabulary.

poses: It puts the client in charge of her own work, guarding against diagnosis. Trina knows more about her problems and needs than I do. Labeling her is not helpful to either of us, although renaming her problems may be. Often, the only characterizations available to people are laced with Pig: "I'm in trouble at work because I'm so slow to learn how to do things," or, "I can't make a relationship work because I'm so angry."

Second, the contract is a tool for accomplishing whatever it is Trina chooses to work toward. It should be something Trina can remember in a moment of choice, an idea that helps her choose a new way of being. Third, the contract is a yardstick. If group is not helping her make recognizable change in fairly short order, then something is wrong and she is encouraged to challenge the process. The presumption is that the problem lies in our way of working together, not in her diagnosable pathology.

On the other hand, the contract is frequently a product of discussion in the group. "Self-esteem," for example, is rarely a useful way of framing a contract; it puts too great an onus on the client, distracting from a more interactive materialist understanding.

"What's wrong with your self-esteem?" I asked Trina that first group. "What exactly is the problem?"

"Well, I lose my nerve when I have to do something hard at work. And I end up feeling bad about myself in relationships and somehow or other mess them up."

Trina presented two problems, joined together by an analytic leap she'd made. Wondering whether that leap was influenced by her Pig, I asked her to give us some examples. Getting the details of the story almost always leads to a more refined statement of the problem.

"I thought I was on top of my part in the new project. I worked and worked and worked on it, and I actually got a pretty good evaluation. But then my closest co-worker complained to our supervisor that I was slowing her down by being too meticulous. I felt terrible. I guess I'm just too slow; it does take me forever to sort through what I'm supposed to do."

"Seems to me," said Sylvia, "that your work is more about handling competition than it is about self-esteem." As we talked more, it appeared that Trina was actually doing fine in terms of work skills, but that she was facing a competitive dynamic fueled, in part, by the bad economy we were in and her co-worker's consequent insecurities.

Trina was still not convinced, though, that she wasn't at fault. So she went on to describe some of the interactions with her lover:

> I just can't keep my mouth shut. Matt's a nice person, but he drives me nuts sometimes. We were at a party, and I could see my friend Shana couldn't get a word in edgewise. Matt just went on and on, telling some boring story. I knew Shana was getting upset. So I just blurted out that he should stop dominating the conversation, that I wanted to hear what was up with Shana.
>
> I could see he was hurt. Afterward, he said I was rude and arrogant, and that those qualities were not attractive in a woman. I felt terrible! I didn't mean to upset him. But I do that sort of thing all the time. What's wrong with me?!

Group members agreed that she could use some better skills for speaking her mind. But they pointed out that Matt had "Pigged" her back, and that he'd hit a very vulnerable spot by using a very sexist accusation. No wonder her self-esteem was shaken.

I ventured a suggestion, tying together both stories, and said:

> Maybe the common thread between work and relationship problems is that you blame yourself instead of figuring out what the problem is. How about starting with a contract to nurture yourself in the face of trouble? To do that, I think you'll have to find ways to understand what's going on in a more self-forgiving way, and in turn that self-nurturing can create a positive climate in which you can learn some interpersonal skills—like telling Matt how you're feeling rather than speaking to him judgmentally.

Identifying a unifying theme in a list of problems to be solved is one approach. Another might be to ask Trina to choose a starting place, either work or love, for instance, with the expectation that whatever dynamics they have in common will emerge no matter where she starts.

Once her contract had been defined, Trina came to group to talk about whatever was most compelling for her in the moment. If the topics on her mind did not relate to the contract she made, we explored the possibility that the contract needed altering, not her emotional selection of material to present.

As group members form relationships and give feedback to each other, the group leader plays several roles. She provides safety by helping people learn to talk honestly without judgment. In this aspect of her work, she is both teacher and facilitator. She gives people tools with which to describe more and more vividly and constructively what they experience. In particular, she teaches approaches to fighting the Pig and provides a powerful force in implementing them.

FIGHTING THE PIG

The theory of internalized oppression posits three forms in which Pig messages appear: as emotions, as body sensations, and as ideas. More often than not, we first become aware of them in their most nonverbal forms. We feel fear or anxiety, depression or unrelieved sadness. We hold pain in the stomach, or tense the jaw against expressions of grief, the shoulders against anger. The first step in group, therefore, is to acknowledge the feelings and identify them with words.

The second step is to analyze what exactly the Pig says, to boil it down to its most essential and, therefore, most forceful statement. "I am not good with numbers and often lose track of time" may become "I'm stupid!" "Why are you always so emotional? Can't you just be sensible for a change?" are rhetorical questions masking a conclusion: "I am crazy." Each of these statements is associated with some form of political dynamic. "Stupid," for instance, is often a class-defining accusation. The definitions of smart that most afflict us derive from the skills of those at the top of the social hierarchy: scientists, lawyers, and executives, for example. These are the people who are trained to think in linear, abstract terms. They also are most commonly White and male, even after decades of progress around professional demography. But intelligence actually takes many forms: intuitive, creative, holistic, and so on (Belenky, Clinchy, Goldberger, & Tarule, 1986; Gardner, 1983).

Similarly "ugly" is often a gender message. Beauty matters for women, socialized to take very seriously the assessing gaze of men. Classically, men choose love objects, women wait. Here again, the rule is outdated; the 1960s liberated women's activism in the pursuit of love, and change has marched steadily on from there. But the feelings accompanying even such newer transactions still track the old gender order. Men's aesthetic, socially infected beyond their recognition, far more often determines their choice of partners than does women's. Men judge others and women judge themselves by appearance, not always and absolutely but in great preponderance. Whereas their own appearance may matter to straight men, gay men report a far more compelling preoccupation with their looks as they, like straight women, respond to narrow standards of physical desirability reflected in the judging gaze of potential male partners. Meanwhile, lesbians may be more protected from "looksism" but still don't always escape its touch. Women attracted to women may still be painfully conscious of appearance as a factor in appeal, sometimes with the added problem of uncertainty about how to initiate romance without replicating gendered dynamics of aggression.

That Pig is an ideology fitting people to particular social locations, and capturing them there, is evident in the area of racial identity. All three of these messages—stupid, crazy, and ugly—lie at the heart of stereotypes that beset African American people, for instance. Combined with accusations of laziness, they form a quadruple phalanx driving racism to the most personal levels. Black rage is judged by the White community to be crazed. Black beauty is still distorted by White ideals of fairness, slenderness, and straight hair. Black smarts are overlooked by White teachers, submerged in perceptions of unruliness or the impermissibility of African American forms of speech. Disadvantage is then blamed on the victim, who is accused of laziness, of failing to work hard enough to succeed. Political and cultural movements seek to defend against these onslaughts, with significant success. But in the context of institutional discrimination, the very necessity to resist constitutes oppression.

Other people of color suffer other assaults on self—Asian women become invisible behind presumptions of the exotic, Latino men are stereotyped as erotic and not seen as formidable in all the other respects that they may be. All stereotypes are a form of Pig, by definition: They are generalizations that distort a dimensional reality and oppress options for power of those who are targeted (as well, I might add, of those who target, although that's a story for another day). All resonate within structural systems of inequality that turn the struggle against them into a dire battle.

Super-heavy assaults of Pig sometimes result in suicidality. Like violence toward others, suicide is also a choice. For some people in extreme despair, suicide may appear as the only relief possible. The idea that the only power left is the power to end life is, in our view, the ultimate victory of the Pig. As long as it appears to be an option, it is very hard to do the work of uncovering and contesting all the other messages of powerlessness that have been learned along the way, and to rebuild a life that truly makes for well-being. So we ask people to choose life, and to make a contract with the group to rule out suicide. On the other side of that contract is a commitment by the group, and especially by the group leader, to be available to help fight the despair at any time it becomes suicidally intense. For me as group leader, that commitment is serious. I give people my cell phone number and promise I'll talk to them night or day, if the need is there. Often, the act of making a contract to stay alive is a turning point and the need for emergency intervention never arises. But when it does, to make the critical phone call is such an act of trust, an exercise of essential human power, that the work moves forward steadily from there.

Depression in general, such a common complaint in modern America, we see not as illness but as an expression of alienation. When large segments of a population suffer the same affliction, there is reason to suspect some common social genesis. In fact, I've come to believe that we collapse a multitude of emotional experiences under the diagnosis of depression. Grief, anger in the context of a sense of powerlessness, immobilizing confusion, and so many other similar experiences are pathologized and medicated. But each of those experiences is, to me, an expression of problems that can be understood and addressed in reality. Isolation from others, as I've said, disempowers people, depriving us of the human connection that makes for the power to make change happen. Why not feel depressed if you feel you cannot change that which is dehumanizing? On the other hand, once we've managed to connect with others we stand a far better chance of identifying causes for distress, both external problems and internalized oppression. With that awareness and support, it is possible to begin a process of making changes, step by step. Action in and of itself relieves depression, defeating the Pig messages of powerlessness, and especially the false notion that the cause lies somewhere inside the individual.

Once the Pig is identified and boiled down to its essentials, the next task is to construct strategies for unlearning it and replacing it with a true sense of self. Approaches vary from one person to another, but there are two commonalties. First is the power of exposure in a group. Once spoken, the effectiveness of the Pig message often diminishes. Moreover, it quickly becomes clear that other people's Pigs lie. If Betsy's belief that she is ugly and stupid is so palpably false, it's hard for Annie to maintain that her Pig, and her Pig alone, tells the truth. Interaction with others is thus a powerful, perhaps an essential, element in making change.

The second force for challenging Pig is "strokes." A stroke is any unit of positive interaction, something once again we borrowed (from Transactional Analysis) and then theorized in political terms. We speak of a stroke economy,[4] a constructed scarcity of compliments, affection, encouragement that drives us to try harder, feel less secure, act more competitively—in general, to consent to an individualistic society. We are severely trained in the Western world to curtail strokes. We're taught not to give them (lest we're thought to be sexually aggressive or trying to get something manipulatively for ourselves), not to accept them (lest we're seen as conceited), not to request them (lest we're seen as needy), not to reject them (lest we contradict some imbedded injunction, such as "You're so sweet!"), and, most of all, not to stroke ourselves (lest we induce unacceptable degrees of competitiveness from others). Breaking these rules is radical business, a powerful force against internalized oppression and a serious means of opening channels to positive connection.

Strokes help to keep relationships in group clear, but so too do other forms of emotional dialogue that enable us to work through conflict. Conflict inevitably arises. We do not see conflict as a deflection from the work; it is its essence. Change happens through conflict, properly conducted. So one aspect of group is teaching people to be in conflict respectfully and productively. These practices (which I won't detail here but are elaborated by Claude Steiner [2001] in *Achieving Emotional Literacy*) are also at the heart of the second form in which much of our work takes place.

---

[4]A term coined by Claude Steiner (1969).

CONFLICT RESOLUTION

Finding ways to address conflict started, as I've said, at the very beginning of Radical Psychiatry, at first as a self-help tool for handling conflicts within the collective. Incorporating elements of labor mediation, notions seeping into the American discourse from neighborhood mediation in China, and whatever tools from Transactional Analysis looked promising, the early members constructed a clearly formulated procedure for intervention.

The process of mediation begins with contracts, the participants articulating their goals for the work. They then are helped to clear the air, telling the stories of their grievances through the use of emotionally oriented statements: "I-statements" in current conflict resolution jargon; "held feelings" in common Radical Psychiatry jargon. Participants take turns saying the things that upset them, without judgment, and also without discussion or argument. The premise here is that what we feel matters. It is an antipathology premise: nobody is crazy, we all feel what we feel for a reason, and the feelings must be spoken if change is to happen. At length, once all the subjective experiences have been voiced, the mediator offers direct feedback. The mediator presents a likely story or analysis of how the various subjective experiences fit together, and then invites the participants to craft revisions until they agree on an understanding of what's going on between them.

At this point, the participants say what they'd like to change, encouraged to imagine an ideal outcome. Where there are differences in the visions, the mediator guides the participants through a negotiation. We work from a theory of negotiation: start with 100% of what you want, lest compromise deprive you of more than you can tolerate giving up. Then look for new solutions that stand to satisfy all the interests expressed. If none can be found (and here's a place where the mediator can be helpful, offering imagination and the accumulated knowledge of other people's successful solutions), then begin to trade compromises. In the end, whatever new terms are set up need to be tested in reality. An onerous agreement is a fragile one. Agreements need to be subject to revision, just so long as that act is not unilateral. If it doesn't work, in other words, renegotiate, don't renege.

Mediation quickly spread from practitioners to consumers. We began mediating other people's interpersonal conflicts as well as our own. Because the individuals who came to therapy were commonly also involved in other communities, often working in social change organizations and institutions of a progressive sort, we began to be asked to mediate larger groups of people. Over the years, we've worked with a great array of cultural, social service, educational, and political groups, as well as with families (it's a dynamite form to use with teenagers; they excel in the dialogue and get important support to renegotiate power with parents) and other social groupings.

The structure I've outlined here is a starting place. As with most things in life, flexibility is necessary. The classic forms are culturally biased. They privilege a certain degree of comfort with verbal expressions of emotion, with face-to-face confrontation, and with an acceptance of direction in manners of speaking. Working in multicultural settings, I often present the structures and tools as possibilities, not necessities, inviting participants to share the work of constructing a culturally appropriate dialogue that fulfills the essential principles of respectful and honest communication in the service of collaborative settlements.

Mediation always involves rearranging power in some form. That process is clearest when generational differences are at issue, but it is true also in organizations. A large part of the work there is sorting out the institutional roots of seemingly interpersonal conflicts. Often two people in what are defined as personality struggles are actually playing out unarticulated problems of hierarchy and role function. By combining attention to individual and transactional power issues with such questions of structure, mediation in organizations crosses the lines between therapy and organizational development. It binds together understandings of power and of emotion with dignity and effectiveness.

The model is simple to state and easy to teach, but it contains some parts that draw on considerable skill. Establishing enough rapport with upset people to be able to guide the discourse in constructive directions is itself an example of the respectful use of power. Formulating an analysis requires a point of view and keen perceptions of transactions as they are described and enacted in the room, skills that come with lots of practice.

Finally, advocacy is a necessary part of addressing power imbalances. Neutrality is not a value in a Radical Psychiatry mediation. When I mediate, I find it easy to feel sympathy with people on all sides of a power divide. Nobody is bad, even though the need for change may be unequally distributed. The job of the mediator is to persuade those with more power to see where their own interests join with their subordinates' in recasting roles and relationships, as well as teaching leaders the difference between the cooperative use of power and its hierarchical abuse.

This last comment suggests the ways in which mediation is not a universally applicable form. It presupposes a will to equality, of rights as well as power. It requires, in other words, that conditions for cooperation exist, for mediation is by definition a cooperative process. Many social change organizations today seek to construct humane hierarchies, eschewing the time and energy demands of consensus for more efficient modes of decision-making. That endeavor is worthy but difficult. It requires a willingness for transparency on the part of the leadership, and for acceptance of the limitations of participation on the part of all others. Leaders must be able to say, Here I'm inviting input but I'll make the decision, and, There you have a real say; we'll come to a decision together.

PARANOIA: THE VALUE OF INTUITION

There is one other tool we use in mediation and elsewhere in our practice that is unusual and unusually helpful. It is a technique for checking out assumptions, in the variety of forms they take. Provocatively, in line with our challenge to traditional psychiatry, we named this class of events "Paranoia," and we reframed paranoia as something positive rather than pathological.

The theory is that human communication takes forms beyond the verbal. We perceive the most subtle of signs—the lift of an eyebrow, the quick dart of an eye, the tensing of a shoulder—and we make meaning, interpreting the significance in the context of a framework of things known, feared, suspected, anticipated, and so on. We create a story to fill in blanks, making sense of that which goes unsaid. In this sense, Paranoia is "heightened awareness," a slogan we coined long ago and that has since, in light of subsequent political events, become a good deal less radical than it seemed at the time. Such meaning making draws on accurate perceptions; people are not crazy, therefore what we pick up is always based on something real.

But the explanations we create can also contain inaccuracies. In essence, we're making a good guess about what another human being is thinking or feeling, but we cannot really know without honest witness from the person involved.

The approach we propose is that people pose their Paranoias directly, running out the story they imagine to be true while implicitly understanding they may not be altogether correct. We sometimes call these stories "Paranoid Fantasies," rhetoric intended to encourage elaboration of assumptions and concerns. The partner to this transaction is then urged to tell the truth, first identifying what is true about the offered version, then correcting any distortions. We urge that particular order of things because we know that people have a strong tendency to defend their perceptions, only giving them up when they've gotten essential validation for the kernel of truth they've intuited. To contest the offered version is to invite an argument. But, like a muscle spasm, the tendency toward defensiveness relaxes in light of an adequate validation.

Paranoia is in a sense a litmus test for power. The more insecure we feel, the more risks we in fact face, the more paranoid we become. Keen intuition is a survival skill. Like a dog sniffing out the subtlest smells of food and foe, we use our nonverbal perceptiveness with more or less alacrity depending on how serious the consequences of missing something important are likely to be. Paranoia also increases with distance. The less we know directly, the more we need to pick up intuitively. It is a dynamic that therefore characterizes race relations in America: The social distance between people of different communities combined with perceptions of danger and disadvantage promote heightened alertness to nuances and symbols. Often, the stories we construct on both sides of a racial divide are simultaneously both accurate and amiss, the distorted part fed by stereotypes and fears. But although Paranoia operates on both sides of the racial divide, there are important differences in its forms and consequences. Members of a dominant group have more power to harm than those in subordinated categories, who are continuously dealing with systemic racism already. Moreover, people of color and others consigned to marginalized social locations classically do more than their share of the work of divining the meanings of mainstream behavior, both because they are more at risk and also because the lives of those in the mainstream are more apparent, overrepresented as they are in popular culture.

IMPLICATIONS FOR SOCIAL JUSTICE

The theory of Paranoia as heightened awareness is one of several ways that Radical Psychiatry can contribute to social justice work. Combined with an analysis of power, it is a tool for understanding commonly divisive dynamics among people of different identities, whether class-based, racial, gendered, generational, or along some other lines.[5]

The conflict resolution work is an instrument for creating greater unity across boundaries that commonly divide social justice activists. From the very beginning, we've declined to mediate across structural power inequities. We do not work in corporations or in prisons, unless some very particular conditions are negotiated

---

[5]I've elaborated this aspect of the work in "For White People, on How to Listen When Race is the Subject" (Roy, 2002).

(they sometimes are in corporations, haven't so far been in prisons). But we have helped many, many progressive organizations learn and grow stronger from otherwise destructive conflicts in their ranks. Mediation in this context is not simply a service to help people avoid damage: It is an opportunity to teach tools and skills for conducting human interaction in a way that models the world so many of us wish to create, where power is transacted humanely, relationships matter as much as outcomes, and emotions are both honored and honorably expressed.

Finally, the work in groups helps to build communities of support well beyond the persons of the group members themselves. The road to the changes people seek—relief from overwork, the enactment of functional love relationships, finding meaningful careers, having a voice in political decisions in the wider world—more often than not traverses a terrain of caring communities. Two single moms may make a child-rearing cooperative that benefits six other families as well as their own. Trina may introduce into her workplace concepts of loving support, lobbying for more praise and less secrecy, and in the process extending notions of cooperation to a wider groups of people. Simon and Wendy could start a co-housing project, where they join with other families, elderly people, young singles, to share the chores of life and build a society of friendliness and fun.

Overall, Radical Psychiatry's approach challenges a psychiatric hegemony that heavily supports the construction of consent to oppressive social structures. If dissatisfactions are diagnosable, if the sources of discontent reside wholly within the individual psyche, then inclinations toward social critique are undermined. The very structure of most therapeutic intervention supports individualist assumptions. One "doctor" and one "patient" in a room alone, however comforting the dialogue may be to both people involved, nonetheless teeters on the brink of replicating the sort of power inequities that may have injured people in the first place. Moreover, the therapeutic relationship, curtained in confidentiality, promotes isolation in a society heavily oriented toward dyads. Clearly, it would be unsafe and unwise for therapists to share information about their clients haphazardly. But when we accept rigid rules of confidentiality uncritically, we are in danger of colluding with judgments, unfortunately so widespread in the greater society, about their distress. Where is the line between hiding the illness of a patient and tacitly agreeing that the world would condemn the patient's plight? In the end, patients may feel ill and alone, and therapists may be deprived of both accountability and support that would flow from a more open dialogue. Here is another argument for group therapy: When the work of an individual with a group leader is witnessed by several other people, there is less risk of power abuse by the therapist. For many years, one criterion for calling oneself a Radical Psychiatrist was that the therapist meet regularly with a peer support collective where the details of practice were disclosed and discussed. We had little use for credentials as a means to maintain quality, feeling that they glorified professionalism and stood to disorient clients' own assessments of the effectiveness of the therapy. (Doesn't that row of diplomas and certificates on the wall suggest the fault lies not with the "expert" therapist but with the client who persists in not "getting better"?) Instead, at the same time that we encouraged clients to maintain critical evaluation of their experience, we relied on knowing each other's work in an on-going way in great detail. If a collective member's work was questionable, it was questioned, immediately and constructively, not to punish but to help.

Better protection and better learning derive from more openness, in an environment where everyone involved is committed to respectful treatment of each other and of all clients. Similarly, group members promise not to talk lightly about each other's work. But we also acknowledge that there is a lot of learning that goes on in the course of one's peers' work, and to prohibit discussion of that learning with intimates outside the group would be counterproductive. If someone wants a particularly stringent vow of confidentiality about a particular story, that is honored. But, in general, we counsel people to use information responsibly and to protect their fellow members from judgment (the Pig lives in the wider community, although these issues tend to broaden the challenge to its dominance). Moreover, group work sometimes leads to the weaving of networks of interaction. People refer their friends and family members. People make new friends, and sometimes family members. These interconnections are positive, but they also require care and cooperation, and we teach and support adequate agreements about how to handle information.

If the object of the exercise is to heal illness, then one doctor—one patient makes sense. But if the objective is to change conditions of isolation and internalized judgment, to heal social injuries to the souls of healthy human beings by building positive relationships in ever-widening circles, then a very different structure is called for.

BUT WHAT ABOUT . . .?

What of mental illness, then? Do we seriously suppose there is no such thing? In our heyday, we provocatively declared just that. Along with R. D. Laing and Wilhelm Reich, we saw those phenomena generally labeled as *mental illness* as an outgrowth of familial and social dynamics. We resisted the new genetic explanations for just about everything.

Today, after 30 years of practice, I would qualify that stance, in this specific way: I do believe there exist conditions that lie beyond the reach of cognition. I can't say I'm convinced by any of the explanations for those conditions. Western thought strongly inclines toward separating mind and body, and then recombining them in one-directional, mechanical ways. First science says it's all in the mind, then it's all in the genes. I believe that emotional life has the power to alter the material body. We secrete chemicals when upset (Taylor et al., 2000). Our emotional lives influence how we eat, sleep, exercise, interact with others, all of which involve biochemical processes. Indeed, there is no thought or emotion that is not composed of chemical interaction. So the mind—body connection is multidirectional: mind reacts to chemistry, chemistry to mind, and both are housed in a mechanical body that tenses and relaxes, grows habits of rigidity and learns new forms of flexibility, provides pleasure and pain, throughout life.

Mental illness, then, is something I believe to affect a very, very small number of people. We don't really know how many, in part because the designation so easily becomes the metaphor for describing—and the program for treating—a vast array of normal human phenomena. Pathologies as widespread as depression and anxiety, for instance, are far better understood in terms of their social functions, and as symptoms of widespread social dysfunction.

Another place we run afoul of conventional wisdom is in our approach to treating substance abuse. First, we do not accept at face value the easy application of the common labels of addict and alcoholic. We ask people to recount the problems associated with their substance use. Do they suffer physical damage? Are their relationships with other people negatively affected? Is their use of the substance out of their control? Having decided to have two drinks, for instance, do they find themselves downing the fifth? These are the most prevalent problems people encounter, and they are reasons to change things.

Commonly, we ask people to stop using for a year, during which time they work in group on whatever problems interfere with their ability to make a clear and controlled choice about how they want to relate to substances. At the end of a year of sobriety, most people can form a healthy relationship to at least some types of substances. Some people may choose abstinence, realizing that the work involved in maintaining a problem-free way of drinking or smoking involves a use of energies they'd rather invest elsewhere. The act of choosing, however, counters stigmatized identities adhering to those who see themselves as suffering a disease or an addictive personality.

There are exceptions, of course. Some drugs are sufficiently addictive on a chemical level that their use is hard to justify. Others, like alcohol or marijuana, can be habit-forming on a psychological level even if not usually on a biochemical one. There are, however, a very small number of people who do seem to have something akin to an allergic reaction to alcohol. A sip of something alcoholic triggers profound alterations, in body odor, behavior, emotion, and in an ability to drink in moderation. Total abstinence is a wise choice for these folks. But their experience is not widely generalizable.

THE CURRENT STATE OF THE ART

After its promising beginnings, Radical Psychiatry ran into all the familiar troubles. At first, there were a dozen collectives meeting together, offering 24-hour drop-in groups free to anyone who needed them, acquiring a building in Berkeley, running strong. Soon, however, theoretical controversies developed. Was it possible to heal souls without first changing the social system? Were we reproducing a hierarchy in our own midst? Who got to decide how the Radical Psychiatry Center should be used? Eventually, splits happened and within a few years the group reduced to a handful of people.

That handful, however, continued meeting for two decades, developing the work, teaching, publishing a quarterly journal (first called *Issues in Radical Therapy*, and later *Issues in Power and Therapy*), holding an annual 4-day event that was half teaching institute, half eclectic conference—and more than half celebration of a growing, national network. All of these activities served to construct an institutional presence for the Bay Area Radical Psychiatry collective (affectionately known as BARP). As newcomers came into the picture and learned the work, they brought new energy and ideas. But some also expressed resentment that we held too much power. We thought they were right, experiencing the other side of their criticism in the form of our own fatigue and overblown sense of responsibility. So we gave away the journal to a group in Colorado and the Institute to a group in San Francisco. We disbanded our institutional form and dubbed ourselves an informal support network, renamed GOOF (for Group of Old Friends). Despite our facetiousness, we were serious in wanting to experiment with avoiding the calcification of power that accrues when organizations exist over a long time. If the theory and practice we promoted had value, we imagined, it would survive. If it failed, well then perhaps that was right, too.

After many years during which we supported and fought with each other, worked through differences in power and bumped up against differences of opinion, we finally disbanded the collective in 1990 (although the collective had resumed more formal shape for a few years before then). The times had changed; living and working in alternative ways had become harder to sustain. Many of us had taken jobs in agencies, and we were hard-pressed for time, not to mention the patience it takes to work consensually. We decided to give it up, each of us taking our form of the work into whatever new and continuing endeavors we embraced.

Today, a handful of people lead formal Radical Psychiatry groups, but many more incorporate principles of the work into a wide variety of practices. Conflict resolution approaches have been widely influenced by our model of mediation. Radical Psychiatry concepts have made their way into diverse realms, from union organizing to pedagogy, from "diversity work" to arts organizations, and much more.

We still sometimes train people in both group work and, in my case, more consistently, in conflict resolution. Students have taken the work in many different directions—starting practices in small towns, integrating it into bodywork modalities, using it in political organizing, and more. Claude Steiner continues to write and teach skills of emotional literacy. My work as a scholar and writer is deeply informed by my experiences in Radical Psychiatry.

Years ago, a conference was convened in the Midwest on the subject of combining therapy and politics. I remember a woman who stood up toward the end and said, "I've been struggling alone in my work for years and I never knew until now that there were others doing the same. I have a name for what I do now: Radical Therapist." She was working very much in isolation, in an African American community in a southern state. What was inspiring about what she said was the realization that good ideas arise in different places when the time is right, in varied forms, but speaking to the same need and vision.

Today, I believe the time is again right. I see whole new movements of people delving into the connections between social justice and psychotherapy. How encouraging that is, not only for the state of a profession, but for the state of the world. If we truly join the political and the personal, as the women's movement proposed, if we work to liberate the human heart from its burden of alienation, then we cannot continue to countenance oppression of any people, anywhere. And that is very good news, indeed.

REFERENCES

Belenky, M. F., Clinchy, B. M., Goldberger, N. R., & Tarule, J. M. (1986). *Women's ways of knowing*. New York: Basic Books.

Birkhoff, J. (2000). *Mediators' perspectives on power: A window into a profession?* Unpublished dissertation, George Mason University.

Bourgois, P. (1995). *In search of respect: Selling crack in el barrio*. Cambridge, England: Cambridge University Press.

Chesler, P. (1989). *Women and madness*. New York: Harcourt, Brace, Jovanovich.

Fanon, F. (1963). *The wretched of the earth*. New York: Grove Press.

Gardner, H. (1983). *Frames of mind: The theory of multiple intelligences*. New York: Basic Books.

Gramsci, A. (1979). *Selections from the prison notebooks*. New York: International Publishers.

Hochschild, A. (1989). *The second shift: Working parents and the revolution at home*. New York: Viking.

hooks, b. (1992). *Black looks: Race and representation*. Cambridge, MA: South End Press.

Rabenold, D. (1988). Love and rescue in lesbian relationships. In B. Roy & C. Steiner (Eds.), *Radical Psychiatry: The second decade* (pp. 169–177). San Francisco: Bay Area Radical Therapy Collective.

Roy, A. (2003). *Confronting empire*. Speech delivered at Porto Alegre, Brazil, at the World Social Forum, January 28. Retrieved August 15, 2006, from http://www.tamilnation.org/intframe/roy/arundhati.2.htm

Roy, B. (2002). For White people, on how to listen when race is the subject. *The journal of intergroup relations, 29*(3), 3–15.

Roy, B., & Steiner, C. (Eds.). (1988). *Radical Psychiatry: The second decade*. San Francisco: Bay Area Radical Therapy Collective.

Scheff, T. (1990). *Microsociology*. Chicago: University of Chicago Press.

Steiner, C. (1969). *A warm fuzzy tale*. Retrieved August 15, 2006, from http://www.emotional-literacy.com/fuzzy.htm

Steiner, C. (2001). *Achieving emotional literacy*. New York: Trafalgar Square.

Taylor, S. E., Klein, L. C., Lewis, B. P., Gruenewald, T. L., Gurung, R. A. R., & Updegraff, J. A. (2000). Female responses to stress: Tend and befriend, not fight or flight. *Psychological Review, 107*(3), 41–429.

HISTORICAL REFERENCES

Steiner, C. (Ed.). (1975). *Readings in Radical Psychiatry*. New York: Grove Press.

Steiner, C. (1981). *The other side of power*. New York: Grove Press.

Wyckoff, H. (1976). *Love, therapy, and politics*. New York: Grove Press.

Wyckoff, H. (1977). *Solving women's problems*. New York: Grove Press.

5

Ethnopolitical Psychology: Healing and Transformation

Lillian Comas-Diaz
Transcultural Mental Health Institute
Washington, DC

Each (wo)man speaks with his father's (mother's) tongue; ask a (wo)man who (s)he is and (s)he names a race.
—Leonard Cohen, *the Favorite Game* (1963)

A national identity helps members of a social group who share a common history, territory, language, religion, customs, and social institutions to recognize and relate biographically to each other (Montero, 1984). As a "nation of immigrants," the United States contends with a central problem of identity (Hoffman, 1989). Multiculturalism threatens the national identity because the darkening of America's face compromises White Americans' ability to recognize and relate biographically to Americans of color. Founded by White Anglo Saxon Protestant "fathers," the United States fears becoming a cultural and racial Babel Tower (Clausen, 2000), where diversity and pluralism threaten a uniform national identity. Addressing these issues, a Presidential Initiative on Race and Racism concluded that race relations constitute a major national problem, challenging Americans to take pride in being members of a multiracial society ("One America in the 21st century" (U.S. President's Commission, 1998).

North American psychology has acknowledged multiculturalism by studying the cultural patterning of human behavior, cognition, motivation, and development (Shweder, 1993). However, mainstream psychology was established on a monocultural foundation (Kennedy, Scheirer, & Rogers, 1985), neglecting the fact that we are dated and embedded in a political context. Albeit some progress has occurred in recognizing culture (American Psychological Association, 2003), psychology continues to be limited in addressing people of color's needs through the neglect of their historical and political context of behavior. Compared to majority group members, visible people of color emphasize relational and contextual values, viewing personal and collective history as aspects of the same reality.

History and politics affect all of us, although their effects depend on our situated reality. For instance, many U.S. Southerners perceive the Civil War differently from

Northerners, as their unresolved anger still permeates their perception of Yankees. Adverse events—particularly, those that affect large numbers of people such as the Great Depression, natural disasters, political violence, terrorism, and social cataclysms (such as assassination of national leaders, accidents, and others)—tend to form an enduring and distinguishing membership affiliation (Elder, 1979). These formative events lead to feelings of shared participation in social experiences that create firm bonds, distinguishing persons who have endured these events from those whom have not. Moreover, having lived through these formative events tends to shape responses to subsequent events. Likewise, similar sociohistorical and political experiences bond people of color, cementing identification, affiliation, and group membership related to racial oppression. Moreover, racism and trauma are formative bonding experiences for many visible people of color. The pain of oppression can be unbearable for individuals residing in a society that prides itself of being classless and open.

In this chapter, I present an ethnopolitical psychological approach designed for people of color in the United States. This approach encourages healing and transformation through the development of critical consciousness and sociopolitical action. Ethnopolitical psychology aims to decolonize people of color, reformulate their ethnic identity, and promote racial reconciliation, personal transformation, and societal change. Examining the relationship between ethnic minorities and other Americans, I emphasize the role of colonization and cultural imperialism and their sequelae, including postcolonization stress disorder and ethnocultural allodynia. Furthermore, I argue that racism is partly based on evolutionary psychological findings and sustained by projection, scapegoating, and preservation of the status quo. Afterwards, I elaborate on an integrative ethnopolitical practice, one that blends mainstream psychology with ethnic indigenous healing. Ethnopolitical practitioners accompany the oppressed, bear witness, increase cultural consciousness, and promote change. Moreover, I discuss how ethnic indigenous psychology reformulates identity by calling back the spirit. Lastly, I elaborate on how cultural consciousness encourages racial reconciliation, and on how sociopolitical action facilitates personal and societal change.

ETHNOPOLITICAL THEORY AND PRACTICE: CONCEPTUAL INFLUENCES

Psychology in the United States tends to limit its study of ethnopolitical factors to issues of warfare and conflict resolution in the international arena. The Solomon Asch Center for the Study of Ethnopolitical Warfare at the University of Pennsylvania—one of the few North American institutions analyzing ethnopolitical conflict—was founded to study the origins of ethnic conflicts and predictors of ethnopolitical warfare, the escalation and its antidotes during conflict, and the assistance and community building after conflict (Chirot, 1998). However, these studies tend to exclude ethnopolitical conflicts within the United States.

I define an ethnopolitical psychological approach to working with people of color as the study of the interaction of ethnicity and political ideology on human behavior within a national arena (Comas-Diaz, 2000). Ethnopolitical psychology acknowledges ethnic, racial, gender, social, and political realities as they converge with socioeconomic, historical, psychological, and environmental factors. It examines oppression, colonization, and cultural imperialism, paying special attention to the effects of racism, racial terrorism, sexism, and political repression on individuals, groups, and society.

Ethnopolitical psychology encourages healing and transformation through the development of critical consciousness and sociopolitical action. It aspires to social justice, racial equity, and solidarity as psychosocial outcomes (Comas-Diaz, 2000). Ethnopolitical psychology aims to decolonize people of color, reformulate their ethnic identity, and promote racial reconciliation, personal transformation, and sociopolitical change. Several conceptual orientations have nurtured its theory and practice. Some of these orientations include psychology of liberation, psychology of colonization, feminism, Black psychology, ethnic indigenous psychology, trauma therapy, pedagogy of the oppressed, evolutionary psychology, and ethnopolitical conflict management. Table 5.1 summarizes these major theoretical influences.

Ethnopolitical psychology integrates liberation psychology (see Ignacio Martín-Baró, as cited in Aron & Corne [1994], and Blanco [1998]) with an ethnic indigenous psychological perspective (Comas-Díaz, Lykes, & Alarcón, 1998). It is grounded in feminism, because the struggle against colonization generated a need to challenge women's subservient position (Dumont, 1994). Psychology of liberation emerged in Latin America as a response to sociopolitical oppression. It is intimately linked to psychology of colonization with its emphasis on the effects of political, economic, and psychological domination on both colonizer and the colonized. Whereas Frantz Fanon (1967) defined the colonial relationship as the psychological nonrecognition of the subjectivity of the colonized, Albert Memmi (1965) described it as the chaining of the colonized to the colonizer through an economic and psychic dependence. Moreover, Octave Mannoni (1991) emphasized the psychological dependence, arguing that European colonizers masked feelings of inferiority by asserting dominance over colonized individuals.

Psychology of liberation is rooted in Paulo Freire's (1970) pedagogy of the oppressed. Paulo Freire coined the term *concientization* or *critical consciousness* to define the process of personal and social transformation that oppressed Latin Americans experienced while they alphabetized themselves in a dialectic conversation with their world. Freire contended that traditional models of education are instruments of oppression, reinforcing and maintaining social inequities. He developed critical consciousness to teach individuals how to read their surrounding circumstances and to write their own reality. His liberation paradigm states that to articu-

TABLE 5.1
Conceptual Influences on Ethnopolitical Psychology

Orientation	Targets	Goals
Psychology of liberation	Repression, oppression	Liberation
Psychology of the colonized	Colonization	Decolonization
Pedagogy of the oppressed	Oppression	Critical consciousness
Feminism	Sexism	Gender equity/empowerment
Indigenous healing	Disharmony	Spiritual transformation
Black psychology	Racism, oppression	Racial equity/liberation
Ethnic psychology	Disconnection	Ethnic identity
Trauma therapy	Victimization	Personal recovery
Political repression and trauma	Terrorism	Personal/social healing
Evolutionary psychology	Thinking racially	Conviviality
Ethnopolitical conflict	Warfare	Reconciliation and peace

late the personal and communitarian liberation language, individuals and groups need to assume control of their lives, overcome their false conscience and achieve a critical knowledge of themselves.

Psychology of liberation attempts to work with people in context through strategies that enhance awareness of oppression and of the ideologies and structural inequality that have kept them subjugated and oppressed. It collaborates with the oppressed in developing critical analysis and engaging in a transforming practice. Psychology of liberation resonates with African American psychology based on Black liberation theology and Africanist traditions (Jackson, 1987). Likewise, psychology of liberation emerged from Latin American liberation theology. Not surprisingly, Ignacio Martin-Baro—architect of the psychology of liberation—was both a psychologist and a priest.

Ethnopolitical practice incorporates an ethnic indigenous psychology. Due to mainstream psychology's monocultural orientation, ethnic psychology challenged dominant approaches with conceptual, methodological, ethical, and political concerns. For instance, Thomas Gordon (1973) exhorted Black psychologists to develop research that emerges from real-life needs rather than from academic discourse. Furthermore, he called for collaboration between African American communities and researchers asking psychologists to complement their scholarship with the roles of advocates, lobbyists, information resource persons, watchdogs, in order to facilitate the advancement of Black collective interests. In addition to combating oppression, ethnic psychology interprets distress as a result of individuals' disconnection from their cultures of origin.

COLONIZATION

"A thousand years of history are more than good intentions"—Jeanne Kilpatrick

Ethnic, racial, political, and economic factors mediate the relationship between the United States government and its communities of color. Many ethnic minorities struggle with the effects of colonization. Indeed, Kenneth B. Clark (1989), the first president of color of the American Psychological Association, compared the situation of African Americans with that of colonized people. As highly visible "Others," people of color bear the mark of subjugation. Color, the sign of the colonized, bonds many people of color, transcending gender, sexual orientation, and class identities (Almquist, 1989), and subordinating such identities to the condition of being colonized. A look at the United States' history unfolds the designation of its people of color as colonized entities (Comas-Diaz, 1994), promoting a collective racial consciousness equating color with subjugation. As a result, the "us and them" mentality is mediated by the history of Native American genocide (Walker & LaDue, 1986) and their condition of being immigrants in their own land, the legacy of the African American slavery, the conquest and subjugation of Mexicans and their territory (Padilla & Salgado de Snyder, 1992), plus the colonization of Hawaii, the Philippines, and Puerto Rico. Few people of color, with the exception of Japanese Americans, witnessed a substantial redress effort for governmental injustices. Although the U.S. Department of Justice's Office of Redress Administration (ORA) awarded financial payments to more than 81,800 Japanese Americans accompanied by a presidential apology letter, many experience a lack of reconcilia-tion (Kashima, 1998). Moreover, the political conflict with Asians during World War II, as well as the Korean and Vietnam wars, engendered an ambivalent rela-tionship with Asian Americans. Indeed, Chalsa Loo and her research colleagues (Loo, Singh, Scurfield, & Kilauano,1998) found that Asian-American Vietnam veter-ans suffered from race-related stress and trauma due to their physical similarity to the Vietnam enemies. Asian American combatants experienced cognitive disso-nance (killing people who look like them), as well as being themselves the victims of friendly fire.

Colonization involves more than the dynamics of dominance and subordination, power and powerlessness, and aggression and identification with the aggressor. It involves a systematic negation of the colonized, with the consequent pervasive identity conflicts for the colonized of color (Fanon, 1967, 1968). Colonization gives birth to the colonized mentality. This mentality comprises emotional and psycho-logical reactions such as alienation, self-denial, assimilation, and strong ambiva-lence (Memmi, 1965). The colonized mentality generates cognitive schema changes, somatic and physiological symptoms, plus developmental and behavioral changes, among others. The cognitive distortions include alterations in the perception of self, others, and the world as a just place, as well as changes in the sense of trust, power, agency, and safety. The colonized mentality's psychological effects include depres-sion, shame, rage, and post-traumatic stress disorder (PTSD). Furthermore, visible people of color are exposed to postcolonization stress disorder.

POSTCOLONIZATION STRESS DISORDER

Postcolonization stress disorder is the result of struggling with racism and cultural imperialism, as well as with the imposition of mainstream culture as dominant and superior (Comas-Diaz, 2000). Postcolonization stress disorder involves internalized and projected racism. Indeed, Grace (1997) suggests that internalized racism is a disorder of the self due to colonization's severe insults to individual and collective self-esteem.

Although postcolonization stress disorder shares several similarities with PTSD, it is a different entity altogether. Mental health professionals working with terrorism and torture survivors in countries where repression is occurring daily view PTSD as a limited diagnostic category that does not capture the magnitude of a traumatic po-litical terrorism (Lira, 1998). They do not consider terrorism and torture survivors as psychiatric patients because these victims experience a normal reaction to an ab-normal stressor (Becker, 1995). Classifying reactions to political trauma and terror-ism as a mental disorder medicalizes a sociopolitical problem (Becker, 1995; Lira, 1998), without considering the historical and political context.

Indeed, "post-traumatic" implies that repression and terrorism were a single iso-lated trauma. However, most terrorism survivors have a history of previous cumula-tive trauma that continues after the episode (Becker, 1995; Reeler, 1994). Moreover, terrorism and torture are a human-made, politically motivated, physical, and psy-chological trauma designed to destroy the political identity of its victims and to in-timidate a segment of society. In my clinical experience, the cumulative exposure to racism is similar to experiencing terrorism on a continuous basis.

CULTURAL IMPERIALISM

People subjected to cultural imperialism and intellectual domination compromise their cultural values (Said, 1994). A contemporary manifestation of colonization, cultural imperialism universalizes and establishes as a norm the dominant group's experience and culture (Young, 1990). Consequently, dominated group members are defined by the dominant others. The differences between the dominant group members and minority members are identified as deviance and inferiority (Young, 1990). Because oppression generates a psychological adaptation to the political realities of domination, victims internalize their imposed condition and feel incapable of resistance (Freire, 1973). Oppressed by cultural imperialism, visible people of color are systematically indoctrinated to see the dominant cultural values as superior to their own. Moreover, many people of color are exposed to the "cultural Stockholm syndrome," a condition where members of an oppressed group accept the dominant cultural values and ideology, including the stereotypes of their own group (DiNicola, 1997). Similar to the Stockholm syndrome, where the kidnapped person exchanges his or her personal alliance for the perpetrator's, the cultural Stockholm syndrome involves being taken hostage by the mainstream culture and perceptions of themselves. Because the dominant culture assigns negative stereotypes to minority group individuals, pressuring them to accept these images, sufferers of the cultural Stockholm syndrome internalize such negative perceptions. An expression of the cultural Stockholm syndrome, internalized racism is further manifested as horizontal hostility, compromising people of color's capacity for developing solidarity with other oppressed individuals.

ETHNOCULTURAL ALLODYNIA

Ethnocultural allodynia is a disturbance in people of color's ability to judge perceived ethnocultural and racial insults and subsequently discern defiant and maladaptive responses from adaptive ones. We borrowed the term from medicine, where allodynia refers to exaggerated pain sensitivity in response to neutral or relatively innocuous stimuli, resulting from previous exposure to painful stimuli (Comas-Diaz & Jacobsen, 2001). Therefore, we coined the term *ethnocultural allodynia* to describe a pain caused by previous racial and ethnocultural injuries as an extreme reaction to neutral or ambiguous stimuli.

The constant exposure to racism increases behavioral exhaustion, psychological affliction, and physiological distress (Clark, Anderson, Clark, & Williams, 1999). It causes confusion, disillusionment (Franklin & Boyd-Franklin, 2000), and racial mistrust. Thus, people of color develop ethnocultural allodynia as a reaction to pernicious racism and as an abnormally increased sensitivity to ethnocultural and racial dynamics associated with past exposure to emotionally painful ethnoracial stimuli.

Cultural imperialism robs the oppressed of their resilience, mastery, and ability for critical analysis. Ethnic, racial, and sociocultural emotional injuries can cause profound changes in the sense of self, altering object relatedness through an increased sensitivity to loss. Like the colonized mentality, ethnocultural allodynia is an injury to the sense of self, wounding healthy narcissism, impairing coping, and obstructing agency. Consequently, ethnocultural allodynia is a maladaptive response in the continuum of responses to racism, where adaptive racial intuition and resilient creativity are at one end of the adaptive range, and ethnocultural allodynia is at the opposite end.

RACISM

Racism permeates the ethnopolitical relationship between the mainstream society and its people of color. Frantz Fanon (1967) noted that racism is a form of colonialism in which oppressors inscribe a mentality of subordination in the oppressed. He stated that the oppressed needed to find their own voice and language to name and describe their condition for liberation.

A form of colonization, as well as an agent of cultural imperialism, racism has the political function to preserve the status quo, maintain the privileges of the dominant group, and silence racial cries for social justice (Comas-Diaz, 2000). Colonized individuals are not only exploited and victimized for the benefit of the colonial power but also serve as the quintessential scapegoats. Within this context, racism is a scapegoating mechanism, partly sustained by the differential power between people of color and dominant group members. Societal projection and scapegoating serve to systemically benefit White people by maintaining large segments of tension and contradiction confined to people of color. In other words, people of color function as collective tension relievers. Moreover, societal projection provides majority group members with a sense of competence, stability, and a lack of confusion (Pinderhughes, 1989). Negative representations are internalized, whereby stereotypes are reinforced through societal projection onto people of color. Moreover, some people of color reinforce this process by behaving as though the stereotypes are true.

In times of economic hardship, national insecurity, and diminishing resources, individuals intensify their tendency to scapegoat, and visible people of color become the Other (Dobbins & Skillings, 2000; Greider, 1991). Whites project onto people of color their disowned aspects (Reeves, 2000), relieving their increasing demands for catharsis by scapegoating ethnic minority groups (von Franz, 1995). For instance, after the September 11, 2001, attacks, many Latinos in the United States were targeted as the enemy because physically they resembled Middle Eastern individuals (Dudley-Grant, Comas-Diaz, Todd-Bazemore, & Hueston, 2004). Indeed, people of color can be targeted as the enemy (Root, 1990) simply because they are highly visible. Acting as external stabilizers of inner control, enemies relieve the frustration inspired by crises (Volkan, 1994).

Societal scapegoating echoes individual repression and projection. Alice Miller (1997) argues that the root of racism is individuals' personal history of abuse and trauma. In other words, racist people who target minorities have not worked through their own feelings of victimization. Societal and individual projections reinforce the asymmetrical power relationship between dominant members and people of color. As a salient visible characteristic, race facilitates the "us and them" mentality, sorting out allies and enemies. Because the collective unconscious stores racial memories (Carl Jung, cited in Rathus, 1990), racism and oppression become an attempt to stabilize our national identity.

THINKING RACIALLY

Racism constitutes a classic example of an "us and them" mentality. Evolutionary psychology may offer an explanation to the human need to categorize people into allies and enemies. Lawrence A. Hirschfeld (1996), a psychological anthropologist, found that we have a race module—an innate and universal propensity for noticing racial differences—leading to thinking racially. In our need to sort people into categories, he asserts, race becomes an easy category to use. Consequently, mentally representing racial groups with remarkable facility, we invest them with significance, and communicate our ideas about them. Our thinking racially arises as early as 3 years of age, as Hirschfeld found, with a concomitant preference for our own group. Nonetheless, cross-cultural studies suggest that young children manifest a racial color bias against dark complexioned people (Williams & Morland, 1976). Racial scapegoating may be responsible for this learned bias.

Based on an evolutionary psychology perspective, Hirschfeld attributed his findings to a model of mind as an assembly of domain-specific modules specialized to handle specific types of information. Indeed, neuroimaging research studying differences between Whites and Blacks demonstrated that when people face individuals of a different race, their amygdala—the brain area helping to detect emotionally charged information such as danger—becomes more activated than when facing individuals of their own race (Hart et al., 2000). Thus, thinking racially may have evolved to help our evolutionary progenitors overcome some crucial challenge to insure survival. Infusing people with a sense of belonging, thinking racially supports the sense of affiliation to one's kind as a product of an evolutionary bioecological imperative. Racism can be perceived as an expression of thinking racially, aimed at preserving members of the same racial clan while destroying other race clan members.

RACIAL TRAUMA

Control and domination of the Other take various forms within civilized societies. Racial discrimination, trauma, and terrorism are methods of control and subjugation. Racism appears to be endemic in the United States. It engenders psychosocial trauma, highlighting the role of power differentials between Black and White people. Racial discrimination contributes to the large differences in outcomes among racial groups in employment, income and wealth, housing, education, criminal justice, health, and other areas, undercutting the achievement of equal opportunity in the United States (Blank, Dabady, & Citro, 2004). Acknowledging the pervasive effect of racial discrimination in the denial of civil, social, educational, political, economic, and health opportunities for people of color, the Committee on National Statistics convened a panel of scholars to assess and measure the extend of racial discrimination (Blank, Dabady, & Citro, 2004). The committee recommended monitoring data on race and ethnicity in order to understand evolving differences and trends in outcomes among the different groups in the United States (Blank, Dabady, & Citro, 2004).

An enforcer of cultural imperialism, racism is omnipresent in the lives of visible people of color, particularly African Americans (Jones, 1991). Relative to Whites, African Americans of all socioeconomic levels report exposure to more stressors like racism and other types of discrimination (Williams, Yu, Jackson, & Anderson, 1997). For instance, empirically assessing discrimination, Thompson Sanders (1991) found that 28% of her African American participants indicated that they had personally confronted significant racial and or ethnic discrimination during adulthood, and 17% reported that they had experienced discrimination during both childhood and adulthood. In 1996, Thompson Sanders empirically found that 33.8% of her research participants had experienced discrimination within 6 months of her study. Of those reporting discrimination, 33.3% described minor experiences (such as name calling, racial slurs and insults), 43.9% moderate experiences (such as refusal of service, unfair job assignments), 16.6% severe occurrences (such as salary and promotion inequities, denial of housing, police mistreatment), and 6% was unclassified.

Growing up in a racist society leaves indelible marks. People of color are exposed to insidious, pervasive, and cumulative racism inflicted on an episodic, acute, and chronic basis (Harrell, 2000). Episodic racism includes direct, aversive, and vicarious discrimination. Research has validated the existence of unconscious negative racial feelings and beliefs. Using response latency measure of bias, cognitive psychology experiments have demonstrated that individuals who in self-report measures appear to be nonprejudiced, have generally negative attitudes toward African Americans (Dovidio, & Gaertner, 1986). This phenomenon, also known as aversive racism, describes the discrimination of White liberals and conservatives against visible people of color in situations that do not implicate racial prejudice as a basis for their actions (Whaley, 1998).

Visible people of color are exposed to racial microaggressions or the assaults inflicted on them on a regular and acute basis solely due to their race and color (Pierce, 1995). Some microaggressions include being harassed in public places, ignored by clerks in favor of White customers, and mistaken for service personnel, experiencing unequal housing policies, and other innumerable racial slights. Racial macroaggressions are assaults at a more systemic in nature: A good example is racial profiling. Statistically studying racial profiling, Lamberth (1998) found that the rate at which Blacks were stopped was greatly disproportionate to their numbers on the road and to their propensity to violate traffic laws. The American Civil Liberties Union showed that racial profiling has national proportions (Drummond, 1999). This agency reported that law-enforcement agencies have systematically targeted travelers of color for search—pedestrians, motorists, and airline passengers—based on the belief that they are more likely to commit crimes than Whites (Drummond, 1999). Racial profiling affects African Americans and Latinos regardless of social class and geographic location (Harris, quoted in Drummond, 1999). Privilege and fame do not protect people of color. Geraldo Rivera (1999)—a Puerto Rican lawyer and TV personality—reported that due to his ethnic look, he is routinely stopped at airports for suspicion of criminal behavior. The September 11, 2001, attacks have heightened and 'validated" such macroaggressions.

RACIAL TERRORISM

Racial trauma graduates into terrorism (Wyatt, 1994). Racial terrorism is the most efficient way to control and disempower people of color. As an instrument of contemporary colonization, racial terrorism deconstructs individual and collective identities. It reenacts colonization dynamics. Similar to intimate terrorism (Miller, 1995), racial terrorism is embedded in the context of political, societal, and historical realities. Progressing from racist slurs to racial murders, terrorism is not an unusual event in the context of war, but rather an everyday occurrence, a "business as usual" event contributing to the erosion of collective identities (Martín-Baró, cited in Aron & Corne, 1994). Indeed, the most common bias motivation behind hate crimes in the late 1990s was race, followed by religion, sexual orientation, and ethnicity (Federal Bureau of Investigation [FBI], 1997). Although cases of individual racial terrorism are punished, as the death sentence of John William King—a supremacist White man who murdered James Byrd, Jr., by dragging him out of the back of his truck—(Cohen, 1999), other types of racial terrorism usually go unchallenged.

Human-made disasters and violence are more pathogenic than natural disasters. Racial terrorism is pathogenic due to its sinister and pervasive features. Racial terrorism is present in most levels of society, including employment, justice system, education, and health care. As health providers, we need to be aware that racial terrorism permeates the medical and mental health system. For instance, in 1999 the *American Journal of Public Health* devoted a special section to human rights and public health. This section concluded that the United States violates the human rights of women of color, particularly in the medical treatment of HIV (Gollub, 1999). Moreover, the *New England Journal of Medicine* provided another example of insidious racial terrorism. It reported that doctors were 40% less likely to order sophisticated cardiac tests for women and Blacks who complained about chest pain than men and Whites with identical symptoms (Schulman et al., 1999; White, 1999). Furthermore, racial differences exist in the prescription and the type of antidepressant medication given to minorities. For instance, in examining Medicare patients, Malfi, Croghan, Hanna, and Robinson (2000) found that African Americans were less likely than Whites to receive an antidepressant, and when prescribed medication, Whites were more likely than African Americans to receive selective serotonin reuptake inhibitors (SSRIs) as opposed to tricyclic antidepressants. This is a critical issue because using SSRIs may provide specific benefit for African Americans who, due to differences in pharmacokinetics when compared to Whites, are particularly sensitive to side effects of TCAs (Strickland, Ranganath, & Lim, 1991).

Systematic racial terrorism operates in a semiofficial way in the United States. Semiofficial systematic terror involves the intimidation and violence conducted by state officials that is not legally sanctioned by the state (Sidanius & Pratto, 1999). For instance, the United States government has used terrorist techniques on its populations of color (Novo, 1999), specifically African Americans, Latinos, and Asian Americans. Amnesty International (1999) denounced, at the United Nations Commission of Human Rights, the United States' violation of human rights of its people of color, arguing that when attacking people of color who are not offering resistance, the police used weapons that, in other countries, would be classified as torture instruments. In this report, victims of police brutality alleged being repeatedly struck with fists, batons, and other torture instruments—often after minor disputes with officers on the streets. The report also documented deaths in custody from excessive force, and shootings in violation of police's own very strict guidelines for the use of deadly force (Amnesty International, 1999). Racial disparities appeared to be most marked in cases involving deaths in custody or questionable shootings. In many of the cases examined, international standards—as well as U.S. law and police guidelines prohibiting torture or other cruel, inhuman or degrading treatment—appear to have been violated with impunity. Consequently, Amnesty International (1999) has called on the federal authorities to maintain national statistics on police shootings and deaths in custody in the United States. Moreover, the police have been charged with acting as forces of occupation in neighborhoods of color (Rivera, 1999).

COMMUNAL CONSEQUENCES OF RACIAL TERRORISM

Racial terrorism shatters minds, bodies, and spirits. Those individuals affected by direct or vicarious racial terrorism develop serious spiritual disturbances. These disorders include questioning the meaning of life, cessation from practice of faith, demoralization, and losing hope. The disconnection from the divinity results in a loss of vitality and aliveness. These spiritual disturbances impact communities of color in a dramatic way, because many people of color view adherence to spirituality as resilience against adversity (Kay, 1998).

Racial terrorism affects communities of color. The cumulative and transgenerationally transmitted racism-related experiences (Harrell, 2000) alter people of color's collective identity, group relational capabilities, and societal worldview. Consequently, racial terrorism changes the development of self-concept and relationships, including the emergence of projected self-hate onto other people of color due to the horizontal hostility that cannot be expressed directly to the ones in power. The concept of "crabs in the bucket"—popularly used to describe intra-antagonism among people of color—is an example of horizontal hostility. This concept describes the futile efforts of crabs at liberating themselves. When crabs are captured and thrown into a bucket, they struggle with each other to get out. After one of them arrives at the top and tries to get out, other crabs attack it, throwing it back into the bottom of the bucket.

Horizontal hostility not only involves intraracial enmity, but it also extends to other oppressed group members, inhibiting the development of solidarity among oppressed people. The communal effects of racial terrorism include breaking the sense of community, a rigid survivalist mode, and a dualistic thinking, such as an "us and them" mentality. Many marginalized communities develop ingrained feelings of difference and suspicion, even hatred of the other due to an ancestral history of endangered survival (Lechner, 1992). Because all serious ethnic conflicts involve threatened identities (Ross & Rothman, 1999), one's own identity can be affirmed only by the negation of the other. Consequently, the crucial defense of one's ethnic self is identified with the destruction of the other, resulting in the interpretation of social reality as a life or death struggle (Lechner, 1992). Thinking racially facilitates this mechanism of defense.

In summary, colonization and cultural imperialism give birth to postcolonization stress disorder and cultural Stockholm syndrome, respectively. Evolutionary psychological findings suggest that racism is a derivate of thinking racially—a survival mechanism destined to protect "us from them." Lastly, a history of political oppression against people of color metamorphoses into racial terrorism. The internalized colonized mentality generates dysfunction in people of color's ability to express aggression towards the dominant perpetrators, projecting self-hate onto other people of color. Ethnocultural allodynia is a reaction to ongoing racial terrorism. Table 5.2 summarized the main ethnopolitical constructs.

ETHNOPOLITICAL PRACTICE: ACCOMPANYING AND BEARING WITNESS

An ethnopolitical practice fosters decolonization by promoting critical consciousness of the colonized mentality. It challenges and corrects cognitive distortions by recognizing the contexts of colonization and postcolonization stress disorder.

TABLE 5.2
Ethnopolitical Constructs

Colonization	Cultural Imperialism
Postcolonization Stress Disorder	Cultural Stockholm syndrome
Thinking racially	Racism
Colonized mentality	Ethnocultural allodynia
Racial terrorism	Horizontal hostility

Ethnopolitical practice reformulates individual and collective ethnic identities, increases dignity, self- and social mastery, and reconnects individuals with their roots by calling back their spirit. It promotes reconciliation by teaching cultural awareness in a critically conscious manner. Moreover, ethnopolitical practice facilitates personal and collective transformation through sociopolitical action (Comas-Diaz, 2000).

Ethnopolitical practitioners "accompany" people of color by working with them, seeking to develop collaborative relations that recognize power inequities, cultural imperialism, and neocolonization within their relationships as well as within the larger society. To accompany is to engage in an active process geared to catalyze individual and collective action, and promote personal and social responsibility. A way of accompanying the oppressed is to bear witness. Bearing witness aims at change by refusing to succumb to the pressure to revise or to repress experience, embracing resistance rather than conformity, and enduring anger and pain rather than submitting to repression (Tal, 1996).

Ethnopolitical practice utilizes mainstream psychological orientations such as psychodynamic, interpersonal, systemic, cognitive-behavioral (CBT), and other psychotherapies. Although many clinicians and researchers of color have questioned the applicability of mainstream psychotherapy to people of color (Matt & Navarro, 1997; Ramirez, 1991; Sue, 1998), others advocate for modifying and adapting Western psychological interventions to the lives of people of color (Hall, 2001). For instance, Bernal and Scharron del Rio (2001) recommended the addition of multicultural awareness and culture-specific strategies to cognitive behavioral, person-centered, and psychodynamic forms of psychotherapy. As an illustration, some psychoanalysts are incorporating clients' diverse social, communal, and spiritual orientations into their practices (Altman, 1995; Foster, Moskowitz & Javier, 1996). In her application of CBT to women of color, Lewis (1994) considered not only the culture of women of color but also the systemic and historical influences in their lives. Likewise, research found interpersonal therapy to be effective in reducing depression in African Americans (Brown, Schulberg, Sacco, Perel, & Houck, 1999) and in Latinos (Rosello & Bernal, 1999), when its application was culturally appropriate. Moreover, cognitive-behavioral approaches were found to be effective in treating depression among Latinos (Organista, Munoz, & Gonzales, 1994; Rosello & Bernal, 1999). Furthermore, CBT was shown to reduce Latinos' panic symptoms in a community medical center setting (Sanderson, Rue, & Wetzler, 1998).

A practitioner following a CBT approach needs to assess the role of racism, sexism, oppression, and history in her client's ability to achieve mastery and agency. Within the cognitive behavioral approach, ethnopolitical practice uses racial stress inoculation (a derivate of stress inoculation described by Foa, Rothbaum, Riggs, & Murdock, 1991), and critical racial stress incident management, to alleviate the wounds of colonization and foster empowerment. Within this approach, the therapist measures racial injuries with the Schedule of Racist Events (Landrine & Klonoff, 1996). This inventory provides data for the therapeutic desensitization by unfolding the client's hierarchy of exposure to racist events. Using these data, the therapist asks clients to visualize racist events and identify their negative emotions. Clients are then taught progressive muscle relaxation for the systematic desensitization process. Guided imagery is used in the inoculation process by introducing a positive cognition after the desensitization and restructuring.

Eye Movement Desensitization Reprocessing (EMDR), a treatment specifically formulated for trauma, had been found to be effective for reducing racial trauma (Rittenhouse, 2000). I have found EMDR to be congruent with many people of color's worldviews, as long as it is culturally appropriate. According to Shapiro (1995) trauma is fixated at the cognitive, behavioral, and neurophysiological levels. She argues that EMDR reprocesses trauma by eye movements and desensitization, while transforming negative beliefs into positive ones. As EMDR emphasizes self-healing, people of color learn techniques such as safe-place imagery, healing visualizations, body scan, plus self-directed eye movements.

Mainstream psychotherapy has not been committed to a justice-oriented agenda (Brown, 1997). In particular, many people of color suspect that the techniques and goals of mainstream psychotherapy are acculturation instruments used by the dominant Western culture (Ramirez, 1991). Indeed, most mainstream psychological techniques tend to promote individualism over collectivism. In order to be culturally appropriate, ethnopolitical practice follows an integrative approach, blending mainstream psychotherapy with ethnic indigenous psychology. Table 5.3 presents an example of such integration.

The future of psychotherapy involves an integration of Eastern traditions with Western psychotherapy (Bankart, Koshikawa, Nedate, & Haruki, 1992) and indigenous healing. Indeed, such integration has been already documented in the mental health literature (Watts, 1961). Current examples of East–West integration include using meditation in psychotherapy (Epstein, 1995), as well as mindfulness (a type of Eastern meditation practice) in the cognitive-behavioral therapy schema work (Bennet-Golman, 2001). EMDR borrowed a healing light-stream technique from yoga (Shapiro, 1995). Guided imagery, another indigenous technique, is commonly used in Jungian psychotherapy (Foote, 1996) as well as in medicine (Rossman, 2000). Indeed, many cultural groups, including the Navajos, ancient Egyptians, Greeks, and Chinese, used imagery well before Carl G. Jung. Indigenous psychology can help people of color increase their personal sense of agency and mastery. In my experience, indigenous healing shares several commonalities with dynamic psychotherapy such as the acknowledgment of the role of unconscious motivation, the need for catharsis, and the therapeutic power of working through. Indigenous healing has

TABLE 5.3
Ethnopolitical Practice

Mainstream Psychotherapy	Ethnic Indigenous Psychology
Cognitive-behavioral therapy	Dichos therapy
Interpersonal therapy	Testimony
Psychodynamic therapy	Calling back the spirit
Family and group therapy	Culture circles

also been compared to psychoanalysis, group psychotherapy, psychodrama, family therapy, and crisis intervention (Comas-Diaz, 1981). Indigenous healing is consonant with collectivist societies because it restores clients' sense of belonging, as opposed to Western psychotherapy, which is organized around clients' value of individuality (Kakar, 1982). Furthermore, emphasizing self-healing, indigenous approaches are congruent with many people of color's worldviews.

Ethnic psychology provides a culturally relevant framework, validating both the importance of racial and ethnic meanings and the historical and political contexts of oppression. Adhering to a social justice perspective, many indigenous psychologies can help in the construction and transformation of a more egalitarian future. Indeed, I strongly believe that ethnic psychology is anchored in a liberation discourse because it provides resources for rescuing ancestry and archetypes by reaffirming and grounding ethnic identity into a collective self. Indigenous, ethnic and non-Western healing approaches are effective in remembering and retelling people of color's cultural memory and thus aiding in identity reconstruction (Comas-Díaz, Lykes, & Alarcón, 1998). They facilitate the psychological redemption of ethnic minorities with the reacquaintance of their history and culture. As an illustration, Black psychology has advocated for alternative modes of treatment, using African American history to repair a collectively damaged African American psyche, while insisting that Eurocentrism does not address African Americans' reality (Early, 1996).

INDIGENOUS HEALING: CALLING BACK THE SPIRIT

Many people of color adhere to a relational worldview that is central to their sense of healing, well-being, and identity (McGoldrick, García-Preto, Hines, & Lee, 1989). Family and interpersonal relationships do not necessary end with death among people of color (Council of National Psychological Associations, 2003; Shapiro, 1994). Indigenous healing predicates the process of "calling back the spirit." In this case "spirit" can be personal, ancestral, ecological, natural, divine, and/or cosmic entities. Indigenous healing is based on a holistic pan-relational worldview and involves ancestral and sacred affiliations in the healing therapeutic (Morones & Mikawa, 1992). Within this worldview, many people of color believe that health is attained through the harmony of mind, body, and spirit (Dudley-Grant et al., 2004; Ho, 1987; Tan & Dong, 2002; Zea, Mason, & Murguia, 2002).

Calling back the spirit is a way of life because spirituality is a major force among many communities of color. Although most religions tend to be patriarchal, spirituality empowers oppressed individuals, particularly females (Bourguignon, 1979). As an illustration, many healers in communities of color are women whose roles as women are radically modified by their healer status (Koss-Chioino, 1992). Their empowered role as healers challenges the traditional gender balance (Hoch-Smith & Spring, 1978). For example, becoming a legitimate healer empowers oppressed Latinas and provides them with respect, agency, and resources within their communities (Espin, 1996).

The APA Guidelines, *Multicultural Education Training, Research, Practice and Organizational Change* (APA, 2003), encourage psychologists to recognize that culture-specific treatment may require nonmainstream interventions. More specifically, Guideline 5 encourages practitioners to develop skills and practices congruent with their clients' worldview by striving to incorporate an understanding of their clients' ethnic, racial, linguistic, spiritual, and cultural background into treatment. Effective psychotherapy with individuals from other cultures needs to endorse a plurality of interventions (Hays, 1995). Thus, psychologists are encouraged to learn about helping practices and healing traditions used in non-Western cultures that may be suitably included in psychological practice. When deemed appropriate, the guideline encourages psychologists to recognize and enlist the assistance of recognized helpers such as indigenous healers. Likewise, the Surgeon General concluded that Western psychological interventions could benefit from incorporating core assumptions and practices of indigenous healing, (Surgeon General, 2000).

In addition to cognitive, aesthetic, social, and political concerns, people of all colors have spiritual needs (Tillich, 1957). In times of crisis, many turn to spirituality and folk healing. With its underlying assumption of spirituality, alternative medicine provides patients with a participatory experience of empowerment, authenticity, and enlarged self-identity when illness threatens their sense of intactness and connection to the world (Kaptchuk & Eisenberg, 1998). The majority of patients appear to be using alternative medicine not so much as a result of being dissatisfied with conventional medicine but largely because they find their health care alternatives to be more congruent with their own values, beliefs, and orientation towards health and life (Astin, 1998). Around 83 million Americans used complementary and alternative healing in 1997, spending $21.2 billion on unconventional medicine, which was more than twice the amount ($9.1) billion of all expenditures for hospital care in that same year (Eisenberg et al., 1998). These figures got the attention of Congress, promoting the establishing of the National Center for Complementary and Alternative Medicine (NCAM, 2001). As many ethnic minorities culturally regress under distress, indigenous healing can offer a cultural holding environment by recovering from trauma, increasing resilience, reconnecting with the mother culture, and promoting transformation (Comas-Diaz, 2003a). Indeed, suffering and injustice are spiritual issues (Wright, Bell, & Watson, 1996). Spirituality helps people of color to cope by addressing the meaning of life, hopelessness, victimization, racism, and demoralization. Combating a long history of oppression, people of color develop resilience by affirming their spirituality (Kay, 1998). Therefore, ethnopolitical practice encourages people of color to call back their spirit by rescuing and utilizing traditional spiritual beliefs to reinforce their cosmic connectedness (Comas-Diaz, 2003a; Ho, 1987). Calling back the spirit refers to helping individuals acknowledge and "remember" their ethnic, cultural, spiritual and historical roots. People of color lose hope when they are cut off from their roots. Calling back their spirit helps them become whole, reconnected, full of spirit, and able to return "home" (Comas-Diaz, in press).

A practical illustration of calling back the spirit involves using rituals to enhance healing and transformation. As signs to the unconscious (von Franz, 1995), rituals facilitate recovery when they are a complement to psychotherapy. Cultural ritualistic practices such as herbal cleansing, sweat lodges, pilgrimages, meditations, and labyrinth walks are useful in dealing with trauma and addressing low self-esteem (Comas-Diaz, 2003a). Particularly for Native Americans, spiritual ceremonies reaffirm ethnic identity grounded in a collective self (Duran & Duran, 1995; Mehl-Medrona, 2003).

The Latino celebration of the Days of the Dead, for instance, can promote healing of complicated bereavement. As an illustration, Jose—an economist at an international bank—entered therapy a year after his mother's death. "I'm stuck," was his chief complaint. Jose expressed his bereavement through angry outbursts. After identifying the source of anger as a reaction to abandonment, the therapist addressed Jose's psychodynamics. His being stuck was both at a personal level as well as in his career, where Jose felt that his racist boss was keeping him from moving forward. As a conjoint treatment, the therapist recommended Jose to participate in a Days of the Dead celebration. Accompanied by his sister, Jose traveled to Mexico for the commemoration. Afterwards, he stated that he "remembered" that as a child he accompanied his mother during Days of the Dead. Working within a psychodynamic and ethnic psychological perspective, the therapist helped Jose to integrate his mother's death with her life. Jose remembered that his mother was an avid supporter of education for the underprivileged. Therapy helped him to move forward in his bereavement. Jose became conscious of the toxic racial climate permeating his place of employment. He decided not to "waste energies in fighting this institutionalized racism." Instead, Jose looked for a new job and used his extra energy to mentor inner-city Latino youth. A 1-year follow-up revealed that Jose was satisfied with his choice. "Life's good," he reported.

Patricia Mathes Cane (2000) described a "calling back the spirit" healing program. Using a holistic approach combined with a liberation framework, Cane found significant results working with victims of violence, indigenous peoples, refugees, prisoners, battered women, and children from El Salvador, Nicaragua, Honduras, and Guatemala. The mind, body, and spirit component included self-healing practices such as Tai Chi, Pal Dan Gum, acupressure, visualization, breath work, ritual, polarity, massage, labyrinth, body movement, and intuition work. The holistic techniques just stated were taught to grass-roots leaders, following Paulo Freire's critical consciousness. The grass-roots leaders shared these practices with their communities. The goal was to empower people to take on their own healing process, because they can learn these body–mind–spirit practices and use them for themselves, their families, and communities. Research methods included quantitative and qualitative methods, such as questionnaires, focus groups, and in-depth interviews. The study's findings showed a lessening of symptoms related to traumatic stress and post-traumatic stress disorder. Moreover, findings showed the benefit of specific practices with different kinds of populations. For instance, Tai Chi, polarity, and acupressure were very effective with Mayan communities in Guatemala. Breath work and Pal Dan Gum exercises were helpful to male and female prisoners in Honduras. Cane concluded that the liberation component was an effective way to promote the inherent healing capacity of the person and the community, and to complement and support community resources, cultural practices, and mental health programs.

DICHOS: AN ETHNIC PSYCHOLOGY

Dichos reconnect Latinos with their cultural ancestry through Spanish proverbs, idiomatic expressions or sayings, and capturing folk wisdom (Aviera, 1996; Zuñiga, 1991). As an ethnic psychology, dichos help Latinos to make meaning out of their reality. They validate the importance of Latino cultural and ethnic representations within the historical and political contexts of oppression. Dichos can be resistant strategies against oppression. For example, *"Buen caballero don dinero"* ("Mr. Money is a good gentleman") denounces the use of financial privilege within a classist society. The dicho *"El que no tiene dinga tiene mandiga"* attacks internalized racism. It literally means that many Latinos have either Indian (dinga) or African (mandinga) roots and therefore cannot pretend that they are White. Moreover, dichos can be subversive responses in that they undermine the ruling of oppressors by finding meaning elsewhere and transferring it to another sphere. For example, *"Valgan las verdes por las maduras"* literally refers to eating green fruits when ripe ones are unavailable. It is used to justify revolutionary behavior within an oppressive situation. Therefore, ripe fruits are a privilege denied to those who cannot afford them. In other words, poor people eat green fruits before ripening, in an attempt to equalize the societal balance.

Dichos psychology therapeutically addresses a wide range of situations from coping with stress and developmental milestones, to depression, anxiety, and even psychosis. Because chronic exposure to oppression can lead to powerlessness, learned helplessness, and posttraumatic stress disorder among Latinos (Vasquez, 1998), dichos therapy is particularly useful when dealing with losses and traumas. In this regard, dichos are similar to cognitive-behavioral therapy, in that they challenge negative cognitions and are anchored in the value of viewing life as a learning experience. Dichos psychology teaches that we are in a constant process of learning and teaching lessons. Life setbacks are perceived as learning experiences with opportunities for growth and improvement. With its educative perspective, dichos are particularly useful in teaching individuals the art of living, not only dealing with losses and traumas but also celebrating life's blessings. Likewise, many people of color view problems as life-long teachers. For instance, most Native Americans believe adversity teaches valuable lessons in living (Mehl-Madrona, 2003). Similarly, some Asian Americans, conceptualize adversity and suffering as path for enlightenment (Tan & Dong, 2002).

Responsive to the here-and-now needs of oppressed Latinos, dichos therapy teaches negotiation of cultural conflicts. For instance, it challenges dysfunctional cultural gender beliefs, such as bearing a cross as a Latina legacy (Garcia Preto, 1990) and learned helplessness. For example, dichos psychology helps with marianismo—the cultural imperative for women to imitate the Virgin Mary. *Marianismo* expects Latinas to adhere to a self-sacrifice and martyrdom doctrine (Comas-Diaz, 2001; Stevens, 1973).

Consider Laura, a Mexican immigrant who was demoted for "not taking initiative" working as an airport clerk. Coping with acculturation stress, Laura ascribed her behavior to the cultural expectation of being a *sufrida* (sufferer) and not being assertive. Labeling her passive-dependent behavior in a traditional marianista gender role, Laura contrasted it with the assertiveness needed to function in the Anglo work force. Laura's *marianismo* was reframed with a dicho *"Ayúdate que Dios te ayudará"* ("God helps those who help themselves").

Bearing witness, the therapist facilitated Laura's unfolding of her negative cognition and self-attribution: *I am inadequate*. The therapist used the dicho *"Matente tranquila, que las grandes batallas se pierden con la mente"* ("Keep relaxed that the biggest battles are lost in the mind") before teaching her mindfulness. *"Muchas veces perdiendo es como se gana"* ("Many times you end up winning when you lose") was used to reframe Laura's feelings of inadequacy. *"El que no sabe es como el que no ve"* ("He who doesn't know is like he who doesn't see") was used to empower Laura and promote her critical consciousness. The therapist added bibliotherapy recommending *The Maria Paradox* (Gil & Vazquez, 1996) to foster critical consciousness. Laura was able to identify her *marianista* traditional behavior and decided to become a new *marianista* (Gil & Vazquez, 1996). She became conscious of her gender oppression and merged her ethnic background with self-reliance and empowerment. Laura mourned and accepted the loss of the old *marianista* role, modified her new gender role, and regarded it as more positive. She restored self-esteem by developing a sense of mastery regarding the demands of the assertive role. Empowered and critically conscious, Laura decided to help other immigrant women and became the spokesperson and advocate in her workers' union.

TESTIMONY

An ethnic psychology, storytelling predicates on people of color's oral legacies. Narratives are effective in remembering and retelling people of color's cultural memory. A cultural style of relating to significant others, narratives facilitate identity reconstruction. They particularly help people of color whose cognitive style is highly reactive to imagery and fantasy. Because oppression often silences the oppressed, narratives are the preferred way to focus on the construction of meaning among people historically outside of the dominant social group (Anderson & Jack, 1991). Storytelling encourages people to become aware of the cultural influences in their lives, creating personal narratives leading to transformation (White & Epston, 1990).

Testimony, an indigenous way of bearing witness, is a special type of narrative that emerged in Chile in response to political repression and terrorism. Testimony chronicles one's traumatic experiences and how these have affected the individual and family (Aron, 1992). In my clinical experience I have found testimony to share elements with interpersonal psychotherapy (Klerman, Weissman, Rounsaville, & Chevron, 1984). Both approaches focus on interpersonal and attachment factors, while targeting grief, disputes, and role transitions among others.

Testimony consists of a verbal journey to the past, allowing individuals to transform painful experiences and identity, creating a new present, and enhancing the future (Cienfuegos & Monelli, 1983). Testimony has been effectively used in psychotherapy with oppressed women, validating their personal experience as a basis for truth and knowledge in an affirming and empowering manner (Aron, 1992). Consider Hanna's vignette. An African American, Hanna was hired by the federal government as an engineer. After she began working, Hanna realized that her sole responsibility was to develop a newsletter. Although Hanna had no previous experience in writing newsletters, her supervisors failed to address her concerns about the assignment. After a year at her position, Hanna entered therapy at the request of her close friends, who were worried about her social withdrawal. Hanna's main complaint was: "I never had emotional problems." Initially, therapy focused on helping Hanna to understand and manage her anger at the distressful situation. After stabilizing her behavior, the therapist invited Hanna to offer a testimony. During her testimony, Hanna recalled a precipitating event: At an agency activity she was asked to sing and entertain her co-workers. Hanna realized that not only was she not allowed to work as an engineer, but she was also the racial token who entertained others. Hired under an affirmative action quota, Hanna confronted that she was a token. Her predicament illustrated the profound emotional toll caused by being a token in a predominantly White environment, with minimal support (Comas-Diaz & Greene, 1994). Testimony helped Hanna to identity the effects of racism on her self-esteem, creating a safe space for decolonization. Critical racial stress incident management uncovered several experiences with racism and a resultant ethnocultural allodynia. Therapy evaluated her ethnocultural allodynia by using the Schedule of Racist Events (Landrine & Klonoff, 1996). After obtaining a baseline of previous racial injuries, the therapist desensitized and inoculated Hanna against future racial stress. Hanna felt more in control. Understanding the politics of affirmative action at her agency helped Hanna to depersonalize the newsletter assignment. Later, Hanna formed a self-help group for professional women victims of tokenism. Later on the group became an advocate voice and lobbied Congress on behalf of victims.

Testimony transforms pain into consciousness and action. Paulo Freire (1970) stated that oppressed people tend to have a clearer vision of reality than their oppressors. Oppressors' realities are clouded by their privilege and thus, distort their perception of themselves and others. Offering testimony, survivors use their clearer vision for empowerment, decolonization, and transformation.

CULTURAL CONSCIOUSNESS

> Just realize where you come from, this is the essence of wisdom.
> —Tao Te Ching

The most serious political effect of systemic aggression is the erosion of collective identities (Lechner, 1992). A major aspect in ethnopolitical practice, thus, is the promotion of cultural consciousness to facilitate people of color's identification, acceptance, and celebration of their ethnicity and culture (Comas-Diaz 2003b). Oppressed individuals need to find their own voice and language in order to name and describe their condition (Freire, 1970). Indeed, the very act of self-definition is a rejection of colonization (Castillo, 1994). People of color reclaim their voice and ability to name themselves by reconnecting to their cultural roots. Cultural consciousness encourages this process by promoting group solidarity and continuity. Increasing awareness and enhancing reflective work, cultural consciousness rescues people of color's legacies, helping them to rediscover and author their history. A "reclaiming identity and restoring dignity" program is an example of fostering cultural consciousness. Through art, folklore, cultural values, literature, and other practices, this approach helps to combat negative stereotypes promulgated by society at large (Comas-Diaz, 2003b; Ho, 1987) while increasing critical consciousness.

Due to colonization, cultural imperialism, and racial terrorism, many people of color contend with fractioned identities. Reconciliation is needed at a personal level to correct negative internalizations and to become whole. Reconciliation is also needed at a communal level to address horizontal hostility, and at societal level to transform dualistic "us and them" thinking into conviviality. Conviviality takes on a specific meaning in ethnopolitical terms. Conviviality means that individual liberation is realized within interpersonal interdependence (Tillich, 1957). Liberation and conviviality go hand in hand because freedom is a plural concept. As Toni Morrison (quoted in Lamott, 1994) argues, the function of freedom is to liberate someone else.

Culture circles are useful in increasing consciousness and conviviality. Based on Paulo Freire's liberation model, Almeida (2003) described culture circles as groups led by a team of therapist and community people for empowerment purposes. First, the therapists train four to six individuals for 12 weeks in critical consciousness. Afterwards, they facilitate the group process. Culture circles topics include racism, privilege (gender, color, socioeconomic, etc.), oppression, homophobia, and discrimination, among others. For more information on culture circles, consult Rhea Almeida's chapter in this volume.

The ethnopolitical perspective emphasizes decolonization by enhancing consciousness of internalized racism, horizontal racism, and thinking racially. As Janet Helms (1995) suggested, the key milestone in people of color's racial identity development is overcoming internalized racism and developing a sociopolitical understanding of race and oppression. Critical consciousness around the "us and them" mentality is paramount to crystallize cultural remembering and to promote solidarity with other oppressed groups. The model of cultural circles is useful to address inter- as well as intraracial and ethnic conflicts. However, it is imperative to include an ethnopolitical education component on coping with racial terrorism, societal projection, the biology of thinking racially, and ethnocultural allodynia. This module also includes ethnopolitical conflict management and resolution. In particular, it attempts to change the psychocultural assumptions about the inevitability of violence, while encouraging the development of a culture of dialogue through its conflict resolution component (Ross & Rothman, 1999). Moreover, ethnopolitical psychology can further study and develop new models of conflict resolutions.

Reconciliation is a goal within an ethnopolitical conflict resolution. Attitudinal healing circles can help achieve racial reconciliation. Abadio-Clottey and Clottey (1998) devised an approach to racial reconciliation involving a 12-step program. Its psycho-spiritual principles included, among others, healing is conquering fear; giving and receiving are the same; we are always learning and/or teaching; and accepting others entails forgiving rather than judging. However, a salient goal of culture consciousness is to promote action. Because oppression relies on a socioeconomic and political system, individuals are encouraged to engage in social action such as community organization, advocacy, and political involvement. Leadership training and political mentoring can be added to culture circles, paying attention to the race, ethnic, gender, and class interaction.

It is imperative that the ethnopolitical approach targets the youth. I recommend cultural awareness programs for children and youngsters in order to develop critical consciousness. Indeed, research has validated the effectiveness of cultural awareness programs. Program evaluation of cultural awareness indicated learning about their culture enhanced Puerto Rican children's self-esteem (Comas-Diaz, Arroyo, & Lovelace, 1982). Creativity is added because the survival artist is a resilient response to colonization (Elsass, 1992). In the creative module, participants are encouraged to express themselves artistically. For example, literature and media have been successfully used to empower Latinos (Bracero, 1998; Ramos-McKay, Comas-Díaz, & Rivera, 1988; Shapiro, 1998). As an illustration, Ramos-McKay and her colleagues (1988) included literature in a group psychotherapy to promote critical consciousness around being an ethnic minority among Puerto Ricans. Likewise, empirical studies compiled in a book (Costantino, Malgady, & Rogler, 1990) have validated the therapeutic use of *cuentos* (stories) as a Latino indigenous technique in mental health treatment. Additionally, photographs have been utilized as an ethnic clinical tool (Comas-Diaz, 2003a; Ho, 1987). Indeed, increased empowerment has been achieved among participants in cultural consciousness groups who took photographs of themselves and significant others during regular activities (Asociación de la Mujer Maya Ixil & Lykes, 2000).

TABLE 5.4
Ethnopolitical Goals

Objectives	Intervention
Decolonization	Critical consciousness
Reformulated ethnic identity	Calling back the spirit
Reconciliation	Cultural awareness
Resilience	Creativity
Personal and societal change	Sociopolitical action

The writing program at Voices of our Nation's Arts (VONA) provides another example of using art as a cultural consciousness tool. Housed at the University of San Francisco, VONA is designed to teach creative writing from the perspective of writers of color. To achieve this, VONA offers writing workshops, poetry, and music performances, in addition to faculty and student readings. Additionally, VONA promotes solidarity with an exercise entitled "I am from the tribe of," where participants introduce themselves by offering testimony describing their ancestry. Differences and similarities are celebrated, fomenting an atmosphere of conviviality and solidarity. Throughout the program, participants are encouraged to create a graphic art project, which they share with all students and faculty. VONA has demonstrated that expressed in a social justice context, creativity helps to reformulate a collective identity and develop a community of writers of color with solidarity and conviviality as ideals.

Table 5.4 outlines the ethnopolitical goals.

ETHNOPOLITICAL ACTION

Be the change you want to see in the world.
—M. K. Gandhi

People of color transform themselves by offering testimony; calling back their spirits; refusing to succumb to racial terrorism; embracing resistance and struggle rather than conforming to the colonized mentality; becoming critically conscious; and developing resistant, resilient, and creative responses to oppression and racism. However, healing and transformation require addressing the whole system—the individual, the family, and the society (Van der Kolk, McFarlane, & Weisaeth, 1996). Countries with exclusionary national identity refuse to treat different racial, ethnic, and religious groups as equal nationals, and eventually generate an ethnopolitical conflict (Chirot, 1998). Therefore, the purpose of ethnopolitical action is to translate critical consciousness into action leading to racial and ethnic justice.

Many trauma victims find healing and transformation in activism. Research shows that an ideological understanding of oppression, in addition to social activism, facilitates women's recovery from sexist discrimination (Landrine & Klonoff, 1996). Likewise, a political consciousness of oppression can promote recovery from racial terrorism, and foster decolonization. Ethnopolitical action promotes political consciousness, helping to catalyze individual and collective action, and encouraging personal and social responsibility. Becoming politically active is no longer an option for people of color; it is imperative for their cultural survival.

Ethnopolitical action facilitates political struggle for the preservation of people of color's personal and collective self. It promotes cultural resilience by addressing racism, racial terrorism, colonization, and intergenerational trauma. Throughout the world, ethnic minorities develop cultural resilience as a response to ethnopolitical trauma. Peter Elsass (1992) defines cultural resilience as a set of values and practices that promote coping mechanisms and adaptive reactions to ethnopolitical trauma within a cultural context. An ethnopolitical action facilitates reconciliation, encouraging conviviality among people of all colors. It enhances cultural resilience by promoting generativity and developing new horizons for future generations.

Ethnopolitical action involves working toward the creation of a safe society. The psychology of place, an interdisciplinary field emerging out of the study of displacement caused by wars and political repression, proposes that individuals require a good enough environment in which to live (Fullilove, 1996). This model posits that people are linked to a good-enough environment through psychological processes such as attachment, familiarity, and identity. Ethnopolitical action targets the rebuilding of a community affected by racial terrorism by helping to develop a society wherein its members can feel that they are attached, familiar, and identified with this society.

Becoming politically active can promote the building of a nonviolent and safe society. An ethnopolitcal psychology offers resources to strengthen people of color's generativity as well as the next generation's capacity to reconceptualize the effects of racism and terror. It promotes solidarity as an antidote against powerlessness. Collectively calling back the spirit provides the communal energy and strength to work towards societal change. Balancing separation with integration, people of color accompany themselves and others while bearing witness to an emerging national multiracial identity.

In conclusion, ethnopolitical psychology promotes people of color's political, social, economic, and cultural rights. It helps to increase their cultural resilience, reclaim their ethnic and cultural roots, and reconstruct their identities within a multiethnic and multiracial society. Critical consciousness and decolonization can ameliorate ethnopolitical conflicts in our country. Because ethnic and cultural conflicts are part of a larger problem of identity, we need to reformulate the national identity.

As partners with other Americans, people of color work toward an egalitarian society with social justice and racial equity. Regardless of color, this egalitarian society will promote its citizens to relate biographically to each other as full members of the same clan. This is the key to achieve the Presidential Initiative on Race's challenge: We will take pride in being members of a multiracial society.

REFERENCES

Abadio-Clottey, A., & Clottey , K. (1998). *Beyond fear: Twelve spiritual keys to racial healing*. Tiburon CA: H. J. Kramer.
Almeida, R. (2003). Creating collectives of liberation. In L. B. Silverstein & T. J. Goodrich (Eds.), *Feminist family therapy: Empowerment in social context* (pp. 293–305). Washington, DC: American Psychological Association.
Almeida, R. (in press). A Social Justice Paradigm in Family Therapy. In E. Aldarondo (Ed). *Promoting Social Justice through Mental Health Practice*.
Almquist, E. (1989). The experience of minority women in the United States. In J. Freeman (Ed.), *Women: A feminist perspective* (4th ed.). Mountain View, CA: Mayfield Publishing Co.

Altman, N. (1995). *The analyst in the inner city: Race, class and culture through a psychoanalytic lens.* Hillsdale, NJ: The Analytic Press.

American Psychological Association (2003). *Guidelines on multicultural education, training, research, practice, and organizational change for psychologists.* Washington, DC: Author.

Amnesty International. (1999). *United States of America: Police brutality and excessive force in the New York City Police Department* (AI Index: AMR available from International Secretariat, 1 Easton Street, London WCX 8DJ, United Kingdom.

Anderson, K., & Jack, D.C. (1991). Learning to listen: Interviews techniques and analyses. In S. B. Gluck & D. Patai (Eds.), *Women's worlds: The feminist practice of oral history.* New York and London: Routledge.

Aron, A. (1992). Testimonio, a bridge between psychotherapy and sociotherapy. *Women & Therapy, 13*(3), 173–189.

Aron, A., & Corne, S. (Eds.). (1994). *Writings for a liberation psychology: Ignacio Martín-Baró.* Cambridge, MA: Harvard University Press.

Asociación de la Mujer Maya Ixil, & Lykes, M. B. (2000). *Voces e imágenes: Mujeres Maya Ixiles de Chajul* [Voices and images: Mayan Ixil women of Chajul]. Guatemala: Victor Herrera de Magan Terra.

Astin, J. A. (1998). Why patients use alternative medicine: Results of a national study. *Journal of the American Medical Association, 279,* 1548–1553.

Aviera, A. (1996). "Dichos" therapy group: A therapeutic use of Spanish language proverbs with hospitalized Spanish-speaking psychiatric patients. *Cultural Diversity and Mental Health, 2*(2), 73–87.

Bankart, C. P., Koshikawa, F., Nedate, K., & Haruki, Y. (1992). When West meets East: Contributions of Eastern traditions to the future of psychotherapy. *Psychotherapy, 29,* 141–149.

Becker, D. (1995). The deficiency of the concept of post-traumatic stress disorder when dealing with victims of human rights violations. In R. J. Kleber, C. R. Figley, & B. Gerson (Eds.), *Beyond trauma: Cultural and societal dynamics.* London: Plenum.

Bennet-Golman, T. (2001). *Emotional alchemy: How the mind can heal the heart.* New York: Harmony Books.

Bernal, G., & Scharron del Rio, M. R. (2001). Are empirically supported treatments valid for ethnic minorities?: Toward an alternative approach for treatment research. *Cultural Diversity and Ethnic Minority Psychology, 7,* 328–342.

Blanco, A. (1998). *Psicología de la liberación de Ignacio Martín-Baró* [Psychology of liberation of Martín-Baró]. Madrid: Editorial Trotta.

Blank, R. M., Dabady, M., & Citro, C. F. (2004). *Measuring racial discrimination: Panel on methods for assessing discrimination.* Washington, DC: The National Academies Press.

Bourguignon, E. (Ed). (1979). *A world of women: Anthropological studies of women in the societies of the world.* New York: Prager.

Boyd-Franklin, N., & Garcia-Prieto, N. (1994). Family therapy. In L. Comas-Díaz & B. Greene (Eds.), *Women of color: Integrating ethnic and gender identities in psychotherapy* (pp. 239–264). New York: Guilford.

Bracero, W. (1998). Intimidades: Confianza, gender, and hierarchy in the construction of Latino–Latina therapeutic relationships. *Cultural Diversity and Mental Health, 4*(4), 264–277.

Brown, C., Schulberg, H. C., Sacco, D., Perel, J. M., & Houck, P. R. (1999). Effectiveness of treatment for major depression in primary medical care practice: A post hoc analysis of outcomes for African American and White patients. *Journal of Affective Disorders, 53,* 185–192.

Brown, L. S. (1997). The private practice of subversion: Psychology as Tikkun Olam. *American Psychologist, 52,* 449–462.

Cane, P. (2000). *Trauma, healing and transformation: Awakening a new heart with body–mind–spirit practices.* Watsonville, CA: Capacitar Inc.

Canino G., & Canino, I. (1982). Culturally syntonic family therapy for migrant Puerto Ricans. *HospComm Psych*(33), 299–303.

Castillo, A. (1994). *Massacre of the dreamers: Essays on Xicanisma.* New York: Penguin.

Castillo, A. (Ed.). (1996). *Goddess of the Americas/La Diosa de las Américas: Writings on the Virgin of Guadalupe.* New York: Riverhead Books.

Chambless, D. L., Sanderson, W. C., Shoham, V., Johnson, S. B., Pope, K. S., & Cris-Christoph, P., et al. (1996). An update on empirically validated therapies. *The Clinical Psychologist, 49,* 5–18.

Chirot, D. (1998, June). *Ethnopolitical warfare: Causes and solutions.* Report on the American Psychological Association conference held in Londonderry/Derry, Northern Ireland.

Cienfuegos, A. J., & Monelli, C. (1983). The testimony of political repression as a therapeutic instrument. *American Journal of Orthopsychiatry, 53,* 43–51.

Clark, K. B. (1989). *Dark ghetto: Dilemmas in social power* (2nd ed.). Middletown, CT: Wesleyan University Publishers.

Clark, R., Anderson, N. B., Clark, V. R., & Williams, D. R. (1999). Racism as a stressor for African Americans: A biopsychological model. *American Psychologist, 54,* 10, 805–816.

Clausen, C. (2000). *Faded mosaic: The emergence of post-cultural America.* Chicago: Ivan R. Dee.

Cohen, A. (1999, March 8). A life for a life. *Time, 153*(9), pp. 28–35.

Cohen, L. (1963). *The favorite game.* New York: Viking.

Comas-Díaz, L. (1981). Puerto Rican *espiritismo* and psychotherapy. *American Journal of Orthopsychiatry, 51*(4), 636–645.

Comas-Díaz, L. (1994). An integrative approach. In L. Comas-Díaz & B. Greene (Eds.), *Women of color: Integrating ethnic and gender identities in psychotherapy* (pp. 287–318). New York: Guilford.

Comas-Díaz, L. (2001). Culturally relevant issues and treatment implications for Hispanics. In D. R. Koslow & E. Salett (Eds.), *Crossing cultures in mental health* (pp. 25–42). Washington, DC: National Multicultural Institute.

Comas-Díaz, L. (2000). An ethnopolitical approach to working with people of color. *American Psychologist, 55,* 1319–1325.

Comas-Diaz, L (2003a). The Black Madonna: The psychospiritual feminism of Guadalupe, Kali, and Monserrat. In L. Silverstein & T. J. Goodrich (Eds.), *Feminist family therapy: Empowerment and social context* (pp. 147–160). Washington, DC: American Psychological Association.

Comas-Diaz, L. (2003b) LatiNegros: Afro Latinos' quest for identity. In M. Root & M. Kelley (Eds), *Multiracial child resource book* (pp.168–177). Seattle: Mavin Foundation.

Comas-Diaz, L. (in press). Our inner Black Madonna: Reclaiming sexuality, embodying sacredness. *Women & Therapy.*

Comas-Díaz, L., Arroyo, A., & Lovelace, J. C. (1982). Enriching self-concept through a Puerto Rican cultural awareness program. *Personnel and Guidance Journal, 60*(5), 306–308.

Comas-Díaz, L., & Greene, B. (Eds.). (1994). *Women of color: Integrating ethnic and gender identities.* New York: Guilford.

Comas-Díaz, L., & Jacobsen, F. M. (2001). Ethnocultural allodynia. *The Journal of Psychotherapy Practice and Research, 10*(4), 1–6.

Comas-Díaz, L., Lykes, B., & Alarcon, R. (1998). Ethnic conflict and psychology of liberation in Guatemala, Perú and Puerto Rico. *American Psychologist, 53*(7), 778–792.

Costantino, G., Malgady, R. G., & Rogler, L. H. (1990). Cuento therapy: A culturally sensitive modality for Puerto Rican children. *Journal of Consulting and Clinical Psychology, 54,* 639–645.

Council of National Psychological Associations. (2003, November). *Psychological treatment of ethnic minority populations.* Washington, DC: The Association of Black Psychologists.

DiNicola, V. (1997). *A stranger in the family: Culture, families and therapy.* New York: Norton.

Dobbins, J. E., & Skillings, J. (2000). Racism as a clinical syndrome. *American Journal of Orthopsychiatry, 70*(1), 14–27.

Dovidio, J. F., & Gaertner, S. L. (1986). *Prejudice, discrimination, and racism.* San Diego: Academic Press.

Drummond, T. (1999, June 14). It's not just in New Jersey. *Time, 153*(23), p. 61.

Dudley-Grant, R., Comas-Diaz, L., Todd-Bazemore, B, & Hueston, J. D. (2004). *Fostering resilience in response to terrorism: For psychologists working with people of color.* Retrieved from http://www.APAHelpCenter.org

Dumont, M. (1994). The campesina's fist. *Readings: A Journal of Reviews and Commentary in Mental Health, 9,* 8–12.

Duran, E., & Duran, B. (1995). *Native American post colonial psychology.* Albany, NY: State University of New York Press.

Early, G. (1996). Understanding Afrocentrism: Why Blacks dream of a world without Whites. In G. C. Ward & R. Atwan (Eds.), *The best American essays, 1996* (pp. 115–135). New York: Houghton Mifflin.

Eisenberg, D. M., Davis, R. V., Ettner, S. L., Appel, S., Wilkey, S., Van Rompay. M., et al. (1998). Trends in alternative medicine used in the United States. 1990–1997. *Journal of the American Medical Association, 280,* 1569–1575.

Elder, G. (1979). Historical change in life patterns and personality. In P. Baltes & O. G. Brim (Eds.), *Life-span development and behavior.* New York: Academic Press.

Elsass, P. (1992). *Strategies for survival: The psychology of cultural resilience in ethnic minorities.* New York: New York University Press.

Epstein, M. (1995). *Thoughts without a thinker: Psychotherapy from a Buddhist perspective.* New York: Basic Books.

Espin, O. (1996). *Latina healers: Lives of power and tradition.* Encino, CA: Floricanto Press.

Fanon, F. (1967). *Black skin, White masks.* New York: Grove Press.

Fanon, F. (1968). The *wretched of the earth.* New York: Grove Press.

Federal Bureau of Investigation. (1997). *Crimes in the United States 1996.* Washington, DC: Author.

Foa, E. B., Rothbaum, B. O., Riggs, D. S., & Murdock, T. B. (1991). Treatment of posttraumatic stress disorder in rape victims: A comparison between cognitive-behavioral procedures and counseling. *Journal of Consulting and Clinical Psychology, 59,* 715–723.

Foote, W. W. (1996). Guided-imagery therapy. In B. W. Scotton, A. B. Chien, & J. R. Battista (Eds), *Textbook of transpersonal psychiatry and psychology* (pp. 355–365). New York: Basic Books.

Foster, R. F., Moskowitz, M., & Javier, R. (Eds.). (1996). *Reaching across the boundaries of culture and class: Widening the scope of psychotherapy.* New York: Aronson.

Franklin, A. J., & Boyd-Franklin, N. (2000). Invisibility syndrome: A clinical model of the effects of racism on African American males. *American Journal of Orthopsychiatry, 70*(1), 33–41.

Freire, P. (1970). *Pedagogy of the oppressed.* New York: Seabury Press.

Freire, P. (1973*). Education for critical consciousness.* New York: Seabury Press.

Fullilove, M. T. (1996). Psychiatric implications of displacement: Contributions from the psychology of place. *American Journal of Psychiatry, 153*(12), 1516–1523.

Garcia-Preto, N. (1990). Hispanic mothers. *Journal of Feminist Family Therapy, 2,* 15–21.

Gehrie, M. J. (1979). Culture as an internal representation. *Psychiatry, 42,* 165–170.

Gil, R. M., & Vazquez, C. I. (1996). *The Maria paradox: How Latinas can merge old world traditions with new world self-esteem.* New York: Putnam.

Gollub, E. L. (1999). Human rights is a U.S. problem, too. The case of women and HIV. *American Journal of Public Health, 89*(10), 1479–1485.

Goodchilds, J. D. (Ed.). (1991). *Psychological perspectives on human diversity in America.* Washington, DC: American Psychological Association

Gordon, T. (1973). Notes on White and Black psychology. *Journal of Social Issues, 29*(1), 87–95.

Grace, C. (1997). Clinical applications of racial identity theory. In C. Thompson & R. Carter (Eds.), *Racial identity theory: Applications to individual, group, and organizational interventions* (pp 55–68). Mahwah, NJ: Lawrence Erlbaum Associates.

Greider, W. (1991, September 5). The politics of diversion: Blame it on the Blacks. *Rolling Stone, 32–33,* p. 96.

Hall, G. N. (2001). Psychotherapy research with ethnic minorities: Empirical, ethical and conceptual issues. *Journal of Consulting and Clinical Psychology, 69,* 502–510.

Harrell, S. P. (2000). A multidimensional conceptualization of racism-related stress: Implications for the well-being of people of color. *American Journal of Orthopsychiatry, 70*(1), 42–57.

Hart, A. J., Whalen, P. J., Shin, L. M., McInerney, S. C., Fisher, M., & Rauch, S. L. (2000). Differential responses in the human amygdala to social outgroup vs. ingroup face stimuli. *Neuroreport, 11*(11), 2351–2355.

Hays, P. (1995). Multicultural applications of cognitive-behavioral therapy. *Professional Psychology: Research and Practice, 26,* 306–315.

Helms, J. (1995). An update of Helm's White and people of color racial identity models. In J. G. Ponterotto, J. M. Casas. L. A. Suzuki, & C. M. Alexander (Eds.), *Handbook of multicultural counseling* (pp. 181–198). Thousand Oaks, CA: Sage.

Hirschfeld, L. A. (1996). *Race in the making: Cognition, culture, and the child's construction of human kinds.* Boston: MIT Press.

Ho, M. H. (1987). *Family therapy with ethnic minorities.* Newbury Park, CA: Sage.

Hoch-Smith, J., & Spring, A. (Eds.). (1978). Women in ritual and symbolic roles. New York: Plenum.

Hoffman, E. (1989). *Lost in translation: A life in a new language.* New York: Penguin.

Jackson, G. G. (1987). Cross-cultural counseling with Afro-Americans. In P. Pedersen (Ed.), *Handbook of cross-cultural counseling and therapy* (pp. 231–237). New York: Praeger.

Jones, J. M. (1991). The politics of personality: Being Black in America. In R. L. Jones (Ed.), *Black psychology* (3rd ed., pp. 305–318). Berkeley, CA: Cobb & Henry.

Jordan, J. V. (2000). The role of mutual empathy in relational/cultural therapy. *Journal of Clinical Psychology, 56,* 1005–1016.

Kakar, S. (1982). *Shamans, mystics and doctors: A psychological inquiry into India and its healing traditions.* Oxford, England: Oxford University Press.

Kaptchuk, T. J., & Eisenberg, D. M. (1998). The persuasive appeal of alternative medicine. *Annals of International medicine, 129,* 1061–1065.

Kashima, T. (1998, August 16). A never-ending hurt for Japanese Americans. *The Washington Post,* p. C3.

Kaslow, F. (1993). Relational diagnosis: Past, present and future. *The American Journal of Family Therapy, 21,* 195–204.

Kay, A. (1998). Generativity in the shadow of genocide: The Holocaust experience and generativity. In D. P. McAdams & E. de St. Aubin (Eds.), *Generativity and adult development: How and why we care for the next generation* (pp. 335–359). Washington, DC: American Psychological Association.

Kennedy, S., Scheirer, J., & Rogers, A. (1985). The price of success: Our monocultural science. *American Psychologist, 39*(9), 996–997.

Klerman, G. L., Weissman, M. M., Rounsaville, B., & Chevron, E. (1984). *Interpersonal psychotherapy of depression.* New York: Basic Books.

Koss-Chioino, J. D. (1992). *Women as healers, women as patients: Mental health care and traditional healing in Puerto Rico.* Boulder, CO: Westview Press.

Lamberth, J. (1998, August 16). Driving while Black. *The Washington Post*, pp. C1, C5.

Lamott, A. (1994). *Bird by bird: Instructions of writing and life.* New York: Doubleday.

Landrine, H., & Klonoff, E. A. (1996). The Schedule of Racist Events: A measure of racist discrimination and a study of its negative physical and mental health consequences. *Journal of Black Psychology, 22,* 144–168.

Lechner, N. (1992). Some people die of fear: Fear as a political problem. In J. E. Corradi, P. W. Fagen, & M. A. Garreton (Eds.), *Fear at the edge: State terror and resistance in Latin America.* Berkeley: University of California Press.

Lewis, S. Y. (1994). Cognitive-behavioral therapy. In L. Comas-Diaz & B. Greene (Eds.), *Women of color: Integrating ethnic and gender identities in psychotherapy* (pp. 223–238). New York: Guilford.

Lira, E. (1998). Commentary: Managing the care of patients with chronic illness and human rights survivors. *Journal of Ambulatory Care Management, 21*(2), 51–55.

Loo, C., Singh, K., Scurfield, R., & Kilauano, B. (1998). Race-related stress among Asian American Veterans: A model to enhance diagnosis and treatment. *Cultural Diversity and Mental Health, 4*(2), 75–90.

Malfi, C. A., Croghan, T. W., Hanna, M. P., & Robinson, R. (2000). Racial variation in antidepressant treatment in a medication population. *The Journal of Clinical Psychiatry, 61*(1), 16–21.

Mannoni, M. B. O. (1991). *Prospero and Caliban: The psychology of colonization.* Ann Arbor: University of Michigan Press.

Matt, G. E., & Navarro, A. M. (1997). What meta-analyses have and have not taught us about psychotherapy effects: A review and future directions. *Clinical Psychology Review, 17,* 1–32.

McGoldrick, M., García-Preto, N., Hines, P. M., & Lee, E. (1989). Ethnicity and women. In M. McGoldrick, C. M. Anderson, & F. Walsh (Eds.), *Women in families: A framework for family therapy.* New York: Norton.

Mehl-Madrona, L. (2003). *Coyote healing: Miracles in native medicine.* Rochester, VT: Bear & Company.

Memmi, A. (1965). *The colonizer and the colonized.* Boston: Beacon.

Miller, A. (1997). *The drama of the gifted child: The search for the true self.* New York: Basic Books.

Montero, M. (1984). *Ideología, alienación e identidad nacional* [Ideology, alienation and national identity]. Caracas: Universidad Central de Venezuela.

Morones P. A., & Mikawa, J. K. (1992). The traditional Mestizo View: Implications for modern psychotherapeutic interventions. *Psychotherapy, 29*(3), 458–466.

National Center for Complementary and Alternative Medicine. (2001). List of NCCAM-supported CAM Specialty Research Centers. Retrieved from http://ncccam.nih.gov

Novo, C. (1999, April 14). *Amnistia International denuncia que la brutalidad policial en EE.UU. es sistematica* [Amnesty International announces that police brutality in the U.S. is systematic]. *Sociedad* (Barcelona, Spain), p. 40.

Organista, K. C., Munoz, R.F., & Gonzales, G. (1994). Cognitive-behavioral therapy for depression in low income and minority medical outpatients: Description of a program and exploratory analyses. *Cognitive Therapy and Research, 18,* 241–259.

Padilla, A. M., & Salgado de Snyder, V. N. (1992). Hispanics: What the culturally informed evaluator needs to know. In M. A. Weston & L. G. Epstein (Eds.), *Cultural competence for evaluators* (pp. 117–147). Rockville, MD: U.S. Department of Health and Human Services.

Pierce, C. M. (1995). Stress analogs of racism and sexism: Terrorism, torture and disaster. In C. V. Willie, P. P. Reiker, & B. S. Brown (Eds.), *Mental health, racism and sexism* (pp. 277–293). Pittsburgh: University of Pittsburgh Press.

Pinderhughes, E. (1989). *Understanding race, ethnicity, and power: The key to efficacy in clinical practice.* New York: The Free Press.

Ramirez, M. (1991). *Psychotherapy and counseling with minorities: A cognitive approach to individual and cultural differences.* New York: Pergamon.

Ramos-McKay, J., Comas-Díaz, L., & Rivera, L. (1988). Puerto Ricans. In L. Comas-Díaz & E. H. Griffith (Eds.), *Clinical guidelines in cross cultural mental health* (pp. 204–232). New York: Wiley.

Rathus, S. A. (1990). *Psychology* (4th ed.). Fort Worth, TX: Holt, Rinehart, & Winston

Reeler, A. P. (1994). Is torture a post-traumatic stress disorder? *Torture, 4,* 59–63.

Reeves, K. M. (2000). Racism and projection of the shadow. *Psychotherapy: Theory, Research, Practice, Training, 37*(1), 80–88.

Rittenhouse, J. (2000). Using eye movement desensitization and reprocessing to treat complex PTSD in a biracial client. *Cultural Diversity and Ethnic Minority Psychology*, *6*(4), 399–408.

Rivera, G. (1999, May 26). Police brutality against minorities [Interview with Katie Couric]. *Today Show*. New York: NBC.

Rof, S., & Grof, C. (1990). *The stormy search for the self*. Los Angeles: Tarcher.

Root, M. P. P. (1990). Resolving the "other" status: Identity development of biracial individuals. *Women & Therapy, 9*, 185–205.

Rosello, J., & Bernal, G. (1999). The efficacy of cognitive-behavioral and interpersonal treatments for depression in Puerto Rican adolescents. *Journal of Consulting and Clinical Psychology, 67*, 734–745.

Ross, M. H., & Rothman, J. (Eds.). (1999). *Theory and practice in ethnic conflict management: Theorizing success and failure*. New York: St. Martin's Press.

Rossman, M.L. (2000). *Guided imagery for self-healing: An essential resource for anyone seeking wellness* (2nd ed.). Tiburon, CA: H. J. Kramer.

Rush, L. L. (1998). Affective reactions to multiple social stigmas. *Journal of Social Psychology, 138*, 421–430.

Said, E. W. (1994). *Culture and imperialism*. New York: Vintage Books.

Sanderson, W. C., Rue, P. J., & Wetzler, S. (1998). The generalization of cognitive behavior therapy for panic disorder. *Journal of Cognitive Psychotherapy, 12*, 323–330.

Schulman, K. A., Berlin, J. A., Harless, W., Kerner, J. F., Sistrunk, S., Gersh, B., et al. (1999). The effects of race and sex on physicians' recommendations for cardiac catheterization. *New England Journal of Medicine, 340*, 618–626.

Shapiro, B. (1996). One violent crime. In G. Ward & R. Atwan, (Eds.), *The best American essays 1996*. Boston: Hougton Mifflin.

Shapiro, E. R. (1994). *Grief as a family process: A developmental approach to clinical practice*. New York; Guilford.

Shapiro, E. R. (1998). The healing power of culture stories: What writers can teach psychotherapies. *Cultural Diversity and Mental Health, 4*, 91–101

Shapiro, F. (1995). *Eye movement desensitization and reprocessing: Basic principles, protocols, and procedures*. New York: Guilford.

Shweder, R. A. (1993). Cultural psychology: Who needs it? *Annual Review of Psychology, 44*, 497–523.

Sidanius, J., & Pratto, F. (1999). *Social dominance: An intergroup theory of social hierarchy and oppression*. New York: Cambridge University Press.

Stevens, E. D. (1973). Marianismo: The other face of machismo in Latin America. In A. Decastello (Ed.), *Female and male in Latin America*. Pittsburgh: University of Pittsburgh Press.

Strickland, T. L., Ranganath, V., & Lim, K. M., (1991) Psychopharmacologic considerations in the treatment of Black American populations. *Psychopharmacology Bulletin, 27*, 441–448.

Sue, S. (1998). In search of cultural competence in psychotherapy and counseling. *American Psychologist, 53*, 440–448.

Surgeon General. (2000). Supplement to "Mental health: A report of the Surgeon General." *Disparities in mental health care for racial and ethnic minorities*. Washington, DC: U.S. Public Health Service.

Tal, K. (1996). *Words of hurt. Reading the literatures of trauma*. Cambridge, England: Cambridge University Press.

Tan, S.-Y., & Dong, N. J. (2002). Psychotherapy with members of Asian American churches and spiritual traditions. In P. S. Richards & A. E. Bergin (Eds.), *Handbook of psychotherapy and religious diversity* (pp. 421–444). Washington, DC: American Psychological Association.

Thompson Sanders, V. L. (1991). Perceptions of race and race relations which affect African American identification. *Journal of Applied Social Psychology, 21*, 1502–1516.

Thompson Sanders, V. L. (1996) Perceived experiences of racism as stressful life events. *Community Mental Health Journal, 32*, 223–233.

Tillich, P. (1957). *Dynamics of faith*. New York: Harper & Row.

United States President's Commission on Race and Racism. (1998). *One America in the 21st century: Forging a new future* (Executive Summary). Rockville, MD: U.S. Government Printing Office.

Van der Kolk, B., McFarlane, A., & Weisaeth, L. (1996). *Traumatic stress: The effects of overwhelming experience on mind, body, and society*. New York: Guilford.

Vasquez, M. J. T. (1998). Latinos and violence: Mental health implications and strategies for clinicians. *Cultural Diversity and Mental Health, 4*, 319–334.

Volkan, V. D. (1994). *The need to have enemies and allies: From clinical practice to international relationships*. Northvale, NJ: Aronson.

von Franz, M.-L. (1995). *Shadow and evil in fairy tales*. Boston: Shambala.

Walker, R. D., & LaDue, R. (1986) An integrative approach to American Indian mental health. In C. Wilkinson (Ed.), *Ethnic psychiatry* (pp. 143–194). New York: Plenum.

Watts, A. (1961). *Psychotherapy East and West*. New York: Pantheon.

Watts, A. W. (1961). *Psychotherapy East & West*. New York: Ballantine Books.

Whaley, A. (1998). Racism in the provision of mental health services: A social-cognitive analysis. *American Journal of Orthopsychiatry, 68,* 47–57.

White, J. E. (1999, March 8). Prejudice? Perish the thought: The most insidious racism is among those who don't think they harbour any. *Time, 153*(9), p. 36.

White, M., & Epston, D. (1990). *Narrative means to therapeutic ends*. New York: Norton.

Williams, D. R., Yu, Y., Jackson, J., & Anderson, N. (1997). Racial differences in physical and mental health: Socioeconomic status, stress, and discrimination. *Journal of Health Psychology, 2,* 335–351.

Williams, J. E., & Morland, J. K. (1976). *Race, color and the young child*. Chapel Hill: University of North Carolina Press.

Wright, L., Bell, J. M., & Watson, W. L. (1996). *Beliefs: The heart of healing in families and illness*. New York: Basic Books.

Wyatt, G. (1994, August 14). *Impact of racism on psychological functioning*. Presentation made at the 102nd Annual Convention of the American Psychological Association, Los Angeles.

Young, M. I. (1990). *Justice and the politics of difference*. Princeton, NJ: Princeton University Press

Zea, M. C., Mason, M., & Murguia, A. (2000). Psychotherapy with members of Latino/Latina religions and spiritual traditions. In P. S. Richards & A. E. Bergin (Eds.), *Handbook of psychotherapy and religious diversity* (pp. 397–419). Washington, DC: American Psychological Association.

Zuñiga, M. E. (1991). "Dichos" as metaphorical tools for resistant Latino clients. *Psychotherapy, 28,* 480–483.

Gay and Lesbian Couples in Therapy:
A Social Justice Perspective*

Robert-Jay Green

Executive Director, Rockway Institute for LGBT Research and Public Policy
California School of Professional Psychology
Alliant International University

Just as our field has no book about the special characteristics of White families in therapy, but excellent books about African American families in therapy (Boyd-Franklin, 2003), Latino families in therapy (Falicov, 1998), and Asian American families in therapy (Lee, 1997), we are not likely any time soon to see a book with the title *Heterosexual Families in Therapy*. This is because the mental health professions tend to suffer from ethnocentrism—taking the White heterosexual majority group's relationships as the standard against which other groups' relationships are to be "understood." From this majority perspective, minority group phenomena stand out either as "exotic" or "problematic" and need to be explained, whereas majority group phenomena blend in as "normal" and need no further explanation.

For example, writers in our field do not feel obliged to consider how heterosexuals' relationships stand out from those of the lesbian/gay crowd. Instead, couples composed of a woman and a man blend in. Their curious heterosexual ways go unnoticed, apparently not needing further dissection because they are so common. However, heterosexual couples and families are no less a subculturally bound, norm-driven, singular group than same-sex couples and families (who are just as diverse in all of the sociodemographic and psychiatric ways imaginable). It takes a "queer eye," as it were, to see heterosexuals and their habits as distinctive, rendering the familiar zone of heterosexuality "foreign" for the purpose of analysis.

Therefore, to think clearly about "therapy with gay and lesbian couples," one must at least tacitly understand that coupled heterosexuality is also a distinct social status (or social role) with expectations, norms, and sanctions affecting a particular population of couples in this society. One must grasp that coupled heterosexuality has certain built-in advantages and stresses, just as does coupled homosexuality. Most important, one has to comprehend the myriad ways heterosexual relationships are shaped by historical traditions, given legal legitimization, and offered

---

*Portions of this chapter were adapted from Green and Mitchell (2002) by permission of the Guilford Press, New York.

widespread social supports, rendering them simultaneously more secure but also more constrained than lesbian/gay relationships.

FOCUS OF THIS CHAPTER

In this chapter, I describe how injustice at the societal and familial levels (in the form of antigay prejudice and discrimination) affects the internal functioning of same-sex couples. Then I present some therapy guidelines that help same-sex couples deal with their unique position in society. This is not to say that one needs a whole new theory of therapy in order to work effectively with same-sex couples. Homosexuality and heterosexuality are not opposites. Distressed couples, regardless of sexual orientation, often present similar kinds of problems. However, because of societal prejudice and discrimination, there are some special challenges facing lesbian/gay couples that, if not mastered by the partners on their own, may become problems.

These *special challenges* facing same-sex couples include: (a) coping with external homophobia in families of origin and the larger society and coping with internalized homophobia in the couple relationship; (b) resolving relational ambiguity in the areas of couple commitment, boundaries, and gender-linked behaviors; and (c) developing adequate social supports (a so-called "family of choice") for the couple relationship. Well-functioning lesbian and gay couples handle these tasks on their own. Prior research on community (nonclinical) samples of lesbian, gay, and heterosexual couples show that, as a group, same-sex couples are generally functioning as well as or better than heterosexual couples (Green, Bettinger, & Zacks, 1996; Kurdek, 1995; Peplau, 1991; Solomon, Rothblum, & Balsam, 2004).

It is important to emphasize at the outset that this chapter focuses on same-sex couples *in distress* (a minority of such couples) and then only on the special problems arising from the unique social justice challenges of being a lesbian or gay couple. Many same-sex couples have adequately mastered these lesbian/gay-specific stresses on their own but may still seek therapy for other problems, identical to the problems of heterosexual couples seeking therapy. In this context, the therapist's first task is to assess whether and to what extent the couple's problems are connected to these special challenges of being lesbian/gay versus to other generic processes such as basic attachment issues, communication patterns, or conflict-negotiation strategies. If, after exploration, a couple's problems seem unrelated to the special issues of being lesbian/gay, the major models of couple therapy (Gurman & Jacobson, 2002) can be used essentially intact as long as the therapist's stance is affirming of lesbian and gay couple relationships.

Thus, some same-sex couples explicitly enter therapy to deal with lesbian/gay issues such as conflicts over how to deal with prejudice in one or both partner's families of origin. Still, other couples come in with common psychiatric symptoms (such as depression in one partner), which seem to be compounded by homophobia at work, ambiguity in a partner's commitment, or lack of social support from friends. In each instance, therapists working with same-sex couples face the twin dangers of either ignoring or exaggerating the importance of lesbian/gay factors. Only a case formulation based on careful, continuous assessment of these special areas and other couple dynamics can guide treatment effectively for a given couple.

Because so much clinical writing presents generic models of couples therapy that can be used with same-sex couples whose problems are not lesbian/gay-specific, I limit my focus below to how therapists can help same-sex partners: (a) deal with homophobia in their environments and in themselves, (b) make their couple commitments and relationship roles less ambiguous, and (c) build a more closely knit network of social support. For each of these issues, I describe problem-specific dynamics and related therapeutic techniques. I then discuss how therapists (especially heterosexual therapists) can prepare themselves personally and professionally for this kind of work.

HOMOPHOBIA AND THE CULTURAL CONTEXT

The most salient characteristic that distinguishes lesbian and gay couples from heterosexual couples as a group is that regardless of their enormous sociocultural diversity, all same-sex couples are vulnerable to similar kinds of prejudice, discrimination, and marginalization by persons and institutions outside of their relationships. In this section, I review this aspect of lesbian/gay people's lives—first defining this prejudice, then looking at its effects on couple relationships, and finally considering how therapists can help couples resist being undermined by homophobia.

Prejudice and Discrimination

Several terms have been coined to describe the specific types of prejudice, discrimination, and related stresses faced by lesbians and gay men. _Homophobia_ has been defined as a person's irrational fear and hatred of homosexuality and of lesbian/gay people. Homophobic attitudes are correlated with conservative social attitudes generally and with gender role traditionalism and fundamentalist religious beliefs in particular (Herek, 1994, 1998). Overall, males tend to be significantly more homophobic than females. Studies reveal that heterosexuals—including couple and family therapists—who have more direct contact with lesbians and gay men as friends, family members, and/or clients express more accepting attitudes about homosexuality (Green & Bobele, 1994; Herek, 1994).

Internalized homophobia occurs when lesbian and gay persons (who also have acquired society's antihomosexual attitudes) direct those negative attitudes toward the self. Internalized homophobia is associated with lesbian/gay persons' devaluation of self (lowered self-esteem), higher rates of concealing sexual orientation, greater depression in response to homophobic prejudice, suicidality, increased HIV risk-taking behaviors, and mental health and substance abuse problems (Malyon, 1982; Meyer & Dean, 1998; Shidlo, 1994).

It is axiomatic that all openly lesbian and gay people, including members of couples, have had to counter and unlearn internalized homophobia to some extent in order to achieve a measure of self-acceptance and to form a same-sex relationship. However, in many couples, one or both partners may continue to suffer from internalized homophobia, which frequently contributes to the demise of couple relationships in direct or indirect ways. In the context of couple therapy, an important aspect of internalized homophobia is that some lesbian and gay clients nihilistically believe the cultural stereotype that enduring love relationships between same-sex partners are wrong or impossible to achieve. Then, they unconsciously sabotage their relationships in a kind of self-fulfilling prophecy, often giving up too quickly, pessimistically, rather than trying to work through the inevitable impasses in any long-term relationship. Therapists can help such clients to challenge negative stereotypes about lesbian and gay relationships and to achieve a greater degree of freedom to commit to same-sex couplehood.

Heterocentrism (sometimes referred to as "heterosexism") consists of assumptions and processes embedded in mainstream society and its institutions that imply human beings are naturally heterosexual and that heterosexual lifestyles are the normal standard against which those of lesbians and gays should be compared in order to be understood and evaluated (Herek, 1998). Heterocentric attitudes lead to the unwitting or intentional marginalization and exclusion of lesbian and gay people, rendering them unequal in terms of access to social opportunities, benefits, and civil rights protections. In the mental health fields, heterocentrism occurs when theories or research based on heterosexuals are automatically assumed to apply to gays, lesbians, and bisexuals, or the assumption that heterosexuality is a better psychological adjustment even though the research evidence does not support that conclusion (Gonsiorek, 1991).

The widespread opposition to same-sex marriage is a clear manifestation of heterocentrism. Despite the various new legal statuses and protections for same-sex couples in Vermont (civil unions as of 2003), California (enhanced domestic partnerships as of January, 2005), and Massachusetts (state-sanctioned marriages as of June, 2004), none of these couple statuses are recognized under federal law or in 40 plus other states, all of which have passed so-called "Defense of Marriage (DOMA) Acts" limiting civil marriage to a relationship between one man and one woman. Refusing to grant same-sex partners the same *1,138* protections, rights, and privileges that are provided to married heterosexual couples under federal law (General Accounting Office, 2004) defines same-sex relationships as less worthy of societal support than heterosexual relationships.

The notion that the existence of same-sex marriage threatens the future of heterosexual relationships or the institution of marriage is nothing short of widespread societal projection. It is the largely heterosexual majority that is hurting lesbian and gay couples by prohibiting access to the privileges of same-sex marriage, rather than heterosexual marriages being hurt. One of the great ironies of social injustice is that its perpetrators frequently view themselves as victims acting in self-defense or as protective, benevolent, "colonial" guardians acting in helpful ways rather than as persecutors of those who are different and hold less power.

Effects of Prejudice on Lesbian/Gay Couples

The combination of these external and internalized sources of prejudice create *minority stress* for all lesbian and gay people at various points in their lives (DiPlacido, 1998). This kind of stress typically reaches a crescendo in adolescence when the individual begins self-identifying as lesbian, gay, or bisexual but still has not disclosed these feelings to others (Savin-Williams, 1996). However, most lesbian and gay people continue to experience some degree of prejudice and fear of discrimination throughout their adult lives, depending on their life circumstances (Bepko & Johnson, 2000).

A couple's sexual orientation affects that couple's relationship to almost all other entities in society—family, work, school, medical care, insurance, the legal system, housing, religious institutions, government, and so on. The very right of same-sex persons to associate with one another in a sociosexual relationship was against the law in many states until recently (the so-called "sodomy" statutes, which were finally overturned by the U.S. Supreme Court, in June, 2003). In most areas of the United States, same-sex couples are still vulnerable to discrimination and harm if they are out and visible, or they live with fear of discovery if they conceal their relationships. Discrimination and fear of discovery each may undermine the couple's relationship if the partners do not have internal ways of countering the social stigma of homosexuality, as well as having a social support system to buffer that stress.

woa.

Lesbian and gay relationships are not supported by tradition, rarely sanctified by mainstream religions, and not generally protected against discrimination by law in the United States. The civil rights of lesbian and gay couples are challenged almost every year by court cases, ballot initiatives, legislative proposals, and regulatory revisions at all levels of government (Hartman, 1996). In most jurisdictions in the United States, it still is entirely legal for lesbian and gay people to be summarily fired from their jobs without cause or discriminated against in hiring decisions and in housing simply because they are homosexual.

Although there are pockets of increasing political support for same-sex couples and the U.S. Bureau of the Census has begun counting households headed by same-sex partners, the overall message from the mainstream of American politics to lesbian and gay couples is something like: "We don't want you to exist, so we simply decline to acknowledge or support your relationships in the way we support heterosexual relationships." In this way, much of heterosexism is presumptive and exclusionary rather than overtly aggressive, and it contributes to a feeling of marginality and invisibility for lesbian and gay couples.

In this context, to engage in a committed couple relationship becomes both a personal and a political act for lesbian and gay people, who were literally outlaws in many states until recently. No matter how mundane their everyday suburban lives, "Rozzie and Harriet's" couplehood is at variance with the dominant social and political status quo. They are caught in a cultural vortex of conflicting attitudes—support from some quarters, neglect from most, overt hostility from some. In most circumstances in the United States and around the world, they still risk being gawked at if they hold hands in public. In some circumstances, they will be verbally or physically attacked for such public displays of everyday couplehood.

The vulnerability to these external dangers renders lesbian and gay couples vigilant for discrimination, especially in unfamiliar surroundings, and it increases stress. If each of the partners has reached a high level of self-acceptance about being lesbian or gay, this external stress is manageable, unless of course it involves physical violence. However, to the extent that partners are still dealing with internalized homophobia themselves, their relationship can be threatened even by subtle forms of prejudice and discrimination and the vigilance necessary to protect against it.

For example, realistic fears about holding hands and being affectionate in certain public contexts can stimulate a partner's internalized homophobia, leaving him or her feeling defective, ashamed, bad, unworthy, sick, sinful, depressed, and so on. Or, in certain work environments, the necessity to self-monitor what one says and how one acts may leave a partner feeling stressed and that his or her gayness is causing this problem rather than locating the problem's cause in society's ignorance. When partners' internalized homophobia is triggered in these ways, it sometimes translates into couple difficulties including: (a) inexplicable arguments (e.g., frustration is *ex of results of internalized...*

displaced onto the partner, or self-hatred turns into criticism of one's partner); (b) sexual desire or performance difficulties (caused by inhibition or guilt); and (c) depression and withdrawal from the partner (feeling unworthy, or feeling ambivalent about committing to a lesbian or gay relationship). For couples in which these dynamics seem to be operating, the stated goals of couple therapy (agreed on collaboratively with the clients) should include a reduction in the partners' internalized homophobia.

Interventions for Countering Homophobia

In a sense, all of the techniques discussed in this chapter can serve to counter clients' internalized homophobia and help them cope with external discrimination. However, I present some very specific strategies in the following section. In this aspect of the work, I make use of feminist, profeminist, gay-affirmative, multicultural, and narrative family systems therapy principles.

The two central ideas in applying feminist and profeminist theories of therapy to same-sex couples are the notions of cultural *resistance* and *subversion,* which were implicit in the early feminist therapy and "radical therapy" movements of the late 1960s and 1970s (Radical Therapist Collective, 1971). Most recently, these notions have been well articulated by Brown (1994):

> . . . In feminist theory, resistance means the refusal to merge with dominant cultural norms and to attend to one's own voice and integrity. . . . Each act of feminist therapy . . . must have as an implicit goal the uncovering of the presence of the patriarchy as a source of distress so that this influence of the dominant can be named, undermined, resisted, and subverted. . . . awareness and transformation mean teaching of resistance, learning the ways in which each of us is damaged by our witting or unwitting participation in dominant norms or by the ways in which such norms have been thrust upon us. (p. 25)

In terms of applying these concepts of resistance and subversion to the treatment of lesbian and gay couples, a therapist must start with the basic awareness that by loving someone of the same sex, lesbians and gay men are violating the most basic gender norms of the society. The therapist engages the clients in an exploration of all the oppressive social influences in their lives, influences that pressure them not to engage in same-sex love and to regard their capacity for same-sex love as bad, sinful, disturbed, inferior, and so on. This includes a careful, detailed deconstruction of all the various messages they got about homosexuality (in their families, in school, in their neighborhood, in their religious institutions, through the media, and more generally from members of their specific racial/ethnic group) as they were growing up.

In the same manner, it is important to examine the clients' internalization of traditional gender norms as well as the overt prejudice and discrimination they continue to face from their current social environments (family, neighbors, coworkers) and from the "impersonal" institutions of society (the media, government, insurance companies, employment settings, health care institutions, and the like). Most important, the therapist should counter these oppressive messages, neutralizing society's condemnation of same-sex love in terms of viewing it as a normal human variation, not reinforcing (in subtle or unsubtle ways) its pejorative framing by the larger society (Mitchell, 1988). The therapist thereby functions as a celebrant and witness of constructive lesbian and gay relationships, giving these relationships therapeutic approval and support.

This approach is roughly equivalent to what has become known as "gay-affirmative therapy." As Malyon wrote in first describing this approach in 1982:

> Gay-affirmative psychotherapy is not an independent system of psychotherapy. Rather, it represents a special range of psychological knowledge which challenges the traditional view that homosexual desire and fixed homosexual orientations are pathological. . . . This approach regards homophobia, as opposed to homosexuality, as a major pathological variable in the development of certain symptomatic conditions. (pp. 68–69)

Thus, gay-affirmative therapy involves actively challenging society's negative attitudes towards homosexuality that are contributing to the problems of a lesbian and gay couple. This approach entails helping the couple to dispute, deconstruct, and subvert society's prejudicial views rather than continuing to internalize or be limited by them. In a sense, the work is similar to what narrative therapists have described as externalizing the problem (in this case, viewing homophobia as the oppressive problem rather than viewing one's sexual orientation as the problem; White & Epston, 1990) and what cognitive therapists have sometimes called "disputation" of irrational beliefs (although in this case the disputation is simultaneously of society's irrational homophobia as well as its internalized manifestations).

In some couples therapy cases, partners are at markedly different levels of accepting their sexual orientations. Individual therapy may be warranted for the partner who suffers from a great deal more internalized homophobia than the other, especially if he or she seems ashamed to explore these aspects of self in the presence of the partner. However, if both partners are at roughly the same stage on this dimension, it is most helpful to see them together in conjoint sessions because both then benefit by self-exploration in one another's presence.

In addition to this work of deconstructing internalized homophobia in the sessions, I frequently encourage clients to engage in various forms of participation in lesbian/gay community organizations, including political activism if it fits their sensibilities (i.e., the cultural "subversion" aspect of liberationist therapies). For example, one client (who had played a musical instrument in her high school band) was encouraged to join the San Francisco Lesbian/Gay Freedom Band, which marches in the local Pride Parade and performs in other venues throughout the city. Another client, because of his skills in advertising research, was encouraged to become active in the local chapter of the Gay and Lesbian Alliance Against Defamation (GLAAD), which monitors media representations of lesbian and gay people. Acts such as these constitute an important way in which lesbian and gay clients who suffer from internalized homophobia can stand up (in unison with others) for their right to exist, meet others who can model high levels of self-esteem and empowerment, and contribute to the reduction of homophobia in the larger society. I view these acts of gay community participation as a form of subversion of the status quo and legitimization of the self, implicitly naming society's homophobia (rather than the self) as the problem that needs to be eliminated.

In concluding this section, I would like to add that feminist and gay-affirmative principles of treatment are being increasingly incorporated into another orientation to psychotherapy sometimes called "multicultural family systems therapy" (see especially Boyd-Franklin, 2003; Falicov, 1998; McGoldrick, 1998; Pinderhughes, 1989). As I have written elsewhere on the topic of "race and the field of family therapy":

> In this new era, we will need to distinguish clearly between matters of minority group *differentness* and matters of minority group *oppression*. . . . Our focus on different cultural patterns *within* groups often obscures our understanding of the oppressive relations *between* groups. Cultural, racial, and sexual orientation differences are *not* problems in and of themselves. Prejudice, discrimination, and other forms of aggressive intercultural conflict based on these differences *are* problems. (Green, 1998a, pp. 99–100).

Similarly, Olkin (1999) has developed a minority group model for treatment of people with disabilities and an approach she refers to as "disability-affirmative therapy":

> We reframe "I can't climb stairs" to "why isn't there a ramp?" . . . This is the crux of the minority model, this shift in focus from personal, individual, and problem in isolation, to group, environment, attitudes, discrimination—from individual pathology to social oppression. (p. 28)

A multicultural family systems approach still can incorporate the more traditional ways of looking at the variability in mental health functioning of individuals, couples, and families within a specific minority group. For example, although all same-sex couples encounter a certain amount of prejudice and discrimination, some of them face a lot more of it than others, and some couples cope with it much more effectively than others.

In particular, when confronted with similar levels of external prejudice, same-sex couples with more internalized homophobia will tend to cope less successfully. Depending on the kind of discrimination same-sex partners face, coping successfully may require: (a) working actively for change in one's current social environment; (b) changing to a different social environment (literally relocating geographically or quitting one's job to escape an intransigent or dangerously homophobic situation); (c) reattributing the cause of one's distress to different factors (e.g., attributing one's distress to external prejudice and ignorance rather than to personal inadequacy); or (d) recognizing that some discriminatory situations cannot be changed and then focusing on other areas in one's life.

RELATIONAL AMBIGUITY

In contrast to heterosexual couples, there are no "givens" in same-sex relationships—no pre-ordained expectations, mutual obligations, or contracts, and few visible models of lesbian and gay couplehood to follow (partly because prior generations remained closeted). Lacking historical traditions or a religious or legal framework for same-sex couplehood, the partners in each same-sex couple have both the freedom and the necessity of developing their own definition of a suitable couple commitment and of their boundaries vis-à-vis the outside world.

This is not to say that same-sex partners do not bring to their relationship many of the "lessons" about couplehood acquired in their families of origin and from observing many heterosexual marriages during their lifetimes (Laird, 1996). However, there is no certainty about the extent to which the customs and assumptions of heterosexual marriages might apply to their own lesbian/gay relationship. Same-sex partners must therefore devote much more time and energy to "negotiations" in order to figure out exactly what it means that they are a couple, especially in the beginning stages of their relationship. Much of this negotiation takes place implicitly through the "permitting" of behavior patterns that neither party challenges. However, some of the negotiations occur explicitly through conversations about the meaning of their commitment and about their mutual obligations.

Without normative traditions and mainstream pressures that unconsciously shape their intimate relationship patterns, lesbians and gay men are freer to invent their own relational configurations, depending more on their individual needs and whatever opportunities arise than on fixed traditions of couplehood. Although many same-sex couples have the skills to create a mutually satisfying and clear structure for their relationship, couples in which the rules and boundaries remain extremely vague, changeable, or contested over time are likely to become distressed and require help.

Boundary and Commitment Ambiguity

A key concept in couple and family systems theory has been the notion of boundaries of subsystems, especially: interpersonal boundaries between individuals; generational boundaries between the partners and their families of origin; and boundaries between the couple and the social network surrounding it. Minuchin (1974) defined family boundaries as: "the rules defining who participates and how" (p. 53). It is just as important to consider who or what is excluded from participation in a subsystem as considering who or what is included.

Also basic to the notion of boundaries is the way a relationship is defined by the participants (What kind of relationship is this? A best friendship? A social acquaintanceship? A romantic involvement? A lifelong primary commitment? A temporary dating relationship? A mainly sexual encounter? A commercial exchange? A temporary separation? A mentoring arrangement? An ongoing affair secondary to a primary relationship? Former-lovers-now-friends, etc.). With lesbian and gay couples in therapy, I frequently observe a lack of clarity in how they define their couplehood to themselves and to others. I believe this is partly because lesbian and gay couples (in contrast to legally married heterosexual couples) lack a socially endorsed, legally framed, normative template for how couplehood should be. Overall, partners do not know what they can expect from a same-sex relationship because there is no socially or legally prescribed kind of couplehood for them and no prevailing way of being a same-sex couple.

Pauline Boss's concept of *"boundary ambiguity"* is very relevant here: "a state in which family members are uncertain in their perception about who is in or out of the family and who is performing what roles and tasks within the family system" (Boss & Greenberg, 1984, p. 536).[1] Boss's own research (1999) has focused primarily on situations of "ambiguous loss" (e.g, families of Alzheimer patients, families of men who were missing in action after combat during war, and families following di-

---

[1]I am indebted to Ramona F. Oswald, University of Illinois at Urbana-Champaign, for the general suggestion that Boss's concept of boundary ambiguity might have utility for understanding the couple and family relationships of lesbians and gay men.

vorce or a death in the family). Her studies have demonstrated convincingly that family members' experiences of boundary ambiguity (in this case, ambiguous loss) are associated with signs of family stress and with dysfunction (e.g., depression; Boss, Caron, Horbal, & Mortimer, 1990).

I extend the concept of boundary ambiguity here to situations that might best be labeled "ambiguous commitment," where one or both partners' intentions or degree of joining in the relationship remain in doubt. Ambiguous commitment is prevalent in lesbian and gay couples in therapy, partly because their decisions to be together are not usually preceded by an extended courtship or engagement phase, demarcated by a commitment ceremony, governed by statutes for legal marriage, approved by the partners' respective families of origin, or (in most cases) solidified by becoming coparents to children.

Relationships that I am characterizing here by the phrase "ambiguous commitment" are closest to having what Boss et al. (1990) describe as "physical presence" but "psychological absence." The partners are physically in the relationship (physically present), but the extent and exact nature of their psychological commitment to the relationship is unclear.

In addition, terminations of lesbian and gay couple relationships are sometimes characterized by ambiguous loss, partly because of the absence of formal divorce proceedings to clearly demarcate the ending. This is not to say that most relationships between lesbian or gay ex-lovers are ambiguous and dysfunctional, or that divorce proceedings are necessarily preferable to informal separations. In fact, one of the most distinctive features of lesbian and gay relationships is that close and constructive friendships between gay or lesbian ex-partners are fairly common, even when no children are involved to keep them connected as coparents (Becker, 1988). This stands in sharp contrast to relationships between formerly married heterosexual spouses who usually sever all ties unless children are involved.

However, the absence of a legal ritual formalizing divorce may increase the likelihood that boundary ambiguity will occur and last longer during transitions out of some lesbian and gay couple relationships. In Boss et al.'s (1990) terms, these relationships are closest to having "physical absence" but "psychological presence." The partners are out of the relationship (e.g., may no longer be living together or defining themselves publicly as a couple), but the extent and nature of their ongoing commitment to the relationship is still in doubt. With some lesbian or gay couples in therapy, this ongoing connection with an ex-partner seems to interfere with starting a new couple relationship or with a new partner's sense of primacy over the former partner.

What is strikingly different for same-sex couples is that almost all of the usual expectations that heterosexuals bring to marriage (monogamy, pooled finances, caring for each other through serious illness, moving together for each other's career advancement, providing and caring for one another's families in old age, mutual inheritance, health care power of attorney rights in the event of a partner's mental or physical incapacity) do not necessarily apply to same-sex couple relationships unless discussed and explicitly agreed to by the partners. Typically, same-sex couples do not clarify these expectations before moving in together, and discrepancies in their visions of the relationship only become apparent when expectations are suddenly breached, which can be shocking and very hurtful to the partners.

For example, it may not be clear if or when same-sex partners' commitment includes the traditional marriage vow "in sickness and in health." For married couples, the wedding ceremony officially signals this transition in level of commitment and stated intent. But, unable to have a legal wedding, what marks it for lesbian and gay couples? Is it when they start seeing each other every day? Is it when they move in together? Three years later? Ten years later? When does Partner A know that Partner B has the intent to stay in the relationship "in sickness and in health till death do us part"?

This issue could be discussed by the partners at any time, but typically such issues do not get explicitly raised until the couple comes face to face with a serious illness or disability like HIV or breast cancer. The same, of course, is true for unmarried cohabiting heterosexual couples, but they have the option of getting legally married to clarify their commitment. In fact, most cohabiting heterosexual couples eventually either separate or get married, suggesting that they are implicitly viewing cohabitation as a trial run before making a lifelong commitment.

Although heterosexual spouses sometimes abandon each other during medical crises despite the marriage vow, spouses are more likely to have the expectation of caregiving during illness because it is built into the template for marriage and is expected of married people by their parents, neighbors, coworkers, physicians, children, and so on. By comparison, at what point does society expect lesbian and gay partners to stay with each other and take care of one another during sickness, injury, or disability? Many lesbian and gay partners remain unclear as to what it will mean pragmatically in the future that their partner is "committed" to them and vice-versa. Is moving in together a lifelong commitment in the same way a marriage is supposed to be?

The same kind of ambiguity may permeate other basic parameters of a same-sex couple's relationship. Does being a "couple" mean that they will be monogamous (Blasband & Peplau, 1985; Campbell, 2000; Kurdek, 1988b)? Does it mean that they will share each other's financial obligations from the time they live together—or pool financial resources completely, partially, or not at all? When they move in together as a couple, will each partner authorize the other to have health care power of attorney to make decisions in a medical emergency? Will each name the partner as the executor and a beneficiary in their will? Or are these privileges going to remain with the partners' families of origin indefinitely, or until the partners reach some greater (but unspecified) level of emotional commitment?

Ambiguity Related to Same-Gender Composition

Being composed of two women or two men, same-sex couples cannot rely on traditional male/female (instrumental/expressive) role divisions to structure their overall interactional patterns. Most same-sex couples go though a long period of trial and error before settling on "who does what" in their relationship (Carrington, 1999). Such couples obviously cannot fall back on the usual gender-linked division of tasks in areas such as financial decision-making, relationship maintenance (talking about feelings and problems), earning money, doing housework, preparing meals, taking the lead in sex, arranging their social life, or taking care of children and elderly relatives if applicable. The fact that both partners are the same sex holds the possibility of greater equality if neither is attached to traditional gender roles (Mitchell, 1996), but it also increases the ambiguity about who is supposed to do what in the relationship and in the management of the household.

Furthermore, to the degree that both partners were socialized into and still adhere to traditional gendered behavior for their sex, they may develop more conflicts or certain deficiencies in their relationship (Roth, 1989). In general, women are socialized for more caring, connection, and cooperation whereas men are socialized for more independence, competition, dominance, and the capacity to separate sexual behavior from emotional involvement (Miller, 1976). Although the majority of lesbians and gay men at least partially defy gender role prescriptions (Green et al., 1996), a minority of lesbians and gay men still conform to traditional gender roles in all respects except for their sexual orientation. Such gender conformity produces predictable problems in this particular subset of same-sex couples: (a) both women try to please the other too much and neglect to communicate their own needs (i.e., the so-called problem of "fusion" in the lesbian relationship; Krestan & Bepko, 1980); (b) neither man will relocate for the other's job offer; (c) both men want to be the leader in sex; (d) neither woman feels comfortable initiating sex; (e) the man who has a lower status job than his male partner acts competitively in other areas of the relationship; (f) the woman who earns more money than her female partner feels guilty and disempowers herself in other areas; or (g) a very traditionally gendered man is domineering toward his less traditional male partner who feels overly dependent on the relationship and depressed (Green, 1998b). In other words, these problems arise not because the relationship is composed of two women or two men but rather because some pairs of women or men fall back on traditional gender roles, which creates conflict or deficits in their relationships.

In sharp contradiction to cultural stereotypes perpetuated by such popular films as *Le Cage aux Folles* (more recently remade as *The Bird Cage* in the United States), only a small minority of lesbian or gay couples nowadays divvy up the relationship roles such that one plays the traditional "husband" role while the other plays the traditional "wife" role. In fact, even in the early 1970s, only about 7% of lesbian and gay couples organized their relationship roles that way (Bell & Weinberg, 1978). As I wrote previously:

> . . . the general public still seems quite convinced of, and scandalized by, what it imagines is the widespread playing of artificial "butch/femme" roles by partners in same-sex relationships. Yet this same public remains largely unconscious . . . about its own problematic conformity to the socially constructed "butch/femme" roles in heterosexual relationships. (Green et al., 1996, p. 218.)

The ideal for most lesbian and gay couples is equality of power and sharing of the instrumental and emotional tasks usually associated with the male or female role (Carrington, 1999).

To achieve this kind of compatibility without fixed complementarity requires a great deal of gender flexibility from both partners. The division of labor has to become a more conscious, deliberative process than it is for heterosexual couples. This is not to say that contemporary heterosexual couples never struggle with such issues but rather that a majority of them still devolve—sometimes despite their egalitarian aspirations—toward traditional gender-linked roles in the areas of housework, childcare, care of elderly relatives, cooking, and so on (Hochschild, 1989). Except for that small minority of same-sex couples adhering to the traditional male/ female (butch/femme) roles of heterosexual marriage, lesbian and gay couples cannot rely on these gender-linked divisions to organize their relationships.

Interventions for Relational Ambiguity

I am not advocating any a priori, formulaic solutions for resolving these ambiguities. Nor do I believe that the outcomes should necessarily look like heterosexual marriages, in which many of these uncertainties are settled by law and tradition. In general, however, a couple tends to function best when there are clear agreements about their commitment and boundaries and when the couple's relationship is put higher priority than any other relationships (in terms of emotional involvement, caregiving, honesty, time, and influence over major decisions). From the therapy standpoint, regardless of the couple's presenting problems, I believe that asking certain kinds of questions and arriving at clear answers can be helpful to many same-sex couples:

1. How do you define being "a couple" (what does it mean to you that you are a "couple")?
2. What has been your history as couple?
3. How did your becoming a couple affect your relationships with other family members, friends, the lesbian/gay community, and the straight community?
4. What are the rules in your relationship regarding monogamy versus sex outside the relationship? What are the rules in terms of safer sex practices with each other and/or with others (being very explicit in terms of exact sexual practices to prevent HIV transmission)?
5. What are your agreements with one another about monthly finances, current or future debts, pooling versus separation of financial resources, ownership of joint property, and other financial planning matters?
6. Who does what tasks in the relationship and the household, and how is this division or sharing of tasks decided? Are you satisfied with the current division or sharing of these tasks?
7. What do you see as your obligations to one another in terms of caring for one another in illness, injury, or disability?
8. Are you viewing this as a lifetime commitment? If so, have you prepared legal health care power of attorney documents and wills to protect one another's interests in case of serious illness or death?

Clarifying the extent and nature of partners' emotional commitments to one another is central to therapy with couples in the early stages of their relationship. Sometimes this clarification involves resolving partners' conflicts of allegiance between the couple relationship and other family members, friends, or ex-partners. At other times, it involves spelling out what promises and reassurances each partner is willing to give the other—caregiving, time, monogamy, or other guarantees—that might increase the partners' sense of security, durability, and potential longevity of the relationship.

If it is in keeping with their sensibilities, couples can be encouraged to have a commitment ceremony and a formal exchange of vows covering some of these issues. A book I recommend for this purpose is *The Essential Guide to Lesbian and Gay Weddings* (Ayers & Brown, 1999). For couples who view their relationships as entailing a lifetime commitment, I strongly encourage drawing up appropriate legal documents (especially health care power of attorney and wills/trusts). The book *A Legal*

Guide for Lesbian and Gay Couples (Hayden, Clifford, & Hertz, 2001) is an excellent resource for this purpose.

If one or both partners' gender conformity is creating problems in a same-sex couple, therapists can help by reviewing the clients' original gender role socialization experiences and by challenging limitations associated with current gender role behavior, much as one might do with heterosexual partners in relationships. If ambiguity or dissension exists about who does what in the relationship, then the therapeutic work includes making sure these emotional and instrumental tasks are clarified and distributed equitably, as well as challenging any polarization of roles or dominance/submission patterns that will be destructive to the relationship over the long run. If ambiguity exists in the monogamy agreement, this also should be spelled out, based on full exploration of the underlying emotions and motivations of the partners. If they choose an open relationship, the specific behavioral rules for sex outside the relationship should be delineated and agreed on in great detail (in terms of who, what, when, where, how often, with how much communication about each encounter, and with what limitations; Blumstein & Schwartz, 1983; Johnson & Keren, 1996; McWhirter & Mattison, 1984).

In dealing with relational ambiguity of the kinds just described, I find that homework assignments or in-session exercises that involve putting unspoken relationship contracts into words can be useful for couples. Such vows (in addition to the legal contracts just mentioned) require that the partners address issues explicitly and negotiate specific behavioral agreements for the future. Any intervention that helps the partners clarify expectations and agreements in contested areas or in areas that have never been discussed (such as finances or monogamy) will help reduce relational ambiguity. This, in turn, will increase partners' feelings of secure attachment and belief in the permanence of their union, anchoring their relationship in tangible definitions of what it means that they are a couple.

SOCIAL SUPPORT

Well-functioning lesbian and gay couples are able to develop and maintain cohesive systems of social support. Distressed same-sex couples in therapy, by contrast, tend to be more isolated and to have smaller and less interconnected sources of support. In the latter cases, therapeutic goals should include helping the partners build a support system that is both closely knit and supportive of their being a couple.

Usually, same-sex couples get more of their social support from their friends whereas heterosexual couples rely more on support from their families of origin. In part, this is because many lesbian and gay couples receive only qualified acceptance of their relationships from their families. To varying degrees, these couples must turn elsewhere to achieve a sense of belonging to an intimate, ongoing group. In the following, I discuss family of origin as a source of emotional support and then turn to nonfamily sources.

Families of Origin

It is impossible to understand the psychological issues for lesbian and gay couples unless one first has a sense of what it is like to grow up lesbian or gay and to be a couple in a heterocentric world. Lesbian and gay people occupy an existential position during childhood unlike any other group in our society. Except in rare instances, lesbian girls and gay boys grow up in families in which they are the only one of their kind—the only lesbian or gay family member. This has profound implications throughout the lifespan of almost every lesbian or gay person.

In most other minority groups (for example, racial, ethnic, or religious minority groups), children and parents typically share the same minority status. These children are able to observe their parents dealing with and discussing minor or major acts of discrimination in everyday life. Many minority group parents and their communities intentionally teach children how to mentally counter society's negative views and maintain a sense of connection and pride in their heritage, through participation in customs, rituals, and cultural or religious organizations. In these ways, parents and children build a strong identification with one another as members of the same minority group. They are on the same side against the potential prejudice and discrimination in society, and parents take a protective stance toward their children in this respect.

Not so for lesbian and gay children. Their parents do not share the same minority group status, do not face the same discrimination, cannot recount the history of the lesbian/gay minority group, and would not be able to prepare their children to cope with homophobia even if they were aware of their child's sexual orientation. In contrast to the parents of other minority children, parents of lesbian/gay children frequently do not side with their child against the oppressive forces in society and, in fact, sometimes become the child's main oppressors. At worst, some lesbian/gay children and adolescents are truly "living with the enemy," risking verbal abuse, physical abuse, and/or ejection from the home if their sexual orientation becomes known (Savin-Williams, 1994).

Parents who suspect their children may be lesbian or gay because of the child's gender nonconformity (Bailey & Zucker, 1995) may react by withdrawing from their child or engaging in aggressive attempts to make the child's behavior more gender-typical (Bell, Weinberg, & Hammersmith, 1981). Parental withdrawal or attempts to reform markedly effeminate male children or markedly masculine female children sometimes begins at a very early age, contributing to basic attachment disorders (insecure attachment, or preoccupied attachment styles), which may have negative consequences in adulthood for the couple relationships of these children (Byng-Hall, 1995).

Even in the best of circumstances, heterosexual parents typically lack exposure to gay life and have no personal experience of being lesbian or gay. It thus remains very difficult for even the most accepting heterosexual parents to concretely imagine and identify with the experience of being a lesbian or gay person in this society, in comparison to the ways they are able to identify with their heterosexual children's life experience. For this level of understanding and mutual identification, lesbian and gay people almost always have to turn to each other rather than to heterosexual family members.

The revelation of homosexuality and the family's adaptation to the news tend to be filtered through the family members' usual coping mechanisms, as well as their specific attitudes about gender and sexuality (Laird, 1996). The family that was mostly distant and conflict-avoidant before the disclosure is likely to remain so afterwards. Parents who were intrusive and critical before the disclosure are not likely to become suddenly more respectful of boundaries and individuality in response to this disclosure. Furthermore, different racial/ethnic/religious groups view homosexuality differently, and the very same news of an offspring's homosexual orientation can be viewed quite differently by parents depending on their cultural context (Chan, 1989, 1995; Greene & Boyd-Franklin, 1996; Liu & Chan, 1996; Morales, 1996).

About 25% of lesbian/gay adults in the United States report *not* being out to their mothers, and almost 50% report *not* being out to their fathers (Savin-Williams, 2001). After the person's disclosure of sexual orientation, only about 10% to15% of parents reject their lesbian or gay child over the long run; about 70% to 75% show varying degrees of acceptance; and the remaining 10% to 15% are fully accepting and reach a high degree of comfort (Savin-Williams, 2001). Most families react very negatively at first but become more tolerant or accepting over time (Crosbie-Burnett, Foster, Murray, & Bowen, 1996; Savin-Williams, 1996, 2001).

I have been concerned that there seems to be a normative ideology among many couple and family therapists that it is always good (i.e., mentally healthy) for lesbian and gay clients to come out to their families of origin, without regard for the sociocultural context (Chan, 1989; Green, 2000b; LaSala, 2000). In some family therapy circles (particularly Bowenian), the decision to keep a major secret like this from one's family is almost inconceivable because coming out to the family of origin is viewed as an essential sign of differentiation of self. However, this maintenance of the secret may have nothing to do with being a "differentiated" or "mentally healthy" person. Staying closeted in the family may have more to do with not needing the family's approval and not wanting to be hassled and burdened with the family's irrational upset. Or it may have to do with the person's basic physical safety and economic survival in the family and community. In more collectivist societies and ethnic groups that value interdependence, an offspring's public declaration of homosexuality reflects on the whole kinship group's public success/failure in society rather than reflecting only on the individual. It thus is a very different kind of act to come out publicly in such a context, and many offspring in collectivist societies choose not to come out for fear of seriously damaging their extended families' social standing and the future prospects of close relatives (Chan, 1995; Liu & Chan, 1996).

In addition, being lesbian/gay and coming out to one's heterosexual family members almost always carries some risk of being "disowned" and losing one's ties to biological kin (Weston, 1991). The quintessential lesbian/gay experience of deciding whether to come out to parents leaves lesbian/gay people very aware that continuation of family of origin relations is entirely voluntary on the part of parents and their adult children. Although, as just described, most parents do not actually reject their children after disclosure, the *possibility* of being completely cut off or marginalized by their families is one that most lesbian/gay persons contemplate seriously:

> Of course, heterosexuals can also be disowned. But when straight people encounter rejection by relatives, that rejection arises on a case-by-case basis, generally in response to something done rather than something fundamental to their sense of self. Self-identified lesbians and gay men, in contrast, experience rejection as an ever-present possibility structured by claiming a stigmatized sexual identity. (Weston, 1991, p. 74)

Because of these possible risks of disclosure, therapists should not assume that keeping such a secret from parents is inevitably going to be deleterious to a client's mental health or couple relationships. For example, a 2-year longitudinal study of 48 lesbian couples found that outness to family of origin members was unrelated to lesbian couples' satisfaction at the start of the study, the couple staying together during the 2-year follow-up period, or level of satisfaction among couples that stayed together (Green et al., 1996).

In my professional experience, family of origin support has been important to couple functioning in some, but not all, cases. For those offspring who decide to come out to their families, acceptance is certainly easier to manage than rejection. However, this does not mean that the act of disclosure automatically leads to greater family support or to better couple functioning, especially for lesbians/gays who are the most reluctant or unwilling to disclose to their families based on what they believe are realistic appraisals of their family members' attitudes toward homosexuality. In fact, coming out to family may lead to less support from the family, or to poorer functioning of the couple, or to no change in couple functioning at all.

The psychological consequences of being out to family members and of the family's acceptance versus rejection depend on the centrality of the family as a source of social support and the availability of nonfamily resources (Green, 2000b). Lesbian and gay people who have little contact with their families of origin, whose self-esteem and decision making are not dependent on family members' approval, and who receive substantial social support from friends or other sources may not be adversely affected by remaining closeted or by receiving rejection from their families following disclosure. The most difficult situations are where a lesbian/gay individual is closely involved with the family, has few or no other sources of social support, is psychologically vulnerable to family disapproval, and either remains closeted or receives rejection from the family after coming out.

Ordinarily, after a lesbian/gay adult has been out to the family for some time and is in a couple relationship, parents are at least cordial toward the partner and frequently accept her or him into their homes on holidays and other occasions. However, there may be crucial ways in which the lesbian/gay person's sexual orientation sets their couple relationships apart in the family. For example, despite inclusion in most or all family of origin events, parents may still treat the lesbian/gay offspring's partner as a sort of temporary "friend of the family" rather than as a bona fide family member like the way son-in-laws or daughter-in-laws are treated (Weinstein, 1996).

In addition to seeking family support, the couple sometimes has to protect its functioning from the intrusion of family members who are unsupportive and who seek to undermine the couple's integrity and cohesiveness. A recent study (LaSala, 2002) showed that gay male couples benefited by setting firm boundaries in relation to family members who were unsupportive of their couple relationship. Basically, this involved insisting that their gay partnerships be acknowledged and treated with respect by family members or by distancing from the family if this level of family acknowledgment was not forthcoming. However, lesbian couple relationships seemed to benefit more by the lesbian daughter playing a mediating, nurturing role between the family and her partner—not distancing from the family or her partner, but continuing to work at a reconciliation based on the family's acceptance of the partner. In both situations, however, the lesbian/gay offspring had to affirm the legitimacy of and commitment to the same-sex partnership, even in the face of family disapproval, or the couple relationship was adversely affected.

To understand family of origin support, there are three factors to consider—family members' general support for the clients as individuals; family members' support specifically related to the clients being lesbian/gay individuals; and family members' support for the same-sex couple as a unit. Toward these ends, the following kinds of questions have proven useful:

1. When did you first become aware that you might be lesbian or gay?
2. How do you think this "differentness" may have affected your relationships with family members as you were growing up?
3. If you have not come out to certain family members, what factors led to this decision? Are there any ways that your remaining closeted with your family is affecting your couple relationship positively or negatively?
4. If you have come out to certain family members, describe the process, including what preceded, happened during, and has followed the disclosure up to the present time?
5. If you have introduced your partner to your family of origin members, how have they treated your partner up until now? How have you responded to their treatment of your partner and of the two of you as a couple?

Although a full discussion of family of origin interventions related to coming out and getting family support is beyond the scope of this couple-focused chapter (see Beeler & DiProva, 1999; Green, 2000b; Herdt & Koff, 2000; LaSala, 2000; and Savin-Williams, 1996, 2001), the first step in any such effort involves helping the lesbian or gay person work through any residual internalized homophobia (as described earlier). When the adult child can accept his or her own sexual orientation and choice of partner, dealing with the family is emotionally much easier. A client can then cope with familial homophobia more dispassionately, planfully, assertively, and with fewer setbacks to the couple's functioning if he or she decides to come out to family members. However, as explained above, sometimes not coming out to family members is a self-differentiated decision, and therapists should never pressure a client to come out who is reluctant to do so. One ultimately must assume that the client knows more about the familial and cultural context in which he or she exists and is best positioned to find a decision that fits the self and circumstances.

If the client decides to disclose his or her sexual orientation, disapproving family members quickly sense any internalized homophobia and often will exacerbate the lesbian/gay person's self-doubts with critical comments and attempts to diminish the importance of the couple relationship. Clients with more internalized homophobia will sometimes collude with this process, not bringing the partner home on visits and rarely mentioning the partner in the family member's presence. Typically, when the lesbian/gay person reaches a high level of self-acceptance and can calmly manifest that level in the family's presence, the family will either adapt to and become more accepting of the individual's sexual orientation and choice of partner, or the lesbian/gay person will make family relationships less salient, sometimes decreasing the amount of contact.

Therapeutic interventions in family of origin relations can include: (a) Bowen-type coaching assignments in which the client takes steps toward differentiation of self in the family of origin without the therapist present (Iasenza, Collucci, & Rothberg, 1996; McGoldrick & Carter, 2001); (b) conjoint family therapy sessions with all family of origin members together in the therapist's office (Framo, 1992); or (c) a combination of both methods. I caution against doing any coaching assignments or conjoint sessions with family of origin until the lesbian/gay person has reached a reasonably sustainable level of self-acceptance. After that point, the client's talking directly with family members about the self and partner issues will be much more successful, regardless of whether the therapist is present during those encounters.

Families of Choice

In a seminal ethnographic study, *Families We Choose: Lesbians, Gays, Kinship,* Weston (1991) highlighted a crucial existential difference in the life experiences of lesbian and gay people as compared to heterosexuals. Because of their heightened awareness of the volitional nature of adult kinship ties, lesbians/gays become more psychologically open than heterosexuals to broadening the notion of "family" so that it can encompass nonbiological relations (families of choice).

Lesbian and gay persons' greater openness to nonkinship sources of social support seems to lessen their dependence on family of origin connections during adulthood. In contrast to most heterosexuals, for example, lesbian/gay adults are continually exposed to peers who have experienced varying degrees of rejection and exclusion from their families of origin but still are functioning well. This exposure underscores the fact that parental emotional support during adulthood may not be as crucial as the heterosexual cultural ideal implies. Furthermore, the social support that may be lacking from one's kin often can be found outside the family.

Support from friendship networks seems exceptionally important for the well-being of lesbian and gay people, and therapists should pay at least equal attention to families of choice as to families of origin as sources of social support for these couples. For example, studies in the United States have found consistently that social support from family of origin is unrelated to the mental health of lesbians/gay individuals in couple relationships, but social support from friends is related to these individuals' mental health and better relationship functioning (Campbell, 2000; Kurdek 1988a; Kurdek & Schmitt, 1986, 1987; Roper, 1997; Smith & Brown, 1997).

In a large-scale national survey (Bryant & Demian, 1994), the sources of social support reported by partners in lesbian and gay male couples included (from most to least support): Lesbian/gay friends; various lesbian/gay organizations and groups; heterosexual friends; coworkers; siblings; boss; mother; other relatives; father; and mainstream church. In this ranking, it is remarkable that coworkers are ranked higher as a source of support than any family members; and parents are ranked lower than bosses. If you ask heterosexuals this same question, they typically will rank family members much higher. It seems that well-functioning lesbian and gay male couples are making up for the lower amounts of social support they receive from family members by getting such support from friends.

As a result of this difference, well-functioning lesbian and gay couples typically form very close friendships (Nardi, 1999; Weston, 1991), and in the optimal situation, these collections of friends have what is called high density—meaning that not only is the couple friends with a number of individuals, but these individuals are also friends with each other. When a friendship network has many close interconnections that last over time, it begins to take on a family-like quality, hence the term "family of choice." For same-sex couples, especially those with less family of origin connection and support, the social density dimension of their friendship networks is extremely important. I believe all couples benefit by being embedded in an ongoing social matrix if that set of relationships is nurturing and reciprocal.

Assessing and Developing Social Support

When assessing a couple's social support, most family therapists in the past have focused almost exclusively on the partners' family of origin relations and neglected to take friendships as seriously. I believe this is a grave oversight when working with lesbian and gay people because both family and nonfamily sources of support can be relevant, and sometimes the friendship sources are more significant. In the following sections, I discuss issues in the assessment and treatment of couples for whom more social support from family and friendship sources might help alleviate their distress and sustain their relationships in the future.

In evaluating a same-sex couple's overall social support from both family and nonfamily sources, it frequently helps to do a sociogram as well as a family genogram to map out the people in the couple's social network. Because the formats for drawing genograms are well-known (McGoldrick, Gerson, & Shellenberger, 1999), I focus here only on a format for doing a sociogram with lesbian/gay couples.

 A <u>simplified sociogram</u> can be drawn as five concentric circles, labeling these circles from innermost to outermost as follows (then writing in the names of the couple's relevant network members in the appropriate concentric rings):

- *The couple* (the innermost circle).
- *Very close/supportive ties* (including usually 2–6 closest people such as best friends or closest family member).
- *Close/supportive ties* (including other close friends or family members).
- *Instrumental ties/acquaintances* (which typically would include ongoing work associates who are not close friends, ongoing acquaintances with whom the partners might get together a few times a year, or perhaps family members with whom the partners do not have very close ties).
- *Others* (the outermost circle—a miscellaneous category that might include the couple's attorney, neighbors who are not friends, members of organizations the couple is connected to, family members from whom the couple is very disengaged, etc.)

After writing the names of relevant network members in the appropriate rings based on the partners' input, lines can then be drawn depicting which network members are also connected to each other (solid lines indicating close/supportive connections, dotted lines indicating loose connections). All the rings together make up the couple's social network. The people in the innermost two or three rings comprise what would be the couple's emotionally supportive relationships. These people would only constitute a social support "system" or "family of choice" if they also were close and supportive with one another (solid lines between them).

When the sociogram and genogram are completed, further assessment of the couple's support system should be based on the criteria listed in the following list, which are adapted from the field of network therapy (Kliman & Trimble, 1983):

1. Size and composition of the support system (number and types of people in the couple's support system such as friends, family members, coworkers, neighbors).
2. Frequency and lengths of contacts.
3. Modes of contact (in person, by phone, mail, e-mail).

4. Type of activities or rituals (recreation, meals, holidays, transition celebrations, and so on; see Imber-Black, Roberts, & Whiting, 1988, for examples).

5. Multiplexity of ties (*multiplex* refers to relationships that have more than one role dimension, such as friends who are also coworkers, coworkers who are also cousins, neighbors who are also in the same religious congregation. Multiplex ties tend to be more enduring than uniplex ones, which have only one role dimension.).

6. Types of support (emotional support, material/financial assistance, or practical support such as childcare, moving, cooking, health-related assistance, pet care).

7. Quality of support (satisfaction with support received).

8. Reciprocity of support (bilateral where both persons give and receive support, or unilateral where one person gives and the other receives).

9. Density of ties (extent to which members of the support system know each other and provide support to one another, including the extent to which close subgroups within the support system have overlapping memberships—"cross-ties." Subgroups could include, for example, a family of origin subgroup, a heterosexual coworkers subgroup, and a lesbian/gay friends subgroup. Single ties—relationships with individuals who are not connected emotionally to others in the support system—tend to be less enduring than multiple ties.).

10. Structural stability of the support system (changing versus stable membership over time due to geographical moves, emotional cut-offs, illness/disability, deaths, divorces/separations, addition of new members, and any patterns in termination of ties).

In general, lesbian and gay couples tend to have fewer interconnected social networks (less density of their support networks) than heterosexual couples. Their lesbian/gay friends and their heterosexual family members and friends may meet only rarely, if at all. Even their lesbian/gay friends may hardly know one another because these friendships usually have to be found outside of everyday mainstream situations like work settings, schools, or churches, where many heterosexuals meet their friends and where these friends already would know one another. The tendency toward social segregation of the straight and gay worlds generally—and between the straight and gay segments of an individual's social network (Oswald, 2001)—usually requires that same-sex couples have to expend more deliberate effort to create an integrated social support system that has family-like qualities. The ideal would be to integrate family members, lesbian/gay friends, and heterosexual friends into a cohesive support system.

In working on social support, therapists should encourage couples to take a very proactive, deliberate stance toward the goal of developing an ongoing social support system consisting of about 8 to 12 individuals (Berger & Mallon, 1993). This goal should be discussed with the couple explicitly, sharing with them some of the research findings on the importance of friendship support for the psychological well-being of lesbian/gay individuals and couples. Many same-sex couples in therapy spontaneously report feeling isolated and wishing they had more and closer friendships, especially with other same-sex couples, and they immediately grasp the importance of developing a stronger support system. Defining some of the traits of a strong social support system for them (size, accessibility, frequency, quality, multiplexity, reciprocity, density, stability) in layperson's terms is itself very helpful in orienting the couple to the task at hand.

There are two basic steps the couple has to take in building a personal support system: (1) developing or maintaining a reciprocally supportive relationship with each individual who would be a member of the couple's support system; and (2) "knitting" these individuals together into an integrated system of support (the density factor) by bringing them together repeatedly over many months and years. The great advantage of the couple meeting new people through existing lesbian/gay organizations is that those organizations already will have some degree of interpersonal density or "groupness" to them, so that the couple may be able to become an integral (rather than peripheral) part of an already existing social support system. Therapists who work with lesbian/gay couples should familiarize themselves with lesbian/gay organizations in their communities, or at least know where to suggest that clients find such information. Obviously, if the 8 to 12 individual relationships are accrued at different times from different settings, more effort has to go into weaving these disparate relationships into a more cohesive unit. The only way to increase the density of a fragmented support system is for the couple to actively and persistently take the lead in physically bringing together the disconnected individuals or subgroups.

What is most remarkable as the therapy progresses is that couples who can sustain this effort find that other members of their support system "spontaneously" start to develop autonomous dyadic friendships, getting together on their own. Ultimately, these members will start organizing ways for the larger support system to be together, along with some of their other individual friends. The two key ingredients for reaching this goal are simply for the couple to maintain the closeness of the individual relationships and then to bring these individuals together as frequently as possible in close circumstances. Given that structure, the emotional interconnections among other members of the support system tend to happen spontaneously starting at around 6 months into the effort. With sustained motivation, a sufficiently strong, interconnected circle of support can be created in about 2 years.

In the ways just described, couple therapists should begin to view friendship sources of social support as being at least as important as family of origin support for lesbian/gay persons' mental health and their couple functioning. Many aspects of the therapy with same-sex couples—taking a history, mapping the relevant people in the couple's life, formulating the problem, setting goals, deciding whom to include in sessions, and referrals to adjunctive therapeutic, educational, and support services—should reflect this expanded social network focus.

THERAPIST ISSUES

I could say this a thousand times in a thousand ways and still not have emphasized it enough: *The single, most important prerequisite for helping same-sex couples is the therapist's personal comfort with love and sexuality between two women or two men.* Therapists who are not comfortable with such love and sexuality may actually increase lesbian and gay clients' minority stress and exacerbate their problems unintentionally.

This statement does not mean a misguided blind approval of everything a lesbian or gay person does or avoidance of dealing directly with destructive patterns of behavior by lesbian or gay couples. It does not mean superficial acceptance, or patronizing overprotectiveness with clients. It requires familiarity with lesbian and gay culture, the ability to empathically identify with (but still remain sufficiently "objective" about) the behavior of lesbian and gay clients, and genuine personal ease ("comfort in your bones") when dealing with lesbian/gay partners' emotions for one another. It also requires an ability to ask and talk about homosexual sex in explicit terms with couples that are having sexual difficulties. I believe that with sufficient good will, motivation, and openness to learning and feedback, most therapists (regardless of sexual orientation) can achieve this level of preparedness for therapy with lesbian and gay couples.

To prepare mental health professionals to work with lesbian and gay clients, the American Psychological Association (2000) recently published a superb set of treatment guidelines, which can serve as starting point for those who wish to learn more. In the field of couple and family therapy, many of the central ideas about lesbian/gay issues can be found in the review by Laird (2003), the edited book by Laird and Green (1996), a special section of the *Journal of Marital & Family Therapy* (Green, 2000a), and two recent books on couple therapy (Bigner & Wetchler, 2004; Greenan & Tunnell, 2002). There also are two excellent publications about straight therapists working with lesbian/gay clients (Bernstein, 2000; Siegel & Walker, 1996).

Although such readings are vital, there is ample evidence that heterocentric stereotypes persist among mental health professionals, even after they presumably know (or should know) the basic information about lesbian and gay issues (Garnets, Hancock, Cochran, Godchilds, & Peplau, 1991; Johnson, Brems, & Alford-Keating, 1995). Didactic information is not sufficient to override unconscious prejudice that has been acquired over a lifetime. Working effectively with lesbian and gay clients involves more than just good intentions, significant reading, and the perfunctory kinds of preparation that are common now in our field. Affective and attitudinal learning is at least as important.

As a rule of thumb, I would suggest that if you would not feel comfortable seeing a competent lesbian or gay therapist for your own problems, then you probably are not optimally prepared to work with lesbian or gay couples yourself. If you are employed in a small community or setting or on a managed care panel where you are essentially the only choice of a therapist for such couples, I recommend that you seek expert consultation on every lesbian and gay couples case you treat until you can answer affirmatively to this rule of thumb criterion. If you do not live in an area with an expert consultant for these kinds of cases, I advise arranging confidential, long-distance telephone consultations with appropriate experts on same-sex couples in therapy.

Guarding Against Heterocentric Bias—Countertransference

If heterocentric biases were fully conscious, therapists could counteract them through rational self-monitoring. Unfortunately, we tend "not to know what we don't know." Hence, some therapists believe they are sufficiently knowledgeable about lesbian/gay issues without having immersed themselves in the clinical and research literature (Green, 1996) and without having received sustained supervision from lesbian/gay-knowledgeable colleagues. Even lesbian and gay therapists are not immune to heterocentric assumptions or homophobic reactions, as those of us who are lesbian or gay know from years of shedding our own internalized homophobia bit by bit. The main advantage lesbian and gay therapists have is extensive exposure to ordinary, nondistressed lesbian/gay persons and relationships, which helps disconfirm prejudicial stereotypes promulgated in the larger society.

The field of family therapy is just beginning to build culturally attuned treatment models for working with lesbian and gay couples and families (Bigner & Wetchler, 2004; Greenan & Tunnell, 2002; Laird & Green, 1996). On a personal level, the first step is to acknowledge that heterocentric assumptions are inevitable for all members of our society, including couple therapists. The goal is to make these assumptions conscious and examine them in light of existing psychological knowledge and professional ethics. In the following, I discuss a few additional steps that every therapist can take.

Examine Unconscious Biases and Assumptions. How do we personally view lesbian and gay people's lives, and do our views fit with recent research findings? What are the emotional cues of bias in this area? In general, the signs of bias among professionals tend to be subtle—consisting of inchoate feelings of discomfort, ambivalence, pessimism, anxiety, or "reactive" eagerness to please and appear "expert" when working with lesbian/gay clients. The antidote to acting-out such bias is to become comfortable with "not knowing," retaining a willingness to learn from clients, taking a collaborative stance, making space for discussion of cultural discrepancies and misunderstandings between you and the clients. The optimal attitude is one of nondefensive humility about the true limits of one's training, personal experience, and expert knowledge, while still retaining one's overall professional integrity and realistic confidence.

Personal Immersion in Lesbian/Gay Culture—Becoming "Bicultural." The research on homophobia and the clinical literature on heterosexual therapists working with lesbian/gay clients both point to the positive effects of more social contact to reduce prejudice (Bernstein, 2000; Green & Bobele, 1994; Siegel & Walker, 1996). Heterosexuals (including therapists) who have more interaction with lesbians/gays as personal friends, colleagues, family members, and clients report significantly fewer heterosexist attitudes. High levels of immersion in lesbian/gay culture involve taking concrete actions to work against heterosexism in our own families, friendships, professional settings, and communities. On the political level, couple therapists can contribute by participating in local chapters of Parents, Families, and Friends of Lesbians and Gays (PFLAG's Web site: www.pflag.org). It is important to keep in mind that although unbiased psychotherapy and psychological research have made positive contributions, the gay civil rights movement has made the single greatest contribution to the psychological well-being of lesbian and gay couples. For lesbians and gay men, the political is very personal, and therapists working toward the elimination of homophobia in their own social networks and community institutions is good preparation for doing therapy with lesbian and gay couples.

Getting Training Through Workshops and Case Consultation. Few practicing therapists have had as much as a semester-long course on lesbian/gay issues or been supervised by an expert on lesbian/gay therapy. In the field of couple and family therapy, most of the literature has presumed a heterosexual status among clients seeking treatment. For example, over a 20-year period, only .006% of articles in the major family therapy journals focused on lesbian/gay issues (Clark & Serovich, 1997; Laird, 1996). The consequence is that large numbers of couple therapists are uncertain about how to conceptualize and intervene actively in the problems of same-sex couples.

Surveys have shown that nearly half of all members of the American Association for Marriage and Family Therapy (AAMFT) report that they do *not* feel competent treating lesbians or gay men in therapy (Doherty & Simmons, 1996). Even so, a very large majority of such therapists (72%) state that at least one out of every 10 cases in their practices involves lesbian or gay issues (Green & Bobele, 1994). The data from these and other studies imply that many mental health professionals are treating same-sex couples without feeling adequately prepared. It is inevitable under these circumstances that some of their lesbian and gay clients will suffer the consequences (Garnets et al., 1991).

At a minimum, clinicians should read the available literature and seek continuing education training workshops to make up for this deficit in their graduate education. Most important, therapists should seek expert consultation early in treatment if they are not knowledgeable about lesbian/gay couples therapy and especially if progress with a couple is slower than seems desirable.

Sharing Power in Sessions. When working with lesbian/gay populations, it is important to continually acknowledge and respect mutual expertise, including sharing the power to interpret. A couple's therapist should be willing to discuss in layperson's terminology all assessment results, treatment goals, and therapeutic plans in a collaborative manner with clients, soliciting the partners' active input. The key is to guard against making unwarranted assumptions and to check out one's perceptions about lesbian/gay issues with the clients themselves. If you believe the therapeutic goals for a given couple should include resolving internalized homophobia, reducing relational ambiguity, and building a family of choice, these objectives should be discussed in layperson's terms with the partners. Their understanding and shared commitment to these stated goals should be achieved before proceeding further.

CAUTIONS ABOUT APPLYING THEORY TO SAME-SEX COUPLES

As a caveat, I wish to emphasize again that generalizations about same-sex couples as a group do not apply uniformly to *all* same-sex couples in therapy. In particular, this chapter did not address the special issues for couples in which one or both members are bisexual, or couples in which one or both members identify as transgendered (for more on these topics, see Fox, 1996; and Lev, 2004). This chapter pertains only to same-sex partners who have particular kinds of problems related to the unique position of lesbians/gays in this society. Readers should keep in mind that such couples in therapy do not represent the majority of same-sex partners, who are not distressed.

In the past, the mental health fields have shown a tendency to blur the distinction between well-functioning and distressed lesbian/gay couples and to assume that all same-sex couples are like the dysfunctional couples described in the clinical literature. For example, the notions of "fusion in lesbian couples" and "disengagement in gay male couples"—which came from clinical work with distressed couples (Krestan & Bepko, 1980)—became a kind of legend about all lesbian and gay couples.

However, research with community, nonclinical samples has since clarified that lesbian couples in general are extremely cohesive but not fused and that gay male couples are actually more cohesive than heterosexual married couples, not more disengaged (Green et al., 1996; Mitchell, 1988). In this light, I wish to reemphasize that although all same-sex couples face special challenges in terms of overcoming prejudice, dealing with greater relational ambiguity, and creating cohesive support systems, most lesbian and gay couples are able to manage these tasks successfully without professional help.

To the extent that I offered generalizations about same-sex couples in therapy above, I also wish to underscore that such statements are valuable only insofar as they serve as initial hypotheses in a new case—ideas to be tested and either retained or discarded depending on one's observations in that particular case. Descriptions of dysfunctional same-sex couples in this chapter should be taken as statements of "possible characteristics you may find" rather than universal truths about lesbian and gay couples in therapy. The particulars of real clients in treatment always should supersede abstract generalizations about categories of clients. Otherwise, therapy with same-sex couples would become little more than the imposition of yet another set of stereotypes about them.

SAME-SEX MARRIAGE AND SOCIAL JUSTICE

As of this writing, the United States is embroiled in controversy concerning the granting of marriage rights to same-sex couples. President George W. Bush, recently elected for a second term, is supporting an amendment to the U.S. Constitution that would prevent all courts and state legislatures from allowing same-sex marriage. In addition, a majority of states has approved anti-same-sex marriage laws through their state legislatures or the ballot initiative process (the so-called "Defense of Marriage" acts). Although public opinion polls have revealed that a strong majority of the U.S. population over age 30 opposes same-sex marriage, a similarly strong majority of younger adults is *not* opposed to same-sex marriage. The seeds of eventual change seem to have been sown. In the meantime, the media airwaves are filled with hyperbolic claims from religious and political conservatives about the dangers to "marriage as an institution" and even to "civilization as we know it" if marriage rights were to be extended to same-sex couples.

Despite these claims, there is no evidence that the granting of civil marriage rights to same-sex couples would have any negative effects on heterosexual marriages. Rather, there is much evidence and logic suggesting that marriage rights would be quite beneficial to lesbian and gay couples. For example, married heterosexuals have been found to be physically healthier, better off financially, more mentally healthy, better insured, and to live longer than unmarried heterosexuals (Waite & Gallagher, 2000). In addition, married women fare better in terms of lower rates of suicidality, depression, substance abuse, and history of psychiatric treatment than unmarried women who are in committed heterosexual relationships (Mathy & Lehmann, 2004). The latter finding suggests there is an advantage of marriage per se, above and beyond being in a committed heterosexual couple relationship. There is no basis whatsoever for concluding that same-sex couples would benefit any less from marriage than heterosexual couples do (Rauch, 2004) or that the existence of same-sex marriage would harm heterosexual marriages.

Given that not every same-sex couple wants to marry and that some are concerned about being co-opted by the conformist aspects of marriage as a cultural institution, there are ways in which *all* lesbian and gay persons might profit from the granting of marriage rights. The advent of same-sex marriage would send a powerful message to lesbian and gay people, their family members, their employers, their co-workers, their neighbors, their children's teachers, and many others with whom they interact that same-sex couple relationships are deserving of the same respect and support as heterosexual relationships. Even so, marriage rights will remain only one piece of a much larger struggle. As Ettelbrick (1997) so aptly cautions:

> We must not fool ourselves into believing that marriage will make it acceptable to be gay or lesbian. We will be liberated only when we are respected and accepted for our differences and the diversity we provide to this society. (p. 124)

Perhaps the greatest changes accompanying same-sex marriage would be in the lesbian and gay community's expectations of, and experiences in, same-sex couple relationships. Nothing short of marriage conveys the same multifaceted symbolic meanings nor evokes the same sense of hopefulness about finding psychological intimacy in a relationship.

"Love and Marriage": In all Western societies, the link between these two is virtually imprinted in the human imagination from early childhood onward. In fact, almost all adults in the United States still wish to marry despite the high prevalence of cohabitation and of divorce. For example, the U.S. Census Bureau currently estimates that approximately 90% of adults in the United States will marry at least once in their lifetimes (Kreider & Fields, 2002). Many same-sex couples are yearning for the same psychological sense of completion and secure attachment that marriage uniquely represents for most people in this culture.

Historically, it may be that lesbian and gay people have demanded much less of their relationships as a result of being excluded from marriage for centuries. With the arrival of same-sex marriage in Massachusetts (and briefly in San Francisco) in 2004, we are just beginning to understand the psychological deprivation such exclusion has created. It now seems that prohibiting lesbian and gay citizens from fulfilling these universal aspirations has had an untold dispiriting effect on their identity development, couple relationship expectations, interactions with their families, and relations in the larger community. Giving lesbians and gay men access to marriage would contribute significantly to a reduction in relational ambiguity and possibly to increased social support from families of origin because same-sex partners would legally become "family members" rather than being viewed as antithetical or ancillary to family life. For these reasons, marriage equality remains among the most important civil rights goals for positively impacting the mental health of lesbian/gay people.

Therapists concerned with social justice must always work on two fronts—helping those suffering the negative effects of injustice, and sociopolitical activism to create a more just society. In terms of the latter, publicly supporting same-sex marriage rights is a contribution that all psychotherapists and counselors can make to improve the mental health and relationships of lesbian and gay persons in this century. The question remains whether this society wants to keep lesbians and gay men in a permanently subordinated position as second-class citizens, or whether some future generation of Americans will deliver on the promise that is inherent in the equal protection clause of the United States Constitution. The psychological well-being of many same-sex couples hinges on the answer.

REFERENCES

American Psychological Association. (2000). Guidelines for psychotherapy with lesbian, gay, and bisexual clients. *American Psychologist, 55,* 1440–1451.
Ayers, T., & Brown, P. (1999). *The essential guide to lesbian and gay weddings.* Los Angeles: Alyson Publications.
Bailey, J. M, & Zucker, K. J. (1995). Childhood sex-typed behavior and sexual orientation: A conceptual analysis and quantitative review. *Developmental Psychology, 31,* 43–55.
Becker, C. (1988). *Unbroken ties: Lesbian ex-lovers.* Los Angeles: Alyson Publications.
Beeler, J., & DiProva, V. (1999). Family adjustment following disclosure of homosexuality by a member: Themes discerned in narrative accounts. *Journal of Marital & Family Therapy, 25,* 443–459.
Bell, A. P., & Weinberg, M. (1978). *Homosexualities: A study of diversity among men and women.* New York: Simon & Schuster.
Bell, A. P., Weinberg, M. S., & Hammersmith, S. K. (1981). *Sexual preference: Its development in men and women.* Bloomington: Indiana University Press.
Bepko, C., & Johnson, T. (2000). Gay and lesbian couples in therapy: Perspectives for the contemporary family therapist. *Journal of Marital & Family Therapy, 26,* 409–419.
Berger, R. M., & Mallon, D. (1993). Social support networks of gay men. *Journal of Sociology & Social Welfare, 20,* 155–174.
Bernstein, A. C. (2000). Straight therapists working with lesbians and gays in family therapy. *Journal of Marital & Family Therapy, 26,* 443–454.
Bigner, J., & Wetchler, J. (Eds.). (2004). *Relationship therapy with same-sex couples.* Binghamton, NY: Haworth Press.
Blasband, D., & Peplau, L. A. (1985). Sexual exclusivity versus openness in gay couples. *Archives of Sexual Behavior, 14,* 395–412.
Blumstein, P., & Schwartz, P. (1983). *American couples: Money, work and sex.* New York: William Morrow & Company.
Boss, P. (1999). *Ambiguous loss: Learning to live with unresolved grief.* Cambridge, MA: Harvard University Press.
Boss, P., Caron, W., Horbal, J., & Mortimer, J. (1990). Predictors of depression in caregivers of dementia patients: Boundary ambiguity and mastery. *Family Process, 29,* 245–254.
Boss, P., & Greenberg, J. (1984). Family boundary ambiguity: A new variable in family stress theory. *Family Process, 23,* 535–546.
Boyd-Franklin, N. (2003). *Black families in therapy: Understanding the African American experience* (2nd ed.). New York: Guilford.
Brown, L. S. (1994). *Subversive dialogues: Theory in feminist therapy.* New York: Basic Books.
Bryant, A. S., & Demian. (1994). Relationship characteristics of American gay and lesbian couples: Findings from a national survey. In L. A. Kurdek (Ed.), *Social services for gay and lesbian couples* (pp. 101–117). Binghamton, NY: Harrington Park Press.
Byng-Hall, J. (1995). Creating a secure family base: Some implications of attachment theory for family therapy. *Family Process, 34,* 45–58.
Campbell, K. M. (2000). *Relationship characteristics, social support, masculine ideologies and psychological functioning of gay men in couples.* Unpublished doctoral dissertation, California School of Professional Psychology, Alameda.
Carrington, C. (1999). *No place like home: Relationships and family life among lesbians and gay men.* Chicago: University of Chicago Press.
Chan, C. S. (1989). Issues of identity development among Asian-American lesbians and gay men. *Journal of Counseling & Development, 68,* 16–20.
Chan, C. S. (1995). Issues of sexual identity in an ethnic minority: The case of Chinese American lesbians, gay men, and bisexual people. In A. D'Augelli & C. Patterson (Eds.), *Lesbian, gay, and bisexual identities over the lifespan* (pp. 87–101). New York: Oxford University Press.
Clark, W. M., & Serovich, J. M. (1997). Twenty years and still in the dark? Content analysis of articles pertaining to gay, lesbian, and bisexual issues in marriage and family therapy journals. *Journal of Marital & Family Therapy, 23,* 239–253.

Crosbie-Burnett, M., Foster, T. L., Murray, C. I., & Bowen, G. L. (1996). Gays' and lesbians' families of origin: A social-cognitive-behavioral model of adjustment. *Family Relations, 45,* 397–403.

DiPlacido, J. (1998). Minority stress among lesbians, gay men and bisexuals. In G. M. Herek (Ed.), *Stigma and sexual orientation: Understanding prejudice against lesbians, gay men, and bisexuals* (pp.138–159). Thousand Oaks, CA: Sage.

Doherty, W. J., & Simmons, D. S. (1996). Clinical practice patterns of marriage and family therapists: A national survey of therapists and their clients. *Journal of Marital & Family Therapy, 22,* 9–25.

Ettelbrick, P. (1997). Since when is marriage a path to liberation? In A. Sullivan (Ed.), *Same-sex marriage: Pro and con* (pp. 118–124). New York: Vintage Books.

Falicov, C. J. (1998). *Latino families in therapy: A guide to multicultural practice.* New York: Guilford.

Fox, R. (1996). Bisexuality in perspective: A review of theory and research. In B. Firestein (Ed.), *Bisexuality: The psychology and politics of an invisible minority* (pp. 3–50). Thousand Oaks, CA: Sage.

Framo, J. L. (1992). *Family-of-origin therapy: An intergenerational approach.* New York: Brunner/Mazel.

Garnets, L., Hancock, K. A., Cochran, S. D., Godchilds, J., & Peplau, L. A. (1991). Issues in psychotherapy with lesbians and gay men: A survey of psychologists. *American Psychologist, 46,* 964–972.

General Accounting Office. (2004). Defense of Marriage Act: Update to prior report, GAO-04-353R. Retrieved October 23, 2004, from http://www.gao.gov/new.items/d04353r.pdf

Gonsiorek, J. C. (1991). The empirical basis for the demise of the illness model of homosexuality. In J. C. Gonsiorek & J. D. Weinrich (Eds.), *Homosexuality: Research implications for public policy* (pp. 115–136). Thousand Oaks, CA: Sage.

Green, R.-J. (1996). Why ask, why tell? Teaching and learning about lesbians and gays in family therapy. *Family Process, 35,* 389–400.

Green, R.-J. (1998a). Race and the field of family therapy. In M. McGoldrick (Ed.), *Revisioning family therapy: Race, culture, and gender in clinical practice* (pp. 93–110). New York: Guilford.

Green, R.-J. (1998b). Traditional norms of the male role. *Journal of Feminist Family Therapy, 10,* 81–83.

Green, R.-J. (Ed.). (2000a). Gay, lesbian, and bisexual issues in family therapy [Special section]. *Journal of Marital & Family Therapy, 26,* 407–468.

Green, R.-J. (2000b). Lesbians, gay men, and their parents: A critique of LaSala and the prevailing "clinical wisdom." *Family Process, 39,* 257–266.

Green, R.-J., Bettinger, M., & Zacks, E. (1996). Are lesbian couples fused and gay male couples disengaged?: Questioning gender straightjackets. In J. Laird & R.-J. Green (Eds.), *Lesbians and gays in couples and families: A handbook for therapists* (pp. 185–230). San Francisco: Jossey-Bass.

Green, R.-J., & Mitchell, V. (2002). Gay and lesbian couples in therapy: Homophobia, relational ambiguity, and social support. In A. S. Gurman & N. S. Jacobson (Eds.), *Clinical handbook of couple therapy* (3rd ed., pp. 546–568). New York: Guilford.

Green, S. K., & Bobele, M. (1994). Family therapists' response to AIDS: An examination of attitudes, knowledge, and contact. *Journal of Marital & Family Therapy, 20,* 349–367.

Greenan, D., & Tunnell, G. (2002). *Couple therapy with gay men.* New York: Guilford.

Greene, B., & Boyd-Franklin, N. (1996). African American lesbians: Issues in couples therapy. In J. Laird & R.-J. Green (Eds.), *Lesbians and gays in couples and families: A handbook for therapists* (pp. 251–271). San Francisco: Jossey-Bass.

Gurman, A. S., & Jacobson, N. S. (Eds.). (2002). *Clinical handbook of couple therapy* (3rd ed.). New York: Guilford.

Hartman, A. (1996). Social policy as a context for lesbian and gay families: The political is personal. In J. Laird & R.-J. Green (Eds.), *Lesbians and gays in couples and families: A handbook for therapists* (pp. 69–85). San Francisco: Jossey-Bass.

Hayden, C., Clifford, R. L., & Hertz, F. (2001). *A legal guide for lesbian and gay couples.* Berkeley, CA: Nolo Press.

Herdt, G., & Koff, B. (2000). *Something to tell you: The road families travel when a child is gay.* New York: Columbia University Press.

Herek, G. (1994). Assessing heterosexuals' attitudes toward lesbians and gay men: A review of empirical research with the ATLG Scale. In B. Greene & G. Herek (Eds.), *Lesbian and gay psychology: Theory, research, and clinical applications* (pp. 206–228). Thousand Oaks, CA: Sage.

Herek, G. M. (Ed.). (1998). *Stigma and sexual orientation: Understanding prejudice against lesbians, gay men, and bisexuals.* Thousand Oaks, CA: Sage.

Hochschild, A. (1989). *The second shift: Working parents and the revolution at home.* New York: Viking.

Iasenza, S., Colucci, P. L., & Rothberg, B. (1996). Coming out and the mother–daughter bond: Two case examples. In J. Laird & R.-J. Green (Eds.), *Lesbians and gays in couples and families: A handbook for therapists* (pp. 123–136). San Francisco: Jossey-Bass.

Imber-Black, E., Roberts, J., & Whiting, R. (Eds.). (1988). *Rituals in families and family therapy*. New York: Norton.

Johnson, M. E., Brems, C., & Alford-Keating, P. (1995). Parental sexual orientation and therapists' perceptions of family functioning. *Journal of Gay & Lesbian Psychotherapy, 2*, 1–15.

Johnson, T. W., & Keren, M. S. (1996). Boundary creation and maintenance in male couples. In J. Laird & R.-J. Green (Eds.), *Lesbians and gays in couples and families: A handbook for therapists* (pp. 231–250). San Francisco: Jossey-Bass.

Kliman, J., & Trimble, D. W. (1983). Network therapy. In B. Wolman & G. Stricker (Eds.), *Handbook of family and marital therapy* (pp. 277–314). New York: Plenum.

Kreider, R. M., & Fields, J. M. (February, 2002). *Number, timing, and duration of marriages and divorces: Fall 1996*. Current Population Reports, P70–80. Washington, DC: U.S. Census Bureau.

Krestan, J.-A., & Bepko, C. S. (1980). The problem of fusion in the lesbian relationship. *Family Process, 19*, 277–289.

Kurdek, L. A., (1988a). Perceived social support in gays and lesbians in cohabiting relationships. *Journal of Personality & Social Psychology, 54*, 504–509.

Kurdek, L.A. (1988b). Relationship quality of gay and lesbian cohabiting couples. *Journal of Homosexuality, 15*, 93–118.

Kurdek, L. A. (1995). Lesbian and gay couples. In A. R. D'Augelli & C. J. Patterson (Eds.), *Lesbian, gay, and bisexual identities over the lifespan: Psychological perspectives* (pp. 243–261). New York: Oxford University Press.

Kurdek, L. A., & Schmitt, J. P. (1986). Relationship quality of partners in heterosexual married, heterosexual cohabiting, and gay and lesbian relationships. *Journal of Personality & Social Psychology, 51*, 711–720.

Kurdek, L. A., & Schmitt, J. P. (1987). Perceived emotional support from family and friends in members of homosexual, married, and heterosexual cohabiting couples. *Journal of Homosexuality, 14*, 57–68.

Laird, J. (1996). Invisible ties: Lesbians and their families of origin. In J. Laird & R.-J. Green (Eds.), *Lesbians and gays in couples and families: A handbook for therapists* (pp. 89–122). San Francisco: Jossey-Bass.

Laird, J. (2003). Lesbian and gay families. In F. Walsh (Ed.), *Normal family processes: Growing diversity and complexity* (3rd ed., pp. 176–209). New York: Guilford.

Laird, J., & Green, R.-J. (Eds.). (1996). *Lesbians and gays in couples and families: A handbook for therapists*. San Francisco: Jossey-Bass.

LaSala, M. (2000). Lesbians, gay men, and their parents: Family therapy for the coming out crisis. *Family Process, 39*, 67–81.

LaSala, M. (2002). Walls and bridges: How coupled gay men and lesbians manage their intergenerational relationships. *Journal of Marital & Family Therapy, 28*, 327–339.

Lee, E. (Ed.). (1997). *Working with Asian Americans: A guide for clinicians*. New York: Guilford.

Lev, A. I. (2004). *Transgender emergence: Therapeutic guidelines for working with gender-variant people and their families*. Binghamton, NY: Haworth Press.

Liu, P., & Chan, C. (1996). Lesbian, gay, and bisexual Asian Americans and their families. In J. Laird & R.-J. Green (Eds.), *Lesbians and gays in couples and families: A handbook for therapists* (pp. 137–152). San Francisco: Jossey-Bass.

Malyon, A. K. (1982). Psychotherapeutic implications of internalized homophobia in gay men. In J. Gonsiorek (Ed.), *Homosexuality and psychotherapy: A practitioner's handbook of affirmative models* (pp. 59–69). New York: Haworth Press.

Mathy, R. M., & Lehmann, B. A. (2004). Public health consequences of the Defense of Marriage Act for lesbian and bisexual women: Suicidality, behavioral difficulties, and psychiatric treatment. *Feminism & Psychology, 14*, 187–194.

McGoldrick, M. (Ed.). (1998). *Revisioning family therapy: Race, culture, and gender in clinical practice*. New York: Guilford.

McGoldrick, M., & Carter, B. (2001). Advances in coaching: Family therapy with one person. *Journal of Marital & Family Therapy, 27*, 281–300.

McGoldrick, M., Gerson, R., & Shellenberger, S. (1999). *Genograms: Assessment and intervention* (2nd ed.). New York: Norton.

McWhirter, D. P., & Mattison, A. M. (1984). *The male couple: How relationships develop*. Englewood Cliffs, NJ: Prentice-Hall.

Meyer, I. H., & Dean, L. (1998). Internalized homophobia, intimacy, and sexual behavior among gay and bisexual men. In G. M. Herek (Ed.), *Stigma and sexual orientation: Understanding prejudice against lesbians, gay men, and bisexuals* (pp. 160–186). Thousand Oaks, CA: Sage.

Miller, J. B. (1976). *Toward a new psychology of women*. Boston: Beacon Press.

Minuchin, S. (1974). *Families and family therapy*. Cambridge, MA: Harvard University Press.

Mitchell, V. (1988). Using Kohut's self-psychology in work with lesbian couples. *Women & Therapy, 8,* 157–166.

Mitchell, V. (1996). Two moms: Contribution of the planned lesbian family to the deconstruction of gendered parenting. In J. Laird & R.-J. Green (Eds.), *Lesbians and gays in couples and families: A handbook for therapists* (pp. 343–357). San Francisco: Jossey-Bass.

Morales, E. (1996). Gender roles among Latino gay/bisexual men: Implications for family and couples relationships. In J. Laird & R.-J. Green (Eds.), *Lesbians and gays in couples and families: A handbook for therapists* (pp. 272–297). San Francisco: Jossey-Bass.

Nardi, P. (1999). *Gay men's friendships: Invincible communities.* Chicago: University of Chicago Press.

Olkin, R. (1999). *What psychotherapists should know about disability.* New York: Guilford.

Oswald, R. (2001, August). *Ritual as the site of family integration and disjunction.* Paper presented at the meeting of the American Psychological Association, San Francisco.

Peplau, L. A. (1991). Lesbian and gay relationships. In J. C. Gonsiorek & J. D. Weinrich (Eds.), *Homosexuality: Research implications for public policy* (pp. 177–196). Newbury Park, CA: Sage.

Pinderhughes, E. (1989). *Understanding race, ethnicity, and power: The key to efficacy in clinical practice.* New York: The Free Press.

Radical Therapist Collective. (1971). *The radical therapist.* New York: Ballantine.

Rauch, J. (2004). *Gay marriage: Why it is good for gays, good for straights, and good for America.* New York: Times Books/Henry Holt & Co.

Roper, K. (1997). *Lesbian couple dynamics and individual's psychological adjustment.* Unpublished doctoral dissertation, California School of Professional Psychology, Alameda.

Roth, S. (1989). Psychotherapy with lesbian couples: Individual issues, female socialization, and the social context. In M. McGoldrick, C. M. Anderson, & F. Walsh (Eds.), *Women in families: A framework for family therapy* (pp. 286–307). New York: Norton.

Savin-Williams, R. C. (1994). Verbal and physical abuse as stressors in the lives of lesbian, gay male, and bisexual youths: Associations with school problems, running away, substance abuse, prostitution, and suicide. *Journal of Consulting & Clinical Psychology, 62,* 261–269.

Savin-Williams, R. C. (1996). Self-labeling and disclosure among gay, lesbian, and bisexual youths. In J. Laird & R.-J. Green (Eds.), *Lesbians and gays in couples and families: A handbook for therapists* (pp. 153–182). San Francisco: Jossey-Bass.

Savin-Williams, R. C. (2001). *Mom, dad. I'm gay: How families negotiate coming out.* Washington, DC: American Psychological Association.

Shidlo, A. (1994). Internalized homophobia: Conceptual and empirical issues in measurement. In B. Greene & G. Herek (Eds.), *Lesbian and gay psychology: Theory, research, and clinical applications* (pp. 176–205). Thousand Oaks, CA: Sage.

Siegel, S., & Walker, G. (1996). Connections: Conversation between a gay therapist and a straight therapist. In J. Laird & R.-J. Green (Eds.), *Lesbians and gays in couples and families: A handbook for therapists* (pp. 28–68). San Francisco: Jossey-Bass.

Smith, R. B., & Brown, R. A. (1997). The impact of social support on gay male couples. *Journal of Homosexuality, 33,* 39–61

Solomon, S. E., Rothblum, E. D., & Balsam, K. F. (2004). Pioneers in partnership: Lesbian and gay male couples in civil unions compared with those not in civil unions and married heterosexual siblings. *Journal of Family Psychology, 18,* 275–286.

Waite, L. J., & Gallagher, M. (2000). *The case for marriage: Why married spouses are happier, healthier, and better off financially.* New York: Broadway Books.

Weinstein, D. L. (1996). No place in the family album. *Journal of Feminist Family Therapy, 8,* 63–67.

Weston, K. (1991). *Families we choose: Lesbians, gays, kinship.* New York: Columbia University Press.

White, M., & Epston, D. (1990). *Narrative means to therapeutic ends.* New York: Norton.

CHAPTER

7

Risk Reduction and the Micropolitics of Social Justice in Mental Health Care

Marcelo G. Pakman
Polytechnic University of Hong Kong

> *Understood in terms of a philosophy of truth, "ethical" should simply describe what helps to preserve or encourage a subjective fidelity as such. The ethical prescription can be summarized by the single imperative: "Keep going!" or "Continue!" for a truth is clearly difficult by definition. . . . By going against the current,. . . against the ""natural" movement of time itself, it is vulnerable to various forms of erosion at every moment of its elaboration. To keep going, then, presumes the ability to identify and resist the various forms of corruption or exhaustion that can beset a fidelity to truth.*
>
> —Hallward, cited in Badiou (2001, p. xi)

Although *social justice* had always been, explicitly or implicitly, an important goal of socially progressive movements, the year 1968 signaled an important turning point in its promotion as a legitimate goal for socially committed professionals within the practice of their professions. As Immanuel Wallerstein (2002) has pointed out, 1968, the year of the May revolt in France, of turmoil in American and Mexican universities, and of the invasion of Czechoslovakia by the Soviet Union after the Prague's Spring movement, among other popular mobilization events, marked the deep dissatisfaction with a central tenet of both revolutionary as well as reform movements, namely: that having the power of the State was a preliminary step to introducing social change. By then, it was becoming clear that neither socialism in the East nor social democracy in both the developed West and the Third World, in spite of having come to power in many countries, were capable, given the mechanisms of power, of initiating from the top down the changes in social structures and institutions necessary in order to reduce social inequalities.

The 1968 social explosions of frustration with the traditional ways of attempting to foster social change had at least two consequences: On one hand, they fueled social movements that, without aiming at gaining state power, were, however, still invested in fostering social change (greens and other environmentalists, feminists, minorities representatives, human-rights groups; Wallerstein, 2002). These movements acquired, from then on, a more central role in the political arena and the social discourses that have informed since politics and policymaking. As Jacques LeGoff said,

151

on the occasion of the 30th anniversary of the May events in France: "If revolutionary political leftism was defeated, cultural leftism triumphed" (LeGoff, 1998). On the
other hand, professionals involved in, or influenced and informed by, these social
movements started to find ways to complement their militancy in those movements
with the introduction of those goals for social justice as legitimate ones for their everyday professional practices. The community mental health movement of the 1970s
was, probably, one major such attempt at formatting professional practice around
social justice goals in the mental health professional arena. The many agendas of
"identity politics" have also since gained a voice—not only in mental health professional organizations, but also as goals to be implemented in mental health practices
that evolved under the progressive will of what started to be known as "social justice." However, there have been voices, not only from the political right but also
from within Marxism (Zizek, 1994), stating that the goals of identity politics, in promoting social justice for particular groups of people (women, lesbian and gay, minorities, etc.) tend to overlook the overall picture of social inequality, in which economic inequality is still the dominant factor. For Zizek, forgetting that "identity
politics" is a historical phenomenon has led him to take a nonproblematic view of
economy, as if capitalism were a natural phenomenon, not to be contested anymore. The promotion of "identity politics," aimed at advancing the interests and
well-being of particular social groups, would have, according to this view, paradoxically sealed the lack of alternatives to capitalism.

   As Michel Foucault theorized (1978, 1980, 1982), the inability of progressive social
movements to implement significant social change when in power was to be expected, as power was mostly exercised following distributed (more than central)
mechanisms. If we wanted to see change at work, we had to explore the everyday
discursive practices through which everything continued to go as expected, and all
the necessary structures were kept in place and at full force. An Orwellian "Big
Brother" (1949) was not necessary anymore to supervise and punish in order to as-
sure compliance. Since then—and especially since the more invisible mechanisms of
the post-Cold War neoliberal policies have become uncontested, ultimate "realities"
to live by—we have seen *procedures* reigning as the preferred way in which the ideology of health as a commodity is smuggled and implemented. Those procedures
channel the actions of professionals, and are increasingly limited in their therapeutic choices and creativity (Pakman, 2003).

   For the social justice movement to play a significant social role, it has to be embodied through concrete practices. More than an abstract and politically correct social justice agenda, it is probably a matter of fostering specific, situated social justice programs. If the battle moved from the political to the sociocultural field and
the mechanisms that perpetuate power are embodied in micropractices and procedures, it would be at that level that the microbattles would have to be fought.

   But there is a preliminary epistemological problem to be addressed regarding
how social justice programs would embody that task, a problem whose scope and
pervasiveness is difficult to underestimate and important not to overlook. If social
justice programs are oriented toward working with disadvantaged populations or
groups, then who is going to decide how to define and delimit the composition of
those groups, the problematic areas on which to focus, the appropriate mechanisms to reach them, and so on? At a time in which universal human rights awareness, an increasing preoccupation with bioethics, and the legal rights of the citizens
and subjects to decide for themselves are advanced, at least in intent, in most dem-

ocratic societies, what is at stake is basically the question of how to balance what scientific knowledge seems to present as advisable for people, and to what extent one group of people has the right to take another group as an "object" to intervene on. The overtones of this problem would not escape the reader at a time in which the issue of "liberating others" and "bringing democracy for other people's sakes" constitute the very atmosphere in which we are living.

In the case of mental health programs, this question takes specifically dramatic forms, given the fact that, on one hand, the ethics of most forms of psychotherapy assumes the active participation of a subject, no matter how determined and restricted in their freedom that subject may be conceptualized to be. On the other hand, public mental health approaches seem to have enough research to support the concept that many life situations (physical or sexual abuse, exposure to domestic violence, early abandonment, etc.) are pathogenic in themselves and are to be avoided in any society that cares for the future potential of its members.

Are social justice programs to be based on the insights of professional people operating on other disadvantaged groups taken as targets for intervention regardless of their own will?

I present here, as a concrete instance, the preliminary steps for a way of working with multiproblem disadvantaged families, which I have implemented during the last 10 years. This program illustrates a possible way of answering the just-mentioned conundrum in the social justice practice of mental health. The position taken in practice by this specific program assumes that:

1. It is a legitimate goal to aim to reduce social inequalities, in terms of access to mental health care for disadvantaged populations, and also to reduce the risk for those populations to be affected by certain mental health conditions or mental health consequences of social inequalities, and focus on those factors in the locality of our range of action as a part of our professional practice of mental health.

2. As distributed forms of power do themselves, we have to integrate programs to the everyday professional transactions, embodied as procedures, without getting lost in paying allegiance to politically correct declarations of good intent.

3. Social justice projects like this one introduce, in practice, a *reflective component* through which professionals can become aware of the strong limitations they face when their best efforts are channeled by those procedures of health insurance companies supported by the new conceptual language of the caste of administrators formatted within the "managed care" ideology (managed care, evidence-based outcomes, streamlining, re-engineering, resource optimization, etc.). Social justice projects may then have a chance then to become *critical social projects* (Pakman, 1998a, 1999), to the extent they rend visible restrictive forces at play both in the lives of clients and the professional lives of mental health care workers.

4. Social justice programs (like the one we present) are designed also as instruments for the well-motivated clinicians to operate effectively reducing the burden of their exposure to the ills of socially disadvantaged people with whom they are committed to work. These workers are increasingly dissatisfied by working with unsolvable binds (and asked to vicariously solve what the State does not solve any more). Viable social justice endeavors should optimize the best use of professional energies and not put workers under more pressure to become responsible for what they cannot ultimately solve.

5. This program stresses the *micropolitical* component of the interventions and not the specific psychotherapeutic techniques of mental health professionals. Under a limited definition, the application of those psychotherapeutic techniques tends to be seen as the exclusive legitimate role of a mental health professional. To stress the micropolitical component (regardless of the therapeutic models used by mental health professionals) aims instead at showing the powerful effects of interventions that are sometimes overlooked, and seen as properly belonging to "social work" more than psychotherapy. Focus on micropolitics is considered central to a systemic approach to mental health, in which *systemic* means not a specific set of psychotherapeutic techniques, but a spirit and a methodology that questions the very concept that the complex problems multiproblem families deal with are exclusive psychological problems, and uses instead multiple lenses to approach them. Micropolitics means also operate and are driven by our professional will and the good intent as committed professional to favor disadvantaged populations, but do not sacrifice the will of the subjects (and not "objects") of the intervention. A delicate balance pendulates between the awareness of trivial mechanisms at work in the lives of people that we want them to know about (in the same way that knowing about and receiving a vaccine for a preventable illness is a human right and a bioethically correct thing to do) and the need to acknowledge the limit that comes from people's right to decide for themselves. A daily practice of complex and seasoned decisions cannot be avoided in this regard, and conversations at multiple levels in democratic societies struggle to address them.

MULTIPROBLEM FAMILIES

In multiproblem patients/families, medical, mental health, and chemical dependence issues are usually combined with difficulties in employment, education, violence, and poverty, as well as with social problems related to welfare, disability, minority status, legal issues and housing problems, and the scarcity of an effective social network. It could be argued that many interventions, specially medical ones, tend to be iatrogenic, and the Zen-inspired principle of nonintervention could be evoked as relevant in this regard. But it seems that the combined impact of problems, when they go beyond a certain critical mass, tends to saturate the *homeostatic* mechanisms of the families and individuals, preventing them from regaining balance. It creates instead a negative circle of mounting difficulties, leading to frequent crises and further deterioration of the quality of life. We can say that, in multiproblem families, a variation of Murphy's Law applies: No matter how bad things are, the chances for them to get worse after a certain period of time are very high. Any difficulty in any of the identified domains is a risk factor for things to get worse in terms of increasing difficulties in the other domains. A frequently compounding problem is that health, mental health, substance abuse, or community workers, when confronted with many demanding cases like these (and often deprived of the time, compensation, education, and the means to be helped in this endeavor) tend to become overwhelmed, and mirror the frustration and despair of the families they intend to serve (Pakman, 1995). Burnout, far from being the exception, becomes a common occurrence, and the rapid turnover of professionals adds to the already stressed structures of the community agencies in charge of providing care.

Although all the problematic domains need attention in order to have an impact on the lives of families, the traditional procedures followed by health and mental health care providers tend to focus almost exclusively on strictly the medical and mental health issues. Furthermore, the focus that disciplinary psychology has promoted to center stage in the individual and systemic interactions tends to be overlooked. If the methods are not sensitive to detect social realities, they tend to fade to the background, becoming "contextual matters" that the mental health professional can consider as an option, but not as a central issue pertinent to the practice of the profession. The overwhelming promotion of psychopharmacology and biology as the most "scientific" way of accounting for mental illness has further obscured the complex intricacy of psychosocial/biological factors that make for a systemic approach of mental health. Thus, all other social issues extremely relevant to the evolution of the health and mental health issues have increasingly receded to the background and tend not to be included as legitimate loci of professional intervention. Social workers and community workers with poor credentialing and levels of education are usually the exception to this rule, but their endeavors frequently suffer from being considered "second-class interventions" among the hierarchies of professional ranking that deeply influence academic standing, as well as allocation of financial resources.

The identification of domains of risk is, then, an important aspect of the professional's ability to intervene in order to reduce the negative impact of those social domains on medical, mental, and substance abuse conditions. Simple interventions to address the actual and current state of affairs, thus reducing possible complications in one domain, tend to have a positive impact to reduce risk in other domains. These interventions are frequently not traditional medical ones and can be implemented by different actors involved in the lives of multiproblem families, by definition, highly punctuated by the interventions of multiple systems in well-developed countries, and more frequently left without protection in underdeveloped ones.

The way of addressing multiproblem families that are presented here can be conceptualized as a "risk reduction integrated program." The modest goal of the program is to reduce the chance of things getting even worse, thus starting a spiral of positive events, and moving to slowly improve quality of life for the multiproblem patients and preventing burnout for the committed health, mental health, and community workers. I developed this approach over years of practice in community mental health, fueled initially by the need to address the common occurrence of "burnout" for professionals overwhelmed by caring for multiproblem families. Although multiple systems (health, mental health, substance abuse care, legal, school, police, housing support, etc.) usually have contact with members of these families, interventions are frequently not coordinated, and even contact among these different systems is often nonexistent or conflictive, mirroring and being mirrored by conflicts among family members or between family members and staff of the agencies representing those systems. The *modus operandi* of these various systems does not allocate actual time for the interaction needed for coordination to be available. Even more, the theoretical training of people working professionally at different levels in health and mental health care has not, in general, prepared them to make significant connections among events that, although not necessarily related directly to health and mental health, are risk factors for things to evolve in a negative direction in those areas.

I have been able to implement different aspects of this program myself while working over many years in different settings in community mental health in the United States; I have been able also to spread this program in teaching about systemic approaches to mental health in North and South America and Europe, where different mental health professionals have taken this programming and applied it to their own contexts introducing their own variations.

The program is designed, then, for interventions, and to reduce the risk of further deterioration in several significant domains in the lives of multiproblem individuals and their families, and other "intimate social networks" (Bloch, personal communication,1999). Besides being a risk-reduction program, it is also aimed at optimizing resources, implementing the concept of *virtual support networks*, and reducing burnout among professionals. As we see, the pragmatics of the program integrate problematic domains, allowing bio-psychosocial interventions at multiple levels, and try to enhance the ability to make significant connections among events for individuals, families, and professionals.

DOMAINS OF RISK

The methodology of the program is rather simple and is based on the concept of domains of risk that mutually influence each other in negative or positive ways. Those domains include:

1. General health
2. Mental health
3. Drug addictions
4. Education
5. Work
6. Housing/transportation
7. Legal issues
8. Violence
9. Ethnic/social dissonance
10. Poverty
11. Social network
12. Welfare/disability

The domains are chosen from what clinical experience shows to be independent risk factors for any other domain: Any difficulty in one of the identified areas is a risk factor for things to get worse, in terms of increasing difficulties in other domains. The multiplying quality of the interactions among these domains configurate both a network that traps members of these families in unending vicious circles of increasingly problematic situations and a security net for the potential development of virtuous circles of progressive and positive events.

Let us consider the case of a prototypical multiproblem family.

Irma is a 23-year-old Puerto Rican woman who had lived in New York between the ages of 8 and 15 years old and came to New England 2 years ago after a short period back in the Caribbean. She has been diagnosed with Type II diabetes, which she acquired during her last pregnancy of her now 3-year-old son Richard. The father of Richard, Jose, a Dominican man, is planning to meet her soon but she is not convinced this is going to be of much help. Although she still likes him, he has never helped her financially; he also hid the fact that he had two other children, for whom he had never provided, with another woman. He has also been incarcerated, and when Irma met him they were using cocaine and alcohol on a regular basis. Irma's drug abuse has been intermittent over the years, to the point of dependency during short periods of time, with a binging pattern most frequently. Now she is living with her sister Leonore, who attends a methadone clinic to treat a long-term heroine dependency. She has also an 8-year-old daughter, Mary, the result of a rape by a cousin of hers. It was that abusive event that forced her to move temporarily back to Puerto Rico years ago (sent by her mother, Delia). She is now distanced from her mother, whom Irma believes had considered more important to protect her relationship with her own sister (the mother of the cousin who raped her) than to stand up for Irma, her own daughter. Irma believes her mother's own sexual abuse from her own father (Irma's grandfather) is a precedent for the position her mother took and an example of the role women in the family have taken regarding abusive men in the past—largely, to somehow protect them instead of protecting the younger generation of women. Her daughter Mary stayed, however, with her mother and was still living with her. Irma decided to come back to the United States to get better services for herself as well as to distance herself from her maternal grandmother with whom she was staying in the island. This grandmother was the protector of her abusive husband, abuser of Irma's mother, as she learned while living with her from some neighbors. Although Irma was now considering bringing Mary to live with her, Mary was reportedly resisting this change and preferred to stay with Irma's mother. Irma has also been diagnosed with depression and started a short-lived therapeutic process. For a while, she took a prescribed antidepressant, but she did not like how it made her feel, so she stopped it. Irma has a good connection with her neighbor Alma, who invited her to attend church. Lately she has been to a few parties where she used some cocaine again. She also engaged in unprotected sex with a man she stopped seeing afterwards because she heard "bad things" (that she did not want to comment about) about him. They live in a very bad neighborhood in which shoot-outs are not uncommon at night, and drug dealing is pervasive. She does not drive and does not know how to use public transportation very well. In fact, she had a panic-like attack the second time she took the bus and ended up in an emergency room at a local hospital, where she was sedated. The whole experience has left her fearful. Since then, she has been avoiding similar and related situations in public settings. Irma dropped out from school at an early age and is functionally illiterate. She does have some debts and cannot organize herself to work; public transportation is poor in her area, and her English is not very good to get around and find a suitable job, given her poor work history. She has learned recently she has a case pending for possession of drugs. Irma started receiving a welfare check recently, mostly as a help for her son, and was told she could apply for disability but has been unable to get help to go to the disability office and fill out the papers.

Let us see some of the interactions among problems in different domains and how they negatively impact each other. When a person like Irma is diabetic and depression is added to the picture, the difficulties of having diabetes (symptoms, crises) and of managing it (dietary measures, pharmacological treatment, hygienic measures to prevent complications) will compound the symptoms of depression and the necessary psychosocial steps necessary to adequately treat it. Depressive symptoms and related crises would also impact the ability for the diabetic condition to be stabilized, given the increased difficulties to follow directions and learn about the condition due to the depressed mood, associated cognitive impairment, lack of interest and energy, insomnia and anxiety, and so on. All types of negative interactions ensue. If we add cocaine and alcohol abuse, these will have further negative impact on the evolution of both diabetes and depression and their treatment, and vice versa. Besides the medical complications of both addictions, they increase the risks of decompensation of the diabetic condition as well as of increasing depressive symptoms, rendering it more difficult to take appropriate measures to treat them.

Regarding other factors, more traditionally seen as social problems out of the realm of the health professional, similar vicious circles develop, interacting with more traditional legitimate medical problems. Poor education will certainly be an obstacle for some aspects of the adequate treatment of her diabetes, depression, and addictions, which will, in turn, make much it more difficult to find adequate energies to overcome the educational handicap. Unemployment and its consequences will further add stress to the situation, being in itself a negative factor for the evolution and treatment of diabetes, depression, addictions, and ability to further education. All these factors would, in turn, make it more difficult to find adequate employment. Poor housing and transportation would certainly increase isolation, a major negative factor to adequately treat all the conditions just noted and psychosocial situations. The loop again closes because all those factors negatively influence the ability to find better housing. Pending legal issues—besides being a stressful factor—further block the ability to find better placement and jobs, and increase the risk of medical and mental complications and relapses of addictive behavior. These may then increase the risk of meeting the requirements of probation status and increase the risk of delinquent behavior, seen as a short-term cop-out strategy related to drug use, if not as a short circuit to obtain money, given the shortage of options. Events of domestic violence, as well as the exposure to the violence usually associated with living in poor neighborhoods, add further stressors feeding, maintaining, or triggering more depressive symptoms and drug-addicted behaviors, making it more complicated to take care of the diabetic condition and its associated crises and complications. This will also reduce the chances to improve education, to get a reasonably paid job, to deal with legal issues, all of which increase the atmosphere of doom associated with domestic violence, as well as taking a risk in living in a dangerous neighborhood.

Ethnic dissonance, which comes with speaking poor English and being an immigrant, makes it much more difficult to navigate the systems that might help with all the other difficulties, and, thus, increases isolation. This dissonance makes people more susceptible to being limited to social relationships that frequently share the same or similar complex web of difficulties, and does not provide a way out of their predicament. The mounting difficulties tend to undermine efforts to become more involved and establish patterns of mutual distrust with the police, schools, the legal system, and the health care system. These patterns of distrust, in turn, increase the ethnic and social dissonance. Many of the difficulties just mentioned in multiple domains are the hallmark of poverty, which can yet be seen as a domain of risk in itself, as defined by consensual sociological parameters of income, which are variously defined in different countries and regions within countries. Poverty, defined as such by these financial parameters, is a shadow that usually comes accompanied by worse health and mental health care, more complications and poor evolution for many physical and mental conditions, and the myriad of problems with associated violence, education, housing, and transportation, and so on that punctuate the everyday realities of life. Needless to say, all these aspects of living in poverty tend to perpetuate living below the poverty line, or even being indigent. A thorough evaluation of the social network (Sluzki, 1995, 1996) is of the utmost relevance, not only because life unfolds embedded in social relationships, but also because poverty of the social network and social isolation make it more difficult to find a catalyst to fuel the process of building aspects of a new identity, a reconstruction essential for the recovery from many physical, mental, and social illnesses. All the other difficulties explored so far would, in turn, lock a patient like Irma in place, perpetuating the limited social resources that a social network represents.

The domain of welfare/disability requires some special considerations. Being functionally disabled is a major handicap in challenging many of the compounded difficulties examined herein, which are, to begin with, the causes of that disability. Inability to get resources from a formally recognized welfare/disability system, due to drug addiction, language difficulties, poor contact with systems of help, and an overall unstable, crisis-filled life denies people like Irma of the necessary help needed to compensate for her many social disadvantages. This should not obscure the fact that the identity of being a disabled person might, in itself, be a double-edged sword, installing the need to maintain the illness in order to maintain a social help that no other systems allows for socially disadvantaged people. The professionals dealing with large volumes of people (mostly minorities) on disability have to contend with the complexity and ambiguity of such a situation. Often, the best intentions of these professionals in joining their clients toward a progressive improvement hits a wall when they discover that one of the traps of the system is that "improvement" is seen as risk; the job of the patient is to remain sick. Social stigma clearly adds to this conundrum, when this behavior is seen as ill-intentioned by those who read it as an expression of the negative, "lazy" qualities of those in need of defending their position in society through maintaining the status of disabled people. In the majority of cases, these people are not consciously trying to cheat the system. The situation is much more complex: They find themselves at such a disadvantage that they identify themselves with their incapacity in order to progress in society. Not having access to social help other than becoming part of the welfare/ disability system, they end up occupying the spot the system has for them, if they are to receive any social help. The price to be paid is that of being "disabled." They do not live, in fact, strictly by the letter of the rules of disability that requires them to fall within a diagnostic category, but struggle with their inability to overcome the overwhelming weight of social disadvantages whose unequal burden they share. Ethical problems ensue when the well-intentioned professional in the mental health domain sees his efforts to do his therapeutic job as a threat to the "welfare" of his patient who sees losing his disability status as an added disadvantage.

RISK REDUCTION

As you can see by observing the list of problematic domains, only the first three cover the traditionally considered appropriate levels of health and mental health interventions. As a part of their training, professionals learn to structure vaguely defined problematic situations to the kind of problems they have techniques to deal with (Schön, 1983). As a result, most health and mental health workers tend not to focus on social issues like those covered in Items 4 to 12, although they can be marginally considered as part of the background information. To make them so predominant as a part of a list of domains of risk, with equal standing to the first, more traditional, health care domains, aims at promoting them to center stage in a professional's awareness, to legitimize them as appropriate loci for interventions, and to make them constitutive of the framing of problematic situations into defined problems.

Although different members of the systems involved in helping or working with the person in each domain may be aware of the difficulties in other domains, there is no clear mechanism to validate each area of difficulty as serious enough to represent a risk factor for other domains, to maintain awareness and focus on these difficulties, and to realize that unattended further complications will arise from each of them, Moreover, there is no clear way to channel the efforts in a coordinated way so as to increase effectiveness, to design and follow up on interventions, to involve the client actively and creatively and to avoid being overwhelmed as a professional with the limitations of our own institutional settings and power to be agents of change.

In order to impact all these areas, I have developed a series of basic questions to explore each of those identified domains, the possible risks that problems in each domain pose for the future, the possible ways to go about reducing the chance for things to get worse, the complications for those preventive plans, and ways to overcome those impediments for preventive action. A description of a clinical case like the one we presented previously would not be obtained unless a professional has a list of significant domains integrated to the routine of the clinical evaluation and exploration (or at hand as a reminder if not integrated yet) of a patient's status. Different variations of this question have been used in different circumstances and settings and I offer them only as guidelines to be used, introducing necessary variations according to the setting in which different professionals may find themselves. The series of question follow a *pattern* that starts out by trying to:

1. Define current status in a given domain, followed by;
2. An exploration of the ways in which the current situation can further deteriorate (risks). From here, it goes on to;
3. Explore the patient's current understanding of the ways to avoid that further deterioration from happening;
4. Obstacles that might appear for those progressive efforts to be undermined; and
5. Ways to overcome those obstacles.

In this way, these questions guide the conversation toward a major, but gentle, reframing of the overall context, going from getting deeper into the difficulties and how these can increase, toward working through concrete steps to start doing simple things to avoid those risks and the obstacles, to making those simple steps happen.

Let us see a possible template of the series of questions in each domain, all following the pattern that embodies the risk reduction context in which the program operates. We also include the results of this evaluation for the case we presented previously.

1. General health

• What conditions have you been diagnosed with?

- What are you currently receiving treatment for?
- Do you have an identifiable provider/site treating you for this(these) condition(s)?
- Do you know of possible complications of the just-described condition(s)? Which ones?
- Do you know how to reduce the chances of having those complications? How would you do that?

Irma knew he was diagnosed with diabetes, but did not understand the different types. She assumed she did not have a "real" case of it because she was not prescribed insulin, and an aunt of hers, the only one in the family with a similar diagnosis, has been on insulin for many years. She was taking "pills for diabetes," but she was not following any special diet and had only a vague recollection of something said about it by a nurse she did not understand very well. There was no clear connection in her mind between dietary measures and progress of diabetes. She was attending a neighborhood health center but could not identify a specific provider and has missed several appointments. She knew diabetes "could make you lose a leg," something that happened to her diabetic aunt, but did not know of other complications, nor that there were any clear ways of avoiding those complications other than "taking the pills." She was overweight and did not like it, but did not know of any connection between obesity and diabetes. She was not trained to check her own sugar and considered she was not going to be able to do it.

2. Mental health

- What conditions have you been diagnosed with?
- What are you currently receiving treatment for?
- Do you have an identifiable provider/site treating you for this(these) condition(s)? Do you know of possible complications of the just-described conditions? Which ones?
- Do you know how to reduce the chances of having these complications? How would you do that?

Irma was told she suffered from *depression,* a term she adopted to refer to a whole set of problems, without understanding clearly what it meant. She did not have any clear idea of a connection between her frequent crying and the label "depression," and her own meaning of the term was connected to "not being able to do things." She has stopped seeing the psychiatrist who prescribed an antidepressant and came back now for a new consultation, after hearing there was a Spanish-speaking psychiatrist and therapist that she could see. It was in this context that I started seeing her as an exploratory mini-project on risk reduction. Irma thought that "depression" could lead to being a "mental patient" and being admitted to a "mental hospital." She remembered a neighbor in Puerto Rico who was "not even able to go to the bathroom" when he came back from such a hospital, and the whole idea of that terrorized her. (This was an elderly man who probably suffered from severe dementia.) She was at a loss regarding what to do to avoid feeling worse.

3. Drug addictions

- Do you use any alcohol? Drugs? Which one(s)? Medications acquired on the street or provided by other people? Which one(s)?

- Have you been told you have a problem with using too much of any substance? Which one(s)? Do you consider yourself dependent on any substance? Which one(s)?
- Are you currently receiving any treatment for drug addiction(s)? Are you making any efforts without treatment to overcome a problem with substances? Which one(s)? Have you received treatment or made efforts by yourself to stop using substances before? For what type of substance? What? When?
- Do you know of any possible complications of substance abuse problems that you have, according to yourself or others?
- Do you know how to reduce the chances of having these complications? How would you do that?

Irma admitted drinking alcohol, using cocaine sporadically, and reluctantly using it frequently during periods of her life. She denied using other drugs or unprescribed medications, although her sister Leonore and her ex-boyfriend Jose did offer her some "pills." She has been occasionally told she did have a drug problem, lately insistently by her neighbor Alma, but she considered that "addicts" were people like her sister, who was now on methadone and had used "needles." She believed she was not dependent and could stop at any moment. Irma was not making efforts to stop using lately; she considered it was only something she did "to relax," and would stop it if told it was bad for her. For the same reasons, she never sought treatment before. Irma knew that "drugs are not good," and that people with addictions to crack or cocaine can die from it, but she could not provide any specific information.

4. Education

- What is the maximum level of education you have completed? Did you attend regular or special education classes? Do you read and write in your native language?
- In the future, is it possible for you to lose some of the skills you have now in any area?
- Are you currently involved in any educational project? Do you have any plans to continue your education in the future? How are you going, or will be going, about doing it?
- What are the obstacles to continue your education now or in the future?
- Do you know how to reduce those obstacles? How would you do that?

Irma dropped out from school when she was 13 years old. She sometimes had difficulties in learning but always remained in a mainstream classroom. She could not write or read well in either English or Spanish lately, although she thought she was better at it years ago. She felt she had too many problems now to think about improving her education and did not see how that could help her with the problems at hand.

5. Work

- Do you have a job now? How long you have had this job? How stable is it? What type of job? If unemployed now: what is the reason? For how long? Is it possible for your current work situation to worsen? How so?

- Work history: How old were you when you had your first job? What was the longest time you have held a job?
- Do you have any plans to restart working or improve your work situation, either now or in the future? Which one(s)? How do you or will you do it?
- What are the obstacles to restart working or improve your work situation?
- Do you know how to reduce those obstacles? How would you do that?

Irma is unemployed now, as she has been in general, with the exception of short periods of time on odd jobs since age 18, that did not last in general more than 2 months. However, she was helping a tailor (a woman who was friends with her grandmother) in Puerto Rico a few years ago for almost a year, and learned enough from her to be able to mend and alter her own, as well as some neighbor's, clothing occasionally. Irma said she would like to go to work but she was not very convinced about it and saw it as very difficult given her current circumstances. She did not know where to start, with all her many problems, to be able to think more seriously about working.

6. Housing/transportation

- In what type of living situation are you now? How long you have been in this situation? Is it stable now? Is it possible for your current housing situation to become more complicated? How so? What are your usual means of transportation? Do you foresee this changing in the near future?
- Housing history: What is the longest time you have lived in one place? If you were ever homeless before, when? For how long?
- Do you have any plans to improve your living situation, either now or in the future? Which one(s)? How do you or will you do it?
- What are the obstacles to improve your living situation?
- Do you know how to reduce those obstacles? How would you do that?

Irma was living with her sister Leonore but could not stay there for long because tension was starting to build between them. She was afraid of becoming homeless and having to go to a shelter, which she considered an unsafe place that could jeopardize her attempts at taking adequate care of her son. She could not insist on having her daughter with her either, as long as her housing situation was so unstable. She was quite isolated, afraid of using public transportation, and did not know how to drive. She lived for many years in the same place while in Puerto Rico, but her housing stability in New York as a child and since coming back to the United States was precarious. Irma heard there were ways to find housing assistance, but did not know how to go about it and was afraid that contacting any "governmental" agency might end up in an ordeal that could compromise her custody of her children. She had heard many stories of children being removed from their parents and did not have a clear idea of the specific situations involved in those cases. Irma wanted to find help but not without first knowing more about the risks of losing her child.

7. Legal issues

- Do you have any legal issues pending? What type? Do you have any legal aid for those issues? Is it possible for your current legal situation to become more complicated? How so?

- History of legal problems: Incarceration? When? For how long?
- Do you have any plans to improve your legal situation, either now or in the future? Which one(s)? How do you or will you do it?
- What are the obstacles to improve your legal situation?
- Do you know how to reduce those obstacles? How would you do that?

Irma was recently notified that she had a case pending for possession of drugs, but was not able to go to court and now received a letter with a new citation. She did not know about any legal counseling she could use, was not informed about any lawyer being assigned by the court, and was overall very intimidated by the situation and felt paralyzed. She had never been incarcerated before, nor had any probation or legal charges. She understood that she needed information about the situation she was in as a preliminary step for further action on her part.

8. Violence

- How you been involved in any violent event (as defined by self or others) in the last 6 months? How so (actively, passively, both)? When? How often? What were the consequences? Is it possible that any or more violent events will happen in the future? How so? Is it possible for the consequences to be worse in the future?
- History of past violent events? When? What was your involvement? Consequences?
- Do you have any plans to prevent or reduce being involved in violent events? How do you or will you do it?
- What are the obstacles to prevent or reduced being involved in violent events?
- Do you know how to reduce those obstacles? How would you do that?

Since coming back to the United States, Irma witnessed neighborhood violence, although she was not a direct victim. She also saw many confrontations between her sister Leonore and a boyfriend she had for a while. These events brought back memories of her own rape as well as some physical abuse she suffered from her mother. She felt it was impossible to put all these experiences in her past, due to the circumstances in which she was now living, and feared the return of her boyfriend as a negative factor, given his past involvement with gangs. Irma suffered with nightmares for years and has had sexual difficulties. She was again starting to have sleeping problems. Moving to a better neighborhood was a dream, but she did not know very well how to go about it. She was not very clear about what changes she could introduce in her life in order to reduce the chance for violence to reoccur around her so pervasively.

9. Ethnic/social dissonance

- Are you an immigrant? When did you come to the country? What were the reasons to leave your country? Are you a political refugee? Do you speak English? What kind of things you are limited to do due to lack of English skills? Do you have a minority status (as defined by you or others)?
- Have you felt discriminated? Was that due to your race? Ethnicity? Language? Gender? Sexual orientation? Illness? Age? Other? How so? Is it possible for those experiences of discrimination or stigma to worsen in any way in the future?

- Do you have any plans to prevent those experiences from happening or to reduce its consequences? How do you or will you do it?
- What are the obstacles to prevent those experiences from happening or to reduce the consequences?
- Do you know how to reduce those obstacles? How would you do that?

Irma did not see herself as an immigrant, but for all practical purposes, she had recently come back to the United States, spoke poor English, and, as we have seen, felt very limited by that in many aspects of her life. Her overall relationship with different social systems was colored by this. She was fearful of further interaction, suspicious of asking for help, and afraid of a bad turn of events for herself, given the many stories she heard every day from neighbors in their dealings with schools, the health and mental health system, the courts, and the police. Irma felt there was no way of reducing these experiences that were part of being a Spanish-speaking person in the United States. She did not think there was anything she could do about it other than winning the lottery to "gain some respect."

10. Poverty

- What is your current yearly income from all sources? What was your income in the last 5 years? Do you consider yourself poor? Is it possible for this income to be reduced in the future? How so?
- What are the consequences of poverty or limited income for your life? What are the areas you or others see affected?
- Do you have any plans to maintain or improve your income? How do you or will you do it?
- What are the obstacles to maintain or increase you income?
- Do you know how to reduce those obstacles? How would you do that?

Irma has spent the little money she brought when she came back to the United States and was now receiving only a welfare check that put her clearly below the poverty line. She was surviving with the help of her sister, who paid for some of her necessities and also for the alcohol and cocaine she has been using lately. Not knowing the rules of welfare aid, she believed she could lose this income at any point and felt pressured to do something about it. She has always considered herself poor while in the United States. In Puerto Rico, she lived in a limited-income area but never saw herself as poor. She was well aware of many of the material things she did not have by being poor. She was less aware of other consequences having to do with her many other problems. She had fantasies about meeting a man that could help her better than José or the boyfriends her sister Leonore has had over the years, but she felt could not have access to those men, whom she saw as "doctors or people with good jobs, men not interested in women like me." She could not explain what she meant by women like her.

11. Social network

- Map your social network (See Table 7.1; Sluzki, 1996):
- Has there been a significant change in your social network in the last 2 years? What was the reason? Did it reduce the frequency or number of contacts? Is it possible for your social network to become more limited in the future?

TABLE 7.1

	Daily Contact	Frequent but not Daily Contact	Occasional Contact	Potential Contact
Family				
Friends				
Work				
School				
Health Care System				
Other social activities (religious, sports, volunteer, etc.)				

- Do you have any plans to increase either the frequency or number of contacts in the future? How are you or will you be doing it?
- What are the obstacles to increase either the frequency or number of contacts in the future?
- Do you know how to reduce those obstacles? How would you do that?

Irma's social network included daily contact with her sister Leonore and her son Richard, and her neighbor and friend Alma. She also had frequent contact with other neighbors: Vilma, Ezequiel, Damary, her mother, her daughter Mary, and with the manager of a grocery store nearby. She had occasional contact with a welfare office worker, Ana; the nurse assistant of the pediatrician who was seeing her son due to frequent asthmatic attacks; the physician who diagnosed her with diabetes; her ex-boyfriend José, the father of her son; some friends of her neighbor Ezequiel with whom she had been using drugs and partying lately; and some other people whose names she did not remember, whom she knew through Alma at church. She named as potential contacts a cousin of hers that she was avoiding because she believed this cousin knew about her being raped by another cousin; an aunt of hers who lived in a nearby town; some friends in Puerto Rico she lost contact with; and a possible relationship with a counselor and myself were mentioned as well. Her social network has changed significantly since her move to the United States, and she feared losing her relationship with her sister Leonore, as well as the return of her ex-boyfriend. She considered becoming more involved with the church Alma was attending, but she knew it was going to be "boring" after a while, as has happened with prior attempts at "being a good girl." She heard about a group of women in the neighborhood taking turns at home to take care of their children, but she thought they were mostly Anglo people who she feared would not want to associate with her. She was at a loss regarding how to optimize her social network so as to open new possibilities.

12. Welfare/disability

- Are you currently on welfare? Since when? How you been on welfare before? When? For how long? Have your parents ever been on welfare during their lifetime? For how long? What was the reason for prior period(s) of receiving welfare benefits to end? Is it possible for your current welfare situation to change in the future?
- Are you currently disabled? What is the reason you have been considered disabled? Since when? What was the reason for past periods of disability to end?

Are there any other household family members receiving disability benefits? Since when? Have your parents ever been on disability? What was the reason? For how long? Is it possible for your current disability situation to change?

- Do you have any plans to change your current welfare/disability situation? How are you or will you try to do it?
- What are the obstacles to change your current welfare/disability situation?
- Do you know how to reduce those obstacles? How would you do that?

Irma has temporarily been on welfare help for her younger child for the last 6 months; her welfare status was up for review. Her mother was on welfare while in New York during Irma's childhood for years. She considered applying for disability, knowing that some neighbors were on it, but did not go to the disability office (although she believed she could or should qualify, given her diabetes and her depression). She has a cousin with similar problems who is currently on disability, according to her sister. She would like to be "helped" for a few years to see if she could organize her life differently, but was quite overwhelmed by her many current problems.

PROCESS

The program impacts all of these areas, starting with the utilization of a *form* as a guideline to work with the client on the exploration of current status and future risks of complications, if things were left to their natural evolution in all the domains just mentioned of risk (Table 7.1). The form can be initiated by either a nurse or a social worker in the health clinic, by a clinician or nurse in the mental health or chemical dependency facility, or by a community worker in a community room. Basic information taken from the evaluation just discussed is written on the column "current status" (see Table 7.2).

TABLE 7.2
Risk Reduction Integrated Program

	Current Status	Future Risk	Intervention	Response	Follow-Up	Follow-Up	Follow-Up
1. General health							
2. Mental health							
3. Substance abuse							
4. Education							
5. Work							
6. Housing/transport							
7. Legal issues							
8. Violence							
9. Ethnic/social dissonance							
10. Poverty							
11. Social network							
12. Welfare/disability							

Note. From Pakman (1995, 1997, 2003). Reprinted with permission.

In the case of Irma the column, for each domain, read:

1. Poor understanding of diabetes; unable to participate in self-care; no identified health care provider; inappropriate diet.

2. Empty use of the term *depression;* poorly consolidated therapeutic relationships; stigma of mental illness.

3. Denial of drug abuse problem; unawareness of complications; use of unprescribed medications.

4. Functionally illiterate; poor motivation and no plans to improve.

5. Poor job history; potential skills to be developed (tailoring); no clear plans.

6. Unstable temporary housing situation; unable to use public transportation; intimidated to ask for housing assistance.

7. Legal case pending; no legal counseling assistance.

8. Violent neighborhood; occasional exposure to domestic violence; history of sexual abuse.

9. Recent relocation (functional immigration); poor English.

10. History of long-term poverty; currently below poverty level.

11. Recent changes due to relocation

12. Temporarily on welfare for her child; no disability; history of mother on welfare for years (see Table 7.3).

TABLE 7.3

Social Network	Daily Contact	Frequent but Not Daily Contact	Occasional Contact	Potential Contact
Family	Leonore (sister); Richard (son)	Mother, Mary (daughter)		Claudia (cousin); Laura (aunt)
Friends	Alma (neighbor)	Vilma, Ezequiel, Damary (neighbors)	José (ex-boyfriend); friends of Ezequiel; church friends of Alma	Friends in Puerto Rico
Work				
School				
Health care system			Pediatric nurse (phone: X); PCP (phone: X)	Counselor and myself (phone: X)
Other social activities (religious, sports, volunteer, etc.)		Raul (store manager)	Ana (welfare)	

From the very beginning, the client is part of reflecting on these issues with the person doing the initial risk evaluation. The form is based on an identified patient, given that (in the United States) it is a requirement for medical documentation and most importantly, for reimbursement for services, to identify a main receptor of services. However, the whole program tries to include all relevant social systems that can help in the process of reducing risk as well as to operate on all significant people close to the identified patient, with the understanding that operating on these other people is essential for the overall recovery of the patient, given the intricacy of the ways in which lives are lived and fates are shared.

Surprisingly, the initial effect of this initial evaluation is far from being emotionally negative as some people predicted. It is also powerful enough to elicit an honest and courageous account of the state of affairs, and shows that the professional was not overwhelmed nor disoriented regarding the difficulties. The evaluation reflects, in causal ways, about events in people's lives, and plans interventions. These interventions are planned with the modest goal of reducing the risk for things to get worse for the patient and his family or "intimate social network" (Bloch, personal communication, 1999). It is significant that in starting from these multiproblem situations, assuming this apparent initial pessimistic outlook (based on our version of Murphy's Law) allows both patients and professionals to recover a sensible and modest (but effective) way of being proactive and working toward improvement no matter how bad and discouraging the initial situation is. The pragmatics of the program builds on, and puts to work, the concept that there is always room for improvement, once improvement is redefined as reducing the risk for things to get worse.

The column "future risks" captures the thorough realistic evaluation about how things may get worse in the near future ("a year from now" is used as a parameter).

In the case of Irma this is how it read for each risk domain:

1. Same or increased weight; complications of diabetes (foot, renal, cardiovascular, eye)
2. Increase of depression (suicidality, further social and cognitive deterioration, crises, hospitalizations); chronic depression; increase of anxiety symptoms (panic attacks); reactivation of post-traumatic symptoms.
3. Increase of alcohol and cocaine abuse; development of dependance; continuous or increased use of unprescribed medications; risk of sexually transmitted diseases and unwanted pregnancy as complications of drug abuse instances.
4. Further cognitive deterioration due to lack of stimulation.
5. Continuous unemployment; loss of ability to develop work opportunities; deterioration of current potential skills.
6. Continuous housing in violent, unsafe neighborhoods; lack of independent mobility.
7. Inadequate solution for legal case; potential reoccurrence of delinquent acts; potential incarceration.
8. Further exposure to domestic and/or social violence.
9. Inability to advance English proficiency; further deterioration of cognitive skills.
10. Chronic poverty and its consequences on her children.
11. Loss of current contacts; increase of contacts with similar problems and drug-related social network; lack of further development of potential contacts; poor evaluation of negative consequences of certain relationships and/or inability to distance herself from those.
12. Loss of welfare support; lack of disability support; negative consequences of chronic welfare and/or disability status.

The evaluation is a vertical snapshot of a therapeutic process aimed at reducing both risk in significant domains of patients' lives and professional burnout and consequent ineffectiveness. Clinicians work, between evaluations, with relevant information gathered during evaluations in order to reduce risk. Their initial goals, based on the initial evaluation, are to design simple interventions in order to reduce the risk of things to get worse in different domains.

The initial goals established with Irma, and listed on the "intervention" column, for each domain, were:

1. Regular contact with a Spanish-speaking nurse, associated with a Primary Care Physician; implementation of simple dietary measures; diabetes education; facilitate basic education on sexual practices, contraception, and prevention of STDs.
2. Regular contact with counselor and psychiatrist; rational simple use of psychotropic medication as needed; develop simple skills to identify stressors and predict crises.
3. Basic socially adequate, nonmoralizing education about drug and unprescribed medication use and abuse; early intervention for relapses.
4. Establish early reinforcement opportunities from health education as a starter for further educational steps.
5. Reactivate tailoring skills using limited resources; establish initial contact for formal basic programs to evaluate and develop those skills.
6. Facilitate contact with housing office through temporary help from support agency for mentally ill people.
7. Facilitate contact with agency for public legal representation; work on early recognition of triggers for delinquent acts (addiction, mental health, relational, financial).
8. Early recognition of risk factors for domestic and social violence (relational, housing, drug related).
9. Establish initial contact for adult literacy programs.
10. Establish trusted relationship to help manage meager resources.
11. Make initial steps to increase contact with potential relationships that can further goals stated in other interventions; establish a system to mobilize her closest network on impending crises.
12. Facilitate temporary welfare help; support getting disability help and a rational and, if possible, temporary use of funding.

Further evaluations illustrate to what extent those simple steps were taken, to what extent they were successful, what unexpected difficulties occurred, and what further simple interventions were again presented as simple steps to be taken in order to further reduce risk, regardless of how bad the situation is and how many new problems may have emerged. These simple steps are always listed in the form presented in Table 7.1.

An essential part of the program is that we encourage the form, a visible outcome of an initial future-oriented relationship, to become a part (as the first page) of the record of the mental health or chemical dependency facility, the primary care facility, and/or the community room.

We also encourage the members of these facilities, during each subsequent encounter with the client (regardless of the reason bringing him there at that particular time), to review the form and update at least a few items to see what is happening with that domain in terms of the interventions designed. The professional or staff member involved then checks and dates the "follow-up" column, so as to inform other providers that the intervention of that domain has been discussed and discussion with the patient and/or family members or significant people from his social network. We multiply the effectiveness of the tool by asking any professional reviewing the form with the patient to facilitate the networking with the appropriate agency, either by motivating the patient or family member, or (if time allows) by making a contact him or herself.

We follow up with the client who carries with him or her the reminders of the goals to reduce risk of complications in a folded simple card that becomes the symbol of the work a virtual team of people (which includes the patient) is doing. Patients are also encouraged to have copies of the working form on display at a visible place at home, or to carry the form with them.

Even for illiterate people, the symbolic force of this document of their efforts as a part of a concerted team adds to the pragmatic value of communication among professionals who are part of that virtual team. In this way, evaluations are deemed to show how active the interventions are in reducing risk remain over time, thus reducing risk in significant domains of patient's lives, and focusing the energies of the therapeutic team in a positive way that prevents patients from being overwhelmed by the usually significant number of problems they face.

The form allows different people who are in touch with the patient to work together, even though they are not an actual "team," nor do they have the time to be one. It is in this way that they become a "virtual team" and, most importantly, they start operating as such in the mind of the patient and the family. They are also a team at the actual level of intervention, without everybody having to share the same information, regardless of their hierarchical position in different organizations, and no matter what level of contact with the client or professional knowledge.

In the case of Irma, across a 3-year evolution, as it is usual, new problems appeared that had to be reintroduced in the evaluation, with further steps which incorporated simple interventions, but the initial goals were mostly achieved. She developed a stable relationship with a nurse and had a diminishing number of diabetes-related episodes of hypoglycemia. She developed some initial evidence of retinal problems and started a pattern of regular visits with an ophthalmologist. She remained slightly overweight, but got involved in an exercise program initiated with other members of church. She did not become an enthusiast of church attendance but she developed good friendships with other people who helped her have resources to take care of her son. Her daughter, who reunited with her a year later, became very close to Irma and stabilized herself in school after an initial period of a stormy relationship. Irma decided not to reunite with her ex-boyfriend, and, after asking help from a public legal representative, was given only 6 months of probation for her drug-possession charges. The drug screens that were mandated as a requirement of her probation proved to be a good reminder of her goals regarding abstinence (in spite of her initial anger at being controlled). During that period of abstinence, she started attending the literacy program and did some simple tailoring jobs for her neighbors. A year later she was able to attend a 6-month course at a local school her daughter attended. Her neighbor Alma became temporarily her representative payee and took care of her son while she attended meetings and did initial steps to further her education. She had a temporary relationship with her neighbor Ezequiel, but ended the relationship after he became physically abusive, and the authorities had to be called in twice. She was not able to move to a better neighborhood. Although she considered moving back to Puerto Rico, she decided against it because she wanted to secure more education for her children. Her daughter was becoming a very good student, which raised her hopes of a different future for her children. She maintained a close connection with a counselor and another one that followed her on her leaving the clinic. She also established a close connection with me and used emergency services when at risk for drug abuse relapses. She became interested in HIV education and considered working for a local agency who needed Spanish-speaking personnel.

In many other (so-called "undeveloped") countries, there are no governmental or governmental-supported agencies to help patients in many domain risks; these functions are largely fulfilled, with equal or better efficacy, by the informal social network or by agents of nongovernmental organizations.

We have seen significant advances in terms of risk reduction, in terms of the level of complications of their conditions (medical, mental, and substance dependence) as well as at the level of the social issues these clients were confronting. So far, we have also observed that although different members of the systems involved in helping or working with the person in each domain may be more or less aware of the difficulties in other domains, this program is a more formal mechanism:

- to validate each area of difficulty as serious enough to represent a risk factor for other domains;
- to maintain awareness and focus on these difficulties;
- to realize that unattended further complications will arise from each of them;
- to channel the efforts in a coordinated way so as to increase effectiveness;
- to design and follow up on interventions;
- to involve actively and creatively the client; and
- to avoid being overwhelmed as a professional with the limitations of our own institutional settings and power to be agents of change.

The revolution within the revolution that "May of 1968" called for and seemed to pre-announce led, paradoxically, not to a deepening of transformative social processes but to the demise of the "Other" of capitalism, opening an era in which, neoliberalism has reigned mostly uncontested as a matter of fact ultimate reality. The call for "imagination to power," as the most famous graffiti on the walls of Paris asked for, did not come to be and, on the contrary, we have seen a commodification of society spread among cultures fueled by technological advances in a process enthusiastically celebrated, until September 11th disclosed the inner contradictions of this post-Cold War world. In implementing programs as the one I presented in this chapter, professionals have, however, a modest but encouraging task at hand in their everyday endeavors. As Hallward states (much in the same way as Badiou) in our epigraph, such projects become then ethical ones. They remind us of Antonio

Gramsci's dictum[1] that "it is necessary to direct one's attention violently towards the present as it is, if one wishes to transform it. Pessimism of the intelligence, optimism of the will" (1973, p. 175). It is this "optimism of will" that is at work in the daily engagement of so many mental health professionals who, without access to the academic lights, struggle with the families they serve to improve their chances of social justice, thus extricating each other toward redefining humanness on more solidary terms. There was, after all, another less-famous graffiti on the walls of Paris in 1968 (Besancon, 1968). It read: "The act institutes the consciousness."

REFERENCES

Badiou, A. (2001). *Ethics: An Essay on the Understanding of Evil.* London and New York: Verso.

Besançon, J. (1968). *Les murs ont la parole. Journal Mural Mai, 68.*

Foucault, M. (1978). *Discipline and punish: The birth of the prison.* New York: Random House.

Foucault, M. (1980). *Power/knowledge: Selected interviews & other writings 1972-1977.* New York: Pantheon.

Foucault, M. (1982). Space, knowledge and power. In P. Rabinow (Ed.), *The Foucault reader.* New York: Pantheon.

Gramsci, A. (1973). *Letters from prison.* New York : Harper & Row.

LeGoff, J. (1998). *Le Monde* [Interview]. May 25.

Orwell, G. (1949). *Nineteen Eighty Four.* London: Sacker & Warburg.

Pakman, M. (1995). Therapy in contexts of poverty and ethnic dissonance: Constructivism and social constructionism as methodologies for action. *Journal of Systemic Therapies, 14*(4).

Pakman, M. (1998a). Education and therapy in cultural borderlands: A call for critical social practices in human services. *Journal of Systemic Therapies, 17*(1), 18–30.

Pakman, M. (1998). *The micro-politics of emotional traditions.* Paper presented at University of Bergamo, Bergamo, Italy.

Pakman, M. (1999). Designing constructive therapies in community mental health: Poetics and micro-politics in and beyond the consulting room. *Journal of Marital and Family Therapy, 25*(1), 83–98.

Pakman, M. (2003). A systemic frame for mental health practices. In P. S. Proski & D. V. Keith (Eds.), *Family therapy as an alternative to medication: An appraisal of pharmland* (pp. 93–110). New York: Brunner-Routledge.

Sluzki, C. (1995). Families, Networks and Other Strange Shapes. In *AFTA Newsletter*, 19.

Sluzki, C. (1996). *La red social: Frontera de la terapia sistemica.* Barcelona: GEDISA.

Wallerstein, I. (2002). New revolts against the system. *New Left Review, 18,* 29–39.

Zizek, S. (Ed.). (1994). *Mapping ideology,* London and New York: Verso.

---

[1]See "On daydreams and fantasies. They show lack of character and passivity. One imagines that something has happened to upset the mechanism of necessity. One's own initiative has become free. Everything is easy. One can do whatever one wants, and one wants a whole series of things which at present one lacks. It is basically the present turned on its head which is projected into the future. Everything repressed is unleashed. On the contrary, it is necessary to direct one's attention violently towards the present as it is, if one wishes to transform it. Pessimism of the intelligence, optimism of the will" (Passato, 1932, p. 6). See also Romain Rolland's maxim, "Pessimism of the intelligence, optimism of the will" (cited in Gramsci, 1973, p. 175) was made into something of a programmatic slogan as early as 1919, by Gramsci in the pages of *Ordine Nuovo.*

8

Foundation Concepts for Social Justice-Based Therapy: Critical Consciousness, Accountability, and Empowerment

Rhea Almeida
Ken Dolan-Del Vecchio
Institute for Family Services, Somerset, NJ

Lynn Parker
University of Denver, Colorado

From its inception, the family therapy movement emerged as a radically different way to address the task of healing in the mental health field (Ackerman, 1937; Bowen, 1978; Haley, 1963; Jackson, 1957; Satir, 1964; Selvini-Palazzoli, Boscolo, Cecchin, & Prata, 1978; Watzlawick, 1976; Whitaker & Bumberry, 1988). This movement built on early social work models that viewed the unit of intervention to be greater than the individual. A variety of systemic models emerged, each offering their unique conceptual and technical contributions (Alexander & Parsons, 1982; Madanes, 1981; Andersen, 1987; Anderson & Goolishian, 1988; Carter & McGoldrick, 1988; de Shazer, 1985; Minuchin & Fishman, 1981; Napier, 1987; White & Epston, 1990). Although some of these models have addressed the impact of social realities connected to gender, race, class, and sexual orientation, few have addressed the systematic ways in which the intersectionality[1] (Crenshaw, 1997) of these factors shape family and community life.

We begin the chapter with a brief review of literature and programs that incorporate social justice principles in therapeutic work. At the request of the book's editor, we describe one comprehensive therapeutic program, the Cultural Context Model, which has social justice as its foundation. We do this with some degree of wariness because it has been our experience that when given a description some practitioners focus so exclusively on the differences between this model and traditional practice structures that they become overwhelmed. They find themselves saying, "A social justice-based model is a great idea, but impractical within my current practice situation." In other words, they lose sight of the fact that the Cultural Context

---

[1]Intersectionality refers to an analysis of the dynamic interplay of one's gender, race, sexual orientation, age, disability status, and other diversity characteristics upon multiple aspects of one's identity; including the resources and lack of resources these differences convey upon the individual within their current societal context. This term is used by scholars of the anti-racist/colonization demography.

Model is *one way* of implementing the foundation principles, but not *the only way*. In short, they release themselves from the fundamental challenge posed by this chapter, the challenge to implement social justice principles within *all practice settings*. Don't let this happen to you.

Next, we describe what we believe to be the fundamental principles of social justice-based practice, providing illustrative examples. It is our hope that readers will use this discussion as a springboard for their initiative as they work to create social justice-based innovations within their own practices.

BACKGROUND: FAMILY THERAPY AND SOCIAL JUSTICE

While there exists an ever-expanding body of scholarship by anti-racist, feminist social theorists (Collins, 1986; Crenshaw, 1997; Jaggar, 1983; Moraga & Anzaldua, 1983; Woo, 1985) the work of these theorists has yet to make an impact upon the ways in which most family therapists and other mental health professionals practice. Why? Clearly we live in conservative times. The family therapy and mental health fields reflect the current social and political climate. Moreover, the field of family therapy, like most academic and professional disciplines, adheres to a worldview that suffers from "patriarchal fragmentation." Patriarchy depends on "this" being separate from "that," as difference and separation provide the rudiments of hierarchy. In other words, the differences between men and Women, Blacks and Whites, and straights and queers must be punctuated and rigidly ordained in order for the pyramid of privilege to stand. The compartmentalizing pedagogy to the world required by patriarchy keeps most family therapists and therapists in general, despite their often avowed systemic perspective, at a distance from the work of sociopolitical theorists. Incorporating progressive social ideology into family therapy and mental health praxis challenges patriarchy on a number of levels, creating second-order changes that benefit everyone.

The simultaneous accounting for current and historical repercussions of oppressive social forces, including sexism, racism, homophobia, and classism is what we term a "postcolonial analysis." It is important to note that the prefix "post" is not meant to imply that colonialism is a past, historical phenomenon, but rather a "meta" perspective. A postcolonial analysis recommends that therapists consistently attend to their clients' diversity of backgrounds, including their communities' experiences of oppression *and privilege*, as a fundamental part of the healing endeavor. We italicize privilege in the previous sentence because the field has made some headway in acknowledging oppression, but we have a long way to go toward acknowledging and challenging privilege.

In critical psychology and social work, postcolonial theory has been strongly influenced by Fanon (1963, 1964), Foucault (1975, 1977, 1979), and Spivak (1991). Duran and Duran (1995) and Yellowbird (1995, 2001) exemplify this analysis in their work with First Nations Peoples. For example, they offer therapeutic practices that emphasize liberation by acknowledging the Native American genocide and its intergenerational impact. More specifically, they connect a client family's experience of domestic violence and substance abuse to their multigenerational history of *violent colonization*. This history includes the community's exile onto reservations and the mass kidnapping of their children into Christian boarding homes, where a myriad of inhuman offenses were perpetrated. Highlighting this history when a family describes the issues for which they have sought therapy authenticates the therapeutic endeavor by bringing it in line with the family's longstanding efforts toward cultural resistance and survival.

Similarly, an examination of domestic violence and/or incest in the African American community should prompt therapists to consider the history of slavery and racism in America. In other words, the holocaust of slavery perpetrated by Whites against African Americans, as well as White America's ongoing assaults against communities of color, need to be acknowledged as part of any credible effort to address domestic or youth community violence within an African American family. Contextualizing the family's presenting crisis within the larger crucible of historical and contemporary public assaults against people of color brings integrity to the helping process and allows the multiple challenges facing each family member to be identified, evaluated, and addressed. Introducing Joy Leary's "post-traumatic slave syndrome" would be one way to begin a discussion of the pressures facing such a family (Leary, 2002).

Acknowledging pressures from outside the family does not discount the existence of patriarchy within the African American community, nor does it mean that perpetrators of abuse are not held accountable. Much of the controversy surrounding incest and domestic violence in the African American community is driven by an either–or approach to gender and race. Inequities related to gender (sexism) are often obscured in the effort to highlight the injustices of racism.

Patriarchy, White supremacy, homophobia, and other oppressions need to be addressed simultaneously so that the safety of women and children is never given less emphasis and priority than the safety of men.

We recommend drawing upon the vast array of scholarship that binds race, gender, and White supremacy to begin this discussion. Toni Morrison's The *Bluest Eye* and *Tar Baby,* bell hooks and Cornell West's *Breaking Bread,* Nathan McCall's *Makes me Wanna Holler,* Maxine Hong Kingston's *Woman Warrior,* Arundati Roy's *Power Politics,* and Isabelle Allende's *House of the Spirits* are just a few examples. Select chapters to read together or ask your clients to read the entire book (depending on their abilities) and then discuss the threads that inform identities and problems.

Present day domination does not occur in a vacuum. Exploitation and domination are part of all national, ethnic, and cultural legacies. Illuminating this reality broadens understanding of the ways we replicate domination. A male Irish employer's domination of his Puerto Rican employee can be placed alongside 500 years of British colonization in Ireland and numerous other countries. The Irish's invitation into "Whiteness" within the United States in order to prevent their alliance with Blacks and First Nations Peoples is another important reference point. Raising these historical realities into conversation and, thereby, consciousness provides employers (and employees) with a more informed and compelling challenge: Will they choose to perpetuate or transform such legacies? In the therapeutic setting, raising these historical realities in a matter-of-fact manner provides a framework for making sense of clients' present day issues. Seeing the connection between individual problems and the broader context helps clients recognize that they are part of a network of domination. This frees them from the burden of individual pathology and instead empowers them toward change through social action.

Prilleltensky (1996) and Fowers and Richardson (1996) argue that an ethical framework promoting justice and collaboration must recognize families as open social systems, interdependent with the larger social environment. They maintain that while

ALMEIDA, DOLAN-DEL VECCHIO, PARKER

family therapists were instrumental in introducing notions of justice and collaboration, they continued the convention of confining interventions to the interior of family interactions. These authors suggest the need for therapists to bring social and community action directly into the work of therapy. This includes discussing extrafamilial realities and including extrafamilial participants as part of the normative therapeutic process. Therapists can accomplish this in part through genogram work as well as the use of power and control wheels, and a list of traditional and expanded gendered norms. All of these tools highlight and begin to name both internal and external forces of power, privilege, and oppression. Liberation both within and beyond family boundaries is both the goal of therapy and the work entailed in healing families.

During the last two decades, family therapy approaches that recognize the importance of gender, sexual orientation, class, culture, and race have emerged (Avis & Turner, 1996; Bograd, 1990, 1999; Boyd-Franklin, 1989; Green & Laird, 1996; Hare-Mustin, 1994; Laird, 1989; McGoldrick, 1998; Pinderhughes, 1989; Walters, Carter, Papp, & Silverstein, 1988; Weingarten, 1991, 1992, 1995, 1998). This scholarship, however, typically privileges one discourse of oppression over others, reflecting the manner in which institutions of domination pit marginalized groups against one another instead of addressing the larger systemic pattern. Readers examine sexism or racism or homophobia but rarely the ways in which these systems of interlocking oppression are interconnected.

There are theorist practitioners around the world who have gone farther toward developing intervention models that address these interlocking oppressions. Unfortunately, their work is unknown to most American family therapists and mental health care providers, who generally look no farther than the publications of mainstream, White, heterosexual, American theorists when seeking edification. We believe it is of crucial importance to give the ideas of those outside the mainstream heightened visibility.

The "Just Therapy" team in New Zealand, represented by Kiwi Tamasese and Charles Waldegrave, is one such group of practitioners. Waldegrave (1990) and Tamasese and Waldegrave (1993) describe a therapeutic paradigm driven by a vision of social justice. The guiding principles of this New Zealand team's work with the Maori, as well as other cultural groups, are spirituality, simplicity, and justice. Tamasese and Waldegrave respond to colonialism, patriarchy, and racism by structuring the agency where they practice in a way that counters these oppressive forces. More specifically, at their agency White staff are held accountable to staff of color and male staff are held accountable to female staff when they enact race and gender-based aggressions. This structural dynamic keeps the group moving toward accountability and liberation, and lessens the tendency of staff to unwittingly or purposely replicate their society's racist and sexist aggressions in their delivery of client services.

A growing body of literature promotes family therapy approaches that address the intertwined ways in which sexism, racism, homophobia, and colonization contribute to family conflicts. This literature describes how dismantling privilege and resisting oppression contribute to relational healing (Almeida, 1993; Almeida, 2003; Almeida, Woods, & Messineo, & Font, 1998; Almeida & Dolan-Del Vecchio, 1999; Almeida & Hudak, 2002; Dolan-Del Vecchio, 1998; Dolan-Del Vecchio & Lockard, 2004; Almeida & Durkin, 1999; Hernandez, 2000; Hernandez, Almeida, & Dolan-Del Vecchio, 2004; Watts-Jones, 2002). According to Almeida (1998), addressing families' health (physical and mental) in context involves taking into account structural issues:

The collective of economic and political power by European and American forces descends from a shared and legitimized process of slavery and colonial expansion. This concentration of economic and political power continues today, albeit in better-organized systems of delivery. This misappropriation occurs through the organized control of job opportunities, housing market, medical benefits, political power, and general control of market resources. This creates life-threatening situations for women of color and their children. (pp. 12–13)

ONE APPROACH TO SOCIAL JUSTICE-BASED THERAPY: THE CULTURAL CONTEXT MODEL

The Cultural Context Model is a social justice-based approach to therapy initiated in 1981 by Rhea Almeida and her team at The Institute for Family Services in Somerset, New Jersey. The model offers a reformulation of both the structure of the service delivery system and the process of therapy in an effort to make therapy a journey of liberation and healing instead of a journey toward renewed compliance and acquiescence to society's everyday oppressive expectations. Parker's (2003) research on this model reflects these transformative patterns. As mentioned earlier, we present a description of the model hoping you will look for ways to replicate or borrow pieces of it, rather than feel defeated by the challenge of recreating it entirely within the structure of your tradition-bound practice institution.

Following the brief overview of the Cultural Context Model, we discuss the model's guiding principles: *critical consciousness, accountability, and empowerment*. We'll provide additional examples of these principles in action within clinical, organizational, and community intervention.

THE CULTURAL CONTEXT MODEL

The Cultural Context Model is an expanded family therapy paradigm that gives clients a new awareness of the societal patterns that contribute to their presenting difficulties. The model offers solutions to families by connecting them to a community that promotes liberation. As clients gain knowledge and support from the community, they work within this collective to challenge the systems of power, privilege, and oppression that are the foundation of many presenting problems.

A guiding premise of the Cultural Context Model is that the liberation of women is intrinsically tied to the accountability of men, and, more broadly, the liberation of oppressed peoples is linked to the accountability of those who oppress them. Therefore, dismantling the power imbalances and restructuring the power that exists between men and women from diverse social locations is a fundamental goal of therapeutic change.

In contrast to the Cultural Context Model, individual, couple, and even most approaches to family therapy limit the experiences of change to the interior of family life. This type of structural change maintains the mythology that pathology and therapeutic change occur within individuals and families in order to support society's healthy status quo.

We believe that the pathologies of sexism, racism, homophobia, classism, capitalism, and the "might makes right" mentality of colonialism are far bigger than any one family. Change, therefore, requires intervention that bridges family members to the larger world in a way that sows the seeds of healing in both. The Cultural Context Model provides the individual woman with a coalition of women, thereby increasing her power. It provides the individual man with a coalition of men who simultaneously challenge and support him as he struggles to adopt attitudes and behaviors that are more loving and relationally responsible than the traditional male patterns he has been socialized to enact. Change occurs at the family/community boundary, positively impacting both.

The model has seven components:

1. Orientation
2. Sponsorship
3. Socioeducation
4. Culture circles
5. Family process
6. Graduation
7. Community advocacy.

Think of these components as strands of thread that together make up the fabric of the model. We have teased those strands apart for the purpose of describing them, but in reality they occur simultaneously and are tightly interwoven. In this chapter we emphasize the first five components: orientation, sponsorship, socioeducation, culture circles, and family process. For a more complete discussion of the Cultural Context Model, see Almeida et al. (1998) and Almeida (2003).

1. Orientation (See Fig. 8.1)

Upon intake, each family is introduced to at least two therapists; one who will be behind the one-way mirror in the viewing room, the other in the consultation room with the family. The therapist in the consultation room is linked by a microphone in his or her ear to the therapist in the viewing room. All therapy is accomplished with at least one therapist in the viewing room—most of the time there is a viewing team that includes multiple therapists and interns (Hernandez, 2004). The viewing team's job is to hold the therapeutic process accountable to the experiences of people across the spectrum of diversity, including people of color, queers, and women. The therapist who is physically present with the family in the consultation room, therefore, receives through the microphone in his or her ear ongoing suggestions from the viewing team.

After a basic genogram is constructed with the entire family present, all family members join small, ongoing groups we call culture circles. Culture circles are same-sex groups made up of members of many client families. Culture circles are the model's primary therapeutic vehicle.

2. Sponsorship

Whenever men are present in a therapeutic session, so are male sponsors. Think of sponsors as a community of mentors and role models who demonstrate a version of manhood we can all live with. These are men who model vulnerability, nurturing, gentleness, and empathy for others. They show support to the other men in a thera-

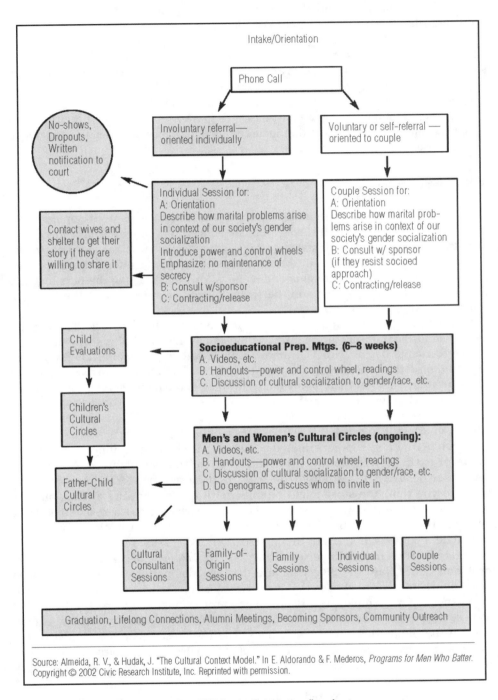

Intake/Orientation

Phone Call

No-shows, Dropouts, Written notification to court

Involuntary referral—oriented individually

Voluntary or self-referral—oriented to couple

Contact wives and shelter to get their story if they are willing to share it

Individual Session for:
A: Orientation
Describe how marital problems arise in context of our society's gender socialization
Introduce power and control wheels
Emphasize: no maintenance of secrecy
B: Consult w/sponsor
C: Contracting/release

Couple Session for:
A: Orientation
Describe how marital problems arise in context of our society's gender socialization
B: Consult w/ sponsor (if they resist socioed approach)
C: Contracting/release

Child Evaluations

Socioeducational Prep. Mtgs. (6–8 weeks)
A. Videos, etc.
B. Handouts—power and control wheel, readings
C. Discussion of cultural socialization to gender/race, etc.

Children's Cultural Circles

Men's and Women's Cultural Circles (ongoing):
A. Videos, etc.
B. Handouts—power and control wheel, readings
C. Discussion of cultural socialization to gender/race, etc.
D. Do genograms, discuss whom to invite in

Father-Child Cultural Circles

Cultural Consultant Sessions

Family-of-Origin Sessions

Family Sessions

Individual Sessions

Couple Sessions

Graduation, Lifelong Connections, Alumni Meetings, Becoming Sponsors, Community Outreach

Source: Almeida, R. V., & Hudak, J. "The Cultural Context Model." In E. Aldorando & F. Mederos, *Programs for Men Who Batter.* Copyright © 2002 Civic Research Institute, Inc. Reprinted with permission.

FIG. 8.1. CCM Intake/Orientation flowchart.

peutic session—and it's a kind of support that includes the expectation that men will be responsible toward their partners and families.

Most sponsors are men who decided at the conclusion of their own therapeutic work to continue their involvement with the program on a volunteer basis. Some sponsors started out as volunteers and received 12 weeks of socioeducational training re: the social forces that constrain people's lives, including institutionalized racism, male dominance, homophobia, and class discrimination.

Sponsors function as nonpaid partners with therapists. They share their own experiences and provide support that includes accountability both inside and outside therapy sessions.

3. Socioeducation

Socioeducation is the presentation of cultural stories (excerpts from popular movies, books, articles, and lyrics from popular songs, as well as power and control wheels; see Appendix) as a starting place for consciousness raising discussions about gender, race, culture, and sexual orientation. Socioeducation shifts clients' focus away from their own thoughts and feelings toward balancing the personal and the political, the intrapsychic and the social, clients' own needs and the needs of those with whom they are bonded.

Consider a vignette from the movie *The Great Santini,* where male domination and female subordination are normalized within family life. The film segment that is shown to clients begins with The Great Santini's wife imploring her children to attend to their father's needs and desires. They salute him upon his arrival from duty at the airstrip. They eat their family dinner with all of the focus, service, and conversation centered on "The Great Santini." After the father, The Great Santini, challenges his 17-year-old son to a game of basketball and loses, he assaults his son and wife in an attempt to regain his sense of masculinity.

Watching the film clip generates discussion that clients can apply to their own lives. For example, after showing this film clip to clients we might ask, "What does this father believe is owed him by his wife, his son, and the world?" And, "In what ways do you think the story might be different if the family were a Black military family or a White family where the father was working class and unemployed?" "What can you take from this film and our discussion to your own lives?" The goal is to initiate a conversation about the intersection of diversity and power.

Socioeducation moves the discussion away from a particular family's presenting problems and toward the bigger picture that includes patterns across many families. Cultural pieces are chosen that initiate discussions relevant to each clients' circumstances. For example, an African American man might say that the history of slavery requires that women honor the status of men to counter the racism experience in the public domain of men's lives. The therapists might present excerpts from films such as *Warrior Marks, Straight out of Brooklyn,* and *Celebration of Our Lives* in order to start a conversation about the experience of dealing with the many forms of oppression simultaneously.

Another commonly presented dilemma involves religion. Many women and men of the Islamic faith argue for the spiritual necessity of veiling or cloistering their adolescent daughters. We use videotapes of our Muslim sponsors and notable Arab feminists who challenge patriarchal interpretations of the Koran. It is important to note that the prophet Mohammed had only daughters and honored each of them. A movie titled *Morning Voices* is also useful. It depicts the dilemmas faced by young women of the Muslim faith struggling to survive in an anti-Muslim Western culture.

The possibilities for sources of socioeducational materials are limited only by the therapist's imagination. The film and video catalogue from Women Make Movies[2] offers a rich array of diverse productions on women from numerous cultures. This is one of a number of great resources for therapists interested in using the medium of film to expand the context of therapy (Almeida, 1998).

4. Culture Circles

Borrowed from Freire (1970), we use the term *culture circle* to describe a heterogeneous helping community that includes members of families who come for treatment, a team of therapists, and sponsors.

We create our culture circles by separating families by gender after the first interview and having them each join a circle. There are women's, men's, children's, and adolescents' culture circles, all containing persons of mixed ages, social classes, races, and sexual orientations.

Members of the same culture circle might happen to have different life circumstances and challenges. Some experience difficulty at work, whereas others may not have work; some experience violence, and others may struggle with single parenthood. We do not assign clients to culture circles according to diagnostic category or presenting problem. It is our belief that segregation in this manner is harmful as it rigidifies clients' identification with problems or diagnoses, compartmentalizing rather than expanding their sense of being.

Most therapy occurs within these same-sex culture circles. Intermittent family or couple sessions are done in the presence of the entire community, consisting of both men's and women's culture circles.

Very generally speaking, women's culture circles empower members by helping them prioritize their needs, dreams, and desires at a level they have been taught to reserve only for others. They are further encouraged to experience the full range of emotions, especially anger, in healthy ways. Empowerment also includes different types of social action that mobilize women in families. This includes women helping one another with legal actions, advocating for improved work conditions, sharing in the daily dilemmas of raising children, and working as a community to better the lives of women and children.

Very generally speaking again, men's culture circles focus the participants on relational responsibilities rather than self-serving initiatives. Participants are encouraged to embrace and experience the full range of emotions, particularly those emotions (e.g., fear, sadness, insecurity) men frequently avoid due to their traditional commitment to stoicism and control. They are also encouraged to become involved with activist efforts toward ending war, racism, domestic and dating abuse, homophobia, and other forms of violence.

---

[2]Established in 1972 to address the underrepresentation and misrepresentation of women in the media industry, Women Make Movies (www.wmm.com) is a multicultural, multiracial, nonprofit media arts organization that facilitates the production, promotion, and exhibition of independent films and videotapes by and about women. The film and video catalogue, a great resource on women's films, is available on request online or from Women Make Movies, 462 Broadway Suite 500WS, New York, New York 10013.

5. Family Process

The Cultural Context model links families to one another (via culture circles), breaking down perceived barriers around each nuclear family. Within this multifamily, multitherapist, community milieu, clients are helped to examine race, gender, class, and other systemic patterns that contribute to their dilemmas.

Numerous family therapy interventions, as well as contributions from feminist family therapists, are utilized within the culture circles. Couple and family sessions take place surrounded by the culture circles that include each family member. Consequently, a broad community comprised of several culture circles holds the family's process. The walls of the therapy room are further extended by inviting other significant persons into the therapeutic process as needed, including community and religious leaders. The model works to dismantle traditional rules about privacy and access to power and social opportunity by creating open dialogues that focus on principles of empowerment and the need for accountability over time. This structure recasts what was considered "private" in personal and family life in order for participants to benefit from the contributions made possible by a more "public" examination and exchange. It also levels power hierarchies between diverse client populations, thus liberating (i.e., providing a legitimate forum for, and thus empowering) the perspectives of traditionally subjugated groups.

Because the Cultural Context Model addresses family issues in the presence of a community of clients and sponsors, learning about the model often raise questions about confidentiality. From our perspective, confidentiality is too frequently used as a way to preserve patriarchal control. This highly regarded ethical–legal value evolved out of mental health systems defined by men for men. We are careful to share information judiciously to ensure safety for all clients. Clients feel safe working within the context of a larger community setting because they develop relationships with community members during the early phase of treatment. Of course, all have consented to this process.

CASE EXAMPLES

Following are two case examples illustrating the Cultural Context Model in action. Please do not mistake the brevity of the case descriptions for simplicity of process. The descriptions are meant to provide a window onto the types of resolutions that can be achieved rather than a comprehensive inventory of the work such changes require of all involved parties. Please note the manner in which the culture circles mobilize resources that would never be available within the confines of traditionally structured practice, as well as the interplay of critical consciousness, accountability, and empowerment in creating healing. The culture circles foster a nonlinear process of healing. There is not a healer and a recipient of healing, but rather a community who strive for healing together, each giving and receiving simultaneously.

Case Example #1. Juan, a Mexican immigrant was being exploited at his work place (a food store) via working extremely long hours and no benefits. Due to his undocumented status, he believed he had no rights. Juan's culture circle, a culturally diverse group of men, supported him by exploring his financial options to open his own store, and providing him with legal options. The exploration with his group helped him acquire a small business loan and open his own store. This big step (i.e., a form of social action, taken in a context of support), which is unheard of in most therapeutic programs, offered Juan the pride and economic stability that he hoped for in his journey to this country.

Case Example #2. Anil, an Asian Indian man, systematically controlled his wife—financially, emotionally, and through requiring her to perform all of the second shift responsibilities for their family. Both of them worked outside of the home, with the wife generating half of their income. In order to right the previous inequity and controlling behavior of the husband, the therapeutic team together with the couple's respective culture circles required that Anil relinquish financial control of 50% of their assets so that the wife could, in partnership with other advisors of her choosing, take a greater share of responsibility for managing the finances. The husband was also required to pay for a list of home improvements that the wife felt were needed as reparation for his controlling behavior, since he had denied her these basic family entitlements throughout their married life. Reparations are viewed as a way that people can bring equity to relationships and begin the process of healing past wrongs. Also essential to the healing of their inequitable relationship was Anil's commitment to become an equal partner in second shift responsibilities (e.g., child, elder, and house care, food shopping and preparation, etc.).

These cases illustrate the benefit of a community treatment format where members can be held accountable to each other as well as the treatment team to create and maintain more just and equitable relationships by dismantling hierarchies of power and dominance. Traditional treatment formats with one therapist for an individual, couple, or family do not afford accountability (i.e., those who will both challenge the status quo and support the changes). These formats do not (cannot) affect justice issues. It takes many people to hold onto the memory of a couple's conflicts, do research that helps partners identify all the options available, check on partners between sessions to see how they are making progress toward agreed-upon changes, listen to partners' discomfort and offer ideas, praise them for following through, and challenge them when they go back on their word. In a community-based approach such as the Cultural Context Model, critical consciousness, accountability, and empowerment go hand in hand.

FOUNDATION CONCEPTS AND MORE ILLUSTRATIVE EXAMPLES

The remainder of the chapter is devoted to describing and providing examples of how to incorporate *critical consciousness, accountability,* and *empowerment,* the guiding principles for a social justice approach to therapy, into therapeutic work,. Because these principles are foreign to most of the institutions that comprise our society, expect resistance to implementing them within all traditional practice settings, including university-based clinical settings, mental health agencies, counseling programs within religious institutions, hospital settings, and managed care funded practices. Implementing social justice-driven practice strategies requires you, therefore, to be a risk taker.

Timing and persistence is often key. One of the authors, for example, was called on to develop and deliver a series of "diversity trainings" for the transnational corporation where he is employed. He took this opportunity to craft a workshop that was quite different from most corporate diversity programs because it included socioeducation on White male heterosexual privilege and its impact upon working groups. The program was well received by workers and middle management, and was therefore eventually delivered to thousands of employees. The author wondered whether those at the highest executive tier of the company would welcome the workshop due to the frank manner in which it addressed privilege. But he also knew that senior executives generally care little about the content of such programs as long as they are well received, minimally expensive, and contribute to the company's "diversity objectives." The senior executives continued to promote the workshops to their work groups and the socioeducation introduced therein sparked changes within the ways several areas functioned. Although the corporation was certainly not fundamentally changed, pockets of resistance to institutionalized inequities were fortified.

Social justice has never been part of the mainstream within our society. Rather it is furthered by the courageous and inventive work of those who are willing to risk upsetting business as usual in order to promote the making of a more just world.

CRITICAL CONSCIOUSNESS: RECOGNIZING THE SOCIOPOLITICAL CONTEXT OF DAILY LIFE

Critical consciousness is an awareness of the sociopolitical context of daily life. It involves illuminating the often taken-for-granted realities about the way the world operates—for example, the manner in which family therapy and mental health service delivery systems are structured according to hierarchies of class, profession, gender, race, sexual orientation, and disability status. Developing critical consciousness is essential for the therapist if he or she wants to resist replicating domination within intervention practices. It is essential for clients to gain a comprehensive (or meta) perspective on the distress they're experiencing.

Families are open systems, and this reality can and should be leveraged in the service of healing. Individual therapy, most forms of family therapy, and traditionally structured group therapies, to which clients are assigned according to presenting problem, preserve the myth that family and mental health problems are essentially bound within the interior lives of individuals and families. When a therapist meets alone in her office with a man to discuss the challenges he faces negotiating a reasonable time to leave work so he can have time and energy for the relationship with his wife and children, the struggle is too often understood to be his alone (or perhaps his family's alone). When a therapist invites this man to meet with three other men, from diverse backgrounds, to discuss the pressures of life within a world driven by (family unfriendly) corporate values, the problem is understood and approached differently. Although there remain individual choices to be made, collective experiences and vision afford this man a much-expanded perspective. We cannot overemphasize the power of linking clients into collectives. Traditional therapeutic structures (e.g., individual, couples, and even family therapy) limit the experience of change to the interior of family (or individual) life, forwarding the notion of change as a force driven by individual action. Accordingly, the changes mostly maintain the status quo within hierarchies of power and privilege.

In contrast, therapists working from a social justice paradigm must challenge themselves to expand the therapeutic context by working with collectives of individuals/families wherever possible and/or by inviting others into sessions who can provide feedback and will act as voices of accountability for the changes family members are attempting to make. In order to heal or change families fundamentally, therapists must address the ways in which institutionalized, daily realities connected to race, gender, class, and sexual orientation shape family life.

What stops therapists from including others in therapeutic settings? Most often it is our own fear and lack of ability to articulate well the benefits of including others. Also, it can be the belief that change is an individual, internally driven enterprise. Much of psychology and even social work and family therapy training are still deeply grounded in individualism. Finally, there is great pressure to conform to the therapist-as-capitalist, beholden to the payor–reimbursement system of insurance companies that pay the highest fee for individual therapy. While family and group therapy advocates more than 20 years ago argued for the inclusion of "more than the individual" in effective treatment, these same activists did not go the step further and demand that the monetary value of individual sessions should be less than or, at most, the same as group and family sessions. The connection between efficacy and reimbursement rate is currently inverted. Research has consistently pointed to the fact that families heal in connection and become more symptomatic in isolation.

Individualism remains a central value within U.S. culture, guiding much of national policymaking. Of course, in all settings, clients must consent to the process of including others in their therapeutic work. However, critical to obtaining consent is the social/political ideology of the therapist. The therapist has to be firmly rooted (or at least intensely interested) in the perspective that holds that personal dilemmas are largely located and can only be effectively solved by addressing the broader social and political systems within which they are embedded. Therapists are wise to consider the ways that the very notion of privacy (a patriarchal mechanism of control) protects not the family members, as it is assumed, but the status quo that continues to oppress them. A good question for clients (and therapists) who are reluctant regarding a collectivist approach is: "what would be the worst imaginable outcome if your personal information were shared with others?" Most answers tend to be some variation on the theme that clients fear they'll loose face or their control over their situation or others. The responses given offer a focus for conversation and insight into why clients currently feel stuck. In other words, trying to save face or maintain control often is part of the problem rather than a liberating solution.

Normal family interaction takes place within a societal context that teaches differential valuing of people according to identity characteristics: skin color, gender, sexual orientation, immigrant status, and class. These variables infuse family interactions with patterns of inequality that are too often unacknowledged and unchallenged. We maintain that unwrapping these patterns is crucial to healing. Because family processes are inextricably linked to their larger social contexts, family intervention must incorporate social systems of accountability and empowerment that are bigger than a single family. It is the linking of multiple family circles, some of whom have gained critical consciousness, which creates a context of accountability and empowerment. This decisive component is missing from most therapeutic models.

A social justice paradigm of family therapy, then, views liberation as a key component in the healing process. In order for liberation to occur for all members of a family, accountability and empowerment need to operate simultaneously. Personal and social liberation can only occur when collectives of individuals and families begin to decipher mechanisms of power, privilege, oppression, and dehumanization (Almeida, 2003; Freire, 1978), understand how power relationships shape people's perceptions and experiences, and identify how they can assume a role in social change. For example, a coalition of women is needed to provide the individual woman an increase in power (empowerment). Simultaneously, the individual man needs a coalition of men who will challenge male privilege and also support him as he struggles to change. These coalitions alter the boundaries and power dynamics that preserve the status quo of family life. Grouping women or men together may seem like a simple intervention. However, the result is powerful when people begin to deconstruct their personal stories and to locate themselves in the social and political world in a conscious community of listeners and responders. Accordingly, we suggest that therapists in all settings should challenge themselves to find ways to expand the treatment unit from a singular one to that of a collective process. This may occur by separating family members into larger gatherings/groups of men, women, and children to emphasize the notion of a family as an open (vs. closed) unit. Or it may occur by inviting in relevant community representatives (e.g., ministers, police officers, someone with a different perspective). Including others shifts expectations for change away from the psychology of individual autonomy to that of collective consciousness. Of course all of this is always done with clients' consent. If therapists are reluctant to include others, clients will also be.

INTEGRATING SOCIOEDUCATION INTO THE PRACTICE OF FAMILY THERAPY

As described earlier, socioeducation alters the perspective with which clients enter therapy. The dynamics of diversity and power will rarely be mentioned by clients because this is not the stuff of polite conversation within our society. Examining these matters is, however, essential to the task of developing critical consciousness and changing family dynamics. For example, a conversation with a middle-aged, socially conservative, Cuban woman who is struggling with her Americanized teenage daughter might be augmented by showing film clips from *Real Women Have Curves*. The film stimulates conversations on a range of topics such as the depiction of Latinas in film, the relationship between mothers and daughters, and the meaning of desire and being desired for women who are thin, fair haired, and fair skinned, as opposed to women who might be moderate to heavy in stature, dark haired and dark skinned. Therapists might inquire about the forces responsible for creating these standards (i.e., men, women, or film capitalists). Then, based on who defines these standards, the therapist might ask, "How can women take back current social definitions for their bodies?"

Films can be used to portray and underline pertinent issues such as domestic violence (e.g., *Sleeping With the Enemy* and *Straight Out of Brooklyn*), gendered expressions of loss and grief (e.g., *Steel Magnolias*), familial and societal oppression of gays (e.g., *Torch song Trilogy*) and the impact of colonization (e.g., *Dirty Pretty Things*). Films vignettes are used jointly with other socioeducational tools (power and control wheels—see Appendix) all of which offer clients and therapists a way to locate the political essence of their personal experience. Viewing the relevant wheel, clients are instructed to identify how they have used or experienced power and control in their intimate (and work) relationships. Incorporating socioeducation into the therapeutic process helps clients (and therapists) see that clinical practice is context bound and inseparable from societal dynamics of dominance and subordination.

CRITICAL CONSCIOUSNESS: THE INTEGRATION OF COLLECTIVISM, SOCIOEDUCATION, AND SOCIAL ACTION

Paulo Freire's (1970) notion of praxis proclaims the power of combining reflection with social action. His concept of "concientización" defines the development of a critical awareness of personal dynamics within the context of social and political situations. Freire's work was mostly used to organize working class communities in Brazil to come together to deal with their social and economic disenfranchisement. Together the workers engaged in collective consciousness raising, which embraced political action. Freire's conceptualization of critical consciousness is useful to social justice workers, though we have expanded the work to include all relevant dimensions of social location: social class, gender, race, sexual orientation, and identity, culture, religion, and physical ability. The main idea is that a collective of people from diverse backgrounds work together toward communal as well as individual healing. Within this crucible of intimate connection to others who are different from themselves, a range of previously unknown perspectives and possibilities are discovered, explored, and practiced, resulting in new experiences of shared power, resources, and healing. Suzanne Pharr, for example, asserts that intervention for domestic violence survivors should center upon empowering them by inviting them into organizing efforts directed at ending sexism, racism, homophobia, and classism. She believes that pathologizing them as agency clients who need mental health services is re-victimization. (Pharr, 1996, 1997).

The process whereby therapists, clients, and communities develop critical consciousness is a first step toward more just relationships. Obtaining a critical consciousness is essential for clients to migrate through the experience of empowerment and accountability—cornerstones for liberation.

Priteltensky's (1997) work on the moral implications of psychological discourse and action is helpful in providing tools to assess the social utility of different mental health approaches. Inherent to a social and economic democracy are notions of mutuality, social obligation, and overcoming oppression. A social justice approach promotes balance between self-determination and distributive justice while at the same time locating individuals within the concrete realities of their communities. For example, the revered older son in an Asian family who is accustomed to shaping and claiming *his* desires can learn in a social justice-oriented therapy through discussion with other men how to counter this self-focus by putting an equal emphasis on the dreams of his young bride. In another example, a self-centered client learns to open his/her heart by being assigned to perform acts of generosity toward others before expecting to receive gifts for him/her self. Simple tasks like these can be assigned to clients that begin to reverse hierarchies of power and privilege. The tasks also articulate the differences between rights and privileges.

When clients bring their presenting problems to therapy, we advocate that they be respectfully yet matter-of-factly asked to engage in a process of consciousness raising. Their personal problems are maintained in a holding pattern while clients participate in an examination of historical/cultural prescriptions for choices they are making in their lives as well as the choices others make that impact them. For example, a White male blue-collar worker in the past 10 to 20 years could live the middle-class American dream if he was supported by a union, received good wages and benefits. Accordingly, he was able to have aspirations for his children. When this same White male blue-collar worker today finds himself jobless, his rage is often directed toward the immigrant workers who have replaced him in the job market by working for even less wages than he earns, no benefits, and certainly NO job security protected by labor unions. Obscured in his consciousness is knowledge of the relationship between transnational corporations and the global capitalist framework. This framework is designed to gather profits instantly for the upper echelons of the corporation. It does not attempt to garner the loyalty of communities and families through valuing employees' longevity in the workforce or the stability of families and communities. All the while, the "wealth" these crimes (i.e., the outsourcing of U.S. jobs and the marginalization of immigrants and third-world nation workers) generate is "shared" in an increasingly limited manner with workers within first-world nations (Chomsky, 1993). The client then is asked to redirect his rage toward learning about the political representation in his community, and toward how he might effectively direct his concerns to policymakers and politicians. Rather than internalizing the issues, he is encouraged to take action in the political and social world. All of this is done simultaneously with assisting his efforts in the job search. And, it is accomplished within a context that holds more than a single individual. Drawing connections between a client's depression and hopelessness in a collective setting that consciously reflects on the broader social and political milieu has an enormous impact. It helps to mobilize the rage and depression, transforming it to healthy anger, dignity, and a demand for equity from those who oppress. Clients may be encouraged to get involved in social action projects relevant to their presenting issues or to do reading or (as mentioned before) watch films pertinent to the issues. Michael Moore's movie, *Roger and Me,* for example, can be recommended (or *The Corporation*), along with follow-up discussions with others who are experiencing similar job outsourcing changes. This film affords another view of colonization, the interlocking systems of oppression, and the creation of a collective in a time of economic disaster for most families.

It is important for therapists to be ever mindful of the world around them and to gain their knowledge of that world from many different sources, especially including those whose perspectives run counter to the mainstream. In order to promote the development of critical consciousness among their clients, it is essential for therapists to be working continuously on developing their own.

Critical consciousness requires an inquiry into the history, status, and future implications of the prevailing capitalist narrative: Who benefits? Who loses? Are there alternative options? Such an effort brings one into stark awareness of the profoundly significant ways in which the current age of corporate globalization for several decades has been reshaping cultural sensibilities across all systemic levels within most societies. It has rapidly shifted institutional, community, family, and individual priorities and values in directions that are proving to be increasingly destructive to all life on our planet (International Forum on Globalization, 2002; Roy, 2003).

The following values guide the culture within many contemporary workplaces:

- Profit motive is sacred.
- Everything, including time and health, is regarded as a commodity.
- What you can get people to believe is more important than truth.
- The costs of social responsibility can and should be avoided.
- Immediate profit gain is prioritized (look no further ahead than quarterly return on investment).
- Knowledge and experience are compartmentalized.
- Accountability goes in one direction only, up the chain of command.
- Rigid hierarchy is the dominant social structure.
- Job security for employees is sacrificed to maximize economic gain for senior executives (and other stockholders)

The effort to foster critical consciousness needs to address the entire matrix of human diversity and social context. This includes not only such matters as the growing hegemony of corporate values and the economic positioning of families, but also the many ways that social realities connected to race, gender, sexual orientation, age, socioeconomic class, and disability status affect presenting problems and the range of available options.

Those who define "reality" most often have powerful social locations and little incentive to explore the experiences of those who are "less fortunate." The process of raising critical consciousness requires that we simultaneously transform ourselves while transforming our relationships with others and our communities. This entails looking at the self only in relation to others, that is, within concrete social and political locations. Accordingly, there is no dichotomy between the personal and the institutional, but rather an awareness of the links between the two. Through dialogue, reflection, social education, and action, families remodel their lives along with their communities.

Case Example. A client who suffered abuse as a child by his priest in his local church would, in addition to deconstructing and addressing his own abuse history in the culture circle, be invited into a broader discussion of how to effectively and respectfully address the children who continue to be victims of sexual abuse within the Catholic Church (i.e., the personal is being connected to a broader social problem). Empowerment (for the man in this case, culture circle members, and others in society) requires a shift that moves beyond responding to individual victims. Systemic violence within the institution of the church must also be acknowledged and addressed and accountability measures developed. As long as individual victims carry the burden of trauma and healing in isolation, while the church institution continues to conceal its ongoing predation, healing and empowerment remain compromised. Keeping the focus on individuals allows us not to see the systemic levels of responsibility. Accountability, and therefore repair of an unjust system that could be achieved through restructuring church practices, is prevented from occurring. To facilitate discussion, reflection, and possible social action, a liberal priest might be invited to join the circle.

Family members need help to critically explore cultural practices (and prejudices) operating within their institutions of faith (as well as their work and leisure arenas). Therapists must initiate and encourage discussion and information sharing among circle members to challenge oppressive belief systems. For example, current rhetoric by fundamentalist Christians concerning the rights of gay and lesbian partners being afforded the same constitutional rights of heterosexual partners (e.g., the right to marry) is often couched in religious ideologies that proclaim heterosexuality as "natural" and the God-mandated foundation of family life. Gay and lesbian relationships are viewed in this ideology as unnatural and a threat to family life. These beliefs are touted as truth despite all the evidence to the contrary. Moreover, many other countries in the world have granted legal benefits to gay and lesbian partners. And interestingly, heterosexuality in those countries has not declined in membership. Family life continues to flourish. Indeed it is strengthened by the legal inclusion of family-minded queers. Uncritical acceptance by therapists of ideologies that privilege some people over others, without deconstructing the cost to those who are marginalized, is in our view unethical at best. Accordingly, reading material can be provided clients to challenge oppressive beliefs regarding the actualities of same-gender partnerships. For example, lesbian and gay couples tend to be more egalitarian than heterosexuals (Green, Bettinger, & Zacks, 1996), and children fare as well in gay and lesbian parent families as they do in heterosexual parent families (Bigner, 1996; Patterson, 1996). Discussion with conscious others is helpful to raising clients' abilities to identify oppressive beliefs and to locate where and how these oppressive beliefs were formed and what purposes they serve.

To recap, developing critical consciousness necessitates a social process—a community of others committed to personal, familial, and social change. The ability to critically question a "reality" develops through a learning process with others, and through the transformation of one's beliefs and experiences with others. In dialogue, people (clients and therapists alike) decode current dynamics of their world and begin to see how domination and oppression operate. Community efforts to build critical consciousness run counter to today's quest for individualism, what W. Parker (2003), terms "idiocy" (p. 2). Parker uses the term, idiocy, as the ancient Greeks did to mean "private, separate, and self-centered-selfish" (p. 2). He contrasts private individuals (idiots) with public citizens who are essential for a well-functioning society (and democracy within it). He writes, "idiots are idiotic precisely because they are indifferent to the conditions and context of their own freedom; they fail to grasp the interdependence of liberty and community" (p. 4).

ACCOUNTABILITY: REPLACING DOMINATION AND PRIVILEGE WITH A CALL FOR RESPONSIBILITY

Families are open systems, vulnerable to all the dimensions of domination and subjugation that operate in the larger society. Therefore, in order to avoid reinforcing oppressive realities within the practice of family therapy, family therapists need to recognize and challenge the ways in which societal patterns of domination are woven into the therapeutic endeavor as well as the fabric of family life. This is far easier said than done because many oppressive patterns are ubiquitous and largely taken for granted by both therapists and client families alike. Moreover, they tend to be invisible to those who hold more power and privilege (e.g., White men and women, heterosexuals, those of middle- or upper-class status, the physically able, Christians, etc.). It is the therapist's job to raise these patterns out of the shadows and into the spotlight of awareness.

Case Example. Consider a heterosexual couple seeking help with parenting their 9-year-old son, who has been labeled with ADHD and medicated. The mother is concerned about the accuracy of the label and the need for medication. The father is passive in his concern and claims that he trusts his wife's judgment. She takes (and has been socially and relationally assigned) responsibility for the children. Accordingly, it is she who attends all the school meetings and car pools the children to all activities and appointments. Therapists rarely question this traditional gender-driven imbalance in responsibility for childcare and second shift duties, especially if the father is present at the session (Parker, 2003, 1997).

In order to help the couple move toward critical consciousness and accountability, a therapist might ask, "How did the two of you decide that the mother would be responsible for most of the people care tasks and the father would take somewhat of a back seat on these issues?" Further, the therapist could inquire into gender roles in the partner's families of origin (e.g., "Is this arrangement similar or different from the way things worked in your family of origin?"). And "what are some solutions you think of when one of you becomes dissatisfied with these assigned roles?"

While the role prescriptions within this family might bring less harm than the more toxic arrangements common within certain cultural groups (genital mutilation, dowries, forced veiling, and class humiliation) it is important to raise them into the realm of awareness and choice.

Moreover, the presenting issues regarding the medication and labeling of this child are issues most therapists would not address. Nor would most therapists initiate a dialogue about the complicity of the medical profession with the pharmaceutical industry when it comes to medicating children. We suggest that therapists do both. Again, the process is not telling others what to do or how to believe, but rather inviting them to engage in a critical inquiry with others about the issues (e.g., the value, or lack thereof, and rationale for labeling and medicating children and adults). The failure to examine is to collude with patterns of inequality.

Moreover, therapists must not stop here, with only destabilizing the gendered status quo (by bringing it to clients' attention). We believe it is important to challenge and support the father toward becoming more actively involved in parenting his son. For example, the father (and culture circle) might be asked, "What kind of relationship do you want with your child? What roles are generally assigned to men (and to women) in regard to children? What consequences do these assignments have, for the child, for the parent? What was your relationship like with your own father? What kind of connection did you have with him?"

Paying attention to accountability requires the creation of equity within all dimensions of the parents' relationship (work, finances, emotional availability, second shift responsibilities, and parenting). This means that the person with more power and privilege, often the man in heterosexual relationships, needs to be held accountable over time for making and maintaining changes. It also means he will likely need to give up some privileges in favor of equity with his partner and increased intimacy with his partner and child. For example, the father may need to take on more of the child-related care—such as scheduling doctor's appointments, driving kids to lessons, getting kids ready for school, laundry, meal shopping and preparation. Patterns related to power and control need to be acknowledged and addressed within therapy in the same matter-of-fact manner as a therapist would gather other basic information (e.g., age, number of children, divorces, etc.).

It is important that therapists seeking to dismantle patterns of domination and subjugation within family life become cognizant of the many, complex, multisystems level manifestations of such patterns. Almeida and Dolan-Del Vecchio (1999) use the term *systemic cultural analysis* to describe this evaluation of power dynamics at many systems levels There are at least three levels of inquiry that need to be pursued within this analysis, each addressing broader institutional levels. The first level addresses the experiences of those oppressed within family life; the second addresses the multiple intersections of power within societal institutional processes; the third addresses global issues through an examination of various economic, immigration, and military policies around the world. Paying attention to these multiple systemic levels forces us to consider the impact of larger systems of domination and entitlement upon families, and the violation of human rights that exists at the center of human pain and suffering in our communities. Consideration of these reciprocally influencing systemic levels invests the family therapy field with an ethical and moral responsibility to place social justice and liberation principles at the center of helping efforts for all families.

For example, a European American and an African American might both be American citizens but in reality occupy two distinctly different social class positions. In U.S. society, what some of us consider basic rights are in fact privileges, granted only to those who have membership in dominant groups. In fact, access to affordable healthcare and housing is mostly unavailable to the working poor. The ability to safely express physical affection in public, or to inherit property, or to visit a dying partner is mostly unavailable to lesbians and gay men. In addition, members of dominant society often assume that much of what they have been granted by virtue of their (racial, skin color, gender, sexual orientation, citizenship status, social class, age, physical ability) privilege is accessible to everyone. Therapists must help clients to deconstruct both their privilege (which is largely invisible to them) as well as the injustices that result from privilege.

The experience of dominance is as ever present as the experience of oppression (Spivak, 1991). For example, children of heterosexual couples are free to invite their friends over and expose the sexual orientation of their parents. In contrast, children of gay couples must be armored against exposing this information freely to their peers and teachers. Doing so could put their parents at risk, as well as expose the children to the prejudice of others, with possible consequences ranging from ostracism to physical assault.

One can identify the privileges one enjoys by identifying the aspects of one's identity that have dominance in our society, considering one's normal activities of daily living (Kivel, 1996; McIntosh, 1988). For example, white heterosexual men may identify some of their privileges as follows:

- When compared to his female counterpart, he often expects and is expected to be less active in childcare, housework, and relationship building, and emotional work.
- Walking out his front door onto the street, a White male of any social class is statistically less likely to be physically attacked, accosted with suspicion by police officers, or followed as a suspected shoplifter when inside a store.
- Later on, during an interview for a new loan application, a White male's gender and skin color are unlikely to cause the loan officer to think twice about his degree of financial understanding or likelihood of remaining gainfully employed.

Although it would seem that each of us should have the right to fairness, safety, and equal opportunity, these examples (as well as the life experiences of multitudes) show otherwise. What ought to be rights turn out to be privileges granted to some and withheld from others.

Individuals do not readily see their role in structures of dominance. Neither do they feel morally obligated to initiate change. Consequently, the ethic of change rests with therapists. Therapeutic work that embraces the continuum from domination to privilege and oppression must engage all clients: heterosexuals and GLBT (gay, lesbian, bisexual, & transgender) clients of all colors and social classes to participate in joint conversations and social change projects. By way of dialogue focused on critical issues of power, privilege, and oppression—who has it, who does not, and under what circumstances—clients and therapists alike can begin to be cognizant of their relative social locations and to confront their experiences of internalized dominance and oppression. The more clearly we choose to acknowledge our own participation in systems of dominance and entitlement within daily life, the more actively we confront and begin to live our moral obligation to interrupt the perpetuation of it.

From this perspective, family therapists and other mental health professionals are morally obligated to hold people accountable for their actions, values, and the institutional traditions they endorse. This is a necessary precursor to deconstructing dominance in family life. Silence and inaction uphold the power and privilege of dominant groups and therefore perpetuate oppression. Our definition of accountability is broader than getting diverse people to talk to each other in therapy groups. It includes building and embracing families in diverse communities (e.g., culture circles) that uphold values and lifestyles for a just and civic community. Crucial to the process is holding those with more power and privilege accountable for change. This includes agencies where the structure of service-delivery constrains innovative models of change (e.g., systems that do not support collective or multi-family interventions). This is markedly different from most therapies where the onus for change is assigned to those with less power and privilege (e.g., clients who are mostly women, people of color, and the poor).

With accountability processes in place, empowerment is a possibility. The third step in a social justice approach to therapy is to dismantle subjugation and empower those with less power and privilege.

EMPOWERMENT: ACTION BASED IN CRITICAL CONSCIOUSNESS AND ACCOUNTABILITY

Empowerment is initiated as clients develop critical consciousness. Liberation is possible as empowerment is paired with the accountability of those with more power and privilege. Said another way, the liberation of women depends on the accountability of men (Almeida, 2003). That is, women and subjugated others are not empowered—their voices will go unheard—unless those with more power and privilege are held accountable. One cannot have empowerment without accountability. In addition, neither is available without consciousness raising. Power and equity disparities (e.g., between genders, various races, sexual orientations, etc.) must be redressed in order for people to achieve liberation.

Consequently, the process of empowerment in the therapeutic process simultaneously includes individual, family, and community conversations, and the linking of these conversations with social action. Empowerment processes are enacted as people change the ways in which they relate to their own communities and become aware of the tools of oppression as well as the areas in which they hold power and privilege. Accordingly, therapeutic interventions must seek to change both individuals and social systems.

Below we posit three possible case scenarios that illustrate the use of empowerment principles in a social justice approach to therapy. Again, each scenario is situated within a community healing process of critical reflection and dialogue focused on accountability and empowerment.

Case Example #1. A Muslim family seeking therapy following the 9/11 tragedy would be involved in a group conversation. Members of many different religious communities would be invited to participate and to share about different forms of Islam as well as different forms of Christianity, Judaism, and Hinduism. The structure and content of this therapeutic conversation would empower and support the integrity of all participants, while also enabling them to critically analyze and hold accountable factions within their own communities of faith whose practices are abusive.

Case Example #2. An African American lesbian who expresses being openly confronted by homophobia within her church community would be invited to become aware of the oppressive norms within her own faith with the support of an embracing and supportive community (e.g., her culture circle). To support this process, an African American heterosexual minister (ideally within the same faith) who shares her concern and can speak openly about homophobia in the church would be sought out and invited into the culture circle as a cultural consultant to challenge this institutionalized homophobia. Although we recognize the value of inviting in a lesbian or gay minister of the same faith, including a heterosexual minister is purposeful as we believe that dominant class members have responsibility for righting and giving voice to oppressive values and practices.

Case Example #3. A Jewish female married to a Christian would be encouraged to discuss the multiple ways in which she is rendered invisible within her partner's religious community. In the culture groups, Christians (who wield more power and privilege in the United States) of all denominations might be asked to generate strategies to help their congregations embrace mixed-faith relationships. Similarly, U.S. Jews may be asked to examine their privilege relative to Palestinians. Deconstructing social location, and relative power and privilege, is fundamental to empowerment. The culture circle members might then be encouraged to create social actions plans to enact in their own places of worship.

PLACING SOCIAL JUSTICE AT THE CENTER OF FAMILY THERAPY PRACTICE

Critical consciousness, accountability, and empowerment are key processes that directly address our therapeutic responsibility to care for families' suffering within a systemic perspective that emphasizes mutuality and justice (see Fig. 8.1). This social justice perspective challenges us to address the issues of both those who suffer and those who perpetuate the suffering, holding those who perpetuate suffering accountable for change. Traditionally, psychological as well as family therapy approaches have focused more on conceptualizing and treating the sufferers, rather than addressing the dynamics of those who perpetuate the suffering. An example of this emphasis on the sufferer's victimization and treatment while neglecting the perpetrator's dynamics occurs in the field of trauma. In this field, there has been a wealth of research on the effects of trauma and the development of posttraumatic stress disorder. However, there is no corresponding research on those who perpetrate, for example, state or nation sponsored violence. Becker (1995) makes a succinct critique of the diagnosis PTSD (posttraumatic stress disorder). He states that people considered threatening to the state or a nation have historically been stigmatized as deviant in various ways. That is, "victimizers in all parts of the world have used the supposed 'disorder' of the victims to justify their acts of cruelty and destruction" (p. 103). A 21st-century example is the rhetoric used by George W. Bush to sell his war in Iraq—labeling whole countries and people as "terrorists" and "evil doers." Too often the innocent victims of war or political repression are labeled as deviant. Moreover, expectable and "normal" [sic] reactions to war and/or political repression (i.e., suffering torture, witnessing assassinations) are labeled as deviant while there is no corresponding examination of the initiators of the violence—in other words, the war opportunists. The term "disorder" might more aptly be applied to perpetrators of violence. In contexts wherein people identify issues of oppression and economic exploitation and also develop political awareness of their situation, labeling is considered yet another tool of oppression. According to Pharr (2002), the notion of organizing women toward liberation is antithetical to the traditional practice of diagnosing, labeling, and thereby pathologizing them. Diagnosing victims of domestic violence with mental health disorders instead of empowering them toward social action is revictimization in the guise of healing. The facilitation of true healing requires that we hold responsible those who perpetuate violence and the legal and social systems that collude with them, while unequivocally supporting efforts to create a world that is safe for all.

Critical consciousness becomes the platform on which interventions are determined. When personal suffering is framed within dominant pathologizing ideologies, privilege is maintained for those with the power to define normality for others. For example, a 13-year-old African American male is diagnosed as "oppositional defiant" because he has been fighting with White boys during school recesses. This boy is also likely to be referred for medication to quell this behavior. Instead, we suggest that the boy's behavior needs to be explored and understood in a social context of racism, and pharmaceutical profiteering where African American boys are more likely to be pathologized and excluded from school. The racial relationships within the school environment need to be explored. Moreover, rather than labeling the boy, which does not lead to solutions and only causes him to be viewed negatively, the school situation might benefit from a critique based on Fordham and Ogbu's (1986) study of *oppositional cultural identity*. These authors use this term to describe the developmental process of African American youth, wherein some youth, in a healthy reaction to a traumatic life condition, often go awry. For example, they found that Black teens denigrated academic achievement by their peers as "acting White." Appropriately contextualizing the issue at hand offers hope and social action (empowerment and accountability) rather than resignation and blame. Rather than pathologizing any of the players, the school needs to be encouraged to look for systemic responses and social pathologies that create tension between diverse groups of all sorts. Solutions need to further consciousness raising of all students. All voices involved in the conflict need to be heard, with the cognizance that the White boys carry more power and privilege in the school system as well as society. White boys have not been required to learn the language of their African American counterparts (or women for that matter). Therefore, the listening needs to be tipped in the direction that requires those with more power and privilege in the system to engage in deep listening with those with less. To respond to an individual case by pathologizing the person(s) in the situation is missing systemic levels of causality where there is potential for overreaching solutions. Acknowledging the fact of racism then requires us to look for its insidious and often hidden presence in mundane situations that appear to be other than that. Are the seeming victims really part of a larger system of victimization? We need to push ourselves to these broader levels of critical inquiry to ferret out solutions that do not further the victimization of some and the privilege of others.

In another example, an English-American woman in a heterosexual marriage finds herself being medicated and diagnosed with anxiety and depressive disorders. She intermittently experiences lesbian fantasies. A traditional therapeutic solution is to increase her medications, assuming these lesbian fantasies are evidence of pathology, rather than take the time to explore her sexual orientation and its meaning within her current life structure. This exploration might be done by encouraging her to attend a series of coming-out groups at her local lesbian, gay, bisexual, and transgender community center and then discuss her experiences and feelings regarding her sexual orientation.

When those who have been victimized develop critical consciousness, they begin to understand how the ideologies of individualism and self-determination attempt to rob them of their collective identity and community ties. Likewise, when people in positions of privilege develop critical consciousness, they come to understand how they automatically take for granted rights and access to resources that are denied to others. They begin to realize that they draw their power from an established collective. People in positions of privilege come to understand that their positions often sanction them to define others and use them to enhance their own class, gender, and ethnic group privileges. As people acknowledge their origins, community identity, and history, and develop a critical consciousness about the ways in which their social location has afforded and constrained privileges, they become aware of the ways in which their lives and those with whom they interact are governed by reciprocity.

Therapeutic approaches that emphasize reciprocity and distributive justice address the accountability dimension of human relatedness. Therefore, helping clients to take responsibility for how they and family members use and abuse power in personal and community relationships is key to a social justice approach.

CONCLUSIONS

The past several decades have seen movement within the field of family therapy to expose gender-based patterns of inequity within family life. However, gender is only one cornerstone of the systemic oppression that structures our society, the practice of family therapy, and our families. Although many approaches to family therapy now acknowledge the significance of gender, as well as other human characteristics, including race, sexual ethnicity, sexual orientation, and class, the work of helping families to challenge the inequities connected to these characteristics is still in its infancy. This reality marks the field of family therapy's complicity with our society's institutionalized patterns of dominance and oppression. Family therapy, therefore, faces a defining moral challenge: Will we continue to be part of the system that marginalizes the many while privileging the few, or will we embrace the challenge of creating therapeutic approaches that realize the connection between social justice and healing? Our experience shows us that developing therapeutic strategies directed toward facilitating collectives of accountability, critical consciousness, and empowerment are fundamental to the necessary and long overdue work that lies ahead. Paradoxically perhaps, we have found that expanding the therapeutic process to include these elements makes the work easier and more enjoyable and energy-producing for practitioners. We encourage readers to move the field forward by creating ways within their unique settings to bring critical consciousness, accountability, and empowerment to the center of family therapy practice.

REFERENCES

Ackerman, N. W. (1937). The family as a social emotional unit. *Bulleting of the Kansas Mental Health Hygiene Society, 12.*

Alexander, J. F. & Parsons, B. V. (1982). *Functional family therapy.* Monterey, CA: Brooks/Cole.

Almeida, R. V. (1993). Unexamined assumptions and service delivery systems: Feminist theory and racial exclusions. *Journal of Feminist Family Therapy, 5,* 3–23.

Almeida, R.V. (1998) The dislocation of women's experience in family therapy. *Journal of Feminist Family Therapy, 10,* 1–22.

Almeida, R. (2003). Creating collectives of liberation. In L. B. Silverstein & T. J. Goodrich (Eds.), *Feminist family therapy* (pp. 293–306). Washington, DC: American Psychological Association.

Almeida, R., & Dolan-Del Vecchio, K. (1999). Addressing culture in batterers intervention: South Asian communities as an illustrative example. *Violence Against Women, 5*(6), 654–683.

Almeida, R., & Durkin, T. (1999). The cultural context model: Therapy for couples with domestic violence. *Journal of Marital and Family Therapy, 25,* 5–32.

Almeida, R., & Hudak, J. (2002). The culture of context model. In E. Aldarondo & F. Mederos (Eds.), *Programs for men who batter: Interventions and prevention strategies in a diverse society* (pp. 108–140). Kingston, NJ: The Civic Research Institute.

Almeida, R., Woods, M., Messineo, T., & Font, R. (1998). The cultural context model: An overview. In M. McGoldrick (Ed.), *Revisioning family therapy: Race, culture, and gender in clinical practice* (pp. 414–432). New York: Guilford Press.

Andersen, T. (1987). The reflecting team: Dialogue and meta-dialogue in clinical work. *Family Process, 26,* 415–428.

Anderson, H., & Goolishian, H. (1988). Human systems as linguistic systems: Preliminary and evolving ideas about the implications for clinical theory. *Family Process, 27,* 371–393.

Avis, J., & Turner, J. (1996). Feminist lenses in family therapy research: Gender politics and science. In D. H. Sprenkle & S. M. Moon (Eds.), *Research methods in family therapy* (pp. 145–169). New York: Guilford Press.

Becker, D. (1995). The deficiency of the concept of post traumatic stress disorder when dealing with victims of human rights violations. In R. J. Kleber., C. R. Figley, & B. P. R. Berthold (Eds.), *Beyond trauma: Cultural and societal dynamics* (pp. 99–131). New York: Plenum Press.

Bigner, J. J. (1996). Working with gay fathers. In J. Laird & R. J. Green (Eds.). *Lesbians and gays in couples and families: A handbook for therapists* (pp. 185–230). San Francisco: Jossey-Bass.

Bograd, M. (1990). *Feminist approaches for men in therapy.* New York: Harrington Park Press.

Bograd, M. (1999). Strengthening domestic violence theories: Intersections of race, class, sexual orientation and gender. *Journal of Marriage and Family Therapy, 25,* 75–190.

Bowen, M. (1978). *Family therapy in clinical practice.* Northvale, NJ: Jason Aronson.

Boyd-Franklin, N. (1989). *Black families in therapy: A multisystems approach.* New York: Guilford Press.

Carter, B., & McGoldrick, M. (1988). Overview: The changing family life cycle. In B. Carter & M. McGoldrick (Eds.), *The changing family life cycle* (pp. 3–28). New York: Allyn & Bacon.

Chomsky, N. (1993). *Year 501: The conquest continues.* Boston: South End Press.

Collins, P. H. (1986). Learning from the outsider within: The sociological significance of Black feminist thought. *Social Problems 33*(6), 14–32.

Crenshaw, K. (1997). Intersectionality and identity politics: Learning from violence against women of color. In M. Lyndon Shanley & U. Narayan (Eds.), *Reconstructing political theory: Feminist perspectives* (pp. 111–132). University Park, PA : Pennsylvania State University Press.

de Shazer, S. (1985). *Keys to solution in brief therapy.* New York: Norton.

Dolan-Del Vecchio, K. (1998). Dismantling White male privilege within family therapy. In M. McGoldrick (Ed.), *Revisioning family therapy: Race, culture, and gender in clinical practice* (pp.159–175). New York: Guilford Press.

Dolan-Del Vecchio, K., & Lockard, J. (2004). Resistance to colonialism as the heart of family therapy practice. *Journal of Feminist Family Therapy, 16*(2).

Duran, E., & Duran, B. (1995). *Native American postcolonial psychology.* Albany: State University of New York Press.

Fanon, F. (1963). *The wretched of the earth.* New York: Grove Press.

Fanon, F. (1964). *Toward the African revolution.* New York: Grove Press.

Foucault, M. (1975). *The birth of the clinic: An archeology of medical perception.* New York: Random House.

Foucault, M. (1977). *Discipline and punish: The birth of the prison.* New York: Pantheon Books.

Foucault, M. (1979). *Un dialogo sobre el poder* [A dialogue about power]. Madrid: Alianza.

Fordham, S., & Ogbu, J. (1986). Oppositional cultural identity.

Fowers, B. J., & Richardson, F. C. (1996). Individualism, family ideology, and family therapy. *Theory and psychology, 6*(1), 121–151.

Freire, P. (1970). *Pedagogy of the oppressed.* New York: Continuum.

Freire, P. (1978). *Education for a critical consciousness.* New York: Seabury Press.

Green, R.-J., Bettinger, M., & Zacks, E. (1996). Are lesbian couples fused and gay male couples disengaged? In J. Laird & R.-J. Green (Eds.), *Lesbians and gays in couples and families: A handbook for therapists* (pp. 185–230). San Francisco: Jossey-Bass.

Green, R. J. & Laird, J. (1996). *Lesbians and gays in couples and families.* San Francisco: Jossey-Bass.

Haley, J. (1963). *Strategies of psychotherapy.* New York: Grune & Stratton.

Hare-Mustin, R. (1994). Discourses in the mirrored room: A postmodern analysis of therapy. *Family Process, 33,* 19–35.

Hernandez, P. (2004). The cultural context model in supervision. *Journal of Feminist Family Therapy, 15*(4), 1–18.

Hernandez, P., Almeida, R. V., & Dolan-Del Vecchio, K. (2004). Critical consciousness, accountability, and empowerment: Key processes for helping families heal. *Family Process.*

Hernandez, M. (2000). Puerto Rican families and substance abuse. In J. Krestan (Ed.), *Bridges to recovery: Addiction, family therapy, and multicultural treatment* (pp. 253–283). New York: Free Press.

International Forum on Globalization. (2002). *Alternatives to economic globalization: A better world is possible.* San Francisco: Berrett-Koehler Publishers.

Jackson, D. D. (1957). The question of family homeostasis. *Psychiatric Quarterly Supplement, 31,* 79–90.

Jaggar, A. (1983). *Feminist politics and human nature.* Totowa, NJ: Rowman & Allanheld.

Kivel, P. (1996). *Uprooting racism: How White people can work for racial justice.* Gabriola Island, B., Canada: New Society Publishers.

Laird, J. (1989). Women and stories: Restoring women's self constructions. In M. McGoldrick, C. Anderson, & F. Walsh (Eds.), *Women in families* (pp. 427–450). New York: Norton.

Leary, J. D. (2002). Discussion of post-traumatic slave syndrome. *The Tavis Smiley Show.* National Public Radio. 12/2/02.

Madanes, C. (1981). *Strategic family therapy.* San Francisco: Jossey-Bass.

McIntosh, P. (1988). *White privilege and male privilege: A personal account of coming to see correspondences through work in women's studies* (Working Paper No.189). Wellesley, MA: Wellesley College Center for Research on Women.

McGoldrick, M. (1998). *Re-visioning family therapy.* New York: Guilford Press.

Minuchin, S., & Fishman, C. H. (1981). *Family therapy techniques.* Cambridge, MA: Harvard University Press.

Moraga, C., & Anzaldua, G. (1983). *This bridge called my back.* New York: Kitchen Table: Women of Color Press.

Napier, A. Y. (1987). Early stages in experiential marital therapy. *Contemporary Family Therapy, 9,* 23–41.

Parker, L. (2003). A social justice model for clinical social work practice. *Affilia* (Vol. 8, No. 3, pp. 272–288). Thousand Oaks, CA: Sage.

Parker, L. (2003). Bringing power from the margins to the center in couples therapy. In L. Silverstein & T. J. Goodrich (Eds.), *Feminist family therapy: Empowerment and social context*. New York: American Psychological Association Press.

Parker, L. (1997). Unraveling power issues in couples therapy. *Journal of Feminist Family Therapy, 9*(2), 3–20.

Parker, W. C. (2003). *Teaching democracy: Unity and diversity in public life*. New York: Columbia University.

Patterson, C. J. (1996). Lesbian mothers and their children. In J. Laird & R.-J. Green (Eds.), *Lesbians and gays in couples and families: A handbook for therapists* (pp. 185–230). San Francisco: Jossey-Bass.

Pharr, S. (1996). *In the time of the right: Reflections on liberation*. Berkeley, CA: Chardon Press.

Pharr, S. (1997). *Homophobia: A weapon of sexism*. Berkeley, CA: Chardon Press.

Pharr, S. (2002, November). *Victimization and/or power: Rethinking our work to end violence against women*. Keynote delivered at New Jersey Coalition for Battered Women.

Pinderhughes, E. (1989). *Understanding race, ethnicity, and power: The key to efficacy in clinical practice*. New York: Free Press.

Prilleltensky, I. (1996). Polities change, oppression remains: On the psychology and politics of oppression. *Political Psychology, 17,* 127–148.

Prilleltensky, I. (1997). Values, assumptions and practices: Assessing the moral implications of psychological discourse and action. *American Psychologist, 52,* 517–535.

Roy, A. (2003). *War talk*. Cambridge, MA: South End Press.

Satir, V. (1964). *Conjoint family therapy*. Palo Alto, CA: Science and Behavior Books.

Selvini-Palazzoli, M., Boscolo, L., Cecchin, G., & Prata, G. (1978). *Paradox and counterparadox*. New York: Jason Aronson.

Spivak, G. C. (1991). Can the subaltern speak? In C. Nelson & L. Grossberg (Eds.), *Marxism and the interpretation of culture* (pp.1–15). Urbana: University of Illinois Press.

Tamasese, K., & Waldegrave, C. (1993). Cultural and gender accountability in the "just therapy" approach. *Journal of Feminist Family Therapy, 5*(2), 29–45.

Waldegrave, C. (1990). Just therapy. *Dulwich Centre Newsletter, 1,* 5–46.

Walters, M., Carter, B., Papp, P., & Silverstein, O. (1988). *The invisible web*. New York: Guilford Press.

Watts-Jones, D. (2002). Healing internalized racism. The role of a within-group sanctuary among people of African descent. *Family Process, 41*(4), 591–601.

Watzlawick, P. (1976). *How real is real?* New York: Random House.

Weingarten K. (1991). The discourses of intimacy: Adding a social constructionist and feminist view. *Family Process, 30,* 285–305.

Weingarten K. (1992). A consideration of intimate and non-intimate interactions in therapy. *Family Process, 31,* 45–59.

Weingarten, K. (1995). *Cultural resistance: Challenging beliefs about men, women, and therapy*. New York: Harrington Park Press.

Weingarten, K. (1998). Radical listening: Challenging cultural beliefs for and about mothers. *Journal of Feminist Family Therapy, 7,* 7–22.

Whitaker, C. A., & Bumberry, W. M. (1988). *Dancing with the family: A symbolic-experiential approach*. New Jersey: Brunner-Routledge.

White, M., & Epston, D. (1990). *Narrative means to therapeutic ends*. New York: Norton.

Women's Conference: Organizing for change: classism, racism, homophobia, cultural imperialism, & violence against women. Cherry Hill, NJ.

Woo. D. (1985). The socioeconomic status of Asian American women in the labor force: An alternative view. *Sociological Perspectives, 28*(3), 307–338.

Yellowbird, M. J. (1995). Spirituality in First Nations story telling: A Sahnish-Hidatsa approach to narrative. *Reflections: Narratives of Professional Helping 1*(4), 65–72.

Yellowbird, M. J. (2001). Critical values and First Nations peoples. In R. Fong & S. Furuto (Eds.), *Culturally competent practice: Skills, interventions, and evaluations* (pp. 61–74). Boston: Allyn & Bacon.

APPENDIX
CCM POWER AND CONTROL WHEELS,
PUBLIC AND PRIVATE CONTEXTS

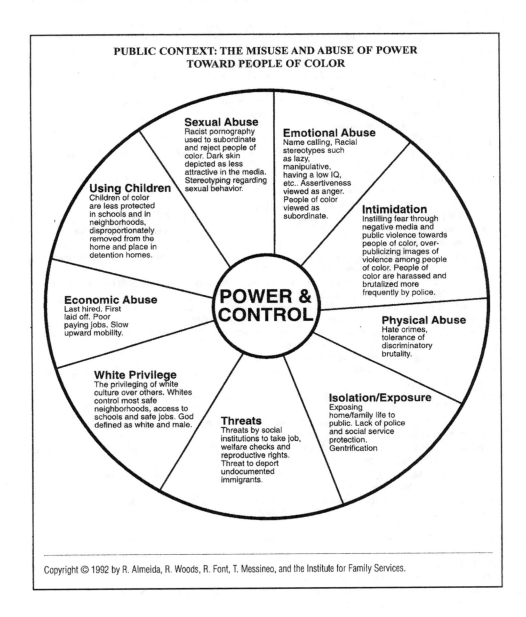

PUBLIC CONTEXT: THE MISUSE AND ABUSE OF POWER
TOWARD PEOPLE OF COLOR

Sexual Abuse
Racist pornography used to subordinate and reject people of color. Dark skin depicted as less attractive in the media. Stereotyping regarding sexual behavior.

Emotional Abuse
Name calling, Racial stereotypes such as lazy, manipulative, having a low IQ, etc.. Assertiveness viewed as anger. People of color viewed as subordinate.

Using Children
Children of color are less protected in schools and in neighborhoods, disproportionately removed from the home and place in detention homes.

Intimidation
Instilling fear through negative media and public violence towards people of color, over-publicizing images of violence among people of color. People of color are harassed and brutalized more frequently by police.

Economic Abuse
Last hired. First laid off. Poor paying jobs. Slow upward mobility.

POWER & CONTROL

Physical Abuse
Hate crimes, tolerance of discriminatory brutality.

White Privilege
The privileging of white culture over others. Whites control most safe neighborhoods, access to schools and safe jobs. God defined as white and male.

Threats
Threats by social institutions to take job, welfare checks and reproductive rights. Threat to deport undocumented immigrants.

Isolation/Exposure
Exposing home/family life to public. Lack of police and social service protection. Gentrification

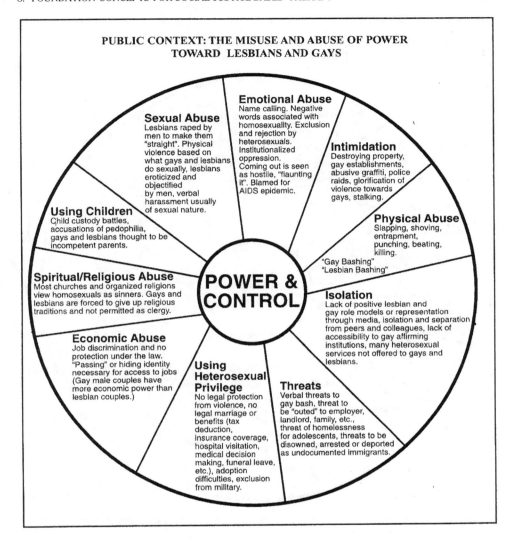

PUBLIC CONTEXT: THE MISUSE AND ABUSE OF POWER
TOWARD LESBIANS AND GAYS

POWER & CONTROL

Emotional Abuse
Name calling. Negative words associated with homosexuality. Exclusion and rejection by heterosexuals. Institutionalized oppression. Coming out is seen as hostile, "flaunting it". Blamed for AIDS epidemic.

Sexual Abuse
Lesbians raped by men to make them "straight". Physical violence based on what gays and lesbians do sexually, lesbians eroticized and objectified by men, verbal harassment usually of sexual nature.

Intimidation
Destroying property, gay establishments, abusive graffiti, police raids, glorification of violence towards gays, stalking.

Using Children
Child custody battles, accusations of pedophilia, gays and lesbians thought to be incompetent parents.

Physical Abuse
Slapping, shoving, entrapment, punching, beating, killing.
"Gay Bashing"
"Lesbian Bashing"

Spiritual/Religious Abuse
Most churches and organized religions view homosexuals as sinners. Gays and lesbians are forced to give up religious traditions and not permitted as clergy.

Isolation
Lack of positive lesbian and gay role models or representation through media, isolation and separation from peers and colleagues, lack of accessibility to gay affirming institutions, many heterosexual services not offered to gays and lesbians.

Economic Abuse
Job discrimination and no protection under the law. "Passing" or hiding identity necessary for access to jobs (Gay male couples have more economic power than lesbian couples.)

Using Heterosexual Privilege
No legal protection from violence, no legal marriage or benefits (tax deduction, insurance coverage, hospital visitation, medical decision making, funeral leave, etc.), adoption difficulties, exclusion from military.

Threats
Verbal threats to gay bash, threat to be "outed" to employer, landlord, family, etc., threat of homelessness for adolescents, threats to be disowned, arrested or deported as undocumented immigrants.

APPENDIX *(Continued)*

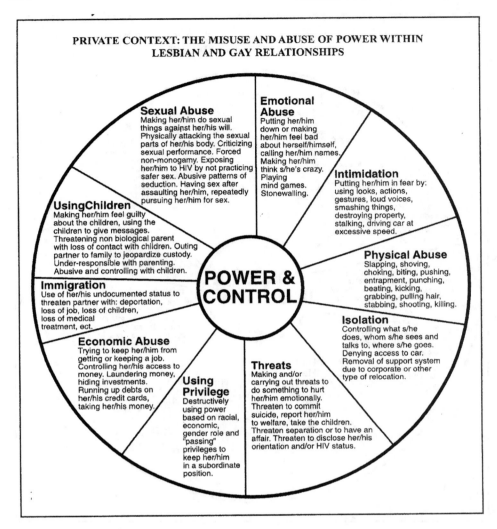

**PRIVATE CONTEXT: THE MISUSE AND ABUSE OF POWER WITHIN
LESBIAN AND GAY RELATIONSHIPS**

Sexual Abuse
Making her/him do sexual things against her/his will. Physically attacking the sexual parts of her/his body. Criticizing sexual performance. Forced non-monogamy. Exposing her/him to HIV by not practicing safer sex. Abusive patterns of seduction. Having sex after assaulting her/him, repeatedly pursuing her/him for sex.

Emotional Abuse
Putting her/him down or making her/him feel bad about herself/himself, calling her/him names. Making her/him think s/he's crazy. Playing mind games. Stonewalling.

Intimidation
Putting her/him in fear by: using looks, actions, gestures, loud voices, smashing things, destroying property, stalking, driving car at excessive speed.

UsingChildren
Making her/him feel guilty about the children, using the children to give messages. Threatening non biological parent with loss of contact with children. Outing partner to family to jeopardize custody. Under-responsible with parenting. Abusive and controlling with children.

Immigration
Use of her/his undocumented status to threaten partner with: deportation, loss of job, loss of children, loss of medical treatment, ect.

Physical Abuse
Slapping, shoving, choking, biting, pushing, entrapment, punching, beating, kicking, grabbing, pulling hair, stabbing, shooting, killing.

**POWER &
CONTROL**

Isolation
Controlling what s/he does, whom s/he sees and talks to, where s/he goes. Denying access to car. Removal of support system due to corporate or other type of relocation.

Economic Abuse
Trying to keep her/him from getting or keeping a job. Controlling her/his access to money. Laundering money, hiding investments. Running up debts on her/his credit cards, taking her/his money.

Using Privilege
Destructively using power based on racial, economic, gender role and "passing" privileges to keep her/him in a subordinate position.

Threats
Making and/or carrying out threats to do something to hurt her/him emotionally. Threaten to commit suicide, report her/him to welfare, take the children. Threaten separation or to have an affair. Threaten to disclose her/his orientation and/or HIV status.

APPENDIX *(Continued)*

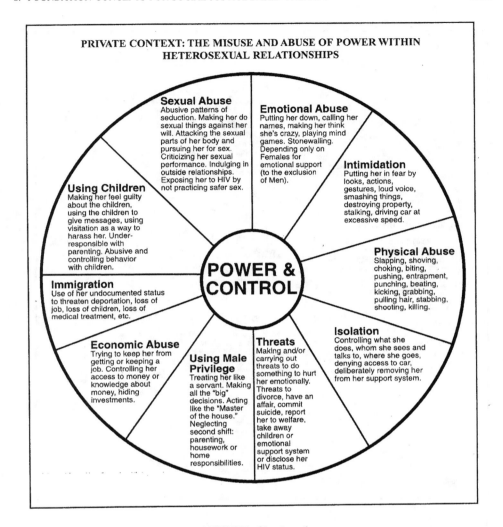

PRIVATE CONTEXT: THE MISUSE AND ABUSE OF POWER WITHIN HETEROSEXUAL RELATIONSHIPS

POWER & CONTROL

Sexual Abuse
Abusive patterns of seduction. Making her do sexual things against her will. Attacking the sexual parts of her body and pursuing her for sex. Criticizing her sexual performance. Indulging in outside relationships. Exposing her to HIV by not practicing safer sex.

Emotional Abuse
Putting her down, calling her names, making her think she's crazy, playing mind games. Stonewalling. Depending only on Females for emotional support (to the exclusion of Men).

Intimidation
Putting her in fear by looks, actions, gestures, loud voice, smashing things, destroying property, stalking, driving car at excessive speed.

Using Children
Making her feel guilty about the children, using the children to give messages, using visitation as a way to harass her. Under-responsible with parenting. Abusive and controlling behavior with children.

Physical Abuse
Slapping, shoving, choking, biting, pushing, entrapment, punching, beating, kicking, grabbing, pulling hair, stabbing, shooting, killing.

Immigration
Use of her undocumented status to threaten deportation, loss of job, loss of children, loss of medical treatment, etc.

Economic Abuse
Trying to keep her from getting or keeping a job. Controlling her access to money or knowledge about money, hiding investments.

Using Male Privilege
Treating her like a servant. Making all the "big" decisions. Acting like the "Master of the house." Neglecting second shift: parenting, housework or home responsibilities.

Threats
Making and/or carrying out threats to do something to hurt her emotionally. Threats to divorce, have an affair, commit suicide, report her to welfare, take away children or emotional support system or disclose her HIV status.

Isolation
Controlling what she does, whom she sees and talks to, where she goes, denying access to car, deliberately removing her from her support system.

APPENDIX *(Continued)*

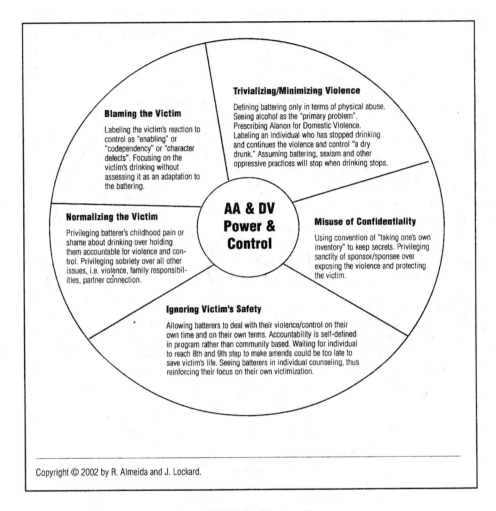

Trivializing/Minimizing Violence

Defining battering only in terms of physical abuse. Seeing alcohol as the "primary problem". Prescribing Alanon for Domestic Violence. Labeling an individual who has stopped drinking and continues the violence and control "a dry drunk." Assuming battering, sexism and other oppressive practices will stop when drinking stops.

Blaming the Victim

Labeling the victim's reaction to control as "enabling" or "codependency" or "character defects". Focusing on the victim's drinking without assessing it as an adaptation to the battering.

Normalizing the Victim

Privileging batterer's childhood pain or shame about drinking over holding them accountable for violence and control. Privileging sobriety over all other issues, i.e. violence, family responsibilities, partner connection.

AA & DV Power & Control

Misuse of Confidentiality

Using convention of "taking one's own inventory" to keep secrets. Privileging sanctity of sponsor/sponsee over exposing the violence and protecting the victim.

Ignoring Victim's Safety

Allowing batterers to deal with their violence/control on their own time and on their own terms. Accountability is self-defined in program rather than community based. Waiting for individual to reach 8th and 9th step to make amends could be too late to save victim's life. Seeing batterers in individual counseling, thus reinforcing their focus on their own victimization.

APPENDIX *(Continued)*

9

Narrative Practice and Culture

Hugo Kamya
Simmons College School of Social Work

My brother, Henry, lay in one corner of the living room in the little house in which I grew up. I vividly remember walking into the house and seeing that everything looked so familiar, yet something looked so different as well. His emaciated body said more than I could ever put into words. He looked at me with piercing eyes. I watched his motionless body and sought to understand the many things he was saying to me, even as he was not saying a word. Many questions raced through my mind. Was he dying? How quickly would this happen? What things did he want to say to me and to those who surrounded him? What was he saying anyway? How much could he ever say? What language was his body communicating? What language was everyone assigning his condition? What remained unspoken? How did his illness, living with HIV, name his reality? Was he living with HIV or dying with HIV? How could this scene reveal yet disguise the obvious? How did his frailty name his reality? What hope, strength, or meaning did this reality speak of?

As I sat and watched his body, I hoped I would see some movement. I wondered about his own emotions and the many other issues this scene represented. I recalled what he once asked of me. "Take care of my children," he had said. What did it all mean now? What stories of pain and resilience did this picture speak of? Whose other stories might this picture evoke? How do these stories gain their significance in the midst of this one story? I looked at my mother sitting next to him. She told me she would not leave his side. I heard in her voice a sense of fear, but also a determination to stay engaged with her son, something she had always done for all her children. I asked myself: Where could my father be in all of this? What messages could my brother's sons and daughters be working through given this picture? How does my brother make meaning of his condition for himself as a man, a father, a husband, a brother? How might this picture speak about larger forces or stories within the family? The culture? What narratives are evoked in this picture? How do these narratives gain dominance over others that are marginalized? What stories of justice or injustice do they pronounce? How does this picture speak about the obligations/responsibilities of richer nations in the face of deprivation?

Such questions only begin to unpack the domain of narrative practice. They reflect the layered and intersecting ways that various discourses shape life experiences and culture. They define what is possible and unpack the webs of meaning that narrative practitioners must engage while seeking to work toward a just practice.

This chapter presents key concepts of narrative practice in the context of culture. First, I discuss key ideas that are often associated with narrative practice. The notion of culture as a dynamic process and its relationship to narrative practice are discussed. The chapter also anchors narrative practice and its evolution in history. The relationship with sociopolitical concerns, as well as notions of liberation and empowerment, is presented and examples from clinical and community practice are employed.

WHAT IS NARRATIVE PRACTICE?

Narrative practice is an evolving approach to clinical work informed by postmodern, feminist, empowerment, and liberation models, all of which give primary importance to the everyday stories of people's lives, the social forces shaping personal narratives, and the ways in which these forces can marginalize, minimize, and obscure our lived experiences. Narrative practitioners help clients articulate multiple aspects of their lived experiences and then aim to identify and amplify indicators of strength and resiliency that clients often fail to recognize when describing their situations. Narrative practitioners describe this process as "thickening" the clients' descriptions (Epston & White, 1992; Morgan, 2000).

Key Concepts of Narrative Practice Text and Narrative Analogies. Narrative practice is distinguished by textual and narrative metaphors (Freedman & Combs, 1996; White & Epston, 1990). Narrative practitioners use texts and narratives as conduits through which people, events, organizations, groups, and communities make sense of lived experiences.

A text analogy helps narrative practitioners to frame people's lives as part of a broader sociopolitical context embedded with power implications (White & Epston, 1990). Narrative practitioners seek to understand the complexity of these lived experiences through the uncovering of dominant and nondominant stories.

Dominant and Subjugated Knowledges. Narrative practice draws heavily from Michel Foucault's work on power/knowledge (White & Epston, 1990). Foucault asserted that society has "normalizing truths" and "unitary knowledges" that have power that constructs people's lives. These normalizing truths create dominant knowledges for those who have power and keep other truths that do not fit these dominant accounts in subjugated positions.

Language. Narrative practice holds the view that reality is constructed and given meaning through language. All lived experience is mediated through language. Language is a non-neutral activity that shapes reality and has political implications. Narrative practice, therefore, maintains that access to language empowers individuals, groups, communities, and organizations.

Sociopolitical Stance. Narrative practice seeks to examine the sociopolitical issues embedded in an interaction. Narrative practice holds that these forces can create power over others, resulting in oppressive ways of being or relating. Narrative practice invites practitioners to accountable practice and self-awareness, especially around issues of oppression and marginalization.

Discourses, Power Relations and Positioning. Drawing on social-constructionist theory, narrative practice employs the notion of discourse in understanding what counts as meaningful. "A discourse refers to a set of meanings, metaphors, representations, images, stories, statements, and so on, that, in some way together, produce a particular version of events" (Burr, 1995). For Freedman and Combs, discourse is a system of words, action, rules, institutions, and beliefs that sustain a particular worldview (Freedman & Combs, 1996). Because no one owns the truth, and no one can claim absolute power, narrative practice strongly acknowledges people, groups, communities, and organizations as vibrant co-authors of their experiences. The experiences that surround individuals, groups, communities, and organizations should be seen not as impediments to growth but as opportunities for growth.

Core Assumptions in Narrative Practice

Poststructuralism. An important influence on narrative practice is poststructuralism. Poststructuralism, as expressed in the work of Foucault (1978), has been concerned with the relationships between language, meaning, power, knowledge, and the abandonment of structured models (White, 1997; 2000). Poststructuralism literally challenged the medieval and modernistic view of life. Meaning was no longer seen as unitary but as multiple, unstable, and open to interpretation (Foucault, 1978). Similarly, language or discourse was viewed as situated rather than neutral.

Language. Within a poststructuralist viewpoint, language is viewed as creating reality. Language is situated in historical, social, and political contexts. Language offers meaning and creates power within these contexts. Foucault argued that knowledge and power are inextricably linked. Foucault questioned the belief that there is a fixed singular order that is true and unmediated. Foucault proposed that categories, definitions, and constructs vary in relation to their particular social, historical, and political milieus. In a poststructuralist view, identity is fluid, changeable, and derived from multiple discourses.

Because meaning is obscured by singular, fixed belief systems, poststructuralism seeks to recover suppressed meanings through a process of questioning known as deconstruction (Derrida, 1978; White, 1990). In so doing, multiple discourses are elevated as meaningful. Similarly, poststructuralism highlights the importance of subjectivity, which is multifaceted and multivoiced depending on the context. In the context of power structures, poststructuralism challenges claims of authority any power would assert to have. Such an approach will claim that there is no inquiry apart from that which is defined by some specific personal and social perspective.

Poststructuralism would also assert that there are dominant discourses. These dominant discourses have been privileged over nondominant discourses. One illustration is the discourse that views illness as an issue of finality rather than as an opportunity or possibility. For example, it is easy to see in Henry a story of a sick and dying man, yet within the same story, a father who loved and cared for his children.

Poststructuralism views power as a process that enables/restricts or promotes/ discourages forms of practice or thought (Adam, 1995, Burr, 1995; Foucault, 1978). As an interpretative paradigm, poststructuralism is characterized by a stance of suspicion toward all grand schemes of meaning, and all ideologies that claim total explanatory power (Hollenbach, 1996). Drawing on this paradigm, narrative practices (White & Epston, 1990) affirm the idea that people's lives and relationships are shaped by the "stories" that they and their surrounding communities create in order to give meaning to their experience. To work with a narrative worldview is to seek "not to privilege specific models, theories, or taken for granted assumptions about human nature, . . . [but to] remain curious and questioning about how people construct their lives and tell their life stories." (Speedy, 2000, p. 365).

POWER AND IDENTITY NARRATIVES

Another influence on narrative practice is the long history of debate by philosophers on the ways we come to know who we truly are within the dialectics of subjectivity/objectivity, or universal empiricism/contextual constructivism. Nietzsche was among the first philosophers of the modern era to challenge the ideas of objective truth or "Cartesian Enlightenment." He instead surfaced the subjugated discourse of "perspectivism" (Irving, 1999, p. 35) as this relates to the search for a "true identity." He described the search for identity as a process that lies within a "movable host of metaphors . . . a sum of human relations" (Nietzsche, 1979, p. 84 as cited in Irving, 1999, p. 33). Nietzsche targeted two inherent flaws within the universal/empirical discourse, which are that: (1) it ignores the importance of language in developing our worldview, and (2) it depends on a flawed assumption that all people perceive the world in the same way (Irving, 1999, p. 34).

Nietzsche's work heavily influenced the postmodern philosophy of Michel Focault. Focault expanded on the ideas of perspectivism, illuminating the function of universal "regimes of truth" (Irving, 1999, p. 36) as a method of gaining and maintaining power and social control. Regimes of truth would relegate explanations to one grand truth. In turn, White and other narrative therapists have integrated the work of Foucault in the development of the narrative therapy conceptual framework. It is through the integration of Foucault's beliefs about the relationship between universal truths and imposed power, and more specifically, their link to increased hierarchy within the clinical relationship, that has led the narrative approach to view this hierarchical approach as further disempowering the individuals and families seen in clinical work (White, 1997, p. 57). The narrative perspective cautions us against the blind application of the prescriptive universal truths systems, identifying a questioning stance as an ethical commitment within psychotherapy (Hoyt & Combs, 1996, p. 37).

INTEGRATION OF CORE IDEAS IN NARRATIVE PRACTICE

Narrative practice acknowledges that people's lives are stories rich with meaning. These stories create facts through which life is lived. The facts, however, are constrained by language and culture. People's lives are seen as multiple stories. Some stories are dominant, whereas others are often nondominant. These nondominant stories tend to be marginalized.

The valuing of people's everyday lives acknowledges the sociocultural/historical context in which these stories are lived and told. These stories create the "facts" in people's lives just as people constantly create the stories. They are indeed formats for self-creation, full of gaps and openings underscoring their complexity and multi-perspectives.

In narrative practice, language is viewed as creating reality. For Freedman and Combs (1996), language constitutes our world and beliefs. Using a social construc-tionist approach, Freedman and Combs' main premise is that:

> The beliefs, values, institutions, customs, labels, laws, divisions of labor, and the like that make up our social realities are constructed by the members of a culture as they interact with one another from generation to generation and day to day. That is, societ-ies construct the "lenses" through which their members interpret the world. The reali-ties that each of us take for granted are the realities that our societies have surrounded us with since birth. These realities provide the beliefs, practices, words, and experi-ences from which we make up our lives. (p. 16)

Narrative practice holds the view that people's lives are not single-storied but multistoried. As such, narrative practice invites people to shift from a single story to a multistory perspective. A consequence of this multistoriedness is narrative's stance to "exoticize" the domestic (White, personal communication, March 25, 2004). Seeing people's lives beyond what is ordinary or familiar opens one to be cu-rious about these lives.

Such a stance also underscores what narrative practice calls unique outcomes. "Unique outcomes are experiences that would not be predicted by the plot of the problem-saturated narrative" (Freedman & Combs, 1996, p. 67). Narrative practitio-ners seek to examine unique outcomes in narratives to allow for the emergence of other narratives that reflect local knowledges and alternative possibilities.

Narrative practice is therefore about opening up and "re-authoring" or "re-storying" conversations. Morgan (2000) writes of stories as consisting of events that are linked in sequence, across time—all of which create meaning according to a plot. The narrative then is the thread that weaves the events together. "No single story can be free of ambiguity or contradiction and no single story can encapsulate or handle all the contingencies of life" (Morgan, 2000, p. 8).

Narrative practice underscores the complex nature of stories in people's lives. These stories have been woven by certain events in a sequence and by the meaning people attribute to them. Narrative recognizes that people have "thin" stories and "thin" conclusions about their lives. Such thin stories may appear in ways that peo-ple represent themselves as incompetent. In narrative practice, the movement is to "thicken" people's stories and to work toward rich story development.

Because life is multistoried, narrative practice honors the many stories that un-fold in people's lives. In narrative practice, no one story can be said to capture the complexity of life. Indeed, narrative practice acknowledges the fact that these sto-ries span all time from the past, to the present, and into the future. These stories could also be contradicting of each other or affirming of each other. The important thing to note is that, in narrative practice, individuals and communities not only are full of stories but also are continually writing new stories.

According to Freedman and Combs (1996), our lives are socially constructed. Indeed, we become who we are through relationships, through how others perceive us and interact with us, and through how we make meaning of those social interactions. Indeed, the story of my brother who lay motionless on the floor may be constructed in a variety of ways. Because HIV is a disease that is terminal, one could view him as dying with AIDS. However, my mother who daily sat with him saw him as living painfully with HIV.

DOMINANT AND NONDOMINANT STORIES

The dominant discourses in our society powerfully influence what gets "storied" and how it gets storied. An outgrowth of the multistoried life is the belief that there are dominant stories and nondominant stories. The dominant are stories that often get privileged over other stories that are marginalized or that may be privileged differently. Some stories become dominant because they are often highlighted at the expense of others. Often these dominant stories "reflect a prevailing structure of social and power relationships" (Madigan & Law, 1992, p. 22). Such an imbalance in the interaction seeks to honor the privileged at the expense of those without power in the interaction. Narrative practice seeks to uncover dominant and nondominant stories in order to examine both. The recognition of both gives rise to an appreciation of alternative stories, all of which add to the rich development of people's lives. Similarly, the surfacing of alternative stories underscores the fact that there are gaps and openings in people's lived stories. It is also an acknowledgment of the multiknowledge perspective in people's lives.

Narrative practice invites mental health professionals to examine their stance in their relationship with those with whom they work. Such a challenge may involve examining the very techniques practitioners use. Practitioners must develop what Schussler-Fiorenza has described as "*hermeneutic* of suspicion" (Schussler-Fiorenza, 1984). A hermeneutic of suspicion is an invitation to be suspicious of our own machinations or techniques. Unchecked or unexamined, they can become oppressive to those we seek to help, creating a new dominant force of ourselves as practitioners in the interaction.

These stories are, therefore, not just performances. They also create facts and knowledges that give meaning to people's lives. Writing about illness narratives, Weingarten (1998) states: "Whether we are aware of a discourse or not, it can powerfully shape the stories we can tell and the stories we can hear. Discourses influence what we can know and not know, see and not see, say and not say, in complex and subtle ways" (p. 4).

Another way practitioners engage in this interaction is through deconstructive listening. In narrative practice, deconstructive listening refers to a type of listening that opens up space for new meaning and understandings. Deconstructive approaches use questioning methods and attend to language construction.

Henry's HIV status illustrates this. For many people all over the world, the diagnosis of HIV sends a clear message that the end is imminent. It echoes the story of finality. However, as I watched Henry surrounded by his family, I sensed his new relationship to life and his optimism to hang on to life.

NARRATIVE PRACTICE AND CULTURE

Another important influence on narrative practice is culture and its constraints. Culture creates the broader social context in which life stories are performed and understood. As Morgan (2000) has put it, "the context of gender, class, race, culture, and sexual preference are powerful contributors to the plot of the stories we live by" (p. 9). Therefore the beliefs, ideas, practices, myths, hopes, dreams, and expectations of the culture play a large part in the meanings we make of our lives. It is also important to note that there are simultaneous influences from other forces both inside and outside the culture. It is therefore necessary to understand story as a dynamic force in people's lives. Cultural forces shape these ideas just as much as these ideas shape cultural forces. With the ever-evolving nature of people's stories, narrative practice deeply values and honors diversity. Narrative practice seeks to deconstruct taken-for-granted norms in order to build an appreciation of diversity in a rapidly evolving context.

TRADITIONAL VERSUS EVOLVING UNDERSTANDINGS OF CULTURE

To understand narrative practice, one must contextualize it in culture. Laird (2000) proposes a metalevel of thinking by raising key questions in exploring the meaning of "culture." In particular, Laird invites practitioners to "learn to think about how to think about culture" (p. 100). For Laird, this metathinking is crucial and useful in practicing responsibly. It is an invitation to move beyond static notions of culture into more dynamic and evolving ways of imaging culture. It is also important to note that, as a dynamic notion, culture is multidimensional and multicontextual.

Static notions of culture view it as unchanging, or something that is learned from books or already existing knowledge. Such a view can be found in several textbooks that seek to offer a deterministic understanding of each specific culture. It is no wonder, then, that one might find statements that offer generalized pictures about different cultures. Although some general statements can be made about a particular situation or group, one can argue that such general statements, at best, are reductionistic because any culture or explanation of it is very complex. It is more than just one thing or one experience. People's experiences are often complicated by history and social locations, all of which continue to offer new ways of understanding any one situation. Indeed, definitive statements about any one culture may only offer a temporary grasp of a situation or a culture. A close examination of such definitions or understandings can reveal stereotypic ways of thinking that do not do justice to the complexity or the ever-evolving nature of issues.

Traditional understandings hold captive the notion of culture. They provide a narrow view of culture that relegates it to something that is knowable. Such traditional understandings may include statements that equate a group to some stereotypic activity. Traditional understandings operate with a modernistic view that seeks to categorize and gain control over knowledge. Although this offers the knower a sense of control, it disadvantages the one whom is sought to be known. In seeking control, one feels grounded, but such grounding often comes at the expense of that other.

Culture is shaping persons, events, circumstances, and situations just as persons, events, circumstances, and situations are shaping culture. Such a view allows for a greater exploration of the complexity of the culture or cultures that are immediately present to us, but also of those cultures that we may not be able to name. Indeed, all cultural notions are "constantly in motion, changing in meanings, and definitions . . ." (Laird, 2000, p. 106). Culture is a multifaceted domain of collective history, beliefs, and practices whose understanding is always evolving. As a dynamic notion, culture resonates well with narrative perspectives.

PROCESS OF NARRATIVE PRACTICE AND SOCIAL JUSTICE

Narrative practice seeks to name injustice and explore power relations. Narrative acknowledges the politics of analysis. Individual stories are influenced by our interactions with others. The making of narrative in shaping identity involves relations of power. The fact that the institutions like the church and government wield so much power in the face of countless helpless individuals goes back to the historical and cultural milieu in which religious and political institutions functioned with and amassed upon themselves unquestioned powers. More specifically, narrative questions various power constructions including gender, race, religion, and patriarchy (Freedman & Combs, 1996; White & Epston, 1990). Men have traditionally had power over women. It is no wonder, then, that the church and most governmental institutions that have been male-dominated continued to oppress women and children, some of the most vulnerable members of society. One example in which power has been abused is the case of the clergy sexual abuse that recently surfaced in the American Catholic Church. Over the years in which the church turned a deaf ear to the abuses allegedly perpetrated by its clergy, distinct gender stories that limited life narratives pervaded people's understanding. The church shied away from the process of deconstructing these limiting stories and bringing forth previously marginalized stories (White, 1990).

Narrative practice values the expertise each person, community, and group brings to any situation. Anderson and Goolishian (1992) have written so eloquently about the client as the expert. They strongly support the stance of "not knowing" one ought to take as one enters into the life of another. They have proposed that a therapist enter the life of clients as an anthropologist who is seeking meaning, rather than as a missionary looking to assign meaning.

It is indeed like opening a book, in some cases seemingly thin and unadorned, binding broken, pages stuck together, torn and missing in what may seem as a first-ever reading of an ignored and obscure work. Working in this mode is like a discovery, perhaps of a new language in a book never before studied, unaccounted for amongst other dominant volumes that have crowded it out. With great care and respect, narrative practitioners work first at just opening the cover, straining to reserve judgment. And then like anthropologists, narrative practitioners glimpse at what might appear at first to be a foreign language. To do so they must embrace a stance of humility as they enter uncharted territories.

Narrative means of understanding therapeutic interaction and effect is derived from an attitude of inquiry rather than instruction. The narrative way is one of co-creation of meaning and interpretation. It is not about the formula of correct questions, but rather about the curiosity with which the practitioner joins the client as the expert in the creation of his or her story.

Socially constructed narratives have real effects in people's lives. For example, the myth that immigrant populations are a drain to the U.S. economy has had negative effects on immigrants—many of whom are contributing to the U.S. economy through hard labor often accomplished in exploitive conditions. Such a view has created policies that have hurt not only those immigrants but also their U.S.-born children. Narrative practitioners must continually question the grand schemes and discourses that continue to alienate these immigrants. Narrative practice must ask questions that invite and open doors rather than make pronouncements that shut doors. In the story of the immigrant, narrative practice must peek and delve further to uncover other, yet-untold stories. Narrative practice must question the injustice to allow for the emergence of other stories. Such a stance helps both practitioners and those they serve to notice the influence of cultural stories that constrain and allow those stories that expand people's experience to develop.

NARRATIVE THERAPY PROCESSES AND TECHNIQUES

The practice of narrative provides new ways of engaging in the therapy process. In particular, it underscores many distinctive features inherent in social justice.

Therapy as a Movement of Resistance

Social inequalities dictated by gender, race, culture, sexual orientation, religion, ethnic background, and ability have a direct impact on the well-being of individuals, groups, communities, and organizations. Narrative therapy as a process echoes the work of liberation theologians. The term *liberation theology,* which has its genesis in the Latin American experience, refers to God's liberation or salvation working on the side of the poor and the oppressed. In a broader sense, it has come to represent the experience of dispossessed people around the world. Although started in the context of the church's response to the poor, the powerless, and the dispossessed, theologies of liberation now speak strongly to institutions of power and their oppressive practices. Indeed, their goal, like that of narrative therapy, is to offer a voice of resistance in the face of powerlessness.

Empowerment models and theology of liberation approaches echo the social justice agenda in narrative practice. Like liberation theology, empowerment theory and narrative practice provide a model for critical reflection and action in the struggle for social transformation. Rappaport (1987) defines empowerment as "a process, a mechanism by which people, organizations, and communities gain mastery over their affairs, and involve themselves in the democratic processes of their community and employing institutions" (p. 122). Narrative therapy process seeks to achieve this social transformation.

Like the work of Freire (1970), narrative therapy process seeks to undermine the oppressor–oppressed dynamic that subjugates those in powerless positions. As a movement of resistance, narrative therapy process assumes that knowledge is not neutral; rather, it is the expression of historical moments where some groups exercise dominant power over others. Oppressed groups of individuals often experience life as objects passively being acted on, rather than as subjects actively living out their lives. Objects often lack certain critical skills essential for influencing the institutions that have control over their lives. People not only have skills for influencing institutions, but also have the opportunity to exercise these skills. Narrative therapy process holds the belief that people can liberate themselves by struggling to transform the conditions that oppress them. Freire (1973) proposed developing a sense of critical consciousness, which, for him, equated to liberation. Critical consciousness is a dialectical process that involves helping individuals name the multiple conditions of their lives, identify the limits imposed on them, and take action toward change. Critical consciousness allows individuals, families, and groups to question the nature of their historical and social situation with the goal of transformation. Narrative therapy process engages people in a critical analysis, reflection, and dialogue into action toward eliminating any oppressive structures. Power issues must be continually examined (Foucault, 1978; McGoldrick,1998; Pinderhughes, 1989; Weingarten,1998; White & Epston, 1990). As a movement of resistance, narrative therapy process values subjugated knowledge and seeks to elevate such knowledges with dignity.

Invitation to Accountability, Problem-Posing and Curiosity

Because therapy can, in itself, create a power dynamic and imbalance, narrative therapy seeks to account for its stance. The process involved is one of co-investigation. Narrative therapists must continually ask themselves how they might be contributing to the oppressive structure that they are fighting against. Indeed, in working toward a socially just world, we must continually be "suspicious" of our own knowledges and examine "sneaky" ways that can make us victim of the force of power and control.

To be accountable we must engage in a "problem-posing" approach (Freire, 1973) in which learning is a mutual process involving therapist and client working together to ask thought-provoking questions. As such, human beings experience interactions as something they do, not something that is done to them. In this approach, individuals and communities are not empty vessels to be filled with facts, or sponges to be saturated with official information. Instead, problem-posing offers a democratic search for knowledge from a variety of situated positions. Conversations then become dialogical rather than monological (Kamya & Trimble, 2002). It also moves people into action as they keep asking critical questions. A narrative stance is a questioning stance that echoes this empowerment approach.

The need to ask more questions is a consequent imperative that seeks to widen new areas of inquiry about a variety of issues that move the therapy process toward social transformation (Kamya & O'Brien, 2000). To not ask questions is to engage a discourse of knowing that forecloses on developing a stance of curiosity and openness. Indeed, it becomes the opportunity for oppression and suppression, both of which beget an unjust society. To do this is to engage in marginalizing narratives. Narrative practice invites people to engage in a serious inquiry of the historical and social context of practice and ideas in order to identify the effects, dangers, and limitations of these practices. The message that narrative therapy process offers is that of continually working toward social justice and social transformation.

Techniques in the Narrative Therapy Process

Narrative practitioners will utilize a number of techniques in the therapy process. Such techniques include a serious scrutiny and appreciation of language from a microperspective to a macroperspective. Narrative practitioners will pay attention to the language that people use to describe themselves and their situations. They will examine the meaning that words carry, both the assigned meanings and the implied meanings. Such a keen eye to language engages in meta-thinking about meanings.

One technique used in narrative therapy is called externalizing conversations. The aim of externalizing conversations is to offer alternative naming of people's problems. Culture has often created ways of naming people's problems. For example, such naming has reflected the psychopathology model of mental illness that has dominated the field of mental health treatment. The dominant discourse has suggested that there is something wrong with the person who struggles with any issue or concern. Engaging in externalizing conversations helps to separate people from their problems. It suggests that people have influences on the problems in their lives just as the problems have influences on them. Narrative practitioners therefore seek to unpack the nature of the relationship a person or organization has with a problem. In so doing, narrative practitioners explore and evaluate the effects of the problem on the person, the meaning of the problem, and ultimately the meaning of the effects the problem has on a person or an organization. In so doing, narrative therapy process identifies the cultural supports for the problem. It further identifies exceptions to the problem's influence and encourages eliciting the meaning of the influence a person or an organization has on a problem. It also aims at clarifying the person's preferences and values that might influence the problem.

Another technique utilized by the narrative process is the plotting of narratives in the "landscape of action and consciousness" (Freedman & Combs, 1996, p. 96). In the landscape of action, the therapist inquires about the specific actions that constitute the preferred narrative, highlighting the agency of persons or communities involved. The landscape of action has clear implications for social justice and social action. The landscape of consciousness invites participants in the process to examine the depth of meaning of actions. One might wonder in the process what it must mean on a larger scale to engage in daily acts of resistance.

The narrative therapy process also uses letters to document new narratives. These documents written by a practitioner and client render a lived experience into a narrative. They also provide local knowledges into a wider circulation underscoring significant shifts in people's lives. Local knowledges refer to people's articulation of their lived experiences that they alone author. They also invite more audiences to witness these new narratives.

The case of Atim illustrates the narrative therapy process and its suspicion of the various meanings assigned to words. Atim, a 25-year-old man who had recently immigrated to the United States, walked into my office as a referral from his physician. He reported that he was very depressed. He described arriving in this country a few months before from an African country where he had seen many of his relatives murdered. He worried for his life and about the possibility that he would be deported. Recently, he had gotten involved with a White American woman who he described as lacking in understanding of his culture:

She cannot understand that I need to call home many times to find out about my relatives. She says she has provided me all that I need. But I do need more. She says I am
depressed because I do not like to eat. I stay awake all night. I am thinking of my family
in Africa. I have to constantly think about them. I do not know exactly what I feel.
Maybe I am very depressed.

A narrative approach would be to examine the various meanings associated with
the depression he reports. Questions such as: What other names would you give depression? What names does depression express? When depression has not been
part of your life, what has your depression felt like to others? Does depression have
other influences in your life? What do you imagine the world would look like without
depression? What supports are there for depression in your life? In other people's
lives? These are externalizing questions that seek to locate the problem outside the
person. They also seek to examine influences and meanings depression might have
in a person's life or a community's life.

Deconstructive listening and questioning has helped the work with Atim. Lately,
he has been able to invite others into his life, widening his influence and his ability
to see himself as agential in his life.

There are many discourses that influence mental health professionals' attitudes
and practices including "discourses about pathology, about normative standards,
and about professionals as experts" (Freedman & Combs, 1996, p. 42). Narrative
practice challenges the concepts of the dominant discourses that pervade people's
lives. In Atim's case, it was important to deconstruct his understanding of depression. Together, Atim and I were able to name a variety of meanings associated with
his feeling "depressed." We were also able to identify how depression served Atim
as he began a new life in the United States. Deconstruction, according to Morgan
(2000), is the narrative practitioner's interest in "discovering, acknowledging, and
'taking apart' (deconstructing) the beliefs, ideas, and practices of the broader culture in which a person lives that are serving to assist the problem and the problem
story" (p. 45). Deconstructing the problematic story in a given issue enables us to
identify the negative social, cultural, and psychological effects associated with it.
Deconstruction often provides a basis for theorists and practitioners to resist the
dominant discourse by creating theories and professional practices that offer alternative nonpathological, health-centered, and client-focused practice models. Narrative practice, therefore, seeks to locate problems in particular discourses and in so
doing, helping people to see themselves as separate from their problems. Once an
individual identifies a problem and its problematic discourse, she or he can oppose
the discourse or choose to construct a different, preferred, discourse.

Situating problems in larger sociocultural contexts always has to do with un-
masking problematic discourses. Narrative practice offers people opportunities to
see themselves as separate from the problems that bind them, and to be hopeful
about managing those problems. One illustration of these benefits of narrative practice is a couple that has been married for five years. Maggie, a 42-year-old woman,
met Jim, a 41-year-old man, six years ago. They both describe falling in love instantly
and deciding to get married. Maggie was plagued by the fear that she would never
get married. She felt "barraged by my mother's insistence that I find a man." When
they came to see me, they reported that they lacked the spark they had when they
first met. Although it was important to do a major history-gathering around family-
of-origin issues and their expectations of themselves and of each other, it became
clear that there were major discourses that directed their understanding of a good

marriage. They both seemed too bound by what their families of origin expected of them. In fact, they were not able to name what they wanted for themselves. Most of their explanations were couched with what others thought about them. Discourses of patriarchy and matriarchy affected them differently.

As our work unfolded, we needed to unpack these discourses and examine the meaning and effects of these discourses on their life together. Lately, they have begun to ask other questions that have allowed them to look beyond culturally expected norms. Indeed, after exploring these issues, Maggie and Jim appreciated the fact that they did not have to have biological children of their own. Maggie finally acknowledged that it was her mother's wish to be a grandmother of Maggie and Jim's biological children. The discourse of having biological children seemed to paralyze Maggie and Jim from imagining other possibilities for themselves. Maggie and Jim have worked to name their own needs in and feelings about their relationship apart from Maggie's mother's interests and dreams for them. They are now considering adopting children.

But Maggie's and Jim's examination of their life as a couple also evoked larger discourses about family and family values. Maggie became an advocate for adoption and welfare services, focusing on international adoption. She and Jim took up their cause for social justice and became lobbyists for international adoptions, seeking to relax restrictions against these adoptions. They turned their individual challenge into a collective cause to provide more for children who needed love and care.

CONCLUSION

Narrative practice encourages individuals to become authors of their own stories. It seeks to work toward social justice. Previously marginalized persons and groups become empowered simply by authoring or co-authoring their own life stories. They can reclaim their right to their own stories. What then matters is the meaning that gets attached to one's life and how that meaning is transformed into larger causes that fight injustice in the world. The making of that meaning is much richer if it is created by individuals, not forced on them by a discourse that has no time or place for an individual's meaning making. Narrative practice further invites individuals and groups to join in promoting social justice and engaging in social change efforts to reduce the effects of oppression. Narrative practice challenges the hierarchical structures that engage in surveillance and monitoring practices that place judgment over others. The narrative practice of promoting the creation and choice of preferred stories, local knowledge, and subjective realities must be seen in contrast to, and as transformations of, pre-constructs, global truths, and objective realities. Narrative practice, therefore, has a voice in larger social justice issues like gender, class, sexual orientation, race, and prejudice. But it also speaks to other concerns like abuse, illness, spirituality, and self-care. Not only does narrative practice empower individuals, it also works towards the greater collective good of society.

REFERENCES

Adam, A. K. (1995). *What is postmodern Biblical criticism?* Minneapolis, MN: Fortress Press.

Anderson, H., & Goolshian, H. (1992). The client is the expert: A not-knowing approach to therapy. In S. McNamee & K. J. Gegen (Eds.), *Therapy as a social construction* (pp. 25–39). Newbury Park, CA: Sage.

Burr, V. (1995). *An introduction to social constructionism*. London: Routledge.

Derrida, J. (1978). *Writing and difference.* London: Routledge.

Epston, D., & White, M. (1992). Consulting our consultants: The documentation of alternative knowledges. In D. Epston & M. White (Eds.), *Experience and contradiction, narrative and imagination: Situated papers of David Epston and Michael White, 1989–1991.* Adelaide: Dulwich Centre Publications.

Foucault, M. (1978). *The archaeology of knowledge.* London: Tavistock.

Freedman, J., & Combs, G. (1996). *Narrative therapy: The social construction of preferred realities.* New York: Norton.

Freire, P. (1970). *Pedagogy of the oppressed.* New York: Seabury.

Freire, P. (1973). *Education for critical consciousness.* New York: Continuum.

Hollenbach, D. (1996). The Catholic university under the sign of the cross. In M. Himes & S. Pope (Eds.), *Finding God in all things* (pp. 27–34). New York: Crossroad.

Hoyt, M. F., & Combs, G. (1996). On ethics and spiritualities of the surface: A conversation with Michael White. In M. F. Hoyt (Ed.), *Constructive therapies* (2nd ed., pp. 33–60). New York: Guilford.

Irving, A. (1999). Waiting for Foucault: Social work and the multitudinous truth(s) of life. In A. Chambon, A. Irving, & L. Epstein (Eds.), *Reading Foucault for social work* (pp. 27–50). New York: Columbia University Press.

Kamya, H., & O'Brien, M. (2000). Interprofessional education in theology and social work: Postmodern and practical theological dimensions. *Journal of Teaching in Theology and Religion, 3*(1), 20–32.

Kamya, H., & Trimble, D. (2002). Response to injury: Toward ethical construction of the other. *Journal of Systemic Therapies, 21*(3), 19–29.

Laird, J. (2000). Theorizing culture: Narrative ideas and practice principles. *Journal of Feminist Family Therapy, 11*(4), 99–114.

Madigan, C., & Law, I. (1992). Discourse not language: The shift from a modernistic view of language to the postmodern analysis of discourse in family therapy. *Dulwich Centre Newsletter, 1,* 31–36.

McGoldrick, M. (1998). *Revisioning family therapy.* New York: Guilford.

Morgan, A. (2000). *An introduction to narrative therapy.* Adelaide: Dulwich Centre Publications.

Phillips, D., & Henderson, D. (1999). Patient was hit in the face by a fist. . . . A discourse analysis of male violence against women. *American Journal of Orthopsychiatry, 69*(1), 116–121.

Pinderhughes, E. (1989). *Understanding race, ethnicity, and power.* New York: The Free Press.

Rappaport, J. (1987). Terms of empowerment—exemplars of prevention: Toward a theory for community psychology. *American Journal of Community Psychology 15,* 2, 121–145.

Schussler-Fiorenza, E. (1984). *Bread not stone: The challenge of feminist Biblical interpretation.* Boston: Beacon Press.

Speedy, J. (2000). The 'storied' helper: Narrative ideas and practices in counseling and psychotherapy. *Journal of Psychotherapy, Counseling and Health, 3*(3), 361–374.

Weingarten, K. (1998). The small and the ordinary: The daily practice of a postmodern narrative therapy. *Family Process, 37,* 3–16.

Weingarten, K. (2001). Making sense of illness narratives: Braiding theory, practice and the embodied life. In D. Denborough (Ed.), *Working with the stories of women's lives* (pp. 111–125). Adelaide: Dulwich Centre Publications.

White, M. (1990). Deconstruction and therapy. *Dulwich Centre Newsletter, 3,* 21–40.

White, M. (1997). *Narratives of therapists' lives.* Adelaide: Dulwich Centre Publications.

White, M. (2000). *Reflections on narrative practice: Essays and interviews.* Adelaide: Dulwich Centre Publications

White, M., & Epston, D. (1990). *Narrative means to therapeutic ends.* Adelaide: Dulwich Centre Publications.

COMMUNITY BUILDING
FOR WELLNESS AND JUSTICE

CHAPTER

10

Families and Therapists as Citizens: The Families and Democracy Project*

William J. Doherty
University of Minnesota

Jason S. Carroll
Brigham Young University

Psychotherapy in its various manifestations would appear to be the quintessentially private profession. People go to therapists to deal with personal problems, and many therapists are drawn to this work because they enjoy intimate psychological dialogue. Therapists are bounded by tighter norms of privacy and confidentiality than most other professionals, and they are expected to avoid relationships with clients outside of the therapy room. It seems a big leap, then, to think of therapists as public citizens engaging in the work of building community and creating social change.

This chapter introduces a new therapeutic paradigm that we hope can move the field past the current gap between ideals and models of public practice. To begin, we set the stage by making a case for the public role of therapists, arguing that dichotomous thinking and misleading beliefs have limited us. We then introduce "family-centered community building" as an emerging arena that combines a family perspective with traditional community perspectives. After a discussion of the special relevance of these ideas to family therapy at this point in its history, we conclude with a discussion of the Families and Democracy Project (FDP). The FDP moves family therapists and other professionals into the community via (1) a critique of traditional provider/consumer models of family services, (2) a set of principles about the civic engagement of families in partnership with professionals, and (3) a set of public practices for working on community problems. We describe the Families and Democracy Model (FDM) and two specific projects that illustrate how it can be applied in real-world settings. We distinguish the model from traditional hierarchical and collaborative models of working with families. And finally, we discuss lessons we have learned so far and our plans to take this work to its next developmental stage.

We begin with a provocative exchange among four leading family therapists that illustrates the gap between training for clinical practice and ideals for social change. Scott Johnson (2001a) argued against what he termed *messianic tendencies* in family therapy, the notion that we have a professional responsibility to bring justice to the world and save the planet. Johnson believes that, because we are trained to work

---

*This chapter is an updated version of Doherty and Carroll (2002a, 2002b).

clinically with individual families, we should be content to make our contributions to human welfare in that way. Our job is to improve human relationships; the more expansive ecological ideals of Gregory Bateson (1972) and subsequent leaders in the field have led us down a path of professional hubris by claiming that family systems theory has the power to save the world.

In a series of commentaries, Carlos Sluzki (2001), Monica McGoldrick (2001), and Ken Hardy (2001) challenge Johnson for limiting the role of the therapist. They argue that matters of social justice, culture, and the larger ecology influence clients' lives and therefore must be fodder for therapy. A poor family's problems are probably related to poverty, which is a social condition stemming from societal inequities, not a clinical condition. The authors fault Johnson for narrowing the role of the therapist after more than two decades of efforts in the field to open it up to this broader context. In his response, Johnson (2001b) notes that he does not mean that therapists should ignore the larger context of clients' lives, but that he rejects the idea that we have the tools and skills, and therefore the responsibility, to directly take on social problems outside of the therapy room. His quarrel, it seems, is not with contextually sensitive therapy but with what he sees as illusions in our rhetoric, which he believes lead to self-righteous, intolerant, and self-deluding thinking.

This exchange illuminates a dilemma for the field at the start of the 21st century. We think that Sluzki, McGoldrick, and Hardy are correct in stressing that therapists must be concerned with larger social issues and must treat clients in the context of these issues. Our agreement with Johnson is more complicated. We are not as disturbed as Johnson is by sweeping rhetoric about changing the world. As long as they avoid intolerance of other worthy approaches to changing the world, professionals' expansive ideas about making public contributions are important and even necessary for a publicly engaged profession. Indeed, as Brint and Levy (1999) found in their historical research on contemporary professions, until the 1930s professional leaders often articulated larger visions of making contributions to the public good and building a democratic nation. In subsequent decades, most professions focused on guild interests and did their "public service" through committees and task forces created to educate the public or advocate for public policies.

But expansive rhetoric has only limited utility without a set of practices for intervening in the public domain. Interestingly, Johnson's critics relied almost exclusively on clinical illustrations, a setting where we now have a set of practices to address the context of clients' lives. But talking with clients about the broader context of their problems, or even intervening on their behalf in local systems, is a far cry from taking direct public action to solve social problems. Helping clients one-to-one is only an indirect way to change the world, especially because only a small minority of people ever see a therapist. (Hillman & Ventura's [1992] book, *We've Had a Hundred Years of Psychotherapy and the World's Getting Worse,* comes to mind here.) In other words, in family therapy we have an inspiring paradigm that calls for social change, but we lack models for how to work on social change beyond helping our own clients in a contextually sensitive fashion.

THE PUBLIC ROLE OF THERAPISTS

All the therapeutic professions—psychiatry, psychology, clinical social work, marriage and family therapy, psychiatric nursing, professional counseling—share assumptions about the nature of professional practice that emerged in the early 20th century (Sullivan, 1995). We divide several of these assumptions into the categories of false dichotomies and misleading conventional beliefs.

False Dichotomies That Shape Therapy's Paradigm

The first dichotomy to be discussed is the *private/public split*, the notion that some problems are purely private and others purely public. (By "public," we mean the larger social, cultural, economic, political and environmental spheres.) Depression in the therapy literature appears almost exclusively as a private problem—depending on your orientation, either a chemical imbalance or psychological disorder or both. Widespread poverty, on the other hand, is seen as a public problem, with societal and economic origins. In our teaching and research, we generally overlook how depression and poverty mutually influence each other, for example, how poverty leads to depression and how depression keeps people mired in poverty. Or take schizophrenia, a prototypically individual medical disorder that often is treated, or not treated, in jails and prisons, which have become the de facto mental health system for many people with serious and persistent mental illness. We know that people with serious mental illness who are abandoned by society have more frequent exacerbations of their illness. Mental illness is a public problem, not just a private one, but the discourse of professional psychotherapy tends to concentrate only on the private domain, leaving the public domain to public health specialists and policymakers. Although it could be argued that clinical social work has a greater community perspective than the other mental health professions, we believe that in everyday practice the work of clinical workers is not very different from that of other clinical professionals.

The second dichotomy is *provider/consumer roles*. This duality runs deep in contemporary American culture (Boyte & Kari, 1996). Individuals are either the providers of a service or the recipient of a service, the former the seller and the latter the buyer. Professional providers are experts on the problems of consumer clients, and consumers are assumed to be concerned only with getting the best service for themselves as individuals, and not with anything related to the common good of a community. Our concern here is not with legitimate differences in roles, or with therapist expertise, but about how the service provider role has come to dominate the way we think about the work of therapists (and other professionals). Missing from our discourse is a way to think of ourselves as citizens, not just providers, as people engaged in partnerships with other citizens to tackle public problems. Also missing is the idea of our clients as citizens with something to contribute to their communities, beyond the "trickle down" effect—the idea that when clients function better personally, they will inevitably be better citizens. The provider/consumer dichotomy leaves out a third alternative—citizen partnerships where we are neither providers nor consumers—which our world sorely needs in an era of widespread disengagement from civic life in the United States and many other industrialized nations of the world (Putnam, 2000, 2004).

The third dichotomy is *individual therapy versus community work*. By individual therapy, we mean work with individuals, families, or small groups, as distinguished from community-based activities for larger groups. Since at least the 1920s, U.S. professions have divided themselves into the majority of providers who work in the individual sphere and a minority who work in the public sphere (Sullivan, 1995; the same split occurs in varying degrees in other countries with which we are familiar).

Examples are clinical medicine versus public health medicine, clinical nursing versus public health nursing, community social work versus clinical social work, and community psychology versus clinical/counseling psychology. When a profession discovers the importance of the community, it generally spins off a subspecialty. In most cases, that community specialty then becomes marginalized from the mainstream of the profession that spawned it (social work is the exception, but in social work, clinical work is often disparaged). In every case we know of, the two groups are cut off from meaningful interaction with each other. In mental health, community-oriented professionals focus on prevention and are often disdainful of the work of clinicians (Albee, 1990), who, in turn, ignore the work of community professionals. In our own work to transcend this dichotomy, we promote the idea that therapists who work with individuals and families could also engage in a citizen project while keeping their day jobs doing therapy. They would do this work in partnership with other community members and with professionals who do community work as their main focus.

Conventional Beliefs That Limit Us

These dichotomies run deep in the paradigm of psychotherapy. They keep us out of the game of public work and civic engagement. The conventional beliefs we turn to next are less central; they don't keep us off the playing field, but they limit our scope and effectiveness as citizen professionals. We don't claim that all therapists hold these beliefs, but we believe they are quite pervasive.

Community Work Is for Low-Income Communities. The assumption here is that only low-income communities are in need of community-based initiatives, as if well-to-do suburbs are not also suffering from a lack of social capital and civic spirit. The upshot is that if a therapist does not have access to the inner city or a poor rural community, there is nothing meaningful to do except to write a check to groups who work with needy communities. The rest of us are off the hook. A more accurate belief, in our view, is that all communities can benefit from organized work of citizens to tackle local problems.

Collaborating With Community Systems Is the Same Thing as Working With Communities. Doherty and Beaton (2000) make a distinction between *community systems* (organized institutions, programs, and agencies) and *communities* (groups of individuals and families that have interlocking relationships and a degree of shared culture and purpose). There are a number of models of collaboration between therapists and community institutions for the benefit of clients (Imber-Black, 1988; McDaniel, Hepworth & Doherty, 1992), but fewer models showing therapists how to work directly with communities themselves, especially outside of clinical context where we might temporarily assemble members of a family's community to help with a clinical case (Speck, 1967). In our observation, many therapists equate "community work" with talking to other professionals about common clients.

A Therapist's Social Responsibility Can Be Adequately Addressed Through Pro Bono Clinical Services. As useful as pro bono services are for those who cannot afford treatment, pro bono work has a number of limitations: the public need for services will never be met this way, it does not alter the provider–consumer dynamic, it does not challenge the private/public split, and it does not transcend the split between individual work and community work.

Students Must Learn Their Clinical Skills First Before Doing Social Justice and Citizen Work. This belief assumes that a therapist is fundamentally a service provider to individuals and that the public dimension is an add-on. The same mistake was made decades ago by medical schools that trained students in anatomy and physiology, including dissecting cadavers, before they learned to interact humanely with patients. The template for professional identity is set from the first day of training. For those of us who came to a public citizen perspective later in our careers, it is tempting to see our own developmental path as necessary for the next generation. But just as a physician can embrace a humanistic, biopsychosocial model from the first day in medical school, so too can therapy students and trainees develop, from the start, an identity as both a personal healer and a community activist.

Public Policy Advocacy Is the Primary Way That Professionals Can Make a Difference in the Public Realm. Professionals who see the limitations of clinical work for social change often assume that the only alternative is public policy advocacy. Although essential to the public contributions of a profession, advocacy also has downsides and limitations as the primary focus of public action by professionals. We outline these here:

- Advocacy often ends up as professional elites talking to political elites about the needs of non-elite people.
- It often does not call on the resources of communities, focusing instead on outside resources and unintentionally communicating the idea that the local community is barren of resources.
- It generally does not engage communities in tackling questions of larger meaning and collective action, focusing instead on specific programs, technical policies, and complex legislation.
- Advocacy is ineffective when viewed by policymakers as predictable, partisan, and guild promoting—characteristics often true of professional advocacy efforts. At the end of the day, most professional advocacy efforts call for more resources for the profession—not necessarily a bad idea, but subject to dismissal for being mainly self-serving.
- Meaningful political change requires a combination of money, votes, and systems of relationships—none of which are delivered well by professional advocacy. Let us be clear that we believe that advocacy by therapists and their professional organizations is important. It is part of being a citizen in a democracy. But it is a selectively powerful tool, not the main way to engage therapists in sustained public action.

Being Socially Responsible Requires Taking Liberal-Left Political Positions. Most therapy organizations that engage issues of social responsibility appear to come from a liberal-left political stance (Redding, 2001). We are concerned about the underlying message this sends to therapists of other political views, and to other citizens we might partner with, that citizen work is inherently liberal or progressive.

Most Americans are political centrists, and many are conservatives. If public work by therapists requires adherence to one subset of political views, then it will always have limited potential for engaging most communities. Our work comes from a populist stance that has no political litmus tests for participants.

We see the inklings of a paradigm shift in new work emerging in family therapy and related fields, a shift away from the splits and misleading beliefs we have outlined here. Next we describe some of this work.

COMMUNITY ORGANIZING AND FAMILY-CENTERED COMMUNITY BUILDING

Since following the pioneering work of Saul Alinsky (1946), the arena of community organizing has developed innovative ways of mobilizing poor communities to tackle local problems. In recent years, Alinsky's Industrial Areas Foundation (IAF) has spread across the United States through alliances with local faith communities (Warren, 2001). (We return later to how the IAF has inspired our own work.) Similar faith-based community organizing groups, such as the Gamaliel Foundation and MI-CAH (Milwaukee Inner-city Congregations Allied for Hope) are also developing innovative community initiatives in low-income communities, often forming partnerships with faith communities in higher income communities (Hart, 2001). Outside of faith-based community initiatives, John McKnight (1995) and his group in Chicago have developed a powerful model of community building through working with the assets of local neighborhoods and other communities. In social work, Kahn (1991) has developed a sophisticated model for mobilizing citizens in neighborhood movements.

For the most part, the existing models of community work have three limitations for family therapists. First, they do not have an explicit focus on families. In some cases, the word "family" is invisible even as an ecological system; the focus is on individuals in their community context, skipping their family context. Second, most of the models have little place for professionals and especially for professional therapists. The IAF, for example, has a historic distrust (probably well-founded) of social workers and other professionals. McKnight (1995) generally sees professionals as part of the problem but not part of the solution to community problems. Although community social work and community psychology have a role for professionals, those fields are cut off from clinicians and appear to have little place for them in the work of building community and solving community problems. And third, community-organizing models tend to focus nearly exclusively on low-income communities, to the exclusion of middle-class communities. (IAF leaders told us recently that they are trying to rectify this limitation by working to organize middle-class families.) Therefore, therapists who lack access to these communities have no models for engaging in community practice.

Family-centered community building has recently emerged as an umbrella term to capture new work that tries to transcend some of the limitations of past ways of thinking of community work. As introduced by former Vice-President Al Gore and his colleagues Martha Farrell Erickson, Richard Louv, Neil Halfon and others, family-centered community building is a wedding of a community consciousness and a family consciousness. Erickson and Louv (2002) describe its core element this way:

Most of all, [Family Centered Community Building] is a movement to put family smack in the middle of community-building, asking at each step of the way, "Does this effort support strong relationships among family members? Does this effort help families do their job of caring for and encouraging all their members? Does this effort bring the whole family and all its members into a greater sense of connection and contribution to community?" (p. 570)

In recent years, family therapists have entered this arena in an important way. In 2002, for example, in our work and in the work of Ramon Rojano (2004) in *The Practice of Community Family Therapy*. These therapists are building on the pioneering contributions of narrative therapists White and Epston (1990) and Madigan and Epston (1995). Indeed, narrative therapists now often call their work "narrative and community work." We think of Charles Walgrave's innovative work with indigenous communities and political action (Walgrave & Tamasese, 1993). Other exciting work is occurring in Pittsburgh where families in faith communities are becoming sources of health promotion (Rogers & Ronsheim, 1998), and in Kentucky where an innovative training program led by Sally St. George and Dan Wulff is combining family therapy and community action.

In addition to theory and practice, there is an emerging research paradigm that seems especially well suited to family-centered community building: participatory action research or action research (Reason & Bradbury, 2001). In action research, the research team forms a collaborative relationship from the outset with community participants to bring about some change or action. In cases when the project begins as a research study, community members are involved in formulating the study questions and the research design, and interpreting the findings. In other cases, the collaborative community initiative adds a research dimension, with constant reflection by all parties about the consistency of what they are building with the democratic model in which they aspire.

THE FAMILIES AND DEMOCRACY PROJECT

Next we describe the Families and Democracy Project, our own effort to move the work of family therapists and other professionals further into the community. Family therapy, from its origin, has been viewed by its advocates as more than a treatment modality or a theory of human functioning in families. Its proponents have boldly asserted the power of viewing people not as psychological soloists but as chorus dancers in a complex family choreography played out on the larger stage of human social life and other ecological systems. Leaders as different as Bateson (1972), Bowen (1976), Auerswald (1968), and Minuchin and his colleagues (1967) tried to understand the larger world that families live in and sought to make a difference in that world. Subsequent pioneers extended this vision of a better world through the lenses of feminism, race, global politics, and narrative therapy (Boyd-Franklin, 1989; Gould & DeMuth, 1994; Hardy, 2001; Hare-Mustin, 1978; Madigan & Epston, 1995; Walters, Carter, Papp & Silverstein, 1988; White & Epston, 1995). Indeed, it seems that the creative edge of family therapy has always pushed the boundaries of the clinical office into the larger world (see review by Doherty & Beaton, 2000). We turn next to the sources of our work outside of the family therapy tradition.

Origins of the Model

The "Families and Democracy" model grew out of the "Public Work" model of the Center for Democracy and Citizenship at the University of Minnesota, as developed by Harry Boyte, Nancy Kari, Nancy Shelton and their colleagues (Boyte & Kari, 1996; Boyte, Kari, Lewis, Skelton, & O'Donoghue, 2000). Harry Boyte, a political theorist who was schooled in the civil rights struggles of the 1960s and the Saul Alinsky tradition of community organizing, moved from a radical-left political philosophy in the 1970s to what he calls a "new populism" in the 1980s and 1990s. The Public Work model brings together strands of American Pragmatism, public realm theorists such as Arendt and Habermas, and philosophical and theological traditions dealing with humans as "homo faber" (constructing the world). Specifically, the Public Work model has three main orientating ideas:

1. *Human beings as producers or co-creators of the world.* Public work is defined as "sustained, visible, serious effort by a diverse mix of ordinary people that creates things of lasting civic or public significance." This is a call for transforming the pervasive provider/consumer dynamic of American culture into a citizen dynamic.

2. *The importance of public life.* The model emphasizes the importance of a public life to a full human life. It rejects the notion of private life cut off from life in the "commons," and posits that the privatization of contemporary life leads to the unhealthy dominance of the market and the state over human affairs.

3. *Democratic, relational power.* Public work stresses the ways that ordinary people working together can influence, through "civic muscle," the world of institutions, professions, and the marketplace. "Democracy" in this sense is not just about voting and volunteering as a private citizen; it's about joining with other citizens to build a robust public world. Although not timid about conflict, the model stresses the development of relationships of mutual interest and collaborative energy to work on public solutions, rather than the traditional politics of protest.

Just as our theoretical work applied the Public Work model to families and family professionals, our practical strategies have been influenced by the contemporary version of the Industrial Areas Foundation (IAF), the community-organizing project created by Saul Alinsky (1946) in the 1940s. The IAF is a national network of multiethnic, interfaith organizations in primarily poor and moderate-income communities. Its goals are the renewal of local democracy; the reorganization of relationships of power and politics; and the restructuring of the infrastructures, physical and civic, of communities (Warren, 2001). From the IAF, we have learned the importance of listening to families to determine what is of most importance to them, mobilizing families around a problem before generating action solutions, doing one-to-one interviews to discover what families think about an issue and what their resources are, and to continually identify and develop new leaders in communities. Thus far, our work has used IAF community organizing principles around family issues among middle-class and working-class families and communities, but with a larger role for professionals than the IAF has allowed in the past. Interestingly, our recent conversations with IAF leaders indicates that the organization is becoming interested in organizing middle-class families and sees one Families and Democracy issue, the problem of overscheduled kids and underconnected families, as particularly ripe for mobilizing middle-class families.

Since the late 1990s, we have been learning to do democratic community organizing with families across a range of settings, and to articulate the theory and skills behind this work. The Families and Democracy Project (FDP) attempts to bring together an understanding of family dynamics, democratic theory, professional roles, and community organizing. We next describe the model and distinguish it from other modes of practice, and then give examples of this work in practice.

Description of the Families and Democracy Model

The model has seven principles and seven general strategies for implementing action initiatives. The model stresses the importance of civic engagement to strengthen family life, the need to transcend the traditional provider–consumer model of health care and professional service delivery, and a vision of families creating public initiatives. It has seven principles:

1. Strengthening families in our time must be done mostly by families themselves, working democratically in local communities.
2. The greatest untapped resource for strengthening families is the knowledge, wisdom, and lived experience of families and their communities.
3. Families must be engaged as producers and contributors to their communities, and not just as clients or consumers of services.
4. Professionals can play an important role in family initiatives when they learn to partner with families in identifying challenges, mobilizing resources, generating plans, and carrying out public actions.
5. If you begin with an established program, you will not end up with an initiative that is "owned and operated" by citizens. But a citizen initiative might create or adopt a program as one of its activities.
6. A local community of families becomes energized when it retrieves its own historical, cultural, and religious traditions about family life—and brings these into the contemporary world of family life.
7. Family and Democracy initiatives should have a bold vision (a BHAG—a big, hairy, audacious goal) while working pragmatically on focused, specific goals.

The Families and Democracy Model is implemented in democratic ways that employ the following strategies, which can be viewed as ways to implement the core principles just described. Along with the families we work with, we keep these strategies in mind in order to avoid the ever-present risk of lapsing back into traditional program and professional service models, and to avoid the typical volunteer approach that involves people as helpers but not as productive citizens.

1. Employ democratic planning and decision making at every step.
2. Emphasize mutual teaching and learning among families.
3. Create ways to fold new learnings back into the community.
4. Continually identify and develop new leaders.
5. Use professional expertise selectively—"on tap," not "on top."
6. Generate public visibility through media and community events.
7. Forge a sense of larger purpose beyond helping immediate participants.

We want to highlight the importance of the fourth item on this list ("new leaders") as something that was not as clear to us at the outset of these initiatives. Everyone's job is to look for people to join the initiative, to add to its energy and resources, and eventually to become leaders. Otherwise, the first round of leaders will get tired, begin to act entitled, or get rigid. We now believe that it takes three "generations" of leaders for an initiative to become mature, that is, the original visioning and planning group, the next wave of participants who come on board to lead action initiatives, and then those who come originally to "consume" a service and then move into leadership. Stopping at the first or second generation does not create transformative change; instead, it substitutes lay service providers for professional service providers.

We turn next to illustrations of this work in practice.

A CITIZEN INITIATIVE IN HEALTH CARE

Other than the military and law enforcement, there may be no more hierarchical institution in the land than the medical care system. It provided an early and valuable test case for our democratic, citizen model. In 1999, Bill Doherty approached an HMO with the offer of pro bono time to start a community-engagement project. We were open to working on any medical problem. The HMO leaders quickly chose Type II diabetes, an illness that frustrates providers, is costly to the medical system, and frequently leaves people with the disease feeling isolated and misunderstood by family members and others around them. We met with clinic staff and held a "public launching event" to recruit lay leaders. The Partners in Diabetes Project involves persons with diabetes, family members, medical and nursing professionals, an HMO administrator, and a family therapist, all working democratically on a mission the group created together: "to improve the lives of patients and families at our clinics whose lives are touched by diabetes." The group decided to create a program in which "diabetes support partners" are nominated as potential leaders by their physicians, receive training, and then reach out through home visits to individuals and families who would like support in dealing with diabetes. The two clinics are in working-class and low-income communities in St. Paul, Minnesota, and serve ethnically diverse populations. The whole group—staff, support partners (including patients and family members)—meets monthly for mutual consultation and decision making on the project.

Unlike the traditional volunteer and paid peer coach models, in which professionals are in charge, Partners in Diabetes works in a democratic, collaborative manner to fashion every aspect of the initiative, from the curriculum for support partners to the procedures for contacting families, to the content and format of information fliers for patients with diabetes. (As we emphasize later, the term *democratic,* as used here, means more than everyone having equal input into decisions; it means collective responsibility for creating and building an initiative that has a public purpose.) The therapist/facilitator is not a content expert, but brings the overarching model and pays careful attention to helping the group achieve a democratic process and avoid a top-down, medical-centered approach, while recognizing that group members—including medical providers—bring different kinds of expertise to the deliberations. The norm is that everyone has something unique to teach and something important to learn.

Through the work of Tai Mendenhall, one of the founders of the initiative, we have used an action research model to study the process of how this project was created and how it is being maintained as a democratic initiative as opposed to a traditional professionally developed program (Mendenhall & Doherty, 2003). The Partners in Diabetes model has spread to several more clinics in Minnesota and in North Carolina, and we believe the model could potentially be used with any medical problem where providers and patients and families agree that the pooling of all their expertise and effort is important. One form of dissemination has already occurred through the work of two group members who have become leaders in their local American Indian community around the issue of diabetes. Inspired by their participation in the Partners in Diabetes Project, they have launched diabetes fairs in their community, for which they recruit the health care professionals and chair the planning meetings. This kind of leadership development is one of the main goals of all Families and Democracy projects.

To give additional flavor to how a Families and Democracy initiative takes hold, here is an extended example of a spin-off of Partners in Diabetes in a different medical setting. The description is adapted from Mendenhall and Doherty (2005). The context is the Department of Pediatrics at Wake Forest University, where providers had been frustrated for some time with how things were going with their adolescent patients with diabetes. Although many kids seemed to do okay—adhering (on their own or at their parents' insistence) to prescribed regimens of diet, physical activity, blood sugar monitoring, and insulin administration—a large proportion of patients were simply out of control. Despite repeated efforts in conventional teaching of important components of diabetes management, hosting diabetes-related fairs and public forums, and persistent warnings regarding long-term consequences related to poor metabolic control, nothing was working. Adolescent patients continued to be brought in by their parents with poor physiological indicators (e.g., hemoglobin A1c levels and weight) and little apparent motivation to change. Parents complained about being "nags" to teenagers who wanted to be left alone. Patients complained about adults who would not "get off their backs" or allow them to have the same spontaneity and freedom as their peers. Providers often felt triangulated into family conflicts—right in the exam room—without any clear idea about what to do other than go over the same old information and cautionary warnings.

Initial conversations between the director of Pediatrics and Tai Mendhenhall (then a marriage and family therapy intern in the Department of Psychiatry) identified new ideas for this old and increasing problem. Having recently been involved in the development of Partners in Diabetes, Mendenhall suggested a new approach that would move beyond traditional and ineffective top-down services. The clinical director, although not familiar with flat-hierarchy interventions involving active patient and family participation, nevertheless mobilized other providers within the hospital to meet, learn about this approach, and decide whether and how to proceed.

Initial meetings with providers addressed how to engage patients as collaborators in the design of supplemental services to standard care. This would tap a variety of resources heretofore untapped, including patients' and families' lived experience and wisdom of living with diabetes on a day-to-day basis. The Families and Democracy Model was introduced as a guiding framework for this work. Six families were invited to meet with providers and discuss ideas regarding the building of a citizenship initiative that would benefit adolescents and parents struggling with diabetes in the local community.

The stage was set to work collaboratively, and a great deal of attention was spent discussing and understanding how these efforts would not follow the conventional provider-led approach. Adolescents and parents alike were enthusiastic about creating something new in democratic partnership with providers, with the larger vision of developing a model of care by and for its citizens with all participants functioning as stakeholders in the process. The group collaboratively identified key areas of concern and developed solutions within the context of the hospital and surrounding community's resources. As adolescents, parents, and providers met over the following months, a new kind of program began to take root.

The group named the project ANGELS (A Neighbor Giving Encouragement, Love, and Support). Adolescents and their parents who have lived experience with diabetes (called "support partners") are connected with other families (called "members") who are struggling with the illness. These efforts begin at the time of diagnosis, which occurs almost universally in the context of emergency hospitalization. It is during this time that the ANGELS want to connect with members, because the motivation to adopt healthy lifestyles is the highest at a time of crisis. After obtaining permission from the family, hospital staff call the support partner families to locate one who is available on short notice to come to the hospital. Support partners and members meet in a variety of combinations (e.g., adolescents with adolescents, parents with parents, families with families), and they continue to meet off hospital grounds (or via telephone or electronic mail) after initial hospitalization. Sometimes members simply need a pep talk; other times ongoing support is offered for several months.

Outcomes following the implementation of the ANGELS program were originally assessed through dialogue between (1) providers directly involved in new patients' emergency hospitalization; (2) new patients and families receiving emergency services and the ANGELS' support; and (3) the patients, parents, and providers directly involved in the creation of the ANGELS initiative. Although most feedback was positive, we made some adjustments (e.g., how to best synchronize standard care provision and ANGELS' meeting and support time, how to most effectively coordinate ongoing support following in-patient care). We are now in the process of assessing changes in quantitative measures of patients' average metabolic control (A1c) between groups receiving support through the ANGELS program in addition to standard care versus *those receiving standard care exclusively*. Anecdotal accounts suggest that the program's usefulness will be further validated as these evaluative efforts are advanced—but only time will tell.

Adolescents and parents in the ANGELS program worked democratically with providers throughout every stage of its development—from initial brainstorming regarding the program's mission, naming process, training design, public-visibility efforts, implementation, and ongoing problem-solving and maintenance. Although functioning under the auspices of an official hospital volunteer program, the ANGELS training reflected citizens' viewpoints regarding how to best prepare for the role of a support partner, going far beyond basic provider-designed training about generic volunteer, health, or diabetes-related topics. Intentionally relying on existing community resources, the ANGELS program has maintained its democratic character and ensured its long-term viability as a resource within its community. Initial efforts are now in process regarding the training of a new generation of support partners—many of whom were members at one time that were connected with this program during their own crisis and early struggles with diabetes. Support partners' sense of personal ownership in the ANGELS programs continues to be reflected in this progression as they are assuming responsibility for components of the training and long-term vision.

The larger vision behind Partners in Diabetes and its spin-offs is to create a transportable model for the democratic engagement of individuals and families as producers of health care for themselves and others in their community and not just as consumers of health care services. Stated differently, we envision health care as work by and for citizens, with all stakeholders bringing something important to the work, and not just as a service delivery system. As in all the Families and Democracy initiatives, the citizen group carrying it out refers to this larger vision from time to time, and has a sense of doing work of great importance. At an early meeting when Bill Doherty said that we are about the work of transforming the way health care is done in this country, one of the support partner members interrupted with, "What about the world?" This is called thinking globally and acting locally.

A COMMUNITY INITIATIVE TO TAKE BACK FAMILY TIME

The second initiative launched in 1999 was "Putting Family First," situated in the suburban community of Wayzata, Minnesota. This project addressed a mounting problem in many middle-class families: overscheduled kids and frantic, underconnected families. Children and youth around the country are increasingly involved in hypercompetitive, time-intensive activities that deprive them and their families of time for meals, trips, and quiet time together as families (Doherty, 2003; Doherty & Carlson, 2002). Our cultural analysis of this problem is that it reflects the ominous invasion of the consumer, market culture into the family, with parenting becoming a form of product development in a competitive, insecure world. After a community talk about this problem, Bill Doherty was approached by a community leader in the Wayzata school district about a return visit to repeat the talk, which he declined but offered to return if the community wanted to tackle the problem collectively. The result was a town meeting and the formation of a leadership group of parents who created the grassroots organization Putting Family First (www.PuttingFamilyFirst.org). Using the Families and Democracy Model and facilitated by a family therapist, the group created a mission statement, a desired future statement, and a set of actions to bring the problem to the consciousness of the community and to begin to turn the cultural tide.

As articulated in Putting Family First documents available on its Web site, the democratic theory underlying this work is that the families can only be a seedbed for current and future citizens if they achieve a balance between internal bonds and external activities, that this balance has become gravely out of whack for many families across our nation, and that retrieving family life requires a public, grass roots movement generated and sustained by families themselves. Putting Family First posits that change must occur simultaneously in communities and in individual families. With a vision of strong, balanced families flourishing in a vibrant democratic community, the group has created a series of initiatives: a Putting Family First Seal for activity groups within the community that do a good job of partnering with families for a balanced life; a Family Consumer Guide to Kids' Activities (a kind of "Consumers Report" on the time and financial demands of local activity group); a structure and process for parent discussion groups; a faith community initiative involving a dozen local congregations (the most religiously diverse group ever assembled in this community); and a local and national media initiative that has generated intensive coverage of the problem in all the major national and local print, radio, and television outlets.

As with all Families and Democracy initiatives, Putting Family First is aiming to have its model spread to other communities, and is in conversation with other community leaders about how to do this. Two communities in New Jersey were inspired enough to launch "Family Night" initiatives in which all community organizations cancelled activities for one evening in order for families to have dinner together and do other family activities. Two other Minnesota communities developed 2-year campaigns to take back family time via family dinners, with more than 1,000 families signing pledges to have four or more family meals per week; the Minneapolis group obtained the active support of the mayor of Minneapolis in the effort. In 2005, parents in the southeastern suburbs of St. Paul, Minnesota, became even more militant by organizing a parent boycott of Sunday youth sports, calling their initiative Taking Back Sundays (see www.balance4success.org). All of these projects required nearly a year of gestation before action steps were taken. And all were intended to be a "stem cell"—a model for generating other initiatives of democratic community building, leadership development, and engagement with challenges facing today's families.

Families and Democracy initiatives have not developed in the linear fashion that the summaries of these projects might imply. The process is often slow and messy, characteristics common to citizen initiatives that use a consensus model and do not rely on the energies of paid staff. There were times when we doubted whether every initiative would take off and that we had the skills to help them take off. Newer initiatives (there are eight initiatives underway on a diverse set of issues) are going more smoothly because of what we have learned, but they are still messy democratic endeavors.

Before turning to conceptual matters, we want to anticipate two common questions and concerns related to time and money. First, this work is not highly time consuming for the therapist/facilitator. We estimate that it took about 6 to 8 hours per month to guide the launching of each initiative. The commitment is more longitudinal than intensive; the projects take at least 2 years to ripen. Second, we did not charge for our time, preferring to see this as both a learning experience and our form of civic engagement. The projects operated with almost no direct funding for a long period of time, after which they began to attract funding in the form of modest but stable institutional support (Partners in Diabetes) and grants (Putting Family First). Seeking significant funding at the outset of a community project before the democratic model is in place can doom it to be a staff-led enterprise and one that is inherently limited to the length of the funding period. Our philosophy has been: Build it and the funds will come.

COMPARISON WITH TWO TRADITIONAL MODELS

Now that we have described and illustrated the Families and Democracy Model, we will distinguish this citizen model from two more traditional models of practice with families: the hierarchical model and the collaborative model. We begin with brief overviews and then explain the three models in the greater detail. See Table 10.1 for the basic elements.

TABLE 10.1
Partnership Models for Family Professionals

Dimension of Practice	Hierarchical	Collaborative	Citizen
Scope of Practice			
What is the scope of practice?	Individual families	Individual families and groups of families	Communities of families
Process Leadership			
What is the family's role?	Passive consumer/ patient/client	Active, engaged but still a consumer/patient/client	Co-creator, producer
Who leads the process?	Professional	Professional leads but shares decision making. Professional always has main responsibility for the process	May begin with collaborative professional leadership, but becomes family-led
Who defines the problems?	Professional, after assessing needs	Professional assesses, consults with families, then co-defines the problems	Communities of families are the main definers, with professional input
Who develops the intervention or curriculum?	Professional	Professional proposes, consults, shares decisions on how to proceed	Jointly generated from the outset
Location and Duration			
Where does the work occur?	Professionally determined site	Professionally determined site, may be tailored to family's needs	Jointly determined sites and locations
What is the time frame for the work?	Tightly bounded appointments. Duration determined by professional	Schedule and duration set by professionals, with consideration of family needs and preferences	Jointly decided meeting times, duration of initiatives often open-ended

The hierarchical model has characterized much of our contemporary thinking about professional roles and ways of practice. In Western culture, it is synonymous with the long history of professional services and interventions with families (Polsky, 1991). The collaborative model of professional partnership, which emerged in the last third of the 20th century, represents an effort by family professionals to deconstruct traditional notions of hierarchy in professional–family interactions in an effort to engage families as active participants in the services they receive. The collaborative paradigm appears to be the primary model aspired to by family professionals today, in values if not always in practice. The citizen model emphasizes democratic partnerships between professionals and families to tackle problems at the community level.

We distinguish the three models on four primary dimensions: (1) scope of practice, (2) processes of leadership, (3) location and duration of the work, and (4) the orienting ideal of the model. We give particular attention to articulating the citizen model of partnership as reflected in the Families and Democracy Model. Our intention in developing this typology is to better articulate how our work differs from other more traditional approaches to family intervention, in particular the collaborative model. This typology should be seen as being primarily descriptive and comparative, rather than evaluative and critical in nature. We recognize that each model in the typology has areas of intervention for which it is particularly suited and that each contributes to the well being of families. Likewise, we acknowledge that professionals work within a variety of settings that constrain the scope and nature of the professional services offered to families. In particular, we are not critical of the collaborative model for clinical practice; indeed, it is our own preferred mode of practice with individual families and small groups of families. It's just that the collaborative model alone will not equip a professional to do citizen work with families.

Scope of Practice

Scope of practice can be defined as who is seen as the unit or system of intervention. Hierarchical models of partnership work almost exclusively with individual patients and families. In fact, most hierarchical systems make a strong distinction between the private and public domains of family life and engage with individuals and their families around private dimensions of their life. Collaborative models also tend to work mostly with individual families, but may also work several families at a time in group therapy or education. A distinctive feature of the citizen model is that the scope of practice is with communities of families. Professional efforts are aimed at facilitating and initiating change at the community level in partnership with families in their role as citizens. We use the term *community* in a broad sense, including a neighborhood, a school district, a medical clinic, a religious congregation, and other types of groups with common interests. In our work we have found that the critical dimension in defining community is a sense of affiliation that sets some boundary and clarifies who is in and out of the community system, along with a sense of common concern about an issue or challenge.

Processes of Leadership

Hierarchical and collaborative models are fundamentally expert-led, but with a difference. In the former, professionals tend to define the problems and challenges families are experiencing and administer professionally developed interventions and curriculums. These interventions are based on professional theories and scientific findings. In collaborative models, practitioners are apt to see themselves as responsible for bringing a treatment model and leading the partnership process—asking the questions, preventing sessions from going awry, protecting vulnerable family members—but less unilaterally responsible for the content of sessions and outcomes. They see themselves as sharing the work with their clients at every stage, until the clients are able to function well without the professional and end treatment. Within a citizen model, the professional is the leader in the early stages—brings the model, facilitates the meetings—but looks to develop new leaders in the group who will take over from the professional after a time. The goal is for the work to become community-led and directed, with the professional serving as a resource. The fundamental shift in paradigm with the citizen model is that of interacting with families as co-creators and co-producers of visible, public work as opposed to being passive consumers as patients, clients, or students (hierarchical model) or active partners in their individual or group treatment or education (collaborative model).

Location and Duration of the Work

Traditional paradigms of partnership with families have tended to define the elements of space (location) and time (duration) in limited, predetermined ways. Most work with families occurs in professional's offices, clinics, and agencies according to professionally determined schedules and session or class durations, or in families' homes if that is what the professionals have decided is best. In citizen work, the group jointly decides where to meet, whether in school buildings, religious institutions, places of employment, homes, or community centers. Thus a defining characteristic of the citizen model is that the location of the work is democratically determined rather than predetermined. Often political considerations go into this decision, such as what kind of message the group wants to send to the larger community by where it meets.

Even more challenging to traditional paradigms around location of family interventions is the citizen model's concept of the duration of the work. In hierarchical and collaborative models, the duration of the intervention (or at least the outside limits) is often known from the beginning. Community-based citizenship work is more fluid in its approach to the duration of the work. Because families are directly involved in defining problems and developing actions, the duration and end point are not known from the beginning, and indeed there may not be an end as the project mutates into something else. This open-ended process is necessary to citizen work.

Orienting Ideal

At their core, all models of professional work are guided by an orienting ideal that inspires their practitioners. This ideal captures what the work is about, what its practitioners are trying to be accomplished for the well being of families. A model's orienting ideal defines good professional practice and suggests the criteria for professional success and competence. We see the orienting ideal of hierarchical partnership as that of taking good care of individual families by helping them receive the best help that professional expertise and knowledge have to offer. For collaborative models of partnership, we see the orienting ideal as a creative partnership to enhance family well-being one family at a time. (When we ask collaborative therapists about their ideals for making the world a better place, they most often refer to improving the world through helping each individual family they work with.) For the citizen model, the orienting ideal is to develop creative partnerships with communities that activate families as builders of their world. Citizen professionals strive to develop an ongoing process of community leadership development and action that will continue to influence families long after their own personal involvement in an initiative has diminished or ended.

KEY LESSONS LEARNED

Several years now into this form of public practice, a number of lessons stand out that were not as apparent when we began, even though our mentors, Harry Boyte and Nancy Kari, emphasized them from the outset. As in any area of practice, the more you do it, the more the first principles become clearer.

- *This work is about identity transformation in the professional as a public citizen.* It's not just about adding a new interest area or set of skills. The new identity is one of "citizen therapist" or "citizen educator" working alongside fellow citizens to make a difference in the public domain.
- *The place to start is with a community where the therapist already has a connection.* Don't go searching for "a community in need." Look for the ones you are part of. This can be the community where you work or live or worship, or where a community leader can sponsor you entering as an outsider. Then you need two more ingredients: an issue that you care deeply about and is of pressing concern to the families in this community, and a mentor to help you launch into citizen work.
- *It's about identifying and developing leaders in the community more than about a specific issue or action.* The issues and action possibilities abound; it takes leaders to mobilize communities around them.
- *It's about sustained initiatives, not one-time mobilizations.* The history of community organizing is filled with brief, shining successes followed by a return to disengagement. The challenge is sustained action.
- *Therapists and other professionals have much to offer, including process and relational skills and credibility on health and familial issues.* But we must learn new ways of thinking and new skills in the craft of public practice.
- *Family therapists and other systemically oriented professionals* are a natural fit for this kind of work because of their ecological focus and their ability to work constructively with competing interests.
- *Although citizen initiatives are often slow and messy in the gestation period, they can be powerful when the time comes for action.* Part of our job is to instill confidence that the "inefficient" democratic process of conversation, mutual influence, and consultation with other citizens will pay off for everyone involved.
- *Citizen initiatives have to engage people personally.* Social change develops momentum when we harness self-interest and public interest; just exhorting people to do good work is not enough. For professionals, this work has to feel personally rewarding and professionally expansive, not like yet another obligation.
- *A professional who is putting too much time into a project is not using the model.* This professional is probably over-functioning, doing work other citizens should be doing. A classic motto of community organizing is to "never say what someone else can say, and never do what someone else can do."
- *External funding for projects at the outset can be a trap.* In addition to the previously mentioned problem of paid staff doing the work, funders require "deliverables" on schedule, which can force the process. Furthermore, well-funded exemplar projects generally cannot be replicated by other communities without the funding, which by definition was a one-time resource. Our approach is to start mostly with citizen effort and available resources, and then attract funding once the conceptual and structural model is in place.
- *Be careful about working mainly with institutional leaders.* Although getting institutional buy-in from administrators and staff is often a necessary step, we follow the model of the Industrial Areas Foundation and seek lay leaders who are not oriented to protecting institutional turf.

- *You can't teach it if you are not doing it.* Before training programs expect students to do this kind of work, faculty will have to get involved first.
- *You can't learn it without mentoring.* This work is like learning to be a therapist; you have to have a coach. We estimate that it generally takes at least 2 years to internalize the model and develop the public craft skills for Families and Democracy work.
- *You need a team with whom to do it.* Our work took off when we formed a team with members working on different projects. Only then could we see the core elements of the model across projects, hone our skills through mutual consultation, and achieve cross-pollination across the initiatives.

FUTURE DIRECTIONS

History is strewn with shining, one-of-a-kind community projects that never endured or replicated. We want to avoid this fate for the Families and Democracy Project. In fact, an explicit goal of our project is to influence the field and its practice in the future. One of our strategies has been to expand our team and our projects in a steady manner, learning as we go, instead of expanding too fast for our resources and ability to learn from our successes and mistakes. In Years 1 and 2 of the Families and Democracy Project, Bill Doherty learned to do this work himself, under the mentorship of Harry Boyte and Nancy Kari, and in Year 3 he learned to mentor students and other local professionals in their own projects. Now the project team is offering mutual mentoring and taking on new learners. A step launched in 2005 was the mentoring of professionals outside our home site of Minnesota. Another step the same year was the launching of the Minnesota Family Formation Project that is engaging low-income, unmarried new parents. The same year we began a depression project with Hmong women.

A key decision we made at the outset was not to aim to create a new full-time specialty practice within family therapy (and related fields) of public work with families—a version of community social work, public health nursing, or community psychology. This approach leads to the marginalizing of public practice in the original field, because most practitioners see it as a sideshow to the clinical work. Full-time public practice also makes its practitioners dependent for their living on the vagaries of public and private funding sources. Instead, we want to train a cadre of therapists and other professionals in unpaid, part-time action in their local communities, in a way that fits into their professional and family lives. Given our experience that the time commitment is more longitudinal than intensive, we think that this level of involvement could be feasible for many practitioners if they do one or both of the following: make a Families and Democracy project their community volunteering activity, perhaps as a substitute for what they are doing now; or reducing their pro bono hours so as to free up time for public practice without losing income and taking too much additional time away from their families and personal life. The key to using limited time well in public practice is to have a disciplined model of working, rather than just plunging into a community to see what good can be done. If public practice fits within their life ecology, professionals can experience an expanded sense of citizenship and broader professional contribution, and a closer relationship to local communities whose members come to regard the professional as a valuable resource for traditional paid professional practice along with unpaid public practice. In other words, we believe this can be highly rewarding work for therapists and other professionals.

As we mentioned before, there are many blips of innovative community work that ended when the founder retired, the funding ran out, a new administration took office, or a brief cultural wave ran its course. In our view, the key challenge will be not one of ideals but of workable practices. In the exchange between Scott Johnson and his critics, described at the beginning of the chapter, the critics won the "ideals" debate: Most of us believe that our work should make a difference outside our offices and beyond the individuals with whom we work. (Johnson's reply showed that he too shares these ideals.) But Johnson won the "where's the beef?" debate: What realistic difference in the larger world can we make if our skills are limited to one-to-one work with individuals and families, enlightened though we may be in that work? (The "trickle-up" effect from personal therapy to social change is likely to be more effective than the famous "trickle-down" effect in politics and economics.) We need new forms of public practice alongside traditional forms of clinical practice, forms of practice for citizen therapists who become involved in their communities while still earning a living as a clinician. And we will have to confront head-on the historic mistake made by the helping professions in the last century—the disconnecting of the work of personal healing from the work of citizenship and democratic action.

We have created a training program for disseminating this work, using the name "Citizen Health Care Program" (the label "Families and Democracy Project" does not translate in health care settings.) We are using community-based participatory research methods for studying our community projects, and we will use this research approach in the training and dissemination process as we develop it (Mendenhall & Doherty, 2005). Along the way, we will be guided by the mission statement we created for the Families and Democracy Project—to develop the theory and practice of democratic public work in the family field—and by our BHAG (Big, Hairy, Audacious Goal)—to renew and transform family science and practice as work by, for, and with citizens. We are aware of standing with one foot on the shoulders of the giants in our field, and the other foot on the shoulders of pioneering public theorists and community organizers who have shared their wisdom with us. The vista from here is inspiring, though much of the path remains to be cleared.

REFERENCES

Albee, G. W. (1990). The futility of psychotherapy. *The Journal of Mind and Behavior, 11,* 369–384.
Alinsky, S. D. (1946). *Reveille for radicals.* New York: Random House.
Auerswald, E. (1968). "Interdisciplinary" vs. "ecological" approach. *Family Process, 6,* 202–215.
Bateson, G. (1972). *Steps to an ecology of mind.* New York: Chandler.
Bowen, M. (1976). *Family therapy in clinical practice.* New York: Aronson.
Boyd-Franklin, N. (1989). *Black families in therapy: A multisystems approach.* New York: Guilford.
Boyte, H. C., & Kari, N. N. (1996). *Building America: The democratic promise of public work.* Philadelphia: Temple University Press.
Boyte, H. C., Kari, N. N., Lewis, J., Skelton, N., & O'Donoghue, J. (2000). *Creating the commonwealth: Public politics and the philosophy of public work.* Dayton, OH: Kettering.
Brint, S., & Levy, C. S. (1999). Professions and civic engagement: Trends in rhetoric and practice, 1875–1995. In T. Skocpol & M. P. Fiorina (Eds.), *Civic engagement: American democracy* (pp. 163–210). Washington, DC: Brookings Institution Press.
Doherty, W. J. (2003). See how they run: When did childhood turn into a rat race? *Psychotherapy Networker,* September–October, pp. 38–46, 63.

Doherty, W. J., & Beaton, J. M. (2000). Family therapists, community, and civic renewal. *Family Process, 39,* 149–161.

Doherty, W. J., & Carlson, B. Z. (2002). *Putting family first.* New York: Henry Holt.

Doherty, W. J., & Carroll, J. S. (2002a). The citizen therapist and family-centered community building. *Family Process, 41,* 561–568.

Doherty, W. J., & Carroll, J. S. (2002b). The families and democracy model. *Family Process, 41,* 579–589.

Erickson, M. F., & Louv, R. (2002). The Family Re-Union Initiative: A springboard for family-centered community building, locally and nationally. *Family Process, 41,* 569–578.

Gould, B. B., & DeMuth, D. H. (1994). *The global family therapist: Integrating the personal, professional, and political.* Boston: Allyn & Bacon.

Hardy, K. V. (2001). Healing the world in fifty-minute intervals: A response to "Family Therapy Saves the Planet." *Journal of Marital and Family Therapy, 27,* 19–22.

Hare-Mustin, R. T. (1978). A feminist approach to family therapy. *Family Process, 17,* 181–194.

Hart, S. (2001). *Cultural dilemmas of progressive politics.* Chicago: University of Chicago Press.

Hillman, J., & Ventura, M. (1992). *We've had a hundred years of psychotherapy—and the world's getting worse.* San Francisco: Harper.

Imber-Black, E. (1988). *Families and larger systems: A family therapist's guide through the labyrinth.* New York: Guilford.

Johnson, S. (2001a). Family therapy saves the planet: Messianic tendencies in family systems literature. *Journal of Marital and Family Therapy, 27,* 3–11.

Johnson, S. (2001b). Saving the planet—or ourselves! *Journal of Marital and Family Therapy, 27,* 23–25.

Kahn, S. (1991). *Organizing: A guide for grassroots leaders.* Maryland: NASW Press.

Madigan, S., & Epston, D. (1995). From "Spy-chiatric Gaze" to communities of concern: From professional monologue to dialogue. In S. Friedman (Ed.), *The reflecting team in action: Innovations in clinical practice* (pp. 257–276). New York: Guilford.

McDaniel, S. H., Hepworth, J., & Doherty, W. J. (1992). *Medical family therapy: A biopsychosocial approach to families with health problems.* New York: Basic Books.

McGoldrick, M. (2001). Commentary on "Family Therapy Saves the Planet." *Journal of Marital and Family Therapy, 27,* 17–18.

McKnight, J. (1995). *The careless society: Community and its counterfeits.* New York: Basic Books.

Mendhenhall, T. J., & Doherty, W. J. (2003). Partners in diabetes: A collaborative, democratic initiative in primary care. *Families, Systems & Health, 21,* 335.

Mendenhall, T., & Doherty, W. J. (2005). *Action and participatory research methods in family therapy.* New York: Guilford.

Minuchin, S., Montalvo, B., Guerney, B. G., Rosman, B. L., & Schumer, F. (1967). *Families of the slums.* New York: Basic Books.

Polsky, S. J. (1991). *The rise of the therapeutic state.* Princeton, NJ: Princeton University Press.

Putnam, R. D. (2002). *Bowling alone: The collapse and revival of American community.* New York: Simon & Schuster.

Putnam, R. D. (2004). *Democracies in flux: The evolution of social capital in contemporary society.* New York: Oxford University Press.

Reason, P., & Bradbury, H. (Eds.). (2001). *Handbook of action research: Participative inquiry and practice.* Thousand Oaks, CA: Sage.

Redding, R. E. (2001). Sociopolitical diversity in psychology: The case for pluralism. *American Psychologist, 56,* 205–215.

Rogers, B. W. & Ronsheim, D. (1998). Interfacing African American churches with agencies and institutions: An expanding continuum of care with partial answers to welfare reform. *Journal of Sociology and Social Welfare, 25,* 105–119.

Rojano, R. (2004). The practice of Community Family Therapy. *Family Process, 43,* 59–77.

Sluzki, C. E., (2001). All those in favor of saving the planet, please raise your hand: A Comment about "Family therapy saves the planet." *Journal of Marital and Family Therapy, 27,* 13–15.

Speck, R. V. (1967). Psychotherapy of the social network of a schizophrenic family. *Family Process, 6,* 208–214.

Sullivan, W. M. (1995). *Work and integrity: The crisis and promise of professionalism in America.* New York: HarperCollins.

Walgrave, C., & Tamasese, K. (1993). Some central ideas in the "just therapy" approach. *Australian and New Zealand Journal of Family Therapy, 14,* 1–8.

Walters, M., Carter, B., Papp, P., & Silverstein, O. (1988). *The invisible web: Gender patterns in family relationships.* New York: Guilford.

Warren, M. R. (2001). *Dry bones rattling: Community building to revitalize American Democracy*. Princeton, NJ: Princeton University Press.

White, M., & Epston, D. (1990). *Narrative means to therapeutic ends*. New York: Norton.

11

The Practice of Community Family Therapy*

Ramón Rojano, M.D.
City of Hartford
Department of Human Services and
Central Connecticut State University

Community Family Therapy (CFT) evolved from the need to develop effective therapeutic interventions with low-income urban families. The approach is based on the premise that dysfunctions and mental health problems commonly seen in economically deprived and socially destitute families are influenced by other variables, including limited access to resources, individual and family underdevelopment, lack of positive experiences, chronic exposure to stressful environments, and disengagement from civic life. CFT is designed as a multi-pronged approach that includes interventions in three different areas of the family and community ecosystem, and builds capacity to simultaneously impact various types of indicators. The intervention not only addresses the issues that motivated the referral for treatment, but also proposes to design a lifelong action plan that includes elements of personal growth, economic development, and leadership training.

Such a comprehensive agenda requires a strong commitment from both therapists and clients. To be successful, CFT requires multi-skilled, flexible, and creative therapists that, in addition to clinical skills, are also competent in implementing comprehensive socioeconomic interventions. Clients need to be ready to learn how to take charge and assume control and responsibility over their own lives. Additionally, both therapists and clients are expected to develop and/or enhance their leadership skills and engage in civic projects that aim to improve the conditions of the surrounding community. Nine years after its official appearance, CFT has grown into a promising therapeutic intervention with the potential for long-lasting positive effects on individuals and families. The following case narrative illustrates how CFT works.

---

*This chapter is reprinted from "The practice of community family therapy," by R. Rojano, 2004, *Family Process, 43*(1), pp. 59–77. Copyright 2004 by Blackwell Publishing Limited. Reprinted with permission.

Rosa was a 39-year-old, married mother of three children, one 19-year-old daughter and two sons, 13 and 7 years old. She had desperately sought counseling following the recent abandonment by her husband, who had left her and moved in with a former friend of Rosa's. "Why is this happening to me?" she repeated during our first session. It had taken her 23 years to find out that her husband was a chronic philanderer who had been intimate with some of her closest friends in the bed they shared. Everyone but her seemed to know the truth. Even her daughter seemed to be aware of his behavior. "I always knew that there was something wrong with him," she said.

The laundry list of clinical issues that emerged in the first two sessions with Rosa and her children was extensive: sadness, frequent crying spells, grief, anger, low self-esteem, recollection of post-traumatic family experiences, fear, insomnia, and insecurity were among them. The initial situation presented enough material for at least one year of individual work. Moreover, in her new role as head of household, she was encountering new problems: her 13-year-old son had become rebellious and confrontational, talking back and associating with people who had a negative influence on him; her daughter had left the house; and her youngest son was constantly fighting with his brother and experiencing nightmares. The family's socioeconomic indicators presented additional concerns: Rosa had neither employment experience nor formal education; her English skills were limited and her sole source of income was the money her husband provided at his whim.

Rosa and her family's situation is an example of the many cases that evolve at the interface between clinical and social matters. Obviously, some traditional therapeutic work was needed to help her deal with her grief and heal. But she needed, also, to grow and gather new resources, which would allow her to become self-reliant and self-sufficient. In a matter of just three months, reality had brought her from the role of a middle class homemaker to a single mother on the brink of poverty. Rosa's case was not uncommon in the inner-city child guidance clinic where I saw her. In fact, approximately 95% of the more than 2000 individuals seen yearly at the clinic live in low income families.

SOCIOECONOMIC CONTEXT:
DANCING AROUND THE POVERTY ISSUE

Willingly or unwillingly, therapists across the country are forced to wrestle with the poverty issue on a daily basis. The litany of socioeconomic stressors suffered by low-income families has been extensively documented. Significant resource and outcome disparities exist between poor and non-poor children. Poor children are more likely to have health problems, live in inferior housing, have lessened access to computers, attend inferior schools, experience child abuse and parental substance abuse, move frequently, and have increased exposure to environmental pollution (Sherman, 1994).

In economically deprived environments, mental health problems and family disruptions tend to be completely embedded in poly-syndromes that include not only physical health and behavioral health issues, but also other major socio-traumatic indicators. The dynamic and strong interdependency that always exists between these indicators represents a major therapeutic challenge, and could explain the

TABLE 11.1
Factors and Signs Frequently Seen in Low-Income Families

External Factors Community problems	Internal Factors Household issues	Systemic Signs Family matters	Individual Signs Personal problems
• Drug dealing	• Poverty	• Poor communication	• Low self-esteem
• Gangs	• Unemployment	• Disorganization	• Hopelessness
• Street violence	• Low education level	• Unclear boundaries	• Low motivation
• Low performing schools	• Domestic violence	• Inconsistency	• Isolation/Withdrawal
• Dilapidated housing	• Child abuse	• Unclear hierarchy	• Depression
• Abandoned buildings	• Alcohol abuse	• Unclear rules	• Impulsivity
• Garbage	• Low productivity	• Low ritualization	• Anxiety and fears
• Graffiti	• Dependency	• Family secrets	• Mistrust/Paranoia
• Visual pollution	• Chronic illness	• Unresolved disputes	• Anger/Resentment
• Segregation	• Teen pregnancy	• Frequent conflicts	• Violent behavior
• Discrimination	• Lack of food	• Verbal abuse	• Addictive behavior
• High unemployment	• Overcrowding	• Physical abuse	• Antisocial behavior
	• Lack of insurance	• Tension	• Low performance

challenge of producing positive therapeutic outcomes in inner city neighborhoods. In reality, across the country urban clinicians frequently report high rates of no-shows, desertion, or poor compliance with "therapeutic recommendations." Kaplan, Saddock, and Grebb (1994) summarize the data as follows, "The preponderance of evidence indicates that both treated mental health disorders and symptoms of psychological discomfort are found most frequently: (1) in the lowest socioeconomic class, (2) among persons without meaningful social ties, (3) among those who do not have useful social roles, and (4) among those who have suffered the traumatic loss of significant social ties" (p. 199). This clearly means that while a condition of poverty can make people more vulnerable to stressors, such vulnerability is only partially related to income and may be primarily generated by other factors that arise in disenfranchised families. Table 1 outlines a number of the external and internal factors frequently seen in low-income and disenfranchised families and the signs or resulting impacts they often have on systemic and individual levels of functioning and well being.

Historical Context: Family Therapy and Poverty

Although family therapy has proven to be a very effective treatment method, in truth, success in this approach, as well as the individual therapy approach, is better among middle class families. In reality, for any form of therapy to be successful a basic socioeconomic foundation and a social support system must be present. Unfortunately, that is not the case in the vast majority of inner-city families.

With its traditional tendency to broaden the scope, family therapy has tried to deal with these issues by grouping individual, familiar, and environmental variables into various systemic paradigms. The first documented attempt to broaden the mental health territory from individual to family dates back to 1937 when a young psychoanalyst, Nathan Ackerman, published the article "The Family as a Social and Emotional Unit" (Guerin, 1976). Eventually, the family therapy field grew, experiencing a major breakthrough with Salvador Minuchin's development of Structural Family Therapy. While Ackerman and other pioneers were able to describe the importance of family history and communication, it was Minuchin (1974) who operationalized and defined the inner and outer boundaries of the family structure. He was able to apply his work to disenfranchised families. In the book *Families of the Slums,* he was able to find that the struggle for survival was the primary quest for low-income families (Minuchin, 1966). Scores of poor families benefited from the structural approach, which enabled them to establish clearer hierarchies and boundaries. However, at the time, structural family therapists did not feel that plugging in socioeconomic supports was a responsibility of the therapeutic team. With a directive approach and a well-defined set of techniques, therapists concentrated on trying to foster family change from within the boundaries of the office-based practice.

In the 1980s, practitioners started to expand the territory further and the larger systems field was developed. By that time, a large web of public and private agencies was providing a large variety of social programs to provide assistance to low-income families. One of the key leaders of this new development was Evan Imber-Black, who described the influence of extended systems in the lives of families. This approach postulated that families and individuals are inherently competent and addressed the need to understand and intervene with the individual, the family, and the larger systems that may create barriers, or bridges, to that competency (Imber-Black, 1988).

Further developments addressed the need to incorporate gender, cultural, and socioeconomic issues into the practice of marriage and family therapy. This movement inspired the development of various new forms of interventions. Besides the larger systems approach, other forms of integrative models were proposed, among them: Multisystems Approach to the Treatment of Black Families (Boyd-Franklin, 1989); Multisystemic Therapy (Henggeler & Borduin, 1990); Metaframeworks (Breunlin, Schwartz, & Kune-Karder, 1992); Medical Family Therapy (McDaniel, Hepworth, & Doherty, 1992); Internal Family Systems (Schwartz, 1995); and Family Therapy Through a Cultural Lens (McGoldrick, 1998). More recently, the Ecosystemic Family Therapy model has tried to refine and better integrate the aforementioned contemporary approaches. As defined by the model, ecosystemic therapists recognize that individuals are part of many systems and take into account the possible relevance of each system to another, as well as to the clients' presenting problem. This recognition could mean collaborating with physicians or social service providers, for example, or bringing additional people into the therapy room (McDaniel, Lusterman, & Philpot, 2001).

Notwithstanding the high level of motivation shown by family therapists to incorporate poverty-related variables into a systemic description, the fact remains that some hard-core problems tend to remain unresolved, presenting an obstacle in achieving positive therapeutic results. Certainly, clear rules and boundaries could be set or creative new narratives could be proposed to low-income families in masterful therapeutic sessions. However, the potential impact of this one-hour-a-week remedy is outbalanced and severely damaged by such mundane but constant variables as an empty refrigerator, an intoxicated and abusive boyfriend, an eviction notice, or a violent gang across the street.

SIMILARITIES AND DIFFERENCES WITH OTHER THERAPY APPROACHES

CFT was developed out of a conviction that therapists' attachment to traditional treatment methods is a fundamental obstacle for working effectively with poor families. Traditional ideas about job descriptions, program protocols, policies and procedures, theoretical approaches, and traditional therapeutic roles and boundaries form the walls of a constricting box that limit effective treatment for urban, low-income families. CFT was developed in response to the need to address five primary factors that are not traditionally considered to be a part of therapists' responsibilities:

1. Moving family income above the poverty line.
2. Increasing availability and access to necessary community resources.
3. Forming an individualized plan for personal and professional growth.
4. Fostering personal responsibility and self-sufficiency.
5. Developing leadership skills and capacity for civic engagement.

The focus on these five indicators marks a difference of CFT from other therapies. CFT calls for a therapist with multiple skills; besides being skilled in therapeutic techniques, clinicians are expected to be familiar with coaching, case management, networking, and economic and job development strategies. Additionally, CFT requires the commitment of both therapists and clients in becoming civically engaged and working actively on finding solutions to key issues in the community where the therapy takes place. Table 2 presents a summary comparison of CFT with several other common therapeutic approaches.

Roots of the Community Family Therapy Paradigm

CFT has its roots in the theories of Erik Erikson, Kurt Lewin, Harry Stack Sullivan, and several family therapy models. Erikson (1950) clearly chartered the sequential process of human development within the life cycle. He defined the "epigenetic principle," explaining that development occurs in progressive life stages. For individuals to be able to move forward, each step needs to be completed. Failure to resolve a particular stage causes cognitive, social, or emotional maladjustment (Kaplan et al., 1994, p. 260). Specifically, Erikson described eight developmental stages, each with a corresponding conflict that needed to be resolved (e.g., trust vs. mistrust, intimacy vs. isolation, etc.). Grounded in this line of developmental theory, CFT recognizes the need for all clients to grow into the role of mature, productive, and successful adults. CFT, also, goes deeper, postulating that the underachievement, low functionality, and psychosocial malfunctions commonly seen in many low-income individuals are rooted in the lack of an appropriate level of human development. For CFT, individual maturation and family growth are seen as required and mandatory components of successful assessment and treatment.

Among the leaders of psychoanalysis, Sullivan (1953) was the first to address the influence that family and social environments had on an individual's developing psyche. Instead of deriving from intrapsychic forces, the so-called "self system" was

TABLE 11.2

CFT Compared to Other Interventions

	Mental Health Issues	Family-Systems Issues	Issues Faced by Families Socio-Economic Issues	Community Issues	Development Issues
Examples	Depression, Personality Disorders	Marital Discord, Communication Problems	Poverty, Unemployment, Homelessness	Lack of Resources, Drug Dealing	Lack of Education and Other Skills
Most Common Therapeutic Interventions					
Individual Therapy	Therapy medication referral	Individual therapy Some: marital therapy	Referral to social work services	Included in the dialogue if brought up by the client.	Included in the dialogue if brought up by the client.
Biological Psychiatry	Medication referral for therapy	Referral for family therapy Marital/Family therapy	Referral to social work services	N/A Included in the dialogue if brought up by the family	N/A Included in the dialogue if brought up by the family
Classical Family Therapy	Individual therapy Medication referral		Referral to social work services		
Larger System Intervention	Individual therapy Medication referral	Marital/Family therapy	Interventions aiming to change the systems	Empowering families in sessions, Advocacy	Referral to education and training programs
Non-Clinical Social Work	Referral for therapy and/or medication	Referral for family therapy	Comprehensive social work intervention	Provides advocacy services	Referral to education and training programs
Case Management	Referral for therapy and/or medication	Referral for family therapy	Wrap around plan conducted	Provides advocacy services	Direct links to education & traning
Community Family Therapy Approach					
Community Family Therapy Approach	Individual therapy Medication referral	Marital/Family therapy	Teams up with other for systemic interventions, Wraparound plan focused on increasng median family income	Calls for leadership training and development and civic engagement of both client and therapist, Advocacy	Always addressed, Life coaching, Comprehensive personal and family life development plan designed and implemented

conceptualized as the outgrowth of interpersonal experiences. According to Sullivan, the primary role of psychotherapy is the study and transformation of the interpersonal realities of clients (Sullivan, 1953). Like Sullivan's approach, CFT concentrates on helping clients develop connections with family members, human service providers, and community groups; all with the focus of building inner-power through healthy and effective interpersonal engagements.

Lewin (1948) adapted the field concept from physics to explain individual and group behavior. According to his "field theory," human behavior is a function of the interaction between people and environment, together making the "life space." The life space is a field that has "valences" or needs to be satisfied (Kaplan et al., 1994, p. 257). Within that field, the group's pressure causes changes in people's behaviors, but, simultaneously, an individual could also contribute to changes in the entire group (Weiner, 1972). One of the guiding paradigms of CFT is that in urban America, low-income people are trapped in the negative pressures of deprived and oppressive "life spaces" or "fields" in which they are "scheduled" to play the roles of underachievers. Major amounts of energy must be generated to satisfy key "valences" so they can transform their lives and foster change at a community level. People either need to be moved from or helped to develop other, more beneficial "life spaces" and social "fields." Empowered individuals then have better chances of influencing their previous field of origin and contributing to its transformation.

Although it is rooted in the psychological theories mentioned above, in practice, CFT evolved from experimenting with several family therapy models. Initially, the approach mixed elements of structural family therapy and social work. Then, strategic and constructivist techniques and larger system strategies were added. In addition, elements of the feminist critique and cultural competency were integrated. From Minuchin, CFT adopted a directive approach and an emphasis on a structured family unit with clear boundaries, authority lines, and roles (Minuchin, 1974). From Haley, CFT incorporated the need to find creative and strategic ways of dealing with problems (Haley, 1976). From Imber-Black's and Sluzki's work came the recognition of the need to facilitate changes in the social support systems and the understanding of the importance of social networks (Imber-Black, 1988; Sluzki, 1996). Additionally, following Carter and McGoldrick, CFT began to emphasize the need to include gender and cultural issues into any type of practice (Carter & McGoldrick, 1989). In the early years of its development, CFT primarily consisted of a mixture of these elements that were commonly present in the mental health field. However, in 1993, the CFT concept was consolidated and moved into its second wave of development. It was at this time, that the approach began to step "outside of the box" and started to include non-mental health interventions aimed at generating leadership skills, family economic self-sufficiency, and political activism.

The search for meaningful and long-lasting systemic change has been the primary quest of family therapy. Traditionally, therapists have sought to foster first and second order types of change. First order change occurs within the existing system, when its rules are kept intact. Second order change requires a change in the system and the introduction of new rules into the existing system (Watzlawick, Weakland, & Fisch, 1974). Nevertheless, for disrupted and depleted family systems, the search for change through first or second order interventions can often result in only a limited effect. In these types of families, a solid transformation will only occur when there is a substantial solution to the problems of urban, poor families outlined in Table 1. CFT proposes a third order type of change in which the individual gets out of the system, gets empowered, and forms or joins other healthier and more functional systems—while simultaneously facilitating the implementation of first and second order changes within the primary system and the surrounding local community.

PRINCIPLES AND OBJECTIVES OF COMMUNITY FAMILY THERAPY

CFT was developed upon the following guiding principles:

1. Mental health problems in poor families are embedded in a tight web of social issues that need to be resolved or at least improved.
2. Well-trained professionals who partner with clients and community agencies can successfully reduce the family level of poverty and other social issues.
3. Personal motivation for change is needed and people should assume responsibility for their own lives.
4. Personal and family problems are strongly related to individual and family underdevelopment.
5. People malfunction because of lack of "voltage" (inner and outer resources).
6. Leadership development and civic engagement contribute to the improvement of emotional and family problems.
7. Civically engaged and highly skilled therapists who provide pro bono services are posed to produce better results in fostering change.

CFT actively pursues the attainment of the following five objectives:

1. *Attaining family income above the poverty line:* A central component of CFT interventions is to move people from poverty to middle class.
2. *Improving availability and access to new sets of resources:* Referring clients to other agencies may not be good enough. A strong agreement with other providers to largely guarantee access to necessary support systems is needed.
3. *Developing an individualized plan for personal and professional growth:* The need for clients to assume control over their own lives is recognized as a mandate. However, for clients to be able to live independent and self-sufficient lives, a solid educational background and specific skill sets are indispensable.
4. *Improving personal responsibility and self-sufficiency:* Institutions and providers cannot remedy people's problems without determining their ability to assume responsibility for their own lives. CFT proposes to help people help themselves. From the onset, clients are informed of their expected role.
5. *Developing leadership skills and civic engagement:* Altruism is a major curative factor. A sense of frustration and impotence to deal with community problems can be effectively conquered with leadership training and civic engagement. Scoring victories at the community level gives clients a sense of agency and empowers them to tackle inner family problems.

ASSESSMENT IN COMMUNITY FAMILY THERAPY

Therapeutic work with low-income families needs to begin with an extensive inventory of problems and assets. CFT aims to quantify the amount of negative "energy" from all past and present problems, measures the amount of positive energy from existing assets, and works on increasing the levels of both intrinsic and extrinsic power to achieve a favorable counterbalance. CFT utilizes a battery of instruments and charts that help organize and classify multiple factors in a practical way. The *Inventory of Strengths and Resources* (see Appendix A) is the primary tool used and includes a graphic sheet not shown here. This inventory contains 30 indicators in three areas—psychological, support systems, and skills and strengths, divided into six sub-categories. Both the therapist and the client(s) complete this instrument, typically after the second or third session. Normally, it is completed in 10 to 15 minutes. Then they both compare notes and seek agreement on the scores. Besides the strengths and resources inventory, CFT also uses other traditional methods, such as psychosocial assessments, genograms, and eco-maps. Also, as an extension of these methods, CFT utilizes "community-grams"—diagrams designed to allow clients to make an inventory of assets and gaps in both the personal-intimate community and the community of resources.

INTERVENTION IN COMMUNITY FAMILY THERAPY

As stated before, CFT focuses on three treatment goals: (a) constructing an autobiography that focuses on strengths and a life plan that invites positive action and self-development, (b) developing a functional and effective community network of personal and supportive resources, and (c) providing for leadership development and civic engagement. These three goals correspond to the three areas covered by the assessment. The therapeutic plan follows accordingly. Namely, therapist and client, after having agreed upon inventory scores, work together to move the scores up. This is accomplished by simultaneously developing three levels of engagement using strategies summarized in Table 3. Our experience is that this type of multi-focused work can typically be completed in 12–25 one-hour sessions in a 1–2 year period. Half of the sessions are used in the initial 2–3 months. The remaining sessions are used bi-weekly or monthly. As individual, family, and community resources are developed, the need for the therapist decreases. However, a multi-year follow-up plan is often useful to sustain improvements.

First Level of Engagement

This part of the intervention seeks to help clients increase the quality of the connection they have with their own personal history, identity, and self-worth, and to improve their overall mental health status. This work can be done through various forms of individual, couple, or family therapy. It is also complemented using educational and training services to remedy basic developmental gaps, to provide opportunities for new skills development, and to give psychological enrichment. Rather than working primarily on solving problems, CFT concentrates on increasing the capacity of individuals and families to deal with existing issues, and design-

TABLE 11.3
Summary of CFT Therapeutic Strategies

Strategy One Engagement of First Level Individual & Family Therapy	Strategy Two Engagement of Second Level Wrap Around Networking	Strategy Three Engagement of Third Level Leadership & Civic Engagement

Dealing with
  CRITICAL ISSUES
	Activating the
	  NUCLEAR NETWORK
		Developing
		  LEADERSHIP SKILLS

Developing
  HEALTHIER PARADIGMS &
  DESCRIPTIONS
	Developing an
	  EXTENDED RESOURCE
	  NETWORK
		Learning
		  SELF-ADVOCACY

Identifying and using
  STRENGTHS
	Reducing and/or removing
	  SOCIAL STRESSORS
		Learning and using
		  CITIZEN's PRIVILEGES

Enhancing
  SELF-ESTEEM
	Meeting
	  BASIC HUMAN NEEDS
		Getting engaged in
		  CIVIC LIFE

Un-learning
  HOPELESSNESS
	Increasing
	  MEDIAN FAMILY INCOME
		Self Helping by
		  HELPING OTHERS

Designing and implementing
  LIFE PLAN TO TAKE CHARGE
  OF ONE'S LIFE
	Taking advantage of
	  OPPORTUNITIES FOR
	  UPWARD MOBILITY
		Helping solve
		  COMMUNITY PROBLEMS

ing power and happiness building strategies that, in some cases, are able to solve critical problems.

Negative representations of personal or environmental facts are frequently embedded in highly influential social constructs or stated another way, "societies construct the 'lenses' through which their members interpret the world" (Freedman & Combs, 1996, p. 16). Issues related to unresolved grief, shame, pain, anger, frustration, and hopelessness need to be deconstructed, proposing new paradigms that not only help reframe past and present realities but also promote forward movement. In CFT semantics, the intervention aims for the re-editing of autobiographies, allowing clients to "inhabit" their own history. This type of work can be done by any of the well-known techniques described by constructivist and/or narrative therapies also. CFT has created its own techniques for this work using video or audiotapes or just asking clients to write a summary of their own history.

Case Illustration of First Level of Engagement. In the case of Rosa, the first task was to develop a therapeutic engagement, conduct a complete assessment, and help her deal with her emotional crisis. She did not meet the diagnostic criteria for a major depression, but had features related to an adjustment disorder and grief reaction. These diagnoses did not require medication, but individual counseling was necessary. Her story contained elements of victimization, defeat, betrayal, humiliation, hopelessness, desperation, frustration, and impotence. Stuck for years in the role of a submissive and dependent housewife, she was personally and professionally underdeveloped. She did not complete high school, could not speak, read, or write English, and never had a job. The therapeutic goals described in Table 3 were followed.

The initial intervention focused on helping her stabilize and re-write her story. The proposed alternative story described a relatively young, well-disciplined, dedicated, and highly respected mother who was able to raise three children who were doing well at school. It also included descriptions of a single parent who was showing signs of endurance, courage, and readiness to do whatever was necessary to help her family survive. The pain of the separation was validated, but this fact was also presented as an opportunity to be free to do the type of things that she was not permitted to do before. Coming from a family of a dominant and rigid father who never allowed her to have male friends, she had married very young, quickly passing from an over-controlling father to an over-controlling husband.

Rosa seemed to be re-energized with the new approach. Her feelings of impotence rapidly evolved to feelings of pride and honor. By the fourth session, she was already verbalizing a determination to show everyone what she was capable of doing. Subsequently, a dreams and vision exercise showed that she actually was very ambitious and had high goals for herself. She accepted the invitation to work on a personal and professional development plan for herself.

Second Level of Engagement

This level seeks to help clients connect or re-connect with the "community of resources" that can offer sources of support and opportunities to meet basic and developmental needs. This work is primarily done through methods most commonly described as case management, outreach, community education, wraparound services, and networking. Also, therapists help clients build/re-build their "nuclear network," the group formed by the mix of their family members and close friends. We refer to this group as the "personalized community" or "real family."

CFT also helps clients develop and mobilize a strong social network. This network has been described by Sluzki (1996) as the sum of family, friends, coworkers or school peers, and community entities such as health care or religious institutions. It is expected that therapists will tailor a special "therapeutic resource network" formed by various types of community service providers. At first, assembling this group is often time-consuming work for therapists. However, part of the operation will not need to be repeated, and the network that is assembled can later be used to assist other clients.

> *Case Illustration of Second Level of Engagement.* Working at the second level, the intervention focused on helping Rosa identify and access the resources necessary to solve problems, generate income, and enhance development. She was connected with the following resources: (a) a local program that assisted women in her situation with free legal services, helping her get the appropriate financial support from her ex-husband, (b) the Office of Adult Education, where she was able to get English classes and complete her GED, (c) a youth agency in the community that could help her with her adolescent son, (d) a neighborhood school where she initially volunteered and was subsequently hired, (e) a community college where she registered and began taking classes, and (f) a local church where she gained new friends and ultimately a new romantic relationship.

THIRD LEVEL OF ENGAGEMENT

CFT works with a dualistic approach in which both client and therapist get civically involved in community life. Third-level engagement refers to the connection of both clients and therapists with the neighborhood and the local sociopolitical community (see Table 4). Indicators targeted in clients and therapists are listed in Tables 5 and 6. This work is done through leadership training, civic engagement, and advocacy methods. Therapists and clients get out of office and seek to transform outside realities in the surrounding ecosystem.

TABLE 11.4
CFT's Dualistic Approach to Client and Therapist Growth and Change

	Level 1 Personal and Family Development	*Level 2 Utilization of Community Resources*	*Level 3 Community Involvement and Action*
CLIENT			
Targeted Outcomes	Commitment to process, Dealing with issues, Problem solving, Healing, Facilitating a process for personal and family change and development	Access and full utilization of community resources—such as, jobs, health services, child care, education, and training	Assuming control of own life, Getting active in the community, Joining civic or charitable groups, Solving community problems
Methods & Practices	Individual and family therapy	Referral and case management	Leadership training-civic engagement and advocacy
THERAPIST			
Targeted Outcomes	Ability to relate well to the clientele, Personal commitment and motivation, Mechanisms to prevent burn out, Personal growth and development	Familiarity with existing support systems and available resources, Personal linkages with other agencies and some of their workers	Familiarity with community issues, Active participation in at least one community project
Methods & Practices	Supervision, Training, Coaching, and/or Therapy	Training, Networking	Leadership training, Civic engagement, Volunteer work

TABLE 11.5
Targeted Indicators and Examples of Developing Capacity in Clients

Indicator	*Examples*
1. Education attainment	a. High school completion
	b. College enrollment
	c. Professional training
2. Employment	a. Well-paid job with benefits
3. Income and wealth	a. Income above poverty line
	b. Retirement plan
	c. Homeownership
	d. Investments
4. Life planning and management	a. Life-long plan
	b. Discipline
5. Leadership	a. Civic engagement
	b. Political literacy
	c. Assertiveness
	d. Self-advocacy
6. Resource management	a. Knowledge of community resources
	b. Learning how to navigate systems
7. Self-sufficiency	a. Independence
	b. Problem-solving skills

TABLE 11.6
Targeted Indicators and Examples of Developing Capacity in Therapists

Indicator	Examples
1. Cultural competency	a. Ability to be effective with different populations
	b. Comfort working with disenfranchised populations
2. Community engagement	a. Familiarity with surrounding community
	b. Relationships with community members
3. Leadership	a. Civic engagement
	b. Political literacy
	c. Assertiveness
	d. Self-advocacy
4. Life coaching	a. Knowledge of life-long planning
	b. Familiarity with personal and family development strategies
5. Economic development	a. Familiarity with employment programs
	b. Familiarity with economic development programs
6. Resource management	a. Knowledge of community resources
	b. Case management skills
	c. Outreach skills
	d. Learning how to navigate systems
	e. Networking
	f. Using resources to manage stress
7. Commitment and volunteerism	a. Motivation to help a particular community
	b. Willingness to do whatever it takes
	c. Willingness to volunteer
	d. Flexibility

The therapeutic expectation is for clients to be able to take control over their lives. This charge could be easy to follow in a perfect world where fairness and opportunities are available for everyone. But in reality, more than 30 million people in the United States live in communities where various forms of social oppression are prevalent. This reality calls for further human development work to help clients use their entire human capital, become self-sufficient, and develop a deeper sense of agency. The idea is to build the capacity for clients to be able to take care of themselves and minimize the need for therapists. This goal can be accomplished by providing leadership development opportunities or connecting clients with volunteer or action groups. For example, they could begin by attending a parent-teacher association or church council meeting, or volunteering to help organize a street festival or a sports league.

Beyond the immediate practical benefits of accessing and exercising political power, social activism has also proven to have a positive impact on both the physical health and mental health of individuals. After conducting extensive research over many years, Putnam (2000) found a strong correlation between social engagement and wellness, noting that, "the single most common finding from a half-century of research on the correlation of life satisfaction, not only in the United States but around the world, is that happiness is best predicted by the breadth and depth of one's social connections" (Putnam, 2000, p. 332).

For clients, the value added by civic engagement can be immense. Volunteer and community action groups can have the same curative effects sought in therapeutic groups or communities, particularly when we consider that these are not systems that have been put together temporarily, but represent real life ecosystems with higher levels of permanency. Belonging to a community action group has the potential to automatically change a client's position in the immediate neighborhood constellation. Moving away from a position of isolation and victimization, the person is now an empowered and committed community member. Shifting from the passive role of user or recipient of the services and the good will of others, the person becomes the helper and provider of assistance to others. Thus, a new sense of usefulness and power is discovered or reinforced. Low self-esteem feelings can become replaced with feelings of self-worth and self-efficacy.

From analysis of past successful cases, there appears to be a correlation between the level of mastery clients have over their immediate environment and their ability to control their emotions and solve personal and family problems (Rojano, 1997). This finding might explain why it is so difficult to motivate some clients to follow treatment recommendations. The emerging hypothesis suggests that when a person is in a "social hollow," with little social support and no leadership role, he or she may feel so disempowered and overwhelmed that he/she lacks the energy or motivation to take action. Metaphorically speaking, we could say that such people malfunction because of a "lack of voltage." It is true that power can be generated from the inside out, but this is only possible when there is a constant input of external nutrients. Intrinsic power can generate extrinsic power and vice versa. Altruism and compassion can be two of the internal forces that generate motivation for self-improvement. In some way, it is easier to take care of the pain in someone else than in oneself. Once a person starts helping others, their "social position" will automatically begin to change. The person becomes a helper and no longer a non-functioning individual.

> *Case Illustration of Third Level of Engagement.* The intervention invited Rosa to consider the possibility of becoming engaged in a volunteer project. Initially she decided to volunteer for the Parent and Teachers Association at her younger son's elementary school. Every morning, she assisted a teacher in a classroom. This volunteer work quickly paid results. Two months later, a part-time teacher's aide position was offered to her, and she accepted her first job. Also, she started attending community meetings led by a local minister. The minister was seeking to organize neighbors to advocate for the construction of a children's playground in a deprived neighborhood of the city. Her giving spirit quickly moved her to a position of leadership within the group. The minister subsequently invited her to his church, where she made new friends. Helping other people seemed to have a highly positive effect on her. Several months later, on a Saturday morning, when she and 20 other volunteers were building the playground a corporation had donated, she was, indeed, a very happy woman.

The Role of the Therapist

Working constantly with destitute urban families is, per se, a very stressful job. In the majority of cases, therapists go through a predictable cycle. New professionals in the field begin with enthusiasm, ready to foster family change by applying the interventions learned in school. But just months later, they begin to recognize that following textbook strategies may not be enough, and subsequently they begin to demonstrate signs of frustration and burnout. Therapists often feel overwhelmed, not only by the multiplicity of problems at hand but also by the absence of appropriate support from supervisors, institutions, and funding sources. As a result, many family therapists across the country now avoid working with disenfranchised populations. Simultaneously, while surviving multiple socioeconomic stressors, many clients do not demonstrate high levels of compliance with appointments or other treatment recommendations. For many, the mismatch between the proposed therapeutic routine and the problems faced at home prevents them from considering family therapy beneficial enough to continue treatment. The result can be absent clients and demoralized therapists.

For therapists to be ready to practice CFT, the following elements are needed: (a) a willingness and desire to work with a particular individual and family; (b) the ability to see the client as equal, deserving the same rights and opportunities as themselves; (c) a knowledge of existing systems and resources; (d) a personal connection with providers of at least 10 different services; and (e) a basic degree of cultural competency. On the last element, the lack of cultural competency has been found to be related to miscommunication, misdiagnosis, inappropriate treatment, ineffective case management, inadequate referrals, and non-adherence to treatment. Leaders of the family therapy field are now openly talking about the need for therapists to self-evaluate and recognize the possible negative influence of their own upbringing. Walsh wrote: ". . . We have become more aware that clinicians—as well as researchers—co-construct the pathologies that they 'discover' in families. . . . This makes it imperative for clinicians to be aware of their own assumptions and cognizant of cultural norms" (Walsh, 1993, p. 46).

In CFT, the therapist serves as the facilitator of a process of personal and familial development, functioning both as therapist and coach. Practitioners are expected to become "citizen therapists," partnering with the community in various forms of social actions. In the late 1990s, the citizen therapist concept was simultaneously included in the CFT approach (Rojano, 1997) and in the Families and Democracy Project (Doherty & Carroll, 2002, 2007). CFT recognizes several stages in the process of becoming a citizen therapist, namely: (a) *awareness*—the therapist needs to be aware of situations where some citizens are actively working on one of more civic projects; (b) *familiarity*—to be civically minded requires detailed knowledge of and specific information about the issues, facts, and other reasons that led to the development of a civic campaign, struggle, or project; (c) *engagement*—therapists must maintain a minimum level of connection with individuals and groups in the community; and (d) *activism*—a citizen therapist is one who is an active volunteer in one or more civic projects.

While a strong code of ethics needs to be always followed, therapeutic boundaries need to be flexible. CFT interventions transcend the confines of the office. They could happen at home, school, or other places. Non-traditional boundaries can be managed effectively by having frequent access to consultation with supervisors and coworkers. Therapists working with poor families frequently show signs of frustration and burnout. They feel overwhelmed by the multiplicity of problems at hand, the relative lack of success, and the absence of appropriate support. Remaining immune to the pressures, pains, and frustrations that clients bring into our offices is an impossible goal. To survive and develop resilience to the pressures of working in difficult environments, practitioners must work in partnership with others, live healthy lives, and enjoy relaxing and enriching experiences. Therapists who work in isolation are doomed to burnout.

ETHICAL ISSUES AND FUTURE DEVELOPMENT OF CFT

CFT goes beyond existing ethical codes and raises the bar of accountability, encouraging therapists to incorporate issues of social justice into their values. Article 6.5 of the American Association of Marriage and Family Therapy (AAMFT) Code of Ethics for Marriage and Family Therapists mandates practitioners to "recognize a responsibility to participate in activities that contribute to a better community and society, including devoting a portion of their professional activity to services for which there is little or no financial return" (Huber, 1999). This article gives a clear mandate. However, to encourage this type of work, supportive and monitoring mechanisms need to be in place. Unfortunately, contemporary reimbursement schemes force therapists into the confinement of office-bound individual therapy, which often seeks quick solutions by manipulating internal variables.

To generate a new cadre of both highly skilled and socially committed professionals, policy changes, institutional support, and regulatory reforms are badly needed. Rewriting program curricula, job expectations, and licensing criteria will certainly provide family therapists with the mandates and resources to be able to work with larger systems and, thereby, hear and respond to all types of voices and expand the scope.

CFT is a replicable model that has been effectively tried by family therapy students and practitioners in different places across the country. Therapists who have used this approach report that they have found it to be useful, but it still has not been formally adopted in its entirety by any institution. It has worked better in environments where at least a minimal level of institutional support for the model was available. Some agencies have mentioned reimbursement schemes, lack of funding for out of office community work, and fear of relaxing traditional therapeutic boundaries as areas of concern. Doing off-hours neighborhood work, bonding with inner-city multicultural communities, and working pro-bono are three challenges that have prevented some clinicians from routinely practicing the approach.

A multiyear follow up of some cases has shown promise of long-lasting effects. However, no formal evaluation of the CFT model has been conducted yet. A thorough evaluation of this approach will require a novel and comprehensive method of assessment. The study of the impact of such variables as empowerment and civic engagement will need to use creative and non-traditional evaluation tools and techniques. Even though some quantitative data could be obtained through pre and post measures of the CFT instrument, this model of therapy seems to be better suited for qualitative, ethnographic, and participatory-action assessments.

CONCLUSION OF CASE ILLUSTRATION

In Rosa's case, therapy worked concurrently in various areas. While she was helped to deconstruct the oppression caused by her husband's discourse of feminine submission and guilt, she hired a lawyer, completed high school (GED), registered in a community college, got a part-time job, and made new friends. The in-office therapy helped her overcome the difficulties she experienced enjoying the attraction and passion she felt for her new boyfriend. However, it was evident that she had already incorporated new positive elements into her ecosystem. Obviously, the change of one indicator could always lead to improvement of others. Social indicators targeted in levels two and three have the potential of positively impacting psychological indicators and vice versa. For example, Rosa has come to appreciate the therapeutic value of a good job, or, figuratively speaking, the healing power of "J-o-b therapy." Simultaneously, knowing that her therapist was engaged in various pro bono projects served as a model for her. Rosa's case shows the positive outcome of a good partnership between therapist and client. Nine months later, in session eleven, she was already having difficulty finding time in her busy schedule to come for therapy. Therapy was no longer the center of her universe.

REFERENCES

Boyd-Franklin, N. (1989). *Black families in therapy: A multisystems approach.* New York: The Guilford Press.

Breunlin, D. C., Schwartz, R. C., & Kune-Karder, B. M. (1992). *Metaframeworks: Transcending the models of family therapy.* San Francisco: Jossey-Bass.

Carter, B., & McGoldrick, M. (1989). *The expanded family life cycle: Individual, family, and social perspectives* (3rd ed.). Needham Heights, MA: Allyn & Bacon.

Doherty, W. J., & Carroll, J. S. (2002). The citizen therapist and family centered community building: Introduction to a new section of the journal. *Family Process, 41,* 561–568.

Doherty, W. J., & Carroll, J. S. (2007). Families and therapists as citizens: The families and democracy project. In E. Aldarando (Ed.), *Advancing social justice through clinical practice* (pp. 223–244). Mahwah, NJ: Lawrence Erlbaum Associates.

Erikson, E. (1950). *Childhood and society.* New York: W. W. Norton & Company.

Freedman, J., & Combs, G. (1996). *Narrative therapy: The social construction of preferred realities.* New York: W. W. Norton & Company.

Guerin, P. J. (1976). *Family therapy: Theory and practice.* New York: Gardner Press.

Haley, J. (1976). *Problem solving therapy.* San Francisco: Jossey-Bass.

Henggeler, S. W., & Borduin, C. M. (1990). *Family therapy and beyond: A multisystemic approach to treating the behavior problems of children and adolescents.* Pacific Grove, CA: Brooks/Cole.

Huber, H. (1999). *Ethical, legal and professional issues in the practice of marriage and family therapy* (2nd ed., p. 110). Upper Saddle River, NJ: Prentice Hall.

Imber-Black, E. (1988). *Families and larger systems: A family therapist's guide through the labyrinth.* New York: Guilford Press.

Kaplan, H., Saddock, B., & Grebb, J. (1994). *Kaplan and Saddock's synopsis of psychiatry.* Baltimore, MD: Williams & Wilkins.

Lewin, K. (1948). *Resolving social conflicts: Selected papers on group dynamics* (Gertrud Weiss Lewin, Ed.). New York: Harper & Brothers.

McDaniel, S. H., Hepworth, J., & Doherty, W. J. (1992). *Medical family therapy: A biopsychosocial approach to families with health problems.* New York: Basic Books.

McDaniel, S. H., Lusterman, D. D., & Philpot, C. L. (Eds.). (2001). *Casebook for integrating family therapy: An ecosystemic approach.* Washington, DC: American Psychological Association.

McGoldrick, M. (Ed.). (1998). *Re-visioning family therapy: Race, culture and gender in clinical practice.* New York: The Guilford Press.

Minuchin, S. (1974). *Families & family therapy.* Cambridge, MA: Harvard University Press.

Minuchin, S., Montalvo, B. G., Guerney, B. G., Rosman, B. L., & Schumer, F. (1967). *Families of the slums: An exploration of their structure and treatment.* New York: Basic Books.

Putnam, R. D. (2000). *Bowling alone.* New York: Touchstone.

Rojano, R. A. (1997). *Four dimensions and three strategies in community family therapy.* Paper presented at the annual meeting of the American Family Therapy Academy. Minneapolis, MN.

Schwartz, R. C. (1995). *Internal family systems therapy.* New York: Guilford Press.

Sherman, A. (1994). *Wasting America's future: The children's defense fund report on the costs of child poverty.* Boston: Beacon Press.

Sluzki, C. E. (1996). *La red social: Frontera de la practica sistemica* [The social network: Frontier of the systemic practice]. Barcelona, Spain: Gedisa.

Sullivan, H. S. (1953). *The interpersonal theory of psychiatry.* New York: W. W. Norton & Company.

Walsh, F. (Ed.). (1993). *Normal family processes.* New York: Guilford Press.

Watzlawick, P., Weakland, J., & Fisch, R. (1974). *Change: Principles of problem formation and problem resolution.* New York: W. W. Norton & Company.

Weiner, B. (1972). *Theories of motivation.* Chicago: Markham.

Wertheimer, R., et al. (2002). *The right start for America's newborns: A decade of city and state trends (1990–1999).* Baltimore: The Annie E. Casey Foundation.

APPENDIX A

INVENTORY OF STRENGTHS & RESOURCES

Name:_____   **Date:__/__/__   Interviewer:**
INSTRUCTIONS: Scores ranging from 0 to 10: 0 = Extremely poor, 10 = Excellent

AREA I: Psychological Clearance & Drive
Response Question: Is there enough emotional drive and clearance to create/enjoy a successful life?

A. Psychological Clearance
____ I-1a.   SELF-ESTEEM: *Thinks and feels positive about self.*
____ I-2a.   CLEAR GOALS: *Clear goals have been decided and established.*
____ I-3a.   JUDGMENT: *Exercises good judgment. Makes sound decisions.*
____ I-4a.   MENTAL HEALTH: *No current incapacitating personal conflict/problem.*
____ I-5a.   SOBRIETY: *No personal problems with substance abuse/alcohol.*

B. Emotional Drive
____ I-1b.   DESIRE: *Desire to improve life and move forward.*
____ I-2b.   ATTITUDE: *Willingness to do whatever it takes to move forward.*
____ I-3b.   ENDURANCE: *Able to endure problems. Good tolerance to frustration.*
              Persistent.
____ I-4b.   DRIVE: *Energy. Vigor.*
____ I-5b.   SELF-HELP HISTORY: *Past and present history of taking action to*
              achieve goals.

Subtotal ____

AREA II: Support Systems
Response Question: Does the person have good/sufficient support systems available?

A. Family & Social Network

____ II-1a.   HOUSEHOLD: *A cohesive, supportive, and friendly family in household.*
____ II-2a.   FRIENDS: *At least two friends who provide unconditional support and*
               good company.
____ II-3a.   EXTENDED FAMILY: *Extended network provides support and company*
               for leisure.
____ II-4a.   PARTNERS: *A group of individuals available to partner with in different*
               projects.
____ II-5a.   MENTORS: *A group of individuals available who nurture and foster*
               personal growth.

B. Financial & Socioeconomic Support
____ II-1b.   FINANCIAL: *Regular income allows for meeting basic financial needs.*
               (Above poverty line).

_____ **II**-2b. JOB (School): *The person has a good job/good working conditions. If minor, good schooling is available.*

_____ **II**-3b. HEALTH SERVICES: *Necessary health services are available and well utilized.*

_____ **II**-4b. SOCIAL SERVICES: *Social services, enrichment programs, and opportunities are available and well used.*

_____ **II**-5b. NEIGHBORHOOD: *Lives in a healthy, safe, and clean neighborhood.*

Subtotal _____

AREA III: Skills & Strengths
Response Question: Does the person have the necessary skills and strengths to be well-positioned in his/her own social environment?

A. Basic Skills
_____ **III**-1a. WORK HABITS & EXPERIENCE: *Good working habits (discipline, etc.) Experience and skills in at least one type of job.*

_____ **III**-2a. EDUCATIONAL BACKGROUND: *Appropriate education for his/her age.*

_____ **III**-3a. FINANCIAL MANAGEMENT: *Financially literate. Has available and implements a financial plan.*

_____ **III**-4a. COMMUNICATION: *Good communication skills. Able to express ideas well.*

_____ **III**-5a. INTERPERSONAL SKILLS: *Good interpersonal skills. (Gets along well with people.)*

B. Leadership and Empowerment
_____ **III**-1b. NETWORKING: *Capable of developing new working relationships and/or friends and join groups.*

_____ **III**-2b. PROJECT MANAGEMENT: *Capable of initiating and completing a project.*

_____ **III**-3b. ADVOCACY: *Knows how to get basic needs met from government or other agencies/institutions.*

_____ **III**-4b. LEADERSHIP HISTORY/CIVIC ENGAGEMENT: *Serves now or has served as a leader of a group or a community project.*

_____ **III**-5b. QUALITY OF LIFE/ RECREATION & LEISURE: *Knows how to relax and enjoy life.*

Subtotal _____

TOTAL SCORE: _____

12

Applying Feminist Theory to Community Practice: A Multilevel Empowerment Intervention for Low-Income Women With Depression

Lisa A. Goodman
Boston College and ROAD

Angela Litwin
Harvard University and ROAD

Amanda Bohlig
Sarah R. Weintraub
Autumn Green
Boston College and ROAD

Joy Walker
ROAD

Lucie White
Harvard University and ROAD

Nancy Ryan
Cambridge Women's Commission and ROAD

We don't have a community anymore. It's gone. ROAD is the kind of thing that makes a community again. The women in the group were initially just part of a group I joined. Now they've become a family I'm a part of. These new-found mothers and sisters have become the wind beneath my wings, keeping me afloat, keeping me away from drugs and the slippery slope that leads to suicide.

—ROAD member

At the heart of a social justice perspective generally, and a feminist perspective more specifically, is a recognition that the individual struggles experienced by so many people are rooted in oppressive social, political, and cultural forces (Atkinson, Thompson, & Grant, 1993; Morrow & Hawxhurt, 1998). According to this view, helping clients from oppressed communities to explore the psychodynamic or cognitive contributors to their emotional difficulties, although potentially valuable, can do no more than help people adjust to an oppressive status quo; feelings of alienation, disempowerment, or despair experienced by so many oppressed people cannot truly be resolved without changing the systems and structures from which they arise (Goodman, Belle, Helms, Latta, & Weintraub, 2004). This idea has placed many social justice-oriented psychologists and social workers in a quandary: How can we, as mental health professionals trained to work with individuals and groups, possibly make a difference in this realm? Should we have become lawyers, community organizers, political advocates instead?

It is our contention that the dichotomy between structural and individual change is a false one. Instead, the two can and should work together dialectically. Just as psychological empowerment and well-being cannot be had without changes to current social structures, working to make those very changes requires a certain level of psychological empowerment. As Martin-Baro (1994), founder of the idea of liberation psychology, wrote, liberation "involves breaking the chains of personal oppression as much as the chains of social oppression" (p. 27). The idea of empowerment must encompass not only psychological sense of power, but also actual control and influence in the social and political realms (Riger, 2002). It is at this intersection that mental health professionals interested in social justice can have the greatest impact.

The recognition of this dialectical relationship between psychological and political or collective empowerment lies at the heart of the ROAD (Reaching Out About Depression) program described in this chapter. ROAD is an ongoing project in Cambridge, Massachusetts, built on the basis of feminist ideas about empowerment and collaboration, and designed to enable women living in poverty to overcome depression through peer support and community activism. Central to ROAD's design and development are the ideas that (1) mental health arises not (only) from intrapsychic exploration but from peer support and political action activities; and (2) psychological issues such as isolation, feelings of helplessness, or lack of agency can keep communities of people from organizing in the first place. Given the inextricability of psychological and political empowerment, sacrificing either one means sacrificing both.

In the first section of this chapter, we describe the context of poverty and depression from which the ROAD idea was born. In the second section, we provide a detailed description of the program itself; and in the third section, we describe the theory of empowerment that animates it. Finally, we return to the question of the role of mental health providers working towards social justice.

POVERTY AND DEPRESSION IN WOMEN'S LIVES

With job opportunities and relative wages at their worst since the Great Depression, the daily stress of poverty is taking its toll on increasing numbers of American families (Price, 2004). In 2003, 35.9 million Americans were living below the poverty line, which is an increase of 1.3 million people from 2002 (U.S. Bureau of the Census, 2004); of these, 41% earned incomes below half of the official poverty line (Mishel, Bernstein, & Schmitt, 1999). These statistics reflect the reality that there are more poor families in the United States than ever before, and that the poor are poorer now than at any time in the last 20 years.

Poverty is not distributed equally across groups in the United States. The major-ity of the poor are women and their children (Proctor & Dalaker, 2003). Indeed, 63% of female-headed households are poor, and ethnic minorities account for 55% of those living below the poverty level (Miranda & Green, 1999). Compared with 26% of White women, 54% of African American women and 56% of Latinas are poor, and 21% of foreign-born women live below the poverty level (Miranda & Green, 1999).

Since the United States restructured and drastically reduced its economic assis-tance programs in 1996, families in need have been left to piece together sufficient income without the help of the state. In 1995, 4.8 million families were assisted by the Aid to Families with Dependent Children (AFDC) program; by 1999, only 2.6 mil-lion families received benefits from the Temporary Assistance to Needy Families (TANF) program, the current manifestation of federal welfare "reform" (Moller, 2002). Individuals must prove destitution in order to qualify for meager amounts of assistance from locally administered and highly stigmatized programs (Abramovitz, 1996). Even if qualified, new restrictions require employable mothers to work within 2 years and states must impose a lifetime limit of 5 years of support (Moller, 2002). Because of this, increasing numbers of women have been forced to rely on jobs in the low-wage labor market, often earning $6 to $7 an hour without benefits, in order to make ends meet (Belle & Doucet, 2003).

Not surprisingly, depression is one of the most consistent correlates of poverty (Belle & Doucet, 2003). Indeed, women living in poverty, especially racial and ethnic minority women, are at higher risk for depression than any other group (Miranda & Green, 1999), with financial hardship almost doubling women's risk for the onset of depression (Brown & Moran, 1997). In a study of homeless women and housed women receiving welfare, Bassuk and colleagues (1996) used structured interview-ing to determine that 10% of the former and 12% of the latter met *DSM–III–R* criteria for major depression, an incidence approximately twice as high as that in the gen-eral population of women. Other studies have found rates of depression as high as 25% among poor women (Miranda & Green, 1999; Siefert, Bowman, Heflin, Danziger, & Williams, 2000).

In a passage from *The Noonday Demon,* author Andrew Solomon (2001) addresses the incidence of depression among the poor:

> In our rage to medicalize depression, we have tended to suggest that "real" depression occurs without reference to external materiality. This is simply not true. Lots of poor people in America suffer from depression—not just the hangdog, low-down feelings of being at the bottom, but the clinical illness whose symptoms include social withdrawal, inability to get out of bed, disruptions of appetite, excessive fear or anxiety, intense irri-tability, erratic aggression, and inability to care for self or others. (p. 336)

An attempt to understand the connection between poverty and depression re-quires attending to not just the biological and intrapsychic realm of traditional psy-chiatric and psychological conceptualizations, but broadening the scope to include the debilitating external factors that burden poor individuals, families, and commu-nities as well as the intricacies of its expression in the lives of women. As the com-monly invoked biopsychosocial model makes clear, the sources of depression can be traced to a complicated etiology that is part biology, part cultural and social ecology, part personal and relational history, and part personality. The interaction of factors at each of these levels creates greater risks among certain populations, such as poor women, producing depression in some, but not all, members of that population (U.S. Department of Health and Human Services, 2001).

To explore how the extrinsic brutalities of poverty are internalized to become the constellation of symptoms Solomon describes, we borrow from a model of the relationship between external and internal oppression articulated by liberation psychologist Geraldine Moane (2003). Moane describes how poor women's experiences of unrelenting daily hardships, marginalization, deprivation, and violence become internalized to form various patterns of psychological distress. These patterns not only maintain oppression by serving as barriers to action and change, but also can develop into what we think of as mental illnesses like anxiety, posttraumatic stress disorder, or depression. This "essential interlinkage" informs our understanding of the multiple determinant nature of depression for poor women.

Determinants of Depression Among Poor Women

Stressful Life Conditions. Examining the injustice of poverty using rates of incidence or percentages of the population living above or below a deceptive and arbitrarily placed "line" does little to illuminate the day-to-day realities of life for low-income women. These insistent daily struggles, often kept out of the way and therefore invisible to middle- and upper-class Americans, contribute powerfully to depressive symptomatology. The dual demands of single parenting and low-wage work, for example, are likely to be especially challenging for poor women who already suffer from emotional difficulties, but these competing demands may also lead to depressive disorders or anxiety as women ill-prepared for employment are required to work (Brown & Moran, 1997, Miranda & Green, 1999).

In addition to single parenthood and inadequate wages, low-income women must contend with substandard housing, unemployment, discrimination in the workplace and in daily living, inadequate access to heath care (Ambert, 1998), and practical problems like lack of child care or transportation, as well as the inflexibility and instability of low-income jobs (Miranda & Green, 1999). Within this stressful context, recent and well-documented increases in demand at food banks and homeless shelters speak to rising levels of deprivation (Burnham, 2002; Green, 2000). Hunger, which has been found to be a significant predictor of major depression, is increasingly a problem for poor women with children, especially poor women of color (Siefert, Heflin, Corcoran, & Williams, 2001). As one ROAD participant described, "I function in a mode of crisis all the time." As a result, paying electric bills or going to the food pantry to secure food for her family often takes precedence over meeting her own physical and mental health needs.

Traumatic Events. On top of the daily indignities and chronic deprivations caused by poverty, poor women are disproportionately at risk for exposure to traumatic events (Brown & Moran, 1997; Miranda & Green, 1999). Violence, whether in the form of childhood physical or sexual abuse, sexual assault, or the ongoing aggression of a coercive and violent intimate partner, is often the most dramatic in a constellation of traumatic circumstances. Bassuk, Buckner, Perloff, and Bassuk (1998), for example, found that among low-income mothers, 83% had had been physically or sexually assaulted during their lifetimes, with more than 40% of women reporting having been sexually molested at least once before adulthood. More than a third had experienced posttraumatic stress disorder. Nearly two thirds of the over-all sample had been severely physically assaulted by intimate partners as adults, with between 20% and 25% receiving medical treatment as a result.

It is important to note that not only do low-income women experience more stressful and traumatic life events than more advantaged women, but they are also offered fewer and less adequate supports and resources to cope with such events. Even when effective and sensitive services are accessible, exposure to trauma may serve as a barrier to seeking mental health care (Miranda & Green, 1999). It is there-fore not surprising that 88% of a recent sample of low-income women with domestic violence histories reported clinical levels of depression (Bell & Goodman, 2001). The experience of violence also has related psychological consequences in the form of fear and anxiety, low self-esteem, isolation, feelings of hopelessness, and difficulty trusting others (Briere & Jordan, 2004; Koss et al., 1994).

Physical Health Problems. It is well documented that poverty contributes to physical health problems as well, which can, in turn, exacerbate or be exacerbated by the experience of depression. Bassuk et al. (1996), for example, found that experi-ences with poverty and violence were highly correlated with debilitating short- and long-term medical sequelae, with one third of the women in her sample reporting at least one chronic health condition such as asthma, anemia, or ulcers. These kinds of chronic conditions are influenced by race, as well, as evidenced by research show-ing that African American women experience higher rates of hypertension, obesity, and diabetes during their childbearing years than do White women (Belle & Dodson, 2004). Given the lack of quality and affordable health care for low-income women, many poor women are living severely impaired lives, and are even dying from health problems that could be prevented through early detection and treatment (Fallik & Collins, 1996).

Substance Abuse. As women negotiate the stress of poverty, violence, and men-tal and physical health difficulties, it is not surprising that many turn to substance abuse as a coping strategy (James et al., 2003). Women in poorer neighborhoods are at high risk for tobacco use and illicit drug use and abuse (Williams, Epstein, Botvin, & Ifill-Williams, 1999), and poor women with depression are at especially high risk for heavy drinking and alcohol dependence (Zilberman, Tavares, Blume, & Nady, 2003). The stress of poverty, the pain of mental illness, and the temporary relief af-forded by substance use interact in cyclical and aggravating ways. As Dodson (1998) points out, although substance abuse is generally understood as pathological, it may represent a self-protective function for poor women.

Stigma. No discussion of the "interlinkage" between poverty and depression is complete without attention to the pervasive impact of stigma and shame. Although the consequences of economic and social inequality are well documented, poverty in America is still conceptualized as a problem with individual people, or races of people, as a result of their character deficits, incompetence, or immorality (Dodson, 1998). As a result, the dominant response by those who do not live in poverty to those who do is one of distancing, devaluing, exclusion, and designation of the poor as "other" (Lott, 2002). These are prime conditions for the development of punitive and shaming intolerance and stigmatization. One need only look to the stereotype of the lazy and defiant "welfare mother" for evidence of this process. Compounded by the lived reality of poverty, stigmatization then perpetuates feelings of shame, isolation, guilt, insecurity, and worry among its targets (Moane, 2003). As a ROAD participant explained, the experience of depression among poor women is compounded by the daily humiliation involved in ensuring that basic needs are met:

> Middle-class women don't pay for their groceries with food stamps and WIC vouchers, they don't pay their rent with Section 8, or micromanage a myriad of ongoing appointments with various social service agencies and programs that are there to support you, but only if you beg just a little. They don't glean other people's scraps collecting food boxes when their food stamps don't last until the end of the month. They don't know the humiliation and self-belittlement involved in going to these offices to ask their agents for help, being treated like dirt in their offices, and then returning to the world to be treated like dirt again when offering the vouchers you had to grovel for in exchange for goods or services.

For low-income women, the experience of depression is embedded within this broader experience of being a poor woman within a society that stigmatizes poor women.

Social Isolation. Beyond individual experiences of psychological symptoms, the experience of poverty also damages the sense of connection between individual and community, hindering women's capacity to fight isolation, organize, and work to change sociocultural conditions (Belle & Doucet, 2003; Moane, 2003). As bell hooks notes (1993), "when wounded individuals come together in groups to make change our collective struggle is often undermined by all that has not been dealt with emotionally" (p. 5, as cited in Moane, 2003).

Responses to Depression Among Poor Women

Clearly, effective intervention strategies are needed to benefit poor women who suffer from depression, as well as their families and communities. In the next few paragraphs, we discuss ways in which, respectively, low-income women themselves and the mainstream mental health system respond to this enormous social problem.

Informal Responses: Social Support. Of course, low-income women utilize their own strategies for countering material hardship, stress, and isolation, devoting considerable effort to constructing mutual aid networks through which they support each other emotionally and instrumentally. (Belle & Doucet, 2003). Indeed, there is ample evidence to suggest that social support plays a critical role in promoting resiliency and reducing depression in the face of poverty (see, e.g. Bassuk et al., 1996; Belle, 1982a; Galaif, Nyamathi, & Stein, 1999; Green & Rodgers, 2001).

But at the same time, social networks can also serve as conduits of stress (Belle, 1982b, Belle, 1983; Eckenrode & Gore, 1981; Edin & Lein, 1997; Stack, 1974), especially when network members are themselves poor and stressed, making stress "contagion" likely (Wilkins, 1974). There is considerable evidence that, for poor women, the costs associated with their social networks may actually outweigh the benefits these networks provide (Belle, 1983). Interestingly, in their analysis of the role of social support, Bassuk et al. (1996) found that the amount of resources that network members have at their disposal is critically related to their capacity to create resilience. The mothers in their study who became homeless, for example, not only had fewer network members, but the network members they did list had more limited resources that network members of the housed mothers. It seems that the breadth of resources shared among network members influences the extent to which a network serves a supportive function.

Formal Responses: Mental Health Counseling. Several treatment approaches, including cognitive-behavioral, interpersonal, psychodynamic, psychodynamic-humanistic, and pharmacological, have been found to be effective in the treatment of depression (Dobson, 1989; Elkin et al., 1989; Hollon, DeRubeis, & Evans, 1996; Jacobson et al., 1996; Lambert & Bergin, 1994; Shapiro & Firth, 1987; Watson, Gordon, Stermac, Kalogerakos, & Steckley, 2003). However, such findings have limited generalizability to real-world settings and populations (e.g., Chambless & Hollon, 1998; Goldfried & Wolfe, 1998), and almost no research focuses specifically on treatment outcomes for low-income women in particular (see Miranda & Green, 1999 for one important exception). Indeed, anecdotal evidence suggests that standard interventions for depression do not work well for low-income women (Poussaint & Alexander, 2000). Traditional mental health interventions are predicated on the notion that mental illness is a product of biological, cognitive, and emotional factors (Fancher, 2003). This decontextualized approach does not reflect the reality of poor women's lives or immediate material needs. Nor does it respond to the sociopolitical conditions that hinder women's well-being.

What is needed instead is a response that simultaneously attends to poor women's psychological and material well-being as well as the structural barriers that inhibit their own efforts to bring about social change. Such an intervention would need to address the limitations of impoverished mutual aid networks by increasing the number of resources network members have to work with; and it would need to address the limitations of existing mental health interventions by focusing on the external (as well as internal) conditions that contribute to poor women's emotional distress. ROAD (Reaching Out About Depression) represents just such a response. As the next section shows, ROAD works to alleviate psychological symptoms through personal empowerment, combat the fragmentation of low-income women's communities through collective empowerment, and address damaging social conditions through sociopolitical empowerment.

DESCRIPTION OF THE ROAD PROJECT

History

ROAD (Reaching Out About Depression), now in its 3rd year, evolved from concerns voiced by participants in the Kitchen Table Project, a support group for low-income women. The Kitchen Table Project itself grew out of a series of focus groups the city of Cambridge conducted with families receiving welfare in the wake of welfare reform. One of the major findings of these focus groups was that the women who attended wanted a place to meet regularly where they could share their daily struggles as mothers trying to raise families within the confines of the ever-shrinking social safety net. As a result, the city began sponsoring weekly dinners where low-income women could come together "around the kitchen table" and talk about their lives and the policies that affect them.

ROAD's original Project Director (the second author of this chapter) began volunteering for the Kitchen Table Project in 2000 through a clinical program at her law school. She was struck by the level of depression in the group and by the openness with which the women discussed mental health issues. As part of a long-term school project, she conducted a series of in-depth interviews with six of the women about the relationship of their depression to work and welfare, and then helped them coordinate a series of depression-related events for the entire Kitchen Table Project. Upon graduation, she met with the women who had been most involved in the Kitchen Table depression work, and they brainstormed the basic outlines of ROAD. Frustrated by their struggles with traditional mental health care services, the participants believed that structured community activism would fulfill their need to meet regularly with peers and change what they perceived to be a flawed system. They decided to create a new group with mental health activism at its core and the following as its mission:

> ROAD is a supportive action group made up of diverse women from the community coming together to learn about, manage, and cope with all types of depression. We will work together to find alternative solutions and develop workshops on depression. We will consult with professionals who will be helping us with the workshops. ROAD will also be putting together a list of good supports and resources outside the group. Our eventual goal is to bring back our ideas and suggestions to the doctors and therapists, so that they can develop better services for our community.—ROAD Mission Statement, written by its founding participants

Operation

ROAD—funded by the Annie E. Casey Foundation, the Boston Women's Fund, and the Boston Jewish Women's Fund and housed in the Cambridge Health Alliance's Department of Community Affairs—builds on the idea that effective management of depression is essential to enabling women to engage in personal development and activism, just as engaging in personal development and activism will, in turn, alleviate depression by giving women a sense of agency and control. ROAD is comprised of two major programs: the supportive action workshop and the resource team.

At the heart of ROAD is the supportive action workshop series, during which low-income women come together for the joint purposes of providing peer support to each other and taking action in the community. This workshop series was created by a "core group" of eight women who met weekly with the Project Director over the course of ROAD's 1st year of operation. Together, they developed the 12-session workshop series on the topic of depression in the lives of low-income women, and trained themselves to facilitate these workshops for other low-income women in the community.

ROAD is currently at the beginning of its 3rd year, and this original core group of women has now administered the workshops to three groups of 10 low-income women each, herein called the "workshop participants." The core group members intend to continue to facilitate workshops indefinitely, with workshop participants being offered the opportunity to join the facilitation team once they "graduate." Bringing the workshop sessions to the wider community in this way is ROAD's primary means of growing its supportive action network.

The ROAD workshop series is composed of 12 two-hour sessions, each designed to stimulate a discussion around a depression-related topic. The issues range from economic inequality to intimate partner violence to motherhood. Within each workshop, the facilitators strike a balance between substantive discussion and depression-related education on the one hand, and, on the other hand, "getting-to-know-you" activities that encourage relationship building and group solidarity. All ROAD workshop meetings include a meal and free child care.

There are four activities that remain consistent across the 12 workshop sessions. First, at the beginning of each meeting, participants and facilitators are invited to add to the "Accomplishment Road," a poster-board road on which the women can write achievements they have accomplished since the last meeting. These achievements can range from larger accomplishments such as beginning an educational program to seemingly smaller items such as having a productive conversation with a teenage daughter. Second, towards the end of each meeting, the entire group brainstorms positive strategies the women can use to manage issues related to the workshop topic in their daily lives. Third, during each session, the group works on building its "Action Road." Each series of 12 meetings culminates with an action event in the community. This could be anything from an educational workshop on poverty and mental health for local health providers, to a depression-awareness gospel concert. A poster with a drawing of a blank road, the Action Road is a means of generating ideas for this activity. As the participants generate action ideas, they are written on poster board "bricks" and transferred to the road. Over the course of the 12 weeks, the group paves their Action Road with ideas. During the last meeting, the group will decide which action activity to pursue. Finally, each session concludes with an "Inspiration," where a workshop leader or participant reads a poem or plays a song.

ROAD has developed its own model of team leadership within the workshop sessions. All core group members work as a team to facilitate each meeting. One or two women take responsibility for each activity during the session, enabling all the women to have a leadership role at each session. This also helps to make running the workshop less intimidating for women new to these roles because nobody is required to shoulder the full load. At the conclusion of each workshop series, ROAD takes a 2-month break, during which workshop participants are encouraged to join the facilitation team and receive training to enable them to participate in leading the next series. ROAD's group facilitation model encourages participants to believe that they are qualified to join the facilitation team during future workshop series.

The second arm of the ROAD project is the Resource Team, composed of a network of counseling masters and law school students who offer comprehensive advocacy and practical support to ROAD participants. Some of the students have joined the resource team as part of a course. Others are working on a volunteer basis. All receive supervision from faculty members who are themselves part of the ROAD Advisory Board (see the following section). The resource team is designed to alleviate some of the immediate and long-term pressures ROAD women experience—stressors such as threatened evictions, loss of benefits, or layoffs. Teams composed of one law student and one counseling masters student are matched with each ROAD participant to help them develop solutions to the urgent practical problems they face. These law/psychology teams are a literal embodiment of the interdisciplinary nature of ROAD. The student teams meet with their ROAD partners in their homes for several hours weekly, and then spend additional time advocating on their behalf in the community. They work with one woman for 9 months, with the goal of making themselves obsolete. That is, they attempt to pass on their advocacy skills to their

ROAD partners. Although in practice Resource Team members spend the bulk of their time working with their ROAD partners directly, the Resource Team also prioritizes the goal of making the community more responsive to low-income women's needs more generally. Through advocating for their individual partners, Resource Team students attempt to make systemic changes that could be beneficial to other community members, as well. These students point out repeatedly that they "get" more from this work than they give. They have gained a deeper understanding of the nature of the struggles of low-income women and of innovative ways to address them. (See Table 12.1 for summary of program components, activities, and expected outcomes of ROAD.)

There are two major actors external to the workshops and the Resource Team that enable them both to take place. First, ROAD has one paid staff member, the Project Director, who facilitated the core group meetings during ROAD's 1st year, provides logistical support for the current workshop series, and handles ROAD's management and support functions, such as budgeting, volunteer recruitment, and development. Second, ROAD has an informal Advisory Board, an interdisciplinary group of women, including activists and academics, who have helped to develop and support ROAD and its participants. (The authors of this chapter are either on the Advisory Board, on the Resource Team, or are ROAD participants. Not all of the members of the Advisory Board or ROAD facilitators are co-authors on this article). This group began solely as an evaluation team, but gradually evolved into a forum for discussing the host of complex issues that arise in developing a project like ROAD. Although members have embraced a wide array of roles (including evaluators, consultants, volunteer supervisors, supporters, providers of information, organizers), the Committee regards its overall mission as one of *accompanying* those living in conditions of oppression (Comas-Diaz, Lykes, & Alarcon, 1998).

Over time, we—that is, the ROAD members, the Director, and Advisory Board members—have built this program based on a set of core values, articulated in more detail by Goodman and colleagues (Goodman et al., 2004). These include: (1) ongoing self-examination, (2) sharing power, (3) giving voice, (4) facilitating consciousness raising, (5) building on strengths, and (6) leaving clients the tools to work toward social change (see Table 12.2).

THEORETICAL UNDERPINNINGS OF ROAD

Levels of Empowerment

Animating the ROAD program is a theory of mutually reinforcing layers of empowerment.[1] ROAD envisions three distinct but interrelated types of empowerment: individual psychological empowerment, sociopolitical empowerment, and collective empowerment (see e.g., Moane, 2003, or Morrow & Hawxhurst, 1998, for similarly structured models). We alluded to the first two types of empowerment in the introduction to this chapter, where we discussed the false dichotomy between individual and sociopolitical change. Building on a focus group conversation in which ROAD participants themselves discussed the multiple meanings of empowerment, we define *individual psychological empowerment* as the capacity to experience emotional

---

[1]This theory should be understood as a working premise rather than an idea borne out by evaluative data. Although ROAD is being evaluated using multiple methods, these data are not yet available.

TABLE 12.1
Program Components, Activities, and Expected Outcomes
of ROAD (Reaching Out About Depression)

Program Component	Program Activities	Expected Outcome for Both Components
ROAD workshop series	12-session workshop series developed and facilitated by core group of ROAD participants on the topic of depression in the lives of low-income women. Culminates with a social action project in the community. All workshop meetings include a meal and free child care. Examples of workshop activities include "Accomplishment Road," positive strategies brainstorm, "Action Road," and "Inspiration." Social action projects include "invite-ins" and depression-related literature drops in local housing projects.	*Individual psychological empowerment:* The capacity to experience emotional well-being, to know oneself and one's worth, to have the confidence to give voice to one's needs, and to have an awareness of the role of oppression in one's life *Sociopolitical empowerment:* The capacity to act on the social environment to create positive change
ROAD Resource Team	Composed of counseling Master and law school student teams who offer advocacy and emotional and practical support to ROAD participants. Pairs of Resource Team members meet with their ROAD partner weekly for nine months. Their goal is to make the community more responsive to the needs of their partners and to make themselves obsolete by passing on advocacy skills to their partners. Activities include working with women around debt and bankruptcy issues; teaching women to use the web to find various resources; linking women to community resources such as nutrition and vocational training programs; and creating a resource book about area services for low-income women.	*Collective empowerment:* The capacity of a group to create psychological and sociopolitical empowerment. Acceptance, belonging, and emotional reciprocity serve as a catalyst for individual psychological empowerment and results in group solidarity that leads to social action.

well-being, to know oneself and one's worth, to have the confidence to give voice to one's needs, and to have an awareness of the role of oppression in one's life. We define *sociopolitical empowerment* as the capacity to act on the social environment to create positive change. This might include activities ranging from community service or public education to, as Martín-Baró (1994) writes, "social confrontation of class and group interests" (p. 65).

Collective empowerment is a form of empowerment in its own right, but it also serves the important functions of mediating between individual and sociopolitical empowerment and facilitating the development of both. We define *collective empowerment* as the capacity of a group to create psychological and sociopolitical empowerment. We envision this type of empowerment evolving out of like-minded individu-

TABLE 12.2
Shared Feminist Values.

Guiding Value	Definition
Ongoing self-examination	Acknowledging the ways in which our identities, values, and biases as Advisory Board, Resource Team, and Core Group members shape our contributions to ROAD.
Sharing power	Acknowledging the barriers that limit low-income women's psychological sense of power and actual sociopolitical influence and working *with* them to address these barriers. Taking care to ensure that all perspectives are considered in the development of the program.
Giving voice	Supporting the expression of women's ideas, feelings, and needs. Advocating on behalf of women's expressed needs in the community.
Facilitating consciousness raising	Helping each other understand the ways in which various forms of distress are rooted in larger social, historical, and political forces.
Building on strengths	Identifying each other's strength and goals, and finding ways to channel these into specific roles within ROAD.
Leaving participants with tools for social change	Facilitating self-help. Using the Resource Team and Advisory Board to leave core facilitators with the leadership skills and resources to continue and expand their work in the community.

als coming together in solidarity to share each other's difficulties and to come up with joint solutions. The dimension of collective empowerment that involves acceptance, belonging, and emotional reciprocity serves as a catalyst for individual psychological empowerment. The dimension of collective empowerment that involves group solidarity can enable social transformation.

However, it is not only the collective type of empowerment that can facilitate and enhance other forms. All three types of empowerment intertwine and serve as catalysts for each other, forming a "virtuous circle." A virtuous circle is the opposite of a vicious cycle. In a virtuous circle, instead of two or more negative factors, such as depression and substance abuse, reinforcing one other and forming a total more challenging than the sum of its parts, two or more positive factors, such as exercise and physical health, reinforce one other and form a total with more possibilities than the sum of its parts. For example, once established, individual and sociopolitical empowerment can become mutually reinforcing contributors to low-income women's mental health and well-being. A rough schematic of the relationship between the levels of empowerment is presented below in Figure 12.1. In the next section, we describe each of these forms of empowerment in more detail.

FORMS OF EMPOWERMENT IN THE CONTEXT OF ROAD

Collective Empowerment. We begin with collective empowerment, because it is, in a sense, an essential catalyst of the other two. ROAD approached its attempt to develop collective empowerment cautiously, due to an awareness of the potential hazards that developing a network of low-income women could create. We were acutely aware of the research cited above, which suggested that low-income women's social networks could be as much of a burden as a help to the individual women within them. (Belle, 1982b; Belle & Doucet, 2003). Mindful of these challenges, we sought to structure ROAD so that it would support the women's development of a positive, capacity-enhancing peer network. We hoped that ROAD would

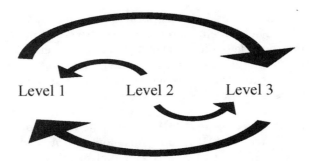

FIG. 12.1. Levels of empowerment.

become a "scaffolding" on which the women's informal networks could build. This scaffolding and our goal of developing collective empowerment are two sides of the same coin. Those features of ROAD that support positive relationships are the same ones that promote group solidarity and enable the group itself to become a positive force in the women lives.

One crucial feature of this support structure is the Resource Team. By helping the women with their practical needs, the Resource Team enables them to build relationships relatively unburdened by each other's struggles to support themselves. The student support enables the women to free up their overburdened personal resources. The time and energy they would otherwise need to spend handling urgent personal matters can now be dedicated to deepening the mutuality and supportiveness of ROAD. For example, with assistance from the Resource Team, one ROAD participant was able to help another woman confront a lawyer who had been taking advantage of her financially. The Resource Team also enables core group members to feel more confident bringing a new group of women into the ROAD community, because they know that the Resource Team can help to support this growing network of women

In addition, several aspects of the core group development and the workshops themselves serve to channel the women's relationships in positive directions and to create a sense of collectivity among ROAD participants. As just mentioned, ROAD began with a core group of eight women who developed the series of workshops. We intentionally started small, so that the group members could truly get to know each other. The weekly meetings were informal, as a way of enabling genuine connection, and yet sufficiently structured so as to provide a framework for positive action. Structuring the meetings around two focused goals that encouraged creativity (workshop development) and strengths (skill development) led to the development of positive, confidence-building relationships and enabled the women to come together in real community. Now that we have created this small community, ROAD is using the workshop meetings as a means of bringing a new group of low-income women within the network of collectivity. As one of the original core group members noted,

> Because ROAD is a participatory action project, we are part of a group that treats us as people. We are doing the group. We created the group. We wrote the workshops. First we were the participants. Now we e facilitators.

The ability of the core group to reach this point over the course of ROAD's first year is a testament, first and foremost, to the strength and dedication of the women themselves; but it also derives from the norm of mutual support established from the start. Both the Project Director and the ROAD core group members themselves spent time together outside of official meetings. They gave each other rides, called each other to encourage reluctant women to attend meetings, and stopped by the homes of women who had missed a few meetings. Core group members have continued to perform these tasks for one other and for the new group of women taking the workshop series.

As the workshops have begun, ROAD also has the benefit of a second support staff member, a volunteer mental health consultant and Advisory Board member (the third author of this chapter). She is a mental health professional who is on hand at the meetings to mitigate crises and make service referrals when mental health issues arise. For instance, if a ROAD participant is triggered by something discussed during a workshop, she might take her aside and talk to her privately about whether she is safe in the short term, and what services she might consider accessing. This enables the core group to feel safe facilitating the workshops and taking risks within their facilitation, because they know that they have a safety net. In addition, this consultant calls the participants between meetings and reminds them about upcoming workshop sessions. This not only builds the group by encouraging attendance, but it also helps participants feel connected to the group and cared for by ROAD as a whole.

There are also specific features of the ROAD workshops that enhance collective empowerment. In designing the workshops, the core group consciously thought about what would make the new ROAD members feel welcome and included. Hence, each workshop begins with a "check-in," which is a chance for participants to talk about their weeks and to receive support from other members of the group. Most of the workshops include a "getting-to-know-you" activity, such as making a group collage or pairing up for an icebreaker. Smaller welcoming touches include applauding when women add achievements to the Accomplishment Road and filling the room with group-created artwork as the workshops progress.

Group members are eloquent in testifying to the power of their collective experience in the ROAD workshop. As one woman summed it up,

> ROAD is a dependable support system. It gives me a lot of comfort that no matter how my week has been, I know that on Sunday I'm coming here to be together with my sisters. Can't nothing happen now because I am here with my sisters.

Individual Psychological Empowerment. As just noted, the sense of acceptance, belonging, and emotional reciprocity that is central to the development of collective empowerment serves as a catalyst for individual psychological empowerment. As one ROAD participant described it, "we raise each other up." A number of components of the ROAD workshop are designed specifically to help women discover their own voices and to feel the confidence to speak out. First, the overall atmosphere of respect, warmth, and mutual regard helps participants become interested in their own feelings and beliefs. Knowing that they won't be shamed for what they have to say, ROAD participants often begin to express ideas, feelings, and needs that have remained hidden, even from themselves. One member explained that ROAD "is a place to feel safe asking for advice. There's no 'you should already know this.'" As women come to recognize and describe their own needs within the group, they also develop the capacity to do so outside ROAD. As one participant noted,

I feel if we as women, mothers, and wives can change our habits and be more able to see our needs, we can become stronger to tell others (our children, too) about our needs and ask if they are willing to help us get those needs.

Second, many ROAD participants have described the sense of psychological empowerment that comes from the sharing of individual stories. As one woman noted, "We can connect stories, and it the same story—just a different version, a different edition." When core group members discuss the development of their own feelings of depression, for example, they characterize themselves as survivors, inspiring workshop participants who have had similar experiences, to believe that the same is possible for them. One woman explained, "I can tell other women 'Yeah, you can live with depression. It is possible. Look at me.'"

Not only does the sharing of stories inspire participants to believe that change is possible, it also serves the purpose of consciousness-raising, enabling participants to understand that they are not alone and that their experiences are not random. Instead, they acknowledge together that their experiences are rooted, in large part, in the social conditions in which they all live, which are, in turn, linked to larger historical, social, and political forces. For example, during meetings ROAD participants have discussed their difficulties with low-wage work, and particularly with rigid employment practices that prohibit their taking time off to care for sick children. In discussing the resultant bind that low-income women face, and the depressive feelings that such structures produce, ROAD participants begin to locate the source of their pain in unjust employment practices rather than in themselves. Making these kinds of connections is often an eye-opening experience for ROAD participants, many of whom have struggled with years of self-blame and self-loathing stemming from their inability to "just get better." Frequently, participants talk about the strength they derive from knowing that, as one woman explains, "it's not just me. It's the society I have to live in."

Fourth, workshop participants gain a sense of psychological empowerment because workshop facilitators focus on the specific strengths and skills of each woman. Women with older children offer others their expertise with parenting. Considered the poet laureate of the group, one participant frequently shares her poetry during ROAD meetings.

Last, specific workshop components were designed to build psychological empowerment within the group. The Accomplishment Road does this in an obvious way. By publicly posting their accomplishments, some of which they may have considered insignificant, the women learn to appreciate themselves and feel encouraged to accomplish additional achievements of which they can be proud. The Positive Strategies activity, where the group brainstorms ways to handle the problems related to the workshop topic in their own lives, is also designed to build psychological empowerment. Positive Strategies brainstorming enables women in the group to see that they—and other women like them—have the ability to identify solutions to many of the problems they face. Whenever the group holds a brainstorming session, the women's ideas are typed up and handed out at the next meeting. This enables the women to see their ideas valued and to keep a copy of the thoughts that they themselves generated. And the Inspiration, read at the end of the workshop, supports individual empowerment by offering comfort, hope, and meaning.

The Resource Team itself also creates psychological empowerment among ROAD members. At the most basic level, Resource Team students help their ROAD partners to get their immediate, daily needs met. They work to maximize women's income by helping them obtain social security income and food stamps, develop a resume, or find vocational training opportunities. They work to lower women's expenses by helping to sort out debts, file for bankruptcy, or find the cheapest grocery stores, which are usually not on subway stops or in low-income neighborhoods. As women's material needs are better met, the stress in their lives is often reduced, and they have the emotional capacity to begin to address their own psychological needs. Further, as the women take small steps and achieve small victories, with the support of their Resource Team partners, they experience that change is really possible; they become empowered to articulate their needs more fully, and to advocate for themselves more vigorously.

Resource Team members also help their ROAD partners with goals that increase longer term success and fulfillment. One Team is working with a ROAD participant who is obese and cannot move around well enough to find or maintain a job. The students are helping to find scholarships to attend Weight Watchers and places to exercise free of charge. Other Resource Teams are researching educational opportunities with their partners, working with them on career planning, or strategizing about life goals more generally. Many are working on ways to overcome or work around the limitations of the mental health system. In these and other ways, they demonstrate that there is hope, and that there are people in the community who care about what happens to poor women. This kind of support goes a long way towards the goal of psychological empowerment.

Sociopolitical Empowerment. As women develop stronger senses of themselves and the power they have as a group, they become poised to create social change in their communities. This is sociopolitical empowerment. Social action is a central part of ROAD. It has guided the conceptualization of the workshop and is built into every meeting. The consciousness-raising component just described helps participants understand the flaws of the social systems that affect them, and how these limitations are connected to their own struggles. As they clarify their own thoughts and ideas and learn to speak up about their concerns, workshop participants become excited to transmit this knowledge to others in their community. As one woman described it, "It makes depression into an active thing, rather than a passive one. Your negativity can be turned into something positive."

Each workshop series culminates with a social action project produced by all of the facilitators and participants. Planning for these kinds of activities begins early on. Towards the end of each meeting, the group generates options for the action project by writing their ideas on poster-board bricks, which are then taped to a poster of the "Action Road." During the final workshop, the entire group decides which activity to pursue and develops a plan for turning the action idea into a reality. The current workshop participants are considering a variety of forms of social activism, such as developing a ROAD cookbook about eating healthy on the cheap, organizing a gospel concert to focus the community on depression awareness, conducting literature drops about depression in local housing projects, creating training sessions for local community mental health providers about how they can better serve low-income women with depression, or doing a depression workshop for kids. As one ROAD member explained, even considering these activities can be a novel experience:

Some of the things we're talking about used to feel like voting—it doesn't make a difference so why bother? But now I think we should give it a try. If we don't at least make our voice heard, they'll just keep letting things slide.

This social action project is an exciting part of the workshop, one that feeds women's sense of psychological and collective empowerment. As one woman noted,

We will be in charge of important things. And also organizing important things and we'll be leading some important things, which is exciting and scary. But I know we'll do it, and I believe that we'll do it well.

Another interesting social action activity in which some have engaged is the "invite-in." Borrowed from the earlier Kitchen Table Project, the support group that preceded and inspired ROAD. Potential allies from high places are invited onto the women's turf to listen to their grievances with respect to the relevant institution and to brainstorm solutions. For example, several heads of department at the Cambridge Health Alliance, the umbrella organization that manages the public health facilities in the city, spoke with the group about how well (or poorly) the Alliance was meeting real community needs. One of the women expressed her frustration with the hours of operation of the public pharmacy, on which many group members relied for affordable medication. She had just left welfare for work and had no flexibility during regular business hours, which were precisely the hours the pharmacy was open. She now had great difficulty getting medication for her disabled son. Horrified to learn about this situation and after a few months of additional behind-the-scenes advocacy, the officials extended the pharmacy's hours into the evening. Ultimately, whatever action project is chosen, participants feel deeply proud of their own attempts to change their communities. They have transmuted helplessness and despair into hope and positive action. As one woman noted, "We get to do something about what we are hollering about."

The Resource Team also serves to create sociopolitical empowerment among ROAD participants. ROAD participants are in a better position to engage in social action because of the instrumental and emotional support they receive from Resource Team members. Resource Team members are also available to help workshop participants with the logistics of the social action project and with the community networking often necessary to make the action successful. In addition, part of the Resource Team's mandate is to make the community more responsive to the needs of poor women and their families. For example, because of their experience with the ROAD participant who struggled with obesity, one pair of students began to advocate for scholarships for poor women in local area gyms, thereby benefiting the ROAD participant and others like her. Another team is putting together a resource book to make area services more accessible to ROAD participants *and* other low-income women in the community.

Integration of Empowerment Levels. Although we have separated them for heuristic purposes, it is clear that each level of empowerment is inextricably linked to the others. We have conceptualized collective empowerment as a catalyst for the others, but it could not exist on its own. As Green and Rodgers (2001) found, low-

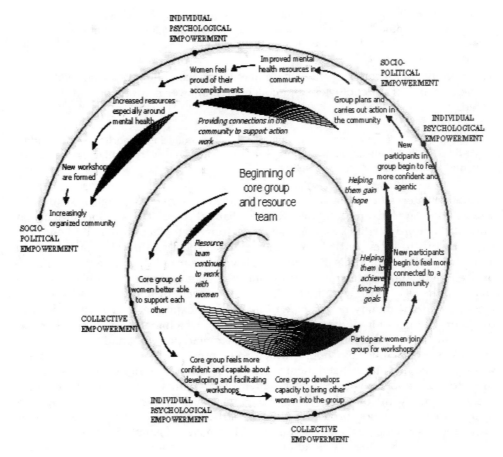

FIG. 12.2. The virtuous circle of empowerment.

income mothers' sense of individual mastery arises from positive experiences with social support. This sense of mastery, in turn, increases subsequent perceptions of having someone to turn to for advice and instrumental assistance. Nor could psychological or sociopolitical empowerment last without each other. In other words, the strength and solidarity of the group gives women the strength to believe in themselves and to create change. At the same time effective management of depression is essential to enabling women to engage in activism, just as engaging in activism alleviates depression by giving women a sense of agency and control. This "virtuous circle" is illustrated in Fig. 12.2.

RETURNING FULL CIRCLE

We began this chapter with a quandary. What are potential roles for mental health providers wishing to work towards social justice? How can we continue to hold on to the notion of empowerment as an animating theme of our work without losing our professional identity as mental health providers? In what ways can mental health practitioners join with others to facilitate the psychological and sociopolitical empowerment of individuals and communities? And what does the example of ROAD tell us?

It is our belief that mental health providers are in an excellent position to enact the model of change embraced by ROAD and to develop new models of intervention in line with social justice principles. Although traditional praxis within the mental health field has focused on individual change, a social justice approach to mental health intervention is consistent with recent feminist and multicultural theoretical conceptualizations of emotional well-being. These theories underscore the need to look outside the person to sociopolitical systems and structures in order to identify some of the contributors to individual suffering (Goodman et al., 2004). As Hill and Ballou (1998) describe, "women's pain cannot be understood outside of the context of women oppression" (p. 2). As just noted, several of us have articulated and illustrated a series of values or principles consistent with this approach (and evidenced in ROAD) that could be used to help practitioners bridge the gap between traditional approaches to intervention and more systemically focused approaches (Goodman et al., 2004; see Table 12.2).

Although these kinds of theoretical advances have far outpaced parallel advances in practice, new programs are developing every year, and there appears to be a rising tide of interest in creating practice in line with the rhetoric. Advances can be seen, for example, in a range of community–university partnerships that are developing in cities across the country (see, e.g., Jensen, Hoagwood, & Trickett, 1999; Ostram, Lerner, & Freel, 1995; Waddock & Walsh, 1999; Walsh et al., 2000; Walsh, Thompson, Howard, Montes, & Garvin, 2000, for examples), in the push towards interdisciplinary and cross-professional collaboration (Brabeck, Walsh, Kenny, & Comilang, 1997; Jensen, Hoagwood, & Tricket, 1999; Walsh & Park-Taylor, 2003), in the movement towards full-service public schools that address, in an integrated fashion, children's and families' material and psychological needs (e.g., Adelman & Taylor, 2000; Coalition for Community Schools, 2000; Greenberg, Domitrovich, & Bumbarger, 1999; Kenny, Waldo, Warter, & Barton, 2002; Kronick, 2000; The Children's Aid Society, 1997), in calls for primary prevention services that target the causes of mental health difficulties rather than their consequences (Conyne, 1991; Elias, 1997; Heppner, 2000; Kaplan, 2000; Romano & Hage, 2000; Vera & Reese, 2000); and in federal mandates that systems address ethnic, race, and class disparities in access to mental health services (e.g., U.S. Department of Health and Human Services, 2000; Prospective Payment Assessment Commission, 1991)

The ROAD project itself illustrates some of the varied roles that can be embraced by mental health providers working towards social justice. Although the core group of ROAD members themselves developed and now implement the ROAD workshops, the ROAD Director and Advisory Board, composed of lawyers, advocates, political scientists, and psychologists (and psychology students), have served key roles in the ongoing work of ROAD. These kinds of roles are critical to the success of a range of community-based endeavors and could be the basis for the development of structured roles for mental health practitioners working in a host of settings with marginalized community groups.

Advisory Board members have shared their knowledge pertaining to grant opportunities, research and evaluation practices, depression and its treatment, group process, leadership development, and organizational growth. They have held focus groups to help ROAD participants flesh out their ideas about empowerment, helped to develop recruiting strategies to find workshop participants, shared their knowledge about mental health and social support, and provided crisis intervention where needed. They have supervised resource team members as they form relationships with, and advocate on behalf of, their ROAD partners. They have worked with individual ROAD core group members on their leadership skills; and they have developed protocols for helping core group members support participants who disclose suicidal thoughts.

Although these activities have served critically important support functions, Advisory Board members have never lost sight of the need for ROAD core group members and participants to determine, ultimately, the shape of the project. From the beginning, they have honored the expertise and knowledge that comes from ROAD participants' lived experiences, and have thought of themselves as accompanying ROAD participants on their journey towards empowerment. As Comas-Diaz, Lykes, and Alarcon (1998) describe this role, accompaniment involves standing alongside oppressed groups, working with them, and seeking to develop collaborative relations with community members that recognize power inequities where they arise.

CENTRAL CHALLENGES

Although we are proud of the ROAD empowerment model and the successes it has engendered, we are also aware of the practical and ethical challenges it presents, both in terms of daily implementation and with regard to the interlocking issues of sustainability and replicability (see Goodman et al., 2004, for a broader discussion of these challenges). A few of these challenges are discussed in this section.

Daily Implementation

Although collaboration across boundaries (e.g. race, class, gender, disciplinary cultures, and approaches to understanding depression) has been a central value in the development of ROAD, putting this value into practice has not been easy. The ROAD Advisory Board, described earlier, is comprised of students and professional from counseling, legal, and community organizing backgrounds. Although this diversity of perspectives, skills and experience has been central to ROAD's success, giving rise to stimulating dialogues and innovative ideas, it also makes for an arduous process. Although we share a common feminist ideology, at different points many of us have had to struggle to lay down "the mantle of specialty recognition" (Palmer, 2004) and work flexibly across disciplines and systems to address the real needs of community members (LaFromboise, 1988).

For instance, Advisory Board members held very different ideas about how to evaluate the ROAD project. Some of us hoped to conduct an evaluation study with a comparison group as soon as possible in order to enable future funding opportunities. Others hoped to focus our energy on program development in order to meet the needs of ROAD participants, and worried that an emphasis on evaluation would detract from program development. After some difficult conversations, we came to realize that we shared a common belief that we should put the current group of ROAD women first (as opposed to a broader group of women who might benefit from future replications), and that any evaluation design we chose should benefit these particular women first, and other women second. Once we had articulated this common understanding, we were able to develop a feminist empowerment model of program evaluation that combines the goals of evaluation and program development (Fetterman, 1999).

In addition to the boundary crossings we navigated within the Advisory Board, we also worked to collaborate across class, race, and professional boundaries that existed between Advisory Board and ROAD core group members. We had to confront a number of challenges, for example, in the writing of this chapter. On reading an initial draft, one author of the chapter voiced concern that the language used was not accessible to her community of low-income women. This raised several questions for us. For whom was this chapter being written? The editor of this book had asked the first author to write the chapter for a mental health practitioner audience. Yet, we wondered, could this piece of writing really represent ROAD when some ROAD members themselves couldn't understand it? In the end, we authors (composed of both Advisory Board members and ROAD facilitators) discussed this issue and arrived at a solution that everyone was satisfied with: In various combinations, we met several times to review every paragraph to make sure that we all understood the chapter in the same way, and that we agreed with its content. We acknowledged that the chapter was not written in a way that would be accessible to all ROAD members and made a commitment to write something else that would be. Negotiating the sharing of power in regard to the representation of ROAD remains a challenge.

We have also found it challenging to balance the day-to-day needs of current ROAD members with the desire to extend our program to others. For instance, ROAD members who work with Resource Team advocates have made clear that they anticipate needing these volunteers in their lives for much longer than the year we initially envisioned. In fact, these women argued that as long as they are dealing with the daily hassles and chronic stress of poverty, they can benefit from the services provided by committed advocates. This idea challenges the underlying goal of the Resource Team, which is to make itself obsolete through the passing on of advocacy skills to the ROAD participants, themselves. Perhaps this expectation is too optimistic considering the insidious effects of poverty and depression in women's lives. But given the scope of our own resources, we cannot keep expanding the number of advocates to meet the needs of new ROAD members. So how do we keep up with the need? This is an issue that we are continuing to discuss as this chapter goes to press.

Sustainability and Replicability

In addition to day-to-day implementation difficulties, we have faced a host of challenges regarding the sustainability of the ROAD project. ROAD represents such a departure from traditional services that it does not currently fit into the mental health system's reimbursement structure. Until state and federal health policies change to allow for more experimentation, private funding is still necessary for ROAD's continued existence. Access to this type of funding is extremely limited, and locating and securing it requires enormous amounts of time and energy. Additionally, private donors are often skeptical about funding a project that combines mental health and political action themes, as many foundations tend to fund either just the former or just the latter. In the meantime, ROAD functions on a limited budget with the ongoing commitment of numerous volunteers. The majority of these volunteers are members of either the Advisory Board or Resource Team, and all maintain numerous commitments to other projects as well. We therefore worry about the sustainability of this particular project, and the chances of replicating it in other parts of the country.

We also wonder about the possibility of replicating the ROAD model in a less services-rich community. Although all community-based models are, to some extent, context-specific, ROAD may be uniquely so. Located in Cambridge, Massachusetts, ROAD benefits from a plethora of services for low-income women that few communities can duplicate. For example, community leaders have eagerly attended "invite-ins," during which they learn from ROAD members how their services impact low-income women, and how to improve them. The responsiveness of these leaders—both with regard to initial attendance and subsequent follow-up—speaks to the dedication of many Cambridge professionals to broad-based community needs. In addition, the Boston area is home to a large number of universities. Indeed, two local universities provide numerous types of in-kind services to ROAD, including student advocates and evaluators. These kinds of resources are central to ROAD's functioning.

We also recognize the hard work it takes to find the kind of community leaders represented by ROAD's facilitation team. The core group members who now facilitate the ROAD workshops struggle with the multiple life stressors associated with poverty and depression; however, at the same time, they display incredible strength and resilience and can be counted on to show up and run the workshops every week. Finding a group of women such as this in other sites will not be easy.

CONCLUSION

Clearly, these challenges are real and significant, but they are by no means insurmountable. Describing the limitations of the mental health system as it is now structured, one ROAD woman poignantly stated,

> Mental health care providers can learn from ROAD that you have to consider people in their circumstances, as whole people. We're not just depressed, or depression-havers. We're people with lives and things in our lives that are affecting our health. You're talking about someone who is being forced to grovel. Talking about our mental health is not the same as someone who feels down sometimes. If you don't have a roof over your head, if you don't have your electric bill paid, then how are you going to take care of your mental health? There is no traditional mental health strategy that gets at that.

We believe mental health practitioners can indeed "get at that" by working with individuals and communities to transform mental health services—bit by bit—to meet the real needs of individuals and communities.

The development of the ROAD project represents one example of this kind of bit-by-bit transformation. It has entailed a slow and careful process of community building. ROAD participants, Advisory Board members, and Resource Team members have created a small community of partners and advocates. As ROAD participants give their series of workshops to other low-income women, supported as they go by a group of dedicated Resource Team partners, they hope to draw greater numbers of low-income women into the network. Buffered by the strength of this continually expanding community, the original group of ROAD participants will serve as models as they reach out to new members. We hope that this process will expand to new communities and are in the process of developing a ROAD workshop manual to make this more likely.

A lot of people think that no matter what, they're not doing anything right. And we have kids to deal with and making it through the day and talking to bosses and driving down the street. When my mother died, I locked myself in the house. ROAD's getting me moving again, getting me back into the things I used to do, seeing people again. It's helping me move back into the world.

ACKNOWLEDGMENTS

We are enormously indebted to the Reach Out About Depression (ROAD) workshop facilitators and Advisory Board members, who poured so much intellectual and emotional energy into the creation and sustenance of the ROAD project. In addition to the fifth and sixth authors of this chapter, the facilitators include: Valarie Ifill, Laverne Jefferson, Rhonda McPherson, Wendy Mizner, Laura Montgomery, Miguelina Santiago, and Claudia Stohrer. In addition to the first four authors of this chapter and the last two, Advisory Board members include: Linda Cundiff, Catherine Glenn, Xenia Johnson, Rachel Latta, Mithra Merryman, Lisa Montouri, Ellen Shachter, and Lynne Tyree.

REFERENCES

Abramovitz, M. (1996). *Regulating the lives of women: Social welfare policy from colonial times to the present.* Boston: South End Press.

Adelman, H. S., & Taylor, L. (2000). Promoting mental health in schools in the midst of school reform. *Journal of School Health, 70*(5), 171–178.

Ambert, A. (1998). *The web of poverty.* Binghamton, NY: Hawthorne Press.

Atkinson, D. R., Thompson, C. E., & Grant, S. K. (1993). A three-dimensional model for counseling racial/ethnic minorities, *The Counseling Psychologist, 21*(2), 257–277.

Bassuk, E. L., Buckner, J. C., Perloff, J. N., & Bassuk, S. S. (1998). Prevalence of mental health and substance use disorders among homeless and low-income housed mothers. *American Journal of Psychiatry, 155*(11), 1561–1564.

Bassuk, E. L., Weinreb, L. F., Buckner, J. C., Browne, A., Salamon, A., & Bassuk, S. S. (1996). The characteristics and needs of sheltered homeless and low-income housed mothers. *Journal of the American Medical Association, 276,* 8.

Bell, M., & Goodman, L. A. (2001). Supporting battered women involved with the court system: An evaluation of a law school-based advocacy intervention. *Violence Against Women, 7*(12), 1377–1404.

Belle, D. (1982a). Social ties and social support. In D. Belle (Ed.), *Lives in stress: Women and depression* (pp. 133–144). Beverly Hills, CA: Sage.

Belle, D. (1982b). The stress of caring: Women as providers of social support. In L. Goldberger & S. Breznitz (Eds.), *Handbook of stress: Theoretical and clinical aspects* (pp. 496–505). New York: The Free Press.

Belle, D. (1983). The impact of poverty on social networks and supports. *Marriage and Family Review, 5*(4), 89–103.

Belle, D., & Dodson, L. (2004). Poor women and girls in a wealthy nation. In J. Worell & C. Goodheart (Eds.), *Handbook of women's and girls' psychological health* (pp. 122–128). New York: Oxford University Press.

Belle, D., & Doucet, J. (2003). Poverty, inequality, and discrimination as sources of depression among U.S. women. *Psychology of Women Quarterly, 27,* 101–113.

Brabeck, M., Walsh, M. E., Kenny, M., & Comilang, K. (1997). Interprofessional collaboration for children and families: Opportunities for counseling psychology in the 21st century. *The Counseling Psychologist, 25*(4), 615–636.

Brown, G. W., & Moran, P. M. (1997). Single mothers, poverty, and depression. *Psychological Medicine, 27,* 21–33.

Briere, J., & Jordan, C. E (2004). Violence against women: Outcome complexity and its implications for assessment and treatment. *Journal of Interpersonal Violence, 19,* 11.

Burnham, L. (2002). Welfare reform, family hardship, and women of color. In R. Albelda & A. Withorn (Eds.), *Lost ground: Welfare reform, poverty, and beyond* (pp. 43–56). Cambridge, MA: South End Press.

Chambless, D. L., & Hollon, S. D. (1998). Defining empirically supported therapies. *Journal of Consulting and Clinical Psychology, 66,* 7–18.

Coalition for Community Schools. (2000, January). *Community schools: Partnerships for excellence.* Washington, DC: Author.

Comas-Diaz, L., Lykes, M. B. & Alarcon, R. D. (1998). Ethnic conflict and the psychology of liberation in Guatemala, Peru, and Puerto Rico. *American Psychologist, 53*(7), 778–791.

Conyne, R. K. (1991). Gains in primary prevention: Implications for the counseling profession. *Journal of Counseling and Development, 69,* 277–279.

Dobson, K. S. (1989). A meta-analysis of the efficacy of cognitive therapy for depression. *Journal of Consulting and Clinical Psychology, 57,* 414–419.

Dodson, L. (1998). *Don't call us out of name: The untold lives of women and girls in poor America.* Boston: Beacon Press.

Eckenrode, J., & Gore, S. (1981). Stressful events and social supports: The significance of context. In B. Gottlieb (Ed.), *Social networks and social support* (pp. 63–68). Beverly Hills, CA: Sage.

Edin, K., & Lein, L. (1997). *Making ends meet: How single mothers survive welfare and low-wage work.* New York: Russell Sage Foundation.

Elias, M. J. (1997). Reinterpreting dissemination of prevention programs as widespread implementation with effectiveness and fidelity. In R. P. Weissberg, T. P. Gullotta, R. L. Hampton, B. A. Ryan, & G. R. Adams (Eds.), *Establishing preventive services* (pp. 253–289). Thousand Oaks, CA: Sage.

Elkin, I., Shea, M. T., Watkins, J. T., Imber, S. D., Sotsky, S. M., & Collins, J. F. (1989). NIMH treatment of depression collaborative research program: General effectiveness of treatments. *Archives of General Psychiatry, 46,* 971–982.

Fallik, M. M., & Collins, K. S. (Eds). (1996). *Women's health: The Commonwealth Fund Study.* Baltimore: Johns Hopkins University Press.

Fancher, R. T. (2003). *Health and suffering in America.* New Brunswick, NJ: Transaction.

Fetterman, D. M. (1999). Reflections on empowerment evaluation. Learning from experience. *Canadian Journal of Program Evaluation, 27,* 5–37.

Galaif, E. R., Nyamathi, A. M., & Stein, J. A. (1999). Psychosocial predictors of current drug use, drug problems, and physical drug dependence in homeless women. *Addictive Behaviors, 24*(6), 801–814.

Goldfried, M. R., & Wolfe, B. E. (1998). Toward a more clinically valid approach to therapy research. *Journal of Consulting and Clinical Psychology, 66,* 143–150.

Goodman, L. A., Belle, L., Helms, J. E., Latta, R., & Weintraub, S. R. (2004). Training counseling psychologists as social justice agents: Feminist and multicultural Principles in action. *Counseling Psychologist, 32*(6), 793–837.

Green, B. L., & Rodgers, A. (2001). Determinants of social support among low-income mothers: A longitudinal analysis. *American Journal of Community Psychology, 29*(3), 419–441.

Green, J. (2000, June 19–July 3). Holding out. *The American Prospect, 33.*

Greenberg, M. T., Domitrovich, C., & Bumbarger, B. (1999). *Preventing mental disorders in school-aged children: A review of the effectiveness of prevention programs.* Washington, DC: U.S. Department of Health and Human Services, Substance Abuse Mental Health Services Administration, Center for Mental Health Services.

Heppner, P. P. (Ed.) (2000). Prevention in counseling psychology [Special issue]. *The Counseling Psychologist, 28*(6).

Hill, M., & Ballou, M. (1998). Making therapy feminist: A practice survey. In M. Hill (Ed.), *Feminist therapy as a political act* (pp. 1–16). New York: Haworth Press.

Hollon, S. D., DeRubeis, R. J., & Evans, M. D. (1996). Cognitive therapy in the treatment and prevention of depression. In P. M. Salkovskis (Ed.), Frontiers of cognitive therapy (pp. 293–317). New York: Guilford.

hooks, b. (1993). *Sisters of the yam: Black women and self-recovery.* Boston: South End Press.

Jacobson, N. S., Dobson, K. S., Truax, P. A., Addis, M. E., Koerner, K., & Gollan, J. K. (1996). A component analysis of cognitive-behavioral treatment for depression. *Journal of Consulting and Clinical Psychology, 64,* 295–304.

James, S. E., Johnson, J., Raghavan, C., Lemos, T., Barakett, M., & Woolis, D. (2003). The violent matrix: A study of structural, interpersonal, and intrapersonal violence among a sample of poor women. *American Journal of Community Psychology, 31*(), 129–141.

Jensen, P. S., Hoagwood, K., & Trickett, E. J. (1999). Ivory towers or earthen trenches? Community collaboration to foster 'real world' research. *Applied Developmental Science, 3*(4), 206–212.

Kaplan, R. M. (2000). Two pathways to prevention. *American Psychologist, 55,* 382–396.

Kenny, M. E., Waldo, M., Warter, E., & Barton, K. (2002). School-linked prevention: Theory, science, and practice for enhancing the lives of children and youth. *Counseling Psychologist. Special Counseling Psychologists and Schools, 30*(5), 726–749.

Koss, M. P., Goodman, L. A., Browne, A., Fitzgerald, L. F., Kelta, G. P., & Russo, N. F. (1994). *No safe haven: Male violence against women at home, at work, and in the community.* Washington, DC: American Psychological Association.

Kronick, R. F. (2000). *Human services and the full service school.* Springfield, IL: Charles D. Thomas.

LaFromboise, T. D. (1988). American Indian mental health policy. *American Psychologist, 43*(5), 388–397.

Lambert, M. J., & Bergin, A. E. (1994). The effectiveness of psychotherapy. In A. E. Bergin & S. L. Garfield (Eds.), *The handbook of psychotherapy and behavior change* (pp. 143–189). New York: Wiley.

Lott, B. (2002). Cognitive and behavioral distancing from the poor. *American Psychologist, 57,*(2), 100–110.

Martin-Baro, I. (1994). *Writings for a liberation psychology.* Cambridge, MA: Harvard University Press.

Miranda, J., & Green, B. L. (1999). The need for mental health services research focusing on poor young women. *Journal of Mental Health Policy & Economics, 2*(2), 73–80.

Mishel, L., Bernstein, J., & Schmitt, J. (1999). *The state of working America: 1998–1999* [Economic Policy Institute Series]. Ithaca, NY: Cornell University Press.

Moane, G. (2003). Bridging the personal and the political: Practices for a liberation psychology. *American Journal of Community Psychology, 31,* , 91–101.

Moller, S. (2002). Supporting poor single mothers: Gender and race in the U.S. welfare state. *Gender & Society, 16*(4), 465–484.

Morrow, S. L., & Hawxhurst, D. M. (1998). Feminist therapy: Integrating political analysis in counseling and psychotherapy. *Women & Therapy, 21*(2), 37–50.

Office of Women's Health (2003). *The health of minority women.* Washington, DC: U.S. Department of Health and Human Services.

Ostram, C. W., Lerner, R., & Freel, M. A. (1995). Building the capacity of youth and families through university-community collaboration: The Development-In-Context Evaluation (DICE) model. *Journal of Adolescent Research, 10*(4), 427–448.

Palmer, L. K. (2004). The call to social justice: A multidiscipline agenda. *Counseling Psychologist, 32*(6), 879–886.

Poussaint, A. F., & Alexander, A. (2000). *Lay my burden down.* Boston: Beacon Press.

Price, L. (2004). The longest sustained labor slump is taking a toll on working families. Retrieved February 15, 2005, from www.epinet.org/webfeatures/viewpoints/1

Proctor, B. D. & Dalaker, J. (2003). *Poverty in the United States: 2002.* Washington, DC: U.S. Government Printing Office.

Prospective Payment Assessment Commission. (1991). *Rural hospitals under Medicare's prospective payment system* (Congressional Report C-91-03). Washington, DC: U.S. Government Printing Office.

Riger, S. (2002). What's wrong with empowerment. In T. A. Revenson & A. R. D'Augelli (Eds.), *A quarter century of community psychology: Readings from the American Journal of Community Psychology* (pp. 395–408). New York: Kluwer Academic/Plenum.

Romano, J. L., & Hage, S. M. (2000). Prevention and counseling psychology: Revitalizing commitments for the 21st century. *The Counseling Psychologist, 28*(6), 733–763.

Shapiro, D. A., & Firth, J. A. (1987). Prescriptive vs. exploratory psychotherapy: Outcomes of the Sheffield Psychotherapy Project. *British Journal of Psychiatry, 151,* 790–799.

Siefert, K., Bowman, P. J., Heflin, C. M., Danziger, S., & Williams, D. R. (2000). Social and environmental predictors of maternal depression in current and recent welfare recipients. *American Journal of Orthopsychiatry, 70*(4), 510–522.

Siefert, K., Heflin, C. M., Corcoran, M. E., & Williams, D. R. (2001). Food insufficiency and the physical and mental health of low-income women. *Women and Health, 32*(), 159–177.

Solomon, A. (2001). *The noonday demon: An atlas of depression.* New York: Scribner.

Stack, C. (1974). *All our kin: Strategies for survival in a black community.* New York: Harper & Row.

The Children's Aid Society. (1997, October). *Building a community school.* New York: Author.

U.S. Bureau of the Census. (2004). Current population reports: Income, poverty, and Health insurance coverage in the United States. Washington, DC: United States Government Printing Office.

U.S. Department of Health and Human Services. (2001). *Healthy People, 2010: Converence edition* (Vols. 1–2). Washington, DC.

U.S. Department of Health and Human Services. (2001). *Mental health: Culture, race, and ethnicity—A supplement to mental health: A report of the surgeon general.* Rockville, MD: Author.

Vera, E. M., & Reese, L. E. (2000). Prevention interventions with school-aged youth. In S. D. Brown & R. W. Lent (Eds.), *Handbook of counseling psychology* (3rd ed., pp. 411–434). New York: Wiley.

Waddock, S. M., & Walsh, M. E. (1999). Paradigm shift: Toward a community-university community of practice. *Journal of Applied Behavioral Science, 7,* 244–264.

Walsh, M. E., Brabeck, M. M., Howard, K. A., Sherman, F. T., Montes, C., & Garvin, T. J. (2000). The Boston College—Allston/Brighton Partnership: Description and challenges. *Peabody Journal of Education, 75*(3), 6–32.

Walsh, M. E., & Park-Taylor, J. V. (2003). Comprehensive schooling and interprofessional collaboration: Theory, research, and practice. In M. M. Brabeck, M. E. Walsh, & R. E. Latta (Eds.), *Meeting at the hyphen: Schools-universities-communities-professions in collaboration for student achievement and well-being* (The 102nd yearbook of the National Society for the Study of Education, Part 2, pp. 8–44). Chicago: University of Chicago Press.

Walsh, M. E., Thompson, N. E., Howard, K. A., Montes, C., & Garvin, T. (2000). The transformative process of action inquiry in a school–community–university partnership. In F. S. Sherman & W. R. Torbert (Eds.), *Transforming social inquiry, transforming social action: Creating communities of practice at the university and in the community* (pp. 93–115). Norwood, MA: Kluwer.

Watson, J. C., Gordon, L. B., Stermac, L., Kalogerakos, F., & Steckley, P. (2003). Comparing the effectiveness of process-experiential with cognitive-behavioral psychotherapy in the treatment of depression. *Journal of Consulting & Clinical Psychology, 71*(4), 773–781.

Wilkins, W. L. (1974). Social stress and illness in industrial society. In E. K. E. Gunderson & R. H. Rahe (Eds.), *Life stress and illness* (pp. 242–254). Springfield, IL: Charles C. Thomas.

Williams, C., Epstein, J. A., Botvin, G. J., & Ifill-Williams, M. (1999). Marijuana use among minority youths living in public housing developments. *Journal of Urban Health: Bulletin of the New York Academy of Medicine, 76*(1), 85–101.

Zilberman, M., Tavares, H., Blume, S. B., & Nady, E. (2003). Substance use disorders: Sex differences and psychiatric comorbidities. *Canadian Journal of Psychiatry, 48*(1), 5–13.

13

Toward a Community
Psychology of Liberation

Julia L. Perilla
Evelyn Lavizzo
Georgia State University

Gladys Ibáñez
NOVA Southeastern University

> *. . . The concern of the social scientist should be not so much to explain the world as to transform it. . . .*
>
> —Martín-Baró (1994, p. 19)

The words of the late social psychologist and Jesuit priest Ignacio Martín-Baró echo loudly as we face the urgent problems of our society. Although his context was the daily reality of the poor in Central America, Martín-Baró's writings have surprising relevance to the plight of Latinos in the United States and to the theoretical and practical applications of community psychology throughout the world. More specifically, the ideas of a psychology of liberation seem exceptionally appropriate as a framework from which to try to understand and—more importantly still—address the issues of Latino immigrant families affected by domestic violence.

Community psychology and liberation theology, two fields from which the principles of a community psychology of liberation arise, both emerged from the tumultuous and changing era of the 1960s and 1970s (Levine & Perkins, 1987; West, 1999). Not surprisingly, their origins were the response—the first academic, the second religious—to the historical and sociopolitical conditions of specific groups at the time. The principles of a community psychology of liberation stem from a confluence of these two streams and are meant to address the current problems of society as well as the role of psychology and psychologists in this endeavor. The language used by many of its proponents—empowerment, ecology, liberation, praxis—is reminiscent of the decades from which the two streams emerged yet is particularly applicable to the current realities of marginalized and oppressed people in the United States and elsewhere. The words also carry a particular significance to the issue of domestic violence in Latino communities. This chapter presents some of the ideas of a psychology of liberation as they have been used by social scientists in Latin America and the United States. It then describes the way in which the principles of a community psychology of liberation have been applied to an intervention program with Latino immigrant families affected by domestic violence in its work to create social change.

CREATING A COMMUNITY PSYCHOLOGY
OF LIBERATION

Community psychology emerged as an attempt to modify existing theories and practices in the field of mental health and make them relevant to the social realities of time, history, geographical location, class, and so on. From the beginning, community psychology has stressed the importance of context in the study of human behavior so that interventions and research are appropriate to the people and situations for which they are designed. At the same time, some social scientists (many of them influenced by the ideas of liberation theology from proponents such as Gustavo Gutierrez, Ernesto Cardenal, Paulo Freire, Juan Luis Segundo, and Beatrice Couch, among others), have advocated for the reformulation of the role of the social sciences in today's societies. They emphasize the potential of the professions as tools for the liberation of oppressed and marginalized people in light of their own realities (Martín-Baró, 1994; Serrano-García, 1990; Watts, Griffith, & Abdul-Adil, 1999). The concepts underlying a community psychology of liberation emerged from a confluence of these efforts.

Martín-Baró (1994), writing about the contribution of psychology as science and praxis to the history of the people of Latin America, suggests that the field as a whole has given little to the plight of the people in that part of the world. Whereas individual psychologists have done some important work on the effects of underdevelopment, oppression, and dependence, psychology as a profession has not produced applications that respond to the needs of the people. It appears that psychology has been most effective in this regard when it has been used in conjunction with other social sciences to advance theories and movements that address immediate social concerns. A prime example of this is Freire's (1978, 1997) use of a fruitful mix of psychology, education, philosophy, and sociology in his formulations of a pedagogy of liberation and his concept of *concientización* (critical consciousness). For Freire (1978) *concientización* is the process of personal and social transformation experienced by oppressed people once they become literate in their world. It is not only understanding the written word, but more importantly, learning to read the reality of our environment and becoming aware of the possibility of writing our own history. *Concientización* has added the social and political dimension to personal consciousness, providing ". . . historical dialectic between knowing and doing . . . individual growth and community organization . . . personal liberation and social transformation." (Martín-Baró, 1994).

In challenging the field of psychology—including community psychology—Martín-Baró (1994) and others have invited psychologists to look more closely at the manner in which Western theories, methods, and practice have left out the reality of the majority of the people of this hemisphere, most especially those who are economically, socially, and politically marginalized. These fundamental principles, they argue, have been derived from the perspective of middle- and upper-class Western society and have claimed universality. If reality is created and changed by the person-environment interactions, one must be aware of the subjective reality of the theorists and practitioners who have created the current social sciences. Proponents of liberation psychology question the assumed relevance and aptness of generally accepted methods to study and intervene with the poor and marginalized, whose voices are not present among theoreticians, researchers, and practitioners.

Martín-Baró (1994) proposes three essential elements for a psychology of liberation: a new horizon, a new epistemology, and a new praxis. Psychology, he suggests, must give priority to its capacity for providing effective services to poor and marginalized populations, rather than concern itself exclusively with its scientific and social status. In the same manner as other psychologists have done (e.g. Bronfenbrenner, 1979; Kelly, 1966; Trickett, 1995), Martín-Baró cautions against psychology's interest in studying individuals as if they were removed from society and history. A person or group's context is essential in understanding their reality and thus in intervening effectively or conducting research that is valid and respectful. In addition, a new epistemology or new ways of seeking knowledge must be used. This knowledge must come from the people who are creating the truth of their reality. As Freire (1997) points out regarding education, *concientización* only happens when the educator and the community enter into dialogue so that people can become critically aware of their reality and learn to write their own history. A psychology of liberation must emerge from the experience of the oppressed so that its truth can be discovered and built. This new perspective does not require that we throw away all of the existing knowledge, however. What must happen is for psychologists to "relativize" that knowledge and critically review it to determine its usefulness and validity for the people with whom we are working. Finally, the new praxis that Martín-Baró (1994) and Freire (1978, 1997) propose has to do with entering reality and in so doing, transform it. For psychologists it is not sufficient to take the perspective of the people, but also to involve ourselves in praxis with community members that will help us understand not just what is, but also what has the potential to be. For this to happen however, we must create more horizontal relationships between researchers and participants. Fals Borda (1988), for example, proposes participatory research as one of the methods with which to do away with the unbalanced relationship between researcher and participant.

In general, psychologists have entered the social process from a position of power, taking the perspective of the powerful in order to attempt scientific purity. Even community psychologists, having designed our research and intervention from within the academic walls, often arrive in the community full of ideas, plans, and money. It is easier for us to place ourselves alongside those with status and power rather than with the marginalized and dispossessed, never leaving our roles as technocrats and experts to work alongside community groups. Martín-Baró (1994) believed it is essential to engage in the praxis by which we transform ourselves as we attempt to transform reality for the liberation of groups of people.

The new praxis brings to the forefront the issue of power and thus the politicization of psychology. To take the perspective of the oppressed is to take sides and thus face the potential of losing scientific objectivity. Martín-Baró points out the confusion that often exists between bias and objectivity. Something biased is not necessarily subjective (e.g. a stand against violence) and must be taken many times as an ethical choice. This brings the idea of values into the picture. As Aldarondo (2001) points out, it is important to acknowledge not only the inevitability but the importance of value-based research. As social scientists working towards social change, our research must be clearly entrenched within the framework of values that enhance the potential for liberation. This must be done in a conscious and systematic manner, so that our stated values are reflected in every aspect of our work. In truth, class membership always carries with it a specific bias. However, values are not always used in a conscious way to make ethical choices that could advance social justice. Fals Borda (1988), for example, suggests that practical knowledge gained through participatory research can lead people to gain power, allowing them to be the writers of their own history and thus effect changes that will benefit all of society.

So how does community psychology become a community psychology of liberation? Because of its historical roots and strong tradition of responding to societal issues, community psychology contains many of the elements necessary for the creation of a community psychology of liberation. As stated in a previous section, the focus on diversity, ecology, empowerment, and social justice provide a strong basis for exploring the effectiveness of some of the ideas and proposals of social scientists in Latin America and elsewhere regarding the role of psychology and the inherent potential for the profession to be used as a tool for liberation. Its ecological approach to research and interventions afford the possibility of creating the "new horizon" Martín-Baró writes about. The connection between personal liberation and social transformation becomes possible when psychology provides the spaces and resources for people to learn to read their environment and thus define for themselves their place in history. As to a new epistemology, community psychology has begun to give more credence and respect to different ways of seeking knowledge, including the everyday experiences of community participants. It is perhaps in the need to engage in a new praxis that community psychology meets its biggest challenge. Despite individual efforts by community psychologists and a stated value that calls for a more balanced approach between scientist and participant, the field is still fraught with pitfalls in the way this value is carried out. Issues of power are more easily seen between men and women, Blacks and Whites, and low- and upper-class groups than those that are present in the interactions between researcher and participant, or between service provider and community member. We are still not able to engage in true dialogue with communities without bringing to the table our unacknowledged historical and professional status. The political and value-laden positions taken by many community psychologists often stop at rhetoric and theory, and the action element of praxis is not present.

A community psychology of liberation necessitates a change of attitude and heart on the part of its proponents, most especially those in the United States. In the 1960s, French psychologists suggested that the role of psychologists at the time was to provide an alternative to social friction by changing the individual to adapt to the existing social order (Martín-Baró, 1994). It appears that half a century later, psychology may still be filling that role. In the United States, for example, psychologists continue to attempt to understand individuals from ethnic "minority" groups (a label that itself carries a great deal of baggage) using the theories, tools, and strategies that were originally designed for mainstream groups. These theories, tools, and strategies seldom take into consideration contextual issues. The stated importance of contextualizing our work requires the design and implementation of methods, procedures, and models that emerge from within such contexts.

DOMESTIC VIOLENCE FROM THE PERSPECTIVE OF A COMMUNITY PSYCHOLOGY OF LIBERATION

From the perspective of our work, what would a community psychology of liberation bring to our understanding—and more importantly, to our intervention—of domestic violence among immigrant Latinos? The ideas contained in a community psychology of liberation offer a more comprehensive conceptual structure from which to explore the issue of domestic violence than what had been possible with existing theories. As a first step, it is essential to acknowledge the importance of the experiences and everyday reality of men who use violence, of women survivors, and of the children in these families, through a careful exploration of their specific cultural and social context—in our case, Latino immigrant communities.

Culture as Context

Latinos are currently the largest and fastest growing minority group in the United States. Latinos are a very diverse group and their level of acculturation varies greatly. Regardless of their degree of acculturation, however, there are certain cultural norms and values that are shared by most Latinos that have special relevance to the dynamics of domestic violence. Among these are the importance of family; distinct, and oftentimes rigid, gender roles; and such cultural scripts as *familismo, machismo,* honor, and *respeto* (for an extensive discussion of this topic see Perilla, 1999).

Familismo refers to the central place that the family has in Latinos/as lives. Families in this culture are usually highly integrated and family members are expected to give support and be loyal to each other, including extended family (Westberg, 1989). Along with its positive, protective, supportive qualities, Abalos (1986), among others, has pointed out that Latino families often provide safety for their members but do not necessarily allow people to be their own selves.

Traditionally, gender roles in the Latino culture have been clearly and rigidly defined. Male and female children were—and in some subgroups, still are—socialized differently from an early age (Triandis, 1983). There are different expectations of what boys and girls can and will do that are directly related to the gender roles they will be expected to carry out when they become adults (Abalos, 1986; Ramírez, 1999). Strict ideas of what tasks are appropriate for each gender often increase gender role inflexibility. However, the socioeconomic status and country of origin may affect this gender role rigidity (Marín & Marín, 1991). Additionally, the process of acculturation in many instances has served to erode the strict gender role differentiation (Coltrane & Valdez, 1997). Economic realities as well as the direct confrontation with majority culture values appear to be affecting the roles and expectations for males and females in Latino communities. Whereas these changes may increase gender role flexibility, they may also affect the stabilizing influence of traditional gender roles on the family, including the values and expectations found in the concept of *machismo.*

Machismo is the term given to a set of expectations for males in the culture. *Machismo* is seen as an expression of the exaggeration of maleness in contrast to femininity; an exaltation of physical superiority and brute force, the legitimization of a stereotype that uses unjust power relations (Lugo, 1985). Díaz-Guerrero (1996) defines it as a ratification of the cultural supremacy of men over women. At the same time, there are also positive attitudes that are equally important expectations for males in the culture. These include being strong and a good provider for his family (Marín & Marín, 1991), and a sense of honor and respect, generosity, and loyalty (Coltrane & Valdéz, 1997). (For a more complete discussion of *machismo* and domestic violence, see Perilla, 1999).

Respeto (respect) is another important cultural script of great relevance for any formulations and understanding of domestic violence dynamics in Latino populations. As children, Latino/as are socialized to show deference and respect for their elders (including parents, grandparents, older siblings, and extended family members) and for people in power. Antonio Ramírez (1999) writes that Latino fathers must be accorded great respect in their families, regardless of their actions. Some Latino social scientists (see, e.g., Abalos, 1986) caution parents against a misunderstood form of respect that supports parents' use of power against their children. Whereas, at times, the issues of respect and fear appear closely linked as a potentially detrimental element in relationships, this cultural script may be also be a valuable contextual element. The respect that must be accorded to people in positions of power (such as clergy and members of the court) can potentially be used to enhance domestic violence interventions with Latino batterers.

DOMESTIC VIOLENCE IN THE CULTURE

A review of the literature (Ruiz, 1998) gives scant and, at times, contradicting data regarding prevalence rates of domestic violence among Latinos, quite possibly due to a number of reasons, including the reporting mechanisms used to gather data, methodological issues, and the heterogeneity of the Latino population. It is believed, however, that Latino prevalence rates may be similar to those for other ethnic groups in the United States (Kaufman Kantor, Jasinski, & Aldarondo, 1994) and more importantly, that there may be important differences among subgroups of Latinos (Puerto Rican, Mexican, and Cuban), based on country of birth and acculturation levels, which are important contextual variables when attempting to establish prevalence rates in this ethnic group.

Regardless of the actual numbers, it is imperative that we understand, as clearly as possible, the circumstances and elements—including the historical, political, economic, spiritual, and social, as well as the individual ones—that serve as precursors of the abuse, maintain and support the dynamics of violence, and impact its aftermath. By including as many contextual elements as possible into our understanding we are not, at any point, attempting to rationalize, minimize, or excuse the violence perpetrated by the batterer. The intention is rather to understand more fully the circumstances of the violence so that our conceptualizations—and more importantly still—our interventions, will reflect as fully as possible the reality of the actors in the drama of violence. For example, the concept of *concientización* in the eradication of this serious and urgent social problem provides a framework from which to understand the transformation process that is a stated goal of intervention programs.

Although men batter for a variety of reasons, it appears that, across cultures, the exercise of power of one person over another is inherent in the dynamics of domestic violence. In much the same way as in political or social situations, intimate partners bring to their relationship resources that make them more or less powerful. The more varied the resources, the more power one has in the relationship. Power is thus the disparity of resources that happen within relationships and that allows, in the case of partnerships in which violence is present, the man's objectives and interests to prevail over those of his partner and/or his children (Perilla, 1999).

Although a great deal still needs to be learned about the texture of violence in Latino couples, it appears that domestic abuse has both universal and culture specific elements. The scientific literature on domestic violence has advanced a number of theories that have served as the basis for programs and interventions. Whereas these have almost exclusively been advanced from a Western middle-class perspective, they have assumed universal relevance and applicability. The voices—and thus the reality—of people of color and of immigrants and refugees in the United States have just recently begun to be included in the discourse. Conceptualizations of domestic violence emerging from the perspective of White, middle-class U.S. populations, for example, may not only *not* serve Latino families affected by domestic violence, but may in fact add to the stress of battered Latinas and their children and even create an unwanted situation of revictimization. For example, the emphasis on individual independence and autonomy that is often the basis for many battered women's interventions has been derived from the stance that *all* women must strive for these characteristics. This philosophy does not take into consideration the cultural norms and scripts that are such a central part of a woman's identity. For many Latinas (as well as members of other ethnic groups who hold strong traditional values regarding gender roles) who have been socialized to believe that their roles as wives and mothers are the most important ones in their lives, the idea of having to leave their partner and become autonomous adds to the stress and trauma of their situation. It may very well be that, in the end, some women may decide that this is exactly what they will do, but each woman must be given the opportunity to decide for herself the direction of her life.

Moreover, as Martín-Baró (1994) points out, psychological theories based on a positivist perspective, by concentrating exclusively on what can be seen and measured, often leave out the potential contained in the person–situation dynamic and thus often fail to provide the entire reality. A positivist perspective, for example, would find that Latino male batterers are simply *machistas*. This negates the complex reality of their being, the manner in which historical, social, economic, and spiritual forces affect their roles as batterers. A contextual and dialectic approach to domestic violence could explore the way in which these forces both maintain and support their violent behaviors and attitudes and also contain rich possibilities for change. This potential change refers not just to their role as batterers, but to their existence as human beings who possess the inherent possibility to become change agents of themselves, their families, and their society. In the same manner, conventional theories and research methods may find Latinas who have been battered only as depressed, dependent women with low self-esteem and suffering from "learned helplessness." A positivist perspective would fail to see their potential for self-definition, for celebration, for wisdom regarding the timing and orchestrating of their lives, and their immense capacity for survival. In terms of Latina/o children who have lived in a home often resembling a war zone, theories based on positivist ideas and methodologies might see only the risk factors present in their lives, the negative behaviors easily observed, rather than the entire reality of their lives and their possibilities, including their resiliency, their need to advance through all developmental stages despite their experience of violence, and their tremendous potential.

The emphasis on individualism of conventional theories of domestic violence also presents a problem for a more complete understanding of this phenomenon. The problem lies on seeing as individual characteristics those that many times are part of the collective, or those that happen only in interpersonal relationships. Individualism can thus reinforce existing structures in society and family, for example, by ignoring their communal existence and considering as personal problems that which should be societal ones (Martín-Baró, 1994). Many psychologists and other social scientists still design studies and interventions as if domestic violence was a personal problem of the woman or of the batterer, or at best a couple dynamic, without analyzing or including the societal structures (including culture and church) that allow violence to thrive. For immigrant Latinos it is important to take into consideration the precarious status in which society has placed them, in addition to the culture of violence and domination from which they have come and the one into which they have arrived. Their history in their countries of origin, their immigration experience, and the conditions of their existence in this country are essential variables in our quest for understanding their roles as perpetrators, victims and witnesses.

A community psychology of liberation would have us go beyond the conventional way of researching and intervening, to create theories and methods that are more respectful and responsive—and thus truly more empowering—for the populations with whom we work. Diversity would not be an add-on variable, but rather the contextual framework from which to advance conceptualizations and theories. The necessary emphasis on the ecological reality of the people would include a central focus on social justice, including elements in the environment that would help or hinder its attainment. Just as importantly, indeed even more so, would be the "change of heart" on the part of psychologists so that we would approach these tasks from an egalitarian stance, being constantly aware of the potential to misuse the power inherent in our professional status. Latino batterers, abused Latinas, and their children would be able to enter into dialogue among themselves, with each other, and with us, to attempt to change the ways they see themselves, as well as their places and roles in the world. The following section describes an intervention and evaluation project with Latino immigrant families affected by domestic violence that is attempting to put to work the ideas of a community psychology of liberation.

CAMINAR LATINO: A DOMESTIC VIOLENCE INTERVENTION AS A TOOL FOR LIBERATION

Conceptual and Philosophical Frameworks

The domestic violence intervention model that we have created—and that continues to evolve as we learn together about this complex phenomenon—attempts to see both what is as well as what can be. Caminar Latino, Inc. (Latino Journey) is a comprehensive intervention program for Latino immigrant families affected by domestic violence, whose main objective is the increased safety of women and children. We conceptualize domestic violence as a violation of the fundamental human rights of women and children that bears remarkable similarity to the dynamics present in acts of terrorism (Perilla, 1999). We have learned from the people that conventional models that looked exclusively at battered women or solely at men who batter did not work for our community. Because of the centrality of family in our culture, the family unit was the most appropriate place in which to intervene. This, of course, meant that children would have to be a central part of our efforts, not simply a peripheral service for abused mothers. Another issue that has become clear is the absolute need to contextualize the phenomenon of domestic violence, not to condone or excuse it, but to understand it more fully from within the framework of our culture and, in so doing, maximize the potential effectiveness of our interventions.

Our program does not consider domestic violence to be an individual problem of the abused woman, the male batterer, or the couple. We see it a social illness that mirrors the violence present in many aspects of society and that plays itself out in many families. As a result, ours is not a counseling or therapeutic intervention. The violence of the men who come to our program is not conceptualized as individual pathology that can be treated by mental health "experts" in one-on-one sessions. In the same manner, we believe that battered women are best served by interactions with groups of real experts, women who have also experienced domestic abuse, rather than in individual sessions with a therapist. We believe that the violence perpetrated by men against women is a behavior that males have learned through modeling at home and in a society in which violence is an accepted way of resolving differences. The inequalities present in many male–female relationships lend themselves to the potential for oppression that mirrors power imbalances throughout society, including those based on class, gender, race/ethnicity, sexual orientation, abledness, education, and so on.

The benefits of an ecological approach to domestic violence have been emphasized in the field (Carlson, 1984; Dasgupta, 2001; Dutton, 1994; Dutton, 1996; Edleson & Tolman, 1992; Heise, 1998; Pence & Paymar, 1993; Perilla, 1999; Perilla, Bakeman, & Norris, 1994) and were the framework used in all of our studies with this population. The issue of cultural contextualization is especially important when working with immigrant populations. In our case, studying the dynamics of abuse in Latino families as if domestic violence happened in a vacuum would quite possibly render our interventions not only ineffective, but dangerous as well. By failing to bring in the universal and culture-specific elements in the environment that affect the occurrence of violence, we could easily fail to recognize that domestic violence is only one of the many forms of oppression with which many immigrants must contend. Furthermore, if we had not entered into a dialogue with the actors (and thus the real experts) in this drama of violence, we could ourselves become oppressors, by attempting to speak about their reality without inviting them to use their own voices.

In recent years, there has been a growing number of voices that have questioned the effectiveness and wisdom of an exclusively punitive approach to domestic violence interventions that are aimed at individual batterers. Cultural and social norms that encourage, permit, or affirm abuse and violence must be identified, studied, and named as an essential culprit in this widespread phenomenon. There appears to be suspicion and reluctance of changes in existing norms and values that may alter the status quo. In terms of immigrant cultures, it is often believed that if we name and speak against phenomena such as domestic violence, we are somehow undermining our cultural traditions and values. As Antonio Ramírez (personal communication, September, 2000) points out, there are many cultural traditions that, as immigrants, we must pass on to our children. There are other beliefs and attitudes, however, which we must leave behind, among them the rigid and misplaced expectations and ideas that make domestic violence possible in our communities. Interventions that aim to change attitudes, expectations, and behaviors may indeed change cultural norms and thus the balance or homeostasis of a society. Based on this premise, our program has chosen to adopt a climate of respect and solidarity in which accountability and responsibility go hand in hand with respect and mutual reformulation of roles and expectations, rather than a punitive stance toward the perpetrators or a blaming attitude toward the victims.

From the perspective of a community psychology of liberation, the recovering of a historical memory is an important element for people to gain a sense of themselves and the entire reality of their culture (Freire, 1978; Martín-Baró, 1994). Latino culture, as all cultures, carries both positive and negative aspects that must be recognized and named collectively so they can be used to construct models of identity that open up possibilities for liberation and fulfillment, rather than for oppression. Latino immigrants seldom have the opportunity to collectively engage in the recovery of historical experiences. Caminar Latino provides safe spaces in which groups of abused Latinas and groups of Latino men who batter can gain important insights into their situation as survivors and perpetrators by exploring their histories and experience and the manner in which these impact their present attitudes and behaviors. In doing so, they are able to create for themselves new identities and roles that will enhance their potential for non-violence.

For this to happen, however, it is imperative that a community dialogue with the people be established (Freire, 1997) so that the understanding emerges from the experience of the people themselves, not from that of those in power. It was both inadequate and dangerous, for example, for our team to use existing theories and methods to intervene with Latino immigrant families affected by domestic violence. We had to go to the people themselves and learn first-hand about the reality of their experiences, their understanding of it, their mechanisms for survival, the beliefs and values that have kept domestic violence in place, and the ways in which changes could be initiated and maintained. For this, we had to accept the fact that we were not the experts and that it was necessary to adopt the interchangeable role of student/teacher–teacher/student (Freire, 1978). It was also clear that we could not simply throw away or dismiss the impressive body of knowledge that already exists about domestic violence in mainstream U.S. communities as well as the emerging knowledge about the topic in Latin America. The program has been enriched by European-American feminist theories and models of domestic violence (e.g. Bograd, 1984; Yllö & Bograd, 1988) as well as by Latin American feminisms. The latter bring into the analyses a wide range of issues in gender relations, including political, historical, social, and spiritual elements (e.g. Lagarde, 1997; Lugo, 1985; Ramírez, 1999). Our ongoing analysis of the issue of domestic violence has allowed us to see it as a phenomenon that emerges from the imbalance of power in relationships, which has deep roots in and is thus supported and sanctioned by oppressive social structures.

What we have set out to do, as Martín-Baró (1994) suggests, was to "relativize" the existing knowledge and critically review it to determine its usefulness for our people. We have learned that, indeed, there appear to be universal dynamics and sequences that are present in the occurrence of domestic violence (e.g. the cycle of violence, low self-esteem and depression on the part of the abused woman, expressions of denial and minimization on the part of the male batterer), and for which existing conceptualizations, educational materials, and resources, and techniques are quite effective. At the same time, it became clear that there are also culture-specific elements that affect the occurrence of violence and that must be identified, named, and brought into any intervention that focuses on a particular population (e.g. history of exposure to social and political violence, gender and family role expectations, immigration status, level of acculturation, within-group diversity, etc.). The contextual analysis of the occurrence of domestic abuse has helped us to explore in depth the effect of Latino cultural values, traditions, expectations, and beliefs (e.g. rigid gender role expectations, supremacy of males over females, importance of preserving the family unit) on the occurrence of this phenomenon in our countries of origin as well as in this country. At the same time, we have also obtained important insights about specific Latino cultural values and scripts (e.g. centrality of family, issues of respect, honor, and responsibility, spirituality) that have served as tools in the process of transformation (see following section for a discussion of this issue). The degree to which we include or fail to include these different elements may help or hinder our understanding as well as the effectiveness of our interventions. Thus, it became vital for us to develop ways that were culturally appropriate to determine the usefulness of existing knowledge as well as to develop new knowledge that would help us understand more fully this social phenomenon. In this manner, we could enhance the possibility to change what has been and to invite the emergence of what has the potential to be.

Program History, Structure, and Approach

From the beginning, *Caminar Latino*'s history and trajectory have been guided by specific needs in the community. The program began in 1990 as a grass-roots response to the realities of abused immigrant Latinas in Atlanta, with the first support group for Spanish-speaking battered women in the state of Georgia. The child care service first offered to the women has evolved into a comprehensive children's program over time. In 1995 a male batterer intervention group was added to the program at the request of the women. Participants argued that their lives would not change in significant ways unless their partner, with whom most of them continued to live, could also get help. The wisdom of the women regarding the reality of their situation supports Freire's (1978) ideas regarding the use of the "knowledge of the people" in program design. The comprehensive family intervention model that emerged as a result of the women's request—although unorthodox by mainstream standards—has proven to be an innovative and appropriate manner to work with Latino families affected by domestic violence.

Caminar Latino was originally a program of the outreach arm of a Catholic hospital that provided services to immigrant and homeless populations. Over the years, the increasing numbers of participant families provided the impetus to seek out other community players who could become partners in this endeavor. For more than 10 years Caminar Latino was a collaborative project of the original sponsor and a Catholic mission and community center serving Latinos, a community of Catholic sisters, and a state university. In 2003, the program incorporated as Caminar Latino, Inc., and obtained its own nonprofit status. In keeping with its program philosophy and history, Caminar Latino's board of directors includes professionals, business people, and community members including women who were formerly part of the survivors' group. Staff members take an active part in all facets of the administration, serving on all standing committees, participating in fundraising activities, decision-making processes, and program goals and objectives.

Individuals and families arrive at Caminar Latino through different routes. Approximately 85% of male participants are court-mandated to participate in a 24-session intervention. Their partners and children are invited to attend the women's and youth programs. Other men are referred to our program by priests, nuns, ministers, mental health professionals, or family members of program graduates. A substantial number of women participants (more than 50%) attend the program without their partners, most of them bringing their children. Children in these families can attend the groups as long as one of the parents is participating.

Caminar Latino currently offers three groups for abused Latinas, two male batterers groups (with a substance abuse component), an adolescent group, two groups for children (4–7 years old and 8–12 years old) and an infant and toddler play-group that meet concurrently once a week for 3-hour sessions at a church-run community center. The program team consists of four full-time and two part-time staff members and approximately 15 to 18 regular volunteers, including a doctoral-level clinical psychologist, as well as graduate and undergraduate students and postdoctoral fellows. Team members represent seven Latin American countries in addition to the United States and the Caribbean. Whereas a collaborative stance between academia and community has proven to be very fruitful for the program, the presence and active participation of community individuals within the intervention team has been the key factor in its effectiveness. The extensive experience and knowledge of the community that these team members bring to the program provide a valuable complement to the skills of the academically trained members.

The location in which the program is held is another key element of the intervention. The church-run community center in which the program is housed is easily accessible by public transportation. Due to the deep respect the overwhelming majority of immigrant Latinos have for the church (regardless of their denomination), the church accords an additional element of safety for women and children. In addition, church staff members are strong supporters of the program, and their visibility and involvement send a strong message regarding their stance on domestic violence as well as the community approach to the intervention.

The group format is ideally suited to the philosophical and theoretical orientation of the program. New participants join existing groups made up of members with different levels of experience in the program. In keeping with the ideas of a community psychology of liberation regarding the need for nonhierarchical approach to interventions, Caminar Latino group facilitators are not the "experts" on issues of violence. Participants who have been in the program for a while teach new members through a sharing of their own experiences and insights regarding their experience of violence. Using Freire's philosophical framework, we believe that if information is merely imparted by "experts" to court-mandated batterers, to battered women, or even to their children about the dynamics, types, and effects of domestic violence, participants may learn the terminology and ideas "deposited" by the facilitators or instructors on participants (see Freire, 1997). However, for real transformation to occur, there must be an opportunity for individuals to experience a safe space in which to critically explore the antecedents, dynamics, and effects of violence. In so doing, we are hopeful that they will also transform the way they view themselves, their role as human beings, and their unique potential.

Women's Program. The abused women's support and reflection groups use a framework informed by third-world feminist theories, in which the women have the opportunity to explore the meaning of their abuse from a social and cultural perspective that takes into account their status as immigrants. During group sessions, women are encouraged to make use of the support provided by other participants, as well as use the awareness and knowledge acquired in the weekly reflections regarding topics of common interest. Group members play an active role in the ongoing development and evaluation of the program and are encouraged to provide input regarding new reflection topics and ways to improve the services.

As we listened to the women, team members became aware that, once more, the women were proving to be the experts regarding their own lives. Women coming into the program are usually in a state of crisis, and their needs and interests are quite different from those of women who have been in the program for a while and whose lives have achieved more stability. As a result of the women's comments and suggestions, the woman's group split into two levels. Women in the first level who are just entering the program participate in groups with a structured format that includes a support component plus a component with basic information on domestic violence (definitions, dynamics, types, effects), as well as topics regarding safety planning, resources, laws, rights, and options. After 10 weeks in the first-level group, women join the second-level group in which they have the opportunity to explore more in-depth issues related to their self-definition, life goals, family dynamics, and so on. This group uses a Freirean approach, in which topics determined by the women are used to create a curriculum that is presented on a cyclic basis. Weekly themes for dialogue and exploration are brought to the group so that relevant ways to address specific issues can emerge from the participants themselves.

Over the years, the evolution of the women's program has reflected the participants' increasing sense of ownership in their groups. For example, the program was originally called "Latino Families at Risk." The name was changed to Caminar Latino (Latino Journey) at the request of the women, who indicated that they wanted a more positive label for the program. In the same spirit, women in the second level group began to keep journals when they indicated that they wanted to document their healing process. They designed the format of the journal to include several art media, so that all women could make use of this tool, regardless of their literacy level. This sense of group ownership and the awareness of untapped potential reflect the collective strength of survivors in their process of concientización.

Men's Program.   The batterers' intervention program uses a 24-session, two-level group format and is based on the Training Center Against Male Family Violence CECEVIM (*Centro de Capacitación Contra la Violencia Intrafamiliar Masculina*) program in San Francisco (Ramírez, 1999) and modified to address the specific needs of the Latino population in Atlanta. All men who join the program, whether they are court-mandated or voluntary participants, sign a contract to attend a minimum of 24 sessions and to do 50 hours of community work. The first-level group consists of 10 sessions that follow a structured class format. Because of the low level of formal education of many of our participants, the program does not use any reading assignments or journal writing. Instead, it uses repetition and discussions of basic concepts directly related to the batterers' responsibility for their violence and their change. The second-level group is comprised of individuals who have not used physical violence with their partners for 10 weeks and who pass a test of the material covered in the first level. In the second level, men have the opportunity to explore, in more depth, issues related to their definition of masculinity, cultural norms regarding gender roles, parenting issues, as well as verbal, emotional, and sexual abuse within their relationships.

To address the importance of substance abuse as a predictor of violence in this population (Hightower & Gorton, 1998; Kaufman Kantor, 1997; Neff, Holamon &

Schluter; 1995; Perilla et al., 1994), the weekly batterers' group has a substance abuse education component in addition to the structured violence reduction curriculum. In lieu of a fee, program participants are required to work 50 hours in projects benefitting the community. This emphasizes the community aspect of the program and the responsibility of the men for the impact their violent behavior has had on society. It also addresses the economic reality of the Latino immigrant community where both men and women are often forced to take two or more jobs in order to meet their family's financial obligations. Community work hours, being the sole responsibility of the batterer, do not affect directly the entire family's economic resources. The ongoing support and contact with staff and the mandatory reporting to the courts seems to be especially well-suited for working with this population.

From the perspective of Caminar Latino, accountability is more than the reparation that men must make for the effects of their violence. The process of transformation into a less violent human being makes the issue of a man taking responsibility for his behavior is a given premise. *Concientización* requires that, beyond reparation, each man begin to make a critical examination of all aspects of himself that may in some way contribute to the beliefs, expectations, and attitudes that have led—and may continue to lead—to violent acts. If critical consciousness takes place, for example, former batterers would decide not to commit future acts of violence not just because of the legal and economic consequences that could ensue, but because in their new understanding of themselves and their place in the world, new acts of violence would compromise their integrity as human beings who are struggling toward nonviolence.

Youth Program. The youth program is a vital component of Caminar Latino's work. Conceptualized as the component of the program that provides primary intervention, the work being done with the children of families in which domestic violence is present is, at once, the most challenging and the most promising. The first children's group began as a child care service for women participating in the support group. It soon became evident, however, that the children's own needs would need to be addressed. As the program continued to grow and the number of children increased, groups for different ages as well as structured activities began to be offered.

The number of very young children who participate in the program is a sobering reflection of the dynamics of domestic violence. In the "honeymoon period" that often occurs after physical abuse has happened, many women become pregnant. Our youngest group for children aged from newborns to 3 years old gives mothers an opportunity to have time for themselves in the women's group while trained volunteers care for their babies and toddlers. During our last 15 years of work with Latino families affected by domestic violence, we have been able to observe closely the tremendous effect on children from an early age. The playgroup for infants and toddlers is structured so that the children have an opportunity to interact with each other and with the adult facilitators in a nonviolent and respectful way. For many children, this means learning to share toys and play equipment in nonaggressive ways as well as experiencing nonviolent boundaries and consequences. For others, the playgroup is a place in which our young participants undergo a remarkable transformation as they begin to reach out to facilitators whom they have learned to trust.

The program curriculum for the three sharing groups contains common themes that are tailored for each age level—living with self, living with family, living with friends, living with(out) violence, living with community, living with culture, and so on. Within each theme, relevant topics are addressed (e.g. self-esteem, anger, feelings, relationships, bullying, violence, safety plans, drugs and alcohol, school, siblings, dreams/options, etc.). In the safe space provided by the groups and through a series of exercises, games, discussions, role-play, and so on, children are encouraged to explore the experience of violence in their families, as well as other issues relevant to their development. The curriculum also includes opportunities to access their cultural roots through dance, music, songs, stories, crafts, presentations, and so on. For children needing additional help, the program also offers referral to other community agencies and resources, as well as liaisons with schools, juvenile justice courts, and other government agencies, tutoring, and individual and family (child/ren and mother) counseling on a limited basis.

The adolescent group and the two children's groups are cofacilitated by a staff member and volunteers who receive ongoing training regarding program philosophy and values, in addition to basic information regarding domestic violence. As in the infant and toddler playgroup, one of the main objectives of the sharing groups is to provide safe spaces for the youth while modeling nonviolent ways of relating to one another. Discipline and limit-setting are thus accomplished in ways that are respectful of the dignity of each child and adolescent and is consistent with the principles being discussed in the women's and men's groups.

As with the adult participants, our work with these children of families affected by domestic violence has given us the opportunity to learn a great deal. Although it was not contemplated in the original conceptualization of the intervention program, the input and ongoing dialogue with adolescents and older children in our program has become a central element of our work. Not surprisingly, teenage members have very clear and strong ideas about the topics that needed to be addressed, as well as activities that would be relevant and fun for their group. For example, the group writes, casts, directs, and presents to other program participants, as well as the community, short plays regarding issues of importance to them, including drugs, alcohol, violence, racism, immigration, ethnic identity, homelessness, school dropout, teenage pregnancy, and suicide. Using lyrics from popular music, the group also explores issues related to gender relations, violence, stereotypes, and so on.

Does This Model Work?

The tenets of a psychology of liberation call for studies and interventions that address the specific needs and realities of Latino immigrants and make use of methods and practices that are respectful and relevant to the participants and invite their voices to the table as equal partners throughout the process. This essential task in our attempt to utilize Caminar Latino as a tool for social change has been at once daunting and exciting.

The evaluation of domestic violence intervention programs is a complex issue, starting with the operationalization of the concept of success. The criminal justice system has, in the past, used recidivism rates as a marker for the effectiveness of batterer intervention programs. We know, however, that part of the danger inherent in these programs is the potential for batterers to acquire knowledge that will allow them to continue to use verbal, emotional, and other type of control tactics that will maintain their dominance, without ever getting back into the criminal justice system.

Additionally, women's and children's advocates are well aware that the cessation of physical violence is only the first step in creating homes in which there is an increased feeling of safety. Gondolf (2001) and others have written about women's feeling of safety as one of the best indicators of whether or not violence will again erupt in that home. The voices of children, however, have seldom been invited to help determine the markers of the effectiveness of intervention programs and services.

In a previous study with couples in this population (Perilla & Bakeman, unpublished manuscript), we had found striking gender differences in the perception of personal and relationship variables. Males and females differed in their reports for all but one of the variables we examined. The remarkable lack of concordance gave support to an ecological approach to the study of domestic violence and to Martín-Baró's critique of the limitations of a positivist approach to research done in community. It became obvious that not only were the reports of both men and women essential to our evaluation strategies, but that voices of the children needed to be included in order to obtain a more accurate understanding of the situation. In addition, Caminar Latino's perspective of domestic violence as a social problem and human rights issue, required a more thorough understanding of the social, political, cultural, and familial realities of this immigrant population within which the violence was occurring, so that we could better contextualize the men and women's perceptions of their situation.

To explore these contextual components of domestic violence, focus groups and qualitative interviews were conducted with Latino and Latina adults and youth, members of the clergy, service providers, and court personnel who work directly with Latino families. The themes that emerged from the focus groups and interviews suggested a strong connection between violence experienced in the home and the direct experience with various types of social violence such as war, violence perpetrated by the police and military, as well as gang and school violence. In terms of the role of culture, participants indicated that there was a strong socialization for men to use violence and women to see violence as part of their lot in life. Gender roles and expectations determined the consequences of violent behavior. Finally, many of the participants indicated that there was very little support from family and church for women who were abused (Perilla, Lavizzo, Ibañez, & Parker, 2000).

The results of the qualitative study were used in the preparation of the evaluation protocol that is currently in use. Long-term women participants and the adolescent and older children in the program served as consultants throughout the process and helped to pilot and fine-tune the questionnaire. The involvement of the survivors (women and youth) has been extremely valuable, giving support to the principles of participatory research, a framework that has guided our study. In addition, their involvement has kept our team conscious of Martín-Baró's insistent question: "for whose benefit?" Conducting research with families traumatized by violence must be more than an academic exercise that will advance scientific knowledge. It must do that, of course. But if we were to stop at this widely accepted goal, we could run the risk of *using* the people with whom we work, rather than *collaborating* with them. It is imperative for us, then, that the research that we conduct together have concrete applicability to the current reality of our families. The results that emerge from our studies must be relevant to the plight of the participants and our interpretations must be done taking into consideration their comments and questions regarding our findings. Our team has learned that the contribution of our participants to the process is essential not only to safeguard our ethical responsibility to them, but also enhance the richness and validity of our data. Current evaluation strategies in Caminar Latino include standard measures, open-ended questions and qualitative data from adult and youth participants and weekly reports from group facilitators.

So, does our program work? In terms of the men, women's reports indicate marked decrease in physical abuse within the first 2 weeks after a man joins Caminar Latino. However, the beliefs, expectations, and attitudes that maintain sexual, verbal, and emotional abuse happening and that have been present for two, three, four, or more decades require a great deal of time and conscious effort to change in a radical way. The 24 weeks to which batterers are mandated by Georgia law are thus only the beginning of a process that requires a lifetime to accomplish. Many women report a decrease in sexual, verbal, and emotional abuse and state that they feel safer in their homes. Others indicate that beyond the cessation of physical violence, the controlling attitudes and behaviors are still present and some opt to leave their partner. Approximately 90% of the men who are court-mandated complete the program (completion rates for men who participate voluntarily is approximately 75%). In addition, at 6-month follow-up, approximately 97% of the men who complete our program have not re-entered the court system. This may be due to a number of reasons, among them the cultural specificity of the program, the respectful and egalitarian approach to the intervention, the extensive connection to community, and the comprehensive family focus of the program. As just stated, it could be argued that program participants do not re-enter the court system because they have learned the extent to which they are able to engage in violent actions and attitudes without getting caught. It could also be that Latinas are reluctant to call the police once they realize the ramifications of their seeking services for domestic violence from police and courts. Although this may be true in isolated cases, we believe that Caminar Latino provides a promising alternative for Latino families affected by domestic violence. We have maintained contact with women whose partners have completed the intervention and their feedback suggests that the improvements gained during the program are still in place 2 and 3 years after completion. We consistently invite men who are completing the program to continue attending the group on a voluntary basis with their families once they have been released from their probationary status. Approximately 25% of the men continue to attend a minimum of five additional classes after completion. Several men continue to come to the program for months and even years. From this group, men who show potential as group leaders and demonstrate an interest in the long-term process are invited to continue their training as future facilitators.

In terms of the women's program, the structure and ongoing dialogue with program participants has already proven its effectiveness. In addition to the sense of group ownership that has made the women's voices become the guiding force for the program, women are gaining an increasing awareness about their rights and options. Many of the women have learned to drive or are attending English or computer classes, some have retrained to work in nontraditional jobs (i.e., taxi drivers, heavy machinery operators), and others are seeking residency status under VAWA guidelines.[1] Their knowledge of services and resources in the community has decreased their isolation and many of the women have become involved in church

---

[1] The Violence Against Women Act (VAWA) provides a remedy for battered women to apply for legal residency on their own, rather than having to rely on their spouse's willingness to apply on their behalf.

and community programs. Women in the second-level group have requested opportunities to explore together issues such as parenting, discipline, education, sexuality, and so on, because of its immediate relevance to their lives and those of their families. In addition, the women's program is a good example of the potential that exists within ethnic communities to develop core groups of trained individuals. Two of the current group facilitators are former members of the original abused Latinas' group. Two other former group members have helped establish small groups for other battered Latinas: one in an Atlanta suburb and the other among migrant farm worker women in South Georgia. Long-term members of the program have spoken at domestic violence rallies and vigils, served on planning committees for a victims' conference, and one served on the board of directors of Caminar Latino, Inc. If success is measured in terms of level of *concientización,* one would have to argue that the women's program in Caminar Latino is remarkably successful.

It is interesting, but perhaps not surprising, to note that it is among the adolescent participants in Caminar Latino that we see the most immediate potential for transformation that reaches beyond the confines of the intervention groups. With the support and encouragement of the adolescent group facilitators (community members and students who are themselves not much older than the participants), several group members have begun to show a genuine interest in social justice issues. For example, they have begun to work with homeless individuals, participated in peace rallies, are actively seeking information regarding political and social issues in Latin America and the United States, and serve as tutors for younger program participants. For the past three summers, adolescent group participants have been eligible to join Caminar Latino staff to work for a week in South Georgia as part of an interdisciplinary team with migrant farmworker families. The youth have the opportunity to serve as interpreters for psychology, nursing, physical therapy, and dental hygiene students and faculty, as well as work directly with migrant children in group settings and activities. This activity has been so positive that it now serves as an incentive for our young participants to do well in school in order to be eligible for the Moultrie experience. We believe that the impetus for this type of *concientización,* at least in part, derives from the opportunity these young people have had in the program to explore together their lives, their options, and their place in the world. It is encouraging to think that out of the disruption and chaos of domestic violence there is the potential for a true transformative praxis.

LESSONS LEARNED

One of the central tenets of Freire's model of transformative education is the dialectical nature of the process. All participants in this common quest become pupil–teacher and teacher–pupils, as we teach and learn from each other simultaneously. The members of Caminar Latino have learned firsthand the accuracy of this statement. Each one of us has been deeply affected by our work with the families we serve and with each other. This has been especially significant for those of us who are academically trained professionals. We have had the unique opportunity of learning a great deal about ourselves, our profession, our limitations, our possibilities, and our responsibilities.

Among the things we have learned from the people with whom we work is to rethink—and challenge—medical models of clinical psychology that would have us fo-

cus on individual pathology by paying exclusive attention to a person's internal es-
tates, rather than looking at domestic violence with an ecological lens that requires
a social and cultural contextualization of the issue. We have been reminded of how,
as mental health professionals, we have attempted to create change from a distance, without joining the community in which we practice, guiding the client in
making changes in his or her environment, while maintaining a distant, objective,
and "nonbiased" stance. We have learned that, in order to facilitate a lasting change
in consciousness in the people with whom we work, it is essential to become part of
the community so that we can obtain knowledge and participate in the process of
liberation from within that context. We have become aware of the limitations of our
profession as a tool for social change when we attempt to have people adapt to oppressive circumstances, without attending to their inherent liberation potential. We
have been challenged about our self-definition as "experts" on the issue of domestic
violence and been forced to redefine our idea of expertise on this topic.

As academically trained professionals, we have learned just how easy it is to take
our privilege, our status, and the power they bring and misuse it in our work in ways
that often go unchallenged. It is easy to fall into hierarchical models that are often
more expedient, but that contradict and weaken the liberation component of our
work. We have learned that as our program name suggests, "caminar" is a journey
that must be undertaken at the pace and time of each person with whom we work,
which very often does not match our own. Over the years, we have become aware
of the challenge of incorporating a psychology of liberation perspective into our
work within the larger society in which hierarchy and bureaucracy are the prevailing models.

These challenges have brought to the forefront the need for ongoing support
from one another because of the isolating nature of the work we are proposing to
do. It would be impossible for one person alone to do this work. Our journey requires fellow travelers and allies who will help us do work that goes against established norms. The task is not easy, but it is remarkably rewarding. Along with the
satisfaction of seeing individuals and families gain a new understanding of their role
in making the world a more peaceful place is the pleasure of observing the emergence of leaders from within the community who will continue the work into the
next generation. There is also the excitement of seeing students become open to
new, broader, and more meaningful opportunities for their chosen careers, as they
incorporate their experiences into their professional identities. The potential for social change at many levels is truly remarkable.

CONCLUSION

The results obtained thus far give us cause for hope. When Latino men who were
former batterers and women who were abused begin to change their lives, they are
often moved to start working with people like themselves in order to change not
just their families but their communities as well. The solidarity found among men
and among women in these circumstances far surpasses any individual gain and enters into the realm of collective action. In terms of the children, we have described
in a previous section the inherent potential not only for a primary intervention that
would enhance the possibility of breaking the intergenerational cycle of violence,
but also for the emergence of a transformative praxis that may impact our commu-

nity in exciting ways. The ideas contained in a community psychology of liberation allow us to see not only the trauma, pain, and challenges inherent in this public health issue, but also the potential of what could emerge out of interventions such as this one. The true collaborative endeavor among researchers, practitioners, and community members is indeed a model that could transform our field and help the cause of liberation and social justice.

REFERENCES

Abalos, D. T. (1986). *Latinos in the United States: The sacred and the political*. Notre Dame, IN: University of Notre Dame Press.

Aldarondo, E. (2001, July). What research has to contribute to ending violence in communities of color. Paper presented at the Multi-Cultural Forum on Violence Against Women, U.S. Department of Health and Human Services, Carolina, PR.

Bograd, M. (1984). Family systems approaches to wife battering: A feminist critique. *American Journal of Orthopsychiatry, 54*(4), 558–568.

Bronfenbrenner, U. (1979). *The ecology of human development*. Cambridge, MA: Harvard University Press.

Carlson, B. (1984). Causes and maintenance of domestic violence: An ecological analysis. *Social Service Review, 58,* 59–587.

Coltrane, S., & Valdez, E. O. (1997). Reluctant compliance: Work–family role allocation in dual-earner Chicano families. In M. Romero, P. Hondagneu-Sotello, & V. Ortiz (Eds.), *Challenging fronteras: Structuring Latina and Latino lives in the U.S.* (pp. 229–246). New York: Routledge.

Dasgupta, S. D. (2001). Towards an understanding of women's use of non-lethal violence in intimate heterosexual relationships. *Applied Research Paper Series* [Online]. Retrieved December 29, 2002, from www .VAWnet.org/VNL/Library/general/AR_womviol.html

Díaz-Guerrero, R. (1996). *Psicología del mexicano: Descubrimiento de la etnopsicología* [The psychology of the Mexican: The discovery of ethnopsychology]. Mexico, DF: Editorial Trillas.

Dutton, D. G. (1994). Patriarchy and wife assault: The ecological fallacy. *Violence and Victims, 9*(2), 167–182.

Dutton, M. A. (1996). Battered women's strategic response to violence: The role of context. In J. L. Edleson & Z. C. Eisikovits (Eds.), *Future interventions with battered women and their families* (pp. 105–124). Thousand Oaks, CA: Sage.

Edleson, J. L., & Tolman, R. M. (1992). *Intervention for men who batter*. Newbury Park, CA: Sage.

Fals Borda, O. (1988). *Knowledge and people's power: Lessons with peasants in Nicaragua, Mexico and Colombia*. New Delhi : Indian Social Institute HN980 FAL.

Freire, P. (1978). *Education for a critical consciousness*. New York: Seabury Press.

Freire, P. (1997). *Pedagogy of the oppressed*. New York: Continuum.

Gondolf, E. (2001). *Batterer intervention systems: Issues, outcomes, and recommendations*. Thousand Oaks, CA: Sage.

Heise, L. (1998). Violence against women: An integrated, ecological framework. *Violence Against Women, 4*(3), 262–290.

Hightower, N. R., & Gorton, J. (1998). Domestic violence among patients at two rural health care clinics: Prevalence and social correlates. *Public Health Nursing, 15*(5), 355–362.

Kaufman Kantor, G. (1997). Alcohol and spouse abuse ethnic differences. In M. Galanter (Ed.), *Recent developments in alcoholism, Volume 13: Alcoholism and Violence* (pp. 57–79). New York: Plenum.

Kaufman Kantor, G., Jasinski, J. L., & Aldarondo, E. (1994). Sociocultural status and incidence of marital violence in Hispanic families. *Violence and Victims, 9*(3), 207–222.

Kelly, G. A. (1966). Humanistic methodology in psychological research. In B. Maher (Ed.), *Clinical psychology and personality: The selected papers of George Kelly* (pp. 133–146). New York: Wiley.

Lagarde, M. (1997). *Género y Feminismo: Desarrollo Humano y Democracia* [Gender and Feminism: Human Development and Democracy]. Madrid, Spain: Horas y Horas.

Levine, M., & Perkins, D.V. (1987). *Principles of community psychology: Perspectives and applications*. New York: Oxford University Press.

Lugo, C. (1985). *Machismo y violencia* [Machismo and violence]. Caracas: Nueva Sociedad.

Marín, G., & Marín, B. V. (1991), *Research with Hispanic populations*. Newbury Park, CA: Sage.

Martín-Baró, I. (1994). *Writings for a liberation psychology*. Cambridge, MA: Harvard University Press.

Neff, J. A., Holamon, B., & Schluter, T. D. (1995). Spousal violence among Anglos, Blacks, and Mexican Americans: The role of demographic variables, psychosocial predictors, and alcohol consumption. *Journal of Family Violence, 10*(1), 1–22.

Pence, E., & Paymar, M. (1993). *Education groups for men who batter: The Duluth model.* New York: Springer Publishing Company.

Perilla, J. L. (1999). Domestic violence as a human rights issue: The case of immigrant Latinos. *Hispanic Journal of Behavioral Sciences, 21*(2), 107–133.

Perilla, J. L., & Bakeman, R. (unpublished manuscript). *Perceptions of domestic violence in relationships: gender differences between Latinas and Latinos.*

Perilla, J. L., Bakeman, R., & Norris, F. H. (1994). Culture and domestic violence: The ecology of abused Latinas. *Violence and Victims, 9*(4), 325–339.

Perilla, J. L., Lavizzo, E., Ibañez, G., & Parker, J. (2000, November). *Caminar Latino: An emerging model for research and intervention in a Latino community.* Paper presented at Latino Psychology 2000: Bridging Our Diversity Conference, San Antonio, TX.

Ramírez, A. (1999). *El hombre y la violencia intrafamiliar* [Man and family violence]. Mexico, DF: Editorial Pax.

Ruiz, R. (1998). *Latino intimate partner violence: Culture, history, socioeconomic status and methodology.* Unpublished manuscript, National Medical Fellowship Inc., Violence Prevention.

Serrano-García, I. (1990). Implementing research: Putting our values to work. In P. Tolan, C. Key, F. Chertok, & L. Jason (Eds.), *Researching community psychology: Issues of theory and methods* (pp. 171–182). Washington, DC: American Psychological Association.

Triandis, H. C. (1983). Some dimensions of intercultural variation and their implications for community psychology. *Journal of Community Psychology, 11,* 285–301.

Trickett, E. J. (1995). Human diversity and community psychology: Where ecology and empowerment meet. *American Journal of Community Psychology, 23*(5), 583–502.

Watts, R. J., Griffith, D. M., & Abdul-Adil, J. (1999). Sociopolitical development as an antidote for oppression—Theory and action. *American Journal of Community Psychology, 27*(2), 255–271.

West, C. (1999). *The Cornel West reader.* New York: Basic Civitas Books.

Westberg, J. (1989). Patient education for Hispanic Americans. *Patient Education and Counseling, 13,* 143–160.

Ylló, K., & Bograd, M. (Eds). (1988). *Feminist perspectives on wife abuse.* Newbury Park, CA: Sage.

14

Striving for Social Justice Through Interprofessional University–School Collaboration*

Maureen E. Kenny
Elizabeth Sparks
Boston College

Janice Jackson
Harvard University Graduate School of Education

The academic achievement, physical health, and psychological well-being of urban youth are a serious concern to the nation. Recent reports reveal that urban youth are less likely to receive a postsecondary degree, are more likely to drop out of high school, and are less likely to meet the minimum standards on national tests of literacy than are suburban youth (Loveless, 2003). Contemporary education reform efforts are challenged by the numerous social issues that proliferate in our communities, including unsafe sex, drug and alcohol abuse, familial and community violence, teenage pregnancy and parenting, lack of job skills, inadequate access to health care, and homelessness (Dryfoos, 1990; Lerner, 1995). Within urban communities, the challenges confronting youth are extensive and complex, with basic health needs often inadequately addressed (Wilson, 1996). In affluent suburban schools, economic resources are used to hire consultants to address social, emotional, and academic problems when they occur; however, in most urban schools, limited resources makes it difficult (if not impossible) to provide much-needed assistance to the many students who are at risk for academic failure (Pittman, 2000). Clearly, significant inequities exist for urban and suburban youth.

Despite the urgent need for interventions that will increase resources for urban youth, efforts are limited not only by budget shortfalls, but by a system of fragmented services in which educational professionals are situated in the schools, and mental health professionals, for the most part, work in community-based facilities and in academia (Walsh, Howard, & Buckley, 1999). Counseling and clinical psychologists have traditionally served urban youth and their families by providing individual and family therapy in community mental health settings. Although these ser-

*This chapter is based on work funded by Grant D40HP01371, Department of Health & Human Services, Bureau of Health Professions, Graduate Psychology Education Program and a grant from the Collaborative Fellows Program, Lynch School of Education, Boston College.

vices benefit many, large numbers of urban youth and their families do not frequent mental health clinics (Baker & Adelman, 1994; Gibbs & Huang, 1997), and psychologists who work in mental health settings do not generally coordinate their interventions with professionals in schools. These psychologists are often isolated from educational professionals and do not fully understand the realities of urban education. Among doctoral-level psychologists, school psychologists are the only specialty that has been primarily based in schools. The roles for school psychologists now include consultation, intervention, prevention, health care and research (National Association of School Psychologists, 2004). Yet, for many years, much of their time was consumed by psychological assessment and special education placement, leaving less time for the development, delivery, assessment and coordination of an array of preventive and remedial services. Despite the efforts of some psychologists to offer services to teachers as consultants, psychological consultants within the schools have traditionally been perceived as "psychological experts"(Caplan, 1970; Dougherty, 2000). The role of expert can create distance between psychologists and teachers, with teachers feeling that their expertise is not recognized or valued.

We contend that the challenges facing urban families and youth, in conjunction with the importance of academic achievement for economic mobility in contemporary life, call for a revised relationship between education and psychology. Psychologists cannot begin to address problems within urban education, nor can they effectively promote positive mental health for urban youth, without understanding the importance of children's educational development. We propose that interprofessional collaboration, which brings together varied professionals seeking to support the development of the whole child across academic, social, career, and health domains (Brabeck, Walsh, Kenny, & Comilang, 1997; Walsh, Brabeck, & Howard, 1999), can effectively contribute to the dialogue concerning urban education. This chapter examines the collaboration among psychologists and educational professionals, who strive to alter some of the inequities experienced by urban youth and, in this way, promote social justice.

THE PROPOSED BENEFITS OF INTERPROFESSIONAL COLLABORATION

There are a number of reasons why interprofessional collaboration within school settings can be a mechanism for promoting social justice. Concerns regarding the effectiveness of public schools are being voiced across the nation, but are particularly prevalent regarding urban schools. Recent educational reform efforts, such as the federal No Child Left Behind Act of 2001 (NCLB), have sought to address these concerns. The stated purpose of NCLB is to ensure that all children reach "challenging" standards in reading and mathematics and to close the achievement gap (Paige, 2002; U.S. Department of Education, 2002). NCLB is grounded in an accountability system that is centered around the requirement for students to pass standardized tests that are based on state-developed academic standards. Teaching to pass these tests has, at times, overshadowed attention to students' psychosocial needs. In many schools, students have been retained when they have failed to attain competence in basic skill areas as assessed by this standardized testing. Academic retention is not an effective educational reform strategy, however (Haney et al., 2004; National Association of School Psychologists, 2003). We suggest that psychologists should join with other professionals, especially educational professionals, to identify effective interventions for enhancing academic achievement.

We suggest furthermore that the complexity of concerns presented by many urban youth and their families cannot be adequately addressed by the knowledge of any single profession (Walsh, Galassi, Murphy, & Park, 2002). Despite the merits of addressing the gaps in academic achievement, recent efforts have tended to neglect the array of social, economic, and psychological factors that present barriers to learning and healthy development (Schorr, 1997; Walsh et al., 2002). We suggest that educational reform efforts that neglect the social and emotional needs of youth and their families are misguided, and that, with appropriate resources, the schools can address both academic and socioemotional development. Because cognitive and social-emotional development are reciprocally interrelated, youth cannot thrive academically when distressed by social and psychological difficulties (Walsh, Howard, & Buckley, 1999), nor can they thrive psychosocially when ill-prepared to function in higher education and gainful employment (Hartung & Blustein, 2002). Addressing educational, socioemotional, and health concerns of youth within schools makes sense additionally because many youth do not access social services within their communities (U.S. Public Health Service, 2000). Because all youth below the age of 16 are mandated by public law to attend school, the public education system offers a setting through which both educational and psychological services can be delivered simultaneously (Kenny, Waldo, Warter, & Barton, 2002). Furthermore, given the stressors prevalent within contemporary education and society, schools need ongoing support services from mental health professionals, rather than sporadic crisis intervention (Youngblood & Spencer, 2002).

Although some urban schools offer mental health interventions, services often focus on deficits and resolving crises, rather than on identifying strengths or promoting skills that will contribute to success in multiple life domains (Dryfoos, 1990; Walsh, Thompson, Howard, Montes, & Garvin, 2000). Consistent with the growing national recognition that comprehensive programming is needed to promote positive youth development (Catalano, Berglund, Ryan, Lonczak, & Hawkins, 1999; The Collaborative for Academic, Social, and Emotional Learning [CASEL], 2003; Elias, 1997), we maintain that interprofessional collaboration should focus not only on resolving crises, but also on offering services that enhance social competencies and maximize opportunities for life success (Kenny, Waldo, et al., 2002; Walsh et al., 2002). Services offered for youth who live in urban communities tend to focus on problem prevention (such as violence prevention; substance abuse prevention; anger management; HIV/AIDS prevention; Yowell, 2002). This is in stark contrast to the array of activities fostering social, academic and artistic growth that are widely available to youth in affluent, suburban communities (Pittman, 2000). Social equity demands that urban youth have access to academic, social, and emotional learning experiences that will enhance their competencies for success throughout life.

Interprofessional collaboration also offers a means for teachers, psychologists, and other professionals to learn from and support one another. The educational system in this country has been under attack by the public and the media. Teachers are under pressure to improve academic achievement as measured by standardized tests and reduce disparities in achievement between majority students and the disenfranchised, such as students of color, second language learners, and students with special needs. Many students arrive at school burdened by psychological and social concerns that present barriers to academic learning (Walsh & Park-Taylor, 2003). Facing tremendous pressures to increase student achievement in the context of numerous obstacles and inadequate resources, teachers can experience discouragement and loss of morale, as well as lowered student expectations (Youngblood & Spencer, 2002). Collaboration between teachers and other professionals might offer an antidote to this discouragement.

Rather than the psychologist as "expert," interprofessional collaboration recognizes the existence of multiple perspectives and knowledge bases and the need for teachers, students, families, psychologists, school administrators, and other professionals to learn from one another (Walsh, Brabeck, & Howard, 1999). Teachers and psychologists bring different areas of expertise that are of equal importance in helping students reach their greatest potential. Too often, the two groups fail to look to each other in their mutual efforts to support students. Through interprofessional co-learning, collaboration can contribute to a more positive and complex understanding of the child and his or her family. We suggest that when professionals have more comprehensive knowledge about the multiple contexts of the child's life and domains of functioning, the capabilities of youth are more apparent and new opportunities for assisting the child's development become evident. A better understanding of an individual student's learning needs can greatly aid teachers in diagnosing problems and implementing strategies that will more likely lead to mastery of the intended content (Tomlinson, 1999). It may also assist teachers in attending to students' successes, not just their failures. Although teachers confront many institutional barriers in their work in schools, interprofessional collaboration from within and outside of the educational system might help to sustain motivation, energy, and morale by offering support, and infusing new ideas and new resources into the system.

We have come to the conclusions just discussed regarding the potential benefits of interprofessional collaboration as a mechanism for promoting social justice as a result of our efforts over the past 10 years as university faculty in developing collaborative partnerships with urban schools. Regrettably, systematic research that examines and documents the impact of interprofessional collaboration remains quite limited (Walsh & Park-Taylor, 2003). Although our experience has given us hope about the positive benefits of such collaborations, it has also made us keenly aware of the obstacles that make the development of effective interprofessional collaborations between universities and urban schools difficult to build and sustain. Through our observations, we have evidence that some of the proposed benefits occur, whereas others are still anticipated. Our experience in training psychology and education graduate students in social justice-oriented interprofessional practice has also contributed to our understanding of the central issues involved in helping students develop the necessary skills to understand issues of social context, and the need for psychologists to engage in practice that increases access to resources for their clients.

This chapter documents the benefits and challenges of interprofessional collaboration as a mechanism for promoting social justice, as well as practices and processes involved in developing interprofessional collaborations and training graduate students for this work. We begin by outlining the theoretical constructs that have informed our work. To exemplify the model and processes, we describe two interprofessional initiatives that we have conducted over the last few years. The first initiative, the Tools for Tomorrow Project, began more than 5 years ago. The second project, the Graduate Interdisciplinary Project, was more recently implemented, and trains graduate students in nursing, social work, and counseling psychology to work as an interprofessional team to provide health prevention programs to children. We assess the status of our collaborations, provide examples that illuminate our progress, and identify key challenges that emerge through social justice-oriented interprofessional collaborations between universities and urban schools. We hope that the story we have to tell and our mutual opportunities to reflect on their meanings will begin to chart a path for professionals interested in collaboration for social justice in urban public schools.

THEORETICAL FOUNDATIONS FOR UNIVERSITY/ SCHOOL INTERPROFESSIONAL COLLABORATION

The developmental-contextual framework (Lerner, 1986, 1991; Lerner, Walsh, & Howard, 1998) provides a theoretical foundation for understanding the proposed benefits of interprofessional collaboration. Walsh and colleagues (Walsh et al., 2002; Walsh & Park-Taylor, 2003) identified four premises derived from this framework. These premises—that development (a) occurs in relation to context, (b) occurs simultaneously across multiple domains within the individual, (c) extends across the life span, and (d) includes the promotion of strengths and healthy resiliencies—provide a compelling rationale for interprofessional collaboration as a component of effective educational and psychological intervention. These premises, in conjunction with attention to the emancipatory communitarian values for personal, relational, and collective wellness (Prilleltensky, 1997; Prilleltensky, Nelson, & Peirson, 2001) have been helpful in guiding our efforts to develop interprofessional collaborations with social justice aims. The implications of emancipatory communitarian values and the developmental-contextual framework for promoting social justice through interprofessional collaboration are outlined in Table 14.1.

The emancipatory communitarian values for personal wellness include caring and compassion, educational and personal development, and self-determination. Accordingly, through interprofessional collaboration, we strive to demonstrate care and compassion for the professionals with whom we collaborate and seek to enhance the level of care and compassion expressed by professionals towards urban youth. We seek to further the academic, social, and vocational development of urban youth, and to involve youth and their teachers in actively defining the goals they hope to achieve and the means to reach them. We recognize that the achievement lags experienced by some urban youth reflect numerous systemic factors, rather than personal deficits. With regard to the emancipatory communitarian value for collective wellness, we seek to provide students with enhanced educational and vocational resources and strengthen the schools, which are a central community structure. With regards to values for relational wellness, we seek to develop culturally sensitive programs through collaborative practice, rather than assuming the role of psychologist as expert.

We find these values to be complementary to the four developmental contextual premises. Developmental contextual theory, for example, recognizes that development occurs as a result of the dynamic relation between an individual and the multiple contexts in which the individual is embedded. Accordingly, optimal development occurs most readily when there is a "good fit" between the individual and the multiple social contexts in which the individual is situated (Lerner, 1986, 1991). This emphasizes the importance of strengthening the contexts that support human development. Certainly for school-aged youth, the schools are a critical developmental context. The developmental-contextual emphasis on context is consistent with the emancipatory communitarian collective wellness value for distributive justice,

TABLE 14.1

Implications of Emancipatory Communitarian Values and Development-Contextual Premises for Interprofessional Collaboration

Emancipatory Communitarian Values	Principles of Interprofessional Collaborative Practice	Developmental-Contextual Framework
Personal Wellness		
Caring and compassion	Professionals support each other Develop holistic understanding of student Treat students with care and compassion	Development across the life span Development across multiple domains
Educational and personal development	Develop student competencies of educational, social, and occupational growth	Promotion of strengths and health resiliencies
Self-Determination	Promote voice of all stakeholders in program development	
Collective Wellness		
Social justice in provision of resources	Add university resources to strengthen school and community	Development occurs in relation to context
Support community structures	Teach students to access resources and negotiate barriers	
Relational Wellness		
Respect for human diversity	Respect cultural background of students and culture of school setting Adapt interventions to fit context	Development occurs in relation to context
Collaboration and democratic participation	Provide opportunities for all stakeholders to participate meaningfully Build on interdependence of needs Develop through connection, cooperation, coordination, and consensus building	Development occurs in relation to context

which states that all children should be provided with adequate resources to support their educational development (Prilleltensky, Nelson, & Peirson, 2001). Attention to context also suggests, consistent with the relational wellness value of respect for human diversity, that interventions should be contextually and culturally sensitive. That is, in order to promote person-environment fit, interventions need to be meaningful in terms of the cultural contexts of students' lives and need to demonstrate respect for school norms. Collaborators need to be aware of their impact on the contexts they are entering and of the dynamic interactions that occur transactionally among teachers, psychologists, and students.

Another developmental-contextual premise maintains that individual development occurs across multiple domains, including the biological, cognitive, emotional, and social. This premise is consistent with the emancipatory communitarian focus on promoting educational and personal development and with recent research suggesting that mental health and learning are often connected and that problems in one domain of functioning are often related to difficulties in another domain (Adelman & Taylor, 2000). Consequently, effective interventions often focus on multiple domains, rather than on isolated aspects of experience (Gottfredson, Fink, Skroban, & Gottfredson, 1997). Programs that simultaneously promote emotional and social health can thus enhance students' abilities to achieve by reducing barriers that interfere with learning (Elias, 1997). Through interprofessional collaborations, the knowledge of multiple disciplines can be integrated and coordinated in a comprehensive manner (Brabeck, Walsh, Kenny, & Comilang, 1997).

A third developmental-contextual premise suggests that change is possible at any time across the life span. Individual, as well as environmental, factors dynamically interact to produce continuing possibilities for change and intervention. Because change occurs among individuals at all phases of the life span, all interventions inevitably impact adults in the school, as well as the children. Teachers, psychologists, school administrators, university professors, and graduate students are part of the dynamic interaction process and should be responsive and open to ongoing change as they learn from each other, students, parents, and community leaders (Kenny, Simon, Kiley-Brabeck, & Lerner, 2002; Walsh et al., 2002).

The developmental-contextual perspective also recognizes that unique patterns of strengths and protective factors make it possible for individuals to develop in adaptive ways, despite the presence of environmental risks (Walsh et al., 2002). Psychoeducational interventions that seek to promote strengths and healthy resiliencies are also resonant with the emancipatory communitarian personal wellness value for educational and personal development. Such interventions also respond to growing national demand for comprehensive efforts to promote positive youth development (Catalano et al., 1999; Walsh et al., 2002). Interventions that focus on promoting positive youth development recognize that merely reducing risks is inadequate preparation for a successful future (Pittman, 2000; Roth & Brooks-Gunn, 2000).

SOCIAL JUSTICE COLLABORATIVE PRACTICE—TOOLS FOR TOMORROW

The Tools for Tomorrow (TFT) intervention represents a university–public school interprofessional collaboration between administrators and teachers in the Boston Public Schools and faculty in Counseling Psychology and in Curriculum and Instruction at the Boston College Lynch School of Education. TFT was developed to strengthen students' understandings of the connection between school and work, thereby enhancing school engagement and decreasing school dropout.

The TFT psychosocial curriculum is delivered to ninth-grade students by a Boston Public School classroom teacher and a counseling psychology faculty or graduate student. The curriculum consists of three instructional units that are integrated into an existing class and are presented once a week over the course of an academic year. The "Who am I?" unit focuses on engaging students in a process of self-discovery and enhancing personal and ethnic identity exploration. "The Connecting School and Career" unit facilitates student exploration of career paths, and helps students to translate knowledge about themselves and their world into academic and career goals. This unit is designed to consolidate students' awareness of the connections and various pathways between school and their educational and vocational futures. The "Identifying Resources and Barriers" unit was designed to help students identify external and internal resources and barriers, develop skills needed to maximize resources and overcome barriers, and develop mentoring relationships.

TFT was developed to encompass a number of the characteristics that we have identified as central to collaborative practice for social justice. The collaboration also reflects applications of the four developmental-contextual principles and emancipatory communitarian values. Consistent with social justice concerns for the equitable provision of resources and the premise that context affects development, for example, the collaboration seeks to enhance the resources of the public schools by bringing mental health professionals into the classroom and applying research knowledge to program development. The collaboration between teachers and counselors is intended to be mutually supportive, and to thereby foster the capacities of professionals within the classroom to treat students with care, compassion, and empathy.

TFT also recognizes the interplay between the academic and psychosocial domains of development. By using a literacy-rich curriculum that includes readings and written assignments, the intervention seeks to simultaneously promote psychosocial and vocational development and develop academic skills. Furthermore, the collaboration between teachers and counselors in delivering the curriculum is intended to expand the knowledge of each profession with regard to the needs of the whole child. The psychologist or psychology student learns about the academic strivings and challenges of the student, while the teacher learns about the psychosocial resources and barriers to learning in the students' experiences beyond the school. As the teacher and the psychologist learn from one another over time, they can support the development of their students in a holistic manner that also shows respect for human diversity. For example, after reading the excerpts "Those Who Don't" and "A Smart Cookie" from *The House on Mango Street* by Sandra Cisneros, students in one class discussed their experiences with racism as they travel to school using public transportation. The classroom teacher later mentioned how that discussion had increased her understanding of how racial stress permeates her students' lives on a daily basis. With regard to development across the life span, TFT seeks to support the development of teachers, psychologists, and future psychologists in training, as well as urban high school students. Optimally, all participants develop personally and educationally, building mutual understanding, respect, empathy, and skills for democratic participation and collaboration.

With regard to attention to healthy resiliencies, TFT seeks to address the risks for school failure and dropout that are associated with the ninth-grade transition

(Department of Research, Assessment, and Evaluation, Boston Public Schools, personal communication, October 25, 1999) by promoting student strengths. TFT focuses students on identifying cultural, familial, and community assets and resources, while also gaining awareness of the structural barriers, including poverty and racism, that place obstacles in their paths to high school completion and further educational and career success. TFT adheres to the premise and a growing body of research, which suggests that school engagement and expectations for future success can be strengthened among low-income students of color when they are provided with specific procedural knowledge that helps them to connect the context of their present lives with their dreams for the future (Oyserman, Terry, & Bybee, 2002; Yowell, 2002). By providing students with a more complex understanding of the steps needed to complete school and enter into higher education and careers that offer advancement in the new global economy (Marshall & Tucker, 1992; Wilson, 1996), we strive to teach urban high school students to "cope more adaptively with the opportunity structure" (Hartung & Blustein, 2002) and offer empowering knowledge that is part of the "social capital" of middle-class society (Blustein et al., 2001). Ultimately, we hope that our efforts will help to reduce the existing bifurcation of educational opportunities based on social class and race and contribute to distributive justice, or a more equal distribution of goods and opportunities across social groups (Blustein et al., 2001).

SOCIAL JUSTICE COLLABORATIVE PRACTICE—GRADUATE INTERDISCIPLINARY TRAINING PROJECT

The Graduate Interdisciplinary Training Project (GIT) was designed to train counseling psychology graduate students in interprofessional collaboration for social justice. Over the years, the authors had attended student support meetings at a number of collaborating urban public schools and were involved with various intervention and staff training activities. Through this work we recognized that there was a need to not only have the university assist with prevention efforts within the schools, but to also train graduate students in the skills necessary to be effective in establishing and maintaining interprofessional collaborations. Through GIT, graduate students in counseling psychology collaborate with nursing and social work students in the implementation of an empirically supported prevention program to address specific areas of high-risk behavior and promote the development of psychosocial competencies among students in low-income urban schools. In addition, graduate students in psychology, social work, and nursing participate in a weekly interdisciplinary seminar. The interface of psychology, nursing, and social work students within the graduate classroom and the urban public schools creates a network of interdisciplinary collaborative training that impacts every aspect of the project.

Similar to TFT, GIT brings increased resources to the public schools, recognizes the interplay between academic and psychosocial development, and seeks to promote strengths and healthy resiliencies among youth. As with the TFT project, we chose to utilize an urban public school as the site for our prevention efforts in order to reach more students than would be possible if we conducted this work in a community-based mental health setting. Our hope is to influence the lives of urban youth as they are learning and developing healthy lifestyles. By partnering nurses, social workers, and psychologists in delivering services within an educational setting, the project also recognizes the interplay of the cognitive, social, emotional, and biological domains of development and the need to prepare professionals who can address the needs of the whole child.

The GIT Project was funded by the U.S. Department of Health and Human Services (Graduate Education in Psychology Program) and the implementation process began in fall, 2003. The initial focus was on formalizing communications with the administration and staff of two target schools (an elementary school and a high school) and developing the interdisciplinary seminar where graduate students learn about the various ecological, family, and intrapersonal factors that contribute to the development of high-risk behaviors in urban youth. Although each of our target schools were interested in participating in the project, it was only possible in the first year to implement the program in the elementary school for a variety of reasons that will be discussed more fully in a later section. The GIT Project addressed the following goals during this first year: (1) to provide counseling psychology graduate students with an opportunity to increase their ability to work with students from other disciplines through the implementation of an evidence-based health prevention program for urban school students; (2) to teach graduate students the skills necessary to conduct a program evaluation of this intervention; (3) to increase the graduate students' cultural competence, while also enhancing their confidence in their ability to pursue careers with high-risk urban youth; and (4) to establish a model that can be used by other psychology programs to train graduate students for collaborative social justice practice.

The interdisciplinary graduate seminar meets on a weekly basis and is facilitated by the GIT Project Coordinator. Students read relevant literature from the three professional disciplines, and faculty supervisors from counseling psychology, nursing, and social work give presentations on relevant topics. The graduate students also critique existing prevention programs to determine which might be appropriate for the students in our target school. The seminar also served as a component of their field supervision. For the counseling psychology graduate students, this experience satisfies one of our 1st-year doctoral requirements, the First Year Experience (FYE). The FYE involves students in community-based sites that provide opportunities to design, implement, and evaluate preventive interventions, participate in systematic interprofessional collaborations with community-based groups, and/or provide advocacy. These experiences broaden their understanding of the roles that professional psychologists may assume in helping individuals, families, and communities improve their lives (Kenny & Gallagher, 2000). For the graduate students in the Schools of Nursing and Social Work, the GIT field experience fulfilled a portion of their required clinical training hours.

There were many different areas of physical/mental health that we could have chosen as the focus of our prevention work. We initially discussed the following eight areas with our public school partners: (1) drug/alcohol use; (2) self-esteem and building resilience; (3) healthy eating behaviors; (4) problem-solving and conflict resolution; (5) healthy sexual behavior; (6) AIDS prevention; (7) the relationship between racial identity and health; and (8) domestic and relationship violence. We selected these particular areas because each represents a critical health risk in poor urban communities in the United States. In fact, a review of the Healthy People report (U.S. Department of Health and Human Services, 2000) furnishes compelling evidence that preventive interventions in each of these areas can provide an important means of reducing high-risk behaviors in disadvantaged communities. Further support for focusing on these areas can be culled from a review of the psychological literature on health behaviors (e.g., Hoffman & Driscoll, 2000; Matarazzo, Miller, Weiss, Herd, & Weiss, 1990; Nicassio & Smith, 1995; Park, Adams, & Lynch, 1998; Wilson, 1996).

Following a discussion with our school partners, we decided to focus our prevention efforts in the area of problem solving and conflict resolution. Our school partners at the elementary level were very eager to implement a social skills program entitled SCORE, which was developed by researchers from the University of Kansas (Vernon, Schumaker, & Deshler, 1993). The SCORE program teaches a set of social skills that are foundational to effective cooperative group work and to building learning communities. The five social skills addressed in the SCORE curriculum are: *S*hare ideas, *C*ompliment others, *O*ffer help or encouragement, *R*ecommend change nicely, and *E*xercise self-control. The rationale for focusing our intervention on the SCORE skills rests with the significance of social skills in enabling youth to establish and maintain appropriate interactions and relationships with peers. The SCORE curriculum lessons mainly focus on teaching students how to become socially strategic. In order for students to become socially strategic and apply appropriate social skills fluently and automatically, they must be systematically taught these skills. Once these skills have been rehearsed and learned, the students should be able to approach tasks by thinking, planning, acting, and evaluating their performance (Vernon et al., 1993). There are a total of seven lessons in the SCORE curriculum sequence that include such procedures as introducing the students to the concept of social skills; teaching them how to effectively share their ideas with others; and modeling ways to engage in prosocial activities such as complimenting others, offering help, and recommending changes in such a way that others respond positively to them. The implementation of the SCORE curriculum began with three groups of children in the elementary school: (1) a group of fifth-grade girls; (2) a group of fifth-grade boys; (3) and a group of boys and girls that met during the after-school program.

DEVELOPING INTERPROFESSIONAL UNIVERSITY/SCHOOL COLLABORATIONS

Our experiences with TFT and GIT exemplify a number of issues central to the development of interprofessional collaborations. From a developmental-contextual perspective, collaboration is a means for expanding resources in ways that can address the complex problems experienced by some urban youth. From an emancipatory communitarian perspective, collaborations that are to achieve social justice aims must simultaneously attend to values of personal, collective, and relational wellness, with a particular focus on self-determination, respect for human diversity, and democratic decision-making. Attention to this array of complex values, however, means that collaborations take a long time to develop, and require ongoing attention and modifications.

As noted by Lawson (2003), the development of an effective collaboration involves a number of time-consuming processes, including connection, communication, cooperation, coordination, and consensus building, which are consistent with emancipatory communitarian focus on democratic participation. Collaborative relationships and partnerships between the Boston Public Schools and the Lynch School of Education that existed prior to the development of the TFT and GIT collaborations offered the initial connection through which these programs were developed. More than 10 years ago, and with substantive involvement of several counseling psychology faculty, administrators and faculty from across the university began meeting to discuss opportunities and mechanisms for interprofessional training and collaboration (Brabeck et al., 1998). Over time, these meetings produced a number of successful grant applications, including receipt of a U.S. Office of Education Fund for the Improvement of Secondary Education (FIPSE) grant that focused on preparing current and future teachers and health/human service professionals to work in partnership with families and schools to address the multiple barriers that limit children's academic achievement. Following the success of these initial efforts and in recognition of the importance of community collaboration, the Boston College Center for Child, Family, and Community Partnerships (CCFCP) was established to provide a university infrastructure that could foster comprehensive university–community initiatives aimed at improving the quality of life for children and families (Brabeck et al., 1998; Fleming & Brabeck, 2002). Several of the developers of TFT and GIT had been involved in aspects of this interprofessional work since its inception. Another of the developers was formerly the Deputy Superintendent in the Boston Public Schools and strongly supported the implementation of school-to-career[1] within the school district. These existing relationships and collaborative partnerships between the Boston Public Schools and faculty from Boston College provided a foundation of mutual trust and positive expectancy between the public schools and the university.

Collaborations often evolve under conditions of interdependence, such that the collaborating parties are able to more effectively achieve their goals when working together, rather than independently. This benefit of collaboration makes it rewarding, despite the time-consuming processes necessary to properly nurture and sustain a collaborative relationship (Lawson, 2003). TFT evolved because it met the mutual needs of all partners. For example, the school-to-career programs of Boston Public Schools were strong, yet the leadership believed that their program could be further enhanced through increased attention to occupational exploration, career planning, and the development of psychosocial competencies. One of the Boston College faculty had recently completed a scholarly review of school-to-career literature (Blustein, Juntunen, & Worthington, 2000) suggesting that school-to-career programming often omitted critical "connecting activities" that are needed to help students understand the relationship between their current education and future vocational opportunities. The findings of this review resonated with the observations of the local public school leaders, who felt that the university professionals could help them to strengthen their programs. The collaborating Lynch School faculty offered professional knowledge in vocational psychology, adolescent development, multicultural issues, and educational curriculum and administration that could be helpful to the school district in enhancing the school-to-career programming. The interest of the school leadership in partnering with the university met the scholarly and social justice agenda of the university faculty who were interested in

---

[1]School-to-Career is a whole school change effort in the district that is the implementation of the federal School-To-Work Opportunities Act of 1994.

designing and evaluating the necessary connecting activities, but who needed the educational expertise and local knowledge of the public school professionals in designing the curriculum, as well as access to the pubic school classrooms in order to carry out this endeavor. Given the complex challenges confronted by urban high school youth, the university faculty also recognized that collaboration among educational professionals would be needed to develop and deliver an effective multifaceted intervention.

The development of TFT curriculum units met the needs of the collaborating schools and teachers. At one of the high schools, for example, a new health and wellness course was to be implemented and the development of TFT units became part of the curriculum for that course. A key teacher in one of the schools was instrumental in enriching the literacy components of the curriculum and in aligning the TFT lessons with the curriculum frameworks and standards of the school district, for whom literacy was a top priority. In a similar way with GIT, the collaboration between the three professional schools at Boston College and the public schools grew out of a recognition of the need to train graduate students to work across disciplines, and a corresponding need to have increased prevention programming for the schools. The selection of the SCORE curriculum was based on input from our public school partner and was deemed appropriate for our purposes because it addressed a critical social developmental area for the elementary school students. An additional incentive for its use was the fact that a member of the Lynch School of Education faculty is a certified trainer for this curriculum and was able to train the GIT Project participants (graduate student, faculty, and public school personnel) in the model.

As noted by Lawson (2003), we have found that communication, cooperation, coordination and consensus building are central to achieving interdependent, trusting and equitable collaborative relationships. In our experience, the development of collaborations requires ongoing conversations through which perspectives are exchanged and consensus and trust are gradually built. After meeting with school administrators to build an initial consensus regarding the goals, structure and location of the TFT program, principals and school-to-career coordinators at the school level identified teachers who might be interested in this initiative. Teachers joined the meetings and began delineating their students' needs and their own needs for resources and support to carry out this type of collaboration. The initial meetings with teachers were important in eliciting, listening to, and incorporating their perspectives so that the collaboration would not be perceived as a top-down central administration initiative in which they had little input or choice. Focus groups were held at one of the high schools to better understand teachers' perspectives on the school-to-career needs of their students. The development of the TFT curriculum sought input from all collaborators, with no single group or individual seeking to dominate the process or product. The school district administration provided time and/or monetary support for teachers, school-to-career coordinators, and student support-team coordinators to attend planning meetings, which was important in engaging the initial "buy-in" from school-based professionals.

For the GIT Program, similar conversations took place with faculty from the three university professional schools in an effort to recognize the unique contributions that students from each of these disciplines would bring to the project. Each discipline has a particular way of training its preservice professionals, and the initial conversations were geared towards identifying ways of integrating the students' experiences that would be mutually beneficial. In addition to working through the interdisciplinary issues in the university, we also needed to include public school personnel (teachers and administrators) in our conversations. It was clear that the schools wanted to have more prevention programs for students, and in general, were very supportive of our efforts to train graduate students for interdisciplinary practice. However, the intervention was perceived as being a "service" that the graduate students would provide to the schools, with only minimal participation from school personnel. This posed a problem for the development of a true collaboration between the university faculty/students and the school personnel, and will be discussed in more detail in a later section of the chapter.

PROGRAM EVALUATIONS

As a result of our university–school collaboration more than 1,500 students have now participated in TFT. A much fewer number of students participated in the GIT project during its first year primarily due to its limited scope and circumscribed implementation plan. Data obtained from ongoing process and outcome evaluation have been valuable in identifying the aspects of the programs that are working well and those that need modification and has thus contributed to a process of continual modification of the curriculum and modes of delivery. We are now in a position to partially reflect on the ways in which we are meeting our social justice goals.

Consistent with the relational wellness values of human diversity, collaboration and democratic participation (Prilleltensky et al., 2001), we have invited students and school personnel to evaluate both of these programs and not to feel bound by our agenda and expectations (Blustein et al., 2001). In TFT, teacher and high school student voices were instrumental, for example, in the addition of a field trip to our campus, where the high school students learn from current college students, including ethnic minority students who attended urban high schools, about their journeys to and experiences at college. A particularly powerful assignment in which TFT students interview a family member or other caring adult about their pathways from school to work/career was an addition to the curriculum suggested by one of the teachers.

The findings from a 6-student focus group of TFT students completed by an external evaluator also suggests that TFT is accomplishing some goals consistent with an emancipatory communitarian approach (Prilleltensky, 1997; Prilleltensky et al., 2001), such as personal wellness values of caring and self-determination and the relational wellness values of respect for community. One student, for example, appreciated the opportunity to give feedback on the TFT program. He enjoyed that students were treated "like young adults instead of little kids." Students experienced the addition of the counselor to the classroom activity as supportive, stating that the person from Boston College seemed to "really care for us." Collaboration and respect among students have also been noted. Some students reported that they learned to understand and work better with their classmates through the class activities. Another student reported making new friends and being less "scared to come to high school." Students also seemed to understand the curricular emphases on connecting school and work, describing the program as emphasizing the importance of planning things out, being prepared for class, and doing homework. Some students even reported that the program changed the way they thought about school, now being "more open minded in thinking about my future goals" and "more serious about high school."

Interviews with school staff revealed that the program was viewed as authentic collaboration and effective team teaching approach, with mutual respect between the teacher and counselor (Department of Research, Assessment, and Evaluation, Boston Public Schools, personal communication, February 12, 2001). In meetings about the project we have been told repeatedly by teachers and administrators that what makes TFT unique is the sustained collaborative partnership between the schools and the university.

Data obtained from quantitative measures in the TFT Program have been helpful in assessing the theoretical premises on which the intervention was developed. For example, our data reveal that urban high school students' perceptions of available support are positively associated with their levels of school engagement and career expectations (Kenny, Blustein, Chaves, Grossman, & Gallagher, 2003). These data affirm the importance of attending to students' relationships with teachers and counselors as we seek simultaneously to enhance their knowledge of self, school, and career. Quantitative data have also served to verify the premise that school engagement and career development are related and that efforts to enhance school engagement by building knowledge of the relationship between school and work are theoretically sound (Kenny et al., 2004). Subsequent quantitative and qualitative efforts in progress will assess the extent to which indices of school engagement and career planning are modifiable as a result of the intervention.

In the GIT Project, the evaluation has consisted primarily of qualitative data from the graduate students' journals and process notes of the groups, as well as summaries of the weekly seminar discussions. We also conducted a focus group meeting at the end of the year where we addressed the students' experiences and perceptions of the interprofessional collaboration among themselves as well as with the school personnel. The graduate students wrote weekly notes on the group sessions and weekly journal entries where they commented on their reactions to the group intervention and seminar discussions. They were asked to focus their reflections in the following areas: (1) interdisciplinary collaboration; (2) adapting the curriculum to the needs of the students; (3) implementing the curriculum; (4) working in an urban school; and (5) individual goals. It is too early in the process to assess the students' learning as they delivered the prevention curriculum. But a preliminary review of their journal entries and group notes suggest that the graduate students are realizing the complexities involved in working as a collaborative team with students from other disciplines, and are gaining a greater appreciation for the challenges the children face across multiple contexts. They also seem to be developing a heightened awareness of some of the structural challenges involved in implementing a prevention program within an urban elementary school. This learning experience reflects the emancipatory communitarian value of enhancing the level of care and compassion expressed by professionals towards urban youth. Our hope is that the graduate students who participated in the project will continue to enhance their knowledge through similar experiential opportunities in the future. Additionally, in order to learn more about the collaborative relationships that were developed between the graduate students and the school staff, we solicited feedback from the school personnel to gain a picture of their experience of the project and the collaboration. By all accounts, the teachers and school administrators seemed pleased with the way that the project developed, and felt that it was helpful for the children who participated in the psychoeducational groups. Although there was no formal assessment with the schoolchildren, they provided many anecdotal comments about their participating in the SCORE groups that suggested that they found the lessons helpful and the skills important ones for them to know.

Our plan for the GIT Project was to use this year as a "pilot" to identify the aspects of the project that were effective in training graduate students for interdisciplinary social justice practice, and which need to be revised. We were also concerned about piloting a prevention intervention that would be effective in increasing skills beneficial to the children's continued growth and development. At this stage in the project, we are a long way from being able to realize our evaluation goals; however, we have made a positive beginning and hope to make some critical revisions in the program so that it can be more effectively implemented in the future.

CHALLENGES TO IMPLEMENTING INTERPROFESSIONAL SOCIAL JUSTICE PRACTICE

Our ongoing evaluation has also made us aware of the obstacles that limit realization of our ideals as we consider future directions for our work. Fiscal and structural constraints represent major challenges.

Fiscal Constraints

As we seek to continue our collaborations, we are challenged by a number of pragmatic considerations. For example, for the TFT project, we need to find a cost-effective way to sustain our work, without hampering the collaborations that we have worked so hard to develop. In the first years of TFT, several university faculty co-facilitated classroom groups at the school on a weekly basis. Over the past several years, faculty have assumed supervisory and research roles. Through grants from the Commonwealth of Massachusetts Department of Education, the Boston Public Schools, the American Honda Foundation, and the Boston College Lynch School of Education Collaborative Fellows Program, we have been able to fund doctoral students as graduate assistants to work in the classrooms and to assist in program evaluation under the close supervision of university faculty. Through one of these sources, we were also able to offer stipends to teachers to attend planning meetings after school. Our current goal is to institutionalize the curriculum in the school so that the TFT program can be sustained without external grants. As we consider alternative models, we are aware that the interprofessional relationships that we have built have profited by the level of sustained commitment, skill, and maturity of the graduate student collaborators from Boston College. We are concerned about being able to continue to provide this type of graduate student involvement with less funding, but have taken on the challenge to identify an innovative and creative solution to the dilemma.

The GIT Project received only 1 year of funding, and we have made the decision not to seek additional funding at this time. The first year of implementation helped us realize that we need to do some revisions to the design of the intervention in order to make it more reflective of social justice collaborative practice. We need to work through the university-based constraints so that the graduate students who participate in the program have sufficient time and training to support the work that they will be doing in the schools. This will require more conversations with faculty in the three professional schools, and administrative support for developing an interdisciplinary seminar for the students. We also need to take additional time to develop the type of collaboration with our public school partners where all parties have significant input in the design of the intervention and implementation plan. Our goal is to seek funding for a redesigned interprofessional collaborative prevention project within the next two years.

Structural Constraints

The school setting, which inevitably involves administrative hierarchy and is bound by federal and state regulations, presents many challenges to implementing social justice collaborative practice from an emancipatory communitarian perspective. With recognition of the complex context in which our work is embedded, we have learned that structural barriers are inevitable and that flexibility is necessary and beneficial. For example, although the TFT intervention is best implemented with relatively small class groups, classes have been very large (almost 40 students) at times as a result of budget cuts and scheduling issues. With larger classes, discipline issues arise and it is more difficult to build the type of caring classroom climate that TFT seeks. With the use of additional graduate student volunteers, we have attempted to break into smaller groups, but space is not always available to make that possible. Budget cuts, large classes, and layoff notices (even when not acted on) also have negative impacts on teacher morale, at least temporarily. Competing activities at the school often means that some of our sessions are cancelled. School-wide standardized testing as mandated by No Child Left Behind and school assemblies are only some of the factors that sometimes reduce our opportunities to work with students. Student use of public transportation to travel long distances to get to school often means that many students are late to their first-period classes in which TFT is sometimes taught. Because we work with students only one day per week, we regret these interruptions to our efforts.

In a very similar way, the GIT project also experienced barriers that were a result of the structure within both the university and the schools. We found it difficult to recruit students from the other professional schools because of the various requirements for their field experiences. The students from both Social Work and Nursing who volunteered to participate in the project were already in placements that met disciplinary requirements, There was not much "space" for their participation in the project, despite their personal interest and that of their university supervisors. This limited how actively they could be involved in some of the planning activities that were critical to the establishment of a true interdisciplinary collaboration among the graduate students. As the project continued, this became less of a problem as the graduate students found time to discuss their cofacilitation responsibilities for the groups. This experience, however, highlighted the need to work out the interdisciplinary aspects of the project very carefully.

Early on in the implementation process of the GIT project, we encountered challenges to implementing the program at the high school level. Although we engaged in a number of discussions with various school professionals, it was ultimately not possible for us to effectively work through the structural barriers at this time. Our initial contact and negotiations were done directly with the high school principal, who was quite supportive of the project and felt that it would be beneficial for the students. When we met to discuss the details of the implementation process, he requested that we coordinate our work with another university-based program that was already established within the school. After a number of failed attempts, the GIT Project Director was able to meet with the director of this program to discuss ways that we could coordinate our work in the school. We learned that they were providing prevention programming to students in grades 10 to 12, and did not seem open to our involvement with the same group of students. We therefore attempted to locate our program within the Ninth-Grade Academy, and began a series of conversations with the Ninth-Grade Coordinator and the Student Support administrator to figure out an effective way for us to engage with the staff and students. Neither of these conversations led to a commitment, and we were then referred to the Character Education coordinator, who seemed very interested in having the graduate students work with her social studies class. In discussing the details, however, it became clear that the type of services she was requesting were not consistent with the goals and focus of GIT. We reluctantly made the decision not to pursue our efforts to implement the program at the high school, and to work exclusively with the elementary school site during this first year. Our experiences at the high school highlight the importance of having a solid collaboration with school personnel, both teachers and administrators. Although we had buy-in from the school principal, we did not have the same type of support or collaborative relationship with the teaching staff. As a result, we were unable to actually implement the program within the school. In the continuation of the project, we hope to remedy this situation and to work hard to reestablish a mutually beneficial and substantive collaborative relationship with the professionals at the high school.

Structural barriers associated with the university setting and the mental health marketplace also challenge our work. As professors, our university administration has expressed a commitment to our collaboration in the schools, which has been evident by the development of the Collaborative Fellows grants and recognition of this work in our annual evaluations. We cannot, however, be confident that future administrators will hold similar values and thus feel vulnerable about our capacity to remain engaged in university–school collaboration over time. This type of work is very time consuming, and all faculty, but especially junior faculty, need to be cognizant of whether this type of service is diminishing the scholarly productivity for which university professors are most clearly rewarded. It is noteworthy that many universities now recognize their responsibility to respond to societal problems (Boyer, 1990) and seek to use their educational and social resources to contribute to a more just society (Kenny, Simon, Kiley-Brabeck, & Lerner, 2002). Nevertheless, as noted by Ivey and Collins (2003), universities remain part of a profit-oriented and market-driven socioeconomic system that challenges social justice commitments and activities. Opportunities for the graduate students we train to engage in interprofessional collaboration within the schools after they become doctoral-level professionals will also depend on the availability of funds to support them in this work. Although we seek to train students with a focus on social justice, we are realistic that they will not be able to support themselves in social justice work unless jobs are available to do this.

The graduate students participating in the GIT project also identified university-related structural barriers that had an adverse effect on their establishing interprofessional collaborative relationships with their team members. The first issue was the way that time constraints hampered dialogue and planning activities. Because of their respective schedules (classes and field placements), the students had very little time to discuss their co-leadership relationship or to plan for the group sessions. Not surprisingly, they found that the co-leadership of the groups ran more smoothly when they had adequate time to plan. The students managed to find ingenious ways to discuss their work together, and by the end of the project, were talking more regularly about the group sessions and activities. The second issue had to do with the often subtle ways that their discipline-specific training influenced their approach to teaching the SCORE curriculum. In discussing the SCORE lessons, they had an opportunity to share perspectives, through which they recognized the ways that training and previous experience shaped their knowledge. The co-leadership teams were able to successfully negotiate any differences in perspective that arose, and the students reported that this process added depth and richness to their knowledge and experience.

CONCLUSIONS

Our efforts in building and sustaining interprofessional university–school collaborations have been both energizing and challenging. Despite the difficulty of this type of work, we believe that complex problems can only be addressed through interdisciplinary strategies. We thus believe that intercollaborative efforts are ultimately worthwhile, although developers need to be prepared to deal with the fiscal and structural constraints. Our experiences documented in this chapter have led us to identify important lessons that we believe are important to the development of university–school interprofessional collaborations.

We have gained profound respect for the professionalism and expertise of K–12 school personnel and recognize that every participant in the collaboration must feel as though his or her "voice" is heard and respected. Schools are under a political microscope at this time, and many teachers are feeling that they are under attack. Interprofessional collaboration provides an opportunity for teachers and other school professionals to come to the decision-making table and be treated as experts. They can participate fully in the design and implementation of programs that will benefit the young people for whom they are responsible.

The challenges of this work are real. Recognition of the challenges of this work suggests that organizations and individuals who approach the process of university–school collaboration need to anticipate the detailed preparation and resources that are needed as a foundation for these efforts. Ample resources, in terms of time and finances, must be garnered to build relationships and support all partners over time. Much of this work depends on grant funding, which can be difficult to secure and sustain. Patience and long-term commitment are necessary. If university partners pull out after encountering initial obstacles, they may do more harm than good.

With regard to the outcomes of our work, initial data suggest that our collaborations are promising, but we cannot say for sure that we are achieving all of our social justice goals. Most critically for TFT, we are concerned about whether teaching high school students how to better prepare themselves and negotiate the "opportunity structure" is enough. We may be changing the schools and classrooms in which we work in a small way, but we cannot claim to be changing social systems and

structures beyond the school. The GIT Project shares similar questions and limitations. Our goal is to train graduate students for effective interdisciplinary practice,
which we feel reflects the tenets of social justice. It is our belief that such collaborative efforts across academic disciplines, and between universities and public
schools, will ultimately produce a shift in the way that education (as an institutional
system) facilitates positive youth development. To date, our collaborations in both
of these projects have been limited to schools and students, and have omitted other
critical contexts of the students' lives, such as family and community. As put forth
by Prilleltensky and Prilleltensky (2003), emancipatory communitarian values are
synergistic and do not operate effectively in isolation. Whereas we have some confidence that in the TFT project we have met student and teacher needs for personal
and relational wellness, we have less evidence that progress is being made towards
collective wellness in terms of distributive justice and economic equality. In the 5
years since we started TFT, we have witnessed large changes in the job market,
where opportunities for employment have diminished across many sectors of the
economy. Although to some extent this means that students need to be even better
prepared to compete for good jobs, it also means that the "opportunity structure"
may be more biased and restricted to those with greater privilege. As university–school collaborators, we cannot ultimately be content with enhancing skills in
high school students, but must consider ways to work beyond the schools to make
sure that the hopes and dreams of urban high school youth are not frustrated.

In the GIT Project, our challenges are similar, but we have had less time to address our concerns. One of our goals for GIT is to increase the graduate students'
awareness of social justice issues inherent in the urban school setting. As they
worked with the children and learned more about their everyday lives, both in
school and at home, the graduate students began to realize that the urban school
context is very different from the predominantly White, middle-class schools that
many had attended as children. They became aware of the limited resources, such
as the lack of funding for materials/supplies for the classrooms, and the spatial limitations within the school building. They found these limitations frustrating, and began to recognize the multiple ways that these issues can adversely affect learning.
As they worked to adapt the curriculum to the needs of the children, the students
began to appreciate that many of the children live in very stressful, multiproblem
family and community situations. They became more sensitive to the challenges
faced in urban education as schools attempt to provide a learning environment that
addresses many of the children's needs. As a result of our experiences we learned
that it is vitally important that we find ways to involve school personnel more actively in the training of our graduate students, and in the actual implementation of
the prevention activities within the schools. We also realized the need to find creative ways of getting the children's parents more involved in our intervention. At
this point, we have many more questions than we have answers, but our plan is to
continue to engage these issues both within the university and within the schools.

We anticipate that the graduate students, at the completion of this and other experiences throughout the remainder of their training, will make a personal commitment to continue social justice-oriented work in their future careers, joining with
other like-minded professionals to actively work towards changing our institutional
systems. Whether our counseling psychology doctoral students will continue their
social justice work as professionals remains uncertain, however. We expect nevertheless that all of our students will have gained a more complex understanding of

the social structures that sustain social injustice in ways that will make them more sensitive mental health professionals and more effective social change agents.

In this chapter, we have provided substantial detail about the rationale and processes of our work and our efforts in striving for social justice. We ultimately believe that interprofessional university–school collaboration is a promising mechanism for extending the resources of the university to the public schools and for preparing future psychologists and educators as social change agents. We hope that our narrative will increase understanding of what is needed to build collaborative partnerships and will enhance dialogue on the role of university–school partnerships in training professionals and in promoting social justice.

REFERENCES

Adelman, H. S., & Taylor, L. (2000). Moving prevention from the fringes into the fabric of school improvement. *Journal of Education and Psychological Consultation, 11,* 7–36.

Baker, L. A., & Adelman, H. (1994). Mental health and help-seeking among ethnic minority adolescents. *Journal of Adolescence, 17,* 251–263.

Blustein, D. L., Jackson, J., Kenny, M. E., Sparks, E., Chaves, A., Diemer, M. A., et al. (2001, March). *Social action within an urban school context: The Tools for Tomorrow project.* Paper presented at the Fourth National Counseling Psychology Conference, Houston, TX.

Blustein, D. L., Juntunen, C. L., & Worthington, R. L. (2000). The school-to-work transition: Adjustment challenges of the forgotten half. In S. D. Brown & R. W. Lent (Eds.), *Handbook of counseling psychology* (3rd ed., pp. 435–470). New York: Wiley.

Boyer, E. (1990). *Scholarship reconsidered: Priorities of the professoriate.* Princeton, NJ: The Carnegie Foundation for the Advancement of Teaching.

Brabeck, M., Cawthorne, J., Gaspard, N., Hurd-Green, C., Kenny, M., Krawczyk, R., et al. (1998). Changing the culture of the university to engage in outreach scholarship. In R. M. Lerner & L. A. K. Simon (Eds.), *Creating the new outreach university for America's youth and families: Building university–community collaborations for the twenty-first century* (pp. 335–364). New York: Garland.

Brabeck, M., Walsh, M., Kenny, M., & Comilang, K. (1997). Interprofessional collaboration for children and families: Opportunities for counseling psychology in the 21st century. *The Counseling Psychologist, 25*(4), 615–636.

Caplan, G. (1970). *The theory and practice of mental health consultation.* New York: Basic Books.

Catalano, R. F., Berglund, M. L., Ryan, J. A. M., Lonczak, H. C., & Hawkins, D. (1999). *Positive youth development in the United States: Research findings on evaluations of positive youth development programs.* Washington, DC: Department of Health and Human Services, National Institute for Child Health and Human Development.

The Collaborative for Academic, Social, and Emotional Learning. (2003). *Safe and sound: An educational leader's guide to evidence-based social and emotional (SEL) programs.* Chicago: CASEL

Dougherty, A. M. (2000). *Psychological consultation and collaboration in school and community settings.* Belmont, CA: Wadsworth.

Dryfoos, J. G. (1990). *Adolescents at risk: Prevalence and prevention.* New York: Oxford University.

Elias, M. J. (1997). *Promoting social and emotional learning: Guidelines for educators.* Alexandria, VA: Association for Supervision and Curriculum Development (ASCD).

Fleming, J. J., & Brabeck, M. (2002). A great labor: Developing knowledge in service to others at Boston College. In M. E. Kenny, L. A., Simon, K. Kiley-Brabeck, & R. M. Lerner (Eds.), *Learning to serve: Promoting civil society through service learning* (pp. 79–96). Norwell, MA: Kluwer.

Gibbs, J., & Huang, L. (1997). *Children of color: Psychological interventions with minority youth.* San Francisco: Jossey-Bass.

Gottfredson, D. C., Fink, C. M., Skroban, S., & Gottfredson, G. D. (1997). Making prevention work. In R. P. Weissberg, T. P. Gullotta, R. L. Hampton, B. A. Ryan, & G. R. Adams (Eds.), *Establishing preventive services* (pp. 219–252). Thousand Oaks, CA: Sage.

Haney, W., Madaus, G., Abrams, L., Wheelock, A., Miao, J., & Grucia, I. (2004). The education pipeline in the United States, 1970–2000. Retrieved February 2, 2004, from http://www.bc.edu/nbetpp

Hartung, P. J., & Blustein, D. L. (2002). Reason, intuition, and social justice: Elaborating on Parson's decision-making model. *Journal of Counseling and Development, 80,* 41–48.

Hoffman, M. A., & Driscoll, J. M. (2000). Health promotion and disease prevention: A concentric biopsychosocial model. In S. D. Brown & R. W. Lent (Eds.), *Handbook and counseling psychology* (3rd ed., pp. 532–570). New York: Wiley.

Ivey, A., & Collins, N. M. (2003). Social justice: A long-term challenge for counseling psychology. *The Counseling Psychologist, 31,* 290–298.

Kenny, M. E., Blustein, D., Chaves, A., Grossman, J., & Gallagher, L. A. (2003). The role of perceived barriers and relational support in the educational and vocational lives of urban high school students. *Journal of Counseling Psychology, 20,* 142–155.

Kenny, M. E., Blustein, D. L., Haase, R. F., Sparks, J., Jackson, J., Perry, J., et al. (2004, July). Setting the stage: Career development and the school engagement process. In D. L. Blustein (Chair), *Ties that bind—Internalizing connections between school and work.* Symposium presented at the 112th annual convention of the American Psychological Association, Honolulu, Hawaii.

Kenny, M. E. & Gallagher, L. A. (2000). Service learning as a vehicle in training psychologists for revised professional roles. In F. S. Sherman & W. R. Torbert (Eds.), *Transforming social inquiry, transforming social action: Creating communities of practice at the university and in the community* (pp. 189–205). Norwell, MA: Kluwer.

Kenny, M. E., Simon, L. A., Kiley-Brabeck, K., & Lerner, R. M. (2002). Promoting civil society through service learning: A view of the issues. In M. E. Kenny, L. A., Simon, K. Kiley-Brabeck, & R. M. Lerner (Eds.), *Learning to serve: Promoting civil society through service learning* (pp. 1–14). Norwell, MA: Kluwer.

Kenny, M. E., Waldo, M., Warter, E., & Barton, K. (2002). School-linked prevention: Theory, science and practice for enhancing the lives of children and youth. *The Counseling Psychologist, 30,* 726–748.

Lawson, H. A. (2003). Promoting and securing collaboration to improve results. In M. M. Brabeck, M. E. Walsh, & R. Latta (Eds.), *Meeting at the hyphen: Schools-universities-communities-professions in collaboration for student achievement and well being* (102nd Yearbook of the National Society for the Study of Education; pp. 45–73). Chicago: University of Chicago Press.

Lerner, R. M. (1986*). Concepts and theories of human development* (2nd ed.). New York: Random House.

Lerner, R. M. (1991). Changing organism-context relations as the basic process of development: A developmental-contextual perspective. *Developmental Psychology, 27,* 27–32.

Lerner, R. M. (1995). *America's youth in crisis: Challenges and options for programs and policies.* Thousand Oaks, CA: Sage.

Lerner, R. M., Walsh, M. E., & Howard, K. A. (1998). Developmental-contextual considerations: Person-context relations as the bases for risk and resiliency in child and adolescent development. In T. Ollendick (Ed.), *Comprehensive clinical psychology, Vol. 4: Children and adolescents: Clinical formulations and treatment* (pp. 1–24). New York: Elsevier.

Loveless, T. (2003, October). *The 2003 Brown Center Report on American Education: How well are American students learning?* Providence, RI: Brown Center on Education Policy.

Marshall, R., & Tucker, M. (1992). *Thinking for a living: Education and the wealth of nations.* New York: Basic Books.

Matarazzo, J. D., Miller, N. E., Weiss, S. M., Herd, J. A., & Weiss, S. (1990). (Eds.). *Behavior health: A handbook of health enhancement and disease prevention.* New York: Wiley.

National Association of School Psychologists. (2003). *Position statement on student grade retention and social promotion.* Bethesda, MD: National Association of School Psychologists.

National Association of School Psychologists. (2004). *What is a school psychologist?* Bethesda, MD: National Association of School Psychologists.

Nicassio, P. M., & Smith, T. W. (1995). (Eds.). *Managing chronic illness: A biopsychosocial perspective.* Washington, DC: American Psychological Association.

Oyserman, D., Terry, K., & Bybee, D. (2002). A possible selves intervention to enhance school involvement. *Journal of Adolescence, 25,* 313–326.

Paige, R. (2002). An overview of American' education agenda. *Phi Delta Kappan, 83*(9), 708–713.

Park, T. L., Adams, S. G., & Lynch, J. (1998). Sociodemographic factors in health psychology research: 12 years in review. *Health Psychology, 17,* 381–383.

Pittman, K. J. (2000, May). *What youth need: Services, supports, and opportunities.* Paper presented at the White House Conference on Teenagers: Raising Responsible and Resourceful Youth, Washington, DC.

Prilleltensky, I. (1997). Values, assumptions, and practices: Assessing the moral implications of psychological discourse and action. *American Psychologist, 52,* 517–535.

Prilleltensky, I., Nelson, G., & Peirson, L. (2001). *Promoting family wellness and preventing child maltreatment: Fundamentals for thinking and action.* Toronto: University of Toronto Press.

Prilleltensky, I., & Prilleltensky, O. (2003). Synergies for wellness and liberation in counseling psychology. *The Counseling Psychologist, 31,* 273–281.

Roth, J., & Brooks-Gunn, J. (2000). What do adolescents need for healthy development? Implications for youth policy. *Social Policy Report, 14*(1), 3–19.

Schorr, L. B. (1997). *Common purpose: Strengthening families and neighborhoods to rebuild America.* New York: Anchor Books/Doubleday.

Tomlinson, C. A. (1999). *The differentiated classroom.* Alexandria: ASCD.

U.S. Department of Education. (2002). *No Child Left Behind: A desktop reference.* Washington, DC: Office of Elementary and Secondary Education.

U.S. Department of Health and Human Services. (2000). *Healthy People 2010: Conference edition* (Vols. 1–2). Washington, DC: Author.

U.S. Public Health Service. (2000). *Report of the Surgeon General's conference on mental health: A national action agenda.* Washington, DC: Department of Health and Human Services.

Vernon, D. S., Schumaker, J. B., & Deshler, D. D. (1993). *The score skills: Social skills for cooperative groups.* Lawrence, KS: Edge Enterprises, Inc.

Walsh, M. E., Brabeck, M. M., & Howard, K. A. (1999). Interprofessional collaboration in children's services: Toward a theoretical framework. *Children's Services: Social Policy, Research, and Practice, 2*(4), 183–208.

Walsh, M. E., Galassi, J. P., Murphy, J. A., & Park, J. (2002). Conceptual frameworks for counseling psychologists in schools. *The Counseling Psychologist, 30,* 682–704.

Walsh, M. E., Howard, K. A., & Buckley, M. A. (1999). School counselors in school–community partnerships: Opportunities and challenges. *Professional School Counseling, 2,* 349–356.

Walsh, M. E., & Park-Taylor, J. (2003). Comprehensive schooling and interprofessional collaboration: Theory, research, and practice. In M. M. Brabeck, M. E. Walsh, & R. Latta (Eds.), *Meeting at the hyphen: Schools-universities-communities-professions in collaboration for student achievement and well being* (102nd Yearbook of the National Society for the Study of Education; pp. 8–44). Chicago: University of Chicago Press.

Walsh, M. E., Thompson, N. E., Howard, K. A., Montes, C., & Garvin, T. (2000). The transformative process of action inquiry in a school–community–university partnership. In F. S. Sherman & W. R. Torbert (Eds.), *Transforming social inquiry, transforming social action: Creating communities of practice at the university and in the community* (pp. 93–115). Norwood, MA: Kluwer.

Wilson, W. J. (1996). *When work disappears: The world of the new urban poor.* New York: Random House.

Youngblood, J., & Spencer, M. B. (2002). Integrating normative identity processes and academic support requirements for special needs adolescents: The application of an identity-focused cultural ecological (ICE) perspective. *Applied Developmental Science, 6,* 95–108.

Yowell, C. (2002). Dreams of the future: The pursuit of education and career possible selves among ninth grade Latino youth. *Applied Developmental Science, 6,* 62–72.

15

The Psychology of Working
and the Advancement of Social Justice

David L. Blustein
Justin C. Perry
Alexandra C. Kenna
David B. DeWine
Boston College

In this chapter, we seek to infuse a sociopolitically informed discussion of the psychology of working into the broader discourse about social justice and mental health that is taking place in our field, which is reflected within the pages of this book. Our position is that a comprehensive discussion of mental health and social justice cannot be complete without a fully informed analysis of the nature of working and the impact of work (and, inversely, lack of work) in relation to individual life and to the welfare of communities and societies. The psychology-of-working perspective that is detailed in this chapter is an outgrowth of historical traditions in vocational psychology coupled with the infusion of literature from the social sciences on work, career, and vocational behavior (e.g., Applebaum, 1992; Gini, 2000; Powell, 1999; Richardson, 1993; Sennett, 1998; Thomas, 1999; Wilson, 1996). In this contribution, we introduce readers to the psychology-of-working perspective, followed by a discussion of the potential of this initiative to inform the social justice agenda within psychology. (See Blustein, 2006, for a more detailed presentation of the psychology-of-working perspective.) The chapter concludes with an overview of the potential implications of an inclusive psychology of working for counseling practice, preventive/systemic interventions, and public policy.

MAPPING THE TERRAIN OF THE PSYCHOLOGY
OF WORKING

In order to accurately map the landscape of the psychology of working, we first describe how our perspective contrasts with other psychologies that have examined careers and organizational behavior. Building on the contributions of Richardson (1993) and Blustein (2001a), the psychology-of-working perspective moves beyond the notion of "career" to include the experiences of all workers as well as those who are unemployed, those who are engaged in caregiving activities with family or loved ones, and those who have been separated from traditional working experiences. By taking a psychological perspective, we seek to focus more attention on individuals' understandings of work, work-related activities, emotions, and beliefs (Blustein, 2006). In adopting a psychological vantage point, we therefore contrast our perspective with studies of working from sociology and anthropology (e.g., Applebaum, 1992; Wilson, 1996); however, as we detail in this chapter, the literatures from the other social sciences that have studied working naturally have been very informative to our thinking. Whereas traditional theories of vocational behavior and career development (e.g., Holland, 1997; Super, 1957) generally have focused on the experiences of people who have the resources, opportunities, and freedom to find a life-long career that best matches their interests and abilities, the psychology-of-working framework seeks to affirm and understand the experiences of the many working-class, poor, and marginalized individuals for whom work is often grueling, uninteresting, and unrewarding. Yet the psychology-of-working perspective is still highly relevant to the lives of those who do have choices with respect to the means by which they earn their livelihoods. Indeed, we view the psychology of working as the overarching framework that may facilitate an integrative understanding of the depth and breadth of psychological experiences pertaining to work.

An expanded vision of a psychological analysis of working reveals a number of common themes and characteristics about the meaning of work within our society. First, working provides individuals with a sense of identity within their external or contextual environment (Blustein, 1994; Erikson, 1968). In a culture that equates work with concepts of productivity, growth, and power, often individuals' sense of self-worth and value is linked in varying degrees to their perceived ability to contribute to society. Second, the efforts and human energy expended through work contribute to the larger social and economic culture (Blustein, 2006). In effect, work functions as an underlying bond between people living in a shared culture. Therefore, work (including caregiving and nonpaid work) is inextricably linked to larger social structures, such as social stratification, racism, sexism, and social class (Blustein, 2001a; Richardson, 1993). Third, work has personal meaning and significance to individuals that is powerfully informative to the construction and expression of identity (Blustein, 2001a, 2006). It is a venue through which we develop meaningful relationships with coworkers and therefore has emotional significance. Fourth, work is a consistent and ongoing reality in our lives that serves to unify members of society (Blustein, 2006; Super, 1957; Wilson, 1996); in effect, working serves as a social web, connecting individuals and groups with shared interests or experiences.

It is important to note that the psychology of working is not intended to serve as a replacement for earlier theories and practices related to career and vocational counseling. In other words, traditional theories of career choice and development (e.g., Holland, 1997; Lent, Brown, & Hackett, 2002; Mitchell & Krumboltz, 1996; Super, 1957) are still relevant in describing the work-related issues faced by those who have the privilege of experiencing varying degrees of volition in their educational and vocational options. In contrast, the psychology-of-working perspective that we are advancing here is an attempt to build on some of their key concepts to construct a broader, and ultimately, more inclusive perspective. In order to understand the context for a psychology of working, we review the historical and cultural influences on the field as a way of understanding how the existing psychologies of career and organizations emerged in the last century and how current trends augur for the development of a broad-based psychology of working.

In the 19th and early 20th centuries, industrialization created vast new work opportunities for both men and women (Hartung & Blustein, 2002). With these new types of jobs, individuals were faced with more complicated decision-making tasks regarding the selection of occupations that would be the best fit for their individual set of attitudes, values, interests, and abilities (Blustein, 2006). Vocational guidance and counseling sprung out of this culture with the intention of helping individuals find a match that would best complement their abilities and interests (O'Brien, 2001). During World War I, the military sought to develop methods to match individuals with positions that would best fit their skills and aptitudes. The personnel needs of the wartime militaries coupled with growing knowledge in psychological testing soon led to the development of personality tests, intelligence tests, and interest inventories, which were designed to help individuals find appropriate career matches.

Super (1957), whose expansive theoretical lens significantly shaped the vibrant community of career development scholars and practitioners, sought to further this work by establishing a model that encompassed the entire life span. Rather than focusing solely on adolescence and early adulthood, Super was interested in how people of all ages explore and negotiate work/career issues and the way in which work and related life roles unfolded and intersected over time. His integration of career issues into the larger context of human development was a monumental contribution to the field. In addition to the life-span and life-space perspectives, vocational psychology was profoundly influenced by contributions from the person–environment fit theories (e.g., Holland, 1997), which emphasized the advantages for people who can obtain occupations that match with their interests and abilities. In addition, the behavioral revolution influenced the development of social learning theory of career development by Mitchell and Krumboltz (1996), which infused more of a contextual perspective into career theory and practice. However, the prevailing focus on a cumulative concept of career (which became the post-World War II trend among vocational counselors in North America), wherein an individual seeks to build the skills and experience necessary to attain fulfilling and rewarding lifelong experiences at work had ramifications for the poor and working classes for whom this sort of working life was not a viable option. The result was that the field of career counseling shifted its focus toward relatively affluent, well-educated people who had the resources and opportunities available to pursue a life-long career.

Industrial/organizational psychology (I/O psychology) developed around the same time frame as vocational counseling, also reflecting changes in the labor market and corresponding economic structures (Landy, 1989). Organizations began to grow in size and complexity with resultant problems in recruiting effective workers, retaining employees, and motivating high levels of performance from the full gamut of an organization's human resources. During World War I, the military wanted to ensure that training was provided to those who would most likely benefit from it. Like career and vocational counseling, I/O psychology also was impacted by the development of psychometric measures, which offered a sense of legitimacy and objectivity to the psychology field in general (Landy, 1989). Whereas career and vocational counseling reflects a focus on the experiences of the individual client, I/O psychology more often takes on the perspective of the employer and the organization. The I/O perspective seeks to create optimal person–environment fit with the overarching goal of enhancing the productivity and competitiveness of a given company or organization. By promoting employee job satisfaction, increased productivity, decreased employee turnover, and overall organizational commitment, I/O psychology sought to help employers maximize their efforts for the company or organization. After World War II, I/O psychology expanded its intellectual net to encompass group dynamics, leadership, and organizational climate and performance (Golembieski, 1993). Despite some wonderful efforts to enhance the experiences of public servants (such as teachers, police officers, nurses, etc.), those working in less prestigious or appealing jobs were generally not included in the efforts of I/O psychology, thereby leading to a further neglect of the experience of the poor and working classes.

The psychology-of-working perspective that we are advancing seeks to expand the impact of psychological research, practice, and policy advocacy beyond the scope of workers who have choices in their selection of occupational pathways. Our goal is to construct a psychology of working that is inclusive across a number of dimensions. First, the psychology of working explicitly seeks to understand the nature of working experiences for individuals who do not have much, if any, volition in their choice of occupations. Second, the psychology of working includes the very real demands of nonpaid work, including caregiving to children, family members, and the elderly. Third, the psychology of working seeks to understand the nature of working via multiple paradigms, including traditional logical positivist methods as well as narrative and postmodern approaches to understanding a given phenomenon. In sum, the psychology-of-working perspective seeks to dignify all aspects of working by affirmatively casting a wider net of inclusiveness that would encompass the experiences of those who have not been on the radar screen of psychologists in recent decades.

In our view, the psychology-of-working perspective is an ideal fit with the social justice mission of psychology that is taking shape in this volume as well as other venues (e.g., Goodman et al., 2004). The argument and rationale for the development of an inclusive psychology of working is based, to a large extent, on a moral position that is very consistent with the growing social justice voice within psychology (e.g., Martín-Baró, 1994; Prilleltensky, 1997; Vera & Speight, 2003). To guide subsequent inquiry and deliberation about the psychology of working, we provide the major attributes of an operational definition of working, which are based on the aforementioned themes of work (pp. 3–4) and have been culled from a book project on the psychology of working (Blustein, 2006).

1. Working is a pervasive constant in our lives; the experience of working unifies human beings across time frames and cultures.
2. Working includes effort, activity, and human energy in given tasks that contribute to the overall social and economic welfare of a given culture. Moreover, working includes paid employment as well as work that one does in caring for others within one's family and community.
3. An individual's conception of working is psychologically constructed, culturally bound, and socially mediated through interactions with others.
4. Work provides people with a clear means of furnishing their identity (i.e., their sense of who they are) in their social interactions.

In sum, the psychology-of-working perspective that we are advancing here is designed to embrace the full scope of human experiences in the work sphere. By maximizing the inclusiveness of working experiences, scholarly, practice, and public policy initiatives emerging from a psychology of working are inherently linked to a social justice agenda. In short, the world of work in most cultures is essentially a place where inequities are often most apparent and most pernicious.

Work/Career and Mental Health

Another major feature of the psychology of working is that this perspective offers a means of reducing the artificial boundaries that have separated considerations of working from analyses of mental health, psychotherapy, and relational life. Although career and work-related issues (and corresponding theories) have been viewed as specialty or niche areas of psychology, we would argue that this trend has limited the scope and impact with which we can view individuals as well as groups within the larger context of their lives. For many people in the Western world, working can occupy as much as one third or more of one's time in adulthood.

Freud (1930) helped to place work on the psychological radar screen by discussing its use as a way of sublimating drives and instincts in order to abide by society's rules. Although he did not view work as inherently gratifying or rewarding, he did consider it as essential to human functioning. Following the rich tradition of psychoanalysis, the world of psychotherapy grew in countless directions with theoretical orientations that encompassed strict behavioral perspectives, humanistic and existential views, as well as more contemporary psychoanalytic approaches. Yet in the diverse tapestry that characterizes the world of psychotherapy theory and practice, surprisingly little attention has been devoted to understanding the psychological meaning of working. Although there are some notable exceptions to this trend (see, e.g., Axelrod, 1999; Lowman, 1993), most theorists within the psychotherapeutic world have viewed work as a secondary or tertiary concern. In fact, issues arising at work often have been viewed from the lens of unresolved developmental processes (e.g., Smelser & Erikson, 1980) or conflictual family relationships (e.g., Chusid & Cochran, 1989).

Theorists within career development and organizational psychology also have tended to circumscribe their considerations of human behavior by focusing almost exclusively on career choice or adjustment issues. Although some theorists, such as Super (1957) and more recently Savickas (2002) and Flum (2001), have been creative and articulate about embedding their thinking about career into the broader fabric of human experience, other theories, such as the Person–Environment fit models (e.g., Holland, 1997) have not fared as well. The tendency to circumscribe considerations of work behavior also has been evident in I/O psychology (see, e.g., Landy's 1989, classic text). Here again, there have been cogent exceptions to this trend, most notably the work of Hall (e.g., 1996) who has effectively integrated relational perspectives into theoretical statements about organizational behavior. By expanding our vision beyond those who have volitional careers to those who have little to no choice in their work lives, we are challenged to think in a more integrative fashion about the nature of the role of work in mental health, psychotherapy, and in the broader social and economic context of life.

Despite the tendency to construct different intellectual and practice worlds for psychotherapy and career counseling, a number of initiatives in the past few decades have sought to bridge this gap (e.g., Savickas, 1995). Blustein and Spengler (1995) outlined a domain-sensitive approach to treatment that in many ways foreshadows some of the ideas that are included in this chapter. The domain-sensitive approach is characterized by the counselor's concerted interest in and awareness of all possible ramifications of a client's psychological experience and its behavioral expression. A critical characteristic of this approach is that the counselor does not treat a set of issues in a given domain as solely a manifestation of problems in other domains. One of the hallmarks of a domain-sensitive approach is that clients can learn and explore new ways of interacting and relating to themselves and others in a domain that is relatively easier to cope with. Once clients have achieved some sense of mastery in the less challenging domain, they may be better able to cope with the difficulties in the more challenging domain. Also, clients can learn about patterns of behavior and relating that are common across domains of life experience. In our view, the domain-sensitive approach is an excellent fit with the psychology of working in that it does not denigrate the working experiences of clients by treating these issues as solely a manifestation of intrapsychic or familial struggles. Rather, work-related issues are viewed as real-life experiences and events that require real-life solutions. Naturally, many of these solutions transcend the experience of individuals and require social and policy changes. For example, a woman who is experiencing pain and trauma related to sexual harassment needs some individual assistance; however, as we learn later in this chapter, the psychology-of-working perspective also would call for systemic change to reduce the incidence of such oppressive working conditions.

The domain-sensitive approach provides a viable means of integrating the psychology of working into social justice-oriented modes of intervention that seek to empower clients. However, we are aware that the focus on changing the individual to accommodate to often unfair and oppressive conditions does not fit with the broader social change orientation that is inherent in many recent initiatives within critical psychology and liberation psychology (e.g., Martín-Baró, 1994; Prilleltensky, 1997). Toward the end of this chapter, we explore the potential within the psychology-of-working perspective to provide the intellectual framework for the development of scholarship that will inform social and public policy change efforts.

THE PSYCHOLOGY OF WORKING AND SOCIAL JUSTICE

As we have discussed earlier, the psychology of working seeks to incorporate the experiences of people previously voiceless (such as the working classes and poor) within psychological analyses of careers, occupations, and vocational life. Although these individuals and their work experiences have been neglected to varying extents, their voice is crucial in understanding how work relates to overall mental health and to human functioning in general. Once we move beyond the privileged world of white-collar workers and professionals, the world of work looks very different. Rather than the focus on individual satisfaction, productivity, or self-efficacy, we see a world in which many people do not have particularly inspiring or rewarding jobs. Moreover, the psychology of working is also concerned with the psychological consequences of unemployment and underemployment, which are already major threats to the quality of human experience and to the welfare of entire communities (e.g., O'Brien, 1986; Wilson, 1996). In addition, the nature of work has changed dramatically as the economy has shifted within many Western nations from manufacturing to services and information technology. These trends have reduced the stability of work for nearly all workers, ranging from unskilled factory workers to high-level management executives (Blustein, 2006; Sennett, 1998). This changing face of work requires that we pay attention to the experience of all who are working and unemployed, not just those who have the resources to pursue careers.

We are currently faced with a huge population of people out of work within North America and indeed, around the globe (Blustein, 2006). The experience of these individuals—whether they have been laid off due to economic changes or cannot find work due to shifts in the nature of the labor market—needs to be considered when thinking about how work and career fit into mental health in general. As Wilson (1996) detailed in his book *When Work Disappears,* the disappearance of blue-collar jobs has led to devastating effects for urban populations, particularly workers of color. Issues related to drug abuse, violent crime, and depression have been linked to joblessness in inner-city communities within the United States (Danziger & Haveman, 2001). Recognizing that a relationship exists between working and social risk, the mental health field must integrate the experiences of the nonworking as well as the working poor if we hope to move toward effective solutions to these social problems.

Without a clear and systemic focus on working, we are ignoring one of the most powerful means of enacting change and empowering people. One's job is inextricably linked to her or his place within the larger social structure and hierarchy. By placing working as the "figure" (instead of its usual role as the "ground" in psychological analyses), we are more likely to understand the effects of working (as well as lack of working) on mental health and other social problems. As Wilson (1996) discusses, work-related issues, such as the availability of jobs, transportation, and training, are inextricably linked to racial reform and social policies. By attending to the unequal distribution of access to education, training, and employment, we are forced to reckon with the very real consequences of racism, sexism, and classism. For any clinician working with marginalized individuals, the effects of these "isms" must be addressed when conceptualizing how clients develop their sense of self-worth and identity within our society.

Shared Assumptions and Values

The psychology of working espouses a social justice agenda, in which value is deliberately assigned to the empowerment of those who do not have much "choice" in their work lives, as opposed to the socially and economically privileged. A psychology of working perspective naturally lends itself to ideologies that extend beyond analyzing the individual person, namely, a sociopolitical rendering of human behavior and wellness. This set of assumptions about the psychology of working can be traced to the influences of the emancipatory-communitarian (EC) approach (Prilleltensky, 1997) and liberation psychology (Blustein, McWhirter, & Perry, 2005; Martín-Baró, 1994). These critical movements have shaped the philosophical underpinnings of the perspectives we propose.

The ideas of Prilleltensky (1997) serve as a bridge between the perspective of working we advocate and traditional models of career counseling. In his EC approach, Prilleltensky (1997) articulated a moral vision for psychological discourse and practice. He sought to enjoin psychologists to clearly explicate their vision of the good life and the good society, and the ways in which such a vision can be translated into action. According to Prilleltensky, an EC approach refers to the process of liberating people from all forms of oppression through the active endorsement of compassion, social obligation, and self-determination. In short, he promoted a way of viewing the self from an interpersonal and sociopolitical frame of reference, thus bringing core attention to systemic factors associated with injustice and suffering.

In this chapter, our underlying premises about the social and psychological meaning of working owe much to the contributions of Prilleltensky (1997). Our thinking is strongly influenced by the notion that psychological functioning is tied to the structural conditions that determine individuals' access to resources in work as well as in other domains of life. As a result, psychological experiences and behavior in working cannot be divorced from the context of advantage (e.g., higher levels of social class, able-bodied) and disadvantage (e.g., lower levels of social class, disabling conditions) in which they are embedded. We maintain that human diversity and distributive justice are values that facilitate the empowerment of people who do not have the luxury of exerting volition in their lives.

Similar to the EC model, the field of liberation psychology (e.g., Martín-Baró, 1994) has left a vital mark on various schools of thought in the social sciences as well as mental health practice. The social resistance efforts of Freire (1970) and Martín-Baró (1994) are the most renowned examples of liberation psychology. Both activists fought to develop a *conscientization* or "critical consciousness" among indigenous people, whose basic rights were being exploited. To that end, they were able to help their fellow citizens transform their awareness of what they had originally taken for granted, that is, the inequities of power and resources. Their personal courage and sacrifice has inspired the thinking and pedagogical practices of educators, psychologists, and social activists around the globe. In short, the goals of liberation psychology are to use the principles and processes of psychological theory, research, and practice to change the structures that perpetuate inequality and oppression. At the same time, liberation psychologists are equally committed to empowering the vast numbers of people who have been marginalized and oppressed by unfair and inequitable social and economic policies (Martín-Baró, 1994).

Consistent with the societal goals and theoretical foci within liberation psychology, the psychology of working is grounded in the premise that opportunities for satisfaction in one's work life are filtered through an asymmetrical system of social group statuses in which some group members are ascribed with more power than others. Traditional person factors (ability, skills, self-efficacy, self-esteem) that help people actualize their occupational interests do not exist in a sociopolitical vacuum. Rather, the world of work operates as part of a social system that tolerates racism, sexism, and classism; moreover, the working world exists in a context that tends to grant some with rewards and opportunities, but not others (Blustein, 2001a, 2006). Typically, these pervasive societal injustices, which collude with those in power, dictate who has better access to acquiring a higher standard of living (Carter & Cook, 1992). From a psychology-of-working perspective, individual assets in work do not overshadow the effects of prejudice and socioeconomic pressures people encounter on a daily basis. This is a reality that underscores (if not understates) virtually every person's work domain in developing countries.

The common theme of viewing individual behavior within a context of communitarian values sets the EC approach and liberation psychology apart from traditional psychological models, including those that have dominated the career development literature (Vera & Speight, 2003). Guided by such paradigms, the psychology of working perspective is not simply based on an empowerment of personal adaptation to discriminating and denigrating conditions, but also one that aims to directly challenge the mechanisms of oppression in work and educational settings. Against this backdrop, we turn to the psychosocial and political roles of work, providing a brief description of their conceptual importance.

In light of the gap between *describing* problems of oppression and *confronting* them in people's daily work lives, Harmon (1994) keenly noted that "the theories we have available do very little to tell us how to practice interventions that will change the experience of those for whom work is a drudgery or not even worth pursuing" (p. 226). In this chapter, three specific functions of work are briefly described that address this criticism: (a) work as a form of survival and power, (b) work as a form of social connection, and (c) work as a form of self-determination. We propose that these functions provide the heuristic tools needed in order to understand and directly impact the people whom Harmon referred to. (For a full description and analysis of the three functions of work, see Blustein, 2006.)

Need for Survival and Power. The first function, survival and power, is a fundamentally different way of viewing one's work life in comparison to the traditional perspectives that have defined vocational psychological thought to date. In brief, work provides people with a means of obtaining the necessary goods and services to be able to eat, have clothing, and be sheltered (Wallman, 1979). Although not a new concept to anthropology and sociology, contemporary discourse in psychology has only recently begun to explore how this key assumption is related to the lives of ordinary working class citizens (e.g., Carter & Cook, 1992; Harmon, 1994; Helms & Cook, 1999). Freud (1930) noted that work was primarily a means of survival, and not a generally pleasant activity. His pessimistic view still holds true for the lives of the vast majority of people who cannot exercise meaningful direction or expression in their working lives.

As human civilization evolved from primitive hunting and gathering to agrarian-based economies, the tasks of work to ensure survival became more complex and differentiated. Societies with advanced technologies gradually transitioned into market-based economies. This major shift in working forced people to move outside of their communal groups, requiring individuals to adopt more complex social roles. More importantly, it changed the way in which needs for survival became associated with social status, privilege, and power; those who were able to master tasks valued by the community were able to generate higher levels of social standing, and thus accrue resources (Donkin, 2001). As societies became increasingly layered with symbolic meaning and complex social mores, it also became important to find ways to designate which people were more capable of controlling the exchange of necessities in life, as well as having access to them. Not every worker was inherently interested in becoming powerful, but working for survival naturally entailed the means to gaining power, as wealth, land, and food had to be distributed in more sophisticated ways.

Although possessing advanced skills and abilities in obtaining resources can lead to the conferment of power to some individuals over others, this is not to suggest that power is simply the consequence of "the fittest" people. The function of power refers to the control and use of resources that allows one to increase his or her social standing, and, at the same time, increases the likelihood of successfully coping with environmental stressors. Given the values of one's community, the power that is associated with working has the potential to be used for both oppressive and liberating purposes.

Need for Social Connections. The second function focuses on the role of work in providing people with a means of social connection. Over the past decade, scholars in vocational psychology (e.g., Blustein, 2001b; Flum, 2001; Hall, 1996) have begun to examine the nature in which the world of work and the world of intimate relationships and social support networks are intertwined. This phenomenon dates back to ancient times (Gini & Sullivan, 1989), as early bands of hunters and gatherers typically worked in mutual collaboration to enhance their chances of obtaining resources (Wallman, 1979).

At a rudimentary level, work fosters direct contact with others, opening space up for developing meaningful connections. From attachment (Bowlby, 1988) and contemporary psychoanalytic (e.g., Josselson, 1992; Mitchell, 1988) perspectives, this inherent assumption is tied to the idea that human beings are "hard-wired" to strive for close emotional bonds fueled by interpersonal connection. According to Sennett (1998), this evolutionary longing is just as relevant in what he refers to as today's "new capitalism." Indeed, the information era and need for rapid change and flexibility have become hallmarks of the 21st-century labor force. Given that the changing nature of the labor market (Arthur & Rousseau, 1996) is increasingly requiring people to become more autonomous, competitive, and exercise greater risk-taking, Sennett contends that this transformation is leaving many with an intense longing for connection, a biologically programmed need that is strained by the individualistic work ethic. With the advent of downsizing and corporate mergers in an uncertain job market, the plight of "workaholism" has taken on a "get ahead" attitude that deeply cuts into one's sense of psychological cohesion and connection to the community. For those who are unemployed, the lack of connection to a social system may foster feelings of alienation and despair that are often numbed by drugs, alcohol, criminal activity, or violence.

The family–work linkage has received the most specific attention in both vocational and organizational psychology with respect to social connections (Blustein, Walbridge, Friedlander, & Palladino, 1991; Googins, 1991). For the most part, the scholarship in this area has explored the ways in which middle-class couples (typically married heterosexual couples) juggle their work and family roles. The movement of women into the paid employment sector of Western societies following World War II stimulated initial interest in the family–work interface, often falling within the purview of "women's issues." In reality, however, the struggle to find ways of relating meaningfully to both work and family life spheres is a challenge for both men and women, albeit, they are expressed and sanctioned in different ways depending on one's cultural context.

As a source of consolidating one's connections with family, loved ones, friends, and co-workers, the work setting takes on central importance in all relationships, which, to some extent, is likely to "spill over" into a number of different life domains. Similarly, the dynamics of social connections have a tendency to be recreated in numerous contexts, including the workplace. Based on a family systems perspective (e.g., Chusid & Cochran, 1989; Patton & McMahon, 1999), individuals are predisposed to reenact or project aspects of their unresolved family issues, for example, in their work lives. Like most lines of inquiry within the social and psychological sciences, this particular literature has assumed that people possess volitional input into the nature of the work they choose. Although this is certainly not true for everyone, such a perspective does add another layer to the richness of relational strivings and connections between work and other life domains.

The relational elements of working can be further demonstrated in the form of caregiving, or efforts devoted to caring for children, the elderly, and other significant people in one's life (Richardson, 1993). This sort of work is not inherently valued, however, by most Western industrialized societies (Fitzgerald & Weitzman, 1992), and is therefore not generally compensated with money or conferred with access to power. Child care in the United States, for instance, is not offered in a systemic or government-sponsored fashion to parents. In our view, caregiving needs to be appreciated as a legitimate form of work, and merits further exploration in research as a way to enhance social connection and foster self-determination.

Need for Self-Determination. The third and final function of working focuses on opportunities for self-determination that exist within many work contexts. In motivational psychology, Deci and Ryan (1985, 2000) advanced a theory of self-determination that conceptualizes motivation as an internal resource that can explain many aspects of human behavior, including tasks that involve activities that are not necessarily intrinsically interesting. According to this theory, intrinsic motivation is the most desirable state of self-determined functioning. When people are intrinsically motivated, they engage in activities out of interest, pleasure, or enjoyment. On the other hand, when people are extrinsically motivated, activities are accomplished for instrumental reasons, typically arising from the need to attain an outcome or meet an environmental demand that is separate from the activity itself. Activities in which the individual is supported relationally and provided with the mean for attaining competence and autonomy are thought to enhance a form of extrinsic motivation that can be self-determined. In other words, if individuals can become self-regulating with respect to a given set of tasks, they are more likely to have greater motivational initiative and greater satisfaction with these tasks.

The self-determination literature provides a rich conceptual lens for understanding how autonomy, competence, and relatedness can help extrinsically rewarding activities become more meaningful experiences, even in the face of social inequity and economic hardship. Specifically, we propose that some working conditions offering very little opportunity for volition may still become internalized positively through the support of others, the achievement of competence, and a personal sense of empowerment. The role of self-determination can therefore be viewed as a psychological process in which people transform an externally regulated value or behavior into an internal one. Our view with respect to the potential value of extrinsic motivation for people without volition in their work lives is not meant to cast the working classes and relatively unskilled workers aside, relegating them to a lifetime of externally regulated work. Indeed, we hope that our society can move toward greater equity in educational and vocational opportunities so that increasingly more workers can enjoy the satisfaction that can result from a job that offers a good fit between individual characteristics and the demands of the occupation. In other words, we would indeed hope that everyone who works can have the opportunity for a congruent person–environment fit as well as a job that offers dignified working conditions (fair wages, humane supervisors, safe environment, etc.). However, the self-determination model by Deci and Ryan (1985) describes specific attributes of a context that can be used to explore ways of enhancing the dignity and rewards of jobs that are extrinsically rewarding, but not intrinsically interesting.

Overall, the psychology of working can be seen as a powerful tool to promote social justice as it is a perspective that addresses the experiences of all individuals, not just those that have access to power and resources. Moreover, it is a framework that seeks to understand the role that economic, political, and social policies play in the way that we view people and distribute services. Although some of these issues are potentially controversial and may be viewed by some as outside of the purview of psychological discourse, we would argue that only by addressing and exploring these difficult questions can we work toward the promotion of social justice.

IMPLICATIONS FOR PRACTICE, PREVENTION, AND PUBLIC POLICY

Although the study of the psychology of working is still in an early stage of development, a number of relevant implications for practice and prevention can be inferred based on the major premises of our perspective coupled with an understanding of social justice issues in the mental health and vocational behavior arenas. First, the psychology of working helps to root mental health practice in the real world. Consistent with Maslow's (1968) classic need hierarchy, the psychology of working would help clinicians to acknowledge that needs for safety and security are critical in life and must be fulfilled if people are going to be able to profit from treatment and if they are going to be attain a state of contentment and satisfaction with life. Second, the psychology-of-working perspective can be used to inform prevention and policy changes devoted to labor policy, educational reform, urban renewal, and rural development.

Psychology of Working and Individual Counseling Practice

As indicated earlier, we propose that the domain-sensitive approach to treatment (Blustein & Spengler, 1995) may have the potential to place work-related issues in the forefront of mental health practice. In the Blustein and Spengler review of the literature examining the degree to which career interventions affect noncareer outcomes, and the degree to which noncareer interventions affect career outcomes, problems with career development and personal adjustment were viewed as influencing each other, but probably not at all points in time. Although considerable overlap was found between career and noncareer domains of behavior, it was also clear that unique areas of functioning exist that require domain-focused interventions, given the client's presenting problems and reasons for referral.

In general, the practice of psychotherapy can benefit from an explicit awareness of the importance of working across the rich array of life experiences. The three major functions that working provides to people, which were detailed earlier, provide a useful means of exploring how working issues can be understood within the realm of direct services to clients.

Working and the Need for Survival/Power. In our view, an inherent advantage of a psychology-of-working perspective in the practice context is its affirmation that people need to earn a living. As employment becomes less steady across the globe due to technological changes and globalization (Arthur & Rousseau, 1996; Sennett, 1998), the reality that clients need to find and sustain work is likely to become more prevalent, even among well-educated populations. However, the most important implication of this attribute of working for clinical practice is its legitimization of the very real need that people have to work in order to survive and to support their families. Clinicians who are informed by the psychology-of-working perspective will ideally be more sensitive to work issues and will seek to become knowledgeable about relevant bodies of knowledge from traditional career counseling that have been used to help people find and sustain work as well as to adjust to work (e.g., Peterson & Gonzalez, 2005).

Working and the Need for Social Connection. The need for interpersonal relatedness that forms the core of this component of working also represents a growing perspective within many models of psychotherapy (e.g., Jordan, Kaplan, Miller, Stiver, & Surrey, 1991; Josselson, 1992; Mitchell, 1988). Indeed, one of the most significant trends in clinical practice in recent decades has been the emergence of relational models, which has encompassed various schools of psychotherapy. The primary assumption of the relational models is that people need interpersonal connection much as we need air, food, and water (e.g., Bowlby, 1988). From the more global perspective of the psychology of working, the role that work plays in connecting people to others can be understood as a human need that is relevant to all workers, not just those with volitional careers. This perspective is also very informative in providing mental health services for clients who are not working. The absence of work often leaves people with few relational resources, thereby enhancing feelings of loneliness and disconnection. Within the psychotherapy context, counselors would benefit from understanding how work functions to connect people to others in a regular, systematic fashion as well as linking people to broader social and cultural contexts. In addition, the role of power and authority within working relationships may be explored productively in therapy, which may have implications for the clients' personal growth, as well as clients' social and political consciousness.

Working and the Need for Self-Determination. The need that people have to determine the course of their own lives has a rich legacy in mental health treatment. As we outlined earlier, the process of self-determination is most likely to occur when individuals are engaged in intrinsically interesting tasks. However, self-determination can also occur if people have an opportunity to internalize many of the motivational factors involved in a given set of extrinsically motivated tasks. In the realm of clinical practice, therapists may find it helpful to use the Deci and Ryan (1985) motivational model in helping clients who are faced with working tasks that are not necessarily intrinsically motivating.

The three contextual factors that support the self-determination process—conditions of autonomy, relatedness, and competence—also have a home within the conceptual world of psychotherapy. In fact, these three qualities have been integral to numerous models of psychotherapy, such as psychodynamic theory (e.g., Mitchell, 1988; Wachtel, 1993) and cognitive behavioral theory (e.g., Bandura, 1997). In addition, the movement toward greater self-regulation and self-determination may foster a greater sense of empowerment by clients in their lives. For many clients, the acquisition of a job and the development of the means of supporting themselves and their loved ones may be a major impetus toward internalizing greater power in their own lives and within their communities.

This brief review of the implications of the psychology of working for counseling practice naturally provides a surface-level analysis. The full impact of a psychology of working in clinical work may not be readily evident until further research and theoretical progress is made. However, the issues that we have noted furnish readers with some important ideas for introducing work-related issues into psychotherapeutic treatment. Moreover, explicit discussions of working may likely move therapy sessions into the sociopolitical space, in which the conversation explores the impact of various social, educational, economic, and political policies on the availability of training and jobs. The degree to which this forms the essence of a therapy session is difficult to assess. Our view is that psychotherapy works best when insights emerge naturally from the fabric of the therapeutic discourse. In this context, we are not necessarily arguing against open discussions of inequities or political issues; rather, we believe that progress on these issues is most likely to ensue when clients are open to this material and when it is inherently related to their treatment goals. We do, however, believe that clients benefit from learning about the nature of the market-based economy, its inherent inequities, and the struggles to deal with racism, sexism, ageism, classism, and ableism. In fact, explicit discussions of working within clients' own lives may be one of the most viable means of helping clients to explore these broader sociopolitical issues in an experience-near fashion.

Another set of practice implications for the psychology of working is in the development of psychoeducational interventions. The following section reviews some of the more prominent exemplars of work-based interventions that are designed at a broader and, at times, systemic level.

Psychology of Working and Intervening in Broader Systems

Mental health practitioners who are versed in the psychology of working stand uniquely poised to develop and practice interventions designed to affect change across the broad contextual systems, which dynamically influence the lives of marginalized people (Blustein et al., 2001). Drawing from a developmental-contextual perspective of human development (Lerner, 2002), we propose that effective systemic interventions must simultaneously address the needs of individuals and the needs of their environment. Through the use of sound theory and best practices, career interventions can and have been implemented to empower underprivileged populations.

Given the theoretical underpinnings of a psychology of working, we propose that "empowerment" serves as an organizing construct for any systemic vocational intervention. To empower individuals with restricted access to work-related resources, counselors and psychologists must be willing to intervene on the individual, as well as the contextual, level (Richardson, 2000). The following section includes examples of interventions, which have been shown to effectively address the needs of underserved populations by addressing the systems that affect them.

The "I Have a Future Program" (IHAF), was designed by D'Andrea and Daniels (1992) to serve Black inner-city youth (14–17 years) residing in urban, low-income housing projects. IHAF is a community-based career development curriculum including an 8-week course in which teens attend 2-hour classes held twice a week. Recognizing the complex barriers inner-city Black teenagers face in regards to their vocational and personal needs, IHAF counselors utilized a "traditional services" approach to vocational development (i.e., promoting career awareness, teaching pre-employment skills, increasing personal discipline, cultivating problem-solving skills) in conjunction with a unique culturally sensitive model proposed by Kunjufu (1984). The IHAF program is infused with an African worldview driven by the seven life principles called "Nguzo Saba." By utilizing small-group counseling methods and culturally relevant activities, counselors assisted participating youth in examining their racial identity while learning important work attainment skills.

Within this culturally sensitive and affirmative framework, IHAF integrated a community counseling approach into the program. Based on a model by Lewis and Lewis (1989), the staff and counselors actively collaborated with elected officials, human service professionals, leaders in the Black churches, public housing officials, community role models, parents, and representatives in the private industry as a means to sustain and amplify the impact of the intervention. By advocating for these youth through direct contact with community agents of change, the IHAF team endeavored to strengthen the goals of their efforts with the expertise and consolidated support of people who bear a systemic and interpersonal influence on them in their daily lives. The IHAF program illustrates the creative ways in which mental health professionals can integrate work-related issues with relevant cultural and community resources to empower individuals to attain new skills.

Two additional examples of how the psychology of working has been applied within urban schools are the Achieving Success Identity Pathways (ASIP; Solberg, Howard, Blustein, & Close, 2002) program and the Tools for Tomorrow Program (TFT; Blustein et al., 2001; Hartung & Blustein, 2002; Kenny, Sparks, & Jackson, this volume). Both of these school-to-work interventions confront the disparity in urban schools by incorporating academic skills development with individual and group activities designed to help students internalize the connection between school, work and the rest of their lives. These programs also recognize the systemic barriers urban youth face and incorporate this information within the context of traditional school-to-work skills training.

The ASIP, developed by Solberg and his colleagues (Solberg et al., 2002), reflects the importance of teaching career development skills to urban students while simultaneously restructuring the environments they live in. The ASIP program consists of structured classroom curricula designed to encourage student interest in "academic and life success" and a teacher-training program that encourages broader investment in the career development needs of students. This multifaceted approach towards urban student achievement incorporates the developmental-contextual approach (Lerner, 2002) to human change by influencing changes in the schools and not just within the students. Evidence by Solberg and his team (e.g., Solberg et al., 2002) suggests that the ASIP intervention is having a positive impact on the students, the teachers, and other individuals involved in the larger system.

Like the ASIP program, the primary goal of the TFT program (Blustein et al., 2001; Kenny et al., chap. 14, this volume) is to help inner-city youth internalize the connection between school, work, and their lives. The TFT program also draws broadly from developmental-contextualism (Lerner, 2002) as well as self-determination theory (Deci & Ryan, 1985) in that it seeks to address the needs of the individual while restructuring the educational environment. The TFT program emphasizes the importance of inner-city youth identifying the unique resources and barriers that influence the development of their individual career pathways. This unique element of the TFT program encourages students to access information from their communities and build individualized "goal maps" that incorporate their cultural worldview. By infusing contextually relevant material into the career pathways curriculum, the TFT program hopes to transition students from an amotivated position with respect to school engagement towards more adaptive and internalized modes of motivation that are self-determined (Deci & Ryan, 2000).

In a career intervention program for adult female offenders, Chartrand and Rose (1996) examined the needs of female perpetrators as opposed to female victims, pointing out how the population of female offenders is expanding at an overwhelming rate, particularly for African American and Hispanic women. The authors noted that for many female offenders, finding employment that can adequately support themselves and their families after release from prison is one of their greatest challenges. Grounded in social cognitive career theory (Lent, Brown, & Hackett, 2002), Chartrand and Rose (1996) operated from the assumption that self-efficacy and positive outcome expectations for many women offenders are underdeveloped and that many have been afforded restricted learning opportunities. In addition, they postulated that various "cognitive deficits" often experienced by offenders may result in self-efficacy estimates that grossly diverge from their ability. Consequently, they proposed that social cognitive career theory is especially appropriate for incarcerated populations in addressing female offenders' cognitive functioning.

In project PROVE (Prevention Recidivism through Opportunities in Vocational Education), Chartrand and Rose (1996) described a 12-week career-development program they originally developed for female offenders who were scheduled to be released into the community. By emphasizing the values of personal mastery and responsibility for creating change, Project PROVE seeks to develop personal performance accomplishments (e.g. woman are asked to list accomplishments that are personally important), create vicarious learning situations (such as undergraduate role models assisting women with program exercises), and teach the offenders the relationship between physiological states and self-efficacy (such as identifying fear and anxiety's impact on job interview behavior and beliefs). To help women identify desired accomplishments and formulate aspirations and goals, Project PROVE asks them to develop a lifeline that includes important past and anticipated events and accomplishments as a means to build educational and career efficacy, as well as to motivate career planning behavior.

One of the common questions that is often raised about social justice and psychotherapy/psychoeducational interventions pertains to the degree to which these sorts of interventions function to "patch" people up rather than actually change systems. In actuality, the aforementioned practice suggestions and preventive/educational interventions are probably not going to engender vast systemic changes. In other words, if we were to end our chapter here, we would likely be guilty of endorsing the same approach that our field has employed for well over a century—that is, to help repair people rather than the aversive contexts that shape individuals in so many powerful and often subtle ways. However, our implications for practice do seek to change one of the most powerful systems within the mental health world—the world of clinicians. Our hope is that by placing work-related issues at the forefront of thinking, at least within this chapter, we have helped to move one of the major sources of power (and marginalization) out of the shadows of neglect and into the active engagement that is increasingly needed in applied psychological contexts. In the section that follows, we follow this path by exploring the potential impact of the psychology of working on the design and implementation of more equitable social and public policy.

Implications for Research and Public Policy

We have integrated the implications for research and public policy in this section for a very important reason. We believe that scholarship emerging from the psychology of working can have a profound impact on the development of public policies that are rooted in the experiences of working. In this section, we outline some of the most important directions for research that ideally will have the potential to impact education, training, and other relevant public policies.

Exploratory Studies on the Nature of Working. First and foremost, we would like to advocate that mental health professionals and other social scientists engage in exploratory studies that will map the terrain of the inner experiences of workers. In the Blustein (2006) book on the psychology of working, many of the inferences that are being derived about working are culled from memoirs, poems, song lyrics, novels, and other forms of discourse that seek to describe how people from various occupations (and from the ranks of the unemployed) understand their working experiences. One of arguments that Blustein (2001a) detailed in his original call for investigations in this area is that far too many of the theories and practices developed within career counseling and I/O psychology have emerged from an experience-distant perspective. In contrast, the psychology of working is based on an assumption that our field is in need of the voices of the working class, poor, and unemployed who have not been adequately represented in our literature to date. Although some important strides are taking place within psychology currently that are seeking to provide a more active and experience-near place regarding working outside of the traditional career models (e.g., Juntunen et al., 2001; Schultheiss, Kress, Manzi, & Jeffrey Glasscock, 2001), far more effort is needed to fully map the psychology of working.

Unemployment. We are also very concerned with a thorough exploration of the impact of unemployment on individual functioning and on the functioning of communities. Research on unemployment, naturally, is not new to our field, or more broadly to the social sciences (e.g., O'Brien, 1986; Wilson, 1996). Indeed, the contribution of Wilson's book may be construed as one of the most compelling research studies about working in that it yielded important implications for both the social sciences and public policy. Following Wilson's work, we believe that research is needed to define the full range of consequences that are causally linked to unemployment and underemployment. The importance of this work is critical as many governments across the globe are faced with difficult choices about how to best manage unemployment. Given the findings reported by Wilson, we imagine that further evidence will be obtained emphasizing the critical nature of working in sustaining a vibrant human trajectory. Moreover, consistent with Wilson's findings that the lack of work was associated with growing problems in urban communities, we envision studies on the psychology of working that will delineate how working functions to support social structures that sustain coherence and stability within families and communities. These findings are actually quite critical, as some government leaders have already accepted unemployment as a natural consequence of a market-based economy, often minimizing the role of government in designing social and economic systems to support full employment.

Working and Mental Health. Another important area for research and policy reform is in the study of the relationships between employment and mental health. In the Blustein and Spengler (1995) chapter, evidence was presented that supported the position that working provides people with a means of warding off mental health problems. We believe that further research is needed that will explicate how working functions to support mentally healthy behavior. For example, studies that will explore the nature, attributes, and consequences of the three functions that work provides may be particularly useful as psychologists and other mental health specialists chart the role of work in supporting positive and affirming lifestyles, and conversely, warding off the aversive life consequences.

In addition, the role that issues pertaining to working play in the psychotherapy process would be important to document. As Blustein and Spengler (1995) noted, psychotherapists have little training or knowledge with which to understand or treat work-related issues in treatment. In this context, it would be useful for scholars to identify how clients tend to present issues relating to working in therapy and how clinicians deal with these issues. Some empirical evidence exists suggesting that clinicians tend to overshadow vocational problems with personal problems of relatively equal severity, thereby suggesting that biases may exists among clinicians that function to distance work-related issues from the core of the treatment process (e.g., Spengler, Blustein, & Strohmer, 1990). As we have noted in this chapter, the discussion of working may in fact provide the conduit to broader conversations about the fundamental issues pertaining to social injustices that are a major contributing factor to many clients' problems. In this context, we believe that one particularly fruitful line of inquiry would be to explore the impact of varied working conditions on the nature of individual well-being and mental health. In general, research and theoretical efforts designed to map the terrain of work-related issues in psychotherapeutic interactions would provide a powerful means of enhancing the inclusiveness and quality of mental health treatment.

Impact of Racism in the Workplace. Following the contributions of Carter and Cook (1992) and more recently Helms and Cook (1999), issues of work and career are central in the psychological experiences of people of color. Whereas many European Americans in North America, for example, tend to consider work-related issues primarily from the perspective of self-determination of their interests, people of color are faced with far more pressing concerns. The vast disproportion of poverty and unemployment among people of color in the United States would suggest that work-related issues ought to be central to socially relevant and effective mental health treatments and prevention efforts. As we have noted, the development of the ability to earn one's living provides a critical means of ensuring that one will have the power and means of surviving. Moreover, the ability to work and have a place at the table where decisions are made about allocations of resources (such as in government, education, business, and public policy) provides an even more potent way to affect systemic social change. The role of work in the empowerment of people of color has had an historic as well as contemporary role in many liberation movements. As such, we advocate research and theoretical developments that will facilitate a broader understanding of how racism functions to inhibit the work-related goals and dreams of people of color. In addition, further research on the impact of racial identity development (cf. Helms & Cook, 1999) would be very productive. Taken together, these scholarly efforts may further inform public policy and educational reform, which is increasingly critical in empowering people of color.

Impact of Sexism in the Workplace. One of the areas in which psychologists have, in fact, developed a knowledge base that has informed public policy in the workplace is in the realm of sexual harassment (Fitzgerald, 2003; Riger, 1991). The study of the psychology of working may further the cause of reducing sexual harassment, particularly as knowledge is developed on the experiences of women from the full gamut of jobs and occupations. Moreover, the continued existence of sexism in education, training, and within the workplace needs far more study. We believe that experience-near investigations that give voice to women who have been subjected to sexism will be very influential in public policy circles, particularly if the research is done in accordance with the rigorous, high standards of ethnographic and qualitative methods (Denzin & Lincoln, 2000).

These specific themes begin to suggest the breadth and depth of studies that can be conducted under the rubric of the psychology of working. As we begin to understand the nature of working, further areas of inquiry may emerge that expand the impact of psychological research. Moreover, studying the psychology of working is likely to yield a natural linkage between scholarship and public policy, which may provide an important voice for the social justice agenda that is articulated in this chapter and others in this volume.

CONCLUSION

Embedding this overview of the psychology of working in a book on social justice is an ideal venue for our work. The social justice mission of enhancing equity and changing systems is a hallmark of the psychology of working (Blustein, 2006); indeed, we believe that an active inclusion of discourse about working is critical in constructing a psychology that will advance a social justice agenda. We hope that the material that we have presented in this chapter furnishes the seeds for the eventual development of a liberation psychology that will explicitly address the potential of working in empowering people and systems so that all individuals may have access to work that offers security, self-determination, and dignity.

REFERENCES

Applebaum, H. (1992). *The concept of work: Ancient, medieval, and modern.* Albany, NY: State University of New York Press.

Arthur, M. B., & Rousseau, D. M. (Eds.). (1996). *The boundaryless career.* New York: Oxford University Press.

Axelrod, S. D. (1999). *Work and the evolving self: Theoretical and clinical considerations.* Hillsdale, NJ: The Analytic Press.

Bandura, A. (1997). *Self-efficacy: The exercise of control.* New York: W.H. Freeman.

Blustein, D. L. (1994). The question of "Who am I?": A cross-theoretical analysis. In M. L. Savickas & R. W. Lent (Eds.), *Convergence in career development theories: Implications for science and practice.* (pp. 139–154). Palo Alto, CA: Consulting Psychologist Press.

Blustein, D. L. (2001a). Extending the reach of vocational psychology: Toward an inclusive and integrative psychology of working. *Journal of Vocational Behavior, 59,* 171–182.

Blustein, D. L. (2001b). The interface of work and relationships: A critical knowledge base for 21st century psychology. *The Counseling Psychologist, 29,* 179–192.

Blustein, D. L. (2006). *The psychology of working: A new perspective for career development, counseling, and public policy.* Mahwah, NJ: Lawrence Erlbaum Associates.

Blustein, D. L., Copman, S., Jackson, J., Kenny, M. E., Mullin, K., Sparks, E., et al. (2001, March). *Social action within an urban school context: The tools for tomorrow project.* Paper presented at the Fourth National Counseling Psychology conference, Houston, TX.

Blustein, D. L., McWhirter, E. H. & Perry, J. C. (2005). An emancipatory communitarian approach to vocational development: Theory, research, and practice. *The Counseling Psychologist, 33,* 141–179.

Blustein, D. L., & Spengler, P. M. (1995). Personal adjustment: Career counseling and psychotherapy. In W. B. Walsh & S. H. Osipow (Eds.), *Handbook of vocational psychology* (2nd ed., pp. 295–329). Mahwah, NJ: Lawrence Erlbaum Associates.

Blustein, D. L, Walbridge, M., Friedlander, M. L., & Palladino, D. E. (1991). Contributions of psychological separation and parental attachment to the career development process. *Journal of Counseling Psychology, 38,* 39–50.

Bowlby, J. (1988). *A secure base: Parent–child attachment and healthy human development.* New York: Basic Books.

Brown, D., & Brooks, L. (1996). (Eds.). *Career choice and development* (3rd ed.). San Francisco: Jossey-Bass.

Carter, R. T., & Cook, D. A. (1992). A culturally relevant perspective for understanding the career paths of visible racial/ethnic group people. In H. D. Lea & Z. B. Leibowitz (Eds.), *Adult career development: Concepts, issues, and practice* (pp. 192–217). Alexandria, VA: National Career Development Association.

Chartrand, J. M., & Rose, M. L. (1996). Career interventions for at-risk populations: Incorporating social cognitive influences. *Career Development Quarterly, 44,* 341–353.

Chusid, H., & Cochran, L. (1989). Meaning of career change from the perspective of family roles and dramas. *Journal of Counseling Psychology, 36,* 34–41.

D'Andrea, M., & Daniels, J. (1992). A career development program for inner-city black youth. *Career Development Quarterly, 40,* 272–280.

Danziger, S. H., & Haveman, R. H. (Eds.). (2001). *Understanding poverty.* Cambridge, MA: Harvard University Press.

Deci, E. L., & Ryan, R. M. (1985). *Intrinsic motivation and self-determination in human behavior.* New York: Plenum.

Deci, E. L., & Ryan, R. M. (2000). The "what" and "why" of goal pursuits: Human needs and self-determination of behavior. *Psychological Inquiry, 11,* 227–268.

Denzin, N. K., & Lincoln, Y. S. (2000). (Eds.), *Handbook of qualitative research* (2nd ed.). Thousand Oaks, CA: Sage.

Donkin, R. (2001). *Blood, sweat, & tears: The evolution of work.* New York: Texere.

Erikson, E. (1968). *Identity, youth, and crisis.* New York: Norton.

Fitzgerald, L. F. (2003). Sexual harassment and social justice: Reflections on the distance yet to go. *American Psychologist, 58,* 915–924.

Fitzgerald, L. F., & Weitzman, L. M. (1992). Women's career development: Theory and practice from a feminist perspective. In H. D. Lea & Z. B. Leibowitz (Eds.), *Adult career development: Concepts, issues, and practice* (pp. 124–160). Alexandria, VA: National Career Development Association.

Flum, H. (2001). Relational dimensions in career development. *Journal of Vocational Behavior, 59,* 1–16.

Freire, P. (1970). *Pedagogy of the oppressed.* New York: Continuum Publishing Company.

Freud, S. (1930). *Civilization and its discontents.* New York: Norton.

Gini, A. (2000). *My job, my self: Work and the creation of the modern individual.* New York: Routledge.

Gini, A., & Sullivan, T. J. (Eds.). (1989). *It comes with the territory: An inquiry concerning work and the person.* New York: Random House.

Golembiewski, R. T. (1993). (Ed.). *Handbook of organizational behavior.* New York: Marcal-Dekker, Inc.

Goodman, L. A., Liang, B., Helms, J. E., Latta, R. E., Sparks, E., & Weintraub, S. R. (2004). Training counseling psychologists as social justice agents: Feminist and multicultural principles in action. *The Counseling Psychologist, 32,* 793–837.

Googins, B. K. (1991). *Work/family conflicts: Private lives—public responses.* New York: Auburn House.

Hall, D. T. (Ed.). (1996). *The career is dead—Long live the career: A relational approach to careers.* San Francisco: Jossey-Bass.

Harmon. L. W. (1994). Frustrations, daydreams, and realities of theoretical convergence. In M. L. Savickas & R. W. Lent (Eds.), *Convergence in career development theories* (pp. 226–234). Palo Alto, CA: CPP Books.

Hartung, P. J., & Blustein, D. L. (2002). Reason, intuition, and social justice: Elaborating Parsons's career decision making model. *Journal of Counseling and Development, 80,* 41–47.

Helms, J. E., & Cook, D. A. (1999). *Using race and culture in counseling and psychotherapy: Theory and process.* Boston: Allyn & Bacon.

Holland, J. L. (1997). *Making vocational choices: A theory of vocational personalities and work environments* (3rd ed.). Odessa, FL: PAR.

Jordan, J. V., Kaplan, A. G., Miller, J. B., Stiver, I. P., & Surrey, J. L. (1991). *Women's growth in connection: Writings from the Stone Center.* New York: Guilford.

Josselson, R. (1992). *The space between us: Exploring the dimensions of human relationships.* San Francisco: Jossey-Bass.

Juntunen, C. L., Barraclough, D. J., Broneck, C. J., Seibel, G. A., Winrow, S. A., & Morin, P. M. (2001). American Indian perspectives on the career journey. *Journal of Counseling Psychology, 48,* 274–285.

Kunjufu, J. (1984). *Developing positive self-images and discipline in Black children.* Chicago: African American Images.

Landy, F. J. (1989). *The psychology of work behavior* (4th ed.). Belmont, CA: Brooks/Cole.

Lent, R. W., Brown, S. D., & Hackett, G. (2002). Social cognitive career theory. In D. Brown (Ed.), *Career choice and development* (pp. 255–311). San Francisco: Jossey-Bass.

Lerner, R. (2002). *Concepts and theories of human development* (3rd ed.). Mahwah, NJ: Lawrence Erlbaum Associates.

Lewis, J., & Lewis, M. (1989). *Community counseling: A human services approach.* New York: Wiley.

Lowman, R. L. (1993). *Counseling and psychotherapy of work dysfunctions.* Washington, DC: American Psychological Association.

Martín-Baró, I. (1994). *Writings for a liberation psychology.* Cambridge, MA: Harvard University Press.

Maslow, A. H. (1968). *Toward a psychology of being.* New York: Van Nostrand Reinhold

Mitchell, L. K., & Krumboltz, J. D. (1996). Krumboltz's learning theory of career choice and counseling. In D. Brown & L. Brown (Eds.), *Career choice and development* (3rd ed., pp. 233–280). San Francisco: Jossey-Bass.

Mitchell, S. A. (1988). *Relational concepts in psychoanalysis.* Cambridge, MA: Harvard University Press.

Neff, W. S. (1985). *Work and human behavior* (3rd ed.). New York: Aldine.

O'Brien, G. E. (1986). *Psychology of work and unemployment.* New York: Wiley.

O'Brien, K. M. (2001). The legacy of Parsons: Career counselors and vocational psychologists as agents of social change. *Career Development Quarterly, 50,* 66–76.

Patton, W., & McMahon, M. (1999). *Career development and systems theory: A new relationship.* Pacific Grove, CA: Brooks/Cole.

Peterson, N., & Gonzalez, R. C. (2005). *The role of work in people's lives: Applied career counseling and vocational psychology* (2nd ed.). Belmont, CA: Brooks/Cole.

Powell, G. N. (Ed.). (1999). *Handbook of gender and work.* Thousand Oaks, CA: Sage.

Prilleltensky, I. (1997). Values, assumptions, and practices: Assessing the moral implications of psychological discourse and action. *American Psychologist, 52,* 517–535.

Richardson, M. S. (1993). Work in people's lives: A location for counseling psychologists. *Journal of Counseling Psychology, 40,* 425–433.

Richardson, M. S. (2000). A new perspective for counsellors: From career ideologies to empowerment through work and relationship practices. In A. Collin & R. A. Young (Eds.), *The future of careers* (pp. 197–211). Cambridge, England: Cambridge University Press.

Riger, S. (1991). Gender dilemmas in sexual harassment policies and procedures. *American Psychologist, 46,* 497–505.

Savickas, M. L. (1995). Current theoretical issues in vocational psychology: Convergence, divergence, and schism. In W. B. Walsh & S. H. Osipow (Eds.), *Handbook of vocational psychology* (2nd ed., pp. 1–34). Mahwah, NJ: Lawrence Erlbaum Associates.

Savickas, M. L. (2002). Career construction: A developmental theory of vocational behavior. In D. Brown (Ed.), *Career choice and development* (pp. 149–205). San Francisco: Jossey-Bass.

Schultheiss, D., Kress, H., Manzi, A., & Jeffrey Glasscock, J. (2001). Relational influences in career development: A qualitative inquiry. *The Counseling Psychologist, 29,* 214–239.

Sennett, R. (1998). *The corrosion of character: The personal consequences of work in the new capitalism.* New York: Norton.

Smelser, N. J., & Erikson, E. H. (Eds.). (1980). *Themes of work and love in adulthood.* Cambridge, MA: Harvard University Press.

Solberg, V. S.. Howard, K. A., Blustein, D. L., & Close, W. (2002). Career development in the schools: Connecting school-to-work-to-life. *The Counseling Psychologist, 30,* 705–725.

Spengler, P. M., Blustein, D. L., & Strohmer, D. C. (1990). Diagnostic and treatment overshadowing of vocational problems by personal problems. *Journal of Counseling Psychology, 37,* 372–381.

Super, D. E. (1957). *The psychology of careers.* New York: Harper & Row.

Thomas, K. (1999). *The Oxford book of work.* New York: Oxford University Press.

Vera, E. M., & Speight, S. L. (2003). Multicultural competence, social justice, and counseling psychology: Expanding our roles. *The Counseling Psychologist, 31,* 253–272.

Wachtel, P. (1993). *Therapeutic communication: Principles and effective practice.* New York: Guilford Press.

Wallman, S. (Ed.). (1979). *Social anthropology of work.* New York: Academic Press.

Wilson, W. J. (1996). *When work disappears: The world of the new urban poor.* New York: Random House.

16

Mental Health Policy
and Social Justice

Barry J. Ackerson
Wynne S. Korr
University of Illinois at Urbana-Champaign

Changes in the treatment of persons with mental illness over the last 200 years can be examined in terms of the promotion of social justice for this marginalized and stigmatized group. For most of those years, the main justice goal was ending inhumane treatment. More recently, the goals have shifted to promotion of a right to treatment and to full inclusion in civil society. Our focus now is on ensuring full human rights for persons with serious mental disorders and securing the resources needed to fulfill those rights.

The movement toward justice for this population has been achieved through policy change. Policies provide goals and directions for provision of services and define the roles of government and the private sector. For example, the federal community mental health legislation of the 1960s and 1970s set a course for community-based care in contrast to the state hospital-based care of the previous century. The federal government set direction and provided service requirements. The legislation required involvement of state governments to define catchment areas and to set priorities for services and client groups. Private sector partners, typically non-profit community-based organizations, were the service providers.

We review some of the major policy changes that characterized the last two centuries with attention to how various actors have pursued social justice goals in mental health. We then discuss a framework for evaluating existing and proposed policies along with practical recommendations for policy advocacy. We conclude the chapter with some critical reflections on broader justice issues pertaining to promotion of prevention and well-being.

HISTORICAL DEVELOPMENTS

Mental health policy developed out of partnerships among social advocates, professionals, and users of mental health services. Several authors have described the development of mental health policy as occurring in a cyclical manner in conjunction with various social justice movements and reform eras (Fellin, 1996; Mechanic, 1999; Rochefort, 1997). These cycles are characterized by drawing attention of the public to the problem, proposals for reform in policies and services, a larger social reform movement that creates an environment favorable for legislative and judicial reforms, followed by the enactment of policies, judicial rulings, and service innovations. Unfortunately, the cyclical nature of mental health policy in the United States also describes a pattern of diminished interest and reduced policy activity following the implementation of reforms. Rochefort (1997) describes this cyclical process as having many components that are congruent with larger social policy issues and others that are unique to the mental health policy sector. Thus, mental health policy in the United States has developed within the context of larger social reform movements, as well as being driven by specific concerns for social justice on behalf of people with serious mental disorders.

Moral Treatment and the Building of Asylums

The first major event in formal mental health policy was the creation of state hospitals and asylums in the early to mid-1800s. Prior to this time, there was no real treatment for persons with any type of mental disorder, including both the "insane" and the "mentally defective" or "imbeciles." Individuals with any type of bizarre behavior, impaired cognitive functioning, or extreme moods were feared or shunned or both. Many of these individuals were either locked away in their homes or were placed into local poorhouses and jails, lacking humane care. In Europe a number of individuals, such as Phillipe Pinel in France and William Tuke in England, began to espouse the development of asylums where those afflicted with mental and emotional problems could seek refuge and "moral treatment" in a protected environment (Grob, 1994). These innovative ideas influenced American doctors such as Benjamin Rush and Thomas Kirkbride, who promoted the idea of moral treatment in asylums.

However, the importation of innovative treatment approaches from Europe was not sufficient to cause major policy change. The role of social policy advocates was crucial to institutionalizing these treatment innovations as long-lasting policy reforms. For example, the first public hospitals for the insane were in the South, but most were primarily custodial, lacking the moral treatment philosophy. These institutions did not significantly influence mental health policies or services in other states. However, in 1830, reformers in Massachusetts successfully advocated for the creation of a state hospital based on moral treatment principles. Dorothea Dix, a Sunday school teacher from Massachusetts, became a strident advocate for the expansion of the hospital in Massachusetts and for the building of similar hospitals across the country. She allied herself with Dr. Benjamin Rush. Her advocacy is credited with the building of state hospitals throughout the country.

From a policy standpoint, the greatest impact of this advocacy was not just the creation of state mental hospitals but the assumption of responsibility by the states for care of individuals with mental disorders and mental retardation. This was made possible because moral treatment was promoted as part of the social justice movement of that era. As state legislators were confronted with the deplorable conditions for their citizens who were "insane" or "feebleminded," they eventually allocated funds to build state-supported facilities for the insane and later provided funding for state schools for the mentally retarded. As the idealized hope of moral treatment faded and public attention waned, state support for these facilities diminished over time leading to the decline and deterioration of these institutions.

Progressive Era Reforms

The next major innovation occurred during the Progressive Era in the late 19th and early 20th centuries. The public health movement and larger social justice reforms served as the backdrop for the "mental hygiene" movement (Rochefort, 1997). Two key figures associated with this era are the famous psychiatrist, Adolph Meyer, and Clifford Beers, a former patient who became a vocal advocate for mental health reform. Although they differed at times, both Dr. Meyer and Mr. Beers advocated for reform of the state hospitals and the creation of new community-based prevention and treatment programs. There was some success in creating new mental health services during this era. Innovations included community child-guidance clinics and smaller, community-based psychopathic hospitals that focused on short-term active treatment in contrast to the custodial care provided in the state facilities. However, no large-scale policy changes occurred during this time on either the state or federal level, due, in part, to the continued dominance of the state hospital system and the growing numbers of patients in those systems despite innovations in community-based services (Grob, 1994). In addition, shifting national priorities because of the Great Depression and World War II overwhelmed other domestic policy issues.

The Community Mental Health Movement

Following World War II, public attention was drawn once again to the plight of individuals with mental illness and development disabilities. The war created a renewed interest in reforms in mental health services by psychiatrists and other mental health professionals. Experiences of soldiers during the World War II, along with observations of psychologists and psychiatrists that prevention and early treatment could prevent more serious mental health problems, led to new ideas about a community-based approach. At the same time, public interest was drawn to the deteriorated conditions in the state hospitals through a series of studies, such as *Shame of the States* by Albert Deutsch (cited in Grob, 1991, p. 71) and exposés in the popular media such as *Bedlam 1946* and the popular novel and movie of the late 1940s, *The Snake Pit* (as cited in Grob, 1991, p. 77). As a result of this increased attention to the deplorable conditions in the states' mental health facilities, social justice advocates as well as mental health professionals were able to advance a reform agenda on the federal level just as advocates a century earlier had promoted reforms that had an impact on the state level.

The postwar reform movement led to the passage of two major pieces of federal legislation that would set the stage for even greater changes in the 1960s and 1970s. The National Mental Health Act of 1946 created the National Institute of Mental Health (NIMH). The establishment of NIMH represented the first involvement of the federal government in mental health policy and services in the United States. Its primary purpose was to promote research and training programs, while also providing grants to improve state and local mental health services. However, the biggest impact that NIMH had in its early years was to promote policies and research that eventually led to the community mental health movement. An example of NIMH's involvement in policy advocacy was its role in the passage of the Mental Health Study

Act of 1955. This legislation called for a comprehensive review of the mental health system in the United States, primarily the state hospitals. The resulting report to Congress proposed substantial changes in mental health services (Rochefort, 1997). These changes included promoting deinstitutionalization and the development of community-based mental health services with the active assistance of the federal government.

The community mental health movement resulted from social advocacy in the both the legislative and judicial arena. Legislative advocacy led to federal action supporting a community-based approach. The Mental Retardation Facilities and Community Mental Health Centers Construction Act (PL 94–63; 1963), more commonly referred to as the "Community Mental Health Centers Act of 1963," ushered in a fundamentally new approach in the provision of mental health services. This Act and its successors were a direct result of a social activist agenda that arose out of the "Great Society" programs of the Kennedy and Johnson administrations. President Kennedy, with a strong personal interest because of a sister with mental retardation, announced this federal legislation as a "bold new approach." The Act was the result of many years of work by NIMH and professional mental health organizations, yet it was also the product of competing advocacy and interest groups. Because it was a compromise between various groups, the 1963 Act funded only the construction of community agencies and fell short of the more radical reforms proposed in the original report to Congress in 1961. The need for funds to staff the services led to a series of amendments to the Community Mental Health Centers Act during the 1960s and 1970s that also expanded the types of services required.

Civil Rights Reform Through Litigation

Federal and Supreme Court decisions were also fundamental to creating this significant shift in mental health policy. These cases had their roots in the Civil Rights movement and the broader concern for social justice on behalf of disadvantaged populations. Civil rights advocates took up the cause of mental patients whom they believed were too often committed to hospitals without regard to due process rights, then held there indefinitely with infrequent review of their status and little or no treatment.

Several landmark rulings addressed civil commitment laws, involuntary hospitalization, and the right to treatment. These rulings resulted in a judicial mandate for deinstitutionalization and for substantial reform of the care provided in state mental hospitals. *Wyatt v. Stickney* (1971) is considered to be the first case to establish a "right to treatment" for involuntarily committed patients. This case was brought by attorneys in Alabama who had been active in civil rights cases of the 1960s and was prompted by a severe reduction in state hospital staff as the result of financial problems that the state was facing at the time. The *Wyatt* case not only established that mentally ill patients who had been involuntarily confined had a right to treatment, it also established basic standards for treatment. This case was followed by *Youngberg v. Romeo* (1982) in Pennsylvania, which extended a right to safety and a more limited right to treatment to persons with mental retardation. The impact of these rulings, along with others that followed in their wake, was to do away with "warehousing" of those with mental illness and developmental disabilities. States now had a legal mandate to substantially improve both the staffing and physical structure of these facilities. Although the CMHC Act provided the "carrot" for developing community-based services, this legal mandate served as the "stick" that promoted deinstitutionalization. Most states realized that they had a financial, as well as humanitarian, incentive to significantly reduce the size and number of their state mental health and mental retardation facilities.

Lessard v. Schmidt (1972) was a federal district court case in Wisconsin that had a profound impact on state civil commitment laws. In *Lessard,* the court ruled that, in order to confine mentally persons against their will, there has to be proof of both mental illness and dangerousness. This case was argued on the civil libertarian grounds that a person's due process rights may not be denied just because they have an illness. In order to confine a person involuntarily, the state must also prove the individual presents a danger to themselves or others. The court ruled that civil commitment procedures must meet the same standards for due process as criminal cases. The *Lessard* ruling led to changes in most states' commitment laws. Involuntary commitment to state hospitals became much more difficult. Other rulings followed, such as *O'Connor v. Donaldson* (1975), that resulted in large numbers of patients being released from hospitals because they were not dangerous and were not receiving active treatment.

The development of psychotropic medication in the 1950s and 1960s, along with establishment of community mental health centers in the 1960s and 1970s, made community-based treatment possible. The judicial reform of civil commitment laws provided strong legal reasons for pursuing deinstitutionalization of mental health services.

A more recent decision, *Olmstead v. L.C.* (1999), made it clear that Title II of the Americans with Disabilities Act (1990) requires states to integrate patients into the community and cannot keep them in hospitals indefinitely by arguing that community resources do not exist. This decision, in essence, completes the shift from focusing primarily on rights related to hospital care to a focus on community integration and inclusion.

Policy Change Through Funding Mechanisms

In the 1980s, mental health policy became more influenced by funding mechanisms. The categorical grants that funded the CMHCs were converted to block grants from the federal government to state governments. This change in funding philosophy was part of the Reagan and Bush administrations' "New Federalism," which promoted reduced federal authority over social service programs such as mental health and substance abuse services. Although the block grants gave the states more autonomy in providing services, they also resulted in a significant reduction in federal support for mental health services. A number of scholars have noted that, during this time, community providers underwent a change in philosophy and adopted a more business-like approach in their operations (Mechanic, 1999). As states assumed greater authority over administration of the block grant dollars, they emphasized serving specific target populations, that is, adults with severe and persistent mental illness and children with serious emotional disorders. Therefore, most community mental health agencies shifted their focus away from prevention and service to the broader community in favor of targeting services to specific populations for whom they received funding.

During the 1980s and 1990s, privatization of mental health services greatly expanded. This occurred in several ways. Because of the shift to community-based care, many individuals with private insurance could now obtain a variety of services in their local communities. This expansion of the private mental health sector also coincided with the emergence of managed behavioral health care and HMOs (Dorwart & Epstein, 1993; Sharfstein, 1993). The emergence of a large private sector led to concerns about further fragmentation of services and a two-tiered system of care. In this system, publicly funded agencies would focus primarily on serving the most severely disabled clients and those covered by public insurance such as Medicaid, whereas the private programs would focus more on clients with private insurance and less severe diagnoses (e.g. depression and anxiety disorders). Furthermore, many states and local agencies in the late 1990s began to emulate the private system by adopting managed care approaches to the funding and delivery of community mental health services (Mazade, 1996; Mechanic, 1999).

During this same time period, family and mental health consumer advocacy groups emerged. The largest of these groups was the National Alliance for the Mentally Ill (NAMI). NAMI and other advocacy groups were concerned about problems they experienced as a result of deinstitutionalization and a lack of coordinated community services. They advocated reducing the stigma of mental illness, better services for those with serious and persistent mental illnesses, and a research agenda that emphasized the neurobiological basis of severe mental disorders. Partly as a response to their advocacy, the federal government passed the State Comprehensive Services Plan Act of 1986. This legislation was complementary to block grant funding. It supported the decentralized funding of services while establishing a federal mandate for development of a continuum of mental health services at the state and local levels. One of the most significant aspects of this legislation was the requirement that families and mental health consumers be represented in each state's planning process, thus guaranteeing a role for these advocacy groups in the development of publicly funded mental health services.

In addition to the fight against stigma and advocacy for services, family and consumer groups became involved in advocating for equity in funding. Because the vast majority of individuals now receive mental health services in community agencies and local hospitals, third-party reimbursement has become a major funding source for community mental health services. For example, in many states, Medicaid reimbursement provides more funds for community mental health agencies than the federal block grant. Individuals requiring hospitalization typically are treated locally with payment coming from Medicaid, Medicare, or private insurance. The availability of private and public insurance for inpatient psychiatric services has contributed to privatization in the mental health sector (Dorwart & Epstein, 1993). An example was the substantial increase in local inpatient psychiatric beds at the same time that states were undergoing drastic reductions in state hospital beds.

As families and consumers began to realize the impact that third-party payment mechanisms had on their ability to receive care, they became increasingly concerned about equity in insurance payments for mental health and substance abuse services in comparison to other health conditions. Funding issues, which had been primarily a concern of policy experts, emerged in the 1990s as an issue of fairness and social justice for those with mental disorders. Advocacy on this issue led to passage of the Domenici-Wellstone Parity Amendment of 1996 (known as the "Mental Health Parity Act"). What is remarkable about this piece of legislation is that it was co-sponsored by a liberal Democrat (Paul Wellstone) and a conservative Republican (Pete Domenici). This represents a significant victory for mental health advocates in creating a bipartisan consensus on behalf of a mental health policy. Unfortunately, the Act expired in 2001. Some provisions were maintained through continuing resolution. The proposed successor legislation, the Paul Wellstone Mental Health Equitable Treatment Act, has not been passed.

As states try to avoid budget deficits, they are experimenting with financing strategies that may redesign mental health service delivery (Miller, 2005; Petrilla, 2001). Both managed care and privatization continue to be tools for controlling costs. Privatization increasingly includes for-profit providers in the service delivery mix. Mental health services traditionally provided by specialty community mental health agencies may move to Medicaid Health Maintenance Organizations (HMOs). Miller advises advocates to be involved in shaping and evaluating these new financing strategies and proposals for reorganizing services.

Barriers to Full Inclusion

Despite all the policy changes of the last 40 years, mental health professionals and advocates recognize significant shortcomings in service delivery and barriers to full inclusion for persons with mental disorders. Barriers remain in accessing known effective treatments, finding affordable housing, and obtaining gainful employment. In 1999, Surgeon General David Satcher issued a major report that highlighted how stigma remains a barrier to accessing treatment, despite the existence of scientifically tested treatments (U.S. Department of Health and Human Services [USDHHS], 1999). A subsequent report highlighted continuing disparities for racial and ethnic minorities in accessing needed mental health treatment (USDHHS, 2001). As mental hospital beds disappeared, jails and prisons became an alternative and these now house large numbers of persons with severe mental illness. Human Rights Watch (2003) and other advocacy groups have documented that correctional facilities use punitive rather than rehabilitative strategies. The enactment of the federal Mentally Ill Offender Treatment and Crime Reduction Act of 2004 was a beginning response to the needs of mentally ill persons in the justice system. It supports the use of mental health courts to divert persons from the justice system and the training of criminal justice system staff to better understand the needs of persons with mental illness.

Recent Developments

In April 2002, President George W. Bush appointed a commission (the New Freedom Commission) to address the problems in the country's mental health system. Bush's charge to the Commission built on the goals of his father's legislation, the Americans with Disabilities Act, and his own belief in the need to enable "freedom" for all persons with disabilities (the New Freedom Initiative announced in 2001). The Commission recommended "fundamentally transforming how mental health care is delivered in America." The Commission identified six intertwined goals as the basis for that transformation:

1. Americans understand that mental health care is essential to overall health.
2. Mental health care is consumer- and family-driven.
3. Disparities in mental health services should be eliminated.
4. Early mental health screening, assessment, and referral to services are common practice.

5. Excellent mental health care is delivered and research is accelerated.

6. Technology is used to access mental health care and information.

More than 2,500 people submitted comments to the Commission. They represented consumers, families, advocates, providers, educators, and researchers—reflecting a deep involvement in policymaking on the part of stakeholders.

FRAMEWORK

As just stated, our focus is on ensuring full human rights for persons with serious mental disorders and securing the resources needed to fulfill those rights. To achieve these social justice goals, we approach policy evaluation with two overarching principles: The policy must promote integration of persons with mental illness into the community and the policy must promote recovery. These principles are reflected in many of the recommendations made by the Bush Presidential Commission. The Surgeon General's Report makes it clear that for policies to be effective, they need to address the problems of stigma and barriers to accessing care. Policies should recognize key stakeholders—individuals who are ill as well as their families.

A framework for formulating and assessing mental health policies was developed by the World Health Organization (WHO) in their 2001 study of world mental health. Their framework is designed to be applied internationally and covers the range of issues from those based on social justice and human rights including rights to health, housing, and employment. The questions posed in the framework that are most relevant to the U.S. context follow:

- Does the policy promote the development of community-based care?
- Does the policy encourage partnerships between individuals, families, and health professionals?
- Does the policy create a system that respects, protects, and fulfills the human rights of people with mental disorders?
- Are evidence-based practices utilized wherever possible?
- Is there an adequate supply of appropriately trained service providers to ensure that the policy can be implemented?
- Are the special needs of women, children, and adolescents recognized?
- Is there parity between mental health services and other health services?
- Does the policy require the continuous monitoring and evaluation of services?
- Does the policy create a system that is responsive to the needs of underserved and vulnerable populations?
- Is adequate attention paid to strategies for prevention and promotion? (WHO, 2001, p. 80).

In addition, WHO considers the importance of the linkages of mental health and other service delivery systems, particularly primary health care.

The congruence of the WHO framework and the goals promulgated by the President's New Freedom Commission on Mental Health (2003) are clear. Both encourage consumer and family involvement and response to the underserved or those experience disparities in treatment, recognize the importance of research and evidence-based practices, and prevention through mechanisms such as early screening. Both the WHO questions and the Commission goals can be used as tools in assessing the value of proposed policies. The focus of the Commission on recovery also leads to a new view on monitoring client outcomes—symptom change and reduction in hospital use are no longer adequate outcome indicators. Indicators of recovery and inclusion such as education and employment must also be included.

Influencing Policy

As we have described, policy can be shaped through legislation, court decisions, finance mechanisms, and structuring of service delivery through administrative action and rules. Any citizens can be involved in influencing these policies. For example, the Commission recommended that consumers "play a significant role in shifting the current system to a recovery-oriented one by participating in planning, evaluation, research, training, and service delivery" (p. 10). Certainly mental health professionals can do the same.

Opportunities for participation are often facilitated through involvement in advocacy organizations such as the National Alliance for the Mentally Ill (NAMI) or through policy initiatives of professional organizations such as the American Psychological Association and the National Association of Social Workers. Given that policy actions occur at the federal, state, and local levels, opportunities for participation can be found at all levels. NAMI, for example, is not only a national organization, but has state and local chapters. Although NAMI is primarily an organization for families and consumers, professional involvement has always been welcome. Their Web site, www.nami.org, offers resources on policy and treatment issues. Many states and some counties have mental health planning boards and advisory committees with opportunities for citizen participation, if not as a member of the board, then as someone who attends meetings and provides input.

The group, Influencing State Policy, has developed a Web site with resources for tracking policy issues at the state level—www.statepolicy.org. This organization assists in providing resources for influencing policy formulation, implementation, and evaluation for social work educators and students. These resources are useful for anyone interested in mental health policy.

CRITICAL REFLECTIONS

We deliberately chose to focus on social justice for persons with severe and persistent mental illness because of the long history of stigmatization this group has experienced and because of the relative successes in policy reform of recent years. However, the focus on illness begs the question: What have we done to prevent mental health problems and promote wellness? Prevention was an important aspect of the Kennedy-era community mental health reforms, yet these reforms have received far less attention in public policy. An effective social justice approach would include prevention.

Prevention of mental health problems takes us into a highly contested terrain regarding the role of government in responding to social problems. For example, poverty is a risk factor for mental health problems. Women, especially poor mothers, have high rates of exposure to both community and interpersonal violence. They also have high rates of depression. One prevention strategy would be to reduce poverty. Conservatives and liberals in the United States have opposing views on how this should be achieved. The liberal approach that a safety net through public assistance is necessary has lost out in recent years to a conservative view that work is the answer. The consensus in the 1990s on how to reduce poverty was to minimize welfare and to promote work. This approach to poverty reduction has not had as many of the disastrous effects liberals predicted, but it also did not lift women and children out of poverty nor reduce the stressors that produce mental health problems. It also did not address the needs of individuals with persistent psychiatric disabilities who have limited capacity for work in competitive employment, or whose work histories may be frequently disrupted due to the episodic nature of their illness.

If we cannot reduce poverty, mental health professionals can advocate for access to treatment for depression and the allied problem of substance abuse for poor and working-class women who often have no health insurance. For many women, access to mental health treatment occurs through their health care providers. Providing better access to health care through more equitable funding mechanisms for health and mental health services is an important component of prevention. Similarly, improved access to quality child care, education, and the building of social capital for disadvantaged populations are examples of community-based approaches to prevention.

Violence and intolerance adversely impact mental health in tangible, concrete ways. For example, being the victim of racial slurs or homophobic attacks increases the risk of depression and suicide. Such attacks are particularly harmful when directed at adolescents. Should we seek a federal policy that reduces bullying as part of our mental health prevention efforts? Congressional support for such activities seems unlikely at this time. However, mental health professionals should ally themselves with parents and teachers to promote safety and respect in schools.

Improving the lives of the most seriously ill is a necessary part of social justice-oriented practice. Promoting policies that create "a system that respects, protects and fulfills the human rights of people with mental disorders" as the WHO framework recommends, demands action against conditions that undermine the worth of ill people as human beings. Advocating for policies that promote the well-being of all people and that reduce illness is a far greater challenge but one which we must confront.

REFERENCES

Americans With Disabilities Act of 1990, 42 U.S.C.A.§ 12101 *et seq.* (West 1993).
Community Mental Health Centers Act, PL 88-164, 164th Congress, 1st Session (1963).
Dorwart, R. A., & Epstein, S. (1993). *Privatization and mental health care: A fragile balance.* Westport, CT: Auburn House.
Fellin, P. (1996). *Mental health and mental illness: Policies, programs and services.* Itasca, IL: F. E. Peacock.
Grob, G. N. (1991). *From asylum to community: Mental health policy in modern America.* Princeton, NJ: Princeton University Press.
Grob, G. N. (1994). *The mad among us: A history of the care of America's mentally ill.* New York: The Free Press.
Human Rights Watch. (2003). Ill equipped: U.S. prisons and offenders with mental illness. Retrieved October 2003 from www.hrw.org/press/2003/10/us10203.htm
Lessard v. Schmidt, 349 F. Supp. 1078 (E.D. Wisc. 1972).

Mazade, N. A. (1996). State mental health agencies: Emerging fiscal and policy issues. *Administration and Policy in Mental Health, 23,* 275–277.

Mechanic, D. (1999). *Mental health and social policy: The emergence of managed care* (4th ed.). Boston: Allyn & Bacon.

Mental Health Parity Act of 1996 (Public Law 104-204).

Mentally Ill Offender Treatment and Crime Reduction Act of 2004 (PL 108-414).

Miller, J. E. (2005, Winter). A brave new world: The coming re-organization of state mental health services. *NAMI Advocate,* 10–11.

New Freedom Commission on Mental Health Care (NFC). (2003). *Achieving the promise: Transforming mental health care in America.* Final report, DHHS Pub. No. SMA-03-3832. Rockville, Md.

O'Connor v. Donaldson, 422 U.S. 563 (1975).

Olmstead v. L.C., 119 S.Ct. 2176 (1999).

Paul Wellstone Mental Health Equitable Treatment Act. (2003), S 486/ HR 953.

Petrilla, J. (2001). From constitution to contracts: Mental disability law at the turn of the century. In L. E. Frost & R. J. Bonnie (Eds.), *The evolution of mental health law* (pp. 75–100). Washington, DC: American Psychological Association.

Rochefort, D. A. (1997). *From poorhouses to homelessness: Policy analysis and mental health care* (2nd ed.). Westport, CT: Auburn House.

Sharfstein, S. S. (1993). Twenty years of mental health policy: Private opportunity and public neglect. *Administration and Policy in Mental Health, 21,* 113–116.

State Comprehensive Services Plan Act of 1986. PL99-660.

U.S. Department of Health and Human Services. (1999). *Mental health: A report of the Surgeon General.* Rockville, MD: U.S. Department of Health and Human Services, Substance Abuse and Mental Health Services Administration, Center for Mental Health Services, National Institute of Mental Health.

U.S. Department of Health and Human Services. (2001). *Mental health: Culture, race, ethnicity—A supplement to Mental health: A report of the Surgeon General.* Rockville, MD: U.S. Department of Health and Human Services, Substance Abuse and Mental Health Services Administration, Center for Mental Health Services.

World Health Organization. (2001). *The World Health Report 2001—Mental Health: New Understanding, New Hope.* Geneva, Switzerland: WHO.

Wyatt v. Stickney, 325 F. Supp. 781 (1971).

Youngberg v. Romeo, 457 U.S. 307 (1982).

TEACHING AND TRAINING
FOR SOCIAL ACTION

CHAPTER

17

Advocacy, Outreach, and Prevention: Integrating Social Action Roles in Professional Training

Elizabeth M. Vera
Suzette L. Speight
Loyola University, Chicago

Social justice and injustice have inextricable links to the mental health and well-being of individuals. Although mental health professionals are often called on to confront the aftermath of oppression and related injustices, it is debatable to what extent training programs have prepared their graduates to confront these issues in the most effective, proactive ways. In this chapter, a brief critique of traditional counselor training models and rationale for an expansion of our roles is provided. Then social action is defined and mental health interventions that advance social justice are described, namely the concepts of prevention, outreach, and advocacy. In the latter part of this chapter, suggestions related to training professionals to engage in such activities are discussed.

CRITIQUING THE STATUS QUO

Traditionally, counseling has primarily sought to change individuals to adapt to and cope with their environments, rather than change the social context and, in so doing, "join the forces that perpetuate social injustice" (Albee, 2000, p. 248). Counseling, by and large, is based on a remedial medical model of service delivery whereby a problem has developed and the counselor works to ameliorate the problem. Albee was highly critical of a reliance on such a model, stating that remedial models of treatment do not seek to end the social conditions that maintain social inequality such as poverty, discrimination, exploitation, and prejudices.

Bemak (1998) echoed such sentiments by claiming that contemporary counseling is markedly deficient in advocating to address the social, political, cultural, and economic problems faced by hundreds of millions of people. The field's predominant emphasis on working with individuals has, in effect, "neutralized social and political concerns, and as a consequence, preserved traditions of neutrality and dominant paradigms" (p. 280). This is not to say that counselors are trained to be oblivious of such systemic concerns, but the emphasis has been to help clients recognize the "causes" of their problems and help them learn to help themselves.

In fact, "improving society" through helping people empower themselves has been a major objective of the counseling profession (Lee, 1998). However, the origins of many mental health problems lie in toxic environmental conditions. This is particularly true for traditionally underserved populations, such as people of color, the poor, and residents of rural and urban communities. To what extent has the profession of counseling prioritized the task of intervening with the systemic factors that result in poor mental health outcomes? Although social action has had a fluctuating presence on the radar screen of our profession, and it is becoming a more frequent focus within the counseling literature, the extent to which the actions of counselors reflect a social action emphasis is fleeting.

Unfortunately, economic trends within the larger society serve to reinforce the pattern of remedial, individual-based service delivery within which the field operates. Systemically, remediation is reimbursed financially to the exclusion of a variety of proactive efforts. Insurance companies do not typically pay for preventative mental health services or client advocacy efforts. Even within the confines of our profession, remediation is the preferred mode of service delivery. Our attention to systemic forces has resulted in attempts to infuse multiculturalism into the curricula of training programs by teaching students to be culturally sensitive in therapeutic and testing contexts (Vera & Speight, 2003).

One could argue that the narrowness of our self-defined roles has constrained mental health professionals from considering proactive, system-focused intervention. There may be a belief that being active in the community or becoming familiar with community resources was somehow outside the realm of the counselor's professional responsibility. Counselors and psychologists are assumed to be therapists whereas other types of professionals (e.g., case managers) are assumed to be responsible for any advocacy, community-level intervention, or accessing community resources for clients. A commitment to social justice requires a redefinition of our roles to include advocacy and other forms of social action-oriented intervention (Vera & Speight, 2003).

Lewis and Arnold (1998) state that "social action on behalf of our multicultural populations should include (a) addressing the inadvertent tendency of the counseling profession to collude with oppression, (b) supporting community empowerment efforts, (c) engaging in political advocacy, and (d) emphasizing the social action agenda of our professional association (p. 54). Yet, clearly such a shift in focus requires a critical examination of the field itself (Brown, 1997).

There are many reasons that the profession has difficulty "looking within." Fox (2003), echoing the criticisms of many psychologists within the "critical psychology" movement, states that mainstream training of mental health professionals often involves a socialization process where learning to work within institutions such as hospitals and schools results in acquiescing to bureaucracies that constrain concerns for justice. Thus, despite the best intentions, practitioners end up reinforcing oppression by being inside the system, unable to see the system's weakness, and therefore are unable to critique the system.

Furthermore, Fox (1993, 2003), among others, believes that our current professional norms were established by practitioners whose race, gender, and class "blinded them to alternatives" (p. 300). Professional critical examination is risky (Prilleltensky & Prilleltensky, 2003) because those who hold the power within the profession feel threatened by such a process. So given the "uphill battle" nature of engaging in professional criticism, at what point do we as professionals take such risks? As graduate students? As untenured professors? Is risking one's success in academia or being accepted by the profession a risk worth taking? Many professionals walk a tightrope where politics are kept private, secluded to our personal activities, and "toeing the line" professionally is perceived as key to keeping our jobs. Only by legitimizing the work of social action as a profession will activism and commitment to social justice become legitimately realized, and no longer viewed as a risky position.

Interventions

If social action is becoming a desirable professional value, when and where do we prepare the professionals of tomorrow to have the skills and attitudes necessary to be active social change agents in their professional work and in their personal lives? There has been a lot of energy put into infusing multiculturalism into our training curricula but perhaps less energy directed at changing what we actually do as mental health professionals (Vera & Speight, 2003). Specifically, the majority of experiential training that students are exposed to continues to be within traditional therapeutic contexts. Professionals in training may learn to conduct therapy or testing with more diverse populations, or adjust their conceptualization strategies to take into account oppression. However, students are infrequently given opportunities to engage in activism, advocacy, or prevention in underserved communities (i.e., outreach efforts).

For example, many programs train their students in on-campus clinics. Many off-campus training sites use students to generate billable hours for their agency. Advocacy, activism, and outreach are often viewed as supplemental experiences when they are available at all. The likelihood of students having supervisors who are experienced in these areas is low. Furthermore, the competitiveness of internship currently forces students to acquire as many testing and therapy hours as they can, leaving little or no time for "alternative" intervention activities.

Clearly, the current model in which we train counseling professionals must change in order for the next generation to reinvent their roles. Social action and social justice agendas will only be advanced by such a redefinition of roles. Fortunately, several scholars have already developed models of service delivery that are instructive for expanding professional roles in the service of oppressed communities (Atkinson, Thompson, & Grant, 1993; Lewis, Lewis, Daniels, & D'Andrea, 1998).

Atkinson et al. (1993) presented a model for a professional integration of roles including outreach work, consultation, facilitation of self-help or indigenous support, and community advocacy as viable alternatives to psychotherapy. Several factors are considered in determining which professional role or activity is most appropriate to the needs of the client: locus of problem etiology, level of client acculturation, and goals of the intervention. A consideration of these three factors determines in what capacity a counselor can best respond to a client. In essence, the planes and intersections of the three dimensions create eight major roles for counselors working with culturally diverse clients: advisor, advocate, self-help group facilitator, facilitator of indigenous support and healing systems, consultant, change agent, counselor, and psychotherapist.

Another model that addresses the importance of role flexibility and issues of social justice was articulated by Lewis et al. (1998). They emphasized many of the direct client service roles outlined in Atkinson et al.'s model (e.g., counseling, outreach) and described indirect client service roles such as consulting and working to influence public policy. Lewis et al. (1998) identified other roles that are targeted at the community, in general, rather than at a particular client. These roles would include advocate, psychoeducator, or collaborator with community leaders (e.g., ministers, folk-healers). The needs of the client determine which services are utilized and, consequently, which roles would be most beneficial.

Social workers have also been trained historically with models that emphasize the importance of community-based work and services other than psychotherapy to enhance clients' quality of life (Mather & Lager, 2000). For example, social work models of service delivery typically emphasize supportive interventions such as respite care, homemaker services, mutual aid groups (self-help), and other wraparound services. Many other scholars have asserted the need for macrolevel interventions, especially in working with women and people of color (Apfelbaum, 1999; D'Andrea & Daniels, 2000; Helms & Cook, 1999; Rawlings & Carter, 1977; Thompson & Neville, 1999; Walters, Carter, Papp, & Silverstein, 1988), that warrants a commitment to social interventions. Parham and McDavis (1987) emphasized the importance of counselors both working to help individuals become empowered to change their behaviors and relationships *and* becoming environmental change agents. Toporek and Reza (2001) argued that advocacy and policymaking roles are critical to multicultural competence. Hence, there is growing support for a refocusing of the scope of professional practice in counseling and psychology.

In order to encourage the infusion of these alternate roles into the training of future counseling professionals, the next section of this chapter outlines the importance of advocacy, outreach, and prevention as being critical components of a social action agenda for counseling professionals.

ADVOCACY

Advocacy has been a recurring theme in the counseling profession's search for an identity. Gottlieb (1975) urged practitioners to play an active role in advancing the rights of their clients when he proposed the addition of an "advocate professional" model to supplement the traditional scientist-professional model. Advocacy has traditionally been defined as the act of speaking up for people whose rights may be in jeopardy (Lewis et al., 1998). Advocacy is one component of social action, involving the process of arguing or pleading a cause or a proposal (Brown, 1988; Lee, 1998). Advocacy activities range from those as simple as making a phone call on someone's behalf to taking legal steps to ensure that a client's rights are not being violated (MacCluskie & Ingersoll, 2001).

Counselors who serve as advocates are willing to challenge (and help their clients to do so) institutional barriers or policies that inhibit quality of life. Advocacy can take three forms: helping clients to advocate for themselves (i.e., empowerment), advocating directly with institutions or policymakers, or advocating indirectly through training or educating professionals who work with underserved populations. Although most counselors feel comfortable working in partnership with their clients, directly confronting institutions or policymakers can be personally and professionally "new ground." Grieger and Ponterotto (1998) stated,

Advocacy and activism challenge us to take a moral and ethical stand with regard to the touchiest issues within our organizations, to publicly articulate our stand, and to risk the displeasure, if not the wrath, of those who hold power and authority. It may mean being unpopular, becoming a lightning rod for the anger and resistance of colleagues, and at times, it may mean being willing to put our jobs on the line in order to do the right thing. (p. 31)

As an example, imagine a client who presents with symptoms of anxiety exacerbated by chronic fears about the safety of his or her children in a neighborhood plagued by community violence. Although traditional treatment options would likely focus on (a) symptom reduction and/or (b) exploring ways the client could relocate to a safer community, a counselor could also encourage a client to participate with other parents in acts aimed at changing public policy (e.g., an organized march against gangs in the neighborhood, participating in meetings with police and other public officials). Furthermore, a counselor functioning in an advocate role could take on the responsibility of organizing such events that would benefit the community as a whole and ultimately enhance the psychological well-being of its members. Although some might argue that the latter activities goes above and beyond the expectations of our roles, and others may believe that they border on "forcing an agenda" on clients, it is equally arguable that such policy and environment-based interventions more adequately address the systemic roots of the problem.

There are instances in which a counselor may have to take a more direct role in advocating when a client lacks the skills to advocate for him or herself and the urgency of the situation requires immediate action. It could be that a client is being ignored or mistreated by a case worker, or is intimidated by some formal process such as a multidisciplinary staffing in a school system. Some members of racial and ethnic groups, especially those who have recently immigrated to the United States, may lack the English-speaking skills, knowledge of health systems, and economic resources to confront barriers raised by social service agencies, legal institutions, school systems, and/or employment agencies (Atkinson et al., 1993). In cases where systemic barriers contribute to mental health problems, it may be appropriate for mental health professionals to intervene because of their professional status in society, and their familiarity with the laws and regulations of this country.

There are some who caution against the use of counselor-led advocacy efforts for fear that such interventions actually prevent clients from feeling empowered (because counselors are doing what clients should be learning to do for themselves). Additionally, there is a concern that advocacy work can overemphasize the importance of external factors in clients' lives. For example, Parham and McDavis (1987) pointed out that by focusing on external factors alone, we suggest that clients lack the mental fortitude to deal effectively with adverse conditions in society. An alternative position, however, is that advocacy can be an important additional tool that can help in minimizing external stressors that affect marginalized clients. In fact, the goal of advocacy is ultimately self-empowerment of the client. Thus, if a counselor attends a school hearing or legal procedure with a client who feels intimidated by the system, the counselor can help to make sure that the client understands what decisions are being made and also can help the client protect his or her rights during the proceedings. Whether the counselor directly participates in the procedure or encourages the client to intervene on his or her own behalf, the counselor's actions model the assertiveness skills the client may be working on developing.

In some cases, neither the counselor nor the client may be qualified or feel able to advocate in a particular situation. This is where knowledge of community resources can be an important component of advocacy work. Counselors can help clients access existing grassroots networks that engage in citizen-based advocacy work (e.g., legal defense funds, community centers; Lewis et al., 1998). These groups are often composed of citizens working to improve the lives of other citizens who are unable to perform activities critical to daily living (Wolfensberger & Zauha, 1973). Clients may not be aware of the advocacy groups that exist in their communities, which is why counselors need to be knowledgeable about the broad range of social services that are available in the community.

Finally, counselors must not underestimate the impact of advocacy in the form of training other professionals. The Virginia Youth Violence Project is an excellent example of how interdisciplinary advocacy with other professionals can have a significant impact on the crucial issue of youth violence in American schools and communities. The goal of this study was to maximize the impact of educators and human service professionals to disseminate antiviolence programs to youth in the community. Violence prevention training programs and courses were delivered to educators and human services professionals working with aggressive and at-risk youths, in order to provide participants with the knowledge and skills to develop violence reduction programs in the community. The program's success was evaluated by tracking the follow-up activities of the participants regarding the development and implementation of violence reduction projects. More than 60 school or community-based violence reduction programs were identified that involved more than 8,700 youth participants throughout the state of Virginia (Sheras, Cornell, & Bostain, 1996). This study demonstrated the breadth of impact that is possible when psychologists work to train community members and advocate for racial and ethnic communities that are disproportionately affected by social problems such as violence. This example illustrates the "larger net" that advocacy can cast in that it reaches more individuals than would traditional counseling efforts.

OUTREACH

Outreach can be broadly defined as a large-scale, direct-service approach to psychological service provision that takes place in the context of a community, designed to address an existing or anticipated obstacle to psychological growth and well-being (Lewis et al., 1998). As the word implies, outreach work requires professionals to leave the office, hospital, or agency environment and make contacts with clients in their natural environment (Gottheil, Sterling, & Weinstein, 1997). The kinds of contacts made via outreach can vary. In some cases, they may involve developing traditional counseling relationships. Home-based therapy is one example of outreach utilized when transportation or session attendance may be problematic. Aside from being more convenient for clients, home-based therapy can be useful when the counselor wants to observe how clients interact in their home setting. However, home-based therapy is often initiated after a client has been referred to a counseling agency. In many cases, clients never find their way to a counselor's office even if the need for counseling exists. This can happen for a variety of reasons both cultural and pragmatic.

For example, in some racial and ethnic communities, the stigma of seeking therapy is perceived as an admission of "weakness" or a violation of cultural norms regarding seeking help from "outsiders." Problems may be addressed more informally (e.g., within the family, through prayer) or by seeking advice from culturally sanctioned individuals (e.g., talking with a minister, elder, or folk-healer; Broman, 1987; Taylor, Hardison, & Chatters, 1996). Another reason such clients may not patronize counseling agencies, particularly recent immigrants, may be a lack of awareness of available services or distrust of the community mental health center, hospital, or university. In some cases, counseling agencies may not be accessible to clients. Inaccessibility may be geographic, as is the case in many impoverished neighborhoods where basic health care services are not present. Inaccessibility may also be due to institutional barriers such as the cost of sessions or a lack of evening appointments. Counseling services may not be culturally "user-friendly," especially to racial and ethnic groups for whom English is a second language (or English is not spoken).

Engaging in outreach efforts, however, is not primarily about "breaking down barriers" so that historically underserved clients will learn to seek out the services of professional counselors. Rather, it involves collaborating in partnerships with existing community organizations to bring services to where the people are. This is easier said than done. In fact, outreach efforts are far from random and will be largely unsuccessful if done without the involvement of the community members from the inception of the idea.

In order to successfully reach out to underserved communities, three essential steps must be followed: relationship building, collaborative efforts, and needs assessment (Lerner, 1995). Although building relationships is the starting point for any counseling work, the relationships made through outreach often are established via collaboration and needs assessment. The three components of outreach work are equally important to the design of an intervention, its implementation, and evaluation. When professionals initially attempt to offer services (e.g., a parenting workshop, facilitation of support groups), it is critical to affiliate with a trusted member (e.g., a minister, school principal, or community activist) or credible establishment in the community (e.g., a church, school, community recreation center). As outsiders, we often have to work very hard to establish our credibility in the community in ways that differ from traditional counseling work. Credibility is based on trust, which is developed over time.

Members of the majority culture are typically strangers to non-White communities. It is naive to expect strangers to be greeted with open arms. Underserved racial and ethnic groups have historically been used and abused by outside researchers and/or professionals, often in the name of scientific progress (i.e., data harvesting) that fails to benefit the community (Reiss & Price, 1996). Building a trusting relationship typically means that counselors have to rely on personal integrity, not professional training and credentials, as proof of trustworthiness. Ongoing commitment and permanence in the community cannot be undervalued (Lerner, 1995). Ongoing collaboration means that as professionals, we avoid "one-shot" interventions in favor of establishing a long-term presence in which we exhibit the flexibility to accommodate the changing needs of the community, even when they fall outside the original design of the intervention.

Although conversation and collaboration are the processes through which we establish relationships and assess needs, we must be able to modify our ideas to fit the realities of the community. Our perspective as professionals may often illuminate some sense of what may be beneficial to a particular community. However, it is essential that our own ideas, hypotheses, or prejudices do not cloud important community goals. In an ideal collaborative relationship, both parties bring valuable expertise to the table.

Lerner (1995) also advocated that developing appropriate outreach initiatives is enhanced by thinking contextually about the causes and solutions to community problems, including as many community voices as possible, and incorporating evaluation as an ongoing part of any intervention. Through collaborative processes of information gathering, program development, and continual feedback, the likelihood that outreach programs are supported by the community will be increased. Paying insufficient attention to collaboration would result in decreased relevance and success of outreach work (Reiss & Price, 1996). Now that the general principles of outreach work have been presented, consider the following example of engaging in outreach. A local university would like to collaborate with a neighborhood middle school (fifth through eighth grades) in designing interventions to enhance the personal and academic functioning of the pupils. The school has a primarily Latino population and there has been a long-standing problem of too many eighth graders failing to successfully transition to high school. The ties with the administrators were established through the primary investigator's previous volunteer work in the school. Given the successful establishment of preliminary ties with the school administration, identifying the key groups likely to be interested in or affected by the program (stakeholders) would be the first step. In this example, students, their parents, and teachers would be included. In order to assess the needs of the community accurately and to establish a collaborative connection, we would conduct focus groups with stakeholders from each of the identified strata. The focus groups would be aimed at identifying circumstances that disrupt transitions to high school and resources that facilitate academic persistence. Questions about hopes, worries, problems, or concerns would generally encourage discussion of both positive and negative school transition issues with school-age children, their parents, and teachers.

Data gathered from the focus groups would be summarized, then presented back to the community to ensure the validity of the process and clarify any miscommunications. If the stakeholders agree with the accuracy of the needs assessment, we can begin designing interventions collaboratively (e.g., asking students what type of activities they enjoy, asking parents and teachers for feedback about content) and tailoring our methods to the racial, cultural, and sociopolitical context of the community. The particular characteristics of the community (racial and ethnic composition, primary language, location, available resources, etc.), as well as general developmental considerations, would guide the choice of materials and activities. The more accurately the outreach program represents the members of the community, the more successful the program will be.

We would also establish methods of evaluation that are meaningful to the community (both short-term and long-term) that would allow us to determine whether the program has made a difference. Long-term goals might be an increase in the percentages of students graduating high school. Short-term goals might be to improve attitudes toward school, to improve parent–teacher communication, and to increase the number of school services (e.g., bilingual tutors, after-school homework clubs) that help youth who exhibit early signs of trouble.

Illustrations of the obstacles encountered in engaging in outreach work in this example can come in the form of constituent needs requiring changes in program content or process. For instance, often during the course of an outreach program, an event in the school or community will occur during the course of the intervention, and the program counselors may be asked to help the participants by interrupting the curriculum and offering crisis management. Other obstacles can be logistical. For example, there may be no uninterrupted periods of time in which to offer the interventions due to other obligations such as state-mandated testing periods, or special events (e.g., graduation practices, eighth grade picture day, etc.). In such situations, although program fidelity might make for better science (i.e., not modifying the proposed curriculum, having regular program intervals), accommodations would need to be made in the interest of maintaining positive, long-term ties with the constituent groups.

It is clear that many populations, but underserved communities in particular, would benefit from professionals who are actively designing and implementing outreach programs. For example, people of color face unique challenges living in the midst of racism and other forms of oppression (Black & Krishnakumar,1998; Fouad & Brown, 2000). In the aforementioned example, students may be in greater need of a drop-out prevention outreach program because racism and classism has contributed to poorer quality public schools or a perception that people of color do not benefit from formal education in the same way that majority individuals do (i.e., receiving high-paying jobs, occupational advancement opportunities). In general, oppression such as racism, sexism, and classism leads to health disparities and overexposure to stressors that compromise the well-being of ethnic and racial people in the United States. Systemic oppression contributes both directly and indirectly to the underutilization of psychological services in such communities. Outreach efforts can be one way in which we actively eliminate barriers that have excluded people of color from benefiting from the services of mental health professionals. When we are successful at "casting a larger net" into the community, counseling professionals extend a hand to clients who may not typically seek out our services.

PREVENTION

The theme of prevention is a natural extension of the topics addressed throughout this chapter because it is closely linked to the goals of advocacy and the philosophy of outreach efforts. As has been previously stated, relying on traditional remedial approaches to counseling does nothing to prevent the emergence of new mental health problems (Albee, 2000). Although prevention approaches are advantageous to all people, they are particularly pertinent to populations where mental health disparities exist. Problems such as drug abuse, violence, school drop-out, and unemployment are overrepresented in communities of color and/or the poor. The reasons for this are multiple, but are undoubtedly tied to the stressors associated with experiencing racism and oppression.

Even though prevention may be justified by a social justice commitment, it is also financially a sensible role for mental health professionals. It is much more economical and less time consuming to provide programs to youth that attempt to prevent drug use and possible addiction, for example, than it is to provide individual rehabilitation services once addiction has occurred (Lewis et al., 1998). Preventing particular disorders before they occur also leads to a decrease in associated problems. For instance, drug addiction can lead to theft, child abuse and neglect, family difficulties, and homelessness. So, prevention interventions not only decrease the identified problem within the community, but may also eliminate the development of related difficulties that occur as a result of their initial problem. Two recent meta-analyses (Tobler, 2000; Wilson, Gottfredson, & Najaka, 2001) provide strong evidence to support the effectiveness of school-based prevention programs in reducing or preventing crime, substance use, dropout/nonattendance, and other conduct problems among adolescent youth. Indeed, prevention has been a historical emphasis of the mental health field (Romano & Hage, 2000) and there have been recent calls to renew our commitment to prevention activities (Vera, 2000). Although medical science has arguably put more of its "money where its mouth is" on prevention issues, not enough attention has been given to research and practice that exemplifies health promotion and optimal life fulfillment. There has been some debate as to what types of activities actually constitute prevention (Vera & Reese, 2000).

Prevention is traditionally dissected into three levels: primary, secondary, and tertiary (Munoz, Mrazek, & Haggerty, 1996). The popularity of the three levels of prevention is represented in their descending order. For example, most counselors are very familiar and comfortable with tertiary prevention. Interventions at the tertiary level involve reducing the incidence of problems and/or eliminating further distress for those individuals and groups who have already experienced dysfunction (e.g., working with battered women to create safe environments and to protect themselves). Psychotherapy is oftentimes synonymous with tertiary prevention.

The second-most popular approach to prevention is secondary interventions. Secondary prevention strategies are centered on populations who are "at risk" for the development of future problems but who have not yet shown signs of impairment. The purpose of such programs is to detect possible problem areas early on and to impede their progress. As one might imagine, such programs can be controversial because they often rely on epidemiological research that focuses on risk factors for particular disorders and not the environmental conditions that might elicit a mental health problem. However, they are utilized because there are data for many problems that demonstrate predictive power (e.g., children of drug addicts are more likely to have their own drug problems or find partners with addictions).

The least common approach to prevention interventions is primary prevention. Primary prevention programs are geared toward groups who have never been affected by a particular problem. The focus here is on promoting competence and resilience in order to prevent dysfunction and foster continued positive development (Black & Krishnakumar, 1998; Vera & Reese, 2000). Primary prevention can be more difficult to justify because the populations with which we work are asymptomatic. Although, in general, there may be support for programs that bolster mental health and adaptive functioning, proving that such programs work or are cost-effective is difficult and often entails longitudinal designs. Instead of relying on evidence that would show an intervention prevented future problems, it may be more feasible to show an increase in skills (e.g., communication skills) or beliefs (e.g., self-efficacy) that are known to be related to positive developmental outcomes (Vera & Reese, 2000).

Positive development involves highlighting preexisting skills and talents and increasing competence. It uses a strengths-building perspective to cultivate protective factors (i.e., factors which reduce "risk") and positive aspects of an individual, group, or community. For example, teaching communication skills to youth and families equips them with alternatives for interpersonal interaction that may not only result in better relationships but prevent the need to rely on aggression and violence in times of conflict. In many cases, the etiology of problem behavior and poor decision-making skills (e.g., premature sexual involvement, drug experimentation) is not uniquely attributable to environmental stress, family dysfunction, or intrapersonal disturbance. But, the combination of these factors can result in suboptimal developmental life paths (Larson, 2000). Prevention efforts that focus on skill building, goal direction, and internal motivation help to prepare individuals to become more productive and conscientious adults, regardless of what risk factors may exist in their environment.

One of the major advantages of prevention interventions is the ease with which they can integrated into existing service delivery models. For example, a client may be referred for traditional remedial counseling services due to drug or alcohol addiction. Therapy for this individual would perhaps involve keeping the client sober, examining issues or stressors that may have contributed to the use of drugs, and also preventing relapses (i.e., tertiary prevention). Additionally, the counselor may bring the client's children into sessions so that information and refusal skills involving drugs and alcohol can be presented because children of chemically dependent parents are at higher risk for having substance abuse problems themselves (i.e., secondary prevention). Although primary prevention may be more difficult to fit into this model, it might be possible for one's agency or hospital to sponsor a mental health fair in the community where substance abuse prevention materials or lectures might be given at churches, community centers, or schools.

A common way in which primary preventive interventions are delivered is through group-based programs located in schools, clinics, or community recreation centers. A therapist may choose to engage in primary prevention through an affiliation and collaborative relationship with other community organizations. For example, developing and implementing a study skills program to reduce the risk of dropout for first-generation college students would be a primary prevention approach. Delivering a violence reduction program in an elementary school setting would be another example. Sometimes local agencies/organizations may wish to contract with counselors to deliver psychoeducational intervention services. Other times, counselors may engage in these activities as part of our regular jobs (e.g., in K–12 schools, college counseling centers, or community mental health clinics). In either case, counselors can commit time and energy to larger scale interventions that attempt to build on existing strengths and maximize clients' potential. Rather than wait for these stressors to take their toll on a person or persons, one can try to work in ways that help people to avoid these difficulties.

Proactive intervention is not a novel concept within the profession of counseling or psychology. However, job analysis studies have found that prevention is much less likely to be the focus of our work than is remediation (Fitzgerald & Osipow, 1986). Integrating prevention efforts in therapy may not be the only way psychologists and counselors can engage in proactive efforts on behalf of client populations. Although many prevention programs rely on direct interventions with client populations, there are also indirect approaches to prevention that attack problems at their environmental core. These latter approaches in many cases resemble advocacy efforts. For example, environment-centered prevention approaches attempt to change important contexts of the client's life such as family, peer groups, or community. For example, some professionals who engage in alcohol and drug prevention work advocate involving individuals in activities that seek to modify community norms regarding substance use.

Examples include designing media campaigns or advocating for the availability of recreational options for youth that do not involve drugs (e.g., midnight basketball leagues, alcohol-free dance parties on weekend evenings). Oftentimes, these more systemically based, environment-centered primary prevention programs allow therapists to intervene in community contexts that may be involved in exacerbating or perpetuating problems. Systemic-based intervention is critical because systemic problems such as poverty, inadequate housing, and discrimination cannot be prevented with crisis-oriented, client-directed programs (McWhirter, McWhirter, McWhirter, & McWhirter, 1998). Whether we use preventive approaches to supplement the work we do within the context of counseling or we create new contexts of service delivery with marginalized communities of color (e.g., through outreach), the long-term benefits of prevention work should not be underestimated.

TRAINING FOR SOCIAL ACTION ROLES

Now that a more detailed picture of advocacy, outreach, and prevention roles has been presented as a component of a social justice agenda, we turn our attention to their integration into the professional identity of counselors. Can one be taught to value social justice through appropriate professional training activities or must one possess a disposition toward social justice that drives one's professional endeavors? Prilleltensky and Nelson (2002) discuss how social justice can be infused into a psychology training curriculum (and we will come back to this point momentarily), but far less literature addresses the process of adopting a social justice-promoting value system.

D'Andrea and Daniels (2000) described various dispositions that White psychologists, trainees, and other professionals possessed regarding their understanding of racism (a form of social injustice). Most of their research participants were found to possess a "liberal disposition" characterized by an openness to talking about racism but an overall sense of apathy about it (i.e., an absence of anger, urgency, or expressed concern). A lack of antiracist action was associated with this disposition. In contrast, research participants who had a principled activist disposition (less than 1% of the sample) demonstrated a more abstract and systematic understanding of cycles of oppression and the various individual, institutional, and cultural changes needed to eradicate racism. These individuals were characterized as social/political activists who consciously worked to empower marginalized populations. Unfortunately, these same individuals reported a general lack of support for their efforts by their colleagues, administrators, and the profession in general. Based on these findings, it is clear that a great deal of work remains in order to socialize the next generation of counseling psychologists to ground their work in social justice.

Other scholars have discussed the components of teaching students to embrace a commitment to social justice in their future professional work (Buckley, 1998). Buckley maintained that education infused with social justice and humanitarianism should produce a student who is characterized by three qualities. The first quality is an affective dimension of social justice; the student should have a sensitivity to injustice and innocent suffering in the world. Typically, exposure to injustice and its examination is what yields this sensitivity. This awareness, however, is not sufficient to ensuring the transformation process. Many students are aware of injustice and only pity those who suffer as a result.

The second quality is an intellectual dimension of justice; the student should know the causes/conditions that result and perpetuate human suffering (i.e., understanding theories of oppression and liberation). The development and application of critical thinking skills and critical consciousness (cf. Freire, 1994) is often a critical component of this second step in training students to become social justice advocates. Critical thinking is essential in analyzing the social conditions and policies that maintain injustices and circumscribe the lives of oppressed people. Critical consciousness is important in the development of self-awareness for mental health professionals who must learn to be aware of their own social statuses, privileges, and cultural identities. This process of critical self-examination, when combined with an examination of social conditions and policies, ultimately leads to a personal and professional commitment to social change. This understanding is critical to motivating the student to engage in work that tries to change these conditions (discussed in further detail by Goodman, 2001). However, a student's motivation to act must be shaped by a civic view of service that emphasizes mutual responsibility as a component of a democracy in contrast with a philanthropic view of service that emphasizes altruism and charity for the "less advantaged" (Barber & Battistoni, 1993). If the community is viewed "as a common group to which we all belong, not as a group outside the university," then a civic mindset is created (Kenny & Gallagher, 2000, p. 195).

The third quality is the pragmatic or volitional dimension of justice; the student must learn tools and skills that will allow him or her to effectively intervene, and in doing so, contribute to a vision of social justice. This last component is important to address because often students who engage in working with underserved communities, via practicum or research endeavors, can leave the experience feeling disillusioned, burned out, or overwhelmed by the enormity of problems that exist in their clients. However, one could argue that this is a result of being trained to rely on individual-level interventions such as therapy as the primary tool of change. Even when therapy is effective, its power is limited by the necessity of helping people one at a time. If students were taught to think more broadly about their potential roles as professionals, they would be in a better position to intervene at multiple levels for clients and communities.

One way to encourage such a broadening is to offer courses that have a direct focus on skill building in alternative roles (e.g., courses in outreach, activism, consultation) or by infusing into existing coursework service-based learning experiences that rely on alternative roles. Service-learning is intended to increase empathy, reduce stereotypes, and contribute to more complex views of social problems and solutions (Wutzdoff & Giles, 1997). For example, a career development class might provide students with an opportunity to go into community colleges, local high schools, or unemployment offices and deliver programs aimed at developing career decision-making skills and opportunities. A research methods class might allow students to access archival data and then develop papers with clear policy implications that demonstrate interpretation skills and application of information to real problems. Human diversity classes might study theories of oppression but also have students engage in a service-based volunteer experience (e.g., tutoring, working in a homeless shelter) that would allow them to not only participate in grass-roots programs but also would give them some experience learning the administrative and political aspects of such programs. Kenny and Gallagher (2000) provide a detailed discussion about the advantages and practical considerations of service learning projects.

ROADBLOCKS TO THE INTEGRATION
OF SOCIAL ACTION ROLES

Service-learning and other community-immersion opportunities can be the training grounds used to integrate advocacy, outreach, and prevention into the emerging identities of our counseling students. However, implicit in this discussion is the assumption that training programs will take the lead in creating such opportunities.

Academic training programs are in the most powerful positions to set the stage for the next generation of mental health practitioners to have identities as social justice advocates. Lerner (2000) discusses the process of transforming universities to foster and sustain outreach scholarship. "Outreach involves using university scholarly expertise for the benefit of the audiences and stakeholders external to the university" (p. 41). Thus, outreach scholarship involves universities collaborating with community partners to identify and attain meaningful goals such as conducting needs assessments, participatory action research, program design and evaluation, grant writing, or offering psychoeducational programs to community members. The outcomes of these efforts must be mutually beneficial. This may mean that the information gathered from a needs assessment is disseminated in ways that are accessible to the community (e.g., newsletters, local publications), then used to develop programs, in addition to being used to generate publications in more traditional academic outlets (i.e., journals; Lerner, 2000).

One major challenge involved in conducting outreach scholarship are the values of the training institution. Traditionally, "there were few if any rewards within this culture to stimulate leaders of higher education institutions to open the doors of their institutions to the voice and values of the community" (Lerner, 2000, p. 47). In other words, neither altruism nor time-intensive community projects have been valued as the bases of research agendas. Lerner argues that a zeitgeist may be emerging to support universities' engagement in socially meaningful contributions.

Going back to the issue of values, one must consider the academic reward structure currently in place. If the value of the university is to promote independent scholarship, then collaboration might not be encouraged (Lerner, 2000). However, within the fields of education and psychology, collaborative research is often the norm, which may put training programs in these areas in a more advantageous position to engage in outreach scholarship. Half the battle may be convincing our own institutions to support outreach scholarship efforts, but the other half is convincing the community members that our interests are legitimate and our investment will be nonexploitive.

Oftentimes, as professionals, we are not warmly welcomed into "real-world" (i.e., outside the ivory tower) communities. There are good reasons for this. First of all, there are many examples of communities being taken advantage of by so-called "data raiders," those academics who collected data from community members and gave nothing in return (Fairfax, 2000). Oftentimes such researchers gain access to the community under false pretenses, saying that they are there to address a community issue, claiming that data gathering will be part of an ongoing process that will cumulate in some type of intervention. However, once the data have been obtained, the intervention never happens, or happens in a way that it much less rigorous than was true of the data collection. How do we confront these issues and make ourselves trustworthy to skeptical community members?

Trustworthiness must be earned, not blindly given, so that leaves the onus of earning trust to the university partners. Often because expectations have been raised and dashed, over and over, universities can leave communities in worse shape than before they arrived (Lerner, 2000). As is true of our relationships with clients in traditional counseling contexts, trust takes time, patience, and commitment. In reality, this can mean that the first stage of relationship building with the community is characterized by "proving ourselves" over time through volunteering to do whatever may be needed (e.g., accompanying children on field trips, attending school-sponsored events). Only after initial trust is established can more elaborate program development be approached.

Collaborative partnerships with community groups can provide training programs with opportunities to engage in socially meaningful social action training efforts while providing the community with a valuable resource. As dependable partners, universities can offer a variety of services that address a host of community needs. Community members can teach our students about the realities of systemic influences on mental health problems. Their strengths can provide our students with ideas for promoting healthy development and designing prevention approaches. In other words, immersion in the real world via service learning or outreach scholarship programs may be the most desirable vehicles for training counseling professionals to expand the scope of their roles and effectively engage in social action.

CONCLUSION

Although we have only highlighted the ways in which our work as counselors can be enhanced by integrating approaches such as outreach, advocacy, and prevention, the most important point to be made is this: a social justice agenda, as defined by social action on the part of counselors, requires us to think "outside the box" and learn to behave professionally in innovative, socially responsible ways. Although advocacy, outreach, and prevention approaches might not yet be emphasized in traditional counseling training programs, they all are consistent with the overarching goals of the field of counseling that should legitimize their place in our professional lives.

A social justice agenda acknowledges an awareness of how oppression operates in our society. Among other serious problems, oppression results in overexposure to negative life stressors, a lack of access to basic physical and mental health services, and the overrepresentation of particular mental health problems within African American, Latino, Asian American, and Native American communities. Because our clients are forced to live with additional systemic burdens, counseling professionals must be prepared to use additional strategies on their behalf. Advocacy gives us an avenue in which to fight against policies and practices that impede quality-of-life issues. Engaging in outreach allows us to help greater numbers of individuals in need, especially those who may not seek out services independently. Prevention allows us to actively work to minimize the emergence of future problems. In combination with counseling and therapy, these activities add to the arsenal of skills we have. By having as many tools as possible, we are in a more advantageous position to improve the mental health of our clients and the quality of life in our communities.

REFERENCES

Albee, G. W. (2000). Commentary on prevention and counseling psychology. *The Counseling Psychologist, 28,* 845–853.

Apfelbaum, E. (1999). Relations of domination and movements for liberation: An analysis of power between groups. *Feminism and Psychology, 9,* 267–272.

Atkinson, D. R., Thompson, C. E., & Grant, S. K. (1993). A three-dimensional model for counseling racial-ethnic minorities. *The Counseling Psychologist, 21,* 257–277.

Barber, B. R., & Battistoni, R. (1993). A season of service: Introducing service learning into the liberal arts curriculum. *PS: Political Science, 26,* 235–262.

Bemak, F. (1998). Interdisciplinary collaboration for social change: Redefining the counseling profession. In F. T. Sherman & W. R. Torbert (Eds.), *Transforming social inquiry, transforming social action* (pp. 279–292). Norwell, MA: Kluwer.

Black, M. M., & Krishnakumar, A. (1998). Children in low-income, urban settings: Interventions to promote mental health and well-being. *American Psychologist, 53,* 635–646.

Broman, C. L. (1987). Race differences in professional help seeking. *American Journal of Community Psychology, 15*(4), 473–489.

Brown, D. (1988). Empowerment through advocacy. In D. J. Kurpius & D. Brown (Eds.), *Handbook of consultation: An intervention for advocacy and outreach* (pp. 5–17). Alexandria, VA: Association for Counselor Education and Supervision.

Brown, L. S. (1997). The private practice of subversion: Psychology as tikkun olam. *American Psychologist, 52,* 449–462.

Buckley, M. J. (1998). *The Catholic university as promise and project: Reflections in a Jesuit idiom.* Washington, DC: Georgetown University Press.

D'Andrea, M., & Daniels, J. (2000). Exploring the psychology of White racism through naturalistic inquiry. *Journal of Counseling and Development, 77,* 93–101.

Fairfax, D. (2000). From data raider to democratic researcher: Learning to become an academic-activist with the Merrimack Valley Project. In F. T. Sherman & W. R. Torbert (Eds.), *Transforming social inquiry, transforming social action* (pp. 11–36). Norwell, MA: Kluwer.

Fitzgerald, L., & Osipow, S. L. (1986). An occupational analysis of counseling psychology: How special is the specialty? *American Psychologist, 41,* 535–544.

Fouad, N. A., & Brown, M. T. (2000). Role of race and social class in development: Implications for counseling psychology. In S. D. Brown & R. W. Lent (Eds.), *Handbook of counseling psychology* (3rd ed., pp. 339–410). New York: Wiley.

Fox, D. (1993). Psychological jurisprudence and radical social change. *American Psychologist, 48,* 234–241.

Fox, D. (2003). Awareness is good but action is better. *The Counseling Psychologist, 31,* 299–304.

Freire, P. (1994). *Pedagogy of hope.* New York: Continuum.

Goodman, D. (2001). *Promoting diversity and social justice: Educating people from privileged groups.* Thousand Oaks, CA: Sage.

Gottheil, E., Sterling, R. C., & Weinstein, S. P. (1997). Outreach engagement efforts: Are they worth the effort? *American Journal of Drug & Alcohol Abuse, 23*(1), 61–66.

Gottlieb, S. C. (1975). Psychology and the "Treatment Rights Movement." *Professional Psychology, 6*(3), 243–251.

Grieger, I., & Ponterotto, J. (1998). Challenging intolerance. In C. Lee & G. Walz (Eds.), *Social action: A mandate for counselors* (pp. 17–50). Alexandria, VA: ACA.

Helms, J., & Cook, D. A. (1999). *Using race and culture in counseling and psychotherapy: Theory and process.* Boston: Allyn & Bacon.

Kenny, M., & Gallagher, L. (2000). Service learning as a vehicle in training psychologists for revised professional roles. In F. T. Sherman & W. R. Torbert (Eds.), *Transforming social inquiry, transforming social action* (pp. 189–206). Norwell, MA: Kluwer.

Larson, R. W. (2000). Toward a psychology of positive youth development. *American Psychologist, 55,* 170–183.

Lee, C. (1998). Counselors as agents of social change. In C. Lee & G. Walz (Eds.), *Social action: A mandate for counselors* (pp. 3–16). Alexandria, VA: ACA.

Lerner, R. M. (1995). *America's youth in crisis: Challenges and options for programs and policies*. Thousand Oaks, CA: Sage.

Lerner, R. M. (2000). Transforming universities to sustain outreach scholarship: A communique from the front. In F. T. Sherman & W. R. Torbert (Eds.), *Transforming social inquiry, transforming social action* (pp. 37–56). Norwell, MA: Kluwer.

Lewis, J. A., & Arnold, M. (1998). From multiculturalism to social action. In C. Lee & G. Walz (Eds.), *Social action: A mandate for counselors* (pp. 51–66). Alexandria, VA: ACA.

Lewis, J. A., Lewis, M. D., Daniels, J. A., & D'Andrea, M. J. (1998). *Community counseling: Empowerment strategies for a diverse society* (2nd ed.). Pacific Grove, CA: Brooks/Cole.

Mather, J. H., & Lager, P. B. (2000). *Child welfare: A unifying model of practice*. Belmont, CA: Wadsworth.

MacCluskie, K. C., & Ingersoll, R. E. (2001). *Becoming a 21st century agency counselor*. Belmont, CA: Brooks/Cole.

McWhirter, J. J., McWhirter, B. T., McWhirter, A. M., & McWhirter, E. H. (1998). *At risk youth: A comprehensive response*. Belmont, CA: Brooks/Cole.

Munoz, R. F., Mrazek, P. J., & Haggerty, R. J. (1996). Institute of medicine report on prevention of mental disorders: Summary and commentary. *American Psychologist, 51,* 1116–1122.

Parham T. A., & McDavis, R. J. (1987). Black men, and endangered species: Who's really pulling the trigger? *Journal of Counseling and Development, 66,* 24–27.

Prilleltensky, I. (1997). Values, assumptions, and practices: Assessing the moral implications of psychological discourse and action. *American Psychologist, 52,* 517–535.

Prilleltensky, I., & Nelson, G. (2002). *Doing psychology critically*. New York: Palgrave.

Prilleltensky, I., & Prilleltensky, O. (2003). Synergies for wellness and liberation in counseling psychology. *The Counseling Psychologist, 31,* 273–281.

Rawlings, E. I. & Carter, D. K. (1977*). Psychotherapy for women: Treatment toward equality*. Springfield, IL: Thomas Books.

Reiss, D., & Price, R. H. (1996). National research agenda for prevention research: The National Institute of Mental Health Report. *American Psychologist, 51,* 1109–1115.

Romano, J. & Hage, S. (2000). Prevention and counseling psychology: Revitalizing commitments for the 21st century. *The Counseling Psychologist, 28,* 733–763.

Sheras, P. L., Cornell, D. G., & Bostain, D. S. (1996). The Virginia Youth Violence Project: Transmitting psychological knowledge on youth violence to schools and communities. *Professional Psychology—Research & Practice, 27*(4), 401–406.

Taylor, R. J., Hardison, C. B., & Chatters, L. M. (1996). Kin and nonkin as sources of informal assistance. In H. W. Neighbors & J. S. Jackson (Eds)., *Mental health in Black America.* (pp. 130–145). Thousand Oaks, CA: Sage.

Thompson, C., & Neville, H. (1999). Racism, mental health, and mental health practice. *The Counseling Psychologist, 27,* 155–223.

Tobler, N. S. (2000). Lessons learned. *Journal of Primary Prevention, 20*(4), 261–274.

Toporek, R., & Reza, J. V. (2001). Context as a critical dimension of multicultural counseling: Articulating personal, professional, and institutional competence. *Journal of Multicultural Counseling and Development, 29,* 13–30.

Vera, E. M. (2000). A recommitment to prevention in counseling psychology. *The Counseling Psychologist, 28,* 829–837.

Vera, E. M., & Reese, L. E. (2000). Prevention interventions with school-age youth. In S. D. Brown & R. W. Lent (Eds.), *Handbook of counseling psychology* (pp. 411–434). New York: Wiley.

Vera, E. M., & Speight, S. L. (2003). Multicultural competence, social justice, and counseling psychology: Expanding our roles. *The Counseling Psychologist, 31,* 253–272.

Walters, M., Carter, B., Papp, P., & Silverstein, O. (1988). *The invisible web*. New York: Guilford.

Wilson, D. B., Gottfredson, D. C., & Najaka, S. S. (2001). School-based prevention of problem behaviors: A meta-analysis. *Journal of Quantitative Criminology, 17*(3), 247–272.

Wolfensberger, W., & Zauha, H. (1973). *Citizen advocacy and protective services for the impaired and handicapped*. Toronto, Canada: National Institute on Mental Retardation.

Wutzdoff, A. J., & Giles, D. E. (1997). Service learning in higher education. In J. Schine (Ed.), *Service learning* (pp. 105–117). Chicago: University of Chicago Press.

18

Toward an Emancipatory Communitarian Approach to the Practice of Psychology Training

Benedict T. McWhirter
Ellen Hawley McWhirter
University of Oregon

The purpose of this chapter is to examine an applied mental health training program from a social justice perspective. Specifically, we present the University of Oregon (UO) doctoral training program in counseling psychology, and reflect on various dimensions of the training program using the lens of Isaac Prilleltensky's (1997) emancipatory communitarian (EC) approach to psychology. We selected the EC approach as our lens because it overtly reflects a strong social justice orientation. In addition, the EC approach has much in common with multicultural, feminist, and empowerment perspectives in psychology; perspectives that have had a strong presence in counseling and counseling psychology literature and practice for may years (e.g., Arredondo & Perez, 2003; Helms, 2003; Ivey & Collins, 2003; McWhirter, 1994; Sparks & Park, 2000; Sue & Sue, 1990; Worell & Remer, 1992). Although the UO counseling psychology program is not based on the EC model, nor does social justice appear in our mission statement, we believe that many characteristics of our program and training model are consistent with an EC approach and with principles of social justice. Writing this chapter has served as a valuable reflection tool for us as faculty members. We hope that it will generate enthusiasm, ideas, and critical thinking among students and faculty in other programs who are committed to increasing social justice through mental health training, science, and practice.

We begin by providing an overview of Prilleltensky's emancipatory communitarian approach. Next, we describe counseling psychology generally as a sub-specialty of applied psychology, and then elaborate on our specific training program. Our current program model was developed with Urie Bronfenbrenner's (1979, 1986, 1989) ecological model of human development as a foundation, and should be understood in this context. As we overview our doctoral training program, we focus on characteristics that are fairly uncommon, that highlight the manner in which the ecological model is reflected in the program, or that reflect consistencies and inconsistencies with an EC approach. Given the ecological model as a foundation, and the EC approach as an aspirational framework, we then discuss how we evaluate training outcomes. Finally, we offer possible directions for enhancing and expanding the emancipatory and the communitarian aspects of mental health professional training programs. In particular, we hope to identify methods and strategies by which our program and other mental health professional training programs might more closely attend to the larger ecology of those served, and to carry out social justice objectives that reflect emancipatory communitarian approaches.

EMANCIPATORY COMMUNITARIAN APPROACH TO PSYCHOLOGY PRACTICE

In his 1994 article entitled "Psychology and the Status Quo," Isaac Prilleltensky articulated how the practice of psychology reflects the values of the dominant culture and as such, perpetuates society's inequities even as it attempts to ameliorate human problems. Although commonly presented as a value-free scientific enterprise, the way in which psychology is practiced actually is value-laden. For example, the relative emphasis on intrapsychic versus environmental factors in the development of mental health problems, and the design of individualistic versus collectivistic interventions, are characteristics that emerge from specific, even if unexamined, values. Although all psychological practice can be construed as for the benefit of ameliorating human suffering or problems, Prilleltensky (1997) makes a strong case for how the practice of psychology easily serves to maintain systems that are unjust instead of altering those systems. The practice of psychology often inadvertently serves a band-aid function rather than healing and preventing further problems in the multiple contexts in which they occur (Martín-Baró, 1994; McClure & Russo, 1996; Steinbock, 1988).

In subsequent work, Prilleltensky (Fox & Prilleltensky, 1997; Prilleltensky, 1997; Prilleltensky & Nelson, 2002) has characterized approaches to psychology practice with respect to the particular values, assumptions, and practices embedded within each approach. In his 1997 article, Prilleltensky proposed an emancipatory communitarian approach to psychology practice and detailed the values, assumptions, and practices that characterize this approach. *Emancipatory* refers to the ultimate goal of this approach, which is the liberation of individuals and communities from all forms of oppression and injustice. Approaches to psychology that are emancipatory are those that articulate the mechanisms, systems, and structures that perpetuate injustice or that prevent or limit liberation from oppression and injustice, and that serve to change those mechanisms, systems, and structures. Approaches to psychological practice that are "Communitarian" are those that emphasize the compassion, social obligation, and mutual-determination that underlie the liberation process. The term *communitarian* suggests that liberation is the goal for all groups and is not pursued by or for one group or individual to the detriment of others. It highlights a balance between rights and responsibilities, and promotion of the common social good. Prilleltensky notes that this approach is largely aspirational, as some existing approaches are highly emancipatory but less communitarian, whereas others are very communitarian, but less emancipatory, in that they do not attempt to alter unjust structures or systems.

An important construct in emancipatory communitarian approaches is the notion of *concientização*, a term coined by Brazilian educator Paolo Freire that refers to, "the process whereby people achieve an illuminating awareness both of the socioeconomic and cultural circumstances that shape their lives and their capacity to transform that reality" (as cited in Prilleltensky, 1994, p. 800). An emancipatory communitarian approach to psychology includes engagement in and promotion of *concientização*. Further, Prilleltensky (1997) writes that psychologists should engage in both "denunciation" of the structures, systems, and practices that oppress or constrain human well-being, and "annunciation," or identifying possible social structures, systems, and practices that optimize human development and well-being. Annunciation is inherently value-laden, it means actively envisioning a "good society," for example, a society which all people are free of oppression, enjoy a basic standard of living, and have the opportunity to participate in shaping the course of their lives. Psychologists' notion of the good life, and the good society, are directly linked with annunciation.

Five values that are embedded in EC practice consist of (a) *caring and compassion*, or the expression of care, empathy, and concern for the well-being of others; (b) *self-determination*, or fostering individuals' ability to pursue and achieve their chosen goals; (c) *human diversity*, or promoting respect and appreciation for diverse social identities; (d) *collaboration and participation*, or that individuals have peaceful, respectful, and democratic processes through which they can influence decisions that affect their lives, and (e) *distributive justice*, or the fair and equitable distribution of goods, resources, responsibilities, and opportunities among social groups in society (Prilleltensky, 1997, pp. 521–522). As compared with other approaches, which may emphasize some of these values at the expense of others, an EC approach attempts to strike a balance among all five values.

Five assumptions that characterize an EC approach have to do with: (a) *knowledge* (that knowledge should serve humanity, that epistemology is laden with power); (b) the *good life* (that a life of meaning and satisfaction requires attention to collective interests, along with individual well being); (c) the *good society* (that it fosters optimal development and well being for all); (d) *power in relationships* (that psychologists and other mental health professionals collaborate with and respect the wisdom and expertise of those they serve); and (e) *professional ethics* (that ethics codes should first protect the client, and should attend to larger social concerns, such as equitable access to services, rather than being restricted to interactions between the service provider and the client).

Finally, Prilleltensky highlighted five aspects of practice in which the aforementioned values and assumptions are manifested. These five aspects of an EC approach to practice pertain to: (a) *problem definition*, in which strong attention is placed on external conditions that cause or contribute to mental health problems, versus an exclusive focus on internal pathology; (b) *role of the client*, in which active participation versus passive acceptance of therapeutic intervention is sought and encouraged; (c) *role of the helper*, which highlights a client-centered, client-directed orientation; (d) *type of intervention*, which, in general, targets systems and ecologies of clients versus exclusive attention on remediation of internal symptoms; and (e) *time of intervention*, which places a strong emphasis on prevention of problems versus exclusive attention to remediation of existing problems.

This description of the values, assumptions, and aspects of practice provides a fairly concise overview of key features of an emancipatory communitarian approach to psychology. Further descriptions can be found in other chapters of this text as well as Prilleltensky (1997), and Prilleltensky and Nelson (2002). As we noted earlier, we see a great deal of consistency between EC approaches to psychology and the values, assumptions, and practices associated with multicultural, feminist, and empowerment perspectives and practices. Given our faculty's long-term commitment to infusion of the principles of multiculturalism, feminism, and empowerment in training, it is not surprising that many aspects of the training are consistent with an EC approach.

COUNSELING PSYCHOLOGY PROGRAM AT THE UNIVERSITY OF OREGON

Counseling psychology is a unique specialty area within applied psychology that is perhaps most similar to the specialty areas of school and clinical psychology. Gelso and Fretz (2001) described the themes that unify counseling psychology as a specialty. These include (a) a focus on intact (as opposed to disturbed) personalities, although with an increasing range in the severity of problems addressed by counseling psychologists, (b) a focus on assets, strengths, and capacity for change regardless of the severity of problems, rather than a focus on pathology, (c) use of relatively brief interventions, (d) an emphasis on person–environment interactions rather than an exclusive focus on intrapsychic processes, and (e) an emphasis on the educational and career development of individuals and on their educational and vocational environments (Gelso & Fretz, 2001). With respect to intervention, counseling psychology is typically characterized as having a strong, concurrent emphasis on preventive, developmental, and remedial interventions (Gelso & Fretz, 2001); however, in training and practice arenas, prevention is often neglected in favor of interventions for existing disorders and problems (Chronister, McWhirter, Kerewsky, 2004; Romano & Hage, 2000). This is likely due in part to institutional reluctance to acknowledge the systemic ways in which large groups of people are marginalized and their mental health is compromised (Ivey & Collins, 2003; McClure & Russo, 1996).

Many of these descriptors are easily linked with EC approaches to practice, in particular, the emphasis on strengths versus individual pathology, person–environment interactions, attention to educational and vocational issues and environments (which, if optimized, lead to increased opportunities to participate in decisions and direct one's life), and attention to prevention. We believe that a stronger emphasis on prevention in counseling psychology would lead to greater emphasis of the subspecialty on community and structural interventions. Unlike school and clinical psychology, counseling psychology also might be more closely associated with the specialty of community psychology if counseling psychology's emphasis on prevention was commensurate with its emphasis on remedial intervention.

The UO Counseling Psychology doctoral program was accredited in 1955 by the American Psychological Association. The program has a long history of preparing psychologists to serve the mental health needs of the public, consistently evolving to address contemporary needs in a manner consistent with the philosophies and interests of the faculty. For example, Dr. Leona Tyler (1906–1993), program cofounder, was known for her activism in the peace movement, and in the 1960s and early 1970s provided counseling to conscientious objectors in nearby forest camps (Fassinger, 2003; Sundberg & Littman, 1994). Current faculty interests in and commitment to multicultural counseling and diversity are reflected in part in the composition of the student community that we select for the program. Among a group that averages around 42 continuously enrolled students during the past 5 years, nearly half of the students have been members of different American ethnic minority groups: 80% are women; about 15% self-identify as lesbian, gay, or bisexual; and many are first-generation college students and/or grew up in lower socioeconomic backgrounds. Most of our incoming students are interested in contributing to their communities through research and practice when they complete their degrees. The diversity and sense of community among our students is a key factor in the quality of the training that we are able to provide.

In the mid-1990s, faculty members associated with the counseling psychology program began a process of changing the training model to better prepare students to engage in prevention and intervention efforts across settings and contexts, improve attention to school-based work commensurate with the mission of the college of education in which the program is housed, and increase attention to work with children and families (although this was the focus of many faculty members at Oregon for years). Bronfenbrenner's (1979, 1989) ecological model (described in detail in the next section) served as the guiding framework for this change. Development of the new training model was based on a series of fundamental assumptions about the role of counseling psychologists in society. The first assumption is that it is critical to train counseling psychologists who are prepared to engage in research and practice within changing environmental contexts, and who are prepared to have a positive impact on various levels or systems within those environments as well as with individuals. The second assumption is that, in addition to remediation efforts, counseling psychologists are responsible for working to reduce or eliminate risk factors, develop protective interventions that contribute to resilience and pro-social adjustment, and support and strengthen aspects of the community that contribute to the psychological well-being of its members (Gelso & Fretz, 2001; McWhirter, McWhirter, McWhirter, & McWhirter, 2004; Vera & Reese, 2000). As such, the work of prevention must include changing the structures that contribute to marginalization, impoverishment, poor mental health, and other negative outcomes (Chronister, McWhirter, & Kerewsky, 2004). The third assumption is that counseling psychologists must take an active role in shaping environments and to do so they must themselves become a conscious part of the system of social forces that define and determine our professional practice (Brabeck, Walsh, Kenny, & Comilang, 1997; McWhirter, 1997; Prilleltensky, 1997; Vera & Speight, 2003). The fourth and final assumption is that preparation of the next generation of counseling psychologists must emphasize multicultural competence, including understanding the dynamics of privilege and oppression and how these dynamics work in peoples' lives (e.g., Ancis & Szymanski, 2001; Ivey, Ivey, D'Andrea, & Daniels, 1997; Neville & Mobley, 2001; Ponterotto, 1998). Basic multicultural competence is foundational to effective and ethical mental health practice and research in all settings, with all client populations, and in every geographic region (American Psychological Association, 2003; Sue, Arredondo, & McDavis, 1992).

There are key features of our training that, as a whole, may distinguish us in varying degrees from other counseling psychology programs and are also consistent with emancipatory communitary practice. In no specific order of importance, these are (1) integration of the ecological model; (2) required readings in coursework and student assistantship experiences that provide a critique of psychology and exposure to diverse and nontraditional roles of psychologists; (3) infusion of human diversity and multicultural competence training throughout the curriculum; (4) an innovative practica sequence; (5) student engagement in community-based intervention research and prevention research; (6) an overtly articulated and broad attention to the environment in which students are trained; and (7) faculty scholarship and service activity that are prevention-focused as well as consistent with the values and assumptions of an emancipatory communitarian approach to psychology. A final key feature of the program is that we ground clinical practice in an empowerment model. We describe the empowerment model in detail in chapter 19 of this book, however, we occasionally refer to the construct of empowerment in this chapter. In the following sections we elaborate on the seven features just listed, highlighting similarities and differences with respect to the EC approach. We begin by describing the ecological model and, in subsequent sections, illustrate how it is integrated throughout our training program.

Bronfenbrenner's Ecological Model

Urie Bronfenbrenner's (1979, 1989) ecological model of human development posits that development occurs in the context of multiple interacting systems. The individual resides at the center of these systems, which include micro-, meso-, exo-, and macrosystems. The *microsystem* consists of the people and communities with whom the individual comes into direct contact. Important microsystems include the family, the neighborhood, the workplace, faith-based communities, and educational settings. Each microsystem influences the individual's development and well-being, and the individual exerts influence in each microsystem. The *mesosystem* refers to the nature and quality of the interconnections and relations between the different microsystems. For example, mesosystemic factors include the relationships between an individual's family and workplace (e.g., whether there are work-based social events that include family members), and between the neighborhood and faith community microsystems (e.g., hostility toward those entering the church, temple, or mosque; a neighborhood petition to re-locate a religious center to another location). The ecological model assumes that an individual's development is enhanced if the mesosystem, that is, the relationships among the microsystems, is positive (Bronfenbrenner, 1979, 1989). For example, better parent–teacher and school–parent communication has been linked with parent involvement in children's schooling and with children's educational achievement (Coleman, 1991; Cummins, 1986; Greenwood & Hickman, 1991; McWhirter et al., 2004).

The *exosystem* consists of the interconnections between one or more settings that do not directly involve the individual. The policies and practices of the parent's work setting, for example, that influence the parent's ability to stay home with a sick child, take vacations, leave work to meet with teachers or attend school performances, are part of the exosystem. Other examples of the exosystem include policies and practices associated with health care, minimum wage, housing, and the labor market. Although an individual does not participate directly in the systems that maintain or alter policies in these arenas, the development and well-being of individuals over their lifetime is influenced by access to health care, quality of education, and housing, and so on. The micro- and mesosystems are affected by, and influence, the exosystem. For example, local union and boycott organizers can influence corporate change.

Bronfenbrenner (1989) describes the *macrosystem* as our social blueprint: cultural values, belief systems, societal structure, gender-role socialization, race relations, and national and international resources. The macrosystem influences all other levels of the system. For example, negative racial stereotypes influence children's perceptions of themselves and others; political ideologies influence the amount, type, and targets of funding for public education. An additional concept is the *chronosystem*, which is defined as the development of interconnections among individuals and their environments over time.

There are three explicit assumptions of the ecological model (Bronfenbrenner, 1979, 1989). First, the individual and his or her environment are continually interacting and exerting mutual influence, and as a result, both are constantly changing. Second, the individual is an active participant in his or her development and so is not merely acted on by the environment but has the potential to exert influence and power within the environment. Third, the ecological model assumes bidirectionality, or the idea that changes in one ecological system may influence changes in systems that are more proximal and distal to the individual. For example, it is apparent that public policy decisions can impact human development in more immediate or proximal ecological systems, including at the mesosystem, microsystem, and individual levels. In the same way, individuals, families, and communities in the micro- and mesosystems can influence public policy decisions (exosystem) by writing their government representatives, speaking at public forums, or protesting (Chronister, McWhirter, & Kerewsky, 2004).

The ecological model is consistent with the EC approach in two primary ways. First, there is clear attention to the social conditions and structures that impede healthy development. Maximizing individual well-being would require intervention across levels of the ecology, in other words, systemic and structural changes. Second, optimal development occurs within multiple, interconnected communities that are characterized by positive interactions. The well-being of the individual is, in large part, influenced by the well-being of the communities and systems of the individual's ecology. The similarities between emancipatory communitarianism and the ecological model can be seen more clearly in several aspects of the UO training program, which we turn to next.

Readings, Coursework, Assistantships: Big Picture Critique

During their first year in the program, students engage with their cohort in critiquing the practice of psychology, with readings in critical psychology (e.g. Prilleltensky 1989, 1997; Martín-Baró's [1994] *Writings for a Liberation Psychology*), critical pedagogy (e.g., Paolo Freire's [1971] *Pedagogy of the Oppressed*), social change techniques (e.g., Saul Alinsky's [1989] *Rules for Radicals*), and qualitative studies of the conditions of impoverished schools and communities in the United States (e.g., Jonathan Kozol's [1991] *Savage Inequalities,* and [1995] *Amazing Grace: The Lives of Children and Conscience of a Nation).* Early in their program, students gain insights into the diverse contexts and ecology in which prevention and treatment research and practice occur. For example, students are exposed to the work of special education faculty who assist teachers, administrators, and other school staff to alter the school microsystem to reduce problem behaviors in school. Violence prevention and decreases in school disruption are accomplished via primary prevention and curriculum integration strategies, and by optimizing the learning environment, particularly for children with special needs (Carr, et al., 2002; Horner & Sugai, 2000; Horner, Sugai, & Horner, 2000). Across multiple courses, roles of class as well as race/ethnicity, education, gender, and region in psychological research and practice are critiqued. We broadly define and discuss issues of diversity in nearly all courses in the program.

Additionally, over the past few years, we have worked with our departmental colleagues who coordinate our undergraduate program in family and human services to provide graduate assistantships to all of our 1st-year and to some of our advanced doctoral students in counseling psychology. Through this work, students are exposed to more than 100 different human service agencies throughout the community—from "birth-to-3" early intervention programs, to juvenile detention, to adult rehabilitation programs—and they serve as "university supervisors" for undergraduate human service students who are completing practica in these agencies. So, early in their doctoral studies our students are exposed to interagency politics, university–community relations, supervision practice, and to the complications of practice that may range from student impairment issues to agency budget crises that affects its capacity to deliver services. More recently, our colleagues have enhanced this assistantship by providing systemized training and required preparatory readings, similar to those just mentioned, to help our students critically evaluate themselves, their training, and human service practice in general, so that they approach their work in a more critically conscious fashion (Kerewsky & Forrest, 2003). Students are also exposed directly and indirectly to a very diverse clientele through their work as human services supervisors.

As a self-critique, an area that still needs further development within the field of counseling psychology and within our program more specifically is the topic of class and classism. Specifically, in contrast with disciplines such as sociology and social work, within counseling psychology and some other helping professions there has long been an absence of dialogue or recognition of the powerful role of social class in human behavior (Fouad & Brown, 2000), to the detriment of training students to provide effective services to clients who are less verbal than university students and who are not middle class. Class is often overlooked in discussions of diversity, and when it is discussed, it is often in a superficial manner. Most textbooks used in counseling psychology training do not give much attention to class issues. Although there has been more recent recognition of the importance of class in counseling psychology research and intervention (Blustein et al., 2002; Fouad & Brown, 2000; Liu, 2001, 2002; Liu, Ali, Soleck, Hopps, & Pickett, 2004), there are few materials available for assisting students in the exploration, understanding, and competence in addressing class issues among themselves, within themselves, and in the context of intervention and research.

Providing opportunities to discuss and critique the challenging readings presented to students is as important as assigning the readings. It is through subsequent discussions in the classroom, in student supervision meetings for those with assistantships as human service supervisors, and in discussions outside the classroom (often, we are told, in late-night student study groups for comprehensive exam preparation), that the nuances of such readings become integrated into students' professional identity and perspectives. Our goal is that students are critical of the practice of psychology and helping professions, as well as critical of the critiques themselves, that is, our goal is to support the continued development of their critical consciousness.

Human Diversity and Multicultural Infusion

Having a diverse group of students is critical to providing training that enhances multicultural competence and critical consciousness. The instructor and the readings provide an important ingredient to the education of students, but it is the community of students in a given classroom, practicum setting, and program that provide the experiences, insights, questions, and critiques that drive and inspire learning. Our program has been particularly successful in recruiting a student body that is ethnically diverse, due in part (we believe) to our valuing of multicultural competence and overt attention to important issues such as White privilege and socioeconomic background. The program was the recipient of the APA 2001 Suinn Minority Achievement Award for our commitment and contribution to training psychologists of color.

Our college-wide Ethnic Diversity Affairs Committee (EDAC; http://counpsych .uoregon.edu), founded by a group of students interested in creating a specific forum in which to discuss issues of human diversity and provide a venue for mutual support and advocacy for students of color, is one example of our programmatic support to enhance human diversity and attention to multiculturalism. EDAC's mission is to provide support to, and advocacy for, students, staff, and faculty of color in the college, attend to recruitment and retention needs of students of color, and to assist college faculty in infusing issues of human diversity into the College of Education curriculum. Among participants, ongoing differences in culture, privilege, leadership styles, ethnic identity, and desired focus (e.g. interpersonal support vs. campus-wide advocacy vs. community advocacy) make the work of EDAC challenging, and necessitate the development and exercise of multicultural competencies. This committee provides one model for how to incorporate support for human diversity and for specific students, faculty, and staff of color, in a more formalized format. EDAC works on its own, but its effectiveness is highly enhanced by the individual, personal commitment of counseling psychology and other faculty members and advanced students to provide ongoing personal and programmatic support for students from diverse backgrounds on a daily basis. This is an essential component of our training environment.

We believe that attention to ethnic, socioeconomic, and other forms of diversity through readings and discussions is a necessary, but not sufficient, element of promoting multicultural competence. The direct practice work that students engage in, student research, and the training environment of the program itself can also serve to stifle and polarize, or to revitalize and enhance the learning of multicultural competencies.

Practica Sequence

Like most programs, our clinical training begins in the first quarter of training with pre-practicum courses. After completing a series of intervention and theoretical foundation courses, including multicultural counseling, students are required to take practica in this order: a year-long practica focused primarily on individual interventions with adults; a year-long child and family practica in which students serve families in home, school, and clinical settings; and a year-long supervision practica that includes didactic and different kinds of practical supervision experience. This overall practica sequence is designed to systematically increase students' understanding of the multiple contexts in which both clients and mental health professionals function. We require all of these practica so that students are challenged to work across a range of presenting problems with different client populations. Some students may have difficulty in one or the other practica because of their skills and preferences for working with one type of population, and we treat these as developmental challenges to be resolved. Although the choice of each student's subsequent internship setting is determined by their specific interests (e.g., community counseling centers, centers that focus on child and family interventions, VA hospitals, university counseling centers, etc.), we require that all students are exposed to in-depth clinical training across a range of populations and interventions so that they can integrate more fully an ecological model by experiencing and trying to understand clients in many different contexts.

For the adult practica, students are placed in the university counseling center or in the local community college counseling center that serves a fairly "nontraditional" and lower SES student population. Emphasis is placed not only on individual therapy within these practice settings but on prevention and community change, consultation with other campus systems, and preventive psychoeducation (such as different types of skills training). In the supervision sequence, after 1 or 2 years of supervising undergraduate human service majors in practicum settings (via paid assistantships), our students supervise (a) 1st-year students in small skills-training groups, (b) trainees learning individual psychological assessment techniques, and (c) pre-practicum trainees working in an in-patient setting. These experiences, in conjunction with the didactic training, promote the learning of diverse supervision methods as well as enhance awareness of the applicability (and limitations) of standard supervision practice. The end result is that students think more critically about the work that they do, and they examine their role in the process more fully so that they can assess whether they are contributing to practice that is liberating or that perpetuates oppression. Although the individual adult practicum and supervision sequence are more common among other counseling psychology programs, we try to integrate a great degree of critical self-reflection along with multiple role experiences, and we work to diversify the types of clinical and supervision experiences and the types of supervisees that our students work with to maximize a broader understanding of the benefits and limitations of therapy and supervision practice. Additionally, what is less common among other counseling psychology programs is our required year-long child and family practicum.

The families served in the child and family practicum typically seek treatment for an identified child who is engaged in externalizing behaviors such as fire-setting, use of knives, theft, or school disruption. The majority of families served in this practicum live near or below the poverty line and experience a number of concurrent crises. Similar to the adult practicum sequence, emphasis is placed on identification and utilization of the strengths of clients rather than on pathology and deficits. The practicum is conducted jointly with the clinical psychology doctoral program. This practicum is highly structured and provides students with an experience in helping families manage problems across multiple domains (home, school, interactions with different social services, etc.). Families that seek services via this practicum begin with the Family Check-Up (Stormshak & Dishion, 2002).

The Family Check-Up (FCU) is a three-step process (Stormshak & Dishion, 2002) derived from Miller and Rollnick's (2002) motivational interviewing model. Motivational interviewing is a brief intervention technique developed for working with problem drinkers that has been successfully applied to a broad range of clinical and healthy intervention settings (Miller & Rollnick, 2002). The first step in the FCU consists of an intake interview conducted in the home. The interview is followed by a multiagent, multimethod assessment. In contrast with traditional models in which assessment is deficit-focused and organized around the presenting problem, the strengths of the child and of the family, as well as the areas of difficulty, are assessed across contexts (home, school, neighborhood) and considered in relation to major developmental domains (e.g. social skills, family management and interaction processes, child characteristics). Student therapists also directly observe and videotape the interactions between the child or children and the parents, talk with teachers and school counselors, and observe school behaviors. These activities provide a comprehensive·picture of the strengths of the child and the family, so as to build on those strengths in designing an intervention plan. The assessment information is integrated and organized around four elements: (a) the centrality of parenting to the child's success and well-being; (b) attending to potentially harmful behaviors first; (c) tailoring feedback to maximize its utility and effectiveness; and (d) supporting the family's motivation to change (Stormshak & Dishion, 2002).

The third phase of the FCU is the feedback phase. This series of sessions begins with a structured parental self-assessment. Student therapists reflect and validate the parents' evaluation and concerns. Next, therapist feedback is presented, clarified, and augmented by parent perspectives. Finally, based directly on the assessment and feedback, student therapists and the family design a menu of possible options for the family to pursue in order to optimize the child's success and the family's well-being. This menu builds on strengths and targets various dimensions of the child's ecology (e.g., parent training classes, academic tutoring for the child, and the development of a collaborative system for consistent home/school communication, family therapy, etc.). Parents are free to select or reject any of the options presented because, consistent with principles of motivational interviewing, if the family is not ready to participate in an option it will likely not be effective for them. The student trainees assist the family in understanding the benefits of each option and in implementing the menu items. In some cases, student trainees directly provide the intervention/family therapy.

Additional clinical activities in the child and family practicum may also include provision of psychoeducational content to elementary school children via puppet shows, staffing school-based parent support and information centers, and providing teacher and staff training in topics such as cultural awareness. Our students who are fluent in Spanish work with families participating in a residential center for survivors of torture. In the child and family practicum, the engagement of the parents' assessment and evaluation, valuing and reinforcement of family strengths, and the consistent attention to enhancing the family's motivation to address the concerns that they bring to or discover in the course of therapy, all serve an emancipatory function in that the family's independence is supported as well as their ability to address their concerns and interrupt patterns that create problems for them. Part of the student clinicans' role includes altering the microsystems as well as strengthening the mesosystem through pursuit of such goals as increasing home–school communication and rapport or increasing consistency in school-based and home-based interventions. As such, this practicum provides students with opportunities to intervene in multiple microsystems as well as to strengthen the client's mesosystem. All of these clinical experiences provide exposure to economic diversity among the clients, but proportionally reflect the demographics of the local community, which is approximately 85% European American. Additionally, unique clinical opportunities for our students are sometimes grant-driven, so when faculty members receive extramural funding, this practicum provides a venue to integrate clinical and research work.

Community-Based Student Research

Of course, along with clinical training, students in the program are trained as researchers and behavioral scientists and are expected to participate in research outside of that required to fulfill their PhD requirements. More specifically, and consistent with the program model, philosophy, and values, students are strongly encouraged to engage in community-based research. That is, students are encouraged to design and carry out research projects that evaluate prevention and intervention programs, illuminate critical dynamics in struggling families or communities, and/or test theoretical relationships salient to prevention and intervention efforts. In the 7 years preceding this writing, no student has utilized a "Psych 101 data pool" to gather data. Only students with a genuine interest in late adolescence or early adulthood among university students have collected data using university samples. For example, in recent years, students have examined emotional ambivalence, affective expression, and connectedness among early adult university students (Townsend, 2003), and perceptions of stigma and mental health service utilization preferences among Asian and Asian American university students (Liang, 2005). Community-based samples with whom students have engaged in research recently include Vietnamese and Cambodian parents of preschoolers (Hayashino, 2003), Latino high school student participants in a Latino family retreat program (Torres, 2003), gay couples (Matchett-Morris, 2003), battered women (Gragg, 2003), male prisoners (Lusk, 2003), adolescent mothers (Hunt-Morse, 2002), youth in juvenile detention (Knott, 2003), VA hospital clients (Martin, 2001), and staff members of residential child treatment facilities (Hart, 2002). In each of these studies, students developed relationships over time, worked to understand the needs and concerns of the research participants and agencies involved, collaborated with other researchers and interventionists, collected their own data, and designed research studies that were practically meaningful to practice and science. (A description of student community-based research can be found at http://counpsych.uoregon.edu/).

Other students foster relationships with local research institutes within and outside of the university whose behavioral scientists are engaged in large-scale prevention and intervention research, which sometimes results in opportunities to carry out dissertation research using complex and often longitudinal data sets. Still others use research data from Counseling Psychology faculty members that is gathered through the support of extramural funding. These resources allow students to address prevention research questions in community samples not otherwise possible for graduate students to pursue, with populations such as incarcerated youth (e.g. Burrow-Sanchez, 2003; Kaufman, 2003; Stent, 2003), high-risk children, families, and siblings (e.g., Shepard, 2003), and youth victimized by bullying (Goodman, 2002).

With respect to research coursework, we require courses in traditional experimental and quasi-experimental research design as well as focused research methodology courses. In these two-term focused methodology courses, students develop competency in either program evaluation or qualitative research. Both include a research practicum in which students carry out a research project in the second term of the sequence that they designed during the first term of the sequence. The faculty members who teach these sequences seek research ideas from local agencies and the university community and propose a menu of possible projects to students. Students then work in small teams and in consultation with the agencies to design and carry out the project. In this way, questions of importance to the agencies are pursued. For example, a recent project evaluated the success of a Valentine's Day "Relationship Check-Up" program provided to the community by the Couple and Family Therapy program in the UO College of Education (an innovative event designed to encourage couples to strengthen their relationships).

One way that student relationships with the community are facilitated early on is via the community prevention and intervention course that students take their first year in the program. One course requirement that helps students integrate science with practice is for students to visit a local agency that engages in prevention work, to conduct an interview, and to write a paper and deliver a presentation detailing the mission and services of the agency. Many students develop relationships with staff of the agency that they visit and subsequently become involved in volunteer service, research, or both, at that site. The early formation of relationships with community agencies increases students' knowledge of the nature of the local mental health service community, as well as political issues, unmet needs, and populations being served. In addition, students have the opportunity to cultivate relationships that can become truly collaborative, resulting in a dissertation, thesis, or other research project that serves the agency and the clients of the agency (e.g., Bamba, 2001). Through their involvement with agencies and research institutes, students have opportunities to learn about consultation, interagency collaboration, how problems are ecological in their etiology and resolution, and prevention and research skills. They also potentially work with agency personnel on developing grants.

Students actually gain the skills for developing grant proposals for funding their research through a college-level grant writing course that is required of all of our doctoral students. Along with having access to large-scale intervention research data from extramurally funded colleagues, students also work on their own proposals for funding that are based on their more specific areas of interest. At times, students are also able to prepare "supplemental" awards on existing faculty grants to extend an existing grant in a way that supports the student and his or her specific research project. These types of awards allow students to examine multiple contextual variables and utilize multiple methods of data collection that they would normally not be able to support without extramural funding. This enhances their ability to engage in research within the community. This course helps students develop grant-writing skills and it improves our program's ability to integrate best-practices in science with practice. Along with the other required research courses, this course also helps our students to prepare themselves for postdoctoral positions in research institutes, universities, and community agencies that are increasingly searching for extramural funding and for employees who possess sound grant-writing skills. Approximately 40% of our students have successfully prepared grants to support their research, from major U.S. Department of Education student awards to small local and/or foundation grants.

Another critical part of research training is the weekly doctoral seminar that occurs during every term of students' residence on campus. Every Friday morning, all students who are not away on internship meet in groups with their advisor. The primary focus of these weekly meetings is the development and completion of research projects, with attention to professional development and the identification and pursuit of training goals. Each faculty member carries out the seminar in a manner consistent with her or his interests, methodologies, and personality. The weekly seminar format allows for ongoing idea exchange, sharing of resources, investment in others' projects, the development of mutual interests, and the development of strong relationships. Students develop skills and resources important in fostering community and agency relationships, collection of data, data entry and analysis, professional writing, providing and receiving critical feedback, and orally presenting their ideas, projects, and viewpoints. Seminars are combined periodically, to provide students with opportunities to present their research to a larger group and, often, as practice runs for the dissertation proposal defense. The 15 or 20 minutes prior to doctoral seminar has evolved into a social event in the department common area, serving as a weekly reunion for students who might not otherwise see each other in classes or work settings.

We find many dimensions of student research to be consistent with the EC approach. Students generally develop a genuine relationship with, and commitment to, the community or group with whom they carry out their research; they strive to return something to the research participants and to engage in research projects that have social merit. Methodologically, although we train our students to think more broadly about research, most utilize postpositivist experimental or quasi-experimental designs. We believe that greater methodological diversity would enhance the quality and contribution of student research efforts. At the same time, qualitative methodologists are in short supply and high demand on our campus, and our own program faculty does not include an expert in qualitative research methods. Thus, for the most part, students do not have the knowledge base or external support to carry out qualitative research. Participatory research models described by Vera and Speight (2003) and Prilleltensky and Nelson (2002) would be a very positive addition to our training.

Program Training Environment

Recognizing the extent to which our program is an important microsystem for students and faculty, we strive to provide a context that is professional, collegial, and challenging; that of a community of scholars. We attempt to reduce faculty–student hierarchy without denying the power differential inherent in an evaluative training program. This seems particularly important given our commitment to facilitating critical consciousness, that is, the program is not run as a democracy and should not be presented as such. There is a clear difference in power based on the fact that faculty evaluate and ultimately bear the responsibility for working with students on their developmental needs, on any required remediation, on helping some students determine whether they should work toward—or even want—a PhD in counseling psychology, or for removing students from the program if, after remediation opportunities, they are judged by the faculty to be unable to adequately meet the demands of training. Although these decisions are difficult, they do represent, at the most substantial level, the power difference inherent in any training program where faculty evaluate students on professional development. So, we have structured our training, curriculum, and program governance in order to enhance collaboration and a sense of community, encourage responsibility-taking, and reflect open decision-making as much as possible in a manner that plainly acknowledges this power differential. Among ourselves as faculty, we utilize a consensus model of decision-making, and although this can be time-consuming, we have actually had very little difficulty achieving consensus in spite of individual differences in our styles and approaches. Our process of consensus decision-making, whenever possible, is also open to students, and we regularly seek student input and feedback about the program on multiple levels.

In brief, in our training program we actively promote an environment in which collaboration is valued, competition is named and minimized, and feedback is continuously sought and utilized toward program and environmental improvement. Open conversations about competition, overt statements of values, and modeling all serve to communicate a set of norms regarding community, and students themselves are the primary source of modeling noncompetitiveness. One of the challenges here lies in providing optimal support and validation for the accomplishments of students without enhancing interstudent competitiveness. Similarly, interactions during classroom discussions take on a competitive flavor at times, or are perceived by some to be competitive whereas others perceive the same interaction as emerging from a "passion for knowing." Negotiating these moments over time with students is often very challenging. This highlights the importance of a community atmosphere, and the importance of faculty being skilled in group facilitation and in multicultural counseling so that discussions of the group dynamic can be productive and enhance respect for differences. The faculty goal is to always increase a sense of trust that when misperceptions, differences, dislikes, and disagreements emerge, they will be addressed directly. We believe that when students feel a greater sense of community with each other and with the faculty, then there are more channels by which faculty receive feedback about the program. When students are more secure with each others' viewpoints, and when students come forth with problems and suggestions more frequently, these enhance early detection and prevention of potential problems and enhance program improvement.

We discuss our training environment openly and articulate to students and to prospective students the kind of environment we work to maintain. This discussion occurs in courses and practica, in each faculty member's doctoral research seminars, via work with student representatives to the faculty, in EDAC, and during our doctoral student selection process. Courses such as "Introduction to Counseling Psychology" and "Introduction to Doctoral Studies Seminar" include not only traditional readings about the discipline of counseling psychology, but also readings and subsequent discussions about the process of training, the kind of training environment we work to achieve, and specific discussions with students about their rights and responsibilities and about trying to maintain a collaborative and noncompetitive environment. We encourage students to critique not only the science and practice of psychology, but also the experiences we provide to them in the program itself.

We set the tone for this ongoing conversation about our training environment even before students begin doctoral study. We conduct interviews of our program applicant finalists on campus. Although the formal parts of the interview occur on a Friday, the experience extends from Thursday to Sunday. Our students initiated and annually organize teams that provide housing, local transportation, and general hosting for each of the approximately 20 candidates who travel to campus for the interview. The program provides several meals for candidates and their student hosts. Early interview offers, the option of having a phone interview, housing, and hosting over a Saturday night makes the interview weekend more affordable, gives applicants a fuller and more realistic experience of what doctoral study (and life) might be like for them at the University of Oregon, and results in a more diverse socioeconomic background in the student body. Our students are at least as invested in this process as the faculty. They model the norms, values, and personality of the program, and frankly address the questions that applicants won't ask the faculty, so that the selection process is two-way and based on multiple sources of information. Ultimately, our students consistently compare with other psychology doctoral students on campus and around the country on traditional criteria (e.g. undergraduate GPAs, GRE scores, etc.) and on important criteria for counseling-related programs (e.g., communication skills, past related experiences, etc.). But, in addition, we believe that the interview weekend format results in a student body that is characterized by a desire to contribute to its communities of origin and/or affiliation, interest in working at the level of policy to improve client welfare and promote social justice, commitment to developing multicultural competence and critical consciousness, interests in contributing to the welfare of schools, and excitement about collaborating with others.

Throughout the course of training, although consistently acknowledging the power differential between students and faculty, we also consistently challenge students to exercise the multidimensional and very real power that they possess. There are challenges associated with this, for example, individual students have taken the position that *less* power means they cannot critique or attempt to change anything, because faculty will—due to their greater power—evaluate them poorly. In responding to such notions, it has been useful as a faculty to discuss with students, as an analogy, the client–therapist dynamics, exploring whether the student–therapist uses the power differential to punish clients who offer critique. Another challenge is in motivating students to participate actively in decision making via their representatives. Elected student representatives serve in an advisory capacity to the faculty and attend and participate in all faculty meetings, except during "executive sessions" dealing with matters of faculty and student personnel. We encourage students to work with their student representatives and to come to faculty directly when they have ideas of improving or enhancing the program.

Finally, for a number of years, faculty have encouraged students to form a graduate student organization. Some students have conveyed to us that as long as their feedback is heard, there is no impetus to devote the energy to such an organization. This is good in the sense that it appears that there is trust and students feel that their voices are being heard. We also realize that EDAC is an important group for many students and much process occurs in that setting as well, such that students may not feel a need for additional meetings. Nevertheless, because we believe that student organizations are important for professional development and we wish to encourage all students to have a forum for expressing their voices, faculty continue to encourage the development of such a student organization.

Faculty Scholarship and Service

The Counseling Psychology faculty at the University of Oregon share a common interest in prevention and community-based interventions, and each faculty member attempts to integrate attention to human diversity in research, service, and scholarship activities. Specialty areas of faculty include domestic and interpersonal violence, professional training issues such as ethical issues associated with impaired trainees, small-group skills-building among high-risk adolescents, college student development, career development of ethnic minority and female adolescents, empowerment in counseling, and prevention and early intervention strategies with younger children and with high-risk families. Overviews of the specific scholarship and service interests of faculty can be found at the program Web site (http://counpsych.uoregon.edu/). All faculty members attempt to integrate—in different ways and with varying degrees of success—many of the values, practices, and assumptions of an EC approach to training, examples of which we briefly illustrate here.

For instance, Dr. Krista Chronister has spent the past few years developing effective interventions for women survivors of domestic violence. Her work has gained national attention (e.g., receiving the American Psychological Association Division 17 Dissertation Research Award in 2001), and her treatment intervention is sought nationally and internationally. Her work contributes to intervention science while attending to the needs of a highly underserved population in the United States, and it provides opportunities for our students to be involved in community-based, empirically supported intervention work while engaging in the social justice applications of counseling psychology. This work also helps students recognize directly the potentially oppressive power that psychology may have with a high-risk population and helps them to see the importance of the mesosystemic level of intervention.

Other faculty members have worked at the exosystemic level. Dr. Linda Forrest, for example, has been involved for much of her career in the development of policy and training practices within our primary professional organization, the American Psychological Association (APA). Her work in multiple areas within Division 17 (Counseling Psychology) as a service provider and as a reviewer and contributor of scholarship (e.g., as associate editor of *The Counseling Psychologist*) illustrates her efforts to create widespread systemic policy change within the professional organization and, thus, within the profession itself. She is among a select team of psychology professionals who advocated vigorously and successfully for years to have multicultural professional competencies adopted by the APA, and intervention at the exosystemic level. Similarly, one of our instructional faculty members (Dr. Shoshana Kerewsky) is highly involved in local and state professional organizations and as such helps our students integrate their work on a theoretical level with professional participation locally. Her connections to community agencies and interest in training practices supports our attempts to integrate an EC approach to training and helps our students understand the need to be active at the exosystemic level locally while they broaden their thinking as part of their training.

Dr. Beth Stormshak, through our required child–family practicum that she developed and through her own research activities, helps our students understand that intervention must necessarily involve the multiple microsystems children experience in their lives. Through this practicum, students actively work with families and children as well as with schools and other community agencies that have contact with their family clients. As such, Dr. Stormshak helps students work at the level of the family microsystem and mesosystem. Her research work also examines the multiple variables that influence families and children at risk.

As authors, we illustrate in "An Ongoing Community Intervention in Chile" one of our own ongoing projects that reflects dimensions of the ecological and empowerment models. The project is based in Peñalolén, a poor neighborhood of Santiago, Chile (see also McWhirter & McWhirter, 2006). As you read the study, you may ask, "In what way is this work—thousands of miles away—related to our training program's ecological model and our attempt to integrate EC values, assumptions, and practices?" The answer is that, as faculty, this cultural immersion, consultation, and

An Ongoing Community Intervention in Chile

Since 1995, we have made yearly trips to Santiago, Chile, to visit Benedict's uncle, a Catholic priest, who has spent more than 40 years serving communities in Chile and Peru. For the past 12 years he has directed the "Family Center" as part of the huge San Roque parish in the very poor community of Peñalolén. This center is dedicated to supporting family faith education, building family relationships, and connecting families to their community. In 2000, after 5 years of learning about the community and after numerous conversations with couples who volunteer at the Family Center, these couples asked us to provide training in psychology to help enhance and support their efforts. Our Spanish fluency, formal interdisciplinary education, and prior immersion experiences in Latin America provided us with a foundation for understanding the history, cultural norms, religious expression, and economic situation of the people of Peñalolén. Our relationship with many of the families and couples themselves was very strong. So we gladly agreed to help and have been doing annual workshops with them ever since.

One of the contexts of our work, and of particular importance to the people of Chile, is that the country was governed by a brutal military dictatorship from 1973 until 1990. Thousands of people were executed or "disappeared" and tens of thousands were tortured or exiled during the dictatorship. Peñalolén was an area severely affected by this reality. Although Chile returned to "democracy" in 1990, the former dictator, Agusto Pinochet, remains a constitutionally approved lifetime senator until his death. The coup, its aftermath, and U.S. involvement in the coup have been well documented (see Kornbluh, 2003), and the devastating effects of 17 years of repression are still very palpable throughout Chilean society today.

Within this context, and based on guidance from a few of the leader couples, the fundamental focus of our work in Peñalolén has been to provide training to strengthen families. We have been most closely involved with the couples who carry out San Roque's family faith education program. This is a program founded on the notion that parents are the ideal faith educators and models for their own children and for other families as well. These "mentor couples" meet with groups of parents for 2 consecutive years in weekly meetings to strengthen parents' faith knowledge base, increase their sense of community with others, and develop their capacity to nurture each other and their families.

Mentor couples have completed the program themselves and have made a 2-year commitment to working with their spouse to deliver the curriculum. Although they are already active members of the community, the mentor couples typically begin the experience with many apprehensions about their ability to be role models and to carry out the program. Among the 40 mentor couples with whom we have worked over the past 5 years, only 5 or 6 people have formal education beyond high school. All of the couples are confronted by severe economic problems. The couples that these mentor couples work with in their religious education groups also seek out the assistance of the mentor couples outside of group meetings with complex problems and crises, and arrive at the weekly group meetings with varying levels of communication and social skills, motivation, and openness. Thus, the mentor couples are faced with numerous challenges, and this was the basis of their request for our help.

We designed the first series of workshops to provide fundamental listening skills and group facilitation skills. In the next level of training we advanced the complexity of the group facilitation skills, provided additional practice, and also included problem-solving models for working with individual couples who come to the mentor couple with specific difficulties. For the third level of training, we focused on working with couples in acute crisis, facilitating couples' motivation to change negative patterns, and on renewing the marital relationships of the mentor couples themselves. Throughout the training, we have drawn on the mentor couples' experiences not only with their specific groups but

---

An Ongoing Community Intervention in Chile *(cont.)*

also with their spouses and children. We have tried to give psychology away: to provide the mentor couples with additional tools, supports, and skills so that they approach their work with greater confidence and are able to provide a higher level of support to the families with whom they work.

Access to formal psychological services is limited among the families of Peñalolén, so increasing the skills of those already working closely with families increases the resources of the community. Because the mentor couples make enormous sacrifices of time and energy to serve their community in the midst of poverty and limited resources, we attempt to enhance their mutual validation throughout the workshops. Nurturing their support networks to sustain their efforts and energy over time is critical.

Like many mental health professionals, we were trained to avoid the intersection of psychology and religion. This is at odds with an empowerment approach and an ecological model, however, since faith communities and participation in organized religion is often a dominant (and sometimes one of few) system of support among our clients. As Catholics ourselves, we approach this project with an understanding of the diversity and universality of Catholic faith practices. Our academic and lived exposure to liberation theology (Berryman, 1987; Gutierrez, 1990) has enhanced our critical appreciation of both the oppressive and the liberatory potential of faith practice. This experience has not obviated the need to consult and gather information on an ongoing basis, and we continually seek to analyze and critique the way we carry out this synthesis of psychology and theology praxis.

Our richest source of feedback for the ongoing service we provide is, of course, the couples themselves. They regularly provide us with feedback regarding methods, content, and utility of the workshops, and work with us to design each next step. As of this writing, we have just ended a 1-year sabbatical in Chile, which provided us with the opportunity to engage in ongoing consultation with the mentor couples, provide direct counseling, and teach a semester-long course in "marriage maturity" to deepen past workshop themes.

Our goals for this ongoing work in Chile are consistent with an emancipatory communitarian perspective. We hope to augment skills and mutual support networks, increase access to useful practices, and overall to strengthen the integrity of all families in the community. We hope that the effects of healthier, more unified, and more engaged families will reverberate throughout their multiple communities. Our role has been to assist the mentor couples in carrying out the work they are already doing. We use a consultative model of training, state our values clearly, and consistently attend to the ecology in which we are working. As a practical example of this, we use about 45 minutes of warm-up activities in our evening seminars in order to accommodate the long Chilean workday, the long commute time in huge Santiago, and a Chilean flexible sense of time, without punishing those who arrive at the designated hour.

Finally, in sharing examples, struggles, and experiences from our own lives as a couple, there is no doubt that we connect on an important level with the couples, but also communicate how our values, practices, and beliefs may be inconsistent at times with those of some of the couples. That is, because we are always at risk of imposing our own cultural norms and overlooking the strengths of the practices, communication patterns, and methodologies of the couples that may be different from our own, we engage in open dialogue with each other and with the couples during our workshops in order to make the training and the cross-cultural experience more valuable for everyone, more effective, and more highly embedded with a critical self-examination that is essential to empowerment.

service experience informs our conversations with students and colleagues about the multiple opportunities and potential pitfalls of cross-cultural work. It also helps us to critically self-reflect on our professional limitations in a different economic and cultural context, and on the limitations of traditional psychology in serving human need. We make every effort to model this critical self-reflection publicly with our students. Additionally, because we have been conducting this work for many years now, we are able to discuss the effects of the specific sociopolitical history of the community in understanding the problems that have emerged and the solutions that people have developed over time. Understanding the historical experience of a people in context is critical for engaging in practice and research that is socially just, and it also helps students conceptualize their research and practice a bit differently. Finally, our community work in Chile is personally and professionally renewing, so it helps us to better conceptualize our research and better guide student community-based research with greater cultural competence.

TRAINING OUTCOMES, EVALUATION, AND CRITIQUE

We have a well-defined program training model and have worked continuously over the past 8 years to improve and refine the quality of the program consistent with that model. So, does it work? Do our graduates possess the expected skills and knowledge? How should graduates of our program differ from graduates of similar programs? In this section, we describe how we address or could address these questions from an EC perspective.

The key sources of information for attending to these questions are current students at each level of the program (e.g., 1st-year students, students preparing for comps, students completing their predoctoral internship, etc.); program graduates; supervisors and instructors of the students from outside of our core program; program faculty (from their perspectives as instructors, clinical supervisors, advisors, doctoral committee members, etc.); clients and research participants of our students; and employers of our students. Currently, we collect information from all of these sources except the last three. We do not formally or informally gather feedback from clients or research participants at the program level. With respect to clients, we do have standard quality-control mechanisms (e.g., live observation, audio and videotape monitoring, case notes, supervision). Confidentiality concerns preclude systematic data collection from the clients our students serve, although we note the promising research on clients' experience of multicultural counseling by Pope-Davis et al., 2003). With respect to research, participants are always provided with opportunities to contact the faculty research supervisor with concerns, as per Institutional Review Board practices, but the absence of contact does not help us understand the quality of the participants' experience. It would certainly be feasible to solicit feedback in the process of data collection for some projects. With respect to employers, our time and resource constraints, along with the lack of a requirement to do so, have combined to preclude large-scale feedback about our graduates in their postdoctoral settings. Ideally, we would want to know how our graduates compare with others, if they are practicing with multicultural competency, if they are clear about how their values influence their practice, if they are committed to prevention work, and so forth. This level of assessment is an obvious next step to take in understanding the effectiveness of our training program.

Practicum evaluations are completed two or three times per academic year. Evaluations for students in the adult practicum sequence systematically and always include items attending to multiple levels of the ecology, dynamics of privilege, diversity with respect to socioeconomic status, religion, age, and ethnicity. We expect our students to develop strong multicultural competence, and they typically receive very positive feedback from their clinical supervisors about their cultural competence. Each year, we ask informal, open-ended questions of our students on internships about how they are similar to, and different from, their fellow interns who are trained in different institutions. Our students report that they typically feel comparable to other interns across most traditional domains of clinical practice, with clear individual variations across different areas depending on the student and training site. But consensus typically emerges around four areas that our students feel sets them apart from their co-interns: understanding and integration of the ecological model in conceptualization, assessment, and intervention; multicultural competence; awareness of and ability to talk about privilege and power; and commitment to social activism, or at least to a broader understanding of the potential roles of psychologists in enhancing positive social change.

After internship, and after graduation, graduates of our program engage in both research and practice, and tend to select positions that allow them to do some of both. Recent graduates have become Counseling Psychology and counselor education faculty members, researcher/practitioners in clinical settings, university counseling and health center staff, staff members in child-clinical hospitals, research coordinators and clinicians in various community mental health agencies, research-practitioners in VA hospitals, and staff members in community college and university–student affairs divisions.

Some of our annual evaluation procedures are part of an ongoing, internal evaluation process that operates across the college in which we are housed. This process includes both quantitative and qualitative data collected from students, faculty, and clinical supervisors and is reviewed by external reviewers who are members of the mental health community. Annual or bi-annual surveys of students generate data on student perceptions of their research and clinical training, their skills development, and other dimensions of program satisfaction. Students receive an annual written evaluation from their advisors, with input from other faculty members. These evaluations address clinical skills, research skills, coursework, multicultural competence, professional development and involvement, and ethical and self-awareness. Comprehensive exam responses have also provided a useful indicator of the breadth and integration of learning. These and other formal evaluation and feedback methods are very useful; however, we generate the greatest amount of critical feedback about programmatic changes and improvements in training that students want to see via regular contact and conversations with students. By far, the greatest number of program changes and developments has come from this informal, yet critical, process. As long as students feel a sense of community, safety, and commitment, we believe that this will continue to be our richest source of information and critique.

Prilleltensky and Nelson (2002, p. 70) delineated a set of applied skills for critical psychology practice and action that are useful in considering the kinds of skills we hope our own students develop. They present skills at three levels: individual, group, and community/society. At the individual level of the ecology, skills that enhance critical psychology practice include personal reflection and consciousness-raising, communication skills, and assessment and intervention skills for multiple settings. Recommended training processes for achieving these skills include personal reflection exercises, emotional expression, connection of personal and political, raising self-understanding, values education and clarification, basic skills training, practical experiences that include supervision, role modeling, mentoring, peer feedback, and respectful challenging. At the group level, skills include group process facilitation and intervention, and organization development skills including process consultation, action research, team-building, program planning, and partnership processes. Important training processes not already noted include group facilitation, group-based training and support groups, building community within the academic or professional unit, and individual and group projects in the community. Finally, at the community/society level, skills include community development and organizing, skills in social action, coalition building and advocacy, and skills in social policy analysis and formulation. Additional training processes to develop these skills include exposure to community and social issues via field trips, speakers, and practical placements; and encouragement of participation in campus and community events. Although our program includes all of the skills and training processes indicated at the individual and group levels, it is in the community/society area that we could improve and expand to be more consistent with an emancipatory communitarian approach to psychology practice. That is, we do not provide training that specifically addresses community development and organizing, social action, coalition building, or social policy analysis. We do, however, utilize the training processes associated with community-level skills. Our students tend to be very involved in the community via volunteer work and agency service, and are systematically exposed to the work of community agencies and issues, such as the conditions of farm workers and the treatment of survivors of torture, because of the personal/professional connections fostered early in the program.

Finally, Vera and Speight (2003) articulated a series of suggestions for incorporating social justice philosophy into counseling psychology training programs. We provide these here as further bases for evaluating our program and other mental health training programs in general. Their suggestions include: expanding the dissemination of research beyond professional journals, utilizing teaching strategies that give students responsibility as learners and co-creators of the classroom environment and dynamics, increasing faculty commitment to and participation in activism, fostering student sensitivity to injustice and suffering, promoting student understanding of the causes of and conditions that support oppression, providing students with tools to carry out prevention and intervention work that contributes to social justice, and exposing students to diverse roles that psychologists can play in society.

The processes of reading, reflecting, discussing, writing this chapter, and reading reviews of this work from doctoral students, have elicited a number of new questions and indicators that we think would help us understand the effectiveness of our program. Here are some questions that may help our and other training programs address more specifically the dimensions of the program that promote an EC approach to psychology practice and training:

- What percentage of student and faculty research is community-based?
- What percentage of students provide something in return for access to research participants, and what is the nature of their contribution (e.g., presenting to schools, in-service skills training, assisting agencies in grant writing, etc.)?

- Are students able to critically describe their level of multicultural competence, the ways in which they are privileged, and how their privilege interacts with their prevention and intervention skills?
- Are students able to articulate the values and assumptions that guide their clinical and research practices?
- Do students intervene at levels of the ecology other than the individual level?
- Do students conceptualize and assess clients in a manner that takes into account the multiple systems within the ecology of clients' lives?
- What strategies do students employ to enhance critical consciousness, and how will they build on those strategies in their future practice and research settings?
- What skills and experiences have students obtained in advocacy, policy change, consultation, and grant writing?
- What percentage of students has engaged, during their training, in activity that directly led to change of a policy or procedure in a way that increased the welfare of others?
- How do students define community?
- How do students conceptualize the roles and responsibilities of counseling psychologists in today's society?

Based on reviews of this chapter from doctoral students in counseling psychology at the University of Miami, we now plan on using this list of questions in focus groups with our students to generate ideas for improving our programmatic attention to training that better reflects an EC approach to psychology practice.

SUMMARY AND CONCLUSION

Although we are excited about and proud of the program we are a part of, and would even say that aspects of the program are exemplary, we by no means see the program as finished, as good as it could be, or complete. There are numerous areas in which we can increase our attention to social justice, enhance our social advocacy, and further the extent to which students engage in liberatory practice that is fundamental to an EC approach to psychology. In addition to the many areas for improvement, we are also aware of the economic issues confronting state universities and the ongoing need to refine, condense, and evolve to meet constraints and demands of the context. Therefore, we expect to continue the process of refinement and change that has been part of this program's long history. What we can say with certainty is that we have a core of faculty and students with a strong commitment to social justice and to improving the welfare of children, youth, and families through the science and practice of psychology. As in any community, the diversity of our styles, opinions, goals, motives, and talents means that progress will evolve in circles, spirals, fits, and seizures rather than in a linear fashion, and at any given time what some of us see as progress, others of us may see as backward movement. Nevertheless, this is a challenge that not only makes training interesting, but which we see as critical for being more oriented toward an EC approach to psychology and for being committed to training socially conscious psychologists who are prepared for the demands of this new century.

ACKNOWLEDGMENTS

We thank Dr. Etiony Aldarondo and the counseling psychology doctoral student reviewers of the University of Miami who helped us improve this chapter through their thoughtful critiques. We particularly thank Dr. Jeff McWhirter, long-time professor of Counseling Psychology at Arizona State University, for the many years of personal and professional mentoring that has contributed to our thinking and training of counseling psychologists.

REFERENCES

Alinsky, S. (1989). *Rules for radicals: A pragmatic primer for realistic radicals.* New York: Vintage Books.

American Psychological Association. (2003). *Code of ethics.* Washington, DC: Author.

Arredondo, P., & Perez, P. (2003). *The Counseling Psychologist, 31,* 282–289.

Ancis, J. R., & Szymanski, D. M. (2001). Awareness of White privilege among White counseling trainees. *The Counseling Psychologist, 29,* 548–569.

Bamba, M. (2001). *An outcome evaluation of the Make Parenting a Pleasure Program.* Doctoral dissertation, University of Oregon, Eugene.

Berryman, P. (1987). *Liberation theology: The essential facts about the revolutionary movement in Latin America and beyond.* New York: Pantheon.

Blustein, D. L., Chaves, A. P., Diemer, M. A., Gallagher, L. A., Marshall, K. G., Sirin, S., & Bhati, K. S. (2002). Voices of the forgotten half: The role of social class in the school-to-work transition. *Journal of Counseling Psychology, 49,* 311–323.

Brabeck, M., Walsh, M. E., Kenny, M., & Comilang, K. (1997). Interprofessional collaboration for children and families: Opportunities for counseling psychology in the 21st century. *The Counseling Psychologist, 25,* 615–636.

Bronfenbrenner, U. (1979). *The ecology of human development: Experiments by nature and design.* Cambridge, MA: Harvard University Press.

Bronfenbrenner, U. (1986). Ecology of the family as a context for human development: Research perspectives. *Developmental Psychology, 22,* 723–742.

Bronfenbrenner, U. (1989). Ecological systems theory. *Annals of Child Development, 6,* 187–249.

Burrow-Sanchez, J. J. (2003). *Adolescent responses to maternal depressive behaviors during family interactions.* Unpublished doctoral dissertation, University of Oregon, Eugene.

Carr, E. G., Dunlap, G., Horner, R. H., Koegel, R. L., Turnbull, A. P., Sailor, W., et al. (2002). Positive behavior support: Evolution of an applied science. *Journal of Positive Behavior Interventions, 4,* 4–16, 20.

Chronister, K. M., McWhirter, B. T., & Kerewsky, S. D. (2004). Counseling prevention from an ecological framework. In R. K. Conyne & E. P. Cook (Eds.), *Ecological counseling: An innovative approach to conceptualizing person–environment interaction* (pp. 315–338). Alexandria, VA: ACA Press.

Coleman, J. (1991). *Parental involvement in education. Policy Perspectives.* Washington, DC: U.S. Department of Education.

Cummins, J. (1986). Empowering minority students: A framework for intervention. *Harvard Educational Review, 56*(1), 19–36.

Fassinger, R. (2001). Using the master's tools: Social advocacy at the national level. In P. Gore & J. Swanson (Chairs), *Counseling psychologists as agents of social change.* Paper presented at the 4th National Conference on Counseling Psychology, Houston, TX.

Fassinger, R. (2003). Leona Tyler: Pioneer of possibilities. In G. Kimble & M. Wertheimer (Eds.), *Portraits of pioneers in psychology* (Vol. 5, pp. 231–248). Washington, DC/Hillsdale, NJ: American Psychological Association/Lawrence Erlbaum Associates.

Fouad, N. A., & Brown, M. T. (2000). The role of race and class in development: Implications for counseling psychology. In S. D. Brown & R. W. Lent (Eds.), *Handbook of Counseling Psychology* (3rd ed., pp. 379–408). New York: Wiley.

Fox, D., & Prilleltensky. I. (Eds.). (1997). *Critical psychology: An introduction.* London: Sage.

Freire, P. (1971). *Pedagogy of the oppressed.* New York: Herder and Herder.

Gelso, C. J., & Fretz, B. R. (2001). Counseling psychology: A growing profession. In B. R. Fretz & C. J. Gelso (Eds.), *Counseling psychology* (2nd ed., pp. 1–25). Fort Worth, TX: Harcourt Brace.

Goodman, M. (2002). *If we build it, will parents come? Parent participation in preventative parenting groups.* Doctoral dissertation, University of Oregon, Eugene.

Gragg, K. M. (2003). *Women, domestic violence, and career counseling: An empirical evaluation of 2 intervention programs.* Doctoral dissertation, University of Oregon, Eugene.

Greenwood, G. E., & Hickman, C. W. (1991). Research and practice in parent involvement: Implications for teacher education. *Elementary School Journal, 91,* 279–287.

Gutierrez, G. (1990). *A theology of liberation.* New York: Orbis Books.

Hart, R. S. (2002). *An investigation of service provider multicultural competence and facility multiculturalism in children's residential treatment facilities.* Unpublished doctoral dissertation, University of Oregon, Eugene.

Hayashino, D. (2003). *A construct development and preliminary validation study of parenting stress among Southeast Asian immigrant and refugee parents.* Doctoral dissertation, University of Oregon, Eugene.

Helms, J. (2003). A pragmatic view of social justice. *The Counseling Psychologist, 31,* 305–313.

Herr, E. L., & Niles, S. G. (1998). Career: Social action on behalf of purpose, productivity, and hope. In C. G. Lee & G. R. Walz (Eds.), *Social action: A mandate for counselors* (pp. 117–156). Alexandria, VA: American Counseling Association.

Horner, R. H., & Sugai, G. (2000). School-wide behavior support: An emerging initiative [Special issue]. *Journal of Positive Behavioral Interventions, 2,* 231–233.

Horner, R. H., Sugai, G., & Horner, H. F. (2000). A school-wide approach to student discipline. *The School Administrator, 57*(2), 20–24.

Hunt-Morse, M. C. (2002). *Adolescent mothers' psychosocial development: Implications for parenting.* Doctoral dissertation, University of Oregon, Eugene.

Ivey, A. E., & Collins, N. M. (2003). Social justice: A long term challenge for counseling psychology. *The Counseling Psychologist, 31,* 290–298.

Ivey, M. B., Ivey, A. E., D'Andrea, M., & Daniels, J. (1997). White privilege: Implications for counselor education multicultural identity. *Association for Counselor Education and Supervision Spectrum, 57,* 3–6.

Kaufman, N. (2003). *Mediating effects of skill growth on treatment efficacy of depression: An evaluation of cognitive-behavioral group treatment for adolescent depression and conduct disorder.* Unpublished doctoral dissertation, University of Oregon, Eugene.

Kerewsky, S. D., & Forrest, L. M. (2003, March). *Counseling psychology student supervisors of human service trainees.* Paper presented at the National Organization of Human Service Educators (NOHSE) conference, Denver, CO.

Knott, J. M. (2003). *Self-efficacy and motivation to change among chronic youth offenders: An exploratory examination of the efficacy of an experiential learning motivation enhancement intervention.* Doctoral dissertation, University of Oregon, Eugene.

Kornbluh, P. (2003). *The Pinochet file: A declassified dossier on atrocity and accountability.* New York: National Security Archive

Kozol, J. (1991). *Savage inequalities: Children in America's schools.* New York: Harper Perennial.

Kozol, J. (1995). *Amazing grace: The lives of children and conscience of a nation.* New York: Harper Perennial.

Liang, J. (2005). *The influence of role activation and sociocultural factors on the mental health attitudes and coping practices of Asian Pacific Americans.* Unpublished doctoral dissertation, University of Oregon, Eugene.

Liu, W. M. (2001). Expanding our understanding of multiculturalism: Developing a social class worldview model. In D. B. Pope-Davis & H. L. K. Coleman (Eds.), *The intersection of race, class, and gender in counseling psychology* (pp. 127–170). Thousand Oaks, CA: Sage.

Liu, W. M. (2002). The social class-related experiences of men: Integrating theory and practice. *Professional Psychology: Research and Practice, 33,* 355–360.

Liu, W. M., Ali, S. R., Soleck, G., Hopps, J., & Pickett, T. (2004). Using social class in counseling psychology research. *Journal of Counseling Psychology, 51,* 3–18.

Lusk, A. (2003). An experimental evaluation of a prison orientation program. Doctoral dissertation, University of Oregon, Eugene.

Martin, V. (2001). *Relationships between learned helplessness factors, child abuse, combat exposure, and severity of chronic combat-related PTSD.* Doctoral dissertation, University of Oregon, Eugene.

Martín-Baró, I. (1994). Writings for a liberation psychology. In A. A. Aron & S. Corne (Eds.), *Writings for a liberation psychology.* Cambridge, MA: Harvard University Press.

Matchett-Morris, G. (2003). *The mediating role of stress in the relationship between social support and couple satisfaction for gay male couples.* Unpublished doctoral dissertation, University of Oregon, Eugene.

McClure, B. A., & Russo, T. R. (1996). The politics of counseling: Looking back and forward. *Counseling & Values, 40*(3), 162–175.

McWhirter, B. T., & McWhirter, E. H. (1998, Spring). An ecological model of counseling psychology training. *Prevention and Public Interest Special Interest Group Newsletter, 5,* pp. 3–".

McWhirter, B. T., & McWhirter, E. H. (2006). Couples helping couples: Empowerment through consultation and training in Peñalolén, Chile. In R. Toporek, L. Gerstein, N. Fouad, G. Roysircar, & T. Israel (Eds.), *Handbook for social justice in counseling psychology: Leadership, vision, and action* (pp. 406–420). Palo Alto, CA: Sage.

McWhirter, E. H. (1991). Empowerment in counseling. *Journal of Counseling and Development, 69*(3), 222–227.

McWhirter, E. H. (1997, April). Empowerment, social activism, and counseling. *Counseling & Human Development, 29(8),* 1–11.

McWhirter, E. H. (1994). *Counseling for empowerment.* Alexandria, VA: American Counseling Association Press.

McWhirter, J. J., McWhirter, B. T., McWhirter, E. H., & McWhirter, R. J. (2004). *At-risk youth: A comprehensive response* (3rd ed.). Pacific Grove, CA: Brooks/Cole.

Miller, W. R., & Rollnick, S. (2002). *Motivational Interviewing: Preparing people of change* (2nd ed.). New York: Guilford.

Neville, H. A., & Mobley, M. (2001). Social identities in contexts: An ecological model of multicultural counseling psychology processes. *The Counseling Psychologist, 29*(4), 471–486.

Ponterotto, J. G. (1998). Charting a course for research in multicultural counseling training. *The Counseling Psychologist, 26,* 43–68.

Pope-Davis, D. B., Toporek, R. L., Ortega-Villalobos, L., Ligiéro, D. P., Britton-Powell, C. S., Liu, W. M., et al. (2003). Client perspectives of multicultural counseling competence: A qualitative examination. *The Counseling Psychologist, 30*(3), 355–393.

Prilleltensky, I. (1989). Psychology and the status quo. *American Psychologist, 44,* 795–802.

Prilleltensky, I. (1997). Values, assumptions, and practices: Assessing the moral implications of psychological discourse and action. *American Psychologist, 52,* 517–535.

Prilleltensky, I., & Nelson, G. (2002). *Doing psychology critically: Making a difference in diverse settings.* London: Macmillan/Palgrave.

Romano, J. L., & Hage, S. M. (2000). Prevention and counseling psychology: Revitalizing commitments for the 21st century. *The Counseling Psychologist, 28,* 733–763.

Shepard, S. (2003). *Gender differences in siblings' contributions to at-risk youths' substance use.* Doctoral dissertation, University of Oregon, Eugene.

Sparks, E. E., & Park, A. H. (2000). The integration of feminism and multiculturalism: Ethical dilemmas at the border. In M. M. Brabeck (Ed.), *Practicing feminist ethics in psychology* (pp. 203–224). Washington, DC: American Psychological Association.

Steinbock, A. J. (1988). Helping and homogeneity: Therapeutic interactions as the challenge to power. *Quarterly Journal of Ideology, 12*(1), 31–46.

Stent, K. (2003). *Sex differences and post-incarceration school and work engagement of adolescent juvenile offenders.* Doctoral dissertation, University of Oregon, Eugene.

Stormshak, E. A., & Dishion, T. J. (2002). An ecological approach to clinical and counseling psychology. *Clinical Child and Family Psychology Review, 5,* 197–215.

Sue, D. W., Arredondo, P., & McDavis, R. J. (1992). Multicultural counseling competencies and standards: A call to the profession. *Journal of Counseling and Development, 70,* 477–486.

Sue, D. W., & Sue, D. (1990). *Counseling the culturally different.* New York: Wiley.

Sundberg, N. D., & Littman, R. A. (1994). Leona Elizabeth Tyler (1906–1993). *American Psychologist, 49,* 211–212.

Torres, D. M. (2003). *An outcome evaluation of a Latino parent program for enhancing educational achievement.* Unpublished doctoral dissertation, University of Oregon, Eugene.

Townsend, K. (2003). *Late adolescent psychosocial adjustment: Roles of individuation, social connectedness, and ambivalence over emotional expression.* Unpublished doctoral dissertation, University of Oregon, Eugene.

Vera, E. M., & Reese, L. E. (2000). Preventive interventions with school-age youth. In S. D. Brown & R. W. Lent (Eds.), *Handbook of counseling psychology* (3rd ed., pp. 411–434). New York: Wiley.

Vera, E. M., & Speight, S. L. (2003). Multicultural competence, social justice, and counseling psychology: Expanding our roles. *The Counseling Psychologist, 31,* 253–272.

Worell, J., & Remer, P. (1992). *Feminist perspectives in therapy: An empowerment model for women.* New York: Wiley.

19

Grounding Clinical Training and Supervision in an Empowerment Model

Ellen Hawley McWhirter
Benedict T. McWhirter
University of Oregon

In this chapter, we present how clinical training, and specifically the supervision of students in training, can be carried out in a manner that reflects and reinforces an empowerment model of counseling. The chapter opens with the particular definition of empowerment in the context of counseling that influences the authors' training and supervision practices. Although much of this content is consistent with practices in the University of Oregon (UO) counseling psychology program, our goal here is less to describe our particular program than to stimulate thinking and offer ideas for supervision and training. The model of empowerment we describe is not the only influence or model utilized in clinical training and supervision in the UO program, nor are we the only faculty who supervise clinical training. We are fortunate to have a program faculty group with remarkably similar and strong commitments to prevention, multiculturalism, and social justice. Thus, the content of this chapter reflects the authors' perspectives and practices, richly influenced by ongoing dialogue and experiences with our colleagues, and also draws on experiences as faculty members in counseling psychology prior to joining the UO faculty.

Our goal in this chapter is to answer the question: What might supervision and training look like if students are being trained to ground their clinical practice in an empowerment model? After describing the empowerment model in the context of counseling, we illustrate the notion of empowerment using a rubric of "5 C's." For each of the "5 C's," we present case examples that apply elements of the definition to the supervision of students in practicum training. Although all identifying information has been altered significantly, the examples we provide reflect work with actual people, and as such are realistic, rather than idealistic, illustrations of the empowerment model. Next, we describe specific strategies and activities that we have used to incorporate this empowerment model into clinical training and supervision. We note that although our emphasis in this chapter is on supervision, we devote considerable time to describing the process of empowerment within counseling in an effort to make very clear the links between the supervision descriptions and the model.

DEFINING EMPOWERMENT IN THE CONTEXT OF COUNSELING

Empowerment is often used to describe the goal of helping relationships. Typically, empowerment is used to refer to increased assertiveness or other self-management skills on the part of the person being helped. We use the term in a manner that is broader in scope than an individual's development of greater skills or more effective behaviors. A review of definitions of empowerment across fields such as counseling, education, social work, feminist and multicultural counseling, and community psychology (McWhirter, 1991, 1994), serves as the basis for the definition that we use in this chapter and in our work in general.

One of the assumptions of an empowerment approach to counseling is that helping relationships are not necessarily helpful, and can actually serve to oppress rather than empower clients. For example, Prilleltensky (1989; Prilleltensky & Nelson, 2002) has argued that interventions based on traditional approaches to psychotherapy can serve to perpetuate the kinds of systemic problems and inequalities that lead clients to seek psychological services, preserving rather than transforming an unjust status quo. Steinbock (1988) suggests that helping relationships are oppressive to the extent that "helpees" embrace a view of themselves as needy and dependent on the helper for solutions to their problems. Further, he contends that problem resolution focuses on the individual rather than on the systems that create the problems, resulting in a very low likelihood of interventions that produce constructive, preventative change (Steinbock, 1988). Caplan (1992) articulates how feminist therapy, explicitly developed to address women's oppression, is also vulnerable to reflecting and preserving the gender inequities of society. The societal pervasiveness of racism and sexism, economic stratification and violence, leaves counseling relationships vulnerable to subtly and even overtly reflecting these and other forms of oppression. For example, counselors who fail to acknowledge the roles that racism and classism play in creating the environment of a low-income client of color may "blame the victim," and counselors ascribing to the values of the dominant culture without examining the influence of their values in counseling may engage in interventions that are inappropriate for their clients (e.g., Katz, 1985; McWhirter, 1994; Prilleltensky & Nelson, 2002; Sue & Sue, 1990). McClure and Russo (1996) note that in spite of many critiques of the counseling profession for decades (e.g., Aubrey, 1983; Chomsky, 1969; Wrenn, 1983), little has changed with respect to addressing the social inequities and injustices that cause or augment mental health problems.

In spite of these limitations to the ultimate usefulness or helpfulness of counseling, an empowerment approach also recognizes a liberatory potential in counseling. That is, counseling also potentially can be a vehicle for assisting people in transforming their lives and the environmental conditions affecting them. The notion of empowerment described in the literature outside of traditional counseling psychology literature captures this liberatory potential. Drawing from the work of psychologists such as Ignacio Martín-Baró (1994) and Julian Rappaport (1981, 1987), social workers such as Elaine Pinderhughes (1983) and Barbara Solomon (1976, 1987), feminist scholar-practitioners such as Donna Hawxhurst and Susan Morrow (1984), as well as educators such as Paolo Freire (1971), we define empowerment as:

> ... the process by which people, organizations, or groups who are powerless or marginalized: (a) become aware of the power dynamics at work in their life context, (b) de-

velop the skills and capacity for gaining some reasonable control over their lives, (c) which they exercise, (d) without infringing upon the rights of others, and (e) which coincides with supporting the empowerment of others in their community. (McWhirter, 1994, p. 12)

We note that there are other definitions and models of empowerment, and numerous strategies for enhancing empowerment. We limit ourselves here to presenting the definition that emerged from our own practice and immersion in the literature, and that has been useful to us over the years. In keeping with this definition, clinical practice that is guided by an empowerment model is not limited to decreasing symptoms of depression or increasing prosocial behaviors, although these certainly might be part of the clinical goals. It is a practice that extends beyond working with individual adults, and extends into the community; it includes direct work with clients as well as advocacy and involvement in social transformation processes at larger levels (B. T. McWhirter, E. H. McWhirter, & J. J. McWhirter, 1988; McWhirter, 1991, 1998). The empowerment model attends to the various levels of the client's ecology, recognizing that the client is embedded within systems, is influenced by those systems, and is simultaneously able to exert varying levels of influence within the systems (Bronfenbrenner, 1979). This might be seen in each component of the definition.

"Become aware of the power dynamics at work in their life context" refers to identifying the most relevant systemic and structural influences on clients' lives at personal, interpersonal, and societal levels. For example, these influences include racism, sexism, heterosexism, inaccessible environments, and ageism. They also include factors such as the structure of welfare and disparities in the U.S. public education system. Power dynamics also manifest within counseling relationships, as both counselor and client are products (and co-producers) of the social, cultural, political, and economic contexts of their own lives. The counselor's critical awareness of power dynamics within the session and in the client's larger ecology is a prerequisite to facilitating the client's awareness.

"Developing the skills and capacity for gaining some reasonable control over their lives" refers to skill acquisition, as well as the motivation and self-efficacy expectations required to exercise those skills. Much of the literature designed to assist counselors in facilitating skill development is rooted in European-American values, worldviews, and norms (Katz, 1985). Thus, counselors must be prepared to explore the nature of each skill and the manner and context in which the skill is practiced, in accord with the client's goals and values, as well as other salient client characteristics such as personal and sociopolitical history, interpersonal style, and cultural identity (Sue & Sue, 1990). Perhaps more important than the development of new skills is the client's understanding and valuing of her or his preexisting skills and resources. These skills sustained the client through life thus far and should be of great assistance in furthering the client's goals.

"Which they exercise without infringing upon the rights of others" reflects the fact that empowerment fundamentally involves integrative power or "power with others" (Hagberg, 1984) rather than power over others, or power "to do to" others. Violating the autonomy or rights of others in pursuit of client goals is fundamentally incompatible with empowerment.

"Coinciding with support for the empowerment of others in their community" can range from interpersonal behaviors such as providing encouragement and support, to community consciousness-raising efforts such as participating in marches and other public methods of consciousness-raising, advocating for legislative change, or helping to organize cultural and educational events. The role of the counselor is to facilitate and support the client's connections with community, and to enhance the client's ability to support the empowerment of others as appropriate for the client's current situation. In our view, empowerment is not a linear process, nor one that concludes with achievement of a particular "empowered state." This means that therapy may end without clients being ready for, interested in, or committed to the empowerment of others. This is not a failure on the part of the client or the therapist. The therapist's job is not to co-opt or pressure the client into community service or action, but to meet clients where they are in the empowerment process, and respectfully work to increase, enhance, or otherwise promote empowerment in additional ways that are consistent with the client's goals. In the next section we elaborate on the meaning of empowerment in counseling using the rubric of "5 C's of empowerment": collaboration, context, competence, community, and critical consciousness (McWhirter, 1997, 2001). Because our main focus is on the supervision and training of counselors, we elaborate each "C" with examples applied to supervision.

"5 C'S" OF EMPOWERMENT

Collaboration

The first "C," *Collaboration* refers to the dynamic relationship between the counselor and the client. This relationship is one characterized by a joint definition of the problems to be addressed, goals of counseling, and possible interventions and strategies for change and growth. Without collaboration, the counselor risks reinforcing passivity and neediness in the client, misunderstanding the nature and meaning of the client's difficulties, and developing interventions that are inconsistent with the client's values, culture, ideology, goals, and skills. Collaboration in the context of our empowerment model means that the counselor–client power differential is minimized, but *without* the pretense that power differences don't exist. Such pretense perpetuates what Steinbock (1988) refers to as the "homogeneity of power" (p. 32). According to Steinbock (1988), when we presume equality of power, we act as if each member of the relationship is equally free to present viewpoints and to initiate change. Such an assumption in the context of a counseling relationship protects the counselor from critique and from having to change their methods, attitudes, and so on. Clients rarely offer critical feedback unless they perceive that the counselor truly wants feedback, that the feedback will not hurt the relationship, that giving such feedback does not violate important cultural and social norms, that the counselor will not dismiss or punish them, and finally, that they believe their feedback has merit and will benefit the counselor and/or themselves. In other words, even in the most egalitarian of counseling relationships, the counselor cannot assume that the absence of negative feedback is evidence of effective and beneficial counseling.

Rather than assuming a false equality, the nature of the relationship and role expectations should be openly discussed (to the extent that this is respectful and consistent with the client's cultural norms), power differences should be freely acknowledged in terms that make sense to the client, and the counselor should present as an expert who considers the client's self-knowledge, existing skills, and life experience as another source of expertise and as essential resources in the education/mutual growth process. There is no formula for this conversation, but we have found it easiest to introduce these notions as the counselor discusses consent, client expectations, counselor expectations, and the nature of counseling.

Infusing clinical training with the notion of empowerment requires that collaboration characterizes relationships not just between counselors and clients, but between students and faculty as well. For example, there is an obvious hierarchy embedded within a mental health training program because one group of people—the faculty—has the responsibility and the authority to remove from a program a student who has not responded to remediation efforts and is not progressing to the required level of skill, knowledge, or competence. However, this clear and unequivocal power difference does not mean that students are powerless. Rather, everyone in the environment is expected to appropriately exercise the power that they possess in order to achieve the goal of becoming, or of producing, competent clinicians. The faculty, in particular, bear the responsibility of creating environmental conditions conducive to the appropriate exercise of power.

To illustrate the dimension of collaboration, we describe the experience of Alicia, a practicum student who was struggling in her clinical work with a recently divorced young woman. Alicia herself had experienced a difficult relationship break-up 2 months prior to intake with this client, and had shared with her peers her strong and ongoing feelings of betrayal and bitterness. In group supervision after one particular session, her peer observers shared with Alicia and the practicum supervisor concerns that her feelings had been surfacing inappropriately during her sessions. In this situation, a collaborative or "power-with" supervisory approach would include letting Alicia know, clearly and directly, that there is a problem, clarifying Alicia's perceptions, identifying possible means to address the problem in her sessions, and outside of sessions, and choosing the optimal course of action. Group supervision around this issue would provide a balance of support and challenge. Alicia would experience the supervisor's interest in her well-being and respect for her point of view. A noncollaborative or "power-over" supervisory approach would involve unilateral definition of the problem and a threat-like solution without an attempt to integrate Alicia's perceptions, ideas, or resources into the problem-solving process. In either case, depending on what has been happening and Alicia's ability to recognize what is inappropriate in her responses to her client, the supervisor might believe that Alicia must get therapy before or concurrent with continuing in practicum, but the process would unfold very differently according to the supervisor's approach. Ways that collaboration may be manifested more globally in mental health training programs (that is, outside of supervision) is through faculty support of active graduate student organizations, the existence of a responsive system for identifying and attending to student concerns, the incorporation of student-driven content into courses, and the treatment of students as colleagues, co-learners and co-teachers in a community of people dedicated to continuous learning.

Context

The second "C," *Context,* refers to actively incorporating the ecological model (Bronfenbrenner, 1979) into clinical work, understanding that the lives of the clients and the therapist are embedded in families, communities, sociopolitical histories, socioeconomic conditions, cultures, and values systems, each with constructions of gender, race, disability, success, achievement, and so on. This ecology must be considered as the therapist and client(s)—together—formulate the nature of the problems faced by the client, and design solutions and alternatives. Recognition of context requires acknowledging how the context contributes to the development, maintenance, and exacerbation of client concerns. Between the extremes of blaming the victim ("you would have left your abusive partner if you really wanted to") and placing all responsibility external to the client ("there is absolutely nothing you can do about these forces impinging on your life") exists a large middle ground in which the client and counselor can explore realistic avenues for change and action. The counselor's factual and experiential knowledge base influences the extent to which context will be accurately assessed. For example, understanding the context of a client who is negotiating the welfare system will be much more difficult for a counselor who knows nothing about welfare legislation, benefits, requirements, and the difference between how welfare works in theory and in reality. Although clients themselves provide a great deal of rich and valuable information that contributes to the counselor's knowledge base, it is the responsibility of the counselor to develop and continuously augment their knowledge. In addition to textbooks and standard training materials, nonstandard materials such as autobiographies and movies, as well as life experiences such as immersion in non-native cultures and languages, friendships, volunteer experience, and noncounseling related work experiences, can all contribute importantly to contextual awareness.

Mental health training programs generally include systematic self-exploration activities that support the development of context awareness, the success of which can be evaluated through the supervision process. In theory, as counselors in training become more aware of how their attitudes, experiences, behaviors, values, and beliefs have been shaped by their own context, they will be better able and more likely to attend to important contextual issues with their clients. There is a growing body of literature on counselor training pedagogy, particularly in the area of multicultural counseling (Carter, 2003; Mio & Awakuni, 2000; Mio & Barker-Hackett, 2003; Sue & Sue, 1990) that we do not review here. One critical topic area that often seems to go unaddressed is the area of socioeconomic status. Although recognized as an important influence on human development and outcomes (Fouad & Brown, 2000; Jarjoura, Triplett, & Brinker, 2002; Liu, 2001, 2002; Luthar, 1999), until recently there has been little in the counselor training or supervision literature to assist in this area. The emerging line of research and scholarship by Liu and his colleagues (Liu, Ali, Soleck, Hopps, Dunston, & Pickett, 2004; Liu & Pope-Davis, 2003; Liu, Soleck, Hopps, Dunston, & Pickett, 2004; Liu & Ali, 2005) attends specifically to understanding social class and its implications for counseling practice and research.

The following illustrates the notion of context. One of the authors supervised a counselor-in-training who was working with a middle-aged White female client. The counselor-in-training was a young Asian American woman ("Sophie"). During supervision after the third session, the counselor-in-training began our session by expressing anger at the client for continually seeking positive feedback.

> I decided I'm just not going to smile at her anymore. Why do I have to be all smiley all the time? She's a grown-up and she shouldn't be wanting my approval. She doesn't do anything about her life, she just sits there. Does she think I'm a cute Asian girl and I'm just going to make her feel good or something? What does she want from me?

This set the stage for an hour-long discussion of contextual issues, in which we considered some of the following: the client's history of abuse in her family of origin and a previous marriage; the client's current estrangement from her daughter, who was then about the age of the counselor; this was the woman's first experience of counseling; Sophie, in fact, rarely smiled at the client or showed any affect; and, ultimately, that Sophie was currently engaged in a struggle with her own mother, who she felt was constantly demanding more attention and energy than the counselor wanted or was able to give. We also explored discrepancies between Sophie's and client's socioeconomic status (the counselor was from a middle-class background and the client, from a lower working-class background), cultural backgrounds, ages, life experiences, and religious beliefs. This supervision session appeared to be a breakthrough for Sophie's understanding of the client. However, the following week, it became apparent that she had moved from disliking the client to pitying the client. The following supervision session was focused not on context but on the critical consciousness and competence dimensions of empowerment. We return to the example of Sophie in the competence section of the chapter.

An important point we wish to highlight is that attention to context must not serve as a reason for inaction. Such a stance by the counselor is incapacitating for the client. Change and action are explored in light of context, not in spite of context. Because so many of the conditions faced by, and that limit, clients are structural and systemic, mental health service providers bear responsibility for taking action to address societal problems. Thus, the context component of empowerment is directly dependent on the critical consciousness component. Without critical consciousness, efforts to address context are likely to be ineffective because understanding context requires the development of critical consciousness.

Critical Consciousness

The third "C" of empowerment is *Critical Consciousness,* a term derived from Latin American liberation scholars such as Paolo Freire (1971, *concientização*), Gustavo Gutierrez (1990, *concientización*), and Ignacio Martín-Baró (1994, *concientización*), and refers generally to individuals' ability to examine themselves within their life contexts, to critically analyze the dynamics of those contexts, and to see themselves as actors in those contexts rather than merely as individuals who are acted on. That is, critical consciousness includes both awareness and action dimensions. In the context of the empowerment framework, critical consciousness requires an ongoing commitment on the part of the therapist (or the faculty supervisor, instructor, or researcher) to better understand the causes, dynamics, and consequences of oppression, privilege, power, and the context in which the clients (or the students, or the research participants) actually carry out their lives, as well as a commitment to act on that awareness.

Critical consciousness involves two complementary processes, power analysis and critical self-reflection (McWhirter, 1997, 2001). *Power analysis* refers to examining how power is distributed in a given situation in terms of, for example, race, gender, education, economics, sexual orientation, or sociopolitical history. Through power analysis, the therapist and client come to a more informed and context-sensitive understanding of beliefs, choices, perceptions, and behaviors. An important component of power analysis is understanding the meaning and effects of privilege.

Privilege is defined in Webster's *New Collegiate Dictionary* as "a right or immunity granted as a peculiar benefit, advantage, or favor." To be privileged means "not subject to the usual rules or penalties because of some special circumstance" (Webster's *New Collegiate Dictionary*, p. 909, 1980). We find it helpful to think of those "special circumstances" in terms of group membership. The "special circumstance" of being born White, in the United States, able-bodied, heterosexual, Christian, and middle class, grants privileges, rights, and immunities that have a particular and peculiar advantage. Of course, people are not usually aware of privilege. It is invisible. Mary Henning-Stout (1994) noted that, in spite of great personal costs to themselves, people are often motivated to say "no" to oppression because their experience of oppression propels them to act out their values and morals and convictions. However, she writes,

> Saying "no" to privilege is an option that rarely crosses the mind of a privileged person. Questioning privilege requires the comfortable to identify their comfort as harmful to others and to work toward balancing the scales, with the likely cost of relinquishing some of the comfort to which they have become accustomed. (p. 270)

Perhaps the most stark example within psychology of someone who did say no to privilege is Dr. Ignacio Martín-Baró. He was a Spanish-born social psychologist, Catholic priest, and faculty member at the University of San Salvador. He believed that psychology as a discipline was serving the privileged upper class while ignoring the vast majority of El Salvador's people who were (and continue to be) very poor. His research identified and illuminated the terrible oppression experienced by the people of El Salvador, as well as the multifaceted effects of that oppression. He continued this work in the face of many death threats. In 1992, he was lined up and assassinated on his university campus, along with five other priests, a woman housekeeper/cook, and her daughter. At any time prior to his assassination, Martín-Baró could have chosen to abandon his commitment to exposing the truth of the life of the poor of his country and focused his research on safer topics. He could have enjoyed the privileges associated with being a Spanish citizen, an educated, respected faculty member and priest, and one of very few psychologists in the country at that time. He would likely be alive today had he made this choice and lived his privilege. Martín-Baró's example anchors one end of a continuum that few traverse, and puts our own struggles with privilege in a larger context.

Critical self-reflection is the process of analyzing what we (as mental health practitioners, highly educated individuals, members of one or more ethnic/racial groups, etc.) and clients (as members of a social class, one or more ethnic/racial groups, etc.) and others contribute to the power dynamics of a situation through behaviors, privilege, assumptions, and interactions. *Critical consciousness* is what happens when power analysis is combined with critical self-reflection and this awareness is translated into action. Critical consciousness changes the way a person views the world, the person's sense of self in the world, and the person's agency for transforming the reality in which he or she lives. Fostering and reinforcing critical consciousness is an important element of the empowerment process; counselors who are not critically conscious are unlikely to assist their clients with this process. We do note, however, that one of us once observed a live counseling session to the contrary. The counselor in training was struggling to think of questions for the client, with long silences between questions. The client interpreted the silences as thoughtful and deliberate, and engaged in an unusually high level of reflection compared to the previous eight or nine sessions. The client used the silences to search for the connection that she thought the counselor was leading her to, and came up with a very powerful connection between her behavior and that of her spouse that (in the following weeks) lead to subsequent, positive changes in her behavior and their marital relationship. Later that day in supervision, the counselor shared that he had had absolutely no connection in mind, that he was feeling extremely distracted during the session, and had been trying to control his anxiety with deep breathing throughout the hour. In this session, the counselor's lack of critical consciousness did *not* hinder the client's development of a greater level awareness!

The work of one of our former clients, "James," illustrates the development of critical consciousness in a client over time. This example can be a useful tool in supervision when used to foster new insights, a point we return to shortly.

James was a middle-aged, married, African American father of five children. He was an engineer. When he entered counseling, he was in the midst of a deep depression. For the previous 6 weeks, he had been eating the equivalent of one meal a day, was unable to go to work some days, cried uncontrollably at night, and had thoughts of suicide. Six weeks earlier, his wife had left, taking the children, and had written to him from another state to tell him that she was never coming home, wanted a divorce, and that she would fight him for custody of the children. She also told him that he was a terrible husband and father. James' self-concept as a good husband was shattered. He was deeply confused and hurt. He didn't drink, swear, smoke, stay out late, or gamble; he was faithful; he went to church with his wife and children every week; he was in love with his wife and believed her to be the best wife and friend that a man could have; he did the dishes; he rubbed her feet. As a father, he worked hard to provide a safe home in a good neighborhood, there was always enough food in the house, he attended most of his children's school events, and he truly loved his children. He had never so much as raised his voice at his wife or children, much less been threatening or abusive. What had gone wrong, and when?

James could not ask his wife these questions, as she controlled all of the communication and would hang up on him if he raised these issues or if she believed he was asking his children about what happened. Eventually she told him where she was, but insisted that he not visit until "things settled down." James absolutely refused to pursue legal assistance or guidance of any kind, and made discussion of legal rights or possibilities a condition for terminating counseling. I, the counselor, was mystified. What was the secret? What had happened that was so terrible that his wife would take the children away without leaving a note? In those initial weeks, I held hypotheses about possible initiating events, or a secret such as physical or sexual abuse, alcohol, drug use, or mental illness on the part of James or his wife.

The first sessions were devoted to assuring that he would not harm himself (which he easily agreed to because of his religious beliefs) and initiating behaviors that improved his physical condition. He made and kept agreements related to eating, journaling, exercising, and resting. His physical safety established, we began exploring his life and his experience more profoundly. Over the course of weeks, a picture emerged of a man who lived by a set of powerful rules that did not accommodate individual preferences, weaknesses, or aberrations. Order and regularity were a priority. The timing of meals, the nature of meals, the relationship between a man and his wife, the way children were raised, were all dictated by his unwavering sense of order. His wife agreed with him on all of these issues, she always had, he assured me. He ruled his home with an authority that was not angry but that was serious, gentle, and propelled by a desire to be the best husband and the best father that God would allow him to be. He did not believe that his wife had ever expressed unhappiness or dissatisfaction. His role as a client was very parallel. He wanted to be the best client, to devote himself to understanding what went wrong so that he could fix it. He was thoughtful, and beneath the weight of his sadness, motivated.

As we reflected on his experience of marriage and I reflected back to him what I was hearing, raising questions and amplifying themes, James began to initiate questions that had never before occurred to him. As close as he felt to his wife prior to her departure, for example, he was unable to describe how she felt about a variety of topics. Had she wanted to work outside of the home? *Good mothers don't, she always believed that.* But did she want to have a job, and chose not to in order to be a good mother? *I don't know.* James loved to read poetry out loud to her. What was her favorite poem? *I think it was the same as mine, she never said. Hey, is that sexism? Is that what I am? That's what they say about Black men but I thought that was just White-talk.* He began to wonder, *Was this relationship a figment of my imagination? Was it all one-way? Was she faking it for years?* We pursued these questions, considering events, conversations, and themes; after exploring the extreme answers, he arrived at the conclusion that it was not his imagination—she had loved him—but that he had been very unaware of many aspects of her as a person. He had idealized her and held a rigid image of who she was, responding to the image instead of to her as a dynamic, changing person. She was a Black woman, a Christian woman, a good mother, a good wife, and he responded to these roles and identities without nuance. As this realization emerged, he began identifying times when she had expressed dissatisfaction, and he had not heard her. He also came to realize that he did not know his children very well at all. These insights produced a great deal of pain, but he consistently framed the pain as something he had to go through so that he could learn from his mistakes, become a better person, and convince her to give him another chance. They were married. Eventually, she had to come home.

James began talking with each child every week on the phone, arranging his calls to be sure that he did not interfere with their study, music, or sport schedules. He began asking them questions that he had never asked before, and to his delight, they began answering. He came to know more about their daily lives, their fears, and their hopes. His wife agreed to let him visit, and he went with hope of a reunion. He came home delighted about the time with his children, and dismayed that his effort to share what he had learned about himself did not result in a reunion. His wife filed for divorce.

James plunged back into depression. For the first time, he expressed anger at his wife. He began to question her behavior. Perhaps she was also at fault. Perhaps it was entirely her fault. Perhaps he was so blinded by love for her that she had been a terrible person all along. What kind of mother would take children from their father? After agonizing with these questions for some time, he arrived at the conclusion that she was not perfect, that in fact she had not been honest with him, and that he was not perfect, and his own rigidity and self-centeredness had prevented him from being honest with her as well. His anger dissipated. The sadness remained. He insisted that he would live alone for the rest of his life, if that was how long it took her to come back, that even though he was beginning to believe that she probably would not, he had to be ready if she did.

Eventually James began planning for a future without his wife, and resigned himself to having his children at Christmas time and during summers. But he would never date, or love, or marry again, because he was still married. This shifted to include the possibility that perhaps, some time, he might date. His sense of humor began to reemerge. He worked, he prayed, he went to coffee shops and occasionally started conversations, he looked up a few old friends, he wrote long letters to his children, and he decided that although he had not yet done so, he would eventually forgive himself for his self-centeredness, and for all he had contributed to the failure of his marriage. God already had, he said, but he needed more time.

James' process of developing critical consciousness including attending to the power dynamics in the life context around himself and his wife. Our exploration included discussion of racism, sexism, and gender-role stereotyping, as well as the relationship between his upbringing, cultural and religious beliefs, and his profound rigidity. There were weeks when he left sessions feeling irritated with me, and he grew increasingly likely to comment on and critique our sessions over time. For example, during a session, he accused me of having led him in a particular direction, which was exactly what I was doing. After discussion of whether I was being manipulative (darn it, yes, a bit), whether this was intentional on my part (not to be manipulative, but I realized I had stronger inclinations to go in particular directions than I was admitting to myself), we agreed that I needed to be more attentive to when I wanted to pursue a particular direction, and check in with him on whether that was acceptable, that is, to make my process more transparent and give him more control. That worked very well. That conversation occurred after about 4 months of working together, after a great deal of trust had been established, and after he had begun to discover the shades of gray in his world. Although I don't know if James lived "happily ever after," I do know that his perceptions of self and others achieved a much greater level of complexity, that he was better able to critique and modify his own behavior, and that when therapy ended, he was much more actively engaged in his relationships with his children and in his work setting, and was constructing his future with a sense of optimism and hope.

This example can be useful for generating reflection and discussion in supervision. How did both James and the therapist grow in awareness over time? With whom does the trainee identify more strongly, James or the therapist? How could the trainee create opportunities to raise new questions and generate further self-awareness (as opposed to waiting for personal crises to provoke growth)? How would the trainee know when an opportunity to increase critical awareness is present? How might therapist biases have influenced the direction of counseling? What is the difference between manipulation and influence in counseling? How do the trainee's assumptions about relationships reflect personal values, culture, and spiritual or religious orientation? How do the trainee and the supervisor assess the trainee's level of critical consciousness in general? Are there areas of highs and lows (e.g., higher level of critical consciousness on religious spiritual issues, lower level of critical consciousness on socioeconomic issues)? How does the supervisor self-assess and enhance critical consciousness? Exploring these and other questions can help deepen understanding of the process of developing critical consciousness.

Competence

The fourth "C" of empowerment, *Competence,* refers to the primary focus on strengths, resources, and competencies throughout the therapeutic process. Sometimes veteran mental health service providers, beginning therapists, and students in training (that is, any of us), fall into a pattern of assessing only client problems, deficits, and maladaptive behaviors. When this happens, case conferences are characterized by a sometimes overwhelming list of things that have gone wrong, are going wrong, and are getting worse. We forget that clients have survived their entire lives thus far, and that no matter how complex the issues they face, they possess a wide range of survival skills. Sometimes privilege prevents us from seeing what the client has accomplished, just as burnout can prevent us from experiencing a sense of hope for the client's future.

Returning to the supervision example we described in the context section, once Sophie, the practicum student, began understanding her client's context, she felt sorry for the client. She began to see the client as someone that the world had treated badly, someone who was rather helpless, and someone who Sophie should, therefore, provide with large amounts of reassurance. In her next session, Sophie smiled a great deal and was responsive to and praising of the client. However, her tone of voice reflected that she was speaking to someone who did not understand things very well, someone less cognitively able to handle information than Sophie. Sophie's affect was cheerful and at times almost cajoling, which was not only condescending but also confusing to the client because of the sharp contrast with Sophie's behavior in the previous sessions. Later, viewing the session on tape, Sophie was surprised by her tone of voice and her cheerfulness, and could see the client's confusion. What was harder to process was Sophie's attitude toward the client. She had translated her new awareness of socioeconomic differences to mean "less intelligent" and "needs more help." She left supervision with the assignment of identifying the skills required to manage four or five of the life crises that her client had negotiated. Next, she compared her list with a list of skills required for the work world. After looking at the second list, she significantly augmented the list of skills her client possessed. This helped Sophie to appreciate the degree to which her client had far greater life experience, and, in a number of areas, far more life skills than Sophie herself possessed. Sophie opened the next client session with a conversation about the client's strengths.

Overlooking existing skills and resources, and failing to utilize them in the counseling process, reinforces the notion that clients need counselors, fosters dependency, and discourages esteem-building. When self-efficacy expectations, or people's confidence in their ability to successfully carry out specific tasks (Bandura, 1986), are low in a given area, people are far less likely to identify the skills they actually possess. That is, a person may not identify public speaking as one of her skills, even though she is quite good at it, because her perception is that she does poorly when speaking in front of others. Therefore, exploration of client skills must include more than asking clients to simply list what they do well. Asking clients to describe a typical day, in detail, can serve as a foundation for identifying and illuminating their skills. Generating data for how well a client did something can also be useful. For example, these questions may be useful: When you gave that speech, what facial expressions did you notice on the listeners? What do you think the nodding meant? Did the person who left give any indication of dissatisfaction? What did people say to you afterwards? Did you complete the speech? Did you faint during the speech? What physical symptoms did you experience? Was there any indication that others present observed your physical symptoms? What could you do to find out more about people's reactions to your speech? What could you do to find out more about how other people felt while giving their own speeches?

Providing honest feedback regarding skill deficits or personal weaknesses is also an important element of supporting client competence. Most clients understand that they have weaknesses, and they often perceive those weaknesses to be more serious than does the counselor. When counselors avoid constructive feedback, it may be harder for clients to believe positive feedback.

In the same way, grounding training and supervision in an empowerment model means that students must identify their own strengths and weaknesses, and develop strategies for addressing their weaknesses without being overly self-critical.

Students are unlikely to truly appreciate the strengths of others if they are unable to appreciate their own competencies, just as they are unlikely to accept others' weaknesses without accepting their own. Accepting compliments, engaging in realistic self-criticism, and the ability to tactfully offer feedback or suggestions to peers without self-deprecating qualifications (e.g., "This may be a dumb idea, but . . .") are important skills that can be developed in the context of group supervision. Consistent attention to these student behaviors reinforces the notion that awareness of competence and the limits of competence is indeed an essential component of empowerment. Faculty modeling of healthy self-critique is important. It is most helpful to have faculty and supervisor models who can discuss weaknesses and strengths, mistakes and successes, without apology or false humility; models who genuinely accept their limitations and do not expect perfection of themselves. Such modeling also conveys faculty "power with" rather than "power over" students and promotes a reduction in the traditional power differential.

Recognition of a client's resources includes acknowledging their social and support networks, as well as skills (such as how to develop and engage support) and experiences that the client may not recognize as important resources. Identification of new skills that the client would like to develop is enhanced when the client has a clear understanding of existing skills. The development of new skills should be considered in relation to the multiple systems in which clients interact and those by which they are influenced. For example, advocacy skills may be particularly useful to a particular client with respect to her goals of changing her ecology; for another client, skills for completing a job interview might be the highest priority.

The following e-mail was sent, as is, to one of the authors. While dealing with her own chronic illness (one that took her life a few years later), "L." accompanied her mother in the manner so poignantly described in the following letter. Before her death, she gave us permission to use this letter in any way that we wished, and we have used it in practicum as a reading that illustrates the nitty-gritty of accompaniment that many caregivers experience. Here, we recommend that this letter from L. be used as an exercise in identifying strengths and resources. Specifically, what strengths and resources are evident, and what are indications of other possible strengths and resources that L. is using or drawing from in the difficult time period she describes?

Subject: Re: Current thoughts and perceptions

Dearest Ellen,

After 2 weeks of learning how my Mom functions now, (mostly without immediate memory, so reminders like to rinse after soaping up in the shower are necessary), has me astonished at how well she has maintained for the past year or more. Tomorrow, she goes into respite (temporary) care so we can begin to pack and move her. Providing her meds get balanced properly, and she is able to function with few or no symptoms, (especially, we hope and need to eliminate the nighttime wandering), then she is welcome in assisted living. If not, then she will need to stay where she is, as they have an Alzheimer's unit geared to keeping her safe. I hope for the former and will accept the alternative if things turn out that way.

It is harder to contemplate moving her this time than it was the last. Then, we were able to keep the core of the home my parents assembled intact. This time, things are flying apart. The bedroom set is being broken up, as everyone who fits a double bed prefers a water bed and everyone else (or their partners) are way too tall. One niece would keep the furniture for her kids to use, but get real. You have to be over 5 feet tall just to struggle onto the bed because it stands so high. I remember my Dad not even wanting me to touch his chest of drawers when I was a child. He'd shudder at the thought of youngsters using it on a daily basis. If nothing else, I'll put it in my "guest" room.

Otherwise, there is absolutely nothing else going on. This change has consumed us night and day, and probably will continue to do so until March first or thereabouts. Once Mom is moved, I plan to stay with her at night for a week, maybe longer. During the days, I'll be emptying her apartment of everything that is not taken away by family members.

The artifacts of life as I knew it growing up will be gone, never to be reassembled. As her mind unravels, so do her belongings, each change mirroring the other facets of disturbance and decay. I see this as an example of when the "experts" say that we manifest our thoughts in the physical world. Her disordered mind is equally present in the disarray of her home.

Feelings of sadness, grief, loss, and mourning accompany my appreciation that I am able to help her when she needs it. And I realize that who she is today is different, radically estranged from the woman who mothered and raised me. While I am here for her in honor of the past relationship, I also know that I am choosing this course because of who I am now. What was, in partnership with what is, will create what will become.

Her daily behavior is unlike anything I've ever seen from her. She has forgotten please and thank you. She expresses no appreciation neither for specific courtesies nor for her over all care and feeding. She demands now; speaks her criticisms without any softening smile, and openly judges everything and everyone without regarding other perspectives nor giving any weight to a person's intention. She pouts, she complains, she trots out ancient grievances as if they were current events. An astrology reading happened to focus on my relationship with my mother, saying that she has something to teach me now, different from when I was a child, that I should spend time with her to learn the wisdom she has gained in the intervening years. Now if I can just figure out what "wisdom" means in the context of a dissembling mind, I'll let you know. . . .

Tomorrow is another day. Its challenges will be enough for me to contemplate. I will be at Mom's beginning tomorrow and expect to be away most of the month. What a joke. In the past, I always wanted to get away in midwinter for a sun break, a reminder of spring and summer. So this time I'll be away getting a reminder of winter in winter!

Hugs and smiles,

L.

Community

Community, the fifth "C" of the empowerment framework, can be defined in terms of members of the same racial/ethnic group, or extended family and friends, or a faith community, or some other common bond. This component pertains to helping clients identify and connect with, or enhance their involvement in communities, and distinguishes empowerment from processes such as increasing autonomy or self-esteem. Communities can enhance client strength, hope, identity, awareness of history, resources, and opportunities. At the same time, communities offer a source of support and challenge, interaction and contribution. Community is fundamental to empowerment in both the provision of these resources to the client, and equally important, in providing an opportunity for the client to contribute to the well-being and empowerment of others. Counselors should explore the client's sense of community, and the extent and quality of client interactions and roles within the identified communities. Keeping in mind that what is adaptive, functional, or healthy with respect to communities is culturally laden, it is often helpful to examine patterns of giving and receiving in the client's communities. When community participation is limited to giving only, or receiving only, dissatisfaction and disconnection are often the consequence. Sometimes clients do not experience a sense of community with any others in their environment, or may belong to communities that undermine their resources and abilities. In such cases it may be most helpful to identify new potential sources of community, help clients develop skills for drawing upon the community's support, or develop skills for contributing to the community. Entering into new communities, or reconnecting with old ones, can be a powerful affirmation and expression of identity.

For students in training, analysis of their own communities, social support networks, and their roles within their communities, can reveal patterns important in self-understanding. Questions to raise could include: What patterns, highs, and lows can you identify in the quality and quantity of support that you have needed, and the support that you have provided to others, over the past 2 years? What do your community memberships say about your current sense of identity? Your values? What has typically been disappointing to you in your various communities? What has been most rewarding? In what ways do you challenge, motivate, provide safety, demonstrate trust, (etc.) in your communities? How do you protect yourself within communities, block intimacy, or decrease your own sense of belonging? Self-exploration of such questions increases the likelihood that counselors will explore them effectively with clients.

We have found that many graduate students in counseling undergo changes in the communities with which they identify or in the way that they perceive and are perceived by their communities as they complete their graduate work. Community issues associated with ethnic and socioeconomic group membership have been particularly challenging. Changes in important others' perceptions about who they are becoming (too White, brown, or Black; too smart; too "ivory tower intellectual"; too different; too scary; too uppity; too busy) combine with changing self-perceptions and awareness ("I need to know more about my Japanese roots"; "Oh no, I'm as rigid about rules as my father!"; "Am I ashamed of my Whiteness?"; "These other students take money for granted, I'm tired of suggesting cheaper places to go eat"; "If I get one more piece of feedback about getting in touch with my feelings, I am going to scream"; "I resent always being the only one willing to bring up racism"; "Will they still accept me back home—can I and do I still want to be one of them?"; "How come when we talk about racism, the brown students always end up reassuring the White students?"; "Maybe I don't really want to help people after all—people really bug me"; "Hey—I'm a good therapist, I really helped that client!") in a manner that often results in expanding, decreasing, asking more of, or distancing themselves from their existing communities. Community changes students have shared with us include, but are not limited to, distancing from friendship networks in which most of the friendships are dysfunctional or unsupportive; renewal of extended and immediate family networks in the context of increased ethnic, cultural, or familial identities; and the addition of new communities based on graduate program membership, professional identity, agency or community organization involvement, activism, or campus group (e.g., Gay/Lesbian/Bi Alliance; Asian-Pacific American Student Union).

We further illustrate the community component of empowerment with the example of a student trainee, "Steven." In the context of a group counseling class, students participated in a nonstructured process group. In this group, they raised questions about course content, applied skills, developed a sense of what it was like to be in a nontherapy group, gave and received feedback, and examined their own group behaviors and attitudes. Steven was several years older than the other nine students in the class, the only male, and one of very few male students in the counseling program. He shared with the group early on that he was introverted and somewhat shy, and asked the group not to interpret his silences as a lack of interest in the group. As the weeks went on, Steven's verbal participation in the group was quite low. During one class session the topic of risk-taking was initiated, and one highly verbal student turned to Steven and said, "I'm starting to resent that I take all these risks and you never take any. You know all about me and I know nothing about you. Maybe you're sitting there thinking that I'm an idiot. What have you got for us? Are you going to say anything in this class or are you just going to keep taking our energy?" Before Steven responded, several others in the group shared similar perceptions, though they each concluded with a softening statement such as, "I'm sure you are listening, but I want to hear what your opinions are too."

Steven responded by reminding them of his shyness and introversion, and affirmed that he felt very connected to the group and listened with interest and respect. The group became highly charged as the original speaker accused him of being unwilling to give anything to the rest of them, and added a passive-aggressive remark about men in general. The next 10 minutes contained tears, confrontation, anger, apologies (on her part and on the part of Steven), and eventually the focus narrowed on Steven's experience of the group as a microcosm of the program, an experience in which he felt very out of place, disconnected, discounted, and alone: Too male. Up to this point, the dynamics of this example are probably consistent with those experienced by many student trainees in experiential process groups, even if the particular issues are not the same. The reason we use this as an example of community is because of how the process continued to unfold. One of the students specifically brought up feeling discounted as a woman of color, as a way of showing her empathy for Steven. She described the importance of joining a group of other ethnic minority students and the effect this had on her self-concept and hopefulness. She said, "We keep talking about how bad racism is but at the same time we are discounting Steven and he can't help it, he's a man!" This produced laughter, then swift recognition of the irony of her remark, and then a productive discussion of how difficult it is to take risks in a group in which one does not feel accepted, and yet risk-taking can be necessary to increase belonging and acceptance. The group asked Steven to help them be more sensitive and aware about their negative male attitudes and began brainstorming about how he could become part of a men's group. A slogan, "It's Good to be a Guy" emerged from that session. What's more, Steven actually began reading men's gender issues literature and became something of a spokesperson in the program for men's issues. He joined two listservs and began forwarding information to his peers. He joined a men's discussion group. His risk-taking and verbal behaviors in the group counseling class increased, and this generalized to other classes as well. Ultimately, the discussion in that group session led to increased sensitivity to targets of humor and the experience of being "the only one," and Steven's subsequent actions increased the scope of these effects to the larger program.

In presenting this example we are not implying that Steven was oppressed, nor are we implying that he became a strident activist. What we do wish to emphasize is that Steven: was challenged to give more to his community, challenged his community to give more to him as well, altered his community (with their cooperative participation), strengthened his own sense of identity as a male, expanded his community via the listserv and men's group, and developed and shared new knowledge and skills in the process.

The community component of empowerment is the one that has generated the greatest number of questions from students trying to implement the empowerment model. We note that although community is ultimately essential to empowerment, it does not mean pushing an already overwhelmed client into taking on community service and activism. Rather, this dimension stems from the notion that humans are social beings, and that belonging and contributing to communities is an essential part of optimal development and well-being. Exploring possible means of contributing to a community is a way of affirming that the strengths, skills, and resources of the client are truly valuable. That is, the counselor is not just saying nice things but has such confidence in the client's value as to believe the client could make a difference in other peoples' lives. Caplan (1992) notes that urging clients to participate in social action is a principle of feminist therapy, but one which many therapists do not practice because some clients just "aren't ready" for social action. Caplan responds:

> Isn't reluctance about bringing up social action a way of infantilizing the client, of therapists taking on themselves the responsibility of deciding what the client is "ready" to handle—and when? The alternative, I would suggest, is to treat her as an equal by presenting as one option an activity that can be dramatically empowering and health-promoting. (p. 10)

In the following section, we illustrate specific strategies and activities that we have used to facilitate learning and applying the empowerment model, with a particular emphasis on the adult practicum course. In the context of practicum, processing these activities contributes to the individual and group supervision process as well as influencing students' direct practice. We hope that these practical activities are useful across other training and supervision contexts.

PRACTICAL ACTIVITIES IN COURSEWORK

The empowerment model is introduced to students during their first term in the doctoral program via a helping-skills course. This course is required for students within our program who have not had a similar course, and for masters students in the college's communication disorders and sciences program. The course is also an elective for school and clinical psychology students. The primary text for the course is Ivey's *Intentional Interviewing. Counseling for Empowerment* (McWhirter, 1994) serves as the secondary text, and Part II of this book is devoted to applying the empowerment model to working with the following: clients who are members of ethnic minority groups; people with disabilities; people with HIV/AIDS; older adults; people who are gay, lesbian, or bisexual; adolescents; and "the nonbeautiful," or people who are struggling with issues of appearance and/or the idealized dominant culture standards of physical beauty. All students read Part I of the text. Jigsaw learning is used to cover Part II; that is, students divide up the chapters among their small group members, and present and lead a discussion of the content to each other. In addition, class time is used to critically discuss the model as a large group.

The empowerment model is reintroduced during students' second year as they complete a year-long practicum in a university or community college counseling center, with supplementary readings, secondary supervision, case conceptualization activities, and writing assignments that require application of the model. Collaboration is emphasized as students begin working with clients, often for the first time. A collaborative approach is very consistent with the approach used in both of the settings in which our students complete their adult practicum: a community college counseling center and a university counseling and testing center. With respect to context, readings designed to increase student awareness of campus ecologies and student development are required, as well as readings attending to the larger ecology of the United States.

In order to raise attention to power dynamics and promote critical self-reflection, we spend time early in the year discussing the contexts in which the practicum students are providing services. One handout that we have used frequently in adult practicum as well as previously in field placement courses, Analysis of Power Dynamics, is included herein. This handout is designed to help students focus on elements of their new setting that they might not normally attend to. I (Ellen, the Adult Practicum instructor for the past 6 years) begin by passing out a photocopy of a single page of my journal from years earlier. On that page, in a desperate attempt to sort out what was happening, I had diagrammed the personal relationships between staff in the Headstart program in which I was then teaching. Lines connected each pair of people, and along the lines are descriptions of my perceptions of the relationships, for example, "J. is very polite to R., but when R. is not there, J. says terrible things about her," "Some days she is warm and other days she refuses to talk to me or look at me." As students examine the web of relationships, I share my initial perceptions that it was a wonderful, happy organization, and my confusion as I started becoming aware of the racism, classism, and politics that were boiling under the surface. Over the course of 2 years, I came to appreciate the complexity of these and other issues, developed a renewed appreciation for the program, and came to realize that the same dynamics were present to greater and lesser extents in all human service agencies. Through deepening friendships with program staff and Headstart families, I also came to know that domestic violence, physical health problems, mental health problems, and marital conflict among the staff were also contributing to the ways in which people were responding to each other. After some discussion of this journal page, I present the following handout:

McWhirter/Practicum

Analysis of Power Dynamics

How is power distributed in your practicum/ field placement setting? What level of respect, power, decision-making, is granted to trainees/counselors/nurses/social workers/psychologists/physicians (consider salary, scheduling, voting ability, office size, office windows, unspoken rules such as "don't interrupt the doctors," etc.)? How are cultural issues manifested and handled? How are class issues manifested and handled?

Are culture and class viewed as separate or lumped together? Gender? Sexual orientation? How does the larger economic picture affect your organization? Does your organization view practitioners with different degrees as more or less valuable (e.g., is an MSW *better* than an MA?). What are the "appropriate" lines of communication—for example, if you have a problem with a staff member—and to what extent are they followed? How do friendships and alliances among staff affect power distribution, decision-making, atmosphere, credibility, and so on?

What types of staff or client issues are viewed as more or less critical? Who defines problems? How do you know, as you are in group supervision or case conferences or staff meetings, what concerns to voice and what concerns not to voice? What concerns are addressed and which are ignored or given lip service? How are clients/patients discussed? How much emphasis is placed on professional development? How is funding allocated?

Consider the following as well. These provide a way of tracking your own sense of empowerment and possible implications within your counseling sessions:

- my own feelings of powerlessness and how I deal with them
- the extent to which my sense of powerlessness is mirrored in clients
- the extent to which I feel *powerless to help* my clients, and how this influences my interactions with them when, for example, the client's time-line is slower than mine (Do I react with frustration?), when I perceive that the client isn't trying very hard (Do I complain to colleagues that I am doing all the work?), or when I label the client as resistant (Do I feel aggravated, demoralized, self-righteous?)
- what I define as "successes" and "failures" in my work with others
- the extent to which interventions meet my needs versus the client's
- the extent to which others perceive me as powerful or influential
- how I use the power I have, and how effectively I use it (in sessions, in my family, among my friends, in the training program, in the community)

Quite often, students respond to the handout by talking about the fact that everyone in their practicum setting is treated as an equal, that there are no power dynamics, and that although there is some hierarchy, it is appropriate. This seems to be a reflection of loyalty and identification with the setting, which speaks well of the settings' commitment to orientation and incorporation of new staff. Later in the year, although (fortunately) students maintain very positive views of their settings, they are also much more attuned to the ways in which power is manifested in the setting. Similarly, although students have difficulty discussing their own sense of power in sessions early on, due in large part to lack of experience, later in the year they are able to discuss these issues more concretely if they are challenged to do so in a developmentally considered fashion.

During the third term of adult practicum, students write the paper that is described here

Evaluate the nature of the helping relationship you have established with one of your clients in terms of empowerment. Select someone you have seen at least four times. Specifically describe how the relationship is consistent or inconsistent with the goal of empowerment, as described in your text, *Counseling for Empowerment*. How do the dynamics of privilege influence this relationship? How are the "5 C's" of empowerment manifested (or not) in your work (collaboration, context, critical consciousness, competence, and community)? Include a description of how your self-awareness of your assumptions and of interpersonal dynamics in session has changed in the context of this therapeutic relationship. What problems and pleasures have you encountered in attempting to facilitate the empowerment of this client?

Finally, we frequently use two additional handouts in the context of Adult Practicum: "Critical Self-Analysis of Privilege and Power," and the "Story of Ladonna." Both are used to generate discussion of the empowerment process.

Critical Self-Analysis of Privilege and Power[1]

In our society, membership in any of the groups below means to enjoy a privileged status in relation to non-members. Generally speaking, the mainstream or dominant culture in the United States views members of these groups as "superior" to nonmembers. Our own membership or lack of membership in each group is profoundly important in shaping our lives, including our attitudes, behaviors, and assumptions. Some of the general ways that members of each group are privileged are listed in the following list (note that these are not exhaustive, nor are they universally applicable).

Young: More likely to be hired; viewed as more capable, powerful, able-bodied; seen as more attractive, more valuable, more able to contribute; viewed as more sexual, more humorous and quick-witted; viewed as more likely to be healthy, more flexible, and open to change.

Free of disability: Can spontaneously decide to go somewhere without planning; free of worries such as, "Will the bathroom or the building be accessible?" "Will the waiter understand me?" "Will people stare at me or ask rude questions?" "Will there be chairs I can sit in?" time spent on self-care a matter of choice (choosing to spend an hour on hair care vs. requiring an hour to dress); can generally use any form of public or private transportation, and without requiring the physical assistance of others; free from burden of assumptions that visible disabilities imply impaired mental functioning.

Healthy: When leaving home, free from concerns such as, "Will I have to stand for long?" "Will people realize I'm sick and act strange, distant, patronizing, or compete by being 'sicker'?" "Will they tell horror stories of their friends who died from what I have?" "Will there be food that I can eat on the menu?" "Will people talk about me as if I'm not there, or talk with extra loud, sweet voices and say 'we'?" "Will I be able to manage the pain enough to enjoy myself (will it be worth it to go)?" can take health for granted, can assume longevity; free from medical bills, insurance company politics.

Higher socioeconomic status: More access to goods, services (including health care) and opportunities; attend better and safer schools with more resources; more contact with professional role models; higher parental, teacher, and self-expectations ("Of course I'll go to college"); no need to worry about next meal or living one financial setback away from homelessness; more leisure options; easier to get loans, credit; less likely to be viewed with suspicion or mistrust; viewed in general as less likely to commit crime, as more intelligent, as more responsible, more "cultured"; as "better."

Educated: More career/work options (especially if White and if more years of formal education); earn more money (especially if male); earn more respect; viewed as intelligent, "wiser," viewed as role model for others; more socialized to norms and

---

[1]Adapted from E. H. McWhirter (1994), *Counseling for Empowerment,* American Counseling Association Press.

values of dominant society (even if not Euro-American and even if person has retained ethnic minority cultural values and traditions); greater exposure to role models, professionals, mentors, opportunities to network; sense of achievement, accomplishment of socially valued goal.

White or Euro-American: Viewed by Whites as more trustworthy; viewed as more intelligent, less likely to commit a crime; higher teacher and parental expectations; more career and educational opportunities (i.e., White high school dropouts are more likely to be hired than ethnic minorities with bachelor's degrees); socialized into mainstream culture (to point of being unable to see it as a distinct culture); more likely to live to adulthood; can assume everyone does or should speak "my" language; unlikely to be hated or "tolerated" by person with greater power because of ethnicity; less likely to be poor; accomplishments more likely to viewed as due to internal characteristics than due to luck or ethnicity ("He only got that job because he was Black").

Male: More likely to be listened to, less likely to be interrupted, more likely to be viewed as smart and competent (especially if White); more likely to be judged on basis of characteristics beyond purely physical; paid better, more promotions, communication/leadership style more consistent with dominant culture; higher career and education expectations from parents, teachers; less likely to be target of sexual assault, or sexual harassment at school or at work; less likely to have housework and child care responsibilities.

Heterosexual: Marriage and other publicly sanctioned rituals mark important events; health benefits for partners; no need for secrecy; public display of affection not a political act; freedom from fear of losing job on basis of sexual orientation or from being outed or outcast by coworkers; free from fear of hate crimes (if White and not Jewish); free from being viewed as sinful on basis of partner's gender; free from attempts to "convert"; less likely (than gay men) to experience death of large numbers of friends or partners due to AIDS; legal rights related to wills, hospital visitation, and decisions related to partner's health care not in jeopardy; not avoided due to misunderstanding and fear of AIDS, no experience of fundamental self-concept of being "different" and negatively so, on basis of sexual orientation.

Discrepancies of privilege are discrepancies of power. Our own privileged status can prevent us from working effectively with clients. Recommendations: (1) practice ongoing critical self-reflection on our attitudes, behaviors, beliefs, and assumptions are shaped by privilege and power; (2) deliberately increase awareness of how discrepancies in privilege and power effect the lives of others in our society; (3) be honest with ourselves and others about our privileged status (without apology—guilt and pity do not empower anybody); and (4) transform our behaviors and attitudes such that we minimize the extent to which we reflect and maintain the discrepancies of privilege; and (5) engage in social action toward a more just society.

Questions for Reflection

1. To what extent do I ignore or downplay the effects of these group memberships in my own life? In the lives of those I help?
2. Of which group memberships am I more knowledgeable, aware, familiar? Which do I take for granted or fail to consider? Why?
3. To what extent do I view nonmembers of any of these groups as inferior? As people with whom I am uncomfortable? As less capable, resourceful, or wise?
4. How can I create opportunities to receive critical feedback on my awareness of the social consequences or correlates of these group memberships?
5. What is one thing I can do *this week* to begin increasing my awareness of the effects of membership in one of these groups? How might this improve my helping?

The Story of Ladonna

Ladonna is a 34-year-old African American heterosexual woman. One year ago, she divorced her husband of 6 years. Ladonna has three children: Karma, age 9; Thomas, age 5; and Joy, age 2. Karma's biological father was killed in a car accident just before she was born. Al, Ladonna's ex-husband, is an IV drug user. Ladonna initiated divorce proceedings when she found out she had contracted HIV from him. They have had no contact for 6 months, and she believes he left town to avoid paying child support and to "find more drugs." She has had all of her children tested for the virus and all tests thus far have been negative.

Ladonna reports she has never used IV drugs and shows no evidence of having done so. She has not told her children, her mother, or any of her friends about her HIV status. She is alternately experiencing depression and panic, and is terrified of what will happen to her children if she becomes symptomatic. She has begun to experience fatigue and reports having a hard time getting up in the morning. Ladonna works full time in a bank and is very concerned that her employer will find out about her HIV status and find a reason to fire her. She is also afraid that if she tells her mother, her mother will stop taking care of Joy (who is at the "drooling-and-constantly-running-nose" stage) while Ladonna works. She feels very alone.

In small groups, answer the following questions:

1. *Collaboration:* How might you define the problem in a way that is consistent with empowerment? What are the problems Ladonna is facing, and how do you think she might order them in importance? Based on what you know, what would be some potentially effective ways to establish a collaborative relationship with Ladonna? What are some typical counseling behaviors that you suspect would decrease collaboration?

2. *Context:* How does Ladonna's context contribute to the difficulties she currently is facing? What aspects of privilege and power seem most salient in Ladonna's life?

3. *Critical consciousness:* What forms of consciousness-raising or education do you think would be appropriate for Ladonna right now? How would you go about exploring her level of critical consciousness? What biases and assumptions related to privileged status, power, race, and AIDS, will you have to monitor in yourself?

4. *Competence:* What are Ladonna's existing skills and resources? What types of skills would help her to deal with her situation most effectively? What new skills do you think would be most helpful in supporting her empowerment?

5. *Community:* What do you think are Ladonna's existing sources of community? What options do you see for her to increase support from her existing community, and what are the possible risks and benefits associated with each option? What additional sources of community might you help her connect with? How might she empower others (now or eventually)?

These activities and strategies for grounding training and supervision in an empowerment model dovetail well with the rest of the counseling psychology curriculum. For example, in practicum foundations, assessment, and advanced intervention courses, critical consciousness of mental health interventions is facilitated as the constructions of mental illness, wellness, and healing are explored and critiqued via autobiographies and other sources. The program's ecological model of training, based on the work of Bronfenbrenner (1979), highlights the context component of empowerment. University, community college, and in-patient practicum settings are examined as important microsystems, as well as the local community. Exosystemic influences such as campus policies on sexual harassment, alcohol use, funding cuts in mental health services, and mental health commitment criteria are also addressed as part of the context. As we noted earlier, our program faculty is characterized by strong common commitments to prevention, multiculturalism, and social justice, which provides an optimal context for training consistent with an empowerment model. In this final section, we focus on the implications of the empowerment model for social action.

IMPLICATIONS FOR SOCIAL ACTION

The empowerment model has implications for the responsibilities of mental health service providers. These responsibilities are consistent with a prevention approach to mental health (Albee, 1990; Romano & Hage, 2000). That is, given our recognition that societal conditions such as (but not limited to) poverty and institutionalized racism contribute to ongoing problems in the arenas of physical and mental health and education, (e.g., Children's Defense Fund, 2001; Garbarino, 1998; Jarjoura, Triplett, & Brinker, 2002), a strong stance of prevention is critical. This means working to alter the systems and conditions that perpetuate oppression and inequity. Oppression is not merely to be "known" but acted on. Although our individual work with clients may contribute to the prevention of greater distress for clients and their families, preventing racism and other forms of oppression requires more of the mental health professional. As Prilleltensky (1997) notes, psychologists and other mental health practitioners need to engage not just in denunciation of what is wrong with society, but also annunciation, providing a vision for how to improve quality of life for all people.

Albee (1990) suggests that the prevention of poverty and the provision of quality health care and education to all members of our society are not unreachable goals, but accomplishing them would require a significant reallocation of resources and priorities. He argued that the nature of the profession obligates psychologists to be involved in solving the problems of the world. Albee contrasted world expenditure for weapons with the expense of vaccination programs and oral rehydration therapy for children. He made the case that at a relatively modest cost—reallocation of some portion of defense spending—the lives of 6 million children worldwide could be saved by preventing five major childhood illnesses and deaths caused by diarrhea. Within the United States, over the past several decades, cuts in funding of federal and state programs have often targeted those geared toward prevention in spite of the evidence that money spent on prevention efforts reduces the amount of money needed for "interventions" such as court costs, incarceration, and the economic losses associated with drug addictions (McWhirter, McWhirter, McWhirter, & McWhirter, 2004). Mental health service providers, as witnesses to what is wrong with society, are well positioned to engage in social action that calls attention to the devastating effects of poverty and other major social problems, that proposes and works to carry out solutions, and that attempts to change the structures and systems that oppress and marginalize large groups of people.

Of course, the problems of the world are quite staggering and it may seem foolhardy to propose that mental health service providers ought to try to fix them. Our point is that mental health service providers are part of a large and informed community, members of professional organizations, and there are many with whom to share the responsibility for change. Any individual has numerous opportunities for taking part in promoting positive change, but it is at the level of groups and organizations that larger efforts can be coordinated and carried out effectively. Membership in organizations dedicated to addressing societal problems, versus operating at the individual level, seems essential to long-term participation in social change efforts.

One of the least emphasized aspects of the empowerment model in our own program is social action. As we indicated in chapter 18 of this text, our students do not complete coursework or engage in systematic practical experiences in policy research and change advocacy. Students have expressed frustration that they leave the program with a deep awareness of structural and systemic problems, and a clear vision of optimal practices for healthy development and well-being, but without a good sense of how to implement that vision within the constraints of a particular postgraduate setting. It would be helpful if we provided more concrete direction on how to incorporate the role of social activist within students' identity as counseling psychologists. We do have good models of social action among our faculty and students. For example, some faculty members have engaged in consciousness-raising and political action through their national and local leadership in psychology organizations. Faculty and students often promote political and educational events that raise consciousness about injustice in the local community and on a larger scale. During the past year, while we (the authors) have been away on sabbatical, program faculty and numerous students have collaborated with community partners to provide intensive consciousness-raising and educational opportunities for our College of Education around issues of race and diversity. These efforts are leading to promising systemic changes as well. Together with our colleagues, we hope to increase systematic attention to social action and social justice in our curriculum in the coming years.

CONCLUSION

We have been discussing, writing about, and working to implement the empowerment model into our professional work for many years. This model was based on the work of many others, and we note the clear connections between this model and ongoing work in the areas of multicultural counseling, feminist therapy, and community psychology. Our purpose here has been to describe the model itself, and to provide activities and share ideas for using this model in clinical training and supervision, rather than to review the rich literature base from which it emerges (McWhirter, 1994). Use of the empowerment model in our clinical training and supervision has provided an organizing framework for counseling that, by and large, does not restrict theoretical orientation or narrow the range of possible intervention strategies. We view the model as one that will change over time, and view our application of the model to be a work in progress. We look forward also to continuing to learn from students, mentors, clients, colleagues, and family members, who model a commitment to empowerment and social justice through their work and their lives.

ACKNOWLEDGMENTS

We thank our clients, our students, and our program colleagues at the University of Oregon for all that we have learned from and with them. We thank Dr. Jeff McWhirter for modeling a philosophy of empowerment throughout his career.

REFERENCES

Albee, G. W. (1990). Suffer the little children. *Journal of Primary Prevention, 11*(1), 69–82.

Aubrey, R. (1983). The odyssey of counseling and images of the future. *The Personnel and Guidance Journal, 62,* 78–82.

Bandura, A. (1986). *Social foundations of thought and action: A social cognitive theory.* Englewood Cliffs, NJ: Prentice-Hall.

Bronfenbrenner, U. (1979). *The ecology of human development: Experiments by nature and design.* Cambridge, MA: Harvard University Press.

Caplan, P. J. (1992). Driving us crazy: How oppression damages women's mental health and what we can do about it. *Women & Therapy, 12*(3), 5–28.

Carter, R. T. (2003). Becoming racially and culturally competent: The racial–cultural counseling laboratory. *Journal of Multicultural Counseling and Development, 31,* 20–30.

Chomsky, N. (1969). *American power and the new mandarins.* London: Chatto and Windus.

Children's Defense Fund. (2001). *Weakening economy and vanishing safety net also clouds news of last year's decline in child poverty.* Retrieved April 17, 2002, from http://www.childrensdefense.org/release010925.htm

Fouad, N. A., & Brown, M. T. (2000). Role of race and social class in development: Implications for counseling psychology. In S. D. Brown & R. W. Lent (Eds.), *Handbook of counseling psychology* (3rd ed., pp. 379–408). New York: Wiley.

Freire, P. (1971). *Pedagogy of the oppressed.* New York: Herder and Herder.

Garbarino, J. (1998). The stress of being a poor child in America. *Child and Adolescent Psychiatric Clinics of North America, 7*(1), 105–119.

Gutierrez, G. (1988). *A theology of liberation: History, politics and salvation.* New York: Orbis.

Hagberg, J. (1984). *Real power.* Minneapolis, MN: Winston.

Hawxhurst, D. M., & Morrow, S. L. (1984). *Living our visions: Building feminist community.* Tempe, AZ: Fourth World.

Henning-Stout, M. (1994). Thoughts on being a white consultant. *Journal of Educational and Psychological Consultation, 5*(3), 269–273.

Jarjoura, R. G., Triplett, G. P., & Brinker, G. P. (2002). Growing up poor: Examining the link between persistent childhood poverty and delinquency. *Journal of Quantitative Criminology, 18*(2), 159–187.

Katz, J. H. (1985). The sociopolitical nature of counseling. *The Counseling Psychologist, 13*(4), 615–624.

Liu, W. M. (2001). Expanding our understanding of multiculturalism: Developing a social class worldview model. In D. B. Pope-Davis & H. L. K. Coleman (Eds.), *The intersection of race, class, and gender in counseling psychology* (pp. 127–170). Thousand Oaks, CA: Sage.

Liu, W. M. (2002). The social class-related experiences of men: Integrating theory and practice. *Professional Psychology: Research and Practice, 33,* 355–360.

Liu, W. M., & Ali, S. R. (2005). Addressing social class and classism in vocational theory and practice: Extending the emancipatory communitarian approach. *The Counseling Psychologist, 33*(2), 189–196.

Liu, W. M., Ali, S. R., Soleck, G., Hopps, J., Dunston, K., & Pickett, T., Jr. (2004). Using social class in counseling psychology research. *Journal of Counseling Psychology, 51,* 3–18.

Liu, W. M., & Pope-Davis, D. B. (2003). Understanding classism to effect personal change. In T. B. Smith (Ed.), *Practicing multiculturalism: Internalizing and affirming diversity in counseling and psychology* (pp. 294–310). New York: Allyn & Bacon.

Liu, W. M., Soleck, G., Hopps, J., Dunston, K., & Pickett, T. (2004). A new framework to understand social class in counseling: The social class worldview and modern classism theory. *Journal of Multicultural Counseling and Development, 32,* 95–122.

Luthar, S. S. (1999). *Poverty and children's adjustment* (Vol. 41; Developmental Clinical Psychology and Psychiatry). Thousand Oaks, CA: Sage.

Martín-Baró, I. (1994). Writings for a liberation psychology. In A. A. Aron & S. Corne (Eds.), *Writings for a liberation psychology.* Cambridge, MA: Harvard University Press.

McClure, B. A., & Russo, T. R. (1996). The politics of counseling: Looking back and forward. *Counseling & Values, 40*(3), 162–175.

McWhirter, B. T., McWhirter, E. H., & McWhirter, J. J. (1988). Groups in Latin America: *Comunidades eclesial de base* as mutual support groups. *The Journal for Specialists in Group Work, 13*(2), 70–76.

McWhirter, E. H. (1991). Empowerment in counseling. *Journal of Counseling and Development, 69*(3), 222–227.

McWhirter, E. H. (1994). *Counseling for empowerment*. Alexandria, VA: American Counseling Association Press.

McWhirter, E. H. (1997, April). Empowerment, social activism, and counseling. *Counseling & Human Development, 29*(8), 1–11.

McWhirter, E. H. (1998). An empowerment model of counsellor training. *Canadian Journal of Counselling, 32*(1), 12–26.

McWhirter, E. H. (2001, March). *Social action at the individual level: In pursuit of critical consciousness*. In P. Gore & J. Swanson (Chairs), Counseling Psychologists as Agents of Social Change. Paper presented at the 4th National Conference on Counseling Psychology, Houston, TX.

McWhirter, J. J., McWhirter, B. T., McWhirter, E. H., & McWhirter, R. J. (2004). *At-risk youth: A comprehensive response* (3rd ed.). Pacific Grove, CA: Brooks/Cole.

Mio, J. S., & Awakuni, G. I. (2000). *Resistance to multiculturalism: Issues and interventions*. Philadelphia: Brunner/Mazel.

Mio, J. S., & Barker-Hackett, L. (2003). Reaction papers and journal writing as techniques for assessing resistance in multicultural courses. *Journal of Multicultural Counseling and Development, 31*, 12–19.

Pinderhughes, E. B. (1983). Empowerment for our clients and for ourselves. *Social Casework, 64*(6), 331–338.

Prilleltensky, I. (1989). Psychology and the status quo. *American Psychologist, 44*, 795–802.

Prilleltensky, I. (1997). Values, assumptions, and practices: Assessing the moral implications of psychological discourse and action. *American Psychologist, 52*(5), 517–535.

Prilleltensky, I., & Nelson, G. (2002). *Doing psychology critically: Making a difference in diverse settings*. London: Macmillan/Palgrave.

Rappaport, J. (1981). In praise of paradox: A social policy of empowerment over prevention. *American Journal of Community Psychology, 9*(1), 1-21.

Rappaport, J. (1987). Terms of empowerment/exemplars of prevention: Toward a theory for community psychology. *American Journal of Community Psychology, 15*(2), 121–145.

Romano, J. L., & Hage, S. M. (2000). Prevention and counseling psychology: Revitalizing commitments for the 21st century. *The Counseling Psychologist, 28*, 733–763.

Solomon, B. B. (1976). *Black empowerment social work in oppressed communities*. New York: Columbia University Press.

Solomon, B. B. (1987). Empowerment: Social work in oppressed communities. *Journal of Social Work Practice, 2*(4), 79–91.

Steinbock, A. J. (1988). Helping and homogeneity: Therapeutic interactions as the challenge to power. *Quarterly Journal of Ideology, 12*(1), 31–46.

Sue, D. W., & Sue, D. (1990). *Counseling the culturally different: Theory and practice* (2nd ed.). New York: Wiley.

Webster's New Collegiate Dictionary. (1980). Springfield, MA: G. & C. Merriam Company.

Wrenn, G. (1983). The fighting, risk-taking counselor. *The Personnel and Guidance Journal, 61*, 323–326.

20

Applying Principles of Multicultural Competencies, Social Justice, and Leadership in Training and Supervision

Patricia Arredondo
Daniel C. Rosen
Arizona State University

Injustice anywhere is injustice everywhere.

—Martin Luther King Jr.

Application of principles of multicultural competencies, social justice and professional leadership begins through education and training, and supervision grounded in these principles. By virtue of our positions, faculty and clinical supervisors possess enormous responsibility and influence to shape the learning and practice of mental health professionals. The models, theories, and research examples that are taught; the actual experiences with clients while in training; and the examples of professionals in roles of authority can and must promote multicultural and social justice competency development. To not do so only perpetuates training that will be irrelevant for empowering marginalized and oppressed constituencies that are most in need of services, and renders future faculty and practitioners unprepared to work in a world where social injustices prevail. These premises about the roles of mental health professionals underscore the importance of the leadership required of educators, supervisors, and other mental health practitioners. Communicating and modeling principles of multiculturalism, social justice, and leadership is not a small task. However, through this chapter, we intend to discuss theoretical frameworks and practical guidelines for educators and supervisors.

Throughout, we use the term *mental health professional* to encompass all individuals from the helping professions, including counselors, psychologists, and social workers. This chapter is designed to address supervision, a clinical practice that does not exist in a vacuum. Rather, it is part of a formal educational process for mental health professionals. Beyond training, supervision and psychotherapy are interdependent processes. When we are discussing graduate training, we will use the terms *training and supervision,* otherwise, the term *supervision* will be used alone.

PURPOSE

The purpose of this chapter is to discuss the relevance and necessity of the multi-cultural counseling competencies (Arredondo et al., 1996; Sue, Arredondo & Mc-Davis, 1992) and principles of social justice (Bell, 1997; hooks, 2000; Vera & Speight, 2003) for training and supervision, and other activities in which mental health professionals may engage. Additional underpinnings are the Ethical Principles of Psychologists and Code of Conduct (American Psychological Association [APA], 2002), Code of Ethics of the American Counseling Association (American Counseling Association [ACA], 1995), Multicultural Guidelines for Education and Training, Research, Practice, and Organizational Change (APA, 2003), and critical race theory (Delgado, 1995; Solorzano & Villalpando, 1998). Tenets of these documents address social justice and the responsibility of professionals to "respect and protect civil and human rights and the central importance of freedom of inquiry and expression in research, teaching, and publication" (APA, 2003, p. 1062). Definitions and examples are drawn from the multicultural counseling, social justice, and leadership literature, and from the authors' personal endeavors.

Tenets

We believe that: (1) Social justice, multicultural, and leadership principles can be taught and learned; (2) self-leadership (Manz, 1992) for developing one's fullest potential as a mental health professional is also a process that can be learned; (3) multicultural counseling competencies and guidelines inform ethical and culturally responsive training and supervision; (4) critical race theory can inform enablers and remove barriers to social justice in organizations; and (5) values of allocentrism, fairness, equity, power-sharing, and respect enable social justice behavior.

For the purposes of this chapter, social justice will be defined by both its attributes and associated behaviors. Among those that have helped to articulate such a definition, Vera and Speight (2003) argued that for mental health professionals, the principles of collective decision-making and community empowerment take on a role of central importance. Rather than merely reallocating or distributing resources, working toward social justice in mental health will require practitioners to support, through direct service and advocacy, those in society who have become disenfranchised, marginalized, and oppressed. Bell (1997) further elucidated a working definition of social justice, arguing that psychologists committed to this goal must ensure the safety, security, and full and equal participation of all individuals within society. Social justice, therefore, occurs when mental health educators and supervisors work to ensure each of these goals through the principles of empowerment and collaboration.

Affirming a Rationale

Why are multicultural competencies, social justice, and leadership essential to training and supervision? The rationale is far-reaching, but at the core of our response, we believe that training and supervision shape the thinking and behavior of prospective academics, researchers, and clinicians. Topics that are omitted or included in graduate, postgraduate, and continuing education signal the value that helping professions place on these topics. According to Bronstein and Quina (1988), psychology has neglected the cultural factor for reasons that include emphasis on biological versus historical and political explanations for an individual's mental health status; fear of the reinforcement of stereotypes; the U.S. principle of egalitarianism; ethnocentrism that promotes the perspective that Euro-American theories and practices are the correct and best ones; and lack of experience, or even contact, with others who are culturally different and marginalized.

Bronstein and Quina (1988), in their text on teaching psychology from culturally inclusive perspectives, introduced the preceding explanation for neglecting the cultural factor. For example, until recently, discussion about culture in mental health training had been limited to one topic on a syllabus or a single multicultural counseling course. Thus, the focus on culture has been restricted or segregated.

The dominance of the medical model in psychology is well known, and this has led to mental health training that focuses on individual pathology rather than on contextual considerations (e.g., poverty, historic oppression based on ethnicity, race, and gender). The *Diagnostic and Statistical Manual of Mental Disorders*, fourth edition, text revision (*DSM–IV–TR;* American Psychiatric Association, 2000) is the tool primarily used to categorize behavior, irrespective of cultural differences. Cultural syndromes were added in the *DSM–IV–TR*, an attempt to be inclusive of culture-specific explanations of mental distress. More recently, the film *The Culture of Emotions,* provided medical and psychiatric perspectives regarding the interaction of culture and mental health. However, taking these cultural perspectives into treatment is not guaranteed. For now, the preparation of mental health practitioners continues to rely on the *DSM–IV–TR* without a direct link to multicultural psychology.

Multicultural mental health texts (Helms & Cook, 1999; Pedersen, Draguns, Lonner, & Trimble, 2002; Sue & Sue, 2003) illustrate that Eurocentric models have been considered the norm for understanding human behavior, thereby perpetuating ethnocentrism or the attitude that the "Western/European" models are the best for mental health training. It becomes incumbent on students and professionals committed to social justice and multicultural-based mental health education and training to recognize these historic barriers to culture in traditional mental health. Omitting discussions of social justice, multicultural competencies, and critical race theory in training and supervision will likely limit the ability of mental health professionals to see the landscape of injustices and barriers in a society that affects clients' psychological well-being. Further, supervision training that focuses only on intrapsychic processes is a disservice to both trainees and clients. This individualistic approach to training and supervision excludes the multiple systems that surround and influence the human condition (Bronfenbrenner, 1979; Lewis, Lewis, Daniels, & D'Andrea, 2003).

The ecological model of Bronfenbrenner (1979) has introduced a systems approach to explaining conditions that may affect individuals' mental well-being and resources to improve their situations. The microsystem, ecosystem, mesosystem, and macrosystem explicate the importance of context, historical data, sociopolitical facts, institutional culture, and other external forces that affect the well-being of the potential beneficiaries—clients (e.g., students, clients, employees). Further, these perspectives allow mental health professionals to see the client within a holistic framework. We argue that using the ecological model is essential to social justice-oriented training and supervision.

TRAINING AND SUPERVISION INFORMED BY MULTICULTURAL COUNSELING COMPETENCIES: SOCIAL JUSTICE PRINCIPLES AND CRITICAL RACE THEORY

Multicultural Counseling Competencies

Fundamental to the work of mental health practitioners are the ethical principles and multicultural guidelines of our professional associations. The multicultural counseling competencies (Arredondo et al., 1996; Sue, Arredondo, & McDavis, 1992) endorsed by the ACA in 2003 and the APA multicultural guidelines endorsed in 2002 (APA, 2003) provide overt linkages to education and supervision that relate to social justice practice.

The multicultural counseling competencies are organized in three interrelated domains of awareness, knowledge, and skills relevant to supervision and training from social justice perspectives. In fact, the competencies are grounded in an historical and sociopolitical rationale that addresses the long-standing forms of interpersonal and institutional oppression that require a call to the mental health profession to institutionalize "counselor training and practices to be multicultural at the core" (Sue, Arredondo & McDavis, 1992, p. 56).

There are 31 competencies and 119 explanatory or behavioral statements that inform education and practice. One awareness competency states: "Culturally skilled counselors (supervisors) possess knowledge and understanding about how oppression, racism, discrimination, and stereotyping affect them personally and in their work. This allows individuals to acknowledge their own racist attitudes, beliefs and feelings" (Arredondo et al., 1996, p. 59). A simple substitution of the word "supervisor," "educator," or "advocate" for "counselor" suggests the importance of this competency for supervisors. If supervisors are lacking in this self-awareness, they will likely be limited in facilitating awareness of these issues for supervisees. As a result, supervisees may unintentionally pathologize clients with labels such as learned helplessness, "victimology," or oppositional labels that do not take into account institutional and societal barriers. It is often these barriers that preclude options for clients and their self-efficacy.

Educator/supervisor awareness and self-knowledge are cornerstones in a process that is designed to promote change and growth for learners and clients. Chen (2001) described supervision as a "primary mechanism for facilitating a counselor's multicultural counseling competencies" (p. 801). The literature also suggests that supervisory relationships are influenced by different social identities of the supervisor and supervisee (e.g., age, ethnicity, gender, disability, religion, and sexual orientation) (Borders, 2001; Helms & Cook, 1999). In their discussion of a new framework to understand social class in mental health practice, researchers (Liu, Soleck, Hopps, Dunston, & Pickett, 2004) recommended that "counselors need to spend time assessing and understanding their own biases and experiences around social class and classism and, then . . . understand . . . the economic context of their clients before acting" (p. 115).

Because supervision takes place in a sociocultural and political context, there are many forces that impinge on the supervisory relationship. These forces include the primary theoretical orientation and accreditation specialty status of the training program (e.g., community or mental health counseling, counseling psychology), the mission of the college or university, be it private, public, religious, and so forth, the region of the country, and the nation's political climate. We believe that to engage in supervision from a social justice orientation, self, other, and contextual biases, realities, and resources need to be made visible. Only then will well-intended counselors be able to manage their biases and assumptions.

A knowledge-oriented competency about a client's worldview indicates: "Culturally skilled counselors (supervisors) understand and have knowledge about sociopolitical influences that impinge on the life of racial and ethnic minorities. Immigration issues, poverty, racism, stereotyping, and powerlessness may affect self-esteem and self-concept in the counseling process" (Arredondo et al., 1996, p. 65) as well as one's opportunities in daily life. At this point in U.S. history, the flow of new immigrants, particularly from Spanish-speaking and Asian countries, is at an all-time high (U.S. Census Bureau, 2003). Xenophobia fuels exclusionary legislation as evidenced by the Patriot Act, passed after September 11, 2001. For the first time in U.S. history, terrorism by foreign nations has occurred in a pronounced and visible manner with the destruction of the World Trade Center Towers. The result has been increased concerns about personal safety, displacement of anxiety on foreign-looking individuals, particularly of Middle Eastern heritage, and restrictions on immigration. Mental health practitioners are affected by these events and media images.

Xenophobia, or the fear of foreigners, has reemerged, enabling dominant voices to unjustly target marginalized groups. In the southwest, Californians voted for Proposition 187, which denied undocumented immigrants access to public health, public education, and public assistance. The motive of this legislation was to quell the burden that immigration was supposedly levying on the economic infrastructure of the state. This scapegoat tactic was in direct contradiction to the need by California agribusiness for workers. Large industrial farms have, through many generations, encouraged "bracero" or temporary labor programs, yet this relatively voiceless constituency was blamed for the state's economic tribulations.

In the midst of anti-immigration sentiment, mental health professionals have to consider strategies to empower themselves and clients. The writings of social justice advocates such as Martín-Baró (1994) outlined three urgent tasks for Latin American liberation psychology that are applicable to practice in the United States. First, he encouraged practitioners to aid in "the recovery of historical memory" (p. 30), a process of drawing out aspects of the client's culture that serves to create a positive relationship to both one's self and one's culture. Second, Baro argued for the importance of "de-ideologizing everyday experience" (p. 31), a task of facilitating a critical examination of the construction of social experience. This requires the ability to refute any deception and alienation propagated by the mass media and to replace it with the original experience of oppressed groups and persons, thereby validating an individual's ability to acquire knowledge. Finally, Baro suggested the importance of "utilizing the people's virtues" (p. 31), supporting the notion that clients possess important strengths that need to be called upon to facilitate the change process. These frames of reference promote empowerment-based interventions by mental health professionals.

The third domain of the multicultural competencies refers to culturally appropriate intervention strategies. In this domain, there are multiple statements that relate directly to social justice principles through supervision. For example, "Culturally skilled counselors/supervisors can describe concrete examples of institutional barriers within their organizations that prevent minorities (or any other historically oppressed group) from using mental health services and share those examples with colleagues and decision-making bodies within the institution" (Arredondo et al., 1996, p. 69). The entire third domain of the multicultural competencies charges supervisors and all mental health professionals to be cognizant of institutional and professional barriers, and to apply advocacy skills on behalf of their clients. For example, agencies that serve a linguistic minority population need to have practices that are language-sensitive. Intake forms, phone messages in the target language, bilingual receptionists and counselors, interpreters, bilingual materials in the waiting room, and bilingual signage are some of the behaviors that demonstrate culture-specific competence. Although overall cultural sensitivity is essential, there are intergroup and intragroup differences that require culture-specific awareness and adaptability when working with individuals of a unique heritage (e.g., Chinese vs. Vietnamese).

References to liberation psychology are most applicable to this third multicultural competency domain (Freire, 1972; Ivey, Ivey, Myers, & Sweeney, 2005; Ivey & Collins, 2003; Martín-Baró, 1994; Prilleltensky & Prilleltensky, 2003; Vera & Speight, 2003). The liberation psychology paradigm suggests that mental health professionals need to step outside of the socialization of our professional fields in order to recognize what needs to be done, and to transform the world (Vera & Speight, 2003). Liberation psychology requires practitioners to engage in becoming aware of social injustice and inequality, and to help facilitate a shift within the worldview of oppressed individuals that offers hope. As explained by Freire (1972), "This work deals with a very obvious truth: just as the oppressor, in order to oppress, needs a theory of oppressive action, so the oppressed, in order to become free, also need a theory of action" (p. 185). It is this theory of action that we must work toward creating with our clients. For mental health professionals, this means enacting interventions that are based on strength versus deficit paradigms and recognition of our privileges as professionals. Making the transition from theoretical knowledge to practical application of the multicultural competencies entails creating professional strategies that integrate these principles into everyday practice. For example, supervisors may possess knowledge that Latinos typically underutilize mental health services and have high dropout rates after the first session (Ancis, 2004). A proactive culturally response supervisor may implement appropriate retention measures, such as an open discussion about the therapy process and issues regarding early termination.

Critical Race Theory

Premises from multicultural counseling and social justice principles specify the role of institutions as barriers or enablers to mental health, and Critical Race Theory (CRT) serves as another explanatory model. This model has been used to explain research findings regarding the lack of academic success of Latinas/os and other ethnic minorities in higher education (Delgado, 1995; Solorzano & Villalpando, 1998). In particular, CRT describes how the forces of racism have become institutionalized in the policies, practices, and structures of institutions of higher education. For example, some universities attract students through 1st-year tuition awards but will not guarantee financial support thereafter. Those who continue financial support may also expect academic excellence in a context with limited social and academic support. Another example is the continued use of standardized tests for college admissions despite research indicating the lack of predictability for college success of such exams. The victims of this practice are typically ethnic minority students.

CRT is an important framework for mental health professionals as well. We too work in settings that prevent access through different policies and practices (Arredondo, 1999). For example, mental health agencies in immigrant neighborhoods often do not have personnel to provide language specific services. Where interpreters are used, quite often, these individuals do not have adequate preparation, if any, in mental health terminology. Here again, the victims of social justice violations are the individuals most in need of services and least prepared to advocate for themselves. Mental health educators, supervisors, and students need to add CRT to their understanding of institutional barriers to mental health.

RAPPROCHEMENT BETWEEN PRINCIPLES OF SOCIAL JUSTICE AND ETHICAL GUIDELINES

The Ethical Principles of Psychologists and Code of Conduct (APA, 2002), and the Code of Ethics of the ACA (1995) provide statements of expected behavior of their members. The Ethical Principles of Psychologists and Code of Conduct (APA, 2002), and Multicultural Guidelines for Education and Training, Research, Practice, and Organizational Change (APA, 2003) address social justice by making clear the responsibility of professionals to "respect and protect civil and human rights and the central importance of freedom of inquiry and expression in research, teaching, and publication" (APA, 2002, p. 1062).

The APA Code (2002) specifies principles of beneficence and nonmaleficence, fidelity and responsibility, integrity, justice, and respect for people's rights and dignity. The ACA Code of Ethics (1995) provides another link to the multicultural competencies and to social justice principles. In "Section A: The Counseling Relationship, A.2 Respecting Diversity," the following statements are made: "Counselors actively attempt to understand the diverse cultural backgrounds of the clients with whom they work. This includes, but is not limited to learning how the counselor's own cultural/ethnic/racial identity impacts her/his values and beliefs about the counseling process" (p. 3).

These are the principles and codes of conduct that are taught to mental health professionals. Oftentimes however, they are used to address primarily clinical practice and research, with less emphasis on social justice issues faced by historically oppressed client groups (e.g., GLBTQ, people with disabilities). The ethical guidelines from both professional associations require enactment. Educators must operationalize the ethical codes and principles for students. Memorization of the codes is insufficient. For example, supervisors can refer to the ethical guidelines as a normal practice when working with supervisees. The supervisor can invite the therapist to discuss how he or she is respecting the client's ethnic background. Has the therapist inquired about their ability to attend sessions, child care, and other personal adjustments? It is the responsibility of the supervisor to be an educator and an advocate for social justice principles.

ENACTING SOCIAL JUSTICE THROUGH PROFESSIONAL LEADERSHIP

The APA approved *Multicultural Guidelines on Education and Training, Research, Practice and Organizational Change* (2003) and other multicultural competency documents (Arredondo et al., 1996; Sue, Arredondo, & McDavis, 1992; Sue et al., 1982) provide starting points for professional leadership and social justice practices. These documents challenge mental health professionals to think broadly and to model culturally responsive behavior, in other words, to be social justice-oriented professional leaders.

Leadership

Leadership is most often discussed in the business literature and from male perspectives. Terms used to define leadership include *visionary, goal-oriented, creative, transformative, inclusive, patriarchal, accountable,* and *inspirational* (Dreher, 1996; Heider, 1985). Terms that are typically absent in association to leadership include *multicultural, respectful,* and *social justice.*

In this context, the term *servant leadership* seems most relevant for mental health professionals working from a social justice multicultural paradigm. Servant leadership describes behavior that takes into consideration the greater community good (Autry, 2001; Greenleaf, 1998; Spears, 1998). Greenleaf first coined the term in 1970, when he stated, "The servant-leader is servant first. It begins with the natural feeling that one wants to serve. Then conscious choice brings one to aspire to lead" (cited in Spears, 1998, p. 1).

The servant leadership concept is derived from the nonprofit world and is emblematic of the principles of human service and social service organizations. Spears (1998) identified 10 characteristics of the servant leader, which included listening, empathy, healing, awareness, persuasion, conceptualization, foresight, stewardship, commitment to the growth of people, and building community. These characteristics are consistent with the preparation of mental health professionals. We enter the field to become helping professionals, but our responsibility goes beyond that of counseling and supervisory experiences. Mental health professions must also contribute to community building on behalf of the powerless. Consider the following: In the workplace, there generally are opportunities for professionals to advocate for students, other employees, and clients. Advocacy is a form of servant leadership, willingness by mental health professionals to step out and take responsibility and to be courageous.

Multicultural Organizational Leadership

Multicultural organizational leadership is synonymous with leadership in some respects but also has a broader emphasis. Mental health professionals, by definition, must be multicultural and social justice oriented and enact practices that are equitable, inclusive, fair, responsible, and respectful (Arredondo & Perez, 2003). In essence, this is a description of multiculturally competent leadership. Quite often, the responsibility for multicultural organizational leadership lies with an agency or training program administrator. However, to limit leadership to one person can be perceived as abdication of professional responsibility.

Counterpoints to this "one-person rule" come from Arizona State University, where program faculty voted to endorse the Multicultural Counseling Competencies (Sue, Arredondo, & McDavis, 1992); *Guidelines on Psychotherapy with Gay, Lesbian, and Bisexual Clients* (APA, 2000); and *Guidelines on Multicultural Education, Training, Research, Practice, and Organizational Change for Psychologists* (APA, 2003). In behavioral health agencies to which the lead author has consulted, agency administrators have established cultural diversity committees to begin to address the gaps in service to their lower socioeconomic and ethnic/racial minority residents. In the latter instance, state mandates, as well as direction from the agencies' board of directors, have precipitated these proactive social justice actions. Without accountability, there is no social justice leadership.

Professional organizational leadership offers examples of social justice on a larger scale. Counselors for Social Justice, a division of the ACA, was established in 1999 to tackle societal issues that affect counselors and clients alike. Members of this organization commit to equity, social justice, and the elimination of oppression, as stated in the mission of the organization. The CSJ motto is "Counselors Transforming Systems One at a Time" (see http://www.counselorsforsocialjustice.org).

The Council of National Psychological Associations for the Advancement of Ethnic Minority Interests (CNPAAEMI) has produced guidelines for culturally sensitive research practices (2000) and culturally appropriate clinical practice (2004) in four ethnic minority communities. These documents, *Guidelines for Research in Ethnic Minority Communities* (2000), and *Guidelines for Clinical Practice in Ethnic Minority Communities* (2004), emanate from the collaboration between the four ethnic minority psychological associations (e.g., Association of Black Psychologists, Asian American Psychological Association, National Latina/o Psychological Association, and the Society of Indian Psychologists). The guidelines supplement the ethical standards (APA, 2002) and are an example of shared multicultural organizational leadership between CNPAAEMI and APA governance.

The nonprofit organization AWARE (www.worldaware.org) exemplifies both social justice leadership and student activism. Founded in 2000 by Dan Rosen, a graduate student at the time, the organization has existed primarily as a grassroots movement driven by a committed group of graduate students in counseling and clinical psychology. The mission of AWARE is to enhance the effectiveness of healing practitioners by providing opportunities for cross-cultural learning and exchange. The vision of the organization is to create international experiential training programs through which practitioners will learn the healing traditions, practices, and needs of the members of various cultures, and the development of community outreach and consultation services.

AWARE was born out of passion and dedication to ensure that all members of society have access to the method and source of support that will optimize holistic health (e.g., physical, mental, spiritual) throughout the life span. Embedded within academia, AWARE serves to unite students, faculty, and practitioners in an exploration of cutting-edge ideas backed by empirical support. The inclusion of such ideas into mainstream psychology and other health fields fulfills the need to transcend Eurocentric conventions of the dominant culture by creating an open and collaborative discussion of all healing traditions. Perhaps most notably, members of AWARE have organized a now annual conference that draws national and interdisciplinary participation.

A final example of multicultural organizational leadership comes from an accounting of the work of the National Institute of Multicultural Competence (NIMC). An ad-hoc group of counselor educators and counseling psychologists, these professionals have engaged in social actions collaboratively since 1993. Among the outcomes of their deliberate strategies are the creation of the Counselors for Social Justice, the institutionalization of multicultural rituals at national ACA opening sessions, engaging professionals and graduate students in social justice leadership development, and the institutionalization of a column titled "Promoting Dignity, Development, & Diversity" that has appeared in the ACA monthly newsletter since 1994. The most recent endeavor of the NIMC is a national tour to promote social justice on college campuses across the country. The tour targets counselor training programs, colleges of education, and local communities that are engaged in social justice initiatives. The tour promotes consciousness-raising about injustices that occur in different types of settings and invites college administrators, faculty, students, and community representatives to collaborate on specific local projects. A full accounting of the NIMC strategic organizational change process for social justice can be found in D'Andrea et al. (2001).

The examples that have been cited are relevant to all mental health professionals. It is apparent that supervisees, students, and community partners can participate in organizations that engage in practices that promote social justice. In so doing, mental health professionals can enact the principles of CRT, multicultural competencies, and social justice.

BARRIERS TO SOCIAL JUSTICE PRACTICES

Unintentional Racism

The elimination of oppression is the goal most commonly stated by social justice advocates. Oppression refers to behaviors, explicit or implicit, that prevent access and opportunities of basic rights to individuals and groups. Common examples of oppression in all organizations include the "isms" of ableism, anti-Semitism, classism, linguicism, racism, and sexism, as well as homophobia and religious persecution. However, even the most well-intentioned mental health professionals may engage in unintentional racism (Ridley, 1995) or other forms of unintentional oppression.

Ridley (1995) described dynamics of racism that can be applied to understanding other barriers to social justice. His model specifies individual and institutional racism in different forms: overt, "always intentional" (p. 35), and covert, intentional, and unintentional. Examples include professors who avoid talking about issues of homophobia, supervisors who assume that a gay client is sexually promiscuous and communicate this assumption to a trainee, or researchers who use English-language instruments with linguistic minority participants. Agencies that fail to provide transportation to clients with financial duress in their area, or HIPPA forms in the language of non-English speaking clients are engaging in oppressive, irresponsible, and unethical practices.

Higher Education and the Status Quo

There are many forms of subtle or unintentional oppression in the training of mental health professionals that become barriers to social justice. Ignoring cultural factors is one example. Perhaps the most heinous barrier to social justice is unwillingness by mental health professionals to take a stand. For many, it is more comfortable to not "rock the boat," to go along teaching courses the way they always have taught them, to supervise based on models that do not consider cultural factors and systems of oppression, and to administer agencies that inadequately serve clients who have been marginalized historically. Sue (1978) wrote more than 25 years ago that "counseling and psychotherapy are perceived by many to be handmaidens of the status quo" (p. 419) because through training, research, and practice, the profession transmits society's values and paradigms of oppression. Thus, educators, researchers, and other mental health professionals have the responsibility to become conscious and deliberate agents of social justice. bell hooks (2000) reminds us that, "The heart of justice is truth telling, seeing ourselves and the world the way it is rather than the way we want it to be. In recent years sociologists and psychologists have documented the fact that we live in a nation where people are lying more and more each day" (p. 23). Enacting social justice leadership involves active listening, more truthtelling, having difficult dialogues, risk-taking, and applying collective empowerment strategies to combat systems of oppression.

Racism and sexism continue to be systemic barriers to social justice and psychological well-being in institutions of higher learning. Because professionals have been socialized or indoctrinated in these systems, we may not be consciously aware of language oppression, dominant, Eurocentric, meritocracy ideologies, the valuing of linear, logical thinking over contextual, qualitative knowledge, and the perpetuation of Western, historical models of social science in teaching. Critical race theorists (Delgado, 1995; Solorzano & Delgado Bernal, 2001) indicate that "race-neutral" laws are a camouflage for policies and practices that perpetuate racism. Mental health professionals need to be aware of how these institutional practices and "race-neutral laws" adversely affect clients and students, the very same systems that state they are there to serve.

SOCIAL JUSTICE STRATEGIES

Professional leadership is an opportunity to be a teacher and a student working from principles of social justice. As mental health professionals, we have made a commitment to the well-being of others from different walks of life. How we enact this commitment is personal, but does manifest interpersonally, through group behavior and in community interactions. Thus, consideration of how to think about and operationalize one's personal social justice paradigm is appropriate. The strategies that follow begin with the self and are stated with the hope that mental health professionals can work from self-understanding to greater community social justice practices.

Strategies

1. Develop your own paradigm for social justice leadership as an educator/supervisor/practitioner/organizational administrator. Remember, enacting leadership through social justice is a life-long process.

Actions: Mental health professionals can begin by familiarizing themselves with readings of social justice advocates, multicultural counseling competencies, and guidelines, previously cited. These readings can provide insights and terminology to better guide one's work.

Actions: Ethical ambition, according to Bell (2002), is noble but not easy to accomplish. Through personal, historical examples, he identifies contributing factors to social justice behavior that include not compromising his beliefs and "challenging policies that enhance consensus" (p. 8). His 6-step plan includes: working with passion and integrity, courage and "assuming risks in honor of others" (p. 39), evolving faith, that means being optimistic and hopeful, advancing relationships, particularly within our own families, humility versus self-righteousness in the midst of challenging social injustices, and ethical inspirations, which require looking to the examples of other social justice leaders such as Martin Luther King Jr.

2. Develop your own paradigm for social justice leadership in consultation with others.

Actions: Allies are needed to support strategies for the greater good. Examples from NIMC, AWARE, and the Southern Poverty Law Center suggest that collective power and resources are essentials. By engaging with one of these associations, it is possible to feel connected to others who believe in similar principles one has about social justice.

3. Commit to engage in visible acts of social justice through social action, particularly at local levels and through professional counseling, psychology, and other mental health associations.

Actions: Collaboration is identified as one of the many skills necessary for social action because our behavior is enacted across groups with different bases of power, information, and credibility. Becoming a member of the Counselors for Social Justice of ACA will provide opportunities to partner with colleagues to give collective voice against different forms of oppression.

Actions: Donate time and/or resources to progressive community-based organizations. Volunteerism is an important link between the professional or university setting and its larger community. Taking action by getting involved in the local community is a powerful link between the principles of social justice at the professional level and the application of those ideologies with the people most affected.

4. Raise consciousness by bringing the topic of social justice into teaching, supervision, clinical practice, and organizational interactions.

Actions: Mental health professionals need to learn the tenets of critical race theory in order to know how and when to intervene. This means recognizing (1) the centrality of race and racism throughout American society, and by extension, all institutions; (2) the need to challenge dominant ideology about color-blindness, race neutrality, and equal opportunities; (3) the links of social justice principles to theory, research, and practice in higher education; (4) the centrality of experiential knowledge in the forms of field-based research, storytelling, *cuentos,* and other forms of oral history; and 5) that historical, sociopolitical, and socioeconomic contexts count.

Actions: Consider applying culture-centered healing practices that promote psychological well-being from indigenous practices. *Ohana,* the Hawaiian concept of the extended family, has been introduced through rituals at various professional conferences. Through simple ceremony, unity and harmony among culturally different individuals is communicated by placing a lei on the shoulders of each person. For those few moments, the sense of spirituality encompasses all involved. This ceremony dignifies the human spirit in the context of conducting professional business and furthers the example of professional leadership to promote social justice.

Actions: Teach and develop course objectives based on the *Multicultural Guidelines* (APA, 2003). The document suggests behaviors to improve a social justice orientation by (1) thinking more in terms of "us" versus "them" or "those people"; (2) seeing people as individuals, as well as members of different social identity groups; and (3) increasing contact with individuals of differing "minority" statuses to better understand their issues and their needs. These three suggestions can be readily introduced in training and supervision.

5. Identify a cause or goal and champion it.

Actions: For example, in your training program, colleagues may need to give dedicated attention to the mutual relevance of the APA Ethical Standards and the *Multicultural Guidelines*. At your site of practice, you may lead advocacy efforts for clients who speak English as a second language by insisting that inappropriate psychological assessments not be used. In your community, you might support clothing drives for families in poverty.

6. Become familiar with social justice-oriented literature referenced in this chapter or from other sources.

Actions: Commit to read an entry by bell hooks, Martín-Baró, or one of the other social justice advocates identified in this chapter.

7. Learn about the advocacy competencies and other social justice paradigms to guide your work.

Actions: Advocacy is another skill learned by mental health professionals in our role as change agents. Advocacy can take place at three levels: (1) interpersonally, in counseling; (2) at the community level, through collaboration; and (3) through social/political contributions, (e.g., financial, volunteerism). There are numerous benefits from advocacy, including information sharing, individual and group empowerment, self-advocacy, using data to challenge the status quo, and systems change.

Actions: Respectful counseling is a paradigm that refers to education, research, and practice (D'Andrea & Daniels, 2001). The premises of this approach reflect social justice principles and can be incorporated into teaching and supervision.

8. Find ways to balance competition and materialism with social justice.

Actions: Slow down, donate time, or find ways that your privilege as an academic, a clinician, or as a student can be directed to others' well-being. Showing up at an event, a march, or fundraiser can be active ways of giving time and energy back to positive causes. Mother Teresa reminded her workers that, "We should learn how to give. But we should not regard giving as an obligation, but as a desire" (in González-Balado, 1996, p. 19). One of her admonishments was that generosity must be based on love and kindness, and not in the form of condescending behavior.

9. Consider the legacy you want to leave behind to family, friends, students, and peers.

Actions: Visualize the statement that will be read about you at your memorial service. How will others describe your social justice leadership as a mental health professional?

Cesar Chávez, civil rights advocate, stated: "Fighting for social justice, it seems to me, is one of the profoundest ways in which man can say yes to man's dignity, and that really means sacrifices" (Chávez, as cited in Griswold del Castillo & Garcia, 1995, p. 115). Learn from the examples of others.

Actions: Read the biographies of social justice leaders who have affected the lives of many by their intentional words and deeds. Rosa Parks, Nelson Mandela, César Chávez, Mother Teresa, Dolores Huerta, Martin Luther King Jr., Chief Joseph, and Mahatma Gandhi are among those individuals who have promoted and taught about social justice through their speeches, writings, and highly visible behavior. These individuals have also educated us about our mandate for responsibility to communities of marginalized groups. We must model and engage in trust-building and empowerment.

The words of César Chávez, leader of the historic migrant farmworkers' liberation movement, provide caution and a helpful reminder that social justice is a lifelong process. He stated: "When I'm out with workers, they teach me every single day. Perhaps it is because I've made more mistakes than anybody else, I've had a chance to learn more than anybody else. But still, the workers teach me every single day as I teach them" (in Levy, 1975, p. 521). As social justice educators and practitioners, we must be willing listeners and learners.

REFERENCES

American Counseling Association. (1995). *Code of ethics and standards of practice.* Alexandria, VA: Author.

American Psychiatric Association. (2000). Diagnostic and statistical manual of mental disorders. (4th ed., text revision). Washington, DC: Author.

American Psychological Association. (1990). *Guidelines for providers of psychological services to ethnic, linguistic, and culturally diverse populations.* Washington, DC: Author.

American Psychological Association. (2000). Guidelines for psychotherapy with lesbian, gay, and bisexual clients. *American Psychologist, 55,* 1440–1451.

American Psychological Association. (2002). Ethical principles and code of conduct. *American Psychologist, 48,* 1597–1611.

American Psychological Association. (2003). Guidelines for multicultural education and training, research, practice, and organizational change for psychologists. *American Psychologist, 58,* 377–402.

Ancis, J. (2004). *Culturally responsive interventions.* New York: Brunner-Routledge.

Arredondo, P. (1999). Multicultural counseling competencies as tools to address oppression and racism. *Journal of Counseling and Development, 77,* 102–108.

Arredondo, P. (2002). Counseling individuals from specialized, marginalized and underserved groups. In P. Pedersen, J. G. Draguns, W. J. Lonner, & J. E. Trimble (Eds.), *Counseling across cultures* (5th ed., pp. 241–250). Thousand Oaks, CA: Sage.

Arredondo, P., & Arciniega, G. M. (2001). Strategies and techniques for counselor training based on the multicultural counseling competencies. *Journal of Multicultural Counseling and Development, 29,* 263–273.

Arredondo, P., & Perez, P. (2003). Expanding multicultural competence through social justice leadership. *The Counseling Psychologist, 31,* 282–289.

Arredondo, P., Toporek, R., Brown, S. P., Jones, J., Locke, D. C., Sanchez, J., et al. (1996). Operationalization of the multicultural counseling competencies. *Journal of Multicultural Counseling and Development, 24,* 42–78.

Autry, J. A. (2001). *The servant leader: How to build creative team, develop great morale, and improve bottom-line performance.* Roseville, CA: Prima Publishing.

Bell, D. (2002). *Ethical ambition.* New York: Bloomsbury.

Bell, L. A. (1997). Theoretical foundations for social justice education. In M. Adams, L. A. Bell, & P. Griffin (Eds.), *Teaching for diversity and social justice: A sourcebook* (pp. 3–15). New York: Routledge.

Borders, L. D. (2001). Counseling supervision: A deliberate educational process. In D. C. Locke, J. E. Myers & E. L. Herr (Eds.), *The handbook of counseling* (pp. 417–432). Thousand Oaks, CA: Sage.

Bronfenbrenner, U. (1979). *The ecology of human development.* Cambridge, MA: Harvard University Press.

Bronstein, P. A., & Quina, K. (1988). *Teaching a psychology of people.* Washington, DC: American Psychological Association.

Chen, E. C. (2001). Multicultural counseling supervision. In J. G. Ponterotto, J. M. Casas, L. A. Suzuki, & C. M. Alexander (Eds.), *Handbook of multicultural counseling* (2nd ed., pp. 801–824). Thousand Oaks, CA: Sage.

Council of National Psychological Associations for the Advancement of Ethnic Minority Interests. (2000). *Guidelines for research in ethnic minority communities.* Washington, DC: American Psychological Association.

Council of National Psychological Associations for the Advancement of Ethnic Minority Issues. (2004). *Guidelines for clinical practice in ethnic minority communities.* Washington, DC: American Psychological Association.

D'Andrea, M., & Daniels, J. (2001). Respectful counseling: An integrative model for counselors. In D. Pope-Davis & H. Coleman (Eds.), *The interface of class, culture, and gender in counseling* (pp. 417–446). Thousand Oaks, CA: Sage.

D'Andrea, M., Daniels, J., Arredondo, P., Ivey, A. E., Ivey, M. B., Locke, D. C., O'Bryant, B., Parham, T. A., & Sue, D. W. (2001). Fostering organizational changes to realize the revolutionary potential of the multicultural movement: An updated case study. In J. G. Ponterotto, J. M. Casas, L. A. Suzuki, & C. M. Alexander (Eds.), *Handbook of multicultural counseling* (pp. 222–254). Thousand Oaks, CA: Sage.

Delgado, R. (Ed.). (1995). *Critical race theory: The cutting edge.* Philadelphia: Temple University Press.

Dreher, D. (1996). *The tao of personal leadership.* New York: Harper Business.

Freire, P. (1972). *Pedagogy of the oppressed.* New York: Herder and Herder.

González-Balado, J. L. (1996). *Mother Teresa.* New York: Gramercy Books.

Greenleaf, R. K. (1998). Servant-leadership. In L. C. Spears (Ed.), *Insights into leadership: Service, stewardship, spirit, and servant-leader.* New York: Wiley.

Griswold del Castillo, R. G., & Garcia, R. A. (1995). *César Chávez: A triumph of spirit.* Norman, OK: University of Oklahoma Press.

Heider, J. (1985). *The tao of leadership.* New York: Bantam Books.

Helms, J. E., & Cook, D. A. (1999). *Using race and culture in counseling and psychotherapy.* Needham Heights, MA: Allyn & Bacon.

hooks, b. (2000). *Feminist theory: From margin to center* (2nd ed.). Cambridge, MA: South End Press.

Ivey, A. E., & Collins, N. M. (2003). Social justice: A long-term challenge for counseling psychology. *The Counseling Psychologist, 31,* 290–298.

Ivey, A., Ivey, M., Myers, J., & Sweeny, T. (2005). *Developmental counseling and therapy: Promoting wellness over the lifespan.* Boston: Lahaska/Houghton-Mifflin.

Levy, J. E. (1975). *César Chávez: Autobiography of la causa.* New York: Norton.

Lewis, J. A., Lewis, M. D., Daniels, J. A., & D'Andrea, M. J. (2003). *Community counseling* (3rd ed.). Pacific Grove, CA: Thomson/Brooks Cole.

Liu, W. M., Soleck, G., Hopps, J., Dunston, K., & Pickett T., Jr. (2004). A new framework to understand social class in counseling: The social class worldview model and modern classism theory. *Journal of Multicultural Counseling and Development, 32,* 95–122.

Manz, C. C. (1992). *Mastering self-leadership: Empowering yourself for personal excellence.* Upper Saddle River, NJ: Prentice-Hall.

Martín-Baró, I. (1994). *Writings for a liberation psychology.* Cambridge, MA: Harvard University Press.

Matsuda, M. J., Lawrence, C. R., Delgado, R., & Crenshaw, K. W. (1993). *Words that wound: Critical race theory, assaultive speech, and the First Amendment.* Boulder, CO: Westview Press.

Pedersen, P., Draguns, J. G., Lonner, W. J., & Trimble, J. E. (Eds.). (2002). *Counseling across cultures* (5th ed.). Thousand Oaks, CA: Sage.

Prilleltensky, I., & Prilleltensky, O. (2003). Synergies for wellness and liberation in counseling psychology. *The Counseling Psychologist, 31,* 273–281.

Ridley, C. R. (1995). *Overcoming unintentional racism counseling and therapy.* Newbury Park, CA: Sage.

Smith, T. B. (Ed.). (2003). *Practicing multiculturalism.* Boston: Allyn & Bacon.

Solorzano, D., & Delgado Bernal, D. (2001). Examining transformational resistance through a critical race and LatCrit theory framework: Chicana and Chicano students in an urban context. *Urban Education, 36,* 308–342.

Solorzano, D., & Villalpando, O. (1998). Critical race theory, marginality, and the experience of minority students in higher education. In C. Torres & T. Mitchell, (Eds.), *Emerging issues in the sociology of education: Comparative perspectives* (pp. 211–224). New York: SUNY Press.

Spears, L. C. (Ed.). (1998). *Insights into leadership: Service, stewardship, spirit, and servant-leader.* New York: Wiley.

Sue, D. W. (1978). Eliminating cultural oppression in counseling: Toward a general theory. *Journal of Counseling Psychology, 25,* 419–428.

Sue, D. W., Arredondo, P., & McDavis, R. J. (1992). Multicultural competencies and standards: A call to the profession. *Journal of Counseling and Development, 70,* 477–486.

Sue, D. W., Bernier, J., Durran, M., Feinberg, L., Pedersen, P., Smith, E., & Vasquez-Nuttall, E. (1982). Position paper: Multicultural counseling competencies. *The Counseling Psychologist, 10,* 45–52.

Sue, D. W., & Sue, D. (2003). *Counseling the culturally diverse* (4th ed.). New York: Wiley.

U.S. Census Bureau. (2003). U.S. Census 2003. Available from U.S. Census Bureau Web site, http://www.census.gov

Vera, E. M., & Speight S. L. (2003). Multicultural competence, social justice, and counseling psychology: Expanding our roles. *The Counseling Psychologist, 31,* 253–272.

21

Educating for Social Change in the Human Service Professions

Linda C. Reeser
Western Michigan University

This chapter presents an innovative course for graduate students in the human services that includes content and methods for helping them understand and participate in social change. It includes curriculum goals, theoretical and ideological perspectives, social change principles, a range of change strategies, and education methods. Interviews with human service practitioners were conducted to inquire about their experience as activists within and outside their practice and to obtain their advice about how schools can prepare students to be effective change agents. The implications of educating students for social change are discussed.

Social work has a long history of social action since its origin in the late 19th century. At the same time the profession has "often been accused of serving as a handmaiden of the status quo" (Abramovitz, 1998, p. 512). The Council on Social Work Education (CSWE) and the National Association of Social Workers' (NASW) Code of Ethics call for social workers to improve social welfare as a professional obligation.

Social work leaders have a long history of exhorting fellow professionals to become more involved in social action and service to the poor. Where is social work today in regard to the poor and social change? Concern has been expressed over social work's focus on client adaptation to the existing environment and the neglect of social change (Miller, 1981; Reeser & Epstein, 1990) and the near-abandonment of the poor (Stewart, 1981; Walz & Groze, 1991). Specht and Courtney (1994) believed that social work has turned away from social problems, practice in the public sector, and community organization in favor of private psychotherapy. They condemn individualistic microinterventions. Fisher and Karger (1997, p. 45) counter that the problem with social work practice is not psychotherapy or individualism, but rather "decontextualized" practice that looks at problem issues as belonging solely to individuals and families and does not connect them to "larger social forces." They support the integrated practice of social action and casework or therapy, as do other theorists (Coates, 1994; Dodd & Gutierrez, 1990). Walz and Groze (1991) regard social work as being at a crossroads during these conservative times and argue that its mission must be movement beyond a "clinical orientation to engage in institution building, broad public education, and political action" on behalf of "economically and socially disenfranchised people" (p. 503). Empirical research has shown there is reason for concern and for hope. Reeser and Epstein (1990) found recent generations of social workers to be much more likely to be engaged in noncontroversial actions such as working in political campaigns and lobbying and are less likely to want to serve the poor primarily or to endorse an activist goal orientation for social work than social workers in the 1960s. Thus, research shows social workers are not becoming less activist, even though the means employed are conventional, but they view social work as a "consenting profession" (Souflee, 1977) supportive of the political and social class system. Wagner's study (1989) of social workers committed at some time in their careers to social change, found that their idealism had diminished and the majority no longer strongly identified with social work as a profession. They viewed social change as having no association with the profession of social work. There were, however, some social workers who strongly identified with social work "who believed that social work is an instrument of social change" (p. 392).

Reisch and Andrews (2001) surveyed and interviewed social workers who identified themselves as radical. These social workers challenge the status quo within and outside the profession, as well as fight oppression. They believe social work practice must change its theory, educational models, and goals into "grass-roots community-based practice aimed at transforming society and its members" (p. 216). The radical social workers were pessimistic about this happening in the profession because of the resistance of many social workers to this goal for the profession. Reisch and Andrews (2001) however, are somewhat optimistic because professional social workers have been proponents of reform within the profession and have made such changes (e.g., incorporation of feminist and culturally sensitive practice models).

Many social work students aspire to careers in private clinical practice (Butler, 1990; Rubin, Johnson, & DeWeaver, 1986). However, contrary to previous reports, many students also tend to place high value on working with disadvantaged populations (Abell & McDonnell, 1990; Butler, 1990). Wolk (1993) found that social workers' sense of efficacy (i.e., the extent to which they felt they could make meaningful changes in the political/social system) was a key motivating factor in staying politically involved.

What are schools of social work doing to provide students with the knowledge and skills important in understanding how systems act to oppress people and the strategies for effective social change? Most social work students in MSW programs choose to concentrate in clinical social work. In response to the clinical orientation in schools and student career interest, Walz and Groze (1991) propose a clinical activist model in which the practitioner seeks to identify and understand the underlying social causes of client's problems and works to redress their causes. Fisher and Karger (1997) underscore the importance of incorporating social change knowledge into social work practice so that race, gender, age, and sexual orientation are discussed when clients' personal stories are told. The result is that the personal is politicized and a vision of social change may emerge. Gil (1990, p. 23) outlines broad topic areas for "social change-oriented education" to help overcome conservative tendencies in social welfare.

Schools of social work need to be committed to all students being able to understand social change, critically analyze it, and understand alternative strategies, their application, and implications. It is important that students become aware of current events, local, state, national, and global links to better understand social problems and issues and their relevance for social work practice. Thus, students have the tools to attack root causes of problems rather than apply Band-Aids. This is just as critical for students in direct service as it is for those who will work at the macro-level. Thus, it is not sufficient to solely provide this information in the macro-policy/planning/administration concentration where it is usually located. It is also extremely difficult to cover this content in social policy courses which all students are required to take, as it is much broader than understanding political action and policy analysis, the change strategies covered in social policy courses.

The Curriculum Policy Statement (Council on Social Work Education, 2001) of the accrediting body of social work degree programs requires them to teach students how to promote economic and social justice. The Code of Ethics (1996) of the National Association of Social Workers includes the pursuit of social justice as a core professional value, and as an ethical norm that social workers "engage in social and political action" (p. 5). This chapter presents course curriculum goals, content, and methods for educating students for social change. This social change course functions to raise the consciousness of students and encourages them to promote social justice. An innovative course that is required of all 1st-year graduate students at the School of Social Work at Western Michigan University is described.

In preparation for this chapter, interviews with human service practitioners were conducted to inquire about their experiences in activism within and outside the profession and to obtain their advice about how schools can prepare students to be effective change agents. Common themes are discussed to provide insights for educators about what practitioners are doing and what they think educational programs should be doing to better prepare them.

STUDENT ATTITUDES

The need for consciousness-raising is illustrated by the author's experiences teaching a social change course in the social work program at Western Michigan University in Kalamazoo and Grand Rapids. The majority of students are White, female, more than 30 years of age with years of working or raising families, and are from the Midwestern region. Most students lack knowledge about social activism, social change theories, ideological perspectives, sources of power, and change strategies. Many have either forgotten about or never learned about social change movements in this country.

Feelings of powerlessness, apathy, and the fear of challenging the status quo are frequent responses of students in these courses. Some students are shocked when they are asked to discuss ideas of people like Karl Marx and Gandhi and their implications for social work practice. Students often report talking with friends and family members about the course content. Many students express anger, shame and disappointment about the degree of inequality in the United States and the policies and practices that perpetuate it. Their naiveté about history and current events is challenged.

Students rethink their own values and ideologies, learn to analyze systems and view them with a critical eye, become more willing to question authority, conventional wisdom, and the media, stop defining themselves as apolitical beings, develop a sense of local and global responsibility to take action, and believe that they can make a difference. Although some students do not fully grasp the relevance of this perspective to their practice, most students, over time, come to appreciate the importance of this framework to them both as mental health professionals and citizens and recommend that the course continue to be a required part of the curriculum.

The course helps social work students understand a person-in-environment paradigm of social work practice in which individual, family, and community problems are viewed as tied to larger structural factors (i.e., economy, politics) and various forms of oppression (e.g., racism, sexism, anti-Semitism). Psychology students who choose to take this course often note the absence of this perspective from their curriculum and express the desire for the inclusion of this material into their training.

CURRICULUM GOALS

A social change curriculum can be designed to assist students to critically think about past and current events and problems, possibilities for change, strategies to promote these changes, and their dual role as professionals and citizens in this process. The goals of such a curriculum for students include (a) increasing their ability to critically evaluate theoretical and ideological perspectives on social change; (b) demonstrating an awareness of current trends and events, their effects on people, the real beneficiaries, and the values and beliefs underlying practice, policies, and proposals to address social change; (c) understanding social change principles regarding the tools, beliefs, and attitudes change agents must possess; and (d) demonstrating understanding of and evaluate the application of a range of social change strategies and their implications for social workers.

THEORETICAL AND IDEOLOGICAL PERSPECTIVES ON SOCIAL CHANGE

Marxist conflict theory (Lauer, 1982; Longres, 1986; Marx & Engels, 1972), systems theory (Anderson & Carter, 1974; Leighninger, 1978), structural functionalism (Lauer, 1982) and the feminist paradigm (Bricker-Jenkins & Hooyman, 1986) are studied to enable students to examine and develop their own world view about change and to understand and evaluate other world views. The theories are analyzed for assumptions about change and stability, answers to questions regarding how change comes about, whether change may generally be viewed as desirable, and their implications for social workers.

For example, systems theory, a commonly used theory in social work practice classes, is analyzed for its strengths and weaknesses for those interested in bringing about social change. Its ability to provide a map for problem solving, to shift attention from the characteristics of individuals to interaction and relatedness to the environment, and to assume that people are self-initiating and able to change behavior or the environment are characteristics supportive of social change. On the other hand, a number of its concepts borrowed from biology (e.g., homeostasis, integration) have a conservative bias against change that may negate structural change (Leighninger, 1978; Longres, 1986). Systems approaches tend to focus on the individual troubles of clients and helping them cope with the environment. Rarely are elements of the environment weighted for power differential or inequities (Fisher & Karger, 1997, p. 47).

An example of how systems theory can be used to contextualize practice and understand the impact of structural dynamics on individuals is reviewing the impact of globalization on families: companies moving operations to low-wage countries and contracting out work in the United States resulting in lower wages, longer working hours, and higher unemployment. This may contribute to substance abuse, domestic violence, juvenile delinquency, lack of political and civic participation, and scapegoating of immigrants and welfare recipients (Collins & Yeskel, 2000).

Marxist conflict theory is presented as a possible alternative theory for social work because it is supportive of liberal reform as well as radical change to end oppressive social systems and reconstruct new ones. The predictions of Marx that have not been realized, especially the expected role of the industrial working class in changing society, are examined. Students often confuse Marxist philosophy with countries that claim to be Marxist, leading to many misconceptions about this philosophy. Studying Marxist theory and his vision of socialist society leads many of them to conclude that socialism is a set of ideas and long-range goals that encourage creativity and dialogue and that socialist societies that currently exist are a distortion of Marxist philosophy. The ideals of socialism are debated and assessed as to possibilities for their operationalization in practice.

The class discusses the usefulness of dialectical thinking for social workers as a tool for critical analysis and a guide to action. Dialectical thinking enables students to see that individuals' private troubles may be public issues, the importance of understanding that people make history and knowledge about history may help them shape the future, and the need to search for and expose contradictions to enable change to occur. It is an optimistic theory that can inspire hope in those with less power. Longres (1986) points out that Marxist theory identifies the concepts of alienation and class conflict that can unify all of social work practice. He argues that the ultimate goals of practice should be the eradication of alienation, the promotion of class consciousness, and collective action of workers and clients to pursue common class interests.

For example, we discuss that social workers are part of the working class, as are many of their clients. Many students in class who have jobs in social work feel alienated from their work in that they have to account for every 15 minutes of their day, have high caseloads to be viewed as productive, do enormous amounts of paperwork while limiting client-contact hours, and take orders from insurance companies about how many times to see a client and what interventions they should use even if it contradicts clinical judgment. Students often conclude that they need to work with their clients for social change that will benefit working- and middle-class people (e.g., national health care).

In order to understand the positions of those individuals who either support or oppose particular social changes, students learn the attitudes, values, and beliefs of those who hold conservative, liberal, or radical ideological perspectives, and this includes their own. This empowers students to be educated about their motivations for change, and the opposition that one may be up against. The subgroups within these categories (e.g., neoliberals, neoconservatives) are addressed to assist students in recognizing differences. It is conveyed to students that social workers need to be concerned about ideological arguments and be able to argue rationally rather than just make their case on humanitarian grounds. They are expected to make logical arguments that recognize their own and others' assumptions. They provide data based on statistics, examples and/or their own experience. It is not just an intellectual exercise because today's intellectual argument may become tomorrow's conventional wisdom. Critical decisions are made based on these debates. Ideologies are compared regarding basic values and beliefs, views of human nature, the causes and solutions of social problems, the role of the state, views of democracy, views of present society, and visions of an ideal society. This enables students to become aware of and evaluate their own ideology, and identify the grounds they would use to argue with those who hold a different ideology.

Students are presented with appropriate learning opportunities to develop critical capacities. They are asked to locate think-tanks and organizations on the Internet from three different ideological perspectives and compare and contrast them in regard to social issues. They are also asked to select a social change issue of interest to research in depth, apply one or more theories to understand the issue, analyze the issue from at least two ideological perspectives, and address the practitioner's role in the change and the impact on those people affected by the change. They are encouraged to do this research as part of a social action project. This experiential component may enable students to view themselves as change agents.

SOCIAL CHANGE PRINCIPLES

There are principles that are particularly critical for a social change curriculum to understand social change, to be effective in bringing about change, and to stay involved in the long run.

The principles are:

1. *Sound conceptual tools.* Conceptual tools are necessary for the analysis of the political, economic, and social structure of society and to understand how these structures lead to oppression. Critical analysis of social change theories and ideological perspectives and their application to current trends and events, as just discussed, provide these tools.[1]

2. *Historical perspective.* Knowledge of the historical record of social change and the role social work has played is essential. Having knowledge of the successful and unsuccessful attempts to reverse or institute change and understanding of conditions that led to change helps to ameliorate students' fear that this conservative era will never end; it helps to sensitize students to the possibilities for change, and to the role social workers can continue to have in effecting change. Readings on the history of social work's attempts to change economic, political, and social structures to provide a more just distribution of resources should include the settlement house movement, the 1920s or the "seedtime of reform" (Chambers, 1963; Costin, 1983) the "Rank and File" union movement (Leighninger, 1987) and the 1960s. Social movements are a powerful strategy for large scale social change and have had the participation of social workers. The study of successful past social movements for change such as the Anti-Vietnam War movement and the anti-nuclear movement provides lessons for so-

---

[1]There are faculty likely to be well-versed in the content in the sections on theories, ideologies, and social change principles. This content may serve to affirm and reinforce what they are teaching. Faculty who are not fully familiar with it may be assisted in integrating social and economic justice content in their courses.

cial workers today. Participation in voting has decreased, and social movements may provide a need for more people to feel empowered. Examining the lifeline of current social movements such as the anti-globalization movement and the movement to end poverty (VanWormer, 2004) enables students to see the enormous accomplishments of people's movements for change and some direction for future change.

3. *Political nature of practice.* Social work practice should be politicized (Gil, 1990; Reisch & Andrews, 2001; Withorn, 1984) and should include a vision of a just society that will foster the provision of peoples' basic needs and promote their full potential as human beings. Withorn argues that being political means social workers must make the connection explicit between their work and the larger socioeconomic political system. They must analyze the role that social services play in reinforcing or challenging the values, institutions, and behaviors on which the present social order rests. Social workers need to ask the question, "How can services be provided in order to alleviate pain and respond to human needs and at the same time be part of a plan to change the system?" Her claim is that, without a broader political vision, social workers are providing charity that supports the status quo and is not meeting needs so that people can reach their full potential as human beings. If social workers were to place the inadequacy of human service funding and what it would take to meet human needs on the political agenda, it may have an impact on reducing budget cuts. The content on politicized practice fosters a lively debate about the appropriate roles of social workers. Is having political discussions with clients and colleagues professional, and is it acceptable to include clients in the struggle for social justice?

4. *The personal–political link.* The personal is political (Fisher & Karger, 1997; Saleeby, 1990). Even the most private problems have political and social dimensions and there are no private solutions. "We change our world by changing ourselves as we change our world" (Bricker-Jenkins & Hooyman, 1986, p. 12). The implication for social workers is that they are accountable to each other for their actions and if they do not work collectively with clients to transform social and political realities, they risk supporting the status quo. In the process of taking action, social workers expose as false the myth that ordinary people are powerless to effect change.

5. *Reflection/action.* Social change-oriented practice is dialogical (Gil, 1990). This is a process goal and involves people reexamining their own experience and searching for the links between their lives and societal dynamics. Out of this process of developing critical consciousness, reality is renamed according to one's experience and one becomes aware of peoples' capacities to shape and change institutions (Bricker-Jenkins & Hooyman, 1986; Freire, 1968; Saleeby, 1990). This method of dialogue between colleagues and between workers and clients should result in questioning conventional wisdom and existing power structures and collective action to change reality. The relationships are characterized as supportive, nonauthoritarian and nonmanipulative. The aim is to wed reflection and action (praxis).

6. *Bottom-up change.* It is necessary to understand the power of ordinary people to change unjust structures and for social workers to be committed to helping empower people to discover and utilize the resources they have (Simon, 1990a; VanWormer, 2004). A continuing theme throughout the curriculum is that change can, and often does, occur from the bottom up. People without formal power can bring about change through collective action (Gil, 1990; Lerner, 1986; Marx & Engels, 1972; Moyer, 2001; Resnick & Patti, 1980). This is illustrated via discussion of social movements as they have become the "primary vehicle of popular participation," and have achieved meaningful progressive change (Flacks, 1990, p. 39). Many current examples of the

success of "people power" are presented to dispel the illusion that social change only occurred in the 1960s (e.g., economic sanctions against South Africa, partial cancellation of Third World debt owed to the IMF, the passing of the Americans with Disabilities Act).

7. *Top-down strategies.* Students need to learn the strategies power holders use to maintain their power and the status quo and ways to counteract that power and gain power (Moyer, 1990). For example, such strategies as having "official" policies that are different from "real" policies, and demonizing and discrediting others to win the public over to their side. Movements may gain power by getting on the public agenda and presenting alternative information. They must win over the public by showing their movement is grounded in American values and beliefs and is patriotic.

8. *Counteract "surplus powerlessness."* It is critically important to understand that people overestimate their powerlessness, and to also analyze and challenge the "advantages" of powerlessness (Lerner, 1986; Moyer, 1990). Lerner (1986) argues that if "surplus powerlessness," the set of feelings and beliefs that make people think of themselves as having less power than they actually have, does not get confronted, social change is doomed to failure in the long run. People act in ways that actually confirm their powerlessness. People learn from childhood, the media, work, and other aspects of their lives that they are to blame for not having a more fulfilling life and that they have no right or power to change history. Class discussions can focus on ways that powerlessness has become internalized, the advantages of powerlessness and failure, and ways to break through passivity and mutual distrust. Moyer (1990) discusses such advantages of victim behavior as "powerlessness allows us to be unaccountable and not responsible for our actions" and "underdogs have moral superiority" (p. 5). Students learn that active involvement in shaping the future is an antidote to the belief that we have neither the right nor the power to bring about change.

SOCIAL CHANGE STRATEGIES

Students learn about and critically analyze a range of strategies for change from the macro- to the microlevel.

A number of the strategies are outside what is traditionally taught in the social work curriculum. Revolution as well as nonviolent direct action is discussed via case examples of other countries (e.g. Nicaragua, South Africa, Russia, and Eastern Europe). The active participation of social workers in these revolutions and the barriers to social work's participation in progressive change in the United States is discussed. A primary goal is to help students develop a global perspective and identify local global links (Sanders, 1989; VanWormer, 2004).

Nonviolent direct action and social movements are two change strategies that can readily be discussed in tandem. Students learn about *satyagraha,* Gandhi's philosophy and methods for nonviolent direct action (Bondurant, 1969) and evaluate its application in social movements. Such social movements as the antiglobalization and Civil Rights movements provide excellent case studies of powerful people's movements for change. There are wonderful films such as *This Is What Democracy Looks Like* (Freidberg & Rowley, 2000) and *Eyes on the Prize* (Blackside, 1986) series that document the successes and failures of these movements.

Students are made aware of the interdependence of social work and social movements. Social work began as a movement by those in the 1880s to improve quality of life by decreasing poverty and discrimination and helping people cope with the difficulties associated with industrialization, urbanization, and immigration. Early social workers, such as Jane Addams and Julia Lathrop, provided leadership in such areas as peace activism to avert or end war and efforts to reduce oppression against women and children (VanWormer, 2004). Social workers have provided direction, resources, expertise, membership and legitimacy to many movements and social reforms (Simon, 1990a). Current social movements are structured in highly decentralized ways that can readily utilize the grassroots organizing skills of social workers. A most helpful analysis of the stages of social movements and the roles of effective and ineffective actors is provided by Moyer (2001).

Direct service is examined as a strategy for change. Empowerment is a theme for social work practice and at its best it provides a dual focus on individuals and their social and physical environments (Simon, 1994) with an emphasis on eliminating oppression via the redistribution of power (Fisher & Karger, 1997). For example, working with clients who have HIV/AIDS may entail individual work to help them cope with their illness and connect them with resources, as well as work to deal with homophobia and lack of affordable adequate health care for all but the affluent.

Alternative views and models to what students generally are exposed to in their practice classes are presented and serve as a basis for questioning and challenging conventional social work wisdom and practices. Withorn's (1984) definition and guidelines for political practice, Bricker-Jenkins (2002) conceptual framework of feminist practice, Galper's (1980) and Longres' (1986) views about radical practice, and Lerner's (1986) model of liberatory psychotherapy are discussed. Students engage in lively dialogue about the possibilities for pushing for such "nonreformist reforms" (Galper, 1980, p. 60) in their agencies and work settings as decentralizing power and control, realizing the values one would want in a desired society, organizing workers and clients or linking them with existing political organizations, and doing political education and consciousness-raising.

Students are introduced to neighborhood organizing/community development strategies as a way to empower individuals, organizations and communities to improve the quality of life in communities. Checkoway (1995) presents a helpful typology of strategies from the more conflictual (mass mobilization, social action) to the more consensual (citizen participation, local services development). Students are challenged to locate the assets within communities, schools, churches, parks, human service agencies and the skills, abilities, and gifts of individuals and find ways to connect them with one another to increase their power and effectiveness (Kretzmann & McKnight, 1996). For example, human service agencies may decide to provide meeting space and computer usage to local community groups, buy their supplies from local businesses, and organize an after-school recreation program for neighborhood youth.

Consciousness raising is the final strategy to be discussed. It is not only discussed as a dialogical process important for one's personal development and practice as a social worker, but also for becoming an informed citizen. There are a number of excellent readings that are eyeopeners about the role the media plays in "manufacturing consent" for the government, corporations, and the upper class (Carey, 1995; Chomsky, 1989; Herman & Chomsky, 1988). Students are exposed to alternative sources of media so that they read or watch with a critical eye and have access to other sources to form their opinions. Strategies for getting alternative views in the media and confronting the manipulation of the public relations industry

(Stauber & Rampton, 1995) are discussed (e.g., cable access, and expressing discontent to journalists and editors).

METHODS FOR EDUCATING STUDENTS FOR SOCIAL CHANGE

The classroom experience, curriculum, and assignments offer opportunities for implementing the curriculum goals discussed, and for developing the awareness and skills necessary to bring about social change. Students are introduced to alternative theories, ideologies, perspectives, strategies, and practice models. The dialogical process in the classroom and the assignments give many of them the permission they need to challenge mainstream thought and rethink their world view. The educational process is based on dialogue between students, and students and teachers. The goal is to "develop people's consciousness of themselves as knowledge producers" (Kaufman, 2003, p. 285). Questions are posed to students so that they can reflect on their lives, discuss their concerns, the roots of the concerns, and ways to do something about them. It enables them to challenge the prevailing "reality." The teaching philosophy in this social change course is androgogy, which is the art and science of teaching adults. Students are active participants in their own learning. The students are "critical co-investigators in dialogue with the teacher" (Freire, 1968, p. 68). The teacher acts as a facilitator, not expert, to promote egalitarianism. Thus, the students feel confident and trusting enough to rename reality according to their experience and are encouraged to act to change reality. Films and speakers are a very effective way for students to be reached affectively. They bring alive the readings. There are excellent films for showing the history of years of struggle for change. For example, *The Inheritance* (Roth, 1997) portrays the intense struggles of labor unions and, through music, conveys the themes that people have an impact on history, there is no change without pain and struggle, and every generation has to continue fighting for justice or lose what was gained in the past. The instructor can bring in a panel of social work activists to discuss how they realize social change within and outside their practice and how they combat feelings of "surplus powerlessness."

Strategies for social change are best learned by direct involvement and so opportunities are provided for students. Descriptions of peace and justice organizations and their meeting dates can be provided to students. Students are encouraged to participate in the local Social Welfare Action Alliance, a progressive social work organization dedicated to social change. Students may choose to do an assignment that involves their participation in social action. One student group researched, developed, and presented a resolution to the City Commission asking it to request that the federal government decrease the military budget and use the peace dividend for social welfare programs. Sharing such experiences with other students reinforces curriculum content and enables all to witness the empowerment that occurs.

MY EXPERIENCE OF TEACHING THIS COURSE

It has been highly gratifying to teach this course because I often hear that it awakens students who have been uninformed about inequality, oppression, and injustice. The anger that many of them feel may spur them to take action to change the status

469

quo or at least to remain informed critical thinkers. Feminist educator bell hooks (1994) regards critical thinking as the "primary element allowing the possibility of change" (p. 204).

Preparing for this course keeps me abreast of current changes and hopeful for the future, as I search globally and nationally for examples of oppressed people who have been successful in wresting power from power holders. I feel inspired to be part of collective change by the examples they set, and I share my passion about what is possible with the students. I have been told my enthusiasm is contagious.

I have received criticism from some students about the course being biased toward the liberal and radical perspectives. The readings and films are primarily from this part of the political spectrum. I inform the students that this is purposeful on my part because the conservative viewpoint is overrepresented in the mainstream media, the liberal view is rare, and the progressive voice is nonexistent. Conservative students are few in number and many feel very alone. All students are encouraged to share their perspectives and engage in healthy respectful debate with one another. The collegial atmosphere in the classroom allows for a trusting atmosphere to develop. I convey that grade is not dependent on one's ideological beliefs and assumptions but rather on one's understanding of all viewpoints and ability to do critical analysis.

INTERVIEWS WITH HUMAN SERVICE PRACTITIONERS

Eleven human service practitioners were interviewed to explore their professional work history, involvement with social change efforts within and outside their practice; their beliefs about being prepared in their professional degree programs to recognize oppression, and implement strategies to ameliorate or eliminate it; and offer their advice about the attitudes, knowledge, and skills students need to be effective social change agents. This query was motivated by a concern that there is a mismatch between what is being taught in schools of social work about advocacy and social change, service to the poor and disenfranchised, the political commitments of social workers to social justice, and the nature of social work practice. Social workers are primarily engaged in individual problem solving and clinical work in their field placements and in their jobs. The micro- and macrolevels of practice are not usually linked. This is a serious dilemma for the profession if social workers are to implement their ethical commitment to address systems that oppress people via policy change, expansion of choice, and opportunities for people, to "ensure services and opportunities they require to meet their basic human needs and to develop fully" (NASW, 1996).

The interviewees came from a variety of practice settings, as most had worked in more than one field of service. The settings represented are mental health (clubhouse, outpatient and inpatient), corrections, child welfare, medical social work, public health, legislation, grassroots community organizing, university education, school social work, and sexual assault. They all had masters' degrees in social work except for one psychologist. They were invited to talk about their experiences because they viewed their practice as a way to challenge the status quo, work towards the elimination of oppression, and empower their clients. The author knows many practitioners because of her former position at a university as director of field education and her participation in professional organizations. Thus, she selected the sample from these networks. Common themes emerged from the interviews and are described in the section to follow. The practitioners recognized the limits and possibilities of human service agencies in regard to their serving as arenas for engaging in social activism.

FRUSTRATION AND EMPOWERMENT

Most of the interviewees are currently administrators and revealed that they left direct service because they felt they could have more of an impact on policy and in making other social reforms as administrators. Some do both direct service and administration so they can remain in closer contact with clients. Those working only in direct service are engaged in prevention work and agency reform. A common theme was the frustration they experienced in their prior direct service jobs. They were critical of the systems and policies that oppressed clients, but they generally felt unprepared by their education to analyze the issues and engage in social action. Some felt powerless to make significant change and, after a few years, quit their jobs. Some spoke up, challenged authority, were fired, and found more satisfying work elsewhere.

One person worked in an inpatient setting in which she felt clients were over-medicated and unprepared to live in a community that was hostile to them and lacking in resources to meet their needs. She left that system and now works in an agency that does prevention to address the root causes of child abuse and neglect, not just treat the symptoms. She feels much less frustrated, and what she can't accomplish in the agency, she works on in task forces in the community, lobbies legislators, and serves in leadership positions in political action organizations, such as the National Organization for Women. She believes social workers need to be involved in "social change as a lifestyle" both within and outside the work setting.

One social worker felt compelled to make changes but was frustrated by the limits of the position. He stated that practitioners may not be able to directly influence formal policy. He believes however, that workers can influence the process and interpretation of policy. They can also create change by testifying and lobbying. He spoke about how uncomfortable it was to make an anonymous complaint against a psychiatrist who was administering electroconvulsive therapy against a patient's wishes. His goal was to change the policy interpretation and have treatment decisions be decided by a team, not one person. He sent the complaint to the state and the psychiatrist. This doctor went around the department saying there was a subversive staff member out to get him by lying. This worker could not come to his own defense as it would reveal his identity. The worker felt satisfied when the outcome of the complaint was positive. Multiple staff must now be involved in the decision when an individual refuses treatment. Systems may simply need a voice raising awareness that restructuring needs to occur.

He believes practice is political and has made an impact in other jobs by trying to influence others with different points of view by building relationships, challenging them in respectful ways, and reframing issues. One example is his advocacy for clients diagnosed as suffering from borderline personality disorder. When he hears clients being denigrated by staff he points out the strength of their survival skills and acknowledges their humanity. He was interested in influencing policy at the state and national levels and thus moved into an administrative position where he periodically meets with state officials and is asked to give input into policies. He has much more visibility and opportunities to exert influence.

Another example of a frustrating first employment experience concerns a worker in foster care. She became incensed by her department trying to attain support payments from an indigent client with many children who could not afford the payments. This worker advocated for the man to not have to pay. When she was ignored, she involved Legal Aid and they challenged the agency in court. The worker was viewed as a "troublemaker" and fired. After a number of direct-service jobs that alerted her to the injustices in these systems, she stated that clients "needs are first and foremost." Social workers need to "challenge the Social Darwinist ideology of sink or swim," which is a common belief in society. She decided to put her energy into community organizing and development. She feels that one of the most important ways for social workers to effect social change is to be part of an organization that has as its primary goal "building the power of low income folks." She believes "we should be at the table with them demanding change when housing is being demolished and schools are doing a terrible job. Clients need to have better options for a decent life. Politicians need to be held accountable, educated, and lobbied by us."

One social worker who became an administrator felt bitter and disempowered during a time of huge budget cuts resulting in the decision to lay off all her workers and contract case management out to existing agencies. She believed this decision to be psychologically harmful to clients. She described herself as not being political, and yet she discussed the many ways in which she "stonewalls" and "wards off evil" from decisions coming from the top of the organization that create onerous paperwork for staff and policies detrimental to the interests of clients. She spoke about "putting her finger in the dike." She has not been able to stop workers from being used to control and pacify clients. She did reveal that she has been successful in organizing her staff to write a proposal to have another organization hire them as the mental health staff. The proposal was accepted, and they will now be able to continue to provide case management services to many of their former clients. She worked behind the scenes to do this as an indirect power source for her staff. Her belief is that social workers need to "get outside the system to meet the system head on!"

One social worker is quite satisfied with her work as trainer and family clinician. She has helped to develop a curriculum to teach consumers with mental illness how to advocate for themselves with their case managers, family, legislators, neighbors, and so on. Consumers can choose to attend a 9-month module that includes personal leadership skills (e.g., conflict resolution, problem solving), community change (e.g., set up meetings with one's neighbors to advocate for more low-income housing) and political strategies (e.g., meet with legislators, write letters, and speak at legislative hearings). She has accompanied clients to public forums to support them in testifying against budget cutbacks in mental health. The cutbacks were reduced as a result of this feedback. She takes a similarly facilitative, partnering educator role when she does family therapy.

These examples underscore the importance of understanding and using power (direct and indirect), analyzing oppression, its roots and strategies to ameliorate it, and employing social and political action strategies within and outside one's agency. The workers I interviewed understand that practice must be political and that frustration and being uncomfortable are expected when systems are challenged. They work on getting unstuck when they reach barriers to change and figure out alternative ways to reach their goals. They also know how invaluable it is for schools to prepare students with the knowledge, skills and attitudes needed to be effective social change agents.

The practitioners interviewed used the strategies they were most comfortable with to make change. The strategies ranged from dialogue and consciousness-raising, filing anonymous complaints within the agency, serving on boards and task forces of social action organizations, engaging in direct conflict with the agency by turning to the legal system, and using political strategies (e.g., lobbying, establishing relationships with legislators).

They were primarily engaged in collaborative consensus strategies related to advocating for individual clients or groups. Very few were involved in mass-mobilization protest actions. They view client/consumer empowerment as a primary thrust of their work. Some define empowerment more broadly as personal, community, and political. Clients/consumers partner with social workers to make changes in the community and influence legislation. Other workers focus just on personal client empowerment. They teach consumer self-advocacy skills and are careful not to enable consumer dependency. This may even mean opposing a consumer's desire to be hospitalized.

ADVICE ABOUT EDUCATION

When the human service professionals were asked about how schools can educate students for social change, they discussed their assumptions and beliefs about change, concepts, and analytic tools to think about social issues and social work practice, cautions and opportunities for the change agent, and action assignments and field placements to prepare students to engage in social action. The following are the themes that emerged:

Assumptions and Beliefs About Change

- The belief that change is possible is necessary to sustain involvement.
- Systems (e.g., human service agencies, policies, power distribution) are not immutable.
- Authority and conventional wisdom must be questioned. Speak the truth and say "the emperor has no clothes on."
- Thinking outside the box and offering alternative solutions are necessary for change to occur.
- Significant change takes a long time, as it involves changing the thinking of others, so change agents must be in for the long haul.

Analysis/Action

- Critical thinking is key to doing analysis of social problems.
- Learning all sides of an issue by reading alternative media sources is important.
- Blaming the victims of oppression is a common ideology that must be discussed to bring awareness of the real roots of problems.

- Person-in-environment paradigm must include analyzing the social/economic/political systems and their impact on clients' lives. Analysis of this view of the environment obligates the worker to see what policies and systems need to be changed for the clients' issues to be resolved.
- Critical reflection and action must be tied together.
- Analysis must be accompanied by activities that enable students to emotionally experience the impact of oppression (e.g., films, simulations) .
- Showing students the relevance of unjust policies, practices, and systems to their own lives assists them in seeing its relevance for clients.

Social Work Practice

- The artificial spilt between clinical practice and administration/policy practice should be eliminated. Students need to learn to do both. The continuum of practice should include psychotherapy, administration, policy community organizing/development, and social action. For example, when practitioners see gaps in services they should write grants.
- A social worker's role is facilitator/partner with clients to attain empowerment. It may mean encouraging the consumer to join an action group or neighborhood organization or be appointed to the mental health board.

Cautions and Opportunities for Social Change

- Be prepared to be fired. This is less likely if one has built support and established a track record as a competent, responsible worker.
- Do not let yourself be used in your agency as a "social control agent" to "cool-out clients" who are angry about policies and practices.
- Learn to be "comfortable with being uncomfortable" when others get upset about challenges to the status quo.
- Hold the agency to its mission and values.
- Know that the pressure to maintain the status quo is strong.
- "Think about working yourself out of a job and what it would take to do this."
- "Keep your passion and idealism" as you "look beyond your job" and build support as you cannot make change alone.

Classroom Action Projects and Field Placements

- Provide case scenarios and role plays in class to give students opportunities to practice speaking up about injustice and using advocacy skills.
- Provide opportunities for social action projects that include research, writing, presentation of findings, and advocacy for an oppressed group. For example, find out about the accessibility of the campus for students with disabilities. Present the findings and recommendations to a university committee, publish the results in the campus newspaper, and follow up to see if changes are made.
- Do simulations in class, such as experiencing the impact of unequal resources.
- Require that students attend and participate in community meetings, task forces, city council, legislative hearings and/or meetings with legislators.

- Have students do dual placements or have two field instructors to gain skills in clinical, administrative, and social action work. For example, a student may be placed at a domestic assault shelter to do counseling and a congressional services office to learn about the political system and advocating for constituents.

CONCLUSION

There is a need to provide human service students with the content for helping them understand social change. Human service students should be able to critically analyze this content from different perspectives, and be aware of the range of alternative strategies, their ability to effect change, and the multiple roles they can play in this process. In these times of increasing inequality and injustice, human service training programs, such as schools of social work, have a responsibility to prepare students for the historical mission of the profession—social reform and service to the poor and oppressed.

The preparation of students for participation in broad social change has been sorely lacking in the predominantly clinical orientation of our training programs. Students learn how to respond to the immediate crisis or problem of individuals or families rather than deal with the systems that precipitate the problems. Students in macro-concentrations tend to be prepared for a more narrow range of roles, such as policy analyst, planner, and administrator than to work for structural changes in communities and the socioeconomic system.

There are opportunities for human service workers to engage in political practice both within and outside their work settings. Social workers with passion, idealism, commitment, and appropriate tools will be ready to seize these opportunities. Making it possible for human service students to master social change content, develop critical analytic skills, and engage in social and political action, are key to educating students for social change. Action projects and internships provide the links in the field to apply knowledge to practice, experience efficacy, and internalize the learning.

Good mental health practice can be reconceptualized as subversive in that it attempts to empower practitioners and clients while promoting the conditions for a just society. Social workers can play a pivotal role in consciousness-raising, community organization, and social movements for change to realize the vision of a new society in which we all can live with dignity and the resources to reach our full potential as human beings.

REFERENCES

Abell, N., & McDonnell, J. R. (1990). Preparing for practice: Motivations, expectations and aspirations of the MSW class of 1990. *Journal of Social Work Education, 26,* 57–65.

Abramovitz, M. (1998.) Social work and social reform: An arena of struggle. *Social Work, 43,* 512–525.

Anderson, R. E., & Carter, I. E. (1974). *Human behavior in the social environment: A social systems approach.* Chicago: Aldine.

Blackside, Inc. (Producer). (1986). *Eyes on the prize: America's civil rights years 1954 to 1965* [Television series]. Boston: Public Broadcasting Service.

Bondurant, J. (1969). *Conquest of violence.* Berkeley, CA: University of California Press.

Bricker-Jenkins, M. (2002). Feminist issues and practice in social work. In A. Roberts & G. Greens (Eds.), *Social workers desk reference* (pp. 131–136). New York: Oxford University Press.

Bricker-Jenkins, M., & Hooyman, N. R. (1986). A feminist world view: Ideological themes from the feminist movement. In M. Bricker-Jenkins & N. R. Hooyman (Eds.), *Not for women only* (pp. 7–22). Silver Spring, MD: CSWE.

Butler, A. S. (1990). A reevaluation of social work student's career interest: Grounds for optimism. *Journal of Social Work Education, 26*, 45–56.

Carey, A. (1995). *Taking the risk out of democracy: Corporate propaganda versus freedom and liberty.* Chicago: University of Illinois Press.

Chambers, C. A. (1963). *Seedtime of reform.* Ann Arbor, MI: University of Michigan Press.

Checkoway, B. (1995). Six strategies for community change. *Community Development Journal, 20*(1), 2–20.

Chomsky, N. (1989). *Necessary illusions.* Boston: South End Press.

Coates, J. (1994). Education for social transformation. *Journal of Teaching in Social Work, 10*, 1–17.

Collins, C., & Yeskel, F. (2000). *Economic Apartheid in America.* New York: The New Press.

Costin, L. B. (1983). *Two sisters for social justice: A biography of Grace and Edith Abbott.* Urbana, IL: University of Illinois Press.

Council on Social Work Education. (2001). *Curriculum policy statement.* Alexandria, VA: CSWE Press.

Dodd, P., & Gutierrez, L. (1990). Preparing students for the future: A power perspective on community practice. *Administration in social work, 14*, 63–78.

Fisher, R., & Karger, J. (1997). *Social work and community in a private world: Getting out in public.* New York: Longman.

Flacks, D. (1990). The revolution of citizenship. *Social Policy Corporation, 21*, 37–50.

Freidberg, J. (Producer), & Rowley, R. (Director). (2000). *This is what democracy looks like* [Motion picture]. Seattle, WA: Independent Media Center & Big Noise Films.

Freire, P. (1968). *The pedagogy of the oppressed.* New York: Seabury.

Galper, J. (1980). *Social work practice: A radical perspective.* Englewood Cliffs, NJ: Prentice-Hall.

Gil, D. (1990). Implications of conservative tendencies for practice and education in social welfare. *Journal of Sociology and Social Welfare, 17*, 5–27.

Herman, E. S., & Chomsky, N. (1988). *Manufacturing consent.* New York: Pantheon Books.

hooks, b. (1994). *Teaching to transgress: Education as the practice of freedom.* New York: Routledge.

Kaufman, C. (2003). *Ideas for Action: Relevant theory for radical change.* Cambridge, MA: South End Press.

Kretzmann, J., & McKnight, J. P. (1990). Assets-based community development. *Clinic Review, 85*, 23–29.

Lauer, R. H. (1982). Structural-functional theories. In R. H. Lauer (Ed.), *Perspectives on social change* (pp. 73–88). Boston: Allyn & Bacon.

Leighninger, L. (1987). *Social work: Search for identity.* Westport, CT: Greenwood Press.

Leighninger, R. D. (1978). System theory. *Journal of Sociology and Social Welfare, 5*, 446–466.

Lerner, M. (1986). *Surplus powerlessness.* Oakland, CA: The Institute for Labor and Mental Health.

Longres, J. (1986). Marxian theory and social work practice. *Catalyst, 20*, 13–34.

Marx, K., & Engels, F. (1972). Manifesto of the Communist Party. In R. C. Tucker (Ed.), *Marx–Engels reader* (pp. 335–353). New York: Norton.

Miller, H. (1981). Dirty sheets: A multivariate analysis. *Social Work, 26*, 268–271.

Moyer, B. (1990). *The practical strategist.* San Francisco: Social Movement Empowerment Project.

Moyer, B. (2001). *Doing democracy.* Gabriola Island, BC: New Society Publishers.

National Association of Social Workers. (1996). *Code of ethics* (Rev. ed.). Washington, DC: NASW Press.

Reeser, L. C., & Epstein, I. (1990). *Professionalization and activism in social work: The sixties, the eighties and the future.* New York: Columbia University Press.

Reisch, M., & Andrews, J. (2001). *The road not taken: A history of radical social work in the United States.* Ann Arbor, MI: Sheridan Books.

Resnick, H., & Patti, R. (1980). *Change from within.* Philadelphia: Temple University Press.

Roth, B. (Director). (1997). *The inheritance* [Motion picture]. Needham, MA: Platinum Disc LLC.

Rubin, A., Johnson, P. J., & DeWeaver, K. L. (1986). Direct practice interests of MSW students: Changes from entry to graduation. *Journal of Social Work Education, 20*, 5–16.

Saleeby, D. (1990). Philosophical disputes in social work: Social justice denied. *Journal of Sociology and Social Welfare, 17*, 29–40.

Sanders, D. S. (1989). Social work perspective in peace and development in the international context. In D. S. Sanders & J. K, Matsuka (Eds.), *Peace and Development* (pp. 3–14). Honolulu, HI: University of Hawaii, School of Social Work.

Simon, B. L. (1990a, February). *Interdependence between social movements and social work: An heuristic legacy.* Paper presented at the Council on Social Work Education Annual Program Meeting, Reno, NV.

Simon, B. L. (1990b). Rethinking empowerment. *Journal of Progressive Human Services, 1,* 27–39.

Simon, B.L. (1994). *The empowerment tradition in American social work: A history.* New York: Columbia University Press.

Souflee, F. (1977). Social work: The acquiescing profession. *Social Work, 22,* 419–421.

Specht, H., & Courtney, M. (1994). *Unfaithful angels: How social work abandoned its mission.* New York: The Free Press.

Stauber, C., & Rampton, S. (1995). *Toxic sludge is good for you.* Monroe, ME: Common Courage Press.

Stewart, R. P. (1981). Watershed days: How will social work respond to the conservative revolution? *Social Work, 26,* 271–273.

VanWormer, K. (2004). *Confronting oppression, restoring justice.* Alexandria, VA: Council on Social Work Education.

Wagner, D. (1989). Fate of idealism in social work: Alternative experiences of professional careers. *Social Work, 34,* 389–395.

Walz, T., & Groze, V. (1991). The mission of social work revisited: An agenda for the 1990s. *Social Work, 36,* 500–504.

Withorn, A. (1984). *Serving the people.* New York: Columbia University Press.

Wolk, J. (1993, March). *Blowing in the wind: Social work and political participation.* Paper presented at the 11th annual conference of the Association of Baccalaureate Social Work Program Directors, Baltimore, MD.

Author Index

Page numbers in italics refer to the reference listings

Subject Index

Note to readers: For a book in which virtually every page speaks to power, oppression, depression, racism, sexism, inequity, poverty, and privilege, as well as empowerment, social justice, multiculturalism, liberation, community, collaboration, training, and proposals for change, it is difficult to produce a meaningful index based on terms alone. This index focuses primarily on significant models, names, case examples, and programs, along with some key terms and general topics that are by no means limited to the cited pages.